THE PRACTICE OF INTERPRETATION IN INTERNATIONAL LAW

Does a unified law of interpretation exist? Can it be applied to all legal rules, regardless of their source, interpreter, or subject matter? This volume offers a comprehensive exploration of how interpretation is practiced across the diverse landscape of international law. Drawing on contributions from leading scholars and practitioners, the book examines interpretation through the lenses of multiple actors, sources, and regimes, revealing three core themes. Unity emerges in shared interpretative methods, rooted in the Vienna Convention on the Law of Treaties and its customary counterparts. Diversity appears in the distinctive approaches found within specialised legal regimes. Evolution is seen in the growing range of materials considered during interpretation. Rich in comparative insights, this volume will be an essential reference for researchers, practitioners, and anyone interested in the dynamic processes that shape meaning in international law. This title is also available as Open Access on Cambridge Core.

SOTIRIOS-IOANNIS LEKKAS is Lecturer in International Law at the University of Sheffield. He was postdoctoral researcher for the ERC-funded TRICI-Law project at the University of Groningen. His DPhil thesis at the University of Oxford, 'Duality of Responsibility in International Law', won the 2019–21 Hellenic Society of International Law Georges Tenekides Prize.

NINA MILEVA is Assistant Professor of International Law at the University of Groningen. She completed her PhD (University of Groningen) in 2023 within the ERC-funded project TRICI-Law. Dr Mileva is a member of the Coordinating Committee of the Interest Group on International Legal Theory and Philosophy (IGILTP) of the European Society of International Law (ESIL).

PANOS MERKOURIS is Professor of International Law at the University of Groningen. His five-year project on The Rules of Interpretation of Customary International Law was awarded an ERC Starting Grant (ERC grant agreement no 759728). Professor Merkouris is a member of the editorial boards of the Netherlands Yearbook of International Law (NYIL) and the International Community Law Review (ICLR). He was also the co-rapporteur of the ILA Study Group on the Content and Evolution of Rules of Interpretation in International Law.

IVO TARIK DE VRIES ZOU has written a doctoral thesis on the use of soft law in treaty interpretation and the determination of customary rules at the University of Groningen. He has also published on issues of international dispute settlement and worked as an academic as well as for practitioners.

THE RULES OF INTERPRETATION OF CUSTOMARY INTERNATIONAL LAW

Established in 2021, the *TRICI-Law Book Series* is a limited series that aims to publish monographs and edited volumes on topics that shed light on legal interpretation in international law, with a particular emphasis on the interpretation of customary international law. Titles appearing in the series examine the interpretation of customary international law from a theoretical and practical perspective, and compare the characteristics of legal interpretation in international law across courts, regimes and sources as they have evolved and continue to do so through time. The *TRICI-Law Book Series* is a joint initiative between Cambridge University Press, the European Research Council and the University of Groningen. The titles in this series are available as Open Access thanks to the generous funding from the European Research Council (ERC) under the European Union's Horizon 2020 Research and Innovation Programme (Grant Agreement No 759728) and the University of Groningen.

THE PRACTICE OF INTERPRETATION IN INTERNATIONAL LAW

Unity, Diversity, and Evolution

Edited by

SOTIRIOS-IOANNIS LEKKAS

University of Sheffield

NINA MILEVA

University of Groningen

PANOS MERKOURIS

University of Groningen

In association with

IVO TARIK DE VRIES ZOU

University of Goningen

CAMBRIDGE
UNIVERSITY PRESS

CAMBRIDGE
UNIVERSITY PRESS

Shaftesbury Road, Cambridge CB2 8EA, United Kingdom

One Liberty Plaza, 20th Floor, New York, NY 10006, USA

477 Williamstown Road, Port Melbourne, VIC 3207, Australia

314–321, 3rd Floor, Plot 3, Splendor Forum, Jasola District Centre, New Delhi – 110025, India

Cambridge University Press is part of Cambridge University Press & Assessment,
a department of the University of Cambridge.

We share the University's mission to contribute to society through the pursuit of
education, learning and research at the highest international levels of excellence.

www.cambridge.org
Information on this title: www.cambridge.org/9781009599085

DOI: 10.1017/9781009599122

First published 2026

Cover image: *Snow Storm: Steam-Boat off a Harbour's Mouth*, J. M. W. Turner, 1842. Image by Universal
Images Group via Getty Images.

A catalogue record for this publication is available from the British Library

Library of Congress Cataloging-in-Publication Data
Names: Merkouris, Panos editor | Lekkas, Sotirios Ioannis editor | Mileva, Nina,
1992- editor | Vries-Zou, Ivo Tarik de editor
Title: The practice of interpretation in international law : unity, diversity, and evolution / edited by Sotirios-
Ioannis Lekkas, University of Sheffield; Nina Mileva, University of Groningen; Panos Merkouris,
University of Groningen; Ivo Tarik de Vries Zou; University of Goningen.
Description: Cambridge, United Kingdom ; New York, NY : Cambridge University Press, 2026. |
Series: The rules of interpretation of customary international law (TRIC) | Includes bibliographical
references and index.
Identifiers: LCCN 2026013937 (print) | LCCN 2026013938 (ebook) | ISBN 9781009599085 hardback |
ISBN 9781009599115 paperback | ISBN 9781009599122 epub
Subjects: LCSH: International law–Interpretation and construction
Classification: LCC KZ1285 .P73 2026 (print) | LCC KZ1285 (ebook)
LC record available at https://lccn.loc.gov/2026013937
LC ebook record available at https://lccn.loc.gov/2026013938

ISBN 978-1-009-59908-5 Hardback
ISBN 978-1-009-59911-5 Paperback

CONTENTS

CONTRIBUTORS

OLYMPIA BEKOU is Professor of Public International Law and Head of the School of Law at the University of Nottingham. She also heads the International Criminal Justice Unit of the University of Nottingham Human Rights Law Centre. Olympia read law at the Democritus University of Thrace in Greece and in 2000 was admitted to the Greek Bar. She completed the LLM in International Law at the University of Cambridge and obtained her PhD in International Criminal Law from the University of Nottingham, for which she had been awarded a NATO Fellowship. Olympia joined the School of Law in September 2002 and currently teaches International Criminal Law. Over the years, Olympia has been a fellow of the Max Planck Institute for Foreign and International Criminal Law in Freiburg, Germany, and she has also held visiting positions at the TC Beirne School of Law; the University of Queensland, Australia; the University of Nantes, France; and Istanbul Bilgi University, Turkey. She has presented her research in over forty countries around the world and is a frequent speaker in expert meetings, workshops, and conferences.

CATHERINE BRÖLMANN is Professor of Public International Law and Head of the Department of International and European Law at the University of Amsterdam.

MARIA GEORGE is a PhD candidate in international law at the Graduate Institute, Geneva. Her research areas are international climate change, trade, and investment law. She has previously worked in international dispute settlement in trade and investment disputes and on domestic legislative drafting. She has also interned at the World Trade Organization in the Economic Research and Statistics Division.

MARLIES HESSELMAN is Assistant Professor at the University of Groningen Faculty of Law and has chaired the Groningen Centre for

Health Law since 2023. She holds an LLB from Leiden University; an LLM International Law, specialisation human rights (cum laude, top 2 per cent); an LLM European Law, spec. human rights; and a PhD in International Human Rights Law on modern energy services access from Groningen University. Dr Hesselman also studied at Copenhagen University and was a funded visiting scholar at the London School of Economics. Dr Hesselman sits on the Scientific Steering Committee of the interdisciplinary Aletta Jacobs School of Public Health and is founder and academic co-coordinator of the Joint Summer School on Global Governance of Health Vulnerabilities in Africain Tanzania. She also recently co-founded the new Working Group on Human Rights & Climate Crisis at the Netherlands Network of Human Rights Research.

SOTIRIOS IOANNIS LEKKAS is a lecturer in International Law at the University of Sheffield School of Law, and the deputy director of the Sheffield Centre for International and European Law (SCIEL). Prior to this position, Sotirios was postdoctoral researcher for the TRICI-Law project (ERC grant agreement no 759728) at the Department of Transboundary Legal Studies of the University of Groningen. He also worked as a judicial fellow at the ICJ and as a tutor in public international law at the University of Oxford, Faculty of Law. He holds a DPhil in Law from the University of Oxford. He has studied law in Athens and London (University College London), where he was awarded the George Schwarzenberger Prize in International Law by the University of London. He is also a (non-practising) member of the Bar in Athens, Greece.

GABRIELLE MARCEAU was nominated as Honorary Professor (Emeritus) at the University of Geneva on 1 April 2025. Professor Marceau was appointed as a lecturer in 2000 and became an Associate Professor in the Department of Public International Law and International Organization at the Faculty of Law at the University of Geneva (UNIGE) in 2005. She teaches World Trade Organization (WTO) law, supervises numerous master's theses and doctoral dissertations, and organises conferences and research seminars. She also created a doctoral seminar. She is also visiting professor at the University of Ottawa, Law Faculty – Hyman Soloway Chair, and at other institutions. Professor Marceau serves on several scientific councils promoting international economic law. She has been the president of the Society of International Economic Law, is a member of the board of directors of the Geneva Society for Law and Legislation, and is a counsellor of the American Society of International Law. Professor Marceau is a specialist in dispute settlement and the legal relationships between international trade and non-commercial considerations (such as environment, human rights, labour, etc.), with more than 125 publications to her name. Gabrielle Marceau has also worked at the Secretariat World Trade Organization for over thirty years, serving as a legal adviser in international disputes, in the cabinet of Director-General Pascal Lamy, and in the Economic Research and Statistics Division.

PANOS MERKOURIS is Professor of International Law at the University of Groningen. His five-year project on The Rules of Interpretation of Customary International Law was awarded an ERC Starting Grant (ERC grant agreement no 759728). He specialises in interpretation, law of treaties, sources of international law, and dispute settlement. Professor Merkouris is currently a member of the editorial boards of the Netherlands Yearbook of International Law (NYIL) and the International Community Law Review (ICLR). He was also the co-rapporteur of the ILA Study Group on the Content and Evolution of Rules of Interpretation in International Law. He is the author of the monograph *Treaties in Motion* (Cambridge University Press 2020, co-authored with Professor Fitzmaurice) and *Article 31(3)(c) of the VCLT, and the Principle of Systemic Integration: Normative Shadows in Plato's Cave* (Martinus Nijhoff 2015). The latter has been cited with approval by a Chamber of the International Criminal Court. He has numerous publications on interpretation, law of treaties, and customary international law.

NINA MILEVA is Assistant Professor of International Law at the University of Groningen. She completed her PhD (University of Groningen) in 2023 within the ERC-funded project TRICI-Law. Prior to this, she obtained an LLM in Public International Law (Utrecht University). Dr Mileva is currently a member of the Coordinating Committee of the Interest Group on International Legal Theory and Philosophy (IGILTP) of the European Society of International Law (ESIL). Her research interests lie in the fields of general international law, legal theory, public interest litigation, and critical approaches to international law. In addition to her PhD monograph entitled *A Theory of Interpretation for Customary International Law*, Dr. Mileva has authored several peer-reviewed papers and chapters in edited volumes.

ELISA MORGERA is UN Special Rapporteur on Climate Change and Human Rights and a Professor of International Law and Sustainability at the University of Durham. She specialises in international biodiversity law and its linkages with human rights, notably the rights of Indigenous Peoples and small-scale fishing communities, everyone's right to a healthy environment, health and science, and business responsibility to respect human rights. She was the director of the One Ocean Hub, a global inter-disciplinary research collaboration of research institutions in the UK, Africa, South Pacific, and the Caribbean, as well as UN agencies and other international partners. The One Ocean Hub pioneered research on human rights and the marine environment with a view to better connecting marine and social sciences and the arts, to support fair and inclusive decision-making for a healthy ocean whereby people and planet flourish.

THOMAS NEKTARIOS PAPANASTASIOU (LLB, LLM, MA, PhD) is an Associate Professor of Public International Law at the Department of Law, School of Law, University of Nicosia (UNIC Athens). He achieved his PhD from Waseda University, Graduate School of Asian Pacific Studies (Tokyo, Japan, specializing in International Investment Law.). His current research interests lie on the protection of foreign investments, the role of human rights in international investment arbitration, the right to property in occupied Cyprus, and the legal framework of offshore energy investments. He is the co-author (with N. Rubins and S. Kinsella) of *International Investment, Political Risk, and Dispute Resolution: A Practitioner's Guide* (Oxford University Press, 2020) and author of two more books and various articles. Thomas worked as a legal expert on the UNIDROIT Principles of International Investment Contracts representing the Law Office of the Republic of Cyprus, as a consultant to the World Bank (WB, Washington, DC) and as a trainee at the Organization for Economic Cooperation and Development (OECD, Paris). He is a scholarship recipient from the Japanese Government (Ministry of Education-MEXT). His dissertation, 'The Legal Protection of Foreign Investments against Political Risk: Japanese Business in the Asian Energy Sector', was awarded with the 2013 Arghyrios Fatouros Prize by the International Law Association (Hellenic Branch). He has also been elected Treasurer of the Hellenic Society of International Law and International Relations (2026–2028) and Vice President of the Cyprus–Japan Friendship Association (2025–2026).

ILIAS PLAKOKEFALOS is an Assistant Professor of Public International Law at the School of Political Science and Public Administration of the

University of Athens. He holds an LLB from the University of Essex, an LLM from Tulane University, and a PhD from the National and Kapodistrian University of Athens. He was post-doctoral researcher at the University of Amsterdam (2012–15) and assistant professor at Utrecht University (2015–17). He has worked as an advisor to the Greek government (2017–19) and at the Greek Parliament (2019–23). He is a fellow at Athens Public International Law Center of the Law School of the University of Athens.

ELLEN POLICINSKI is an ICRC legal advisor working on the project to update the Commentaries on the 1949 Geneva Conventions and their 1977 Additional Protocols. She has previously held a number of positions at the ICRC at headquarters and in the field, including editor-in-chief of the *International Review of the Red Cross*, an academic journal produced by the ICRC and published by Cambridge University Press. Prior to joining the ICRC, she worked on the IHL team at the American Red Cross and as a consultant at the Center for Civilians in Conflict. She has an LLM from the Geneva Academy of International Humanitarian Law and Human Rights and a JD from the University of Villanova Charles Widger School of Law.

YANNICK RADI is Professor of Public International Law at the Faculty of Law of UC Louvain and an invited professor at the Hague Academy of International Law. He is also a member of the ICSID Panel of Arbitrators and he is on the List of Trade and Sustainable Development Experts, for dispute settlement panels under EU Trade Agreements. His areas of expertise include State responsibility and the law of treaties, international dispute settlement, international investment law, and sustainable development. He is the author of several publications in these fields, notably *Rules and Practices of International Investment Law and Arbitration*, a textbook published by Cambridge University Press in 2020.

VISHAKHA RAJ is a lawyer from India with a master's degree in international trade and investment law from the World Trade Institute, University of Bern. She is based in Bern and works at Besso AG, a company that leverages artificial intelligence to simplify trade regulations for businesses.

LEILA NADYA SADAT is James Carr Professor of International Criminal Law and long-time director of the Whitney R. Harris World Law

Institute at Washington University School of Law. She has served as the Special Adviser on Crimes Against Humanity to the International Court Prosecutor since 2012 and was a member of the US Commission on International Religious Freedom from 2001 to 2003. In AY 2021, she was a senior research scholar at Yale Law School and is currently a visiting fellow at Yale's Schell Center for Human Rights. Sadat is an authority in the fields of public international law, international criminal law, human rights, and foreign affairs, and has published more than 165 books and articles in leading journals, academic presses, and media outlets throughout the world, including leading casebooks on international criminal law and public international law; a monograph, *The International Criminal Court and the Transformation of International Law: Justice for the New Millenium*, and several edited volumes. Sadat directs the Crimes Against Humanity Initiative, a ground-breaking project launched in 2008 that wrote the world's first global treaty on crimes against humanity and continues to spearhead global efforts to negotiate this important new treaty. Closer to home, she has been working on a project on gun violence and human rights, recently publishing "Torture in Our Schools?" with the *Harvard Law Review*, that addresses the crisis of mass shootings in US schools. She was the first woman to receive the Alexis de Tocqueville Distinguished Fulbright Chair in Paris, France (2011) and received an Honorary Doctorate from Northwestern University as well as the Arthur Holly Compton Faculty Achievement Award from Washington University in 2017. Sadat is the chairwoman of the International Law Association (American Branch), chair of the American Association of Law Schools Section on International Law, and a member of the American Law Institute and the US Council on Foreign Relations. Sadat holds law degrees from Columbia Law School, Tulane Law School, and the University of Paris I – Sorbonne

JURE VIDMAR is Chair of Public International Law at Maastricht University. He is also member of the Permanent Court of Arbitration in The Hague, member of the OSCE Court of Conciliation and Arbitration in Geneva, and serves as Judge ad hoc of the European Court of Human Rights. Prior to coming to Maastricht, he held teaching and research positions at Oxford University, Harvard Law School, University of Amsterdam, and University of Nottingham.

INETA ZIEMELE is a judge of the Court of Justice of the EU since 2020, the former president of the Latvian Constitutional Court, and former judge and section president of the European Court of Human Rights. She is Professor of International Law and Human Rights at the Riga Graduate School of Law (Latvia). Judge Ziemele obtained a law degree from the University of Latvia in 1993, which she supplemented that year by a postgraduate study of the American legal system, the law and politics of the European Communities, and political science (University of Aarhus, Denmark). She went on to obtain a master's degree in international law at the University of Lund (Sweden) in 1994 and completed her studies at Cambridge University, where she received her PhD in law in 1999. She began her professional career as a parliamentary assistant at the Latvian Parliament from 1990 to 1992, before working as a consultant to the Foreign Affairs Committee of the Parliament from 1992 to 1995. She has been an adviser to the prime minister of Latvia in 1995 on issues of international and European law. From 1999 to 2001, she worked at the Directorate General of Human Rights of the Council of Europe in Strasbourg (France). Judge Ziemele's academic career began in 1993. She was first a university assistant in the Legal and Political Theory Department and the International Law and Law of the Sea Department at the University of Latvia. She went on to work as a lecturer in International Law and European Law until 1999. In 1995, she founded the Human Rights Institute at the University of Latvia, of which she was the director also until 1999. In 2001, she was elected to the Söderberg Chair for the purposes of teaching international law at the newly established Riga Graduate School of Law (Latvia). From 2001 to 2005, she also taught at the Raoul Wallenberg Institute at the University of Lund as a visiting professor. In 2025, she was elected full member of the Academy of Science of Latvia to which she contributes through her legal research, resulting in numerous books and articles in international law, constitutional law, and EU constitutional law. She is the founder and co-editor-in-chief of the *Baltic Yearbook of International Law* and the author of one of the leading books in the field, *State Continuity and Nationality: The Baltic States and Russia* (2nd rev. ed., Brill, 2025).

TABLE OF CASES

International Court of Justice

Ahmadou Sadio Diallo (Republic of Guinea v Democratic Republic of the Congo) (Preliminary Objections) [2007] ICJ Rep 582

Ahmadou Sadio Diallo (Republic of Guinea v Democratic Republic of the Congo) (Merits) [2010] ICJ Rep 639

Application of the Convention on the Prevention and Punishment of the Crime of Genocide (Bosnia and Herzegovina v Serbia and Montenegro) (Judgment) [2007] ICJ Rep 43

Application of the Interim Accord of 13 September 1995 (the Former Yugoslav Republic of Macedonia v Greece) (Judgment) [2011] ICJ Rep 644

Application of the International Convention for the Suppression of the Financing of Terrorism and of the International Convention on the Elimination of All Forms of Racial Discrimination (*Ukraine v Russian Federation*) (Judgment) [2024] ICJ Rep 78

- Separate Opinion Judge Iwasawa [2024] ICJ Rep 261
- Separate Opinion Judge Charlesworth [2024] ICJ Rep 270
- Separate Opinion ad hoc Judge Pocar [2024] ICJ Rep 289

Application of the International Convention on the Elimination of All Forms of Racial Discrimination (*Qatar v United Arab Emirates*) (Preliminary Objections) [2021] ICJ Rep 71

- Dissenting Opinion of Judge Robinson [2021] ICJ Rep 146
- Dissenting Opinion of Judge Bhandari [2021] ICJ Rep 133
- Dissenting Opinion Judge Sebutinde [2021] ICJ Rep 117
- Declaration of President Yusuf [2021] ICJ Rep 111

Barcelona Traction, Light and Power Company, Limited (Belgium v Spain) (Judgment) [1970] ICJ Rep 3

Case Concerning Pulp Mills on the River Uruguay (*Argentina v Uruguay*) (Judgment) [2010] ICJ Rep 14

- Joint Dissenting Opinion of Judges Al-Khasawneh and Simma [2010] ICJ Rep 108
- *Case Concerning the Gabčikovo Nagymaros Project (Hungary/Slovakia)* (Judgment) [1997] ICJ Rep 7

- Memorial of the Republic of Hungary [2 May 1994] Vol 1
- Memorial of the Slovak Republic [2 May 1994] Vol 1

Certain Activities Carried Out by Nicaragua in the Border Area (Costa Rica v Nicaragua) and Construction of a Road in Costa Rica along the San Juan River (Nicaragua v Costa Rica) (Judgment) [2015] ICJ Rep 665

- Separate Opinion of Judge Donoghue [2015] ICJ Rep 782

Corfu Channel (United Kingdom v Albania) (Merits) [1949] ICJ Rep 4

East Timor (Portugal v Australia) [1995] ICJ Rep 90

Interpretation of the Agreement of 25 March 1951 between the WHO and Egypt (Advisory Opinion) [1980] ICJ Rep 73

Jurisdictional Immunities of the State (Germany v Italy: Greece intervening) (Judgment) [2012] ICJ Rep 99

Kasikili/Sedudu Island (Botswana/Namibia) (Judgment) [1999] ICJ Rep 1045

LaGrand (Germany v United States of America) (Judgment) [2001] ICJ Rep 466

Legal Consequences arising from the Policies and Practices of Israel in the Occupied Palestinian Territory, including East Jerusalem (Advisory Opinion of 19 July 2024) [101] <www.icj-cij.org/case/186/advisory-opinions>

Legal Consequences of the Construction of a Wall (Advisory Opinion) [2004] ICJ Rep 136

Legal Consequences of the Separation of the Chagos Archipelago from Mauritius in 1965 (Advisory Opinion) [2019] ICJ Rep 95

Legal Consequences for States of the Continued Presence of South Africa in Namibia (South-West Africa) notwithstanding Security Council resolution 276 (1970) (Advisory Opinion) [1971] ICJ Rep 16

Legality of the Threat or Use of Nuclear Weapons (Advisory Opinion) [1996] ICJ Rep 226

Legality of the Use by a State of Nuclear Weapons in Armed Conflict (Advisory Opinion) [1996] ICJ Rep 66

Military and Paramilitary Activities in and against Nicaragua (Nicaragua v United States of America) (Merits) [1986] ICJ Rep 14

North Sea Continental Shelf Cases (Federal Republic of Germany/Netherlands; Federal Republic of Germany/Denmark) (Judgment) [1969] ICJ Rep 3

Obligations of States in Respect of Climate Change (Request for Advisory Opinion) General List No 187 (29 March 2023)

Oil Platforms (Islamic Republic of Iran v United States of America) (Judgment) [2003] ICJ Rep 161

Question of the Delimitation of the Continental Shelf between Nicaragua and Colombia beyond 200 Nautical Miles from the Nicaraguan Coast (Nicaragua v Colombia) (Preliminary Objections) [2016] ICJ Rep 100

Reservations to the Convention on Genocide (Advisory Opinion) [1951] ICJ Rep 15

Right of Passage over Indian Territory (Portugal v India) (Preliminary Objections) [1957] ICJ Rep 125

Territorial Dispute (Libyan Arab Jamahiriya v Chad) (Judgment) [1994] ICJ Rep 6

Arbitration

Abaclat and others (formerly Giovanna A Beccara and others) v the Argentine Republic (Decision on Jurisdiction and Admissibility of 4 August 2011) ICSID Case No ARB/07/5

Abaclat and others v the Argentine Republic (Dissenting Opinion of Georges Abi-Saab to Decision on Jurisdiction and Admissibility of 28 October 2011) ICSID Case No ARB/07/5

Aeroport Belbek LLC and Mr Kolomoisky v Russia ('Aeroport Belbek') (Interim Award Addressing Certain Issues of Jurisdiction and Admissibility of 24 February 2017) PCA Press Release, 9 March 2017

Ambiente Ufficio SPA and others v the Argentine Republic (Decision on Jurisdiction and Admissibility of 8 February 2013) ICSID Case No ARB/08/9

Ambiente Ufficio SPA and others v the Argentine Republic (Dissenting Opinion of Santiago Torres Bernárdez to Decision on Jurisdiction and Admissibility of 2 May 2013) ICSID Case No ARB/08/9

Archer Daniels Midland Company and Tate & Lyle Ingredients Americas, Inc v United Mexican States (Award of 21 November 2007) ICSID Case No ARB(AF)/04/05

Award in Arbitration Regarding the Iron Rhine Railway Between the Kingdom of Belgium and the Kingdom of the Netherlands (Decision of 24 May 2005) 27 RIAA 35

Bayview Irrigation District et al v United Mexican States (Award of 19 June 2007) ICSID Case No ARB(AF)/05/1

Bureau Veritas, Inspection, Valuation, Assessment and Control, BIVAC BV v The Republic of Paraguay (Decision of the Tribunal on Objections to Jurisdiction of 29 May 2009) ICSID Case No ARB/07/9

Burlington Resources Inc v Republic of Ecuador (Decision on Liability of 14 December 2012) ICSID Case No ARB/08/5

Ceskoslovenska Obchodni Banka, as v the Slovak Republic (Decision of the Tribunal on Objections to Jurisdiction of 24 May 1999) ICSID Case No ARB/97/4

CSOB v The Slovak Republic (Decision on Objections to Jurisdiction of 24 May 1999) ICSID Case No ARB/97/4

Deutsche Bank AG v Democratic Socialist Republic of Sri Lanka (Award of 31 October 2012) ICSID Case No ARB/09/2

Deutsche Telekom AG v India (Interim Award of 13 December 2017) PCA Case No 2014-10

Enron Corporation v Argentina (Decision on Jurisdiction of 14 January 2004) ICSID Case No ARB/01/3

Everest Estate LLC et al v Russia ('Everest Estate') (Decision on Jurisdiction of 20 March 2017) PCA Press Release, 9 August 2016

Fedax NV v Republic of Venezuela (Decision on Objections to Jurisdiction on 11 July 1997) ICSID Case No ARB/96/3

Fedax NV v The Republic of Venezuela (Award of 9 March 1998) ICSID Case No ARB/96/3

First Award under the Convention between Costa Rica and Nicaragua of 8 April 1896 for the Demarcation of the Boundary between the two Republics (1897) 28 RIAA 215

Garanti Koza LLP and Turkmenistan (Dissenting Opinion of Laurence Boisson de Chazournes to the Decision on the Objection to Jurisdiction for Lack of Consent of 3 July 2013) ICSID Case No ARB/11/20

Giovanni Alemanni and others v the Argentine Republic (Decision on Jurisdiction and Admissibility of 17 November 2014) ICSID Case No ARB/07/8

Gold Reserve Inc and Bolivarian Republic of Venezuela (Award of 22 September 2014) ICSID Case No ARB(AF)/09/1

Grand River Enterprises Six Nations Ltd v United States of America (Award of 12 January 2011) Arbitral Tribunal (North American Free Trade Agreement Chapter 11)

Impregilo SpA v Argentine Republic (Concurring and Dissenting Opinion of Brigitte Stern to Award of 21 June 2011) ICSID Case No ARB/07/17

International Thunderbird Gaming Corporation v The United Mexican States (Separate Opinion of Thomas Wälde of 1 December 2005 to Award of 26 January 2006) <www.italaw.com/sites/default/files/case-documents/ita0432.pdf>

JSC CB PrivatBank v Russia ('PrivatBank') (Interim Award Addressing Certain Issues of Jurisdiction and Admissibility of 24 February 2017) PCA Press Release, 9 March 2017

Lac Lanoux (Espagne, France) (1957) XII UNRIAA 281

Limited Liability Company Lugzor et al v Russia ('*Lugzor*') (Tribunal's letter dated 29 August 2017) PCA Press Release, 13 December 2017

NJSC Naftogaz of Ukraine, PJSC State Joint Stock Company Chornomornaftogaz, PJSC Ukrgasvydobuvannya and others v The Russian Federation ('Naftogaz') (Award on Jurisdiction and Liability of 22 February 2019) PCA Case No 2017-16

Oschadbank v Russia ('*Oschadbank*') (Judgment of the Paris Court of Appeal dated 30 March 2021)

Philip Morris Brands SARL, Philip Morris Products SA and Abal Hermanos SA v Oriental Republic of Uruguay (*Philip Morris v Uruguay*) (Award of 8 July 2016) ICSID Case No ARB/10/7

PJSC DTEK Krymenergo v the Russian Federation, PCA Case No 2018-41

PJSC Ukrnafta v Russia ('Ukrnafta') (Awards on Jurisdiction of 26 June 2017) PCA Press Release, 4 July 2017

RosInvestCo UK Ltd v The Russian Federation (Award on Jurisdiction of October 2007) SCC Case V 079/2005

Sanum Inv Ltd v Lao People's Democratic Republic (Award on Jurisdiction of 13 December 2013) PCA Case No 2013-13

SGS Société Générale de Surveillance SA v Pakistan (Decision on Objections to Jurisdiction of 6 August 2003) ICSID Case No ARB/01/13

SGS Société Générale de Surveillance SA v Paraguay (Decision on Jurisdiction of 12 February 2010) ICSID Case No ARB/07/29

SGS Société Générale de Surveillance SA v Republic of the Philippines (Decision of the Tribunal on Objections to Jurisdiction of 29 January 2004) ICSID Case No ARB/02/6

Sociedad General de Aguas de Barcelona SA (Agbar) v Argentine Republic (Decision on Jurisdiction of 2 May 2006) ICSID Case No ARB/03/17

Stabil LLC et al v Russia ('Stabil) (Awards on Jurisdiction of 26 June 2017) PCA Press Release, 4 July 2017

Tecnicas Medioambientales Tecmed SA v The United Mexican States (Award of 29 May 2003) ICSID Case No ARB(AF)/00/2

The South China Sea Arbitration (Philippines v China) (Award of 12 July 2016) PCA Case No 2013–19

Total SA v Argentine Republic (Decision on Liability of 27 December 2010) ICSID Case No ARB/04/1

Trail Smelter (United States, Canada) (1941) III RIAA 1905

International Tribunal for the Law of the Sea

Case Concerning Land Reclamation by Singapore in and around the Straits of Johor (Malaysia v Singapore) (Provisional Measures) [2003] ITLOS Rep 10

MOX Plant (Ireland v United Kingdom) (Provisional Measures) [2001] ITLOS Rep 95

Request for an Advisory Opinion Submitted by the Commission of Small Island States on Climate Change and International Law (Advisory Opinion) 21 May 2024 <www.itlos.org/fileadmin/itlos/documents/cases/31/Advisory_Opinion/C31_Adv_Op_21.05.2024_corr.pdf>

Responsibilities and Obligations of States Sponsoring Persons and Entities with Respect to Activities in the Area (Advisory Opinion) [2011] ITLOS Rep 10

International Criminal Court and International Criminal/Military Tribunals

Judgment of the Nuremberg International Military Tribunal of 1 October 1946 (1947) 41 AJIL 172

Prosecutor v Abd-Al-Rahman (Decision on the Defence 'Exception d'incompétence') ICC-02/05-02/20 (17 May 2021)

Prosecutor v Abd-Al-Rahman (Decision on the Defence Appeal against the "Decision on the Defence 'Exception d'incompétence'") ICC-02/05-02/20 (1 November 2021)

Prosecutor v Abd-Al-Rahman (Prosecution's Response to the Defence Appeal against the "Decision on the Defence 'Exception d'incompétence') ICC-02/05-02/20 (29 June 2021)

Prosecutor v Akayesu, (Trial Chamber I Judgment) ICTR-96–4-T (2 September 1998)

Prosecutor v Al Bashir (Pre-Trial Chamber I, Decision on the Prosecution's Application for a Warrant of Arrest against Omar Hassan Ahmad Al Bashir) ICC-02/05–01/09 (4 March 2009)

Prosecutor v Al-Bashir (Written Observations of Professor Claus Kreß as *amicus curiae*, with the Assistance of Ms Erin Pobjie, on the Merits of the Legal Questions presented in 'The Hashemite Kingdom of Jordan's Appeal against the "Decision under Article 87(7) of the Rome Statute on the Non-compliance by Jordan with the Request by the Court for the Arrest and Surrender [of] Omar Al-Bashir of 12 March 2018 (ICC-02/05- 01/09-326)"' ICC-02/05-01/09 OA2 (18 June 2018)

Prosecutor v Anto Furundzija (Judgment) IT-95–17/1-T (10 December 1998)

Prosecutor v Bemba Gombo (Judgment Pursuant to Article 74 of the Statute) ICC-01/05–01/08 (21 March 2016)

Prosecutor v Bosco Ntaganda (Judgment) ICC-01/04-02/06 (8 July 2019)

Prosecutor v Dominic Ongwen (Judgment) ICC-02/04-01/15 (4 February 2021)

Prosecutor v Duško Tadić (Decision on the Defence Motion for Interlocutory Appeal on Jurisdiction) IT-94–1-T (2 October 1995)

Prosecutor v Duško Tadić (Appeal Judgment) IT-94–1-A (15 July 1999)

Prosecutor v Duško Tadić a/k/a/ "Dule" (Decision on the Defence Motion for Interlocutory Appeal on Jurisdiction) IT-94–1-T (2 October 1995)

Prosecutor v Kaing Guck Eav alias Duch (Judgment) 001/18-07-2007/ECCC/TC (26 July 2010)

Prosecutor v Katanga (Judgment Pursuant to Article 74 of the Statute) ICC-01/04–01/07 (7 March 2014)

Prosecutor v Kunarac, Kovac and Vukovic (Appeals Chamber Judgment) IT-96–23/1-A (12 June 2002)

Prosecutor v Kupreškić et al (Trial Chamber Judgment) IT-95–16-T (14 January 2000)

Prosecutor v Lubanga Dyilo (Appeals Chamber, Judgment on the Appeal of Mr Thomas Lubanga Dyilo against the Decision on the Defence Challenge to the Jurisdiction of the Court Pursuant to Article 19 (2)(a) of the Statute of 3 October 2006) ICC-01–04/01–06 (14 December 2006)

Prosecutor v Lubanga Dyilo (Decision on the Admissibility of the Appeal of Mr Thomas Lubanga Dyilo against the Decision of Pre-Trial Chamber I entitled 'Décision sur la confirmation des charges of 29 January 2007') ICC-01/04–01/06 (13 June 2007)

Prosecutor v Milanovic, Sainovic, Ojdanic (Decision on Dragoljub Ojdanic's Motion Challenging Jurisdiction – Joint Criminal Enterprise) IT-05–87-PT (21 May 2003)

Prosecutor v Norman (Decision of Appeals Chamber on Preliminary Motion Based on Lack of Jurisdiction (Child Recruitment) SCSL-2004–14-AR72I (31 May 2004) Dissenting Opinion of Judge Robertson

Prosecutor v Ruto and Sang (Judgment on the Appeal of the Prosecutor against the Decision of Trial Chamber V(a) of 18 June 2013 entitled 'Decision on Mr Ruto's Request for Excusal from Continuous Presence at Trial') ICC-01/09–01/11–1066-Anx (25 October 2013) Joint Separate Opinion of Judge Kourula and Judge Ušacka

Prosecutor v Šainović et al (Appeal Judgment) IT-05–87-A (23 January 2014)

Prosecutor v Tadić (Judgment) IT-94-1-A (15 July 1999)

Request under Regulation 46(3) of the Regulations of the Court (Pre-Trial Chamber I, Decision on the 'Prosecution's Request for a Ruling on Jurisdiction under Article 19(3) of the Statute') ICC-RoC46(3)-01/18 (6 September 2018)

Situation in the Democratic Republic of Congo (Judgment on the Prosecutor's Application for Extraordinary Review of Pre-Trial Chamber I's 31 March 2006 Decision Denying Leave to Appeal) ICC-01/04-168 (13 July 2006)

Situation in the Republic of Kenya (Decision Pursuant to Article 15 of the Rome Statute of the Authorization of an Investigation into the Situation in the Republic of Kenya) ICC-01/09 (31 March 2010)

European Court of Human Rights and European Commission of Human Rights

Al-Saadoon and Mufdhi v the United Kingdom (2 March 2010) Application no 61498/08, ECHR 2010-IL, 61

Belilos v Switzerland (29 April 1988) Series A no 132

Demir and Baykara v Turkey [GC] (12 November 2008) Application no 34503/97

Gürdeniz v Turkey [CC] (18 March 2014) Application no 59715/10

Hassan v the United Kingdom [GC] (16 September 2014) Application no 29750/09, ECHR 2014-V1 1

Ireland v the United Kingdom (19 January 1978) Series A no 25

Kokkinakis v Greece (25 May 1993) Application no 14307/88

Loizidou v Turkey (Preliminary Objections) (25 March 1995) Series A no 310

Loizidou v Turkey [GC] (18 December 1996) Application no 15318/89

MS v Croatia [CC] (2 February 2015) Application no 75450/12

Peraldi v France [CC] (7 April 2009) Application no 2096/05

Soering v the United Kingdom (7 July 1989) Series A no 161

Standard Verlagsgesellschaft mbH v Austria (no 3) [CC] (21 December 2021) Application no 39378/15

Tyrer v United Kingdom [CC] (25 April 1978) Application no 5856/72

Ukraine and the Netherlands v Russia [GC] (25 January 2023) App nos 8019/16, 43800/14 and 28525/20

Valentin Câmpeanu v Romania [GC] (7 July 2014) Application no 47848/08

Court of Justice of the European Union

C-1/96, *R v Maff, Ex parte Compassion in World Farming* (19 March 1998) EU.C:1998:113 [1998] ECR 1-1251

C-104/16 P, *Council v Front Polisario* [GC] (21 December 2016) EU:C:2016:973 [2016] OJ C 111

C-156/21, *Hungary v Parliament and Council* (16 February 2022) ECLI:EU:C:2022:97
C-157/21, *Poland v Parliament and Council* (16 February 2022) ECLI:EU:C:2022:98
C-181/73, *Haegeman v Belgian State* (30 April 1974) EU:C:1974:41 [1974] ECR 449
C-188/23, *Conti 11 Container Schiffahrt II* (21 January 2025) EU:C:2025:26
C-188/88, *NMB v Commission* (10 March 1992) EU:C:1992:114 [1992] OJ C 81/4
C-240/09, *Lesoochrandrske zoskupenie (Slovak Brown Bear)* [GC] (8 March 2011) EU:C:2011:125 [2011] ECR I-1255
C-266/16, *Western Sahara Campaign UK* [GC] (27 February 2018) EU:C:2018:118 [2018] OJ C 142/3
C-284/16, *Achmea* [GC] (6 March 2018) EU:C:2018:158
C-337/95, *Parfums Christian Dior v Evora* (4 November 1997) EU-C:1997:517 [1997] ECR 1-6013
C-344/04, *IATA and ELFAA* [GC] (10 January 2006) EU:C:2006:10 [2006] ECR 1-403
C-366/10, *Air Transport Association of America (ATAA) and Others* [GC] (21 December 2011) EU:C:2011:864 [2012] OJ C 49/7
C-402/05 P and C- 415/05, *P Kadi and Al Barakaat International Foundation v Council and Commission* [GC] (3 September 2008) EU:C:2008:461
C-511/13, *Philips Lighting Poland and Philips Lighting v Council* [GC] (8 September 2015) EU:C:2015:553 [2015] OJ C 263/4
Joined cases 21 to 24/72 International Fruit Company (12 December 1972) EU:C:1972:115 [1972] ECR 1219
Opinion 1/91 (14 December 1991) EU:C:1991:490 [1991] ECR 1-06079 (Opinion pursuant to Article 228 of the EEC Treaty)
Opinion 2/13 Accession of the EU to the ECHR (18 December 2014) EU:C:2014:2454
Opinion 2/15 (16 May 2017) EU:C:2017:376 [2017] OJ C 239/3 (Opinion pursuant to Article 218(11) TFEU)

Inter-American Court of Human Rights and Inter-American Commission of Human Rights

Case of the Kaliña and Lokono Peoples v Suriname (Merits, Reparations and Costs) IACtHR, Series C No 309 (25 November 2015)
Case of the Saramaka People v Suriname (Interpretation of the Judgment on Preliminary Objections, Merits, Reparations and Costs) IACtHR, Series C No 185 (12 August 2008)
Case of the Saramaka People v Suriname (Preliminary Objections, Merits, Reparations and Costs) IACtHR, Series C No 172 (28 November 2007)
Request for an Advisory Opinion Submitted by the Commission of Small Island States on Climate Change and International Law (Advisory Opinion) 21 May 2024 <www.itlos.org/fileadmin/itlos/documents/cases/31/Advisory_Opinion/C31_Adv_Op_21.05.2024_corr.pdf>

African Court on Human and Peoples' Rights and African Commission on Human and Peoples' Rights

Centre For Minority Rights Development and Another v Kenya (25 November 2009) [2009] ACHPR 102, Communication no 276/2003

WTO

WTO Appellate Body Report, *Argentina – Safeguard Measures on Imports of Footwear* (14 December 1999) WT/DS121/AB/R

WTO Appellate Body Report, *Brazil – Export Financing Programme for Aircraft* (2 August 1999) WT/DS46/AB/R

WTO Appellate Body Report, *Brazil – Measures Affecting Desiccated Coconut* (21 February 1997) WT/DS22/AB/R

WTO Appellate Body Report, *Canada – Certain Measures Concerning Periodicals* (30 June 1997) WT/DS31/AB/R

WTO Appellate Body Report, *Chile – Price Band System and Safeguard Measures Relating to Certain Agricultural Products* (23 September 2002) WT/DS207/AB/R

WTO Appellate Body Report, *China – Measures Affecting Imports of Automobile Parts,* (15 December 2008) WT/DS339/AB/R, WT/DS340/AB/R, WT/DS342/AB/R

WTO Appellate Body Report, *China – Measures Affecting Trading Rights and Distributing Services for Certain Publications and Audiovisual Entertainment Products* (21 December 2009) WT/DS363/AB/R

WTO Appellate Body Report, *European Communities – Conditions for Granting of Tariff Preferences to Developing Countries* (7 April 2004) WT/DS246/AB/R

WTO Appellate Body Report, *European Communities – Customs Classification of Frozen Boneless Chicken Cuts* (12 September 2005) WT/DS269/AB/R, WT/DS286/AB/R

WTO Appellate Body Report, *European Communities – Customs Classification of Certain Computer Equipment* (5 June 1998) WT/DS62/AB/R, WT/DS67/AB/R, WT/DS68/AB/R

WTO Appellate Body Report, *European Communities – Measures Affecting Asbestos and Products Containing Asbestos* (12 March 2001) WT/DS135/AB/R

WTO Appellate Body Report, *European Communities – Measures Concerning Meat and Meat Products* (16 January 1998) WT/DS26/AB/R, WT/DS48/AB/R

WTO Appellate Body Report, *European Communities – Regime for the Importation, Sale and Distribution of Bananas – Second Recourse to Article 21.5 of the DSU by Ecuador* (26 November 2008) WT/DS27/AB/RW2/ECU

WTO Appellate Body Report, *European Communities – Regime for the Importation, Sale and Distribution of Bananas – Recourse to Article 21.5 of the DSU by United States* (26 November 2008) WT/DS27/AB/RW/USA

WTO Appellate Body Report, *European Communities – Trade Description of Sardines* (26 September 2002) WT/DS231/AB/R

WTO Appellate Body Report, *European Communities and Certain Member States – Measures Affecting Trade in Large Civil Aircraft* (18 May 2011) WT/DS316/AB/R

WTO Appellate Body Report, *Guatemala – Anti-Dumping Investigation regarding Portland Cement from Mexico* (2 November 1998) WT/DS60/AB/R

WTO Appellate Body Report, *India – Quantitative Restrictions on Imports of Agricultural, Textile, and Industrial Products* (23 August 1999) WT/DS90/AB/R

WTO Appellate Body Report, *Japan – Measures Affecting Agricultural Products* (22 February 1999) WT/DS76/AB/R

WTO Appellate Body Report, *Japan – Taxes on Alcoholic Beverages* (4 October 1996) WT/DS8/AB/R, WT/DS10/AB/R, WT/DS11/AB/R

WTO Appellate Body Report, *Korea – Definitive Safeguard Measure on Imports of Dairy Products* (14 December 1999) WT/DS98/AB/R

WTO Appellate Body Report, *Mexico – Tax Measures on Soft Drinks and Other Beverages* (6 March 2006) WT/DS308/AB/R

WTO Appellate Body Report, *Peru – Additional Duty on Imports of Certain Agricultural Products* (20 July 2015) WT/DS457/AB/R

WTO Appellate Body Report, *Philippines – Taxes on Distilled Spirits* (21 December 2011) WT/DS396/AB/R, WT/DS403/AB/R

WTO Appellate Body Report, *United States – Anti-Dumping Act of 1916* (28 August 2000) WT/DS136/AB/R, WT/DS162/AB/R

WTO Appellate Body Report, *United States – Antidumping Measures on Certain Hot-Rolled Steel Products from Japan* (24 July 2001) WT/DS184/AB/R

WTO Appellate Body Report, *United States – Certain Countries of Origin Labelling (COOL) Requirements* (29 June 2012) WT/DS384/AB/R, WT/DS386/AB/R

WTO Appellate Body Report, *United States – Countervailing Duties on Certain Corrosion-Resistant Carbon Flat Steel Products from Germany* (28 November 2002) WT/DS213/AB/R

WTO Appellate Body Report, *United States – Definitive Anti-Dumping and Countervailing Duties on Certain Products from China* (11 March 2011) WT/DS379/AB/R

WTO Appellate Body Report, *United States – Final Countervailing Duty Determination with Respect to Certain Softwood Lumber from Canada* (19 January 2004) WT/DS257/AB/R

WTO Appellate Body Report, *United States – Import Prohibition of Certain Shrimp and Shrimp Products* (12 October 1998) WT/DS58/AB/R

WTO Appellate Body Report, *United States – Measures Affecting the Cross-Border Supply of Gambling and Betting Services* (7 April 2005) WT/DS285/AB/R

WTO Appellate Body Report, *United States – Measures Affecting the Production and Sale of Clove Cigarettes* (4 April 2012) WT/DS406/AB/R

WTO Appellate Body Report, *United States – Measures Concerning the Importation, Marketing and Sale of Tuna and Tuna Products* (16 May 2012) WT/DS381/AB/R

WTO Appellate Body Report, *United States – Standards for Reformulated and Conventional Gasoline* (29 April 1996) WT/DS2/AB/R

WTO Appellate Body Report, *United States – Subsidies on Upland Cotton* (3 March 2005) WT/DS267/AB/R

WTO Panel Report, *China – Measures Affecting the Protection and Enforcement of Intellectual Property Rights* (26 January 2009) WT/DS362/R

WTO Panel Report, *Dominican Republic – Safeguard Measures on Imports of Polypropylene Bags and Tubular Fabric* (31 January 2012) WT/DS415/R, WT/DS416/R, WT/DS417/R, WT/DS418/R

WTO Panel Report, *European Communities – Measures Affecting the Approval and Marketing of Biotech Products* (29 September 2006) WT/DS291/R, WT/DS292/R, WT/DS293/R

WTO Panel Report, *European Communities – Regime for the Importation, Sale, and Distribution of Bananas, Complaint by Guatemala and Honduras* (22 May 1997) WT/DS27/R/GTM, WT/DS27/R/HND

WTO Panel Report, *European Communities and its member States – Tariff Treatment of Certain Information Technology Products* (16 August 2010) WT/DS375/R, WT/DS376/R, WT/DS377/R

WTO Panel Report, *India – Export Related Measures* (31 October 2019) WT/DS541/R

WTO Panel Report, *Indonesia – Certain Measures Affecting the Automobile Industry* WT/DS54/R, WT/DS55/R, WT/DS59/R, WT/DS64/R

WTO Panel Report, *Russia – Measures Concerning Traffic in Transit* (5 April 2019) WT/DS512/R

WTO Panel Report, *Turkey – Restrictions on Imports of Textiles and Clothing Products* (31 May 1999) WT/DS34/R

WTO Panel Report, *United States – Anti-Dumping Act of 1916, Complaint by Japan* (29 May 2005) WT/DS162/R

WTO Panel Report, *United States – Import Prohibition of Certain Shrimp and Shrimp Products* (15 May 1998) WT/DS58/R

WTO Panel Report, *United States – Measures Relating to Shrimp from Thailand* (29 February 2008) WT/DS343/R

WTO Panel Report, *United States – Origin Marking Requirement* (21 December 2022) WT/DS597/R

Domestic Cases

Cour de Cassation of France, *Arrêt du 24 novembre 2021*, Cass Crim, Pourvoi n° 21-81.344, ECLI:FR:CCASS:2021:CR01269 <www.courdecassation.fr/en/decision/619de43eb458df69d4022a18>

District Court of Jerusalem, *Attorney General of the Government of Israel v Adolf Eichmann* (1968) 36 ILR 18

High Court of Australia, *Commonwealth v Tasmania* (1983) HCA 21 – 158 CLR 1

Israel Supreme Court, *Attorney-General of the Government of Israel v Eichmann* (1962) 36 ILR 277

Supreme Court of France, Criminal Law Chamber, *The Prosecutor v Klaus Barbie* (Judgment of 20 December 1985) 86-92714

Swiss Federal First Civil Law Court, *Russian Federation v PJSC Ukrnafta* (Judgment of 16 October 2018) 4A_396/2017

Swiss Federal First Civil Law Court, *Russian Federation v Stabil LLC* (Judgment of 16 October 2018) 4A_398/2017

US Court of Appeals 2nd Cir, *Chubb Son, Inc v Asiana Airlines* (2000) 214 F 3d 301

US Court of Appeals 2nd Cir, *Eahrlich v American Airlines* (2004) 360 F 3d 366

US Court of Appeals, 11th Cir, *US v Belfast* (2010) 611 F.3d 783

US Supreme Court, *Penn Central Transportation Co v New York City* (1978) 438 US 104

US Supreme Court, *The Antelope* (1825) 23 US 66

TABLE OF INTERNATIONAL TREATIES AND DOCUMENTS

Treaties

1907 Geneva Convention for the Amelioration of the Condition of the Wounded and Sick in Armies in the Field (adopted 6 July 1906, entered into force 9 August 1907) 11 LNTS 440

1920 Statute of the Permanent Court of International Justice (adopted 16 December 1920, entered into force 8 October 1921) 6 LNTS 389

1929 Geneva Convention for the Amelioration of the Condition of the Wounded and Sick in Armies in the Field (adopted 27 July 1929, entered into force 19 June 1931) 118 LNTS 303

1929 Geneva Convention relative to the Treatment of Prisoners of War (adopted 27 July 1929, entered into force 19 June 1931) 118 LNTS 343

1945 Agreement for the Prosecution and Punishment of the Major War Criminals of the European Axis (adopted 8 August 1945, entered into force 8 August 1945) 82 UNTS 279

1945 Charter of the International Military Tribunal in Agreement for the Prosecution and Punishment of the Major War Criminals of the European Axis (signed and entered into force 8 August 1945) 82 UNTS 280

1945 Charter of the United Nations (adopted 26 June 1945, entered into force 24 October 1945) 1 UNTS XVI

1945 Statute of the International Court of Justice (adopted 26 June 1945, entered into force 24 October 1945) 33 UNTS 993

1946 Charter of the International Military Tribunal for the Far East (adopted 19 January 1946, amended 26 April 1946) 4 Bevans 20

1946 Charter of the International Military Tribunal for the Far East (adopted 19 January 1946, entered into force 19 January 1946) 20 TIAS 1589

1949 Geneva Convention (I) for the Amelioration of the Condition of the Wounded and Sick in Armed Forces in the Field (adopted 12 August 1949, entered into force 21 October 1950) 75 UNTS 31

1949 Geneva Convention (II) for the Amelioration of the Condition of Wounded, Sick and Shipwrecked Members of Armed Forces at Sea (adopted 12 August 1949, entered into force 21 October 1950) 75 UNTS 85

1949 Geneva Convention (III) relative to the Treatment of Prisoners of War (adopted 12 August 1949, entered into force 21 October 1950) 75 UNTS 135

1949 Geneva Convention (IV) relative to the Protection of Civilians in Time of War (adopted 12 August 1949, entered into force 21 October 1950) 75 UNTS 287

1959 Treaty between the Federal Republic of Germany and Pakistan for the Promotion and Protection of Investments (signed 25 November 1959; entered into force 28 April 1962) <https://investmentpolicy.unctad.org/international-investment-agreements/treaty-files/1387/download>

1965 Convention on the Settlement of Investment Disputes between States and Nationals of Other States (adopted 18 March 1965, entered into force 14 October 1966) 575 UNTS 159

1968 Convention on the Non-Applicability of Statutory Limitations to War Crimes and Crimes Against Humanity (adopted 26 November 1968, entered into force 11 November 1970) 754 UNTS 73

1969 Vienna Convention on the Law of Treaties (adopted 23 May 1969, entered into force 27 January 1980) 1155 UNTS 331

1973 Convention on International Trade in Endangered Species of Wild Fauna and Flora (adopted 3 March 1973, entered into force 1 July 1975) 993 UNTS 243

1977 Protocol Additional to the Geneva Conventions of 12 August 1949, and relating to the Protection of Victims of International Armed Conflicts (Protocol I) (adopted 8 June 1977, entered into force 7 December 1978) 1125 UNTS 3

1977 Protocol Additional to the Geneva Conventions of 12 August 1949, and relating to the Protection of Victims of Non-International Armed Conflicts (Protocol II) of 8 June 1977 (adopted 8 June 1977, entered into force 7 December 1978) 1125 UNTS 609

1978 Protocol relating to the International Convention for the Prevention of Pollution from Ships, 1973 (adopted 17 February 1978, entered into force 2 October 1983) 1341 UNTS 3

1979 Convention on Long-Range Transboundary Air Pollution (adopted 13 November 1979, entered into force 16 March 1983) 1302 UNTS 217

1979 Convention on the Protection of Migratory Species of Wild Animals (adopted 23 June 1979, entered into force 1 November 1983) 1651 UNTS 333

1982 United Nations Convention on the Law of the Sea (adopted 10 December 1982, entered into force 16 November 1994) 1833 UNTS 3

1985 Vienna Convention on the Protection of the Ozone Layer (adopted 22 March 1985, entered into force 22 September 1988) 1513 UNTS 293

1986 Statutes of the International Red Cross and Red Crescent Movement (adopted 31 October 1986, entered into force 8 November 1986, amended 21 June 2006), reproduced in , ICRC and the International Federation of Red Cross and Red Crescent Societies, *Handbook of the International Red Cross and Red Crescent Movement* (14th edn, ICRC and the International Federation of Red Cross and Red Crescent Societies 2008) 519

1990 Agreement on the Promotion and Protection of Investments between Argentina and Italy (adopted 22 May 1990, entered into force 14 October 1993) <https://edit.wti.org/document/show/5b96aa7a-a6d0-4fa5-be70-660428ddcb86>

1991 Convention on Environmental Impact Assessment in a Transboundary Context (adopted 25 February 1991, entered into force 10 September 1997) 1989 UNTS 309

1991 Convention on Environmental Impact Assessment in a Transboundary Context (adopted 25 February 1991, entered into force 10 September 1997) 1989 UNTS 309

1992 Convention on Biological Diversity (adopted 5 June 1992, entered into force 29 December 1993) 1760 UNTS 79

1992 Convention on the Transboundary Effects of Industrial Accidents (adopted 17 March 1992, entered into force 19 April 2000) 2105 UNTS 457

1992 United Nations Framework Convention on Climate Change (adopted 7 May 1992, entered into force 21 March 1994) 1771 UNTS 107

1994 Marrakesh Agreement Establishing the World Trade Organization (adopted 15 April 1994, entered into force 1 January 1995) 1867 UNTS 154

1994 Marrakesh Agreement Establishing the World Trade Organization (concluded 15 April 1994, entered into force, 1 January 1995) UNTS 1867

1994 Understanding of the Rules and Procedures Governing the Settlement of Disputes (adopted 15 April 1994, entered into force 1 January 1995) 1869 UNTS 401

1995 Agreement Concerning Reciprocal Promotion and Protection of Investments between Turkey and Italy (adopted 22 March1995, entered into force 2 March 2004) <https://edit.wti.org/document/show/4cf0850e-3460-4238-9b9c-f9391198a4fc>

1998 Agreement Concerning the Encouragement and Mutual Protection of Investments between Russia and Ukraine (adopted 27 November 1998, entered into force 27 January 2000) <https://investmentpolicy.unctad.org/international-investment-agreements/treaty-files/2233/download>

1998 Rome Statute of the International Criminal Court (adopted 17 July 1998, entered into force 1 July 2002) 2187 UNTS 3

1998 Rotterdam Convention on the Prior Informed Consent Procedure for Certain Hazardous Chemicals and Pesticides in International Trade (adopted 10 September 1998, entered into force 24 February 2004) 2244 UNTS 337

2003 Singapore-United States, Free Trade Agreement (adopted 6 May 2003, entered into force 1 January 2004) <www.ustr.gov/sites/default/files/uploads/agreements/fta/singapore/asset_upload_file708_4036.pdf>

2004 Stockholm Convention on Persistent Organic Pollutants (adopted 22 May 2001, entered into force 17 May 2004) 2256 UNTS 119

2005 Protocol Additional to the Geneva Conventions of 12 August 1949, and relating to the Adoption of an Additional Distinctive Emblem (Protocol III) (adopted 8 December 2005, entered into force 14 January 2007) 2404 UNTS 261

2010 Colombia-United Kingdom, Bilateral Agreement for the Promotion and Protection of Investments (adopted 17 March 2010, entered into force 10 October

2014) <https://investmentpolicy.unctad.org/international-investment-agreements/treaty-files/3253/download>

2010 Nagoya Protocol on Access to Genetic Resources and the Fair and Equitable Sharing of Benefits Arising from Their Utilization (adopted 29 October 2010, entered into force 12 October 2014) 3008 UNTS 3

2013 Supplemental Arrangement to the Status of Forces Agreement between the United Nations and the Government of the Republic of Mali concerning the Treatment of Individuals Detained and Handed over to the Government of Mali by the United Nations Multidimensional Integrated Stabilization Mission in Mali (MINUSMA) (signed and entered into force 1 July 2013) 2933 UNTS 25

2014 Agreement between the European Union and the Central African Republic Concerning Detailed Arrangements for the Transfer to the Central African Republic of Persons Detained by the European Union Military Operation (EUFOR RCA) in the Course of Carrying out its Mandate, and Concerning the Guarantees Applicable to such Persons [2014] OJ L251/3

2015 Acuerdo de Cooperacion y de Facilitation de las Inversiones Entre la Republica Federativa del Brazil y los Estados Unidos Mexicanos (signed 26 May 2015; entered into force 7 October 2018) <https://investmentpolicy.unctad.org/international-investment-agreements/treaty-files/4718/download>

2015 Paris Agreement (adopted 12 December 2015, entered into force 4 November 2016) 3156 UNTS 79

2016 Agreement Between the Slovak Republic and the Islamic Republic of Iran for the Promotion and Reciprocal Protection of Investments (signed 19 January 2016; entered into force 30 August 2017) <https://investmentpolicy.unctad.org/international-investment-agreements/treaty-files/3601/download>

2016 Comprehensive Economic and Trade Agreement (CETA) between Canada, of the one part, and the European Union and its Member States, of the other part (signed 30 October 2016) <https://investmentpolicy.unctad.org/international-investment-agreements/treaty-files/3593/download>

2018 Agreement Between Canada and the Government of the Republic of Moldova for the Promotion and Protection of Investments (signed 12 June 2018; entered into force 2 May 2020) <https://investmentpolicy.unctad.org/international-investment-agreements/treaty-files/5806/download>

2018 Regional Agreement on Access to Information, Public Participation and Justice in Environmental Matters in Latin America and the Caribbean (adopted 4 March 2018, entered into force 22 April 2021) 3388 UNTS 195

2018 Treaty Between the Republic of Belarus and the Republic of India on Investments (signed 24 September 2018; entered into force 5 March 2020) <https://investmentpolicy.unctad.org/international-investment-agreements/treaty-files/5724/download>

2019 Agreement Between the Government of Hungary and the Government of the Republic of Cabo Verde for the Promotion and Reciprocal Protection of

Investments (signed 28 March 2019; entered into force 2 May 2020) <https://investmentpolicy.unctad.org/international-investment-agreements/treaty-files/5916/download>

2023 Agreement under the United Nations Convention on the Law of the Sea on the Conservation and Sustainable Use of Marine Biological Diversity of Areas beyond National Jurisdiction (adopted 1 August 2023, not yet in force) UN Doc A/77/L.82

2023 Agreement under the United Nations Convention on the Law of the Sea on the Conservation and Sustainable Use of Marine Biological Diversity of Areas beyond National Jurisdiction (adopted 19 June 2023, not yet in force) UN Doc A/CONF.232/2023/4

2023 Ljubljana-The Hague Convention on International Cooperation in the Investigation and Prosecution of the Crimes of Genocide, Crimes Against Humanity, War Crimes and Other International Crimes (adopted 26 May 2023, opened for signature on 14 February 2024, not yet in force) <www.gov.si/assets/ministrstva/MZEZ/projekti/MLA-pobuda/The-Ljubljana-The-Hague-MLA-Convention.pdf>

International Documents

General Assembly & Security Council

UNGA, 'Res 3201 (S-VI): Declaration on the Establishment of a New International Economic Order' (1 May 1974) UN Doc A/RES/S-6/3201

UNGA, ' Res 60/1: 2005 World Summit Outcome' (16 September 2005) UN Doc A/Res/60/1

UNGA, 'Crimes Against Humanity: Draft Written Summary' (11 April 2024) UN Doc A/C.6/78/L.22/Add1

UNGA, 'Crimes Against Humanity: Report of the Secretary-General' (12 January 2024) UN Doc A/78/717

UNGA, 'Declaration on Principles of International Law concerning Friendly Relations and Co-operation among States in accordance with the Charter of the United Nations' (24 October 1970) UN Doc A/RES/25/2625

UNGA, 'Human Rights Defenders - Report of the Special Rapporteur (Margaret Sekaggya) on the Situation of Human Rights Defenders' (28 July 2011) UN Doc A/66/203

UNGA, 'Report of the Preparatory Committee on the Establishment of an International Criminal Court, Volume I' (1996) UN Doc A/51/22

UNGA, 'Report of the Preparatory Committee on the Establishment of an International Criminal Court: Volume 2, Compilation of Proposals' (13 September 1996) UN Doc A/51/22

UNGA, 'Report of the Special Rapporteur in the Field of Cultural Rights, Farida Shaheed: the Right to Enjoy the Benefits of Scientific Progress and its Applications' (14 May 2012) UN Doc A/HRC/20/26

UNGA, 'Report of the Special Rapporteur on the Issue of Human Rights Obligations relating to the Enjoyment of a Safe, Clean, Healthy and Sustainable Environment' (24 January 2018) UN Doc A/HRC/37/59

UNGA, 'Res 3314 (XXIX): Definition of Aggression' (14 December 1974) UN Doc A/RES/29/3314

UNGA, 'Res 60/1: 2005 World Summit Outcome' (16 September 2005) UN Doc A/RES/60/1

UNGA, 'Res 64/292: The Human Right to Water and Sanitation' (28 July 2010) UN Doc A/RES/64/292

UNGA, 'Res 68/262: Territorial Integrity of Ukraine' (27 March 2014) UN Doc A/Res/68/262

UNGA, 'Res 70/1: Transforming Our World: The 2030 Agenda for Sustainable Development' (25 September 2015) UN Doc A/RES/70/1

UNGA, 'Res 76/300: The Human Right to a Clean, Healthy and Sustainable Environment' (1 August 2022) UN Doc A/RES/76/300

UNGA, 'Res 79/122: United Nations Conference of Plenipotentiaries on Prevention and Punishment of Crimes against Humanity' (12 December 2024) UN Doc A/Res/79/122

UNGA, 'Resolutions and Decisions Adopted by the General Assembly During Its 64th Session' (25 December 2009 – 14 September 2010) UN Doc A/64/49 (Vol III)

UNGA, 'Rio Declaration on Environment and Development' (12 August 1992) UN Doc A/Conf.151/5/Rev.1

UNGA, 'Situation of Human Rights Defenders – Report of the Special Rapporteur (Michel Forst) on the Situation of Human Rights Defenders' (3 August 2016) UN Doc A/71/281

UNGA, 'Standing Mandate for a General Assembly Debate When a Veto is Cast in the Security Council' (20 April 2022) UN Doc A/76/L.52

UNGA, 'Transforming our World: the 2030 Agenda for Sustainable Development' (21 October 2015) UN Doc A/RES/70/1

UNGA, 'Workshop on a Convention on the Prevention and Punishment of Crimes Against Humanity: Notes by Secretariat' (19 April 2023) UN Doc A/C.6/77/INF/3

UNSC 'Report of the Secretary-General on the Establishment of a Special Court for Sierra Leone' (4 October 2000) UN Doc S/2000/915

UNSC, 'Final Report of the Commission of Experts Established Pursuant to Security Council Resolution 780 (1992)' (27 May 1994) UN Doc S/1994/674

UNSC, 'Provisional Verbatim Record of the 3217th meeting' (25 May 1993) UN Doc S/PV 3217

UNSC, 'Report of the Secretary-General Pursuant to Paragraph 2 of Security Council Resolution 808' (3 May 1993) UN Doc S/25704

UNSC, 'Report of the Secretary-General Pursuant to Paragraph 5 of Security Council Resolution 955' (13 February 1995) UN Doc S/1995/134

UNSC, 'Resolution 808 adopted by the Security Council at its 3175th Meeting' (22 February 1993) UN Doc S/Res/808

UNSC, 'Resolution 955 adopted by the Security Council at its 3453rd Meeting' (8 November 1994) UN Doc S/Res/955

UNSC, 'Statute of the International Criminal Tribunal for Rwanda' (8 November 1994) UN Doc S/RES/955

UNSC, 'Statute of the International Criminal Tribunal for the former Yugoslavia' (3 May 1993) UN Doc S/25704

International Law Commission

ILC 'Draft Articles on the Law of Treaties with Commentaries' (4 May–19 July 1966) UN Doc A/CN.4/191, reproduced in [1966/II] YBILC 187

ILC, 'Articles on Prevention of Transboundary Harm from Hazardous Activities with Commentaries' [2001/II – Part Two] YBILC 144

ILC, 'Documents of the Second Part of the Seventeenth Session and of the Eighteenth Session Including the Reports of the Commission to the General Assembly' (19 July 1966) UN Doc A/CN.4/SER.A/1966/Add.1

ILC, 'Draft Articles on Prevention and Punishment of Crimes Against Humanity' (29 April – 7 June and 8 July – 9 August 2019) UN Doc A/74/10 reproduced in [2019/II – Part Two] YBILC 23

ILC, 'Draft Articles on Responsibility of International Organizations' (26 April–3 June and 4 July–12 August 2011) UN Doc A/66/10, reproduced in [2011/II – Part Two] YBILC 46

ILC, 'Draft Articles on Responsibility of States for Internationally Wrongful Acts with Commentaries' (23 April–1 June and 2 July–10 August 2001) UN Doc A/56/10, reproduced in [2001/II – Part Two] YBILC 31

ILC, 'Draft Articles on the Effects of Armed Conflicts on Treaties' (26 April–3 June and 4 July–12 August 2011) UN Doc A/66/10, reproduced in [2018/II – Part Two] YBILC 107

ILC, 'Draft Code of Crimes against the Peace and Security of Mankind' (6 May – 26 July 1966) UN Doc A/51/10 reproduced in [1996/II – Part Two] YBILC 15

ILC, 'Draft Code of Crimes against the Peace and Security of Mankind. Titles and Texts of Articles Adopted by the Drafting Committee' (5 July 1989) UN Doc A/CN.4/L.459

ILC, 'Draft Conclusions on Identification and Legal Consequences of Peremptory Norms of General International Law (Jus Cogens), with Commentaries' (2022) UN Doc A/77/10

ILC, 'Draft Conclusions on Identification of Customary International Law, with Commentaries' (30 April–1 June and 2 July–10 August 2018) UN Doc A/73/10, reproduced in [2018/II – Part Two] YBILC 91

ILC, 'Draft Conclusions on Subsequent Agreements and Subsequent Practice in Relation to the Interpretation of Treaties, with Commentaries' (30 April–1 June and 2 July–10 August 2018) UN Doc A/73/10, reproduced in [2018/II – Part Two] YBILC 16

ILC, 'Draft Statute for an International Criminal Court' (2 May–22 July 1994) UN Doc A/49/10 reproduced in [1994/II – Part Two] YBILC 27

ILC, 'Fifth Report on Peremptory Norms of General International Law (*jus cogens*) by Dire Tladi, Special Rapporteur' (24 January 2022) UN Doc A/CN.4/747

ILC, 'First Report on Subsequent Agreements and Subsequent Practice in relation to Treaty Interpretation' (19 March 2013) UN Doc A/CN.4/660, reproduced in [2013/II – Part One] YBILC 51

ILC, 'First Report on Subsidiary Means for the Determination of Rules of International Law by Charles Chernor Jalloh, Special Rapporteur' (13 February 2023) UN Doc A/CN.4/760 ILC Secretariat, 'Memorandum prepared by the Secretariat: Subsidiary Means for the Determination of Rules of International Law' (17 January 2024) UN Doc A/CN.4/765

ILC, 'Fourth Report on Crimes Against Humanity, by Sean D Murphy, Special Rapporteur' (18 February 2019) UN Doc A/CN.4/725

ILC, 'Fourth Report on Subsequent Agreement and Subsequent Practice in Relation to the Interpretation of Treaties, by Georg Nolte, Special Rapporteur' (7 March 2016) UN Doc A/CN.4/694

ILC, 'Fragmentation of International Law: Difficulties Arising from the Diversification and Expansion of International Law: Report of the Study Group of the International Law Commission' (13 April 2006) UN Doc A/CN.4/L.682

ILC, 'Fragmentation of International Law: Difficulties Arising from the Diversification and Expansion of International Law: Report of the Study Group of the International Law Commission' (18 July 2006) UN Doc A/CN.4/L.702

ILC, 'Guiding Principles Applicable to Unilateral Declarations of States Capable of Creating Legal Obligations with Commentaries Thereto' (2006) UN Doc A/61/10, reproduced in [2006/II – Part Two] YBILC 160

ILC, 'Principles on the Allocation of Loss in the Case of Transboundary Harm Arising Out of Hazardous Activities, with Commentaries [2006/II – Part Two] YBILC 56

ILC, 'Report of the International Law Commission on the Work of its 72nd Session' (26 April–4 June and 5 July–6 August 2021) UN Doc A/67/10

ILC, 'Report of the International Law Commission on the Work of its Sixty-third Session' (26 April – 3 June and 4 July 12 August 2011) UN Doc A/66/10, reproduced in [2011/II] YBILC 1

ILC, 'Report of the International Law Commission on the Work of its First Session' (12 April 1949) UN Doc A/CN.4/13 and Corr 1-3 reproduced in [1949/I] YBILC 282

ILC, 'Report of the International Law Commission, Seventy-fourth Session' (24 April – 2 June and 3 July – 4 August) UN Doc A/78/10

ILC, 'Report on the Sixth Session of the Asian-African Legal Consultative Committee (Cairo, February-March 1964) by Eduardo Jiménez de Aréchaga, Observer for the

Commission' (21 May 1964) UN Doc A/C N.4/172, reproduced in [1964/II] YBILC 119

ILC, 'Second Report on Subsequent Agreements and Subsequent Practice in Relation to the Interpretation of Treaties, by Mr Georg Nolte, Special Rapporteur' (26 March 2014) UN Doc A/CN.4/671 124

ILC, 'Second Report on Subsidiary Means for the Determination of Rules of International Law by Special Rapporteur Charles Chernor Jalloh' (30 January 2024) UN Doc A/CN.4/769

ILC, 'Text of the Draft Conclusions on General Principles of Law adopted by the Commission on first Reading' in ILC, 'Report of the International Law Commission on the Work of its Seventy-Fourth Session' (24 April–2 June and 3 July–4 August 2023) UN Doc A/78/10

ILC, 'Text of the Draft Conclusions Provisionally Adopted by the Drafting Committee on First Reading' (12 May 2023) UN Doc A/CN.4/L.982

ILC, 'Third Report on Identification of Customary International Law by Michael Wood, Special Rapporteur' (27 March 2015) UN Doc A/CN.4/682

ILC, 'Third Report on Subsidiary Means for the Determination of Rules of International Law by Special Rapporteur Charles Chernor Jalloh' (29 January 2025) UN Doc A/CN.4/781

ILC, 'Titles and Texts of Draft Conclusions 1 to 3 Provisionally Adopted by the Drafting Committee on the Topic of Subsidiary Means for the Determination of Rules of International Law' (2 June 2023) UN Doc A/CN.4/L.985

International Law Association

ILA, 'Final Report on the Impact of Findings of the United Nations Human Rights Treaty Bodies of the Committee on International Human Rights Law and Practice' (Berlin Conference 2004)

ILA, 'ILA Study Group on the Content and Evolution of the Rules on Interpretation – Final Report' (2020) 79 ILACR 914

Institut de Droit International

Institut de Droit International, 'IV. Délibérations de l'Institut en séances plénières: Quatriéme Question – De l'interprétation de traités' (1956) 46 AIDI 317

Other International Documents

1863 Instructions for the Government of Armies of the United States in the Field (Lieber Code) (24 April 1863) <https://ihl-databases.icrc.org/en/ihl-treaties/lieber code-1863>

1991 Arrangement for the Transfer of Enemy Prisoners of War and Civilian Internees from the Custody of the British Forces to the Custody of the American Forces (31 January 1991) reproduced in P Rowe (ed), *The Gulf War 1990–91 in International and English Law* (Routledge 1993) Appendix I, 348

1991 Memorandum of Understanding on the Application of International Humanitarian Law between Croatia and the Socialist Federal Republic of Yugoslavia (27 November 1991) reproduced in M Mercier, *Crimes without Punishment: Humanitarian Action in Former Yugoslavia* (East Haven 1996) Appendix, Document IV, 196

1998 Comprehensive Agreement on Respect for Human Rights and International Humanitarian Law between the Government of the Republic of the Philippines and the National Democratic Front of the Philippines (16 March 1998)

2004 Treaty Between the Government of the United States of America and the Government of [. . .] concerning the Encouragement and Reciprocal Protection of Investment <https://investmentpolicy.unctad.org/international-investment-agreements/treaty-files/2872/download>

2006 ICSID Arbitration Rules <https://icsid.worldbank.org/sites/default/files/ICSID%20Convention%20English.pdf>

2007 Arrangement for the Transfer of Detainees between the Government of Canada and the Government of the Islamic Republic of Afghanistan (3 May 2007)

2007 Memorandum of Understanding between the Ministry of Defence of the Islamic Republic of Afghanistan and the Ministry of Defence of the Kingdom of Denmark concerning the transfer of persons between the Danish Contingent of the International Security Assistance Force (ISAF) and Afghan authorities (8 June 2005, as amended on 1 May 2007)

2009 Updated European Union Guidelines on Promoting Compliance with International Humanitarian Law (IHL) [2009] OJ C303/12

2011 Arrangement between the Government of Canada and the Government of the United States of America concerning the Transfer of Persons between the Canadian Forces and the US Forces in Afghanistan (18 November 2011)

2013 Arrangement between the Government of the United Kingdom and the Government of the United States of America concerning US support for the Transfer of UK-held Detainees from UK Detention to the Afghan Authorities (2 May 2013)

2015 India Model <https://investmentpolicy.unctad.org/international-investment-agreements/model-agreements>

2017 Colombia Model <https://investmentpolicy.unctad.org/international-investment-agreements/model-agreements>

2019 Morocco Model <https://investmentpolicy.unctad.org/international-investment-agreements/model-agreements>

2022 ICSID Arbitration Rules <https://icsid.worldbank.org/rules-regulations/convention/arbitration-rules/chapter-x-publication%2C-access-to-proceedings-and-non-disputing-party-submissions>

Assembly of States Parties, 'Strengthening the International Criminal Court and the Assembly of States Parties' (9 December 2021) ICC-ASP/20/Res.5 [132] <https://asp.icc-cpi.int/sites/asp/files/asp_docs/ASP20/ICC-ASP-20-Res5-AV-ENG.pdf>

CBD, 'Decision VII/11: Ecosystem Approach' (13 April 2004) UN Doc UNEP/CBD/COP/DEC/VII/11

CBD, 'Decision VII/16: Article 8(j) and Related Provisions' (13 April 2004) UN Doc UNEP/CBD/COP/DEC/VII/16

CBD, 'Decision VIII/28: Voluntary Guidelines on Biodiversity-Inclusive Impact Assessment' (9 January 2006) UN Doc UNEP/CBD/COP/8/27/Add.2

CBD, 'Decision XI/18: Marine and Coastal Biodiversity: Sustainable Fisheries and Addressing Adverse Impacts of Human Activities, Voluntary Guidelines for Environmental Assessment, and Marine Spatial Planning' (5 December 2012) UN Doc UNEP/CBD/COP/DEC/XI/18

CBD, 'Decision XV/4: Kunming-Montreal Global Biodiversity Framework' (19 December 2022) UN Doc CBD/COP/DEC/15/4

CESCR, 'General Comment No 15: The Right to Water (Articles 11 and 12 of the Covenant)' (20 January 2003) UN Doc E/C.12/2002/11

Committee on the Rights of the Child, 'General Comment No 26 on Children's Rights and the Environment with a Special Focus on Climate Change' (22 August 2023) UN Doc CRC/C/GC/26

FAO, 'Voluntary Guidelines for Securing Sustainable Small-scale Fisheries in the Context of Food Security and Poverty Eradication' (adopted at the 31st Session of the Committee on Fisheries, 9-13 June 2014) <https://openknowledge.fao.org/server/api/core/bitstreams/edfffbfc-81e5-4208-a36f-334ff81ac10f/content>

FAO, One Ocean Hub, and Office of the High Commissioner for Human Rights, 'Policy Brief: Applying Coherently the Human Rights-based Approach to Small-scale Fisheries for Achieving Multiple Sustainable Development Goals' (2023) <www.fao.org/3/cc3251en/cc3251en.pdf>

HRC Advisory Committee, 'Impact of New Technologies Intended for Climate Protection on the Enjoyment of Human Rights' (10 August 2023) UN Doc A/HRC/54/47

HRC, 'General Comment No 24, Issues Relating to Reservations Made upon Ratification or Accession to the Covenant or the Optional Protocols thereto, or in Relation to Declarations under Article 41 of the Covenant' (11 November 1994) UN Doc CCPR/C/21/Rev.1/Add.6

HRC, 'Opinion No 83/2021 concerning Ahmed Samir Santawy (Egypt)' (28 January 2022) UN Doc A/HRC/WGAD/2021/83

HRC, 'Opinions adopted by the Working Group on Arbitrary Detention at its Ninety-second Session' (*OHCHR*, 15–19 November 2021) <www.ohchr.org/en/special-procedures/wg-arbitrary-detention/opinions-adopted-working-group-arbitrary-detention/opinions-adopted-working-group-arbitrary-detention-its-92nd-session>

HRC, 'Report of the UN Special Rapporteur (J Knox) on the Issue of Human Rights Obligations relating to the Enjoyment of a Safe, Clean, Healthy and Sustainable Environment' (19 January 2017) UN Doc A/HRC/34/49

HRC, 'Res 5/2: Code of Conduct for Special Procedures Mandate Holders of the Human Rights Council' (8 June 2007) UN Doc A/HRC/RES/5/2

HRC, 'United Nations Declaration on the Rights of Peasants and Other People Working in Rural Areas' (8 October 2018) UN Doc A/HRC/RES/39/12

HRCttee, 'General Comment No 33: Obligations of States Parties under the Optional Protocol to ICCPR' (5 November 2008) UN Doc CCPR/C/GC/33

ICC, 'Amendments to Article 8 of the Rome Statute' (10 June 2010) RC/Res.5

ICRC, 'Preventing and Repressing International Crimes: Towards an 'Integrated' Approach Based on Domestic Practice: Report of the Third Universal Meeting of National Committees for the Implementation of International Humanitarian Law', Vol I (*Czech Red Cross*, 2014) 12 <www.cervenykriz.eu/files/files/cz/nsmhp/setkaniNKMHP.pdf>

ICRC, 'Statement of 8 July 1998 Relating to the Bureau Discussion Paper in Document A/CONF.183/C.1 /L.53' (8 July 1998) UN Doc A/CONF.183/INF/10

IPBES, 'Global Assessment Report of the Intergovernmental Science-Policy Platform on Biodiversity and Ecosystem Services' (2019) <www.ipbes.net/global-assessment>

IPCC, 'Special Report on the Impacts of Global Warming of 1.5°C above Pre-industrial Levels and Related Global Greenhouse Gas Emission Pathways, in the Context of Strengthening the Global Response to the Threat of Climate Change, Sustainable Development, and Efforts to Eradicate Poverty' (2018) <www.ipcc.ch/site/assets/uploads/sites/2/2022/06/SR15_Full_Report_HR.pdf>

Morgera E, Switzer S and Tsioumani E, 'Study into Criteria to Identify a Specialized International Access and Benefit-sharing Instrument, and a Possible Process for Its Recognition' (29 May 2018) UN Doc CBD/SBI/2/INF/17

OECD, 'Resolution of the Council on the Draft Convention on the Protection of Foreign Property' (2025) OECD/LEGAL/0084 <https://legalinstruments.oecd.org/public/doc/242/242.en.pdf>

OECD, 'The Multilateral Agreement on Investment: Draft Consolidated Text' (22 April 1998) OECD Doc DAFFE/MAI(98)7/Rev1

OHCHR, 'Key Human Rights Considerations on the Impact of Seabed Mining' (2023) <www.ohchr.org/sites/default/files/documents/issues/climatechange/information-materials/ohchr-seabed-mining-10-july.pdf>

OHCHR, 'Manual of Operations of the Special Procedures of the Human Rights Council' (11 August 2008) 76 <www.ohchr.org/sites/default/files/Documents/HRBodies/SP/Manual_Operations2008.pdf>

Permanent Mission of Mexico to the United Nations, 'Intervención de México en el debate sobre el Tema 80: "Crímenes de lesa humanidad"' (11 October 2023) <www.un.org/en/ga/sixth/78/pdfs/statements/cah/10mtg_mexico.pdf>

Permanent Mission of Romania to the UN, 'Statement Delivered by Ms Alos Lungu, Legal Adviser' (2 April 2024) <www.un.org/en/ga/sixth/78/pdfs/statements/cah/40mtg_romania_2.pdf>

Permanent Mission of the Republic of Cameroon to the UN, 'Declaration du Cameroun faite par NYANID Zacharie Serge Raoul, PhD, Ministre Plénipotentiaire' (October 2023) <www.un.org/en/ga/sixth/78/pdfs/statements/cah/10mtg_cameroon.pdf>

Permanent Mission of the Republic of Sierra Leone to the UN, 'Statement by HE Mr Amara S Sowa' (12 October 2023) <www.un.org/en/ga/sixth/78/pdfs/statements/cah/11mtg_sierraleone.pdf>

Permanent Mission of the State of Eritrea to the UN, 'Statement Delivered by the Delegation of Eritrea' (11-12 October 2023) <www.un.org/en/ga/sixth/78/pdfs/statements/cah/10mtg_eritrea.pdf>

Permanent Representative of Denmark to the UN, 'Statement on behalf of the Nordic Countries' (April 2024) <www.un.org/en/ga/sixth/78/pdfs/statements/cah/39mtg_nordic_2.pdf>

Preparatory Committee on the Establishment of an International Criminal Court, 'Decisions Taken by the Preparatory Committee at its Session Held from 1 to 12 December, Annex I: Report of the Working Group on Definitions and Elements of Crimes' (18 December 1997) UN Doc A/AC.249/1997/L.9/Rev.1

UN Committee on Economic, Social and Cultural Rights, 'General Comment No 25 (2020) on Science and Economic, Social and Cultural Rights (Article 15(1)(b), (2), (3) and (4) of the International Covenant on Economic, Social and Cultural Rights' (30 April 2020) UN Doc E/C.12/GC/25

UN Conference on the Human Environment, 'Stockholm Declaration on the Human Environment' (5-16 June 1972) UN Doc A/Conf.48/4 and Corr.1

'UN High Commissioner for Refugees Responds to U.S. Supreme Court Decision in Sale *v* Haitian Centers Council' (1993) 32(4) ILM 1215

UN Secretariat, 'Secretary-General's Bulletin: Observance by United Nations Forces of International Humanitarian Law' (6 August 1999) UN Doc ST/SGB/1999/13

UN Secretariat, *Repertory of Practice of United Nations Organs: Supplementary No 10 (2000–2009)*, vol 2, advanced version available at <https://legal.un.org/repertory/art18/english/rep_supp10_vol2_art18.pdf>

UN Secretary-General, 'Survey of International Law in Relation to the Work of Codification of the International Law Commission' (10 February 1949) UN Doc A/CN.4/Rev.1

UN Sixth Committee, 'Comments of the Government of the People's Republic of China Concerning the Draft Articles on Prevention and Punishment of Crimes Against Humanity and the Related Recommendation of the International Law Commission' (*United Nations*, 28 November 2023) <www.un.org/en/ga/sixth/78/cah/china_e.pdf>

UN Sixth Committee, 'Crimes Against Humanity (agenda item 80): Oral Report of the Co-facilitators Ms Anna Pála Sverrisdóttir (Iceland), Mr Nizhan Faraz Bin Rizal

(Malaysia), Mr Edgar Daniel Leal Matta (Guatemala)' (*United Nations*, 5 April 2024) <www.un.org/en/ga/sixth/78/pdfs/english/cah_oral_report.pdf>

UN Sixth Committee, 'Written Comments by the European Union on the International Law Commission's Draft Articles on Prevention and Punishment of Crimes Against Humanity' (*United Nations*, 2023) <www.un.org/en/ga/sixth/78/cah/eu_e.pdf>

UN, 'Step Up: A Joint Commitment by Heads of United Nations Entities to Promote the Right to a Healthy Environment of Children and their Participation in Climate Justice Decision-making at all Levels' (June 2021) <https://wedocs.unep.org/handle/20.500.11822/41648>

UNCTAD, 'The Impact of International Investment Agreements on Foreign Direct Investment: An Overview of Empirical Studies 1998-2004' (IAA Issues Note – Working Draft 2014)

UNCTAD, 'International Investment Agreements: Flexibility for Development' [2000] UNCTAD Series on Issues in International Investment Agreements UNCTAD/ITE/IIT/18

UNECE, 'Decision VII/9 on a Rapid Response Mechanism to Deal with Cases Related to Article 3(8) of the Convention on Access to Information, Public Participation in Decision-making and Access to Justice in Environmental Matters' (18–20 October 2021) UN Doc ECE/MP.PP/2021/CRP.8

UNEP, 'Goals and Principles of Environmental Impact Assessment' (1987) UNEP Resolution GC 14/25

UNEP, 'Guidance Note for United Nations Resident Coordinators & Country Teams: Supporting Governments to better Respect, Promote and Protect Environmental Human Rights Defenders' (*UNEP*, November 2023) <www.unep.org/resources/policy-and-strategy/united-nations-guidance-note-environmental-human-rights-defenders>

UNFCCC, 'Glasgow Climate Pact' (13 November 2021) Decision 1/CMA.3

UNHCR, 'Executive Committee Documentation' (*UNHCR*, 2025) <www.unhcr.org/about-unhcr/governance-and-oversight/executive-committee/excom-plenary-sessions/executive-committee>

UNHRC, 'Res 7/22: Human Rights and Access to Safe Drinking Water and Sanitation' (28 March 2008) UN Doc A/HRC/RES/7/22

World Bank, 'Legal Framework for the Treatment of Foreign Investment: Survey of Existing Instruments – Vol 1' (Progress Report And Background Studies 24, World Bank 1992) <https://documents1.worldbank.org/curated/en/790571468782168106/pdf/multi-page.pdf>

World Bank, 'Development Issues: Presentations to the 41st Meeting of the Development Committee, 1991' (*World Bank*, 1991) <https://documents1.worldbank.org/curated/en/301731468765567295/pdf/multi-page.pdf>

World Commission on Environment and Development, 'Our Common Future' (October 1987) <https://sustainabledevelopment.un.org/content/documents/5987our-common-future.pdf>

WTO, 'Accession of the Russian Federation, Decision of 16 December 2011' (16 December 2011) WT/MIN(11)/24

WTO, 'Analytical Index – Annex 2: Dispute Settlement Understanding, Article 3' (*WTO*, 2023) 10 <www.wto.org/english/res_e/publications_e/ai17_e/dsu_art3_jur.pdf>

WTO, 'Argentina, Schedule of Specific Commitments – Supplement I' (7 May 1997) GATS/SC/4/Suppl.1/Rev.1

WTO, 'Canada, Certification of Modifications and Rectifications of Schedule V' (16 December 1994) WT/LET/536

WTO, 'Canada, Schedule V' (12 May 2020) WT/LET/1469

WTO, 'Summary Record of the Third Meeting' (20 April 2012) WT/MIN(11)/SR/3

ABBREVIATIONS

ACHPR	African Commission on Human and Peoples Rights
ADA	Anti-dumping Agreement
AIDI	Annuaire de l'Institut de Droit International
AJCL	American Journal of Comparative Law
AJIL	American Journal of International Law
AL	letter of allegation
API	Protocol Additional to the Geneva Conventions of 12 August 1949, and relating to the Protection of Victims of International Armed Conflicts (Protocol I) of 8 June 1977
APII	Protocol Additional to the Geneva Conventions of 12 August 1949, and relating to the Protection of Victims of Non-International Armed Conflicts (Protocol II) of 8 June 1977
APIII	Protocol Additional to the Geneva Conventions of 12 August 1949, and relating to the Adoption of an Additional Distinctive Emblem (Protocol III) of 8 December 2005
ARSIWA	Articles on Responsibility of States for Internationally Wrongful Acts
Art(s)	Article(s)
ASIL Proc	American Society of International Law Proceedings of the Annual Meeting
ASIL	American Society of International Law
Aust ILJ	Australian International Law Journal
Aust YBIL	Australian Yearbook of International Law
BBNJ Agreement	Agreement under the United Nations Convention on the Law of the Sea on the Conservation and Sustainable Use of Marine Biological Diversity of Areas beyond National Jurisdiction
BIT	Bilateral Investment Treaty
BYBIL	British Yearbook of International Law

CAN	Climate Action Network
CasWResJIntL	Case Western Reserve Journal of International Law
CBD	Convention on Biological Diversity
CDDH	Steering Committee for Human Rights
CEDAW	Convention on the Elimination of All Forms of Discrimination Against Women
CERD	Convention on the Elimination of Racial Discrimination
CESCR	Committee on Economic, Social and Cultural Rights
CESCR	Committee on Economic, Social and Cultural Rights
CETA	Comprehensive Economic and Trade Agreement
cf	confer
ch	chapter
Ch(s)	chapter(s)
Chinese JIL	Chinese Journal of International Law
CIL	Customary International Law
cir	circuit
CITES	Convention on International Trade in Endangered Species of Wild Fauna and Flora
CJEU/ECJ	Court of Justice of the European Union
ColJTransnatlL	Columbia Journal of Transnational Law
Cornell IntlLJ	Cornell International Law Journal
DePaul LR	DePaul law Review
e.g.	exempli gratia
ECHR	European Convention on Human Rights
ECLI	European Case-Law Identifier
ECLR	European Constitutional Law Review
ECR	European Court Reports
ECtHR	European Court of Human Rights
ed(s)	editor(s)
edn	edition
EFTA	European Free Trade Association
EIA	Environmental Impact Assessment
EJIL	European Journal of International Law
Emory IntlLRev	Emory International Law Review
EP&L	Environmental Policy and Law
ESIL	European Society of International Law
esp	especially
FAO	Food and Agriculture Organisation
FDI	Foreign Direct Investment
FET	Fair and Equitable Treatment
ff	and the following
Fordham IntlLJ	Fordham International Law Journal

FYBIL	Finnish Yearbook of International Law
FYROM	Former Yugoslav Republic of Macedonia
GATT	General Agreement on Tariffs and Trade
GC	Grand Chamber
GCI	Geneva Convention (I) for the Amelioration of the Condition of the Wounded and Sick in Armed Forces in the Field of 12 August 1949
GCII	Geneva Convention (II) for the Amelioration of the Condition of Wounded, Sick and Shipwrecked Members of Armed Forces at Sea of 12 August 1949
GCIII	Geneva Convention (III) relative to the Treatment of Prisoners of War of 12 August 1949
GCIV	Geneva Convention (IV) relative to the Protection of Civilians in Time of War of 12 August 1949
GCRF	Global Challenges Research Fund
Geo LJ	Georgia Law Journal
GPL	General Principles of Law Originating from Domestic Legal Orders
GroJIL	Groningen Journal of International Law
HarvILJ	Harvard International Law Journal
HE	His/Her Excellency
HHRJ	Harvard Human Rights Journal
HILJ	Harvard International law Journal
HLR	Harvard Law Review
Houston JIntlL	Houston Journal of International Law
HRBs	Human Rights Bodies
HRC	Human Rights Council
HRCtee	Human Rights Committee
HRLJ	Human Rights Law Journal
HRLR	Human Rights Law Review
HS	Harmonised System
i.e.	id est
IACtHR	Inter-american Court of Human Rights
Ibid	Ibidem
ICC	International Criminal Court
ICCPR	International Covenant on Civil and Political Rights
ICES	International Council for the Exploration of the Sea
ICESCR	International Covenant on Economic, Social and Cultural Rights
ICISS	International Commission on Intervention and State Sovereignty
ICJ	International Court of Justice

ICJ Rep	International Court of Justice Reports
ICLQ	International & Comparative Law Quarterly
ICLR	International Community Law Review
ICRC	International Committee of the Red Cross
ICSID	International Centre for Settlement of Investment Disputes
ICTR	International Criminal Tribunal for Rwanda
ICTY	International Criminal Tribunal for the former Yugoslavia
IEL	International Environmental Law
IHL	International Humanitarian Law
IHRL	International Human Rights Law
IIA(s)	International Investment Agreement(s)
IJGLS	Indiana Journal of Global Legal Studies
IJHR	International Journal of Human Rights
IJMCL	International Journal of Marine and Coastal Law
ILA	International Law Association
ILARC	International Law Association Conference Reports
ILC	International Law Commission
ILM	International Legal Materials
ILR	International Law Reports
ILS	International Law Studies
IMFTE Charter	Charter of the International Military Tribunal for the Far East
IMLI	International Maritime Law Institute
IMT Charter	Charter of the International Military Tribunal at Nürnberg
IMT(s)	International Military Tribunal(s)
IOLR	International Organizations Law Review
IOs	International Organisations
IPBES	Intergovernmental Science-Policy Platform on Biodiversity and Ecosystem Services
IPCC	Intergovernmental Panel on Climate Change
IRRC	International Review of the Red Cross
ISAF	International Security Assistance Force
IsraelLR	Israel Law Review
ITLOS Rep	International Tribunal of the Law of the Sea Reports
ITLOS	International Tribunal of the Law of the Sea
IYBIL	Italian Yearbook of International Law
JCSL	Journal of Conflict and Security Law
JEL	Journal of Environmental Law

JHRE	Journal of Human Rights and the Environment
JHRP	Journal of Human Rights Practice
JICJ	Journal of International Criminal Justice
JIDS	Journal of International Dispute Settlement
JIntArb	Journal of International Arbitration
JIS	Journal of International Studies
JWT	Journal of World Trade
JYBIL	Japanese Yearbook of International Law
LDCs	Least Developed Countries
LJIL	Leiden Journal of International Law
LNTS	League of Nations Treaty Series
LOSC	United Nations Convention on the Law of the Sea
LPICT	Law and Practice of International Courts and Tribunals
LSI	Law and Social Inquiry
MARPOL	International Convention for the Prevention of Pollution from Ships
MEAs	Multilateral Environment Agreement(s)
MFN	most-favored-nation
MichJIntlL	Michigan Journal of International Law
MINUSMA	United Nations Multidimensional Integrated Stabilization Mission in Mali
MJIL	Melbourne Journal of International Law
MLLWR	Military Law and the Law of War Review
MPEiPro	Max Planck Encyclopedia of International Procedural Law
MPEPIL	Max Planck Encyclopedia of Public International Law
MPYBUNL	Max Planck Yearbook of United Nations Law
NCLR	New Criminal Law Review
NGO(s)	Non-governmental Organisation(s)
NIEO	New International Economic Order
NILR	Netherlands International Law Review
NJCM	Nederlands Juristen Comité voor de Mensen-rechten
NJIL	Nordic Journal of International Law
No	number
Notre Dame LRev	Notre Dame Law Review
NQHR	Netherlands Quarterly of Human Rights
NYBIL	Netherlands Yearbook of International Law
OECD	Organisation for Economic Co-operation and Development
OHCHR	Office of the High Commissioner for Human Rights
OJLS	Oxford Journal of Legal Studies

PCA	Permanent Court of Arbitration
PCIJ	Permanent Court of International Justice
POW	prisoner of war
PYBIL	Polish Yearbook of International Law
QIL	Questions of International Law
RdC	Recueil des Cours de l'Académie de Droit International
RECIEL	Review of European, Comparative and International Environmental Law
RIAA	Reports of International Arbitral Awards
RTA(s)	Regional Trade Agreement(s)
SCC	Stockholm Chamber of Commerce
SCM Agreements	Subsidies and Countervailing Measures Agreements
SCSL	Special Court for Sierra Leone
SDGs	Sustainable Development Goals
SingLR	Singapore Law Review
SPS Agreement	Agreement on the Application of Sanitary and Phytosanitary Measures
Stanford EnvtlLJ	Stanford Environmental Law Journal
STLP	Studies in Transnational Legal Policy
TBT	Technical Barriers to Trade
TED(s)	Turtle Excluder Device(s)
TEL	Transnational Environmental Law
TEU	Treaty on the European Union
TFEU	Treaty on the Functioning of the European Union
TIAS	Treaties and Other International Acts Series
tr	translation
TRIMS	Trade Related Investment Measures
TWQ	Third World Quarterly
UA	Urgent Appeal
UK	United Kingdom
UKRI	UK Research and Innovation
UN	United Nations
UNCTAD	UN Trade and Development
UNEP	United Nations Environmental Programme
UNFCCC	United Nations Framework Convention on Climate Change
UNFSA	UN Fish Stocks Agreement
UNGA	United Nations General Assembly
UNHCR	United Nations High Commissioner for Refugees
Uniform LR	Uniform Law Review
UNSC	United Nations Security Council

UNTBs	United Nations Human Rights Treaty Monitoring Bodies
UNTS	United Nations Treaty Serries
US/USA	United States of America
v	versus
VCLT	Vienna Convention on the Law of Treaties
VJIL	Virginia Journal of International Law
WashUGlobalStudLRev	Washington University Global Studies Law Review
WGAD	UN Working Group on Arbitrary Detention
WHO	World Health Organisation
WTO	World Trade Organization
YaleJIntlL	Yale Journal of International Law
YBIEL	Yearbook of International Environmental Law
YBILC	Yearbook of the International Law Commission
ZaöRV	Zeitschrift für ausländisches öffentliches Recht und Völkerrecht – Heidelberg Journal of International Law
ZöR	Zeitschrift für öffentliches Recht – Austrian Journal of Public Law

Introduction

1

Shifting Landscape of Interpretation in International Law

Sources, Actors, Subject Matters

SOTIRIOS IOANNIS LEKKAS, NINA MILEVA,
AND PANOS MERKOURIS

1.1 Theme of the Volume

Interpretation is part and parcel of every juridical endeavour. In international law, the law and methods pertaining to the process of interpretation continue to vex international legal theory and practice – in fact, increasingly so.[1] The provisions of the Vienna Convention on the Law of Treaties (VCLT) on treaty interpretation reflect three premises that can have broader implications for the practice of interpretation in international law.[2] First, they reinforce the idea that interpretation is, or at least can be, a formal process based on legal rules.[3] Second, this process determines the content of rules that are 'in force' and is thus legally and analytically distinct from the processes of identification, modification,

[1] For an indicative bibliography see, e.g. A Kemmerer, 'Sources in the Meta-Theory of International Law: Hermeneutical Conversations' in S Besson and J d'Aspremont (eds), *The Oxford Handbook on the Sources of International Law* (Oxford University Press 2017) 469, 469.

[2] Vienna Convention on the Law of Treaties (adopted 23 May 1969, entered into force 27 January 1980) 1155 UNTS 331 ('VCLT'), arts 31–33.

[3] E.g. R Gardiner, *Treaty Interpretation* (2nd edn, Oxford University Press 2015) 5; M Villiger, *Commentary on the 1969 Vienna Convention on the Law of Treaties* (Martinus Nijhoff 2009) 424; more generally, e.g. A Bianchi, 'Textual Interpretation and (International) Law Reading: The Myth of (In)determinacy and the Genealogy of Meaning' in PHF Bekker, R Dolzer, and M Waibel (eds), *Making Transnational Law Work in the Global Economy – Essays in Honour of Detlev Vagts* (Cambridge University Press 2010) 34, 35.

amendment, and termination of rules.[4] Third, these legal rules can have a general scope of application in the sense that they can apply regardless of the nature or subject matter of the rule to be interpreted and irrespective of who performs the interpretation. That is to say, the VCLT envisages the possibility of a law of interpretation that forms essentially 'a unity'.[5]

At the same time, the process of interpretation in international law takes place within a diverse and constantly evolving doctrinal, epistemological, and institutional landscape. From a doctrinal perspective, whilst the process of interpretation has a formally articulated role and content in the law of treaties, its operation within, and interplay with, the broader theory of sources of international law remains largely underexplored and unsystematised.[6] For instance, the relatively recent works of the International Law Commission (ILC) on customary international law and general principles of law purport to focus exclusively on the identification of rules of unwritten international law without any systematic guidance about how to interpret these rules once identified.[7] In the works of the ILC, rules of interpretation with respect to rules emanating from sources other than treaties remain underdeveloped,[8] notwithstanding the fact that the ILC has alluded to the existence of such rules for all sources

[4] *Compare* art 31(1) VCLT *with* Part II, IV, and V VCLT; see e.g. ILA, 'ILA Study Group on the Content and Evolution of the Rules on Interpretation – Final Report' (2020) 79 ILACR 914, 916.

[5] ILC 'Draft Articles on the Law of Treaties with Commentaries' (4 May–19 July 1966) UN Doc A/CN.4/191, reproduced in [1966/II] YBILC 187, 220 [8]; ILC, 'Draft Conclusions on Subsequent Agreements and Subsequent Practice in Relation to the Interpretation of Treaties, with Commentaries' (30 April–1 June and 2 July–10 August 2018) UN Doc A/73/10, reproduced in [2018/II – Part Two] YBILC 25, 29–30 [15]; see also e.g. J Crawford, *Brownlie's Principles of Public International Law* (9th edn Oxford University Press 2019) 356.

[6] E.g. P Merkouris, *Interpretation of Customary International Law – Of Methods and Limits* (Brill 2024) 1–2.

[7] ILC, 'Draft Conclusions on Identification of Customary International Law, with Commentaries' (30 April–1 June and 2 July–10 August 2018) UN Doc A/73/10, reproduced in [2018/II – Part Two] YBILC 91, 122 ff; ILC, 'Text of the Draft Conclusions on General Principles of Law adopted by the Commission on first Reading' in ILC, 'Report of the International Law Commission on the Work of its Seventy-Fourth Session' (24 April–2 June and 3 July–4 August 2023) UN Doc A/78/10 [40].

[8] ILC, 'Guiding Principles Applicable to Unilateral Declarations of States Capable of Creating Legal Obligations with Commentaries Thereto' (2006) UN Doc A/61/10, reproduced in [2006/II – Part Two] YBILC 160, 173 ff, Guiding Principle 7 and accompanying commentary; ILC, 'Draft Conclusions on Identification and Legal Consequences of Peremptory Norms of General International Law (Jus Cogens), with Commentaries' (2022) UN Doc A/77/10, Draft Conclusion 20 and accompanying commentary.

of international law.[9] In this context of uncertainty, the question arises whether the process of interpretation constitutes 'a unity' regardless of the source of the rule to be interpreted or, inversely, whether there are principled reasons for diversification.

In parallel, a well-recorded tendency in the development of international law is the emergence and increased sophistication of specialised rules or bodies of rules, institutions, and spheres of legal practice, such as international 'trade', 'investment', 'criminal', 'human rights', 'humanitarian', or 'environmental' law and their accompanying bureaucracies or constituencies.[10] In this context, there is certainly the risk for international legal theory and practice to be sliced up into specialised areas of knowledge and expertise in which interpretative practices are tailored to cater to specialised audiences with special interests and ethos.[11] Besides, new challenges emerging from political shifts, unforeseen catastrophes, or technological advancements also invite further reflection on the content of existing law of interpretation and its limitations. Still, even within this complex epistemological and institutional landscape, the authority of interpretative claims often hinges on the premise that such claims are based on a limited set of permissible reasons at the exclusion of other reasons.[12] When multiple actors or institutions compete for interpretative authority over a specified set of rules or when multiple legal regimes intersect in light of a specific situation, there is a strong disincentive to use interpretative arguments or base interpretative decisions on special methods or styles of interpretation designed to fit only a specific audience or a specific case.[13] More generally, whilst the goals or

[9] ILC, 'Draft Conclusions on Identification and Legal Consequences of Peremptory Norms . . .' (n 8) Draft Conclusion 20 and commentary [5]; ILC, 'Text of the Draft Conclusions . . .' (n 7) Draft Conclusion 11(3) and accompanying commentary.

[10] E.g ILC, 'Fragmentation of International Law: Difficulties Arising from the Diversification and Expansion of International Law: Report of the Study Group of the International Law Commission' (13 April 2006) UN Doc A/CN.4/L.682 [8].

[11] J Pauwelyn and M Elsig, 'The Politics of Treaty Interpretation' in JL Dunoff and MA Pollack (eds), *Interdisciplinary Perspectives on International Law and International Relations – The State of the Art* (Cambridge University Press 2013) 445, 467–68; for the broader point, M Koskenniemi, 'The Politics of International Law – 20 Years Later' (2009) 20 EJIL 1, 9.

[12] I Venzke, 'Sources in Interpretation Theories: The International Law-Making Process' in S Besson and J d'Aspremont (eds), *The Oxford Handbook on the Sources of International Law* (Oxford University Press 2017) 401, 406. See also L Lo Giacco, *Judicial Decisions in International Law Argumentation* (Hart 2022) 41-57.

[13] E Bjorge, 'The Convergence of the Methods of Treaty Interpretation: Different Regimes, Different Methods of Interpretation?' in M Andenas and E Bjorge (eds), *A Farewell to*

considerations that guide the process of interpretation may differ in whole or in part in each field of international law or may change through time, normative and practical reasons might militate in favour of at least a common frame of reference.

Against this background, the edited volume maps out current trends in the practice of interpretation in international law. The contributions in the volume are the outcome of the conference *The Practice of Interpretation in International Law* that took place in December 2022 in the Hague. The overarching question the volume addresses is whether and, if so, to what extent the international practice of interpretation points to the existence of a unified law of interpretation that applies to all legal rules irrespective of their source and content. The volume is particularly concerned with identifying points of unity and diversity between, on the one hand, the methods of treaty interpretation codified in the VCLT and, on the other hand, the methods employed to interpret rules emanating from other sources of international law. Furthermore, the volume aims at uncovering whether patterns of similarity or difference can be extrapolated from interpretation as practiced by different actors and across different subject matters. Finally, the volume is also aimed at uncovering evidence of the evolution of rules or methods of interpretation or the field of interpretation as a whole.

1.2 Practice of Interpretation in International Law: Sources, Actors, Subject Matters

The edited volume aims to identify points of unity or diversity in the process of interpretation of international law and to track its evolution over time. Across its diverse chapters, the nature and function(s) of the process of interpretation, as well as the methods and means, reflected in the provisions of the VCLT serve as a point of reference for comparison but also as an object of critique.[14] As a preliminary point, the chapters of this volume bring together contributions by authors from diverse professional backgrounds and subject matter expertise. However, subject matter is only one out of multiple factors that bear on the content and

Fragmentation: Reassertion and Convergence in International Law (Cambridge University Press 2015) 498, 534.

[14] D Peat and M Winsdor, 'Playing the Game of Interpretation: On Meaning and Metaphor in International Law' in A Bianchi, D Peat, and M Winsdor (eds), *Interpretation in International Law* (Oxford University Press 2015) 3, 3.

configuration of the process of interpretation in international legal practice. During the editorial process, it became apparent that some contributions can be understood as instantiations of broader ambiguities as to the role of interpretation within the practice of sources of international law or the configuration and composition of interpretative communities in international legal practice, notwithstanding their apparent focus on a specialised area of international legal practice and expertise.[15] Based on these observations, the edited volume is organised along three parts, each dealing with different forces that drive the practice of interpretation towards unity, diversity, and evolution: sources, actors, and subject matters, respectively.

Part I: Unity, Diversity, and Evolution of Interpretation across Sources of International Law

A force that drives the evolution of interpretation in the practice of international law is its multifarious and interdependent relationship with the rules comprising the theory of sources of international law. In the context of treaty interpretation, the VCLT rules coexist alongside methods, maxims, and practices that might not fit neatly into the means and methods of interpretation envisaged in the VCLT or might expose real or apparent blind spots in those rules. Equally, the fact that interpretation is a process legally and analytically distinct from the process of identification does not mean that it operates in clinical isolation from the broader theory of sources of international law.[16] Interpretation presupposes identification: how practice approaches one process necessarily has ripple effects on the other. On the one hand, interpretation has the capacity to alleviate (or amplify) the challenges posed by the piecemeal formation of international law, such as norm-conflict or legal incompatibility or uncertainty.[17] On the other hand, differences in the process of

[15] For a similar framework of 'substantive', 'institutional', and 'methodological' fragmentation, see M Andenas and E Bjorge, 'Introduction: From Fragmentation to Convergence in International Law' in M Andenas and E Bjorge (eds), *A Farewell to Fragmentation: Reassertion and Convergence in International Law* (Cambridge University Press 2015) 1, 4–12.

[16] E.g. DB Hollis, 'Sources in Interpretation Theories: An Interdependent Relationship' in S Besson and J d'Aspremont (eds), *The Oxford Handbook on the Sources of International Law* (Oxford University Press 2017) 422, 423–24.

[17] See, e.g., ILC, 'Draft Conclusions on Identification of Customary International Law . . .' (n 7) Commentary to Conclusion 2 [5]; 'ILC, 'Draft Conclusions on Identification and Legal Consequences of Peremptory Norms . . .' (n 8) Draft Conclusion 20; ILC, 'Text of the Draft Conclusions . . .' (n 7) Draft Conclusion 11(3).

identification of rules of international law, like their unwritten nature, might militate for differentiation in terms of the process of interpretation as well, such as the unavailability of certain means of interpretation.[18] The contributions in this part draw upon these broader themes.

In the opening contribution of this part (Chapter 2), Jure Vidmar reflects on the role of general principles of law, *jus cogens*, and *erga omnes* obligations in the practice of interpretation of international law. Vidmar starts from the premise that international law formation through treaties and customary international law is inherently based on a private law paradigm characterised by bilateralism and consensualism. For the most part, this private law paradigm permeates into the process of interpretation as reflected in Articles 31–33 VCLT. That said, the principle of 'systemic integration' enshrined primarily in Article 31(3)(c) VCLT and its customary counterpart presumes a systemic structure of international law. In this context, obligations *erga omnes*, *jus cogens* norms, and, to some extent, general principles of law provide for at least a rudimentary public law framework, which dilutes consensualism and enables a certain degree of systematisation of treaty and customary law. Such systematisation then takes places through the process of interpretation and, more specifically, systemic integration. Underlying Vidmar's analysis is the claim that the rule of interpretation requires the systemic integration of the rules of international law 'regardless of the source from which these rules may be stemming'.[19]

In Chapter 3, Yannick Radi similarly examines practices of interpretation across different sources of international law, with a focus on the interpretation of international investment agreements (IIAs). In this chapter, Radi posits that international investment law is a regime in search of its identity. At the core of this search, a central role is played by 'comparativism' (or comparative reasoning) as a method of interpretation employed by investment tribunals. The chapter explores how comparative reasoning fits into the theory of sources and how this method is used by arbitral tribunals to convince their audience. Radi finds that arbitral tribunals regularly rely on customary international law, general principles of law, as well as previous judicial decisions, when interpreting IIAs provisions. However, in doing so, arbitral tribunals display a selectivity in the choice of domestic rules or systems considered for this purpose. Relatedly, when relying on previous judicial decisions, they do not always enquire sufficiently into the similarity (or lack

18 See, e.g., Merkouris (n 6) 82 (Guiding Principle 9(1)).
19 See Jure Vidmar (Chapter 2) in this volume.

thereof) between the past judicial decisions and the present issue at hand. As these trends raise issues from the standpoint of legitimacy, Radi observes that arbitral tribunals rely on comparative reasoning to strengthen or justify the choices made in the course of interpretation.

Finally, in Chapter 4, Ilias Plakokefalos focuses on the interpretation of customary international environmental law (IEL) before international courts. Through a study of the jurisprudence of the International Court of Justice (ICJ), Plakokefalos shows that the range of methods that courts can use for the interpretation of customary law is in principle no different than that applicable to other sources of international law and that these methods roughly correspond to those enumerated in Articles 31–33 VCLT. At the same time, the question is raised whether all these methods are suitable to the interpretation of customary rules of IEL. Plakokefalos submits that it is difficult, and perhaps even fruitless, to interpret customary environmental rules by reference to their object and purpose, given the multiple (at times even contrasting) objects and purposes that these rules can have. This is the main reason why most environmental rules have by their inception an inherent constraint with regard to teleological interpretation as they yield to a number of considerations beyond simply the protection of the environment. Against this background, Plakokefalos finds that international courts and tribunals have interpreted customary environmental rules in expansive as well as regressive ways, oscillating between these two tendencies. When interpreting expansively, courts take into account developments that appear to affect the rule in question and push it to an interpretive point where it catches up with these developments. In contrast, regressive interpretation involves a backward looking approach where the courts are content with offering an interpretation that diverges from the standards surrounding the rule and renders a more conservative version of it.

Part II: Unity, Diversity, and Evolution of Interpretation of International Law across Actors

It is often said that the best way to learn about the art of interpretation in international law is to look at the practice of international courts and tribunals.[20] Undeniably, the practice of international courts and tribunals, especially the Permanent Court of International Justice (PCIJ) and

[20] M Waibel, 'Demystifying the Art of Interpretation' (2011) 22 EJIL 571, 572; M Wood, 'Foreword to the First Edition' in Gardiner (n 3) xvi.

the ICJ, has been instrumental for the codification of rules of interpretation for treaties and unilateral acts.[21] In this context, one of the most theorised aspects of the formal approach towards interpretation in international law has been the extent to which such rules can have a *limitative* function, that is, influencing actors to arrive at certain interpretative conclusion.[22] However, an often neglected aspect of rules of interpretation in international law is their *enabling* function: they specify *how* international law will be interpreted without posing any restrictions as to *who* will interpret them.[23] As a result, a variety of actors including international organisations, expert bodies, or non-governmental organisations can raise claims about the meaning of international law and, in this way, contribute to the development of international law.[24] The contributions included in this part zoom into the neglected interpretative practice of actors besides international courts and tribunals. How do these interpretative practices feed into the evolution of the process of interpretation, and do they drive it towards unity or diversification?

This part kicks off with Chapter 5 by Catherine Brölmann, dedicated to the interpretation of customary international law (CIL) in an institutional context. The 'institutional context' in this chapter refers to the institutional environment of an international intergovernmental organisation, and the chapter focuses on the interpretation of CIL by international organisations. Brölmann maps all the different scenarios when the institutional context is relevant in the interpretation of customary international law, including: (i) instances of an organisation applying and interpreting CIL on par with other international actors; (ii) instances when the interpretation of organisations contributes to the formation of

[21] See, e.g. commentaries to ILC's draft articles on interpretation that contain almost exclusively references to PCIJ and ICJ judgments: ILC 'Draft Articles on the Law of Treaties with Commentaries' (n 5) 217–26 (at fns 125–56); similarly, ILC, 'Guiding Principles Applicable to Unilateral Declarations . . .' (n 8) 164–65 (fns 920–26).

[22] E.g. ILC, 'Draft Articles on the Law of Treaties . . .' (n 5) 218–19 (para. 5); Institut de Droit International, 'IV. Délibérations de l'Institut en séances plénières: Quatriéme Question – De l'interprétation de traités' (1956) 46 AIDI 317, 321; U Linderfalk, 'Is Treaty Interpretation an Art or a Science? International Law and Rational Decision Making' (2015) 26 EJIL 169 ff; G Hernández, 'Law's Determinability: Indeterminacy, Interpretative Authority, and the International Legal System' (2022 69 NILR 191 ff; D Peat, 'Disciplining Rules? Compliance, the Rules of Interpretation, and the Evaluative Dimension of Articles 31 and 32 of the VCLT' (2022) 69 NILR 221 ff.

[23] See e.g. arts 31–33 VCLT.

[24] I Ventzke, *How Interpretation Makes International Law: On Semantic Change and Normative Twists* (Oxford University Press 2012) 16.

customary law; (iii) instances when international organisations apply and interpret CIL within their institutional order; and (iv) instances when soft law produced by international organisations co-creates customary international law. Based on the overview of these different scenarios, Brölmann draws a number of tentative conclusions about the interpretative practice of international organisations. Firstly, the separate institutional sphere of an organisation adds a layer of normativity and authority next to that of general international law. Therefore, it may happen that instruments created by the organisation would have normative effect within the institutional framework but not per se in general international law. Conversely, a rule of customary international law could be of uncontested validity but not have automatically normative force within the institutional framework. Secondly, within the institutional framework, conduct of the organisation may not be readily distinguishable from the conduct of member states. This may then influence the identification of potentially new customary rules. Finally, it seems that the institutional context is conducive to the teleological method of interpretation. Brölmann traces this trend both in the interpretation of constitutive treaties and customary rules.

In Chapter 6 by Ellen Polcinski, we find an overview of the interpretative practice of yet another international actor – the International Committee of the Red Cross (ICRC). In her chapter, Polcinski positions the ICRC as the 'guardian' of international humanitarian law and treats the Commentaries to the Geneva Conventions produced by the ICRC as authoritative guidance on how these treaties are to be interpreted. Thus, in Polcinski's analysis, the ICRC represents an actor whose interpretation is authoritative on its substantive merit. Chapter 5 studies the interpretative methodology behind the Commentaries of the ICRC, eventually concluding that although the methodology has evolved, it has done so apace with the evolution of the rules of treaty interpretation in general public international law – culminating in the adoption of the VCLT. Polcinski considers this as decisive proof that the rules of international humanitarian law (IHL) are subject to the same interpretive rules as other international rules. A further observation that may be drawn from her analysis is that the use of the general rules of interpretation by the ICRC – an actor who is not formally bound by these rules – points to a broader systemic feature of interpretation in international law.

Continuing in a similar vein, Chapter 7 by Marlies Hesselman analyses the interpretative practice of Human Rights Bodies (HRBs). HRBs in this context refer to the human rights supervisory bodies established by the nine core human rights treaties. Their interpretative practice considered in the chapter includes the consideration of individual or inter-State complaints, periodic State reports, and the more general guidance provided by these bodies on the content of treaty norms (e.g. General Comments). At the outset of her analysis, Hesselman notes that when engaging in interpretation, HRBs may follow specific methods of treaty interpretation – including those derived from Articles 31–32 VCLT – or not. However, Hesselman's analysis goes one step further and examines how the interpretative pronouncements of HRBs are themselves considered as authoritative in the subsequent interpretation of treaties or other sources of international law. This is done under the framework of 'pronouncements of expert bodies', as examples of either subsequent practice in the interpretation of treaties within the meaning of Articles 31–32 VCLT, or as 'subsidiary means' for the determination of rules of international law in the sense of Article 38 ICJ Statute. Hesselman concludes that, given the expertise and volume of interpretative pronouncements of HRBs, they need to be taken seriously when it comes to the determination of content of human rights rules. However, at present it is not yet clear whether these pronouncements can be relied on as means of interpretation via the formal avenues available in international law.

Finally, Part II concludes with Chapter 8 by Elisa Morgera, dedicated to the collective interpretative practices of non-judicial actors. In her analysis, Morgera relies on the example of the *One Ocean Hub*, an inter- and transdisciplinary ocean research network that engages academic and non-academic stakeholders, including local decision-makers and representatives from international organisations, civil society, and affected communities, to co-develop mutually supportive interpretations of international environmental law, the law of the sea, and international human rights law. Morgera argues that the interpretative practice of the One Ocean Hub related to the protection of human rights that are dependent on a healthy ocean is an example of collective interpretation whose authority comes from the expertise of the involved practitioners. She examines how this interpretative practice can be institutionalised under the law of treaties, with a view to embedding it in the work of relevant treaty bodies.

Part III: Unity, Diversity, and Evolution of Interpretation across Subject Matters of International Law

A necessary corollary of a formal approach to interpretation is that rules of interpretation, like any other legal rule, are amenable to evolution by being themselves subject to interpretation, amendment, or displacement by other rules of interpretation. The diversification of international legal practice into distinct areas of knowledge and expertise based on subject matter can potentially pose a destabilising effect. In the context of treaty interpretation, the almost unanimous acceptance of the VCLT rules in legal practice does not necessarily entail that they are the final or even clear word on the matter. On the one hand, the entrenchment of interpretative practices along the lines of subject matter expertise is often expressed as a distinctive understanding of the internal relationship between the means of treaty interpretation envisaged in Articles 31–33 VCLT.[25] On the other hand, specific regimes might lay down special rules of interpretation that bring to the fore the external relationship of the VCLT with such special rules. This part draws upon these broader themes.

Part III opens with Chapter 9 by Gabrielle Marceau, Maria George, and Vishakha Raj, analysing the application of the general rules of interpretation in the Dispute Settlement System (DSS) of the World Trade Organization (WTO). In their contribution, Marceau, George, and Raj analyse the 'principle of single undertaking' as a unique feature in the WTO context and reflect on the effect of this principle on the interpretative practice in the WTO DSS. The 'single undertaking' here refers to the fact that the WTO treaty comprises several agreements all of which bind WTO members simultaneously and cumulatively, thus requiring implementation as a single undertaking. Marceau, George, and Raj argue that to maintain coherence within this single undertaking, the WTO DSS has engaged in horizontal cross-fertilisation of jurisprudence across agreements. This, they conclude, is done by reliance on the tools and methods of treaty interpretation as defined by the VCLT rules of interpretation and their customary counterparts.

Continuing in a similar vein, Chapter 10 by Thomas Nektarios Papanastasiou focuses on the interpretation practice of international investment tribunals, using the territoriality requirement in international investment arbitration as a case study. Papanastasiou identifies various interpretative methods that international investment tribunals employ when interpreting the scopes *ratione loci* and *ratione materiae* of investment treaties. In doing so, he finds that on many occasions arbitral tribunals use methods interpretation that favour the object and purpose of treaties over other elements of interpretation envisaged in Articles

[25] See, e.g., ILC, 'Draft Conclusions on Subsequent Agreements and Practice in Relation to the Interpretation of Treaties' (n 5) 29–30 (para 15).

31–33 of the VCLT. When applied to the interpretation of the territoriality requirement, Papanastasiou finds that arbitral tribunals interpret the requirement based on the intention of the contracting parties to create favourable conditions for the promotion of investments and economic cooperation. Such an interpretive approach creates an expansive tendency of the territorial application of investment treaties.

In Chapter 11, Olympia Bekou turns to the examination of international criminal law and the interpretative practice with respect to the Rome Statute of the International Criminal Court (ICC). Interestingly, in Bekou's chapter, interpretative practice refers to the adoption of national legislation implementing the Rome Statute in national legal orders. In the process of national implementation, Bekou argues, states offer their interpretation of the Rome Statute. Her analysis is then focused on the interface between national implementation as interpretation by states and the interpretation of the Rome Statute by the ICC. In particular, Bekou examines instances when these two interpretations of the Rome Statute diverge, with a view to determining how divergent interpretations by states might influence the way the ICC interprets the Rome Statute. As an international treaty, the interpretation of the Rome Statute is governed by the rules of interpretation as enshrined in the VCLT. Against this background, Bekou identifies several different ways in which the divergent interpretations of the Statute by states might need to be taken into account by the ICC when it interprets the Statute (e.g. as subsequent agreement within the meaning of Article 31(3)(b) of the VCLT). Ultimately, Bekou concludes that while it remains necessary to distinguish between an interpretation within the scope of the existing law and modification of the text of a treaty, judges of the ICC may rely on the VCLT rule of interpretation in order to account for the interpretative practice of states.

Finally, in Chapter 12 Leila Sadat reflects on the development of crimes against humanity in international law and the interpretative approaches of states in this process. Sadat provides a detailed genealogy of the development of the crime, from its nineteenth-century natural law origins through its codification in the Rome Statute and finally its possible recodification in a new treaty. She then traces the interpretative approaches of states towards the current draft proposal about a specialised treaty, ultimately concluding that states' attitudes may fall into one of three categories – unity, evolution, or diversity. Unity refers to states who advocate for the new treaty to be a horizontal add on to the Rome Statute, making the two instruments consistent as a matter of text and application. Evolution refers to states who advocate for the progressive interpretation of existing provisions, with a view to adjusting the definition of crimes against humanity consistently with new development or expanding the list of crimes that fall in this category. Diversity, finally, refers to the possibility of states to continue developing the law even after codification, through evolutions in customary law or diversity in national codification.

The overall volume concludes with a contribution by Judge Ineta Ziemele of the Court of Justice of the European Union, reflecting on the theme of unity, diversity, and evolution in the practice of interpretation in international law. This contribution is an adjusted transcript of the keynote speech Judge Ziemele gave at the Hague Conference. In her contribution, Judge Ziemele reflects on the systemic function that interpretation performs in international law. International law, like any other legal system, must ensure legal certainty. This task is all the more important for international law in light of the constant criticism advanced towards the nature of this legal system. Thus, Judge Ziemele argues, one of the key tools to ensure legal certainty is a consistent and coherent application of rules based on a method of interpretation, where that method serves as the backbone of a judgement. The legal system and an act of application of a specific rule gain persuasiveness and legitimacy where the use of the method of interpretation of a rule is consistent from one case to another. Indeed, it is against this background that the overall theme of this volume becomes even more important. While the various contributors to this volume reflect on different actors as interpreters in international law, Judge Ziemele's contribution zooms in specifically on judicial interpretation. Judges, she argues, are the guarantors of the resilience of law in the sense that it is in their power to ensure its impartial and uniform application, which in turn counters allegations of inefficiency or bias of that system of law. All these considerations about the systemic features of interpretation and the role of judges as interpreters play towards at least a perception of the rule of law in the legal system. Therefore, Judge Ziemele concludes, the general rule of interpretation of international law is a central element in the international rule of law.

1.3 Unity, Diversity, and Evolution: Some Common Themes

The investigations presented in this edited volume were motivated by the overarching question of whether the process of interpretation in international law constitutes a 'unity' regardless of the source of the rule to be interpreted, the author of the interpretation, or the regime specificity in which the interpretation is taking place. The answers provided by the different contributors point to three themes that emerge from the practice – unity, diversity, and evolution.

Across different sources, actors, and regimes, the contributions identify a unity in the methods employed for interpretation, which are in turn (loosely) derived from the VCLT rules and their customary law counterparts. For some contributors, this is evidence that interpretation is a systemic feature of international law, which unites and centralises the whole legal system,[26] or specific sub-regimes of it.[27] Notably, this may also point to a key function that interpretation plays when it comes to the maintenance of the international rule of law.[28]

At the same time, some contributors identify points of diversity when it comes to practices of interpretation across different regimes. Examples of this include the 'principle of single undertaking' that guides the interpretation process in the WTO DSS,[29] or the 'rule of strict construction' of the crimes established in the Rome Statute for the International Criminal Court.[30] While these do not amount to different and regime-specific practices of interpretation, they point to divergent tendencies. Thus, it may be said that while interpretation represents a unified formal process in international law, one can expect some divergence in how different actors or institutional contexts will apply the methods of interpretation.

Finally, studies from the regimes of human rights law and international institutional law point to notable evolution. For instance, pronouncements by quasi-judicial bodies such as the HRBs are having an increasing impact on the interpretation of human right rules, so much so that they might have a *sui generis* character when it comes to their authoritativeness in subsequent interpretation.[31] In a similar vein, the interpretative practice of actors such as international organisations[32] or specialised NGOs[33] may play an increasing role in the determination of

[26] See Chapter 2 by Jure Vidmar.
[27] See Chapter 3 by Yanick Radi and Chapter 4 by Ilias Plakokefalos.
[28] See Chapter 13 by Judge Ineta Ziemele.
[29] See Chapter 9 by Gabrielle Marceau, Maria George, and Vishakha Raj.
[30] See Chapter 11 by Olympia Bekou.
[31] See Chapter 7 by Marlies Hesseleman.
[32] See Chapter 5 by Catherine Brölmann.
[33] See Chapter 6 by Ellen Polcinski and Chapter 8 by Elisa Morgera.

content of international rules despite their subordinate role in the formal doctrine of sources.

Despite these potential divergences and evolution, it is evident that the text of the VCLT has an undeniable 'gravitational pull' when it comes to the practice of interpretation. It is telling that many of the aforementioned actors rely on the VCLT or methods of interpretation derived from the VCLT, perhaps as a way of strengthening the authoritativeness or accuracy of their interpretations. The degree of sophistication and extent of adherence to the VCLT might differ depending on the composition, mandate, agenda, and output of each actor: from the faithful and systematic approach of the ICRC Commentary to the more selective and instrumentalist approach of international organisations, HRBs, and interdisciplinary and stakeholder networks.[34] Nonetheless, to the extent that the goal is to impact legal practice and judicial decision-making, the VCLT continues to constitute the standard against which interpretative claims are measured.[35] This in turn lends further support to the observation that the process of interpretation in international law constitutes a unity, with common methods of interpretation forming its core.

Ultimately, all contributions underscore the undeniable reality that the widespread use of international law of interpretation by diverse actors, across varying sources and subject matters, continues to propel its progressive development and refinement. Whether this process has a definitive endpoint or will persist indefinitely is of little consequence. What remains essential is ongoing reflection on the practice of interpretation, as it both reveals and influences broader transformations in the structure of international law and the direction it is taking – or ought to take.

[34] See Chapter 5 by Catherine Brölmann, Chapter 6 by Ellen Polcinski, Chapter 7 by Marlies Hesseleman, and Chapter 8 by Elisa Morgera.

[35] See e.g *Application of the International Convention on the Elimination of All Forms of Racial Discrimination (Qatar v. United Arab Emirates)* (Preliminary Objections) [2021] ICJ Rep 71 [101].

content of a [illegible] despite their subordinate role in the formal doctrine of sources.

Given these potential divergences and evolution, it is evident that the text of the VCLT has an undeniable [illegible] when it comes to the practice of interpretation. [illegible] standard [illegible] the VCLT or methods of interpretation derived [illegible] accuracy of their interpretations. The degree of sophistication and extent of adherence to the VCLT [illegible] depending on the [illegible] mandate, agency, and [illegible] of each actor [illegible] of the [illegible]

[illegible]

[illegible] endpoint [illegible]

[illegible]

PART I

Unity, Diversity, and Evolution of Interpretation across Sources of International Law

2

Systemic Integration and Public Law Elements in the Sources of International Law

JURE VIDMAR

2.1 Introduction

The rules of interpretation in international law are closely associated with the Vienna Convention on the Law of Treaties (VCLT), particularly Articles 31, 32 and 33 of the Convention.[1] The VCLT context creates an impression that interpretation is a concept peculiar to international treaties, that is, written sources of international law with a textual basis and drafting history.[2] However, the work of Panos Merkouris demonstrates that the rules of interpretation also operate beyond treaty law.[3] Although customary international law and general principles of law are mainly unwritten sources, this does not mean that they are not subjected to any rules of interpretation and that they do not have a role in the interpretation techniques.[4] Obligations *erga omnes* and *jus cogens* norms pose an additional challenge to the interpretation techniques. It is not entirely settled where these concepts are derived from and what their relationship is with the formal sources of international law, as reflected in Article 38(1) of the Statute of the International Court of Justice (ICJ).[5]

Some scholars have called general principles systemic elements of international law that determine the scope and applicability of the rules

[1] Vienna Convention on the Law of Treaties (adopted 22 May 1969, entered into force 27 January 1980) 1155 UNTS 331, arts 31, 32, 33 (VCLT).

[2] See e.g. C Greenwood, 'Sources of International Law: An Introduction' (*United Nations Treaty Collection*, 2008) <https://legal.un.org/avl/pdf/ls/greenwood_outline.pdf> (last accessed 1 June 2025).

[3] P Merkouris, 'Debating Interpretation: On the Road to Ithaca' (2022) 35 LJIL 461, 463. See also P Merkouris, 'Interpreting Customary International Law: You'll Never Walk Alone' in P Merkouris, J Kammerhofer and N Arajärvi (eds), *The Theory, Practice, and Interpretation of Customary International Law* (Cambridge University Press 2022) 347.

[4] See e.g. Merkouris, 'Debating Interpretation: On the Road to Ithaca' (n 3) 465.

[5] Statute of the International Court of Justice (adopted 26 June 1945, entered into force 24 October 1945) 33 UNTS 993, art 38(1) (ICJ Statute).

stemming from treaties and custom,[6] while the origins of contemporary *jus cogens* are derived from the idea of *jus strictum* and *zwingendes Völkerrecht* ('compelling law' as opposed to 'voluntary law').[7] The idea of *jus cogens* thus also presupposes the existence of a systemic structure in international law.[8] The systemic rule of general principles and *jus cogens* are closely linked to the VCLT rules on interpretation and, in particular, to the interpretation technique known as systemic integration.[9] As Lekkas and Merkouris demonstrate, general principles of law indeed played a very central role in the drafting history of Article 31(3)(c) VCLT.[10] Indeed, in his seminal work on the law of treaties, Arnold McNair argued that treaties need to be 'applied and interpreted against the background of the general principles of international law';[11] and Campbell McLachlan has noted:

> A treaty will normally be capable of interpretation and application according to its own terms and context. But in hard cases, it may be necessary to invoke an express justification for looking outside the four corners of a particular treaty to its place in a broader framework of international law, applying general principles of international law.[12]

This chapter is concerned with the role of the general principles of law, obligations *erga omnes* and *jus cogens* norms in the rules of interpretation of the sources of international law. In particular, the chapter considers the function of general principles, obligations *erga omes*and *jus cogens* in the interpretative method commonly known as systemic integration of

[6] See C Eggett, 'General Principles as Systemic Elements of International Law' (PhD thesis, University of Maastricht 2021). See also A Kozłowski, 'Systematicity of General Principles of (International) Law – An Outline' (2017) 37 PYBIL 225.

[7] See S Kadelbach, *Zwingendes Völkerrecht* (Dunker and Humblot 1992). J Frowein, 'Ius Cogens' (2013) MPEPIL 1437. See also A Verdross, 'Jus Dispositivum and Jus Cogens in International Law' (1966) 60 AJIL 55, 55, arguing 'the question is whether all norms of international law have the character of *jus dispositivum* or if there exists some norms having the character *of jus cogens* too'. Verdross took a stance against the position that international law is entirely 'voluntary law' or *jus dispositivum* and argued that the law-making powers of states are limited by certain norms that do not emanate from the voluntary law-making powers of states.

[8] See ILC, 'Fifth Report on Peremptory Norms of General International Law (*jus cogens*) by Dire Tladi, Special Rapporteur' (24 January 2022) UN Doc A/CN.4/747.

[9] See C McLachlan, 'The Principle of Systemic Integration and Article 31(3)(c) of the Vienna Convention' (2005) 54 ICLQ 279.

[10] S-I Lekkas and P Merkouris, 'Interpretation of International Law: Rules, Content, and Evolution' (2022) 69 NILR 183.

[11] A McNair, *The Law of Treaties* (Oxford University Press 1961) 466.

[12] McLachlan (n 9) 281.

international law. This method is most notably reflected in Article 31(3)(c) VCLT[13] but also has a life outside of the VCLT and outside of treaty law in general. The chapter argues that the interpretation techniques of the VCLT in general, and Article 31 of the Convention in particular, presume a systemic structure of international law. This systemic structure is underpinned by certain public law concepts, which operationalize the otherwise inherently private law nature of international treaty and customary law.

The private law paradigm in principle makes international law a network of bilateral obligations between states. However, as James Crawford noted, 'at least some obligations are universal in scope, and cannot be reduced to bundles of bilateral interstate relations'.[14] It is argued in this chapter that general principles of law, obligations *erga omnes* and *jus cogens* norms provide for at least a rudimentary public law framework, which enables an application and systematization of treaty and customary law. Such an application and systematization takes places through the process of interpretation.

This chapter does not primarily deal with the interpretation techniques pertaining to customary international law. With respect to custom, this chapter largely subscribes to the position taken in the previous work of Merkouris in the framework of the TRICI-Law project.[15] This chapter rather explores related concepts, as the line between custom, general principles, obligation *erga omnes* and *jus cogens* norms indeed remains fuzzy. To illustrate, it has been argued that *jus cogens* may be both: customary international law and a general principle of law.[16] The concept of customary international law therefore remains important for this contribution, but the chapter does not delve into the theoretical underpinnings of custom and its interpretation techniques.

The chapter outlines the idea of an international legal system and argues how the inherently private law system of public international law had to borrow certain public law principles in order to be able to function as a system. Subsequently, the chapter considers the vertical relationship between the international community and its subjects. In so doing, the chapter seeks to demonstrate how such vertical elements created a systemic legal structure.

13 VCLT (n 1) art 31(1)(c).

14 J Crawford, 'Responsibility to the International Community as a Whole' (2001) 8 IJGLS 307.

15 See Merkouris (n 3).

16 See T Meron, 'On a Hierarchy of International Human Rights' (1986) 80 AJIL 1, 14

2.2 Outlining an International Legal System

In the *Oil Platforms* case, the ICJ reasoned:

> [U]nder the general rules of treaty interpretation, as reflected in the 1969 Vienna Convention on the Law of Treaties, interpretation must take into account 'any relevant rules of international law applicable in the relations between the parties' (Art. 31, para. 3 *(c)*). The Court cannot accept that Article XX, paragraph 1 *(d)*, of the 1955 Treaty [of Amity between the United States and Iran] was intended to operate wholly independently of the relevant rules of international law on the use of force, so as to be capable of being successfully invoked, even in the limited context of a claim for breach of the Treaty, in relation to an unlawful use of force. The application of the relevant rules of international law relating to this question thus forms an integral part of the task of interpretation entrusted to the Court.[17]

In *Oil Platforms*, the ICJ operationalized Article 31(3)(c) VCLT and the systemic nature of international law. The provisions of international treaties should not be read in a legal vacuum – they ought to be interpreted with other rules of international law in mind. In this sense, the ICJ had previously established in *Right of Passage* that treaties ought to be 'interpreted as producing and as intended to produce effects in accordance with existing law and not in violation of it'[18] and in the *Namibia* Advisory Opinion that 'an international instrument has to be applied within the framework of the entire legal system prevailing at the time of the interpretation'.[19] This section seeks to outline the systemic nature of international law and the importance of systemic integration. In so doing, the section situates the VCLT rules on treaty interpretation within the broader theoretical debate on the fragmentation and systemic coherence of international law.

2.2.1 *The Systemic Nature of Interpretation*

From the doctrinal standpoint, the interpretation of the sources of international law usually begins with the rule on treaty interpretation

[17] *Oil Platforms (Islamic Republic of Iran v United States of America)* (Judgment) [2003] ICJ Rep 161 [41].

[18] *Right of Passage over Indian Territory (Portugal v India)* (Preliminary Objections) [1957] ICJ Rep 125, 142.

[19] *Legal Consequences for States of the Continued Presence of South Africa in Namibia (South-West Africa) notwithstanding Security Council resolution 276 (1970)* (Advisory Opinion) [1971] ICJ Rep 16 [53].

codified in Article 31 of the VCLT.[20] This provision provides that international treaties shall be interpreted in good faith and in accordance with the ordinary meaning of the terms used in the treaty.[21] At the same time, the object and purpose of the treaty are also relevant, and the preamble and possible annexes ought to be taken into account.[22] Furthermore, Article 31 provides that any subsequent treaties between the parties, the practice developed later in the interpretation of relevant obligations and any other rules of international law that bind the treaty parties shall be taken into account.[23] Moreover, as McLachlan argues, the Article 31(3)(c) formulation 'refers to rules of international law in general. The words are apt to include all of the sources of international law, including custom, general principles, and, where applicable, other treaties.'[24]

The provisions of Article 31 appear to be logical: it is necessary to start with the underlying text; the words used in this text should not be attributed any unusual meanings; the treaty provisions should be contextualized within the treaty as a whole, while somehow maintaining a balance between the intentions of the treaty parties at the time of the conclusion of the treaty and the subsequent practice. This is where a problem can arise: how to correctly determine the balance between the intention of the treaty parties at the time of the conclusion of the treaty and contemporary practice.

There seems to be no general rule regulating this, and the balance depends on the particular treaty in question. The European Convention on Human Rights (ECHR) is interpreted as a 'living instrument' whereby the intentions of the original parties seven decades ago no longer play any role,[25] while the Charter of the United Nations (UN) is largely still interpreted in accordance with the intentions of the parties at the end of the Second World War.[26] At the same time, it should be noted that Article 32 VCLT provides that the *travaux préparatoires* shall also be considered. With respect to some treaties, for example, the UN Charter,

[20] VCLT (n 1) art 31.
[21] ibid, art 31(1).
[22] ibid, art 31(2).
[23] ibid, art 31(3).
[24] McLachlan (n 9) 290.
[25] See e.g. G Letsas, 'The ECHR as a Living Instrument: Its Meaning and Legitimacy' in A Føllesdal et al (eds), *Constituting Europe: The European Court of Human Rights in a National, European and Global Context* (Cambridge Univeristy Press 2013) 106.
[26] See S Kadelbach, 'Interpretation of the Charter', in B Simma et al (eds), *The Charter of the United Nations: A Commentary*, vol 1 (3rd edn, Oxford University Press 2012) 71.

this is regularly done decades after their conclusion, while in others, the practice can quickly outgrow the framework of the original text and thus the *travaux* quite soon become largely irrelevant.

It clearly follows from Article 31 VCLT that no international treaty is an isolated system of rules. When interpreting treaty provisions, it is necessary to take into account the other international obligations of the treaty parties and other relevant rules of international law. In other words, one should not put a treaty or its individual provisions at the top of the hierarchy and subordinate to it either other treaties or other sources of international law, such as customary international law and general principles of law. The rules of interpretation under Article 31 require a systemic integration of the rules of international law, regardless of the source from which such rules may be stemming.[27]

To illustrate, sometimes the question arises of whether international human rights law even applies in armed conflict.[28] The preferred view nowadays appears to be that human rights law still applies in armed conflict; it only needs to be systematically integrated with the rules of international humanitarian law.[29] The scope of the relevant rules of human rights law can thus change, mostly becoming narrower, but this does not create a hierarchy or superiority of one treaty regime over another.

It is worth emphasizing that for systemic integration in the sense of Article 31(1)(c) VCLT, treaty interpreters are needed who (still) operate within the system of international law, that is, the interpreters who have not already placed themselves outside the system or see themselves in it with only one foot. An example of such an interpreter would be the Court of Justice of the European Union,[30] but to a lesser extent also the panels in the framework of the World Trade Organization (WTO).[31] When the interpreter no longer sees itself in the system of international law, this leads to fragmentation and so-called self-contained regimes and hierarchical placement of one treaty regime above the rest of international law. As noted by the Study Group of the International Law Commission (ILC) in the Fragmentation Report, there is a need

[27] McLachlan (n 9) 290.

[28] N Lubell, 'Challenges in Applying Human Rights Law to Armed Conflict' (2005) 87 IRRC 737.

[29] ibid 740.

[30] See e.g. J Vidmar, 'Unilateral Revocability in Wightman: Fixing Article 50 with Constitutional Tools' (2019) 15 ECLR 359.

[31] See A Rachovitsa, 'The Principle of Systemic Integration in International Human Rights Law' (2017) 66 ICLQ 557, 574.

> to carry out interpretation such that the rules are seen in the light of some comprehensible and coherent objective, so as to prioritize concerns that are more important at the cost of less important objectives. This is all that article 31, paragraph 3 (c), requires: the integration into the process of legal reasoning – including reasoning by courts and tribunals – of a sense of coherence and meaningfulness. Success or failure here is measured by how the legal world views the outcome.[32]

However, as Adamantia Rachovitsa cautions:

> the principle of systemic integration – either allegedly derived from Article 31 (3)(c) VCLT or as a stand-alone principle – cannot remedy the international courts' fragmented lens. The purpose of interpretation is not to integrate treaties into a coherent whole, but to introduce into the process of interpreting a treaty any relevant rules and to offer interpretive guidance (Article 31(3)(c) VCLT being one tool for accomplishing this).[33]

Indeed, systemic integration is no panacea. It is not a solution that would harmonize international law or even constitutionalize it. Nevertheless, systemic integration can provide for certain conceptual solutions and rudimentary public law tools for the interpretation of private law type of legal obligations. While a number of doctrinal writings have assumed that a system can only function if it is constitutionalized or otherwise hierarchical in nature,[34] McLachlan explains that 'the importance of the rules of customary international law and general principles of law . . . [in the systemic integration process] is not in their overriding character'.[35] Indeed, systemic integration is not about hierarchy and overriding, it is about reconciling two or more obligations and shaping their scopes by reading one into another.

2.2.2 *From Fragmentation to Systemic Coherence*

In his seminal work *The Concept of Law*, H. L. A. Hart argued that international law was a simple set of primary rules without any systemic

[32] See ILC, 'Fragmentation of International Law: Difficulties Arising from the Diversification and Expansion of International Law: Report of the Study Group of the International Law Commission' (13 April 2006) UN Doc A/CN.4/L.682 [419] (Fragmentation Report).

[33] Rachovitsa (n 31) 560.

[34] For an overview see E de Wet, 'The International Constitutional Order' (2006) 55 ICLQ 51; D Shelton, 'Normative Hierarchy in International Law' (2006) 100 AJIL 291.

[35] McLachlan (n 9) 313.

coherence significant for municipal legal orders.[36] The Report of the Study Group of the ILC on Fragmentation of International Law came to a similar conclusion: 'The international legal system has never enjoyed the kind of coherence that may have characterized the legal orders of States.'[37]

The lack of systemic coherence can lead to problems in the practical application of the rules of international law. As the Study Group of the ILC further observed:

> [T]he emergence of conflicting rules and overlapping legal regimes will undoubtedly create problems of coordination at the international level. But . . . no homogenous, hierarchical meta-system is realistically available to do away with such problems. International law will need to operate within an area where the demands of coherence and reasonable pluralism will point in different directions.[38]

International legal scholarship has tried to overcome the lack of systemic coherence by introducing certain concepts and principles from municipal legal systems. The project on international constitutionalism has been particularly prominent in this regard. Its proponents have indeed tried to conceptualize international law as a constitutionalized 'homogenous, hierarchical meta-system.'[39] But critics have pointed out that any instances of a hierarchy of norms in international law are merely perceived, while the practical application of legal norms remains non-hierarchical in nature.[40] This line of thought originates in the Hartian description of international law as a *non*-system, and then seeks to achieve at least some systemic coherence through the development of the so-called conflict rules.[41] These are the rules that resolve conflicts between different norms and sub-regimes of the international legal order. This chapter challenges the assumption that no homogenous meta-system is available to ensure a systemic coherence of the international

[36] HLA Hart, *The Concept of Law*, (3rd edn, Oxford University Press 2012) ch 10.
[37] Fragmentation Report (n 32) [493].
[38] ibid.
[39] ibid; cf de Wet (n 34); J Klabbers et al, *The Constitutionalization of International Law* (Oxford University Press 2009).
[40] See E de Wet, 'Paradigmen in der internationalen Praxis: Normenhierarchie versus systemische Integration' in B Fassbender et al, *Paradigmen im internationalen Recht: Implikationen der Weltfinanzkrise für das internationale Recht: mit Diskussion* (Müller 2012) 81; N Krisch, *Beyond Constitutionalism: The Pluralist Structure of Postnational Law* (Oxford University Press 2010).
[41] See the Fragmentation Report (n 32) [249–56].

legal order. But such a meta-system does not need to be hierarchical in nature, and the overarching systemic framework does not need to be constitutionalism or constitutional theory.

International law is a legal system derived from states. This is not to say that actors other than states do not exist in this system. But states are the actors that have the full international legal capacity. This also follows from the formal sources of law: it is states that conclude international treaties in the sense of the VCLT;[42] and it is state practice, combined with *opinio juris* (again derived from states) that forms customary international law.[43] From a purely international perspective, international law as law between states operates in a horizontal paradigm. However, the inter-state legal obligations are only one level of international legal regulation.

International law-making is reminiscent of the concept of creation of legal obligations in municipal private law. For example, international treaty obligations are conceptually similar to contractual obligations domestically. Indeed, some languages do not even employ separate terms for contracts and treaties, and it is understood that treaties are in their essence contracts between states. Some treaties even use the term high *contracting* parties. Despite these private law foundations of international law, certain public law concepts have nevertheless been introduced into the international legal order. Yet it remains ever-elusive how these concepts operate. In the *Barcelona Traction* case, the ICJ pronounced that certain obligations are 'the concern of all States. In view of the importance of the rights involved, all States can be held to have a legal interest in their protection; they are obligations erga omnes'.[44] Following this logic, when certain norms are breached, it is not a single state but the international community as a whole who is injured. This is well-illustrated also in the position of the Study Group of the ILC on Fragmentation of International Law: 'If a State is responsible for torturing its own citizens, no single State suffers any direct harm . . . such action violates some values or interests of all, or . . . [of] the international community as a whole.'[45]

[42] VCLT (n 1) art 1.

[43] See *Military and Paramilitary Activities in and against Nicaragua (Nicaragua v United States of America)* (Merits) [1986] ICJ Rep 14 [184] (*Nicaragua*).

[44] *Barcelona Traction, Light and Power Company, Limited (Belgium v Spain)* (Judgment) [1970] ICJ Rep 3 [33].

[45] Fragmentation Report (n 32) [393].

Indeed, as Sarah Thin has explained:

> The international community interest is at the centre of this global community structure. It both complements and strengthens it. Secondary rules protecting the community interest as such, like those relating to obligations *erga omnes* and *jus cogens*, integrate certain substantive shared values and common interests within this overarching legal structure. Furthermore, some of the foundational principles or aims that underlie this legal order – the principle of legality, the rule of law – can be seen as part of the international community interest. None of these community interest norms would be possible without the recognition that there are some rules which extend beyond basic bilateral structures. The notion that there can exist forms of legal responsibility that engage the interest of the community as a whole, rather than merely an injured state, are fundamental to the existence and recognition of that community itself.[46]

At least theoretically, international legal doctrine has thus established a distinction between horizontal bilateral legal relations between states and vertical legal relations between the state and the international community. This is similar to the methodological divide between private law and public law known in municipal legal systems. Private law governs the horizontal legal relations between different persons of law (contract and torts),[47] while public law regulates vertical relations between the community (the state) and the subjects of law, as well as the relations between the organs of this public community (constitutional law, administrative law, criminal law).[48]

In international law, the distinction between private and public international law means something quite different. Public international law has traditionally developed as a system of rules governing obligations between states, which are for the most part reminiscent of contracts and torts domestically. Private international law has developed as a system of rules governing the relationship between the individual and foreign law/foreign states (e.g. marriage concluded by nationals of different states). The divide between public and private international law is therefore conceptualized on the basis of the identity and nature of actors in a

[46] S Thin, *Beyond Bilateralism: A Theory of State Responsibility for Breaches of Non-Bilateral Obligations* (PhD thesis, Maastricht University 2022) 229.

[47] See H Dagan and B Zipursky, 'Introduction: The Distinction between Private Law and Public Law' in H Dagan and B Zipursky (eds), *Research Handbook on Private Law Theory* (Edward Elgar 2020) 1.

[48] ibid 3.

municipal legal system. To put it simply, where the rules govern relations between states, they are called public and where they regulate relations between individuals (e.g. application of foreign law), they are called private.

A theoretical divide between private law and public law akin to the one known in municipal legal systems also exists within the normative framework of the international legal order. In other words, the public/private law divide exists even within the set of rules traditionally – and somewhat misleadingly – termed as public international law. Yet this divide has not been thoroughly constructed in international legal theory. This is where the chapter turns next. It will be argued that international law functions as a system precisely because the private law type of obligations stemming from international treaties and custom are interpreted in line with certain systemic elements that provide for a rudimentary public law umbrella in the system of international law.

2.3 The Relationship between the 'International Community' and Its Subjects

Thus far, it has been established that public international law operates within a private law paradigm. States make treaties and states can breach those treaties. An individual state can only breach a treaty to which it is a party. We are essentially operating within a contractual logic. Meanwhile, multilateral treaties, the concept of customary international law and some other concepts, such as *jus cogens* and obligations *erga omnes*, have introduced certain elements of public law or at least certain elements of public law reasoning within this private law paradigm. This section considers where the limits of the public law paradigm are in public international law, where the international legal system operates beyond the strict contractual logic and how interpretation and systemic integration indeed operationalize the contractual logic of international treaties.

2.3.1 Vertical Elements in a Horizontal System

In municipal settings, public law and political theorists have been investigating the relationships between (i) institutions of the state and (ii) the state and the individual. This is necessarily different in international law where the actors involved differ from those at domestic level. Arguably, the relationship between the institutions of the international community have been addressed by the studies on fragmentation of international law.[49] These studies have addressed the problem of the relationship between the different regimes of international law built around different institutions (e.g. WTO law, international criminal law, international human rights law, international investment law) and have proposed a robust system of conflict rules to regulate the relationship between these regimes.[50] At the same time, the vertical relationship between the state and the individual has remained either understudied or overtly influenced by municipal theories that are not always readily transposable to the international level.

Inspired by the rise of international human rights law and international criminal law after the Second World War, some scholars have started to place the individual in the centre of the international legal system and have conceptualized a domestic-like vertical relationship between the individual and the international community.[51] But international human rights and international criminal law are still derived from the law-making powers of states. The scope of these legal regimes depends on whether or not a particular state is a party to a certain treaty, whether it has filed reservations to that treaty and sometimes also on how states have voted in the UN Security Council. A good example is the Rome Statute of the International Criminal Court (ICC). While the court was set up to deal with criminal responsibility of individuals, its jurisdiction depends on the will of states and is governed by certain treaty-law mechanisms (e.g. ratification of the Rome Statue, non-party acceptance of jurisdiction, UN Security Council referral). In other words, the position of the individual in international law is not regulated by a 'public law of the international community' but by a private law system of treaty-created obligations between states.

If a 'public law of the international community' exists, the vertical relationship in this system is the one between the international community and the state. On the international plane, it is the state that takes the position of the individual in a municipal public order. International human rights and international criminal law may well play an important role in the political theory governing the vertical relationship between the international community and the state, but this is because the protection

[49] See Fragmentation Report (n 32) [493].

[50] ibid [116–37].

[51] See R McCorquodale, 'An Inclusive International Legal System' (2004) LJIL 477, 486. See also A Peters, 'Humanity as the A and Ω of Sovereignty' (2009) 20 EJIL 513.

of human rights and punishing international crimes belong to the fundamental values of the international community as a whole.

International human rights and international criminal law in this public law model do not operate from the level of an individual but from the overarching level of the community vis-à-vis the state. It needs to be asked whether the notion of 'the international community as a whole' can be conceptualized as a legal fiction to represent an international sovereign authority and develops a political theory of international law that defines the vertical relationship between the fictitious international sovereign – the international community as a whole – and the state.

2.3.2 The Public Law Concepts in the International Legal Order

The use of phrases such as 'the international community as a whole' may be seen as a silent adoption of the idea of public law within the international legal order. Such phrasings introduce a sense of a community, but does this have any implications for how international law operates? The debate seems to have been squeezed between two somewhat difficult concepts: obligations *erga omnes* and norms of *jus cogens*.[52] The norms most commonly associated with these two concepts are the prohibitions of torture, slavery, racial discrimination, aggression, genocide and the right of self-determination (or rather prohibition of colonialism).[53] Instead of looking for hierarchical – or even constitutional – superiority of these concepts,[54] international legal theory needs to identify their theoretical foundations and ask what these foundations tell us about the idea of public law that is lingering in the background.

In one explanation, all non-bilateral obligations have an *erga omnes* character.[55] This view is problematic as it ignores the ICJ's reference to the 'importance of the rights involved', contained in the *Barcelona Traction* dictum. The 'importance' is a substantive issue and can only

52 See E de Wet, '*Jus Cogens* and Obligations *Erga Omnes*' in D Shelton (ed), *The Oxford Handbook of International Human Rights Law* (Oxford University Press 2013) 541.

53 ILC, 'Draft Articles on Responsibility of States for Internationally Wrongful Acts with Commentaries' (23 April–1 June and 2 July–10 August 2001) UN Doc A/56/10, reproduced in [2001/II – Part Two] YBILC 31, Commentary to art 26 (ARSIWA). See also ILC (n 8) Conclusion 23.

54 cf E de Wet and J Vidmar (eds), *Hierarchy in International Law: The Place of Human Rights* (Oxford University Press 2012).

55 C Annacker, 'The Legal Régime of *Erga Omnes* Obligations in International Law' (1993) 46 ZöR 131, 136.

be defined by the special character of the obligations at stake. Maurizio Ragazzi argues that the obligations of this character have two components: 'the moral content' and the 'required degree of support by the international community'.[56] The concept of obligations *erga omnes* thus reflects the notion of a value-loaded international community interest. However, when establishing importance for the international community as a whole, the ICJ has only given circular references and rather generally invoked norms and principles of international law. In *East Timor*, the Court accepted the *erga omnes* character of the right of self-determination by arguing that self-determination was 'one of the essential principles of contemporary international law'.[57] *East Timor* thus defines the 'importance' identified in *Barcelona Traction* as something that is 'essential'. Such circularities are of little help where one needs to explain which norms are the concern of the 'international community as a whole', why that is so, and how is that manifested in the international legal *system*.

The ICJ has also been unable to identify obligations *erga omnes*, their content and underpinnings, on the basis of the formal sources of law alone. As Maurizio Ragazzi has put it, obligations *erga omnes* reflect 'an exceptionless [*sic*] moral norm (or moral absolute) prohibiting an act which, in moral terms, is intrinsically evil (*malum in se*)'.[58] According to Ragazzi, obligations *erga omnes* are binding not only because states agree that they are, but even more importantly, 'because nobody can claim exceptions from moral absolutes'.[59] The second claim, that 'moral absolute' operates as a direct source of international law, remains debatable. It is nevertheless undisputed that the concept of obligations *erga omnes* has its underpinnings in strong moral values and it is these underpinnings that shape international law-making.

Although the concept of obligations *erga omnes* is value-loaded, it is not seen as a hierarchically superior international law. The Report of the Study Group of the ILC on Fragmentation of International Law defines the concept along the following lines:

> A norm which is creative of obligations *erga omnes* is owed to the 'international community as a whole' and all States – irrespective of their

[56] M Ragazzi, *The Concept of International Obligations Erga Omnes* (Clarendon Press 1997) 163.

[57] *East Timor (Portugal v Australia)* [1995] ICJ Rep 90 [29].

[58] Ragazzi (n 56) 183.

[59] ibid.

> particular interest in the matter – are entitled to invoke State responsibility in case of breach. The *erga omnes* nature of an obligation, however, indicates no clear superiority of that obligation over other obligations. Although in practice norms recognized as having an *erga omnes* validity set up undoubtedly important obligations, this importance does not translate into a hierarchical superiority.[60]

Obligations *erga omnes* may thus be seen as a legal manifestation of certain shared community values in the international community, or of an international public order. While the concept may encompass 'moral absolutes', it does not take any hierarchical precedence over other rules of international law. The legal effects of these obligations remain unclear. It thus also remains unclear how these shared community values (the international public order) are accommodated within the international legal system. It does appear that obligations *erga omnes* and their community interest are conceptual in nature; they reflect a sense of a system and community values that stretch beyond the pure bilateral or contractual logic of international law.

There is a great deal of criticism that, after introducing obligations *erga omnes* in *Barcelona Traction*, the ICJ did not develop this concept further and its normative effects thus remain unclear.[61] Although no specific rule may follow from the concept of *erga omnes* obligations directly, the concept introduces a systemic way of thinking and creates a vertical relationship between the states and the community. This element of public law influences the interpretation of treaties and custom: the obligations they generate are not necessarily only bilateral in nature, and international law also imposes certain systemic, community-oriented boundaries on the creation and interpretative scope of international legal obligations.

A strong sense of an international community is also inherent in the concept of *jus cogens*. For a long time, the ICJ had been reluctant to employ the term *jus cogens* and was referring to an *erga omnes* character as virtually a synonym for *jus cogens*.[62] It is now somewhat difficult to

[60] Fragmentation Report (n 32) [380].

[61] See C Eggett and S Thin, 'Clarification and Conflation: Obligations Erga Omnes in the Chagos Opinion' (*EJIL: Talk!*, 21 May 2019) <www.ejiltalk.org/clarification-and-conflation-obligations-erga-omnes-in-the-chagos-opinion/> (last accessed 1 June 2025).

[62] For more on the relationship between *jus cogens* and obligations *erga omnes*, see C Tams, *Enforcing Obligations Erga Omnes in International Law* (Cambridge University Press 2005) 157; de Wet (n 34) 57; S Kadelbach, '*Jus Cogens*, Obligations *Erga Omnes* and other Rules: The Identification of Fundamental Norms' in C Tomuschat and JM Thouvenin

separate the two concepts. The ICJ has not explored the content of obligations *erga omnes* beyond the overlap with *jus cogens*, which is itself a somewhat mysterious concept.[63]

It is in the nature of *jus cogens* norms that they have an *erga omnes* effect.[64] Indeed, we are talking about jus cogens *norms* and erga omnes *obligations*. Arguably, *jus cogens* violations trigger *erga omnes* obligations – for the international community as a whole. Yet not all obligations *erga omnes* are to be found on the flipside of *jus cogens*.[65] Which obligations have an *erga omnes* but not *jus cogens* character remains unclear. Christian Tams concludes that '*[e]rga omnes* outside *jus cogens* is likely to remain uncharted territory until States begin to invoke the concept more commonly in formalised proceedings'.[66] Obligations *erga omnes* may be seen as a legal manifestation of the international community interest. To the extent of their overlap with norms of *jus cogens*, they may also be seen as an enforcement mechanism of the latter. It is wrong, however, to see obligations *erga omnes* as hierarchically superior law. What implications does this have for the idea of an international public order?

As explained by Sarah Thin:

> If one state violates the prohibition of aggression by invading another state, there is indeed an injured state, but the exclusivity of the bilateral model fails to reflect inter alia the rights of other states to invoke responsibility. These structures that we have developed around community interest norms and obligations, from erga omnes to jus cogens, break apart the exclusivity of the bilateral model and impose an extra-state interest. As such, this traditional relationship-based model is no longer sufficient to describe the responsibility that arises from such breaches.[67]

Erga omnes obligations and *jus cogens* norms thus reflect a shift of paradigm from a strictly bilateral private law–like international law to a more systemic and community-oriented model, which adds at least a very basic vertical relationship between states and the international community.

(eds), *The Fundamental Norms of the International Legal Order:* Jus Cogens *and Obligations* Erga Omnes (Martinus Nijhoff 2006) 21, 21–26; M Byers, 'Conceptualising the Relationship between Jus Cogens and Erga Omnes Rules' (1997) 66 NJIL 211, 213–19.

[63] For a survey of obligations for which the ICJ has established that they are of *erga omnes* character, see Tams (n 62) 117–18.

[64] See de Wet (n 34) 61.

[65] ibid.

[66] Tams (n 62) 157.

[67] Thin (n 46) 96.

2.3.3 International Community Values and Limitations on Contractual Freedom

In the VCLT, the concept of *jus cogens* was for the first time unequivocally mentioned in international treaty law.[68] However, even in this instance it was only given a rather narrow power to void treaties. The Convention also remained silent on the content of the concept. Article 53 of the VCLT, *inter alia*, provides that 'a peremptory norm of general international law is a norm accepted and recognized by the international community of States as a whole'.[69] The concept of peremptory norms thus also rests on the presumption of the existence of an international community of states with a shared interest. It is notable, however, that the VCLT qualified the notion of the international community with states, while the ICJ a year later, with regard to obligations *erga omnes*, only referred to the international community. The Court known for its restrictive interpretations of international law certainly did not omit 'states' accidentally.

In the Article 53 definition, a peremptory norm is subject to acceptance – by the international community of states as a whole – of the normative content as well as its peremptory character. Does this mean that *jus cogens* is an inherently treaty law concept? The concept indeed predates the 1969 VCLT and was invoked by writers even in the pre-Second World War era.[70] At the time, it was unclear whether or not it was a concept generally operating in international law. This has now been generally accepted.[71] Even the VCLT reference to 'general international law' suggests that *jus cogens* is a concept grounded outside of treaty law but is capable of having systemic effects on the conclusion and interpretation of treaties.

Any norm of customary international law requires its acceptance by states through state practice and *opinio juris*. However, the acceptance of the special peremptory character, not only normative content, by 'the international community of states as a whole' points to the strong ethical

[68] VCLT art 53.

[69] ibid.

[70] For a detailed account on the early writings on *jus cogens* see Shelton (n 34) 297–99.

[71] There are currently 116 state parties to the Vienna Convention. Many of its provisions are nevertheless binding on non-parties to the Convention via customary international law. Although some states have refrained from ratification precisely because of Article 53, there is little doubt that the article has customary international law status. Indeed, the status of permanent objector to *jus cogens* has not been accepted by the international community of states.

underpinning of these norms.[72] Sandesh Sivakumaran argues that *jus cogens* represents a minimum threshold of the international value system.[73] The strong community-oriented ethical underpinning of *jus cogens* norms has implications for law-making. International law is, in principle, a consensus-based legal system. States create treaty obligations for themselves and at free will. It is *state* practice and *opinio juris* that leads to the emergence of customary norms of international law, from which states again have an escape route through the concept of a persistent objector. In principle, it is only new states that become automatically bound by pre-existing customary law and even automatically accede to certain treaties previously governing their territory (e.g. human rights treaties).[74] Yet the peremptory status of certain norms, encompassing the minimum threshold of the international value system, also overrides some fundamental tenets of a consensus-based international law-making.

The ethical underpinning of the peremptory norms can compensate for deficiencies in universal acceptance of these norms. In this context, three examples appear to be particularly instructive: (1) the right to the freedom from torture is supported by very strong *opinio juris*, yet state practice is rather weak. There is nevertheless little doubt that the freedom from torture has a *jus cogens* status.[75] (2) Apartheid South Africa claimed that it was a persistent objector to the prohibition of racial discrimination. This claim was universally rejected on the basis that unlike ordinary customary law, peremptory law does not allow for the persistent objector's status.[76] (3) France used to claim that it had never consented to the concept of *jus cogens* as such.[77] This argument was

[72] de Wet (n 34) 57.

[73] S Sivakumaran, 'Impact on the Structure of International Obligations' in M Scheinin and M Kamminga (eds), *The Impact of Human Rights Law on General International Law* (Oxford University Press 2009) 146.

[74] See A Rasulov, 'Revisiting State Succession to Humanitarian Treaties: Is There a Case for Automaticity?' (2003) 14 EJIL 141.

[75] See R Garnett, 'The Defence of State Immunity for Acts of Torture' (1997) 18 Aust YBIL 97, making the following argument: 'It may be argued . . . that the absolute nature of the conventional prohibitions, when coupled with the near universal *opinio juris* amongst states as to the illegality of the practice, may be a sufficient basis for concluding that torture is prohibited as a peremptory norm.'

[76] Byers (n 62) 222.

[77] ibid 229.

rejected and now even France has accepted the binding nature of these norms in terms of both content and character.[78]

These examples reveal that with regard to peremptory norms, international law-making may work differently. As Robert McCorquodale argues, 'some human rights create legal obligations on a state irrespective of whether it has ratified a particular treaty, either because the human right is part of customary international law and so binding on all states or by virtue of a rule of *jus cogens*, which no state can derogate from or evade by contrary practice'.[79] Moreover, in *Furundzija*, the International Criminal Tribunal for the former Yugoslavia (ICTY) reasoned: 'Because of the importance of the values [which the prohibition of torture] protects, this principle has evolved into a peremptory norm of *jus cogens*, that is a norm that enjoys a higher rank in the international hierarchy than treaty law and even "ordinary" customary rules.'[80]

Despite this judicial pronouncement, hierarchical superiority of *jus cogens* remains a contested issue, particularly so after the ICJ's *Germany v Italy* decision on jurisdictional immunities.[81] Yet *jus cogens* can have interpretative effects on the system of international law even in the absence of its hierarchical superiority. Notably, neither Article 38(1) ICJ Statute nor Article 31 VCLT create a pre-determined hierarchy of sources and/or norms. The concept of *jus cogens* has its value as an interpretative systemic element that reflects community values and overrides state centrism and certain classical tenets of international law-making. The concept changes the traditional paradigm of international law as voluntary law and introduces a set of norms that can be legally binding on states even in the absence of their consent. It thus manifests a

[78] See A Pellet, 'Comments in Response to Christine Chinkin and in Defense of *Jus Cogens* as the Best Bastion against the Excesses of Fragmentation' (2006) 27 FYBIL 83, 85.

[79] McCorquodale (n 51), 486.

[80] *Prosecutor v Anto Furundžija* (Judgment) IT-95-17/1-T (10 December 1998) [153].

[81] *Jurisdictional Immunities of the State (Germany v Italy: Greece intervening)* (Judgment) [2012] ICJ Rep 99. Consider ibid [93], where the ICJ provided the following reasoning with regard to the question of whether *jus cogens* takes precedence over immunities because of its special character. The ICJ noted that '[t]his argument . . . depends upon the existence of a conflict between a rule, or rules, of jus cogens, and the rule of customary law which requires one State to accord immunity to another'. The ICJ found that 'no such conflict exists'. This is so because '[t]he two sets of rules address different matters. The rules of State immunity are procedural in character and are confined to determining whether or not the courts of one State may exercise jurisdiction in respect of another State. They do not bear upon the question whether or not the conduct in respect of which the proceedings are brought was lawful or unlawful.'

strong sense of the international community interest that prevails over the will of individual states. However, they have not been given any effects of hierarchical superiority in international judicial practice.

When *jus cogens* norms are breached, the concept does not create remedies that would trump other international legal obligations.[82] What *jus cogens* does is that it prevents a certain obligation to develop either by law-making or subsequent interpretation. For example, Article 53 VCLT would void a treaty by virtue of which two or more states create an obligation to torture, for example, a terrorism suspect. Moreover, *jus cogens* prevents that the positive obligation under the right to life could be interpreted as an obligation to torture in order to extract information in the so-called ticking bomb scenario.[83] Such a conclusion would also be in line with Conclusion 20 of the ILC Report on *Jus cogens* which reads: 'Where it appears that there may be a conflict between a peremptory norm of general international law (*jus cogens*) and another rule of international law, the latter is, as far as possible, to be interpreted and applied so as to be consistent with the former.'[84]

International legal doctrine has thus introduced certain concepts that imply the presence of a 'hierarchical meta system',[85] but it appears that Dino Krtitsiotis is right when he concludes that international law does not know how to accommodate these concepts. He argues: 'Our "international community" is "deep" enough to have conceived of the idea of *jus cogens* but not deep enough to know what to do with it. It is caught in the perennial mire of something called *erga omnes* (or obligations owed to the "community" as a whole), and continues to inch toward so-called crimes and offences against the "international order".'[86] The problem is that all these concepts envisage a strong sense of community and its values. While such a community sense may well limit the treaty-making capacity of states and influence the interpretation of treaty and customary obligations, these public law elements in international law remain rather limited. It appears that the value-loaded concepts of *jus cogens* and *erga omnes* serve a similar purpose as limitations on the freedom of contract in municipal law. In other words, it may well be the case that

[82] ibid.
[83] See M Farrell, *The Prohibition of Torture in Exceptional Circumstances* (Cambridge University Press 2013) 82.
[84] ILC (n 8) Conclusion 20.
[85] cf Fragmentation Report (n 32) [493].
[86] D Kritsiotis, 'Imagining the International Community' (2002) 13 EJIL 961, 990.

international law remains a rather shallow system that lacks complexity; but systemic elements are there and shape the interpretation and application of legal obligations stemming from treaties and custom.

2.3.4 The Systemic Elements

General principles of law are a formal source of international law under Article 38(1)(c) of the ICJ Statute.[87] Unlike obligations *erga omnes* and *jus cogens* norms, general principles thus have a clear textual basis for their legal authority as a formal source of international law. Their normative value nevertheless appears to be somewhat undefined. Writers have particularly questioned whether general principles directly generate any international legal rules and obligations.[88] International treaty and customary international law can create an obligation in the sense that state A shall not do X, and state B shall do Y. It would be difficult to derive such obligations from a general principle of law only and exclusively. As argued by Gleider Hernandez, 'general principles normally enter judicial reasoning without formal reference or label'.[89] In other words, general principles of international law are often in the background of reasoning when other sources of international law are interpreted but do not generate direct legal obligations.

In that sense, Hersch Lauterpacht wrote that the concept of general principles of law is 'in essential harmony with the attitude . . . of every legal community'.[90] Notably, Lauterpacht thus saw general principles are an element that underpins the sense of a legal community in international law. The reference to a legal community is very similar to what we understand nowadays under the term systemic integration. International law lacks coherence and characteristics of a legal system if it does not adopt certain internal rules that ensure at least a minimum threshold of its coherence.[91]

Craig Eggett notes in this regard:

> The mode of creation of general principles of law is one of the issues where the lack of clarity in comparison with treaties and customary rules becomes very clear. For treaties, the rules of the . . . [VCLT] set out the

[87] ICJ Statute art 38(1).

[88] C Eggett, 'The Role of Principles and General Principles in the "Constitutional Processes" of International Law' (2019) 66 NILR 197.

[89] G Hernández, *International Law* (Oxford University Press 2019) 33.

[90] H Lauterpacht, *The Function of Law in the International Community* (Oxford University Press 1933) 74–75.

[91] Fragmentation Report (n 32) [15].

> formal procedures for signature and ratification, and provide for certain conditions of validity. For the ascertainment of customary rules, the ICJ has built a body of case law stating and clarifying the well-known elements of state practice and *opinio juris*. There is as yet no such guidance for the ascertainment of general principles of law. Seeking to establish the criteria for the ascertainment of general principles can contribute the establishment of constitutional features in at least two ways. First, there is scope to rely on the concept of the 'international community' as a basis for the recognition of general principles. Increased clarity as to international lawmaking processes enhances its systemic coherence. Second, greater reliance on this source could allow for the creation of rules that are not exclusively dependent on the consent of states, and so seek to serve the interests of the community as opposed to solely those of states.[92]

It has been argued in this chapter that obligations *erga omnes* and *jus cogens* norms provide for a very rudimentary systemic public law element in the private law structure of public international law. Both concepts are built on the understanding of there being an international community underpinned by a minimum threshold of public community values. The role of general principles of law is even more complex in this regard. They bring elements of both public and private law into the international legal *system*.

International judicial bodies had to import to international law a great deal of procedural principles in order to be able to exercise their judicial function.[93] The underlying treaties that create such judicial bodies do not and cannot anticipate every possible procedural issue that may arise in the future, and reliance on the general principles of international procedural law is thus instrumental. International criminal tribunals need to resort to general principles of criminal law in their work.[94] With respect of international treaties, certain private law analogies (e.g. general principles of contract law) maybe used in the process of interpretation and application.[95]

Discussing the rule of law principle, Thin argues that systemic integration of this principle:

> [O]pens the door to a very different role for international courts and tribunals. The end point of this reasoning is to see international courts and tribunals, or at least some particular courts and tribunals, as organs of

[92] Eggett (n 88) 208.

[93] Eggett (n 6) 141–44.

[94] ibid; See also P Palchetti, 'Making and Enforcing Procedural Law at the International Court of Justice' (2019) 61 QIL 5.

[95] H Lauterpacht, *Private Law Sources and Analogies of International Law* (Longmans, Green and Co 1927).

> the international community. They perform a systemic role in the interest of the community in the rule of law rather than purely in furtherance of individual state interests. This way we see the court(s) as above and beyond the will of states; as a form of public authority. Suddenly, the purpose of the judicial body is not only the settlement of the dispute, but also to ensure and enforce compliance with the law more generally .... Such an aim could underlie broader functions, such as the existence of a broader advisory capacity or even judicial law-making in a gap-filling capacity.[96]

In other words, the application of general principles of law enables international courts and tribunals to act as systemic judicial bodies of the international community rather than mere dispute settlement mechanisms akin to private law arbitration.

Eggett argues that 'general principles of law play a central role in the operation of the international legal system, so much so that they constitute systemic elements of international law'.[97] Indeed, it is well-established in doctrine and practice that individual sources of law cannot be read in isolation and need to be interpreted in line with other applicable sources in a particular situation.[98] The general principles of law are instrumental in the process of fitting the puzzle pieces together. It is sometimes difficult to distinguish the effects of the general principles of law in the sense of Article 38(1)(c) of the ICJ Statute from those under treaty or even customary international law. This is because a number of general principles are in any case also elaborated in treaties or have also become customary (e.g. *pacta sunt servanda* and *lex specialis*) under the VCLT and customary law of treaties. But it is not uncommon in international law that a certain legal rule or doctrine may follow from more than one source of law. After all, it is quite common that multilateral treaties overlap with custom. Although Article 38(1)(c) of the ICJ Statute is not their only point of entry into the international legal system, the general principles of law have an important systemic function in the interpretation and application of the rules and obligations of international law.

The ILC has made an interesting terminological choice in Draft conclusion 2 of the Draft Report on General Principles of Law, which

[96] Thin (n 46) 201.
[97] Eggett (n 6) 169.
[98] See e.g. *Oil Platforms* (n 17) [41].

reads: 'For a general principle of law to exist, it must be recognized by the community of nations.'[99] The ILC explained that

> Draft conclusion 2 employs the term 'community of nations' as a substitute for the term 'civilized nations' found in Article 38, paragraph 1 (c), of the Statute of the International Court of Justice, because the latter term is anachronistic. The term 'community of nations' is found in article 15, paragraph 2, of the International Covenant on Civil and Political Rights, a treaty to which 173 States are parties and which is thus widely accepted . . .. By employing this formulation, the draft conclusion aims to stress that all nations participate equally, without any kind of distinction, in the formation of general principles of law, in accordance with the principle of sovereign equality set out in Article 2, paragraph 1, of the Charter of the United Nations.[100]

The ILC's terminological choice is thus not accidental but derived from certain other international legal instruments. The terminological choice of the ILC seeks to stress the diversity of legal systems represented in the world:

> The use of the term 'community of nations' is not intended to modify the scope or content of Article 38, paragraph 1 (c), of the Statute of the International Court of Justice. In particular, the term does not seek to suggest that there is a need for a unified or collective recognition of a general principle of law, nor does it suggest that general principles of law can only arise within the international legal system. Furthermore, the term 'community of nations' should not be confused with the term 'international community of States as a whole' found in article 53 of the Vienna Convention on the Law of Treaties, relating to peremptory norms of general international law (*jus cogens*).[101]

The ILC here clearly subscribed to there being an idea of a community at the international level. The distinction between the 'community of nations' and 'international community of States as a whole' seeks to stress that general principles of law can be derived from all legal systems of the world, and the uniformity of state practice and/or general acceptance requirement is inapplicable to this source of international law. The concept of general principles of law in the doctrine of sources of

[99] ILC, 'Text of the Draft Conclusions Provisionally Adopted by the Drafting Committee on First Reading' (12 May 2023) UN Doc A/CN.4/L.982.

[100] ILC, 'Report of the International Law Commission on the Work of its 72nd Session' (26 April–4 June and 5 July–6 August 2021) UN Doc A/67/10, 162.

[101] ibid.

international law thus reflects the idea of an international public community and supra-national law-making beyond state-centrism.

2.4 Conclusions

Public international law operates in a private law paradigm. In its essence, this is a system of contract-like and tort-like relations between states. The word 'public' in public international law is a misnomer. A comprehensive public law framework is absent in this system. In order for the system to function, however, some rudimentary elements of public law have been introduced to help regulate the private law relations between states. The interpretation technique of systemic integration is a tool for building a rudimentary public law structure in the system of international law. The systemic public law concepts at work here are general principles of law, obligations *erga omnes* and *jus cogens* norms.

It remains debatable whether the general principles of law as a source of international law are able of generating any direct legal rules and obligations. Their function has been said to be primarily systemic in nature. They are often lurking in the background when other sources of international law are applied and interpreted. They also provide coherence to international law and mitigate against Hart's assertion of international law being a non-system. Reliance on general principles has been particularly important in those situations where treaty and customary law was rather thin (e.g. to prevent *non liquet* in international adjudication)[102] or two or more obligations stemming from either treaty or custom appear to be in conflict.[103] As Thin argues

> Despite Hart's rather infamous comments to the effect that international law is better described as a 'mere set' of rules rather than a system, there is increasing acceptance of the systemic nature of international law. The comparative lack of institutional development and coherence is no longer as great a barrier, and the essential 'rules of the game', as noted above, are increasingly accepted as equivalent to the source of essential authority found in domestic systems.[104]

The concept of *jus cogens* is probably nothing different than an international analogy to public law limitations on the freedom of contract.

[102] Eggett (n 6) 79.
[103] ibid 149.
[104] Thin (n 46) 232–33.

They provide for a limitation on state consent and prevent that certain obligations could develop that would offend against the minimum threshold of an international public order. Obligations *erga omnes* presume the existence of an international community or international society and create a vertical (public law type) relationship between states and the community. This relationship, however, is rudimentary and not underpinned by a comprehensive political and constitutional theory the way this is ordinarily done in municipal settings.

It is thus at least premature to analyze international law through the lens of constitutionalism. What international law does have, however, are certain very rudimentary elements of public law without which the interpretation and application of treaties and custom would be difficult in practice. Such elements are not derived from a comprehensive constitutional and political theory of the international community. They rather come from the concept of general principles of law, obligations *erga omnes* and *jus cogens* norms, and enter international legal reasoning through the interpretative technique of systemic integration. International law is certainly not a very comprehensive legal system, but general principles, *erga omnes* obligations and *jus cogens* norms add certain systemic qualities to it and ensure that international law is not a non-system.

3

Comparative Reasoning in International Investment Law and Arbitration

YANNICK RADI

3.1 Introduction

International investment law and arbitration is a regime that is in search of its identity. As further explained below, this is well illustrated by the debates across arbitration practice and legal scholarship on technical legal issues and, more generally, on the nature of the system as a whole. At the core of this search, comparativism – which can be broadly defined as an 'intellectual activity with law as its object and comparison as its process'[1] plays an important twofold role.

From a systemic standpoint, comparativism enables stakeholders to build and justify the identity, that is, the legal nature and features, that they intend to confer to the regime. In this respect, it is worth flagging that comparative reasoning is not a neutral process. In that sense, this type of reasoning has been said to be a means to an end rather that an end in itself, an opinion that entails that the politics of these ends are inevitably at work in the choice of analogies.[2] That being said, comparativism has no doubt the potential to overcome that politics in the long run by establishing a 'transversal' legal dialogue and discourse that can

[1] K Zweigert and H Kötz, *Introduction to Comparative Law* (T Weir tr, 3rd edn, Oxford University Press 1998) 2. Comparativism is referred to in this chapter as a methodology, not as a legal field nor a discipline. The key tenets of that methodology are stressed across the chapter. For a discussion of comparativism as a legal field and a discipline see e.g. T Lundmark, *Charting the Divide Between Common and Civil Law* (Oxford University Press 2012) (chapter 1: 'The Discipline of Comparative Law'). In this chapter, 'comparativism' is used interchangeably with 'comparative reasoning'.

[2] V Vadi, *Analogies in International Investment Law and Arbitration* (Cambridge University Press 2016) 249, referring to M Adams and J Bomhoff, 'Comparing Law: Practice and Theory' in M Adams and J Bomhoff (eds), *Practice and Theory in Comparative Law* (Cambridge University Press 2013) 6.

contribute to conferring an identity to international investment law and arbitration.[3]

From a practical point of view, comparative reasoning is an important tool often used by arbitral tribunals, be it explicitly or implicitly, in order to perform their task. This holds true in particular as regards the interpretation of international investment agreements (IIAs), the determination of customary international law (CIL), and the identification of general principles of law originating from domestic legal orders (GPL).[4] Comparativism has therefore a significant impact on the content-determination of a broad scope of rules pertaining to the substantive protection of foreign investors and to arbitration.

The present chapter focuses on the use of comparative reasoning in the interpretation of – vague – IIA provisions, be they of a substantive or of a procedural nature. Doing so, it also discusses the role played by comparative reasoning with regard to CIL and GPL inasmuch as both sources are relevant in IIAs' interpretation.

More precisely, the chapter addresses the matter from two perspectives – that is, legality and legitimacy – which are both necessary to capture the diversity of issues that comparativism raises in the field. As for legality, it examines how comparative reasoning fits into the theory of sources and into the canons of treaty interpretation under public international law (Section 3.4). As regards legitimacy, it enquires into the potential of comparative reasoning to help arbitral tribunals convince their audience (Section 3.4). To pave the way for the discussion of those two perspectives, the chapter starts by briefly formulating some remarks on the 'why' and 'what' of comparative reasoning. It first explains the reasons why comparative reasoning is used in international investment law and arbitration (Section 3.2), before discussing the materials of comparativism in this field (Section 3.3).

3.2 The Reasons for Relying on Comparative Reasoning

There are two main reasons that explain why arbitrators, counsels, and academics conduct comparative reasonings – namely, legal indeterminacy

[3] Likewise, Sabino Cassese considers that comparativism brings a 'transnational' legal discourse. See S Cassese, 'Beyond Legal Comparison' [2012] Annuario di Diritto Comparato e di studi legislativi 387, 388.

[4] On general principles of law, see ILC, 'Draft Conclusions on General Principles of Law, with Commentaries' (24 April–2 June and 3 July–4 August 2023) UN Doc A/78/10, 13, Conclusion 5 (2) (hereinafter Draft Conclusions on General Principles).

and hybridity. More precisely, hybridity has a twofold dimension, with the interaction between them amplifying this hybridity. The first dimension pertains to the legal nature, features, and components of the regime. The second one relates to the characteristics of the international investment law and arbitration epistemic community. For didactic purposes, those two dimensions are respectively called, in what follows, 'hybridity *ratione materiae*' and 'hybridity *ratione personae*'. Both dimensions are discussed in turn before the chapter addresses the issue of legal indeterminacy.

3.2.1 Ratione Materiae *Hybridity*

As detailed in Section 3.3 in relation to the materials of comparativism in international investment law and arbitration, the nature of this field is disputed among its stakeholders who are involved in dispute settlement. Such a controversy exists also in academia. Face-to-face, one finds in particular the proponents of the 'public paradigm' against those who are supporting and promoting the 'private paradigm'. Whatever the significance of this controversy, it is worth noting that *ratione materiae* hybridity does not originate only from dispute settlement and legal scholarship. It also proves to be the outcome of law-making in the field. The hybridity that derives from that process has both a synchronic dimension and a diachronic one, both contributing to explaining the use of comparative reasoning in the field.

Looking at the matter from a synchronic standpoint first, it is fair to say that *ratione materiae* hybridity is not specific to our time. It has always been a feature of international investment law and arbitration. At all the stages of its history, the regime and its component parts have proven to display diversity, a diversity due to the various legal orders and disciplines it has been connected to. Focusing on the genesis of the regime, for instance, such a characteristic is reflected in the sources of rights and obligations.[5] Customary international law, notably the minimum standard of treatment,[6] attached the field to the (public)

[5] On the sources of rights and obligations in international investment law and arbitration, see e.g. T Gazzini and E de Brabandere, *International Investment Law – The Sources of Rights and Obligations* (Brill 2012).

[6] On the customary law minimum standard of treatment, see e.g. P Dumberry, 'The "Minimum Standard of Treatment" in International Investment Law: The Story of the Emergence, the Decline and the Recent Resurrection of a Concept' in K Polackova van der Ploeg, L Pasquet, and L Castellanos-Jankiewicz (eds), *International Law and Time – Narratives and Techniques* (Springer 2022) 381.

international legal order. On the other hand, the *lex mercatoria* connected it to a transnational legal order.[7] The debate about the legal order in which contracts concluded between host states and foreign investors ('state contracts') are grounded provides another illustration of the *ratione materiae* hybridity of the regime at that time.[8] This diversity of the sources of rights and obligations also reveals that hybridity in the field is a consequence of the choice that is left therein to the parties to choose the law applicable to the settlement of their disputes. Unavoidably, the reference to domestic law, international law, or the *lex mercatoria* leads the regime in different directions. This contributes to its *ratione materiae* hybridity and, more generally, this encourages or justifies the use of different analogies as part of comparative reasoning.

This *ratione materiae* hybridity has also a diachronic dimension, which has impacted both IIAs' substantive rules and the features/nature of the settlement of investor-state disputes. Evolving views and approaches among policymakers have led to evolutions of key components of the substantive protection conferred by IIAs to foreign investors. This has notably been the result of the politics of bilateral investment treaty (BIT) models. European models[9] that were originally predominant have later shared the 'policy floor' with other models from developed and developing countries.[10] All this is well illustrated by the evolution of the expropriation provision. In this respect, it is worth flagging the approach

[7] On the *lex mercatoria*, see e.g. E Gaillard, 'Thirty Years of *Lex Mercatoria*: Towards the Selective Application of Transnational Rules' (1995) 10 ICSID Review – Foreign Investment Law Journal 208.

[8] See e.g. P Mayer, 'Le mythe de l'ordre juridique de base (ou *Grundlegung*)' in P Fouchard, P Kahn, and A Lyon-Caen (eds), *Le droit des relations économiques internationales – Etudes offertes à Berthold Goldman* (Litec 1982) 199; P Weil, 'Problèmes relatifs aux contrats passés entre un Etat et un particulier' (1969) 128 RdC 94.

[9] In this respect, it is noteworthy that European policymakers prepared their BIT models relying on the 1967 OECD Draft Convention on the Protection of Foreign Property, following thereby the OECD Council, which had expressed the view that 'the Draft Convention will be a useful document in the preparation of agreements on the protection of foreign property'. OECD, 'Resolution of the Council on the Draft Convention on the Protection of Foreign Property' (2025) OECD/LEGAL/0084 <https://legalinstruments.oecd.org/public/doc/242/242.en.pdf> (last accessed 1 June 2025).

[10] In addition to the US BIT Model mentioned below, see, for instance, the 2015 India Model, the 2017 Colombia Model, and the 2019 Morocco Model, available on the website of the UNCTAD Investment Policy Hub <https://investmentpolicy.unctad.org/international-investment-agreements/model-agreements> (last accessed 1 June 2025). For analyses of treaty models, see C Brown, *Commentaries on Selected Model Investment Treaties* (Oxford University Press 2013).

adopted on the matter by the US in their 2004 BIT Model, which,[11] as regards expropriation, is directly influenced by the case-law of the US Supreme Court.[12] Since then, this approach has spread across treaty practice.[13] Such an influence of domestic constitutional law evidences, not only how the regime has developed a *ratione materiae* hybridity over time but also how – again – this encourages or justifies the use of different analogies as part of comparative reasoning.

Investor-state arbitration, and more generally the settlement of investor-state disputes, has also experienced a *ratione materiae* hybridity throughout its history. While originally modelled on commercial arbitration and inter-state arbitration, the former being often said to be a 'private' type of justice, investor-state arbitration has developed 'public' features as of the 2000s. The move away from confidentiality and the increase in transparency, initiated by the International Centre for Settlement of Investment Disputes (ICSID) Secretariat,[14] illustrates this diachronic dimension of *ratione materiae* hybridity. The diversification of the methods used to settle investor-state disputes offers another illustration. This diversification materialises, for instance, in the choice

[11] Treaty Between the Government of the United States of America and the Government of [...] concerning the Encouragement and Reciprocal Protection of Investment (2004) <https://investmentpolicy.unctad.org/international-investment-agreements/treaty-files/2872/download> (last accessed 1 June 2025).

[12] See i.e. US Supreme Court, *Penn Central Transportation Co v New York City* (1978) 438 US 104. As evidenced by Annex 6 of the US BIT Model, the case-law of the US Supreme Court has been very influential as regards the list of factors to be taken into account to determine whether a measure constitutes an indirect expropriation. The notion of 'distinct, reasonable investment-backed expectations' is key in this respect. On this notion, see e.g. JA Kupiec, 'Returning to Principles of "Fairness and Justice": the Role of Investment-Backed Expectations in Total Regulatory Taking Claims' (2008) 43 Boston College Law Review 865.

[13] See e.g. Agreement Between the Slovak Republic and the Islamic Republic of Iran for the Promotion and Reciprocal Protection of Investments (signed 19 January 2016; entered into force 30 August 2017) <https://investmentpolicy.unctad.org/international-investment-agreements/treaty-files/3601/download> (last accessed 1 June 2025).

[14] ICSID has led that process in the context of the revision of its arbitration rules, notably by incorporating *amicus curiae* in the 2006 version of the Arbitration Rules (Rule 37) <https://icsid.worldbank.org/sites/default/files/ICSID%20Convention%20English.pdf> (last accessed 1 June 2025). This mechanism is provided in Rule 66 of the 2022 version of the Rules <https://icsid.worldbank.org/rules-regulations/convention/arbitration-rules/chapter-x-publication%2C-access-to-proceedings-and-non-disputing-party-submissions> (last accessed 1 June 2025). On transparency in that latest version of the Rules, see e.g. GJ Shaw, 'The 2022 ICSID Rules: a Leap Toward Greater Transparency in ICSID Arbitration' (2023) 38 ICSID Review – Foreign Investment Law Journal 54.

made by some treaty parties to favour 'the return of the State'[15] and to opt for inter-state arbitration at the expense of investor-state arbitration.[16] Such a choice has notable consequences as regards the debate about the direct or derivative nature of investors rights and the comparisons that can be drawn (or not), for instance, with international human rights law.[17] As it appears here again, all this encourages or justifies the use of different analogies as part of comparative reasoning.

3.2.2 Ratione Personae *Hybridity*

As mentioned above, this form of hybridity pertains to the international investment law and arbitration epistemic community.[18] It allows us to understand and assess how the profile of the members of that community contributes to hybridity in the field and to the reliance on comparative reasoning therein.

As evidenced by the programmes of conferences, the websites of law firms, or the composition of tribunals made public, professionals in the field have a very diverse scientific background. As detailed below in Section 3.3 regarding the discussion of the materials of comparative reasoning, those backgrounds are manifold. This diversity pertains to legal traditions, legal orders, and legal disciplines, which can all vary – according to various combinations – from one of those professionals to the other. Looking at the literature and arbitral practice, it appears that those scientific backgrounds at least partially explain the diverse

15 On this phenomenon, see e.g. J Alvarez, 'The Return of the State' (2011) 20 Minnesota Journal of International Law 268.

16 This approach is promoted in particular by Brazil, see e.g. Acuerdo de Cooperacion y de Facilitation de las Inversiones Entre la Republica Federativa del Brazil y los Estados Unidos Mexicanos (signed 26 May 2015; entered into force 7 October 2018) <https://investmentpolicy.unctad.org/international-investment-agreements/treaty-files/4718/download> (last accessed 1 June 2025). On this approach, see e.g. R Polanco, *The Return of the Home State to Investor-State Disputes – Bringing Back Diplomatic Protection?* (Cambridge University Press 2019).

17 On this debate, see e.g. M Paparinskis, 'Investment Treaty Arbitration and the (New) Law of State Responsibility' (2013) 24 EJIL 617 and the debate with Anastasios Gourgourinis on the matter. A Gourgourinis, 'The Nature of Investor's Rights under Investment Treaties: A Rejoinder to Martins Paparinskis' (*EJIL:Talk!*, 31 October 2013) <www.ejiltalk.org/the-nature-of-investors-rights-under-investment-treaties-a-rejoinder-to-martins-paparinskis/> (last accessed 1 June 2025).

18 On this issue, see e.g. A Bianchi, 'Epistemic Communities in International Arbitration' in F Ortino and T Schultz (eds), *Oxford Handbook of International Arbitration* (Oxford University Press 2017) 569.

analogies and comparative reasonings conducted in the field.[19] Arbitral practice about the most-favoured-nation clause seems to confirm this influence.[20] At the systemic level, those diverse backgrounds generate diverging epistemic forces, which greatly contribute to the *ratione materiae* hybridity of the regime.

That being said, one should not conclude that scientific backgrounds govern *ipso facto* reasonings. There are many reasons for not drawing such a conclusion.

First of all, asserting the opposite basically may lead one to deny the ability of arbitrators to take some distance from their own background and to focus, as they shall do, on the factual and legal specifics of the cases they are called upon to decide.[21] In relation to this, such a radical view tends to negate the benefit of the collegiality that characterises most arbitral tribunals.[22] Indeed, according to this view, there is simply no room for an open-minded discussion and argumentation within the tribunal. There exists no possibility that the dynamics at play between the arbitrators, in the frame of the factual and legal specifics of cases, lead them to broaden their epistemic horizon.

Secondly, it is also of great import not to oversimplify the epistemic landscape and legal practice in our field. Indeed, diversity has not only a collective dimension but also an individual one. A number of stakeholders in international investment law and arbitration have, themselves, a diverse scientific background, rooted in different legal traditions, orders, or disciplines. This is simply the result of the inter-disciplinary and transnational education and experience acquired by those stakeholders.[23]

Thirdly, it is worth realising that comparative reasoning is not only a matter of scientific background and knowledge, but that it is also one of

[19] In that sense, see also A Roberts, 'Clash of Paradigms: Actors and Analogies Shaping the Investment Treaty System' (2013) 45 AJIL 45, 48.

[20] This is well illustrated by the number of dissenting opinions written on the matter. See e.g. Y Radi, *Rules and Practices of International Investment Law and Arbitration* (Cambridge University Press 2020) 131.

[21] About the importance of being open-minded in arbitration, see e.g. Global Arbitration Review, 'Q&A with Professor Pierre Lalive' <https://cdn.arbitration-icca.org/s3fs-public/document/media_document/media012319104758800008_10_14_gar-pla_interview.pdf> (last accessed 1 June 2025).

[22] On the matter, see e.g. CA Rogers, 'Reconceptualizing the Party-Appointed Arbitrator and the Meaning of Impartiality' (2023) 64 HarvILJ 137, 165–67.

[23] On this phenomenon, see e.g. E Darian-Smith, 'Transnational Legal Education' in P Zumbansen (ed), *The Oxford Handbook of Transnational Law* (Oxford University Press 2021) 1153.

interests and capacities. The role that each of the international investment law and arbitration professionals plays in the system impacts (or in any case should impact) on the extent to which she builds her work on her background. Acting as an arbitrator in proceedings is a different exercise than writing an article as a scholar. Also, obviously, acting as a counsel and the interests that one is called upon to defend in that capacity inform if and how one relies on one's own background. Likewise, it indicates the type of comparative reasoning that one conducts.

All these considerations should be taken into account when considering the *ratione personae* hybridity that no doubt characterises and impacts on the regime, notably in the context of its legal indeterminacy.

3.2.3 Legal Indeterminacy

Legal indeterminacy has been typical of IIAs' provisions since the adoption of the first IIA between Germany and Pakistan in 1959.[24]

More precisely, among all forms of indeterminacy,[25] they have been characterised by the indeterminacy of language as notably theorised by Hart.[26] He made notably a distinction between 'easy cases' and 'hard cases', in relation respectively to the 'core' and the 'penumbra' of legal rules. In easy cases, which involve the core of legal rules, their application does not raise any specific difficulty as their meaning appears to be relatively clear in relation to the facts. On the contrary, there is no such linguistic clarity in hard cases that pertain to the penumbra of legal rules. In those hard cases, several plausible interpretations exist, the issue – discussed in Section 3.4 – being then to select one among them. Of course, legal rules and their application can hardly be divided into two clear-cut categories; yet they constitute no doubt the two extreme sides of a sliding scale along which the degree of linguistic indeterminacy

[24] Treaty between the Federal Republic of Germany and Pakistan for the Promotion and Protection of Investments (signed 25 November 1959; entered into force 28 April 1962) <https://investmentpolicy.unctad.org/international-investment-agreements/treaty-files/1387/download> (last accessed 1 June 2025).

[25] For a review and an analysis of those forms, see e.g. CA Miles, 'Indeterminacy' in J d'Aspremont and S Singh (eds), *Concepts for International Law – Contributions to Disciplinary Thought* (Edward Elgar 2019) 447.

[26] See i.e. HLA Hart, 'Positivism and the Separation of Law and Morals' (1957–58) HLR 593, 606–15; HLA Hart, *The Concept of Law* (3rd edn, Clarendon 2012) 160–61.

varies.[27] IIA provisions have traditionally been characterised by a pretty high degree of indeterminacy. Well-known examples are the fair and equitable treatment (FET) and indirect expropriation. What do fairness and equity mean and cover as regards the former?[28] What are the criteria and circumstances to be taken into account to determine the occurrence of an indirect expropriation?[29] These are key questions and challenges that academics and, most importantly, counsels and arbitrators have been facing. To deal with this indeterminacy, notably when international law rules of interpretation fail to deliver a clear meaning, they often rely on paradigms, legal systems, or specific rules that they deem relevant, be it for functional or strategic reasons. This is well illustrated by the practice of arbitral tribunals concerning expropriation. They have relied on various legal systems, rules, and principles in the process of applying that provision and appraising the existence of indirect expropriations.[30] Reference has been made in particular to customary international law in relation to the police power doctrine,[31] or to the European Court of Human Rights case law in relation to the proportionality doctrine.[32]

Of course, drafting has evolved in the IIAs that have been adopted since the 2000s. Treaty provisions in those agreements are often more detailed than they used to be in older ones. Criteria to be taken into account to identify instances of indirect expropriation are included in some treaties,[33] while a distinction between expropriatory measures and regulatory measures is made in many of those newly adopted treaties.[34]

[27] In that sense, see i.e. N MacCormick, *Legal Reasoning and Legal Theory* (Clarendon 1978) 234–35.

[28] See e.g. G Ünüvar, 'The Vague Meaning of the Fair and Equitable Treatment Principle in Investment Arbitration and New Generation Clarifications' in AL Kjaer (ed), *Language and Legal Interpretation in International Law* (Oxford University Press 2022) 271.

[29] See e.g. Radi (n 20) 164–74.

[30] For a critical account, see e.g. J Calamita, 'The Principle of Proportionality and the Problem of Indeterminacy in International Investment Treaties' [2014] Yearbook of International Investment Law and Policy 157.

[31] See e.g. *Philip Morris Brands SARL, Philip Morris Products SA and Abal Hermanos SA v Oriental Republic of Uruguay* (*Philip Morris v Uruguay*) (Award of 8 July 2016) ICSID Case No ARB/10/7 [290–301].

[32] See e.g. *Tecnicas Medioambientales Tecmed SA v The United Mexican States* (Award of 29 May 2003) ICSID Case No ARB(AF)/00/2 [116].

[33] See supra (n 11) and (n 12).

[34] Here again, this evolution is based on the approach initiated by the US in its 2004 BIT model (Annex B) (n 11). It is worth noting that, while making a similar distinction, some treaties depart from this approach by excluding that regulatory measures may constitute expropriatory measures in some rare circumstances, see e.g. Treaty Between the Republic

Likewise, recent treaty practice appears to be much more specific as regards the content of the FET, be it by listing the components of that standard,[35] by attaching it to the customary law minimum standard of treatment,[36] or by providing information about its content. For instance, with regard to legitimate expectations, which is strongly connected to domestic administrative law,[37] some treaties specify that expectations can only originate from specific representations or commitments.[38]

This trend in treaty practice will no doubt limit the need to rely on analogies and comparative reasoning in the future. That being said, one should remember that the vast majority of the treaties that are the object of current disputes before tribunals form part of the old generation characterised by legal indeterminacy. More fundamentally, that old generation of IIAs is still massively predominant among the treaties currently in force, the new generation constituting only a minority. As a result, comparativism will very likely remain paramount in the reasoning of arbitrators and tribunals in the years to come. It is then very much needed to address the issues that comparativism raises in international investment law and arbitration. Before doing precisely this, it is first

of Belarus and the Republic of India on Investments (signed 24 September 2018; entered into force 5 March 2020) (art 5.5) <https://investmentpolicy.unctad.org/international-investment-agreements/treaty-files/5724/download> (last accessed 1 June 2025).

35 See e.g. Agreement Between the Government of Hungary and the Government of the Republic of Cabo Verde for the Promotion and Reciprocal Protection of Investments (signed 28 March 2019; entered into force 2 May 2020) (art 2 Promotion and Protection of Investments) <https://investmentpolicy.unctad.org/international-investment-agreements/treaty-files/5916/download> (last accessed 1 June 2025).

36 See e.g. Agreement Between Canada and the Government of the Republic of Moldova for the Promotion and Protection of Investments (signed 12 June 2018; entered into force 2 May 2020) <https://investmentpolicy.unctad.org/international-investment-agreements/treaty-files/5806/download> (last accessed 1 June 2025).

37 It is noteworthy that most arbitral tribunals have failed to justify the reliance on that notion. On this issue, see e.g. G Potestà, 'Legitimate Expectations in Investment Treaty Law: Understanding the Roots and the Limits of a Controversial Concept' (2013) 28 ICSID Review – Foreign Investment Law Journal 88; Radi (n 20) 88–89. For an exception, see e.g. *Total v Argentina* in which the Tribunal expressed the view that 'a comparative analysis of the protection of legitimate expectations in domestic jurisdictions [was] justified [. . .]'. *Total SA v Argentine Republic* (Decision on Liability of 27 December 2010) ICSID Case No ARB/04/1 [128].

38 See e.g. Comprehensive Economic and Trade Agreement (CETA) between Canada, of the one part, and the European Union and its Member States, of the other part (signed 30 October 2016) (art 8.10.4) <https://investmentpolicy.unctad.org/international-investment-agreements/treaty-files/3593/download> (last accessed 1 June 2025).

necessary to introduce the materials that arbitrators and tribunals rely on when conducting comparative reasonings.

3.3 The Materials of Comparative Reasoning

The materials of comparative reasoning are manifold. To address them and for didactic purposes, a distinction can be made between two types of materials, which are here referred to as forming part of *systemic comparative reasoning* and *specific comparative reasoning*.[39] Each is discussed in turn, the focus being put on the former as, in addition to its intrinsic value, it greatly influences the latter.

3.3.1 Systemic Comparative Reasoning

This type of comparative reasoning consists in the comparison of the international investment law and arbitration regime with other legal systems and paradigms. While this comparison most of the time leads arbitrators and scholars to focus on and favour one of them, they sometimes adopt a pluralistic approach as they consider the regime as a hybrid system. As a result, they rely on various legal systems and paradigms that are seen as being each relevant for different aspects of international investment law and arbitration.[40] Whatever the approach used by those stakeholders, the choice of either of those systems and paradigms is dictated by the analogy that they establish between the situation and problems that arise in international investment law and arbitration and those that arise in those other systems and under those paradigms. This is well illustrated by those who make a comparison between, on the one hand, the foreign investor–host State relationship and, on the other hand, the relation between private persons and the executive.[41] Sometimes, this is the analogy in terms of legal structure and substance that drives comparative reasoning, as is illustrated by those

[39] For *mutatis mutandis* similar distinctions, see Roberts (n 19) 46 and Vadi (n 2) 137 and 175.

[40] See e.g. J Arato, 'The Private Law Critique of International Investment Law' (2019) 113 AJIL 1, 10.

[41] See e.g. the Separate Opinion by Thomas Wälde in *International Thunderbird Gaming Corporation v The United Mexican States* (Separate Opinion of Thomas Wälde of 1 December 2005 to Award of 26 January 2006) [12–13] <https://www.italaw.com/sites/default/files/case-documents/ita0432.pdf> (last accessed 1 June 2025).

who draw an analogy between international investment law and arbitration and international human rights law.[42]

Those legal systems and paradigms that are relied upon in international investment law and arbitration are well-known, in particular the public-private law paradigms. They have already been studied in great detail in the literature.[43] While they are well-known, one should yet be cautious when looking at the systemic and paradigmatic landscape to ensure that one catches all its nuances. This matters as oversimplifying that landscape deprives us from the possibility of getting a sound understanding of systemic comparative reasoning and, most importantly, can lead in practice to making wrong analogies. Two main reasons call for such a cautiousness.

From a methodological point of view, first, the landscape appears to be actually messy. This is mainly due to the fact that there are different ways, in particular in the literature, to map the systemic and paradigmatic landscape. Notably, to develop their typology, some focus on the 'nature' of the body of law, that is, public or private, or on, so to speak, the 'localisation' of the legal order, that is, domestic, international, transnational. For instance, some authors who rely on or discuss the public-private divide put under the paradigmatic umbrella of the 'public' both domestic public law and public international law.[44] On the contrary, others make a distinction between them.[45] Likewise, classifications are based, explicitly or implicitly and alternatively or in combination, on the nature of investment arbitration and on the functions that it performs.[46]

The second reason that calls for cautiousness consists in the fact that those systems and paradigms display, themselves, diversity. This is well illustrated by the public international law paradigm. It encompasses analogies with general public international law,[47] international human

[42] See e.g. M Paparinskis, *The International Minimum Standard of Treatment and Fair and Equitable Treatment* (Oxford University Press 2013) 175–80.

[43] See e.g. Roberts (n 19); C Titi, 'Investment Treaty Arbitration Caught in the Public-Private Law Divide' (2024) 45 MichJIntlL 441.

[44] See e.g. J Alvarez, 'Is Investor-State Arbitration "Public"' (2016) 7 JIDS 534.

[45] See e.g. Roberts (n 19) 63–64.

[46] See Titi (n 43) 449–50.

[47] This approach is well summarised in CJ Tams, S Schill and R Hofmann 'Radiating Effects: The Gentle Impact of International Investment Law on General International Law' in CJ Tams, S Schill, and R Hofmann (eds), *International Investment Law and General International Law – Radiating Effects* (Edward Elgar 2023) 2, 13–16.

rights law,[48] or WTO law.[49] This diversity matters as the analogy with each of them can lead to different outcomes in international investment law and arbitration. This is well illustrated by the debate about the derivative or direct nature of investors rights by analogy with the traditional model of diplomatic protection and human rights, respectively,[50] which has an impact on concrete issues such as the characterisation of IIAs breaches as countermeasures.[51]

Irrespective of the need to approach the matter cautiously, it is worth insisting that systemic comparative reasoning is not a mere academic exercise. The choice of either of those systems and paradigms has substantive practical consequences. A very telling example is provided by the issue of state consent to arbitration. The way it is construed by arbitrators depends largely on the paradigm they rely on. And this greatly contributes to explain the diverse and conflicting views they adopt on specific legal issues, such as the status and nature of pre-conditions to arbitration, or the application of the most-favoured-nation clause to IIAs' dispute settlement provisions.[52]

3.3.2 *Specific Comparative Reasoning*

While systemic comparative reasoning pertains to comparisons with other legal systems and paradigms considered as a whole, specific comparative reasoning consists in the comparison with specific principles, rules, judicial decisions, and practices forming part of such other legal systems. As it appears, the latter is closely connected to the systemic understanding that international investment law and arbitration's stakeholders have of the regime. For instance, those who make an analogy

48 See e.g. Paparinskis (n 17).

49 See e.g. J Kurtz, *The WTO and International Investment Law: Converging Systems* (Cambridge University Press 2016).

50 See Section 3.2.2 on *ratione personae* hybridity, in particular (n 19).

51 See e.g. *Archer Daniels Midland Company and Tate & Lyle Ingredients Americas, Inc v United Mexican States* (Award of 21 November 2007) ICSID Case No ARB(AF)/04/05 [110-80].

52 For views grounded in public international law, see e.g. the Concurring and Dissenting Opinion of Brigitte Stern in *Impregilo SpA v Argentine Republic* (Concurring and Dissenting Opinion of Brigitte Stern to Award of 21 June 2011) ICSID Case No ARB/07/17 [53] as well as the Dissenting Opinion of Laurence Boisson de Chazournes in *Garanti Koza LLP and Turkmenistan* (Dissenting Opinion of Laurence Boisson de Chazournes to the Decision on the Objection to Jurisdiction for Lack of Consent of 3 July 2013) ICSID Case No ARB/11/20 [5–7].

between international investment law and international human rights law will have a strong tendency to turn to the case law of human rights courts.

Specific comparative reasoning is seen here in the context of the interpretation of IIAs' provisions, which constitutes the focus of the chapter. In that context and as discussed in Section 3.4, the materials of that reasoning can be used for various purposes that need to be distinguished as they raise different issues. At this stage, it suffices to say that they are mainly called upon to play a role in evidencing the existence and/or the content of international law rules. This is true notably when materials, notably past judicial decisions, are relied on directly in the process of determining the content of those IIAs' provisions. But this holds true also in those situations where materials are relied upon in relation to other sources, which are themselves used in the interpretation of IIAs' provisions. For instance, domestic rules and principles are used to determine GPL but also as state practice for the identification of customary international law.

Before that, it is worth noting that arbitral tribunals often do not specify or justify how and why they can rely on those materials and sources. Yet, most of the time, it suffices to refer to the gateways that public international law and international arbitration offer to make this possible. Article 31(3)(c) of the 1969 Vienna Convention on the Law of Treaties is one of them as it provides that, when interpreting a treaty, 'there shall be taken into account ... any relevant rules of international law which is applicable in the relations between the parties'.[53] Referring to judicial decisions as a subsidiary means for determining rules of law – as coined in Article 38 of the International Court of Justice Statute – is also relevant in this respect.[54] *Last but not least*, the applicable law chosen by the disputing parties – when international law is part of it – or the law applicable pursuant to Article 42(1) of the ICSID Convention are also of interest to justify the reliance on those materials and sources.[55]

[53] 1969 Vienna Convention on the Law of Treaties (adopted 23 May 1969, entered into force 27 January 1980) 1155 UNTS 331.

[54] 1945 Statute of the International Court of Justice (adopted 26 June 1945, entered into force 24 October 1945) 33 UNTS 993.

[55] Art 42(1) provides that, in case of absence of agreements between the parties, the tribunal shall apply the law of the Contracting State party to the dispute and such rules of international law as may be applicable; Convention on the Settlement of Investment Disputes between States and Nationals of Other States (ICSID Convention) (adopted 18 March 1965, entered into force 14 October 1966) 575 UNTS 159.

3.4 The Issues Raised by Comparative Reasoning

The issues raised by comparative reasoning in international investment law and arbitration can now be addressed in light of the above, with a focus on investor-state arbitration. At the outset, it is worth stressing that some of the issues faced by this judicial forum are actually faced by all judicial fora. Those issues are mainly methodological in nature. They pertain to the determination of the terms of the comparison, to their similitude (or lack thereof), and to the comparison *stricto sensu*. Although they are intertwined with those methodological issues, additional issues are proper to investor-state arbitration, as they pertain to the application of IIAs' provisions. They arise notably in relation to the canons of treaty interpretation and to the theory of sources. To fully grasp those issues, the discussion is conducted here from a twofold perspective – that is, legality and legitimacy, starting with the former.

3.4.1 Legality Perspective

As explained above, the theory of sources, and what it teaches us about the determination of the rules of international law, is highly relevant for the purpose of this chapter as all international law sources play a role in the interpretation of IIAs' provisions. Instances where rules emanating from those sources have been relied on by tribunals in that interpretative process are manifold. Customary international law has been used, for example, in the course of the interpretation of expropriation provisions in applicable IIAs,[56] or in the context of the interpretation of fair and equitable treatment provisions in relation to the minimum standard of treatment.[57] GPL have been relied on, for instance, in that latter context in relation to legitimate expectations.[58] As for the case-law, it has been used – often implicitly – as a subsidiary source in the context of the interpretation of many provisions, such as the umbrella clause[59] or the most-favoured-nation clause.[60] Relying on those sources requires to

[56] See e.g. *Philip Morris v Uruguay* (n 31) [289–90].

[57] On the relation between both, see e.g. Paparinskis (n 42).

[58] See e.g. *Gold Reserve Inc and Bolivarian Republic of Venezuela* (Award of 22 September 2014) ICSID Case No ARB(AF)/09/1 [576].

[59] See e.g. *Bureau Veritas, Inspection, Valuation, Assessment and Control, BIVAC BV v The Republic of Paraguay* (Decision of the Tribunal on Objections to Jurisdiction of 29 May 2009) ICSID Case No ARB/07/9 [138].

[60] See e.g. *RosInvestCo UK Ltd v The Russian Federation* (Award on Jurisdiction of October 2007) SCC Case V 079/2005 [49].

make comparisons between state practices, domestic rules and principles, and past 'judicial' decisions, respectively. Let us appraise the practice of tribunals thereon, focusing successively on the comparisons between judicial decisions and between domestic rules/principles.

Among the judicial decisions rendered by international courts and tribunals, past arbitral awards or decisions are by far the main type of 'judicial' decisions relied on by tribunals in investor-state arbitration. Depending on the case at hand, tribunals rely on one precedent, on a few of them, or on *jurisprudence constante*, which are made of series of precedents.[61] In all those situations, the issue of similarity arises. More precisely, the issue is twofold. First of all, it is worth flagging that similarity does not amount to identity. This begs the question of the degree of similarity or, to put it differently, the question of the conditions under which similarity is deemed to be sufficient. Secondly, it matters to realise that similarity should characterise two sets of relations. Past awards/decisions should first display similarity between themselves. Also, they should be (sufficiently) similar to the factual and legal specifics of the case at hand, in particular to the IIA provision being interpreted.

A review of arbitral practice shows that tribunals hardly ever enquire into similarity in practice. This holds true as regards the similarity that should characterise the two sets of relation mentioned above. *Ipso facto*, this also applies to the degree of similarity. Such a trend is obviously an issue in methodological terms. But, more fundamentally, this is an issue inasmuch as this may lead to situations where the interpretation that derives from relying on precedents conflicts with the intent of treaty parties, by failing to respect the textual, the teleological, or the contextual specifics of the treaty at hand.[62]

Turning to the discussion of arbitral practice pertaining to the reliance on domestic rules and principles, attention should first be drawn to selectivity. Tribunals most of the time refer to a very limited number of domestic legal orders and rules thereof in the process of interpreting

[61] On the debate among arbitrators about whether precedents should be followed despite the absence of *stare decisis* in international (investment) law see e.g. *Burlington Resources Inc v Republic of Ecuador* (Decision on Liability of 14 December 2012) ICSID Case No ARB/08/5 [187]. As regards the absence of *stare decisis* in international investment law, see i.e. ICSID Convention (art 53) (n 55).

[62] On the risk that relying on precedent may lead to disregard the relevant texts and the applicable law see e.g. G Guillaume, 'The Use of Precedent by International Judges and Arbitrators' (2011) 2 JIDS 5, 23.

IIAs' provisions.[63] Also, they usually hardly enquire into the similarity between those rules and principles. Is it an issue? The lack of discussion about similarity is no doubt one, as this is a *conditio sine qua non* to testify of their collective substantive significance. As for selectivity, the answer to the question depends actually on the function assigned to relying on those domestic rules and principles. When the intent is to fill a gap by trying to evidence the existence of a GPL, this seems to be an issue indeed. It is so because the theory of sources teaches us that such general principles should be widespread across domestic legal systems and be characterised by representativeness.[64] On the contrary, when the intent of the tribunal is to confirm an interpretation reached on other grounds, it is less of a concern as those domestic rules and principles relied upon do not aim at evidencing such a general principle.[65] Such a reasoning does not run against the theory of sources, which appears to be irrelevant in that context. From a legality point of view, nothing prevents such a use of domestic rules and principles. On the other hand, this appears to be more problematic seen from the standpoint of legitimacy, to which the chapter now turns to fully grasp the issues raised by comparative reasoning in investor-state arbitration.

3.4.2 Legitimacy Perspective

Legitimacy – understood here as the acceptance of a power exercised by an entity – does matter when appraising the use of comparative reasoning in arbitral practice, as it does more generally as regards the existence and functioning of arbitral tribunals.[66] This results from the power that they exercise and that impacts on disputing parties and beyond, in particular on local populations. This power consists primarily in the settlement of the disputes submitted to tribunals. But it also materialises into the law-making function that they are *de facto* called

[63] On this issue see J Ellis, 'General Principles and Comparative Law' (2011) 22 EJIL 949, 955–58.

[64] See i.e. ILC, 'Report of the International Law Commission, Seventy-fourth Session' (24 April–2 June and 3 July–4 August 2023) UN Doc A/78/10 'Text of the draft conclusions on general principles of law adopted by the Commission on first reading' (Conclusion 5.2). For a critical approach to representativeness, see e.g. Ellis (n 63) 955–58.

[65] In that sense, see e.g. D Peat, 'International Investment Law and the Public Law Analogy: The Fallacies of the General Principles Method' (2018) 9 JIDS 654, 675–76.

[66] See e.g. N Grossman, HG Cohen, A Follesdal, and G Ulfstein (eds), *Legitimacy and International Courts* (Cambridge University Press 2018).

upon to perform when interpreting vague IIAs' provisions.[67] Indeed, their legal indeterminacy, discussed in Section 3.2.3, requires from tribunals to make choices as regards the substance that they give to those provisions in light of the facts of cases. To beef up the acceptability of those choices – and more generally of the power they perform – tribunals have to provide arguments in support thereof. As it appears, this *de facto* law-making function, and interpretation in the context of which this function is formally exercised, boils down to an argumentative practice that is intended to convince the tribunal's audiences of the soundness of the choices made.[68] Comparative reasoning being one method used by tribunals to exercise this *de facto* law-making function, the way it is conducted should contribute to convince the tribunals' audiences.

This is where, in particular, the selectivity of arbitral tribunals as regards the domestic principles or rules that they use can be seen as an issue. Even though such a selectivity cannot be challenged from a legality standpoint when they are relied upon to confirm an interpretation, a 'pick and choose' approach opens a Pandora's box of criticism from that legitimacy point of view. Critics denounce notably the legal hegemony and the cultural biases across the investment law and arbitration community that this selectivity reflects.[69] All this undermines the acceptability of the choices made by tribunals, the acceptability of awards or decisions, and, more fundamentally, the acceptability of investor-state arbitration.

Beyond the academic debate among comparativists between the proponents of functionalism and culturalism as regards the significance of

[67] See e.g. SW Schill, 'System-Building in Investment Treaty Arbitration and Lawmaking' (2011) 12 German Law Journal 1083.

[68] In that sense, see e.g. I Venzke, 'The Practice of Interpretation in International Law: Strategies of Critique' in J Dunoff and MA Pollack (eds), *International Legal Theory: Foundations and Frontiers* (Cambridge University Press 2022) 305. See also CW Tindale, *The Philosophy of Argument and Audience Reception* (Cambridge University Press 2015).

[69] See e.g. Vadi (n 2) 247. In this respect, it is worth noting disagreements in legal scholarship about the representativeness of Western legal orders, both civil and common law ones. On the one hand, some argue that they have spread from their European roots to many other countries across all the continents, be it because of colonialism or legal reforms. On the other hand, other argue that Western ideas of law are not any longer accepted as a primary yardstick. In support of the former approach, see e.g. SW Schill, 'International Investment Law and Comparative Public Law – an Introduction' in SW Schill (ed), *International Investment Law and Comparative Public Law* (Oxford University Press 2010) 29; in support of the latter, see e.g. J Husa, 'Research Designs of Comparative Law – Methodology or Heuristics?' in M Adams and D Heirbaut (eds), *The Method and Culture of Comparative Law* (Hart 2014) 64, cited in Vadi (n 2) 247.

cultural specificities,[70] the difficulty in investor-state arbitration is obviously that the audience is diverse.[71] Distinctions can be made between disputing parties and a broader audience and between states and investors. Another distinction can be made between states depending on whether they belong to the Global South or the Global North. Local populations and civil society are also seen as constituting an additional audience of arbitral tribunals.[72]

This diversity of the audience brings a diversity of expectations. Its component parts often have diverse and sometimes conflicting expectations of arbitral tribunals and, more generally, of international investment law and arbitration. In relation to the discussion conducted in Section 3.3.1 about systemic comparative reasoning, it appears that those expectations are governed by the respective system or paradigm those component parts of the audience rely on. In light of that context, arbitral tribunals seem to have little chance, when conducting their systemic comparative reasoning, to succeed in convincing all of them that they made the right choice in their interpretation of vague IIAs' provisions.

3.5 Conclusion

The discussion conducted in this chapter flags up methodological flaws that exist in the use of comparative reasoning by arbitral tribunals in the process of interpreting vague IIAs' provisions. If these flaws cannot all be criticised from a legality point of view, they have yet the potential, from a legitimacy standpoint, to undermine the acceptability of their awards

[70] Functionalists consider that all societies are faced with the same challenges. In the view of functionalists then, all domestic laws address those same challenges, their rules and concepts being compared because of the analogous function that they perform. On the contrary, the proponents of culturalism believe that societies are confronted with diverse challenges and that domestic law reflects this diversity. Accordingly, they consider that comparativism should take into account that societal and legal diversity. On this issue, see e.g. JC Reitz, 'How to Do Comparative Law (1998) 46 AJCL 617, 626. See also Vadi (n 2) 19–34.

[71] This audience can of course vary from one case to the other, depending notably on the subject matter of the disputes. On those issues, see e.g. JA Maupin, 'Differentiating Among International Investment Disputes' in Z Douglas, J Pauwelyn, and JE Vinuales (eds), *The Foundations of International Investment Law: Bringing Theory into Practice* (Oxford University Press 2014) 466.

[72] On the rise of civil society in investor-state arbitration, see e.g. N Bernasconi, MD Brauch, and H Mann, 'Civil Society and International Investment Arbitration: Tracing the Evolution of Concern' in T Schultz and F Ortino (eds), *The Oxford Handbook of International Arbitration* (Oxford University Press 2010) 304.

and, beyond, of investor-state arbitration as a whole. From that latter point of view, it was also argued that the argumentative strength of comparative reasoning faces limits due to the diversity of the audience of arbitral tribunals.

Those findings sound pretty negative. But there are actually reasons to conclude on a positive note. First, the way tribunals conduct comparative reasoning can improve. In particular, they can pay greater attention to the issue of similarity and be less selective. More fundamentally, there are reasons for being optimistic because of the current evolution of the regime. This is due to the fact that, incrementally, international investment law and arbitration is developing new traits that – in the long run – will make the use of comparative reasoning less pressing and, in any case, will certainly rationalise the way it is used.

First of all, as touched upon in Section 3.2.3 in relation to legal indeterminacy, recent treaty practice shows that IIAs' provisions are much more detailed than they used to be in the agreements adopted in the past.[73] This means that relying on comparative reasoning to interpret those provisions will not be necessary in the future, or in any case less necessary. Secondly – and more importantly– one can conclude on a positive note because of the identity that the regime is progressively acquiring. Why and how? In a nutshell, because it increasingly enables people to be informed and to express their opinions and arguments. This clearly appears in the various mechanisms and fora that have recently been set up to allow various stakeholders to formally contribute to law-making and to dispute settlement,[74] in particular at ICSID.[75] As illustrated by the reform of investor-state arbitration, this contribution – and the exchange of views it permits – allow the regime to make progress in building its own identity. Even if one is less optimistic, one may consider at least that the regime is being equipped to build that identity.

[73] On this process, see e.g. F Ortino, 'Refining the Content and Role of Investment "Rules" and "Standards": a New Approach to International Investment Treaty Making' (2013) ICSID Review – Foreign Investment Law Journal 152.

[74] See e.g. E Shirlow, 'Three Manifestations of Transparency in International Investment Law: A Story of Sources, Stakeholders and Structures' (2017) 8 Gottingen Journal of International Law 73. On the role of civil society outside formal channels, see e.g. J Cavert, 'Civil Society and Investor-State Dispute Settlement: Assessing the Social Dimensions of Investment Disputes in Latin America' (2018) 23 New Political Economy 46.

[75] See supra (n 12).

In the end, one should not forget that international investment law and arbitration, as we know it, is still a pretty young legal regime. Identity being certainly a result more than a given, it is unsurprising that the regime is still building a proper one. The procedural mechanisms and existing fora help in this process. They speed up and streamline that process, which otherwise would certainly have been more chaotic and slower. That being said, one should realise that getting an identity does not amount to the disappearance of hybridity; international investment law and arbitration will no doubt remain hybrid to a certain degree. Is that a problem and could it be any different? Certainly not, as hybridity appears to be inherent to our legal systems.[76] This is the common fate that they all face, especially as a result of globalisation and of the ever-growing interaction between cultures and legal systems.[77]

[76] R Banakar, 'Power, Culture and Method in Comparative Law' (2009) 5 International Journal of Law in Context 69, cited in Vadi (n 2) 73.

[77] Ellis (n 63) 966.

4

Interpretation of Customary International Environmental Law before International Courts

ILIAS PLAKOKEFALOS

4.1 Introduction

International environmental law (IEL) is a fairly recent addition to public international law.[1] International courts and tribunals so far have had few opportunities to discuss its customary aspects, yet they have, in recent years, ruled on some issues central to IEL. This chapter focuses on the interpretative efforts of, mainly, the International Court of Justice (ICJ) but also looking into *ad hoc* tribunals when necessary, that is, whenever they venture into customary international environmental law. An analysis of all international environmental law judgments would clearly yield some useful results but it cannot be successfully undertaken within the confines of these chapters. Another choice that limits the scope of the chapter is to look at two customary IEL obligations: the no-harm rule and the obligation to conduct an environmental impact assessment (EIA). Therefore, it is far more useful for our purposes to focus on those rules that have been discussed by the ICJ and by tribunals with general international law jurisdiction

Having delimited the chapter's content regarding IEL, it is apposite to also sketch the theoretical contours of the chapter regarding interpretation. The starting point on any discussion on interpretation of customary rules is to distinguish it from the process of identification of these rules.[2] After they identify the existence a customary rule (such as no-

[1] The first text of universal ambit, albeit a soft law one is the Stockholm Declaration of 1972. It is not the first text on environmental law, but it can be safely claimed that it marked the beginning of the discipline within international law. UN Conference on the Human Environment, 'Stockholm Declaration on the Human Environment' (5–16 June 1972) UN Doc A/Conf.48/4 and Corr.1 (Stockholm Declaration).

[2] R di Marco, 'Customary International Law: Identification versus Interpretation' in P Merkouris, J Kammerhofer and N Arajärvi (eds) *The Theory, Practice, and Interpretation of Customary International Law* (Cambridge University Press 2022) 416;

harm or EIA),[3] courts also often – but not always – engage with the determination of its content.[4] Arguably, this shows that there are two steps in the process: step one is the identification of the existence rule as custom and step two is the determination of its content. This step can be regarded as interpretation of the rule.[5] The chapter focuses on this second step.

It looks like, at least at first sight, that identification of the existence of the rule (that is the first step) is simply a snapshot of the rule at a particular point in time. Then the question becomes what are the possibilities that a court has to determine regarding its content and what normative weight each of them carries. A first option is the possibility that the court has identified the rule and, in so doing, it has also determined its content. Another, more convincing, possibility is that the court identifies the rule and has to give it some meaning, has to explain it, in order to apply it to the facts of the case. This is the interpretative process.[6] Such an approach means that there are some elements of the rule that cannot be considered as part of the identity of the rule but as interpretation of the rule, and it is the interpretation that gives the rule its content. One can think of a case where the rules of customary EIA are being fleshed out by courts through references to the rich material to be found in the Conference of the Parties of IEL treaties, for example.[7] This construct can prove to be particularly useful especially since IEL is a technical and rather fast evolving area of law, and courts can take the opportunity to enrich their enunciation of a customary rule through interpretation that conforms to the accepted IEL standards.

P Merkouris, 'Interpreting the Customary Rules on Interpretation' (2017) 19 ICLR 126, 127.

3 There is a considerable body of literature that engages with the difficulties of custom identification see, among many others, S Talmon, 'Determining Customary International Law: The ICJ's Methodology between Induction, Deduction and Assertion' 26(2) EJIL 417.

4 The identification of the rule and the identification of its content often appear simultaneously, therefore there is no absolute need for the one to follow the other, see di Marco (n 2) 417.

5 Merkouris (n 2).

6 Di Marco (n 2) 423.

7 On the nature of the Conference of the Parties in IEL treaties, see RR Churchill and G Ulfstein, 'Autonomous Institutional Arrangements in Multilateral Environmental Agreements: A Little-Noticed Phenomenon in International Law' (2000) 94 AJIL 623; S Rioseco, 'Conferences of the Parties Beyond International Environmental Law: How COPs Influence the Content and Implementation of their Parent Treaties' (2023) 36 (3) LJIL 699.

It appears that international courts in the interpretative process of IEL often oscillate between evolutive and regressive interpretations of the relevant customary rules. This requires some explanation. The evolutive interpretation takes into account developments that appear to affect the rule in question and push it to an interpretive point where it catches up with these developments.[8] Regressive interpretation involves a backward-looking approach where the courts are content with offering an interpretation that diverges from the standards surrounding the rule rendering a more conservative version of it.[9] Both interpretative methods form, among others, a central finding of the chapter.

The chapter proceeds by accepting the idea that customary international law can be interpreted, for the most part, using the methods of interpretation propounded in the Vienna Convention on the Law of Treaties.[10] The range of methods the courts can use in interpreting customary IEL is no different than that applicable to other branches of international law.[11] Of course, the distinct possibility that the development of a rule through time may not simply affect its interpretation but may yield a new rule through fresh practice and *opinio juris* is acknowledged.

In the second section, the chapter sets the stage by introducing IEL and its peculiarities in relation to customary law. The third section is divided in two parts. The first one discusses customary law interpretation of the no-harm rule while the second part analyzes the interpretation of the obligation to conduct an EIA. The fourth section presents some concluding remarks showing that international courts do not have a consistent

[8] On evolutive interpretation generally, see, among many others, P Merkouris, 'The Principle of Systemic Integration' [2021] MPEiPro 2866. See also, in the context of the European Court of Human Rights, LA Sicilianos, 'Evolutive Interpretation of the ECHR and Beyond: Recent Developments in the Case-Law of the European Court of Human Rights' (2020) 40 HRLJ 1.

[9] LR Helfer and E Voeten, 'Walking Back Human Rights in Europe?' (2020) 31(3) EJIL 797, 802–5, 817–19.

[10] Vienna Convention on the Law of Treaties (adopted 22 May 1969, entered into force 27 January 1980) 1155 UNTS 331, arts 31, 32, 33 (VCLT). On interpretation of international environmental law in general, and mainly of treaty law, see Y Tanaka, 'Reflections on Time Elements on the International Law of the Environment' (2013) ZaöRV 139; N Mileva and M Fortuna, 'Environmental Protection as an Object of and Tool for Evolutionary Interpretation' in G Abi-Saab et al (eds), *Evolutionary Interpretation and International Law* (Hart 2019) 123.

[11] For a forceful argument on the dilution of the identity of environmental norms, see D Kysar, *Regulating from Nowhere: Environmental Law and the Search of Objectivity* (Yale University Press 2010).

approach to the interpretation of international environmental law. They rather oscillate between expansive and restrictive interpretative efforts.

4.2 The Peculiar Case of IEL

Before embarking on the analysis of the ICJ's attempts at interpretation of customary IEL, it is necessary to place the primary rules of IEL in the framework of international dispute settlement procedures. Every branch of international law (or any kind of law for that matter) tends to be treated as a 'special case' by the literature devoted to that branch.[12] For the purposes of this chapter, it is irrelevant why this happens, maybe it is simply the manifestation of a natural knack for differentiation or for carving a separate niche within the broader picture of public international law. It is most probably a corollary of the development of specific areas of international law. With that caveat in mind, it is submitted that IEL has some attributes that, at least for the purposes of the subject matter of this chapter, distinguish it from most of the other branches of public international law.

The most obvious one is that IEL is mainly law produced through written agreement. Depending on the source, the number of IEL treaties varies, but it is safe to say that it lies in the thousands.[13] That is counting everything from bilateral treaties regulating the use of a shared resource (e.g. the River Uruguay in *Pulp Mills*)[14] to global instruments with near universal acceptance (e.g. Convention on Biological Diversity).[15] It is true that many of these instruments sometimes eschew clear-cut categorization. Is the Convention on International Trade of Endangered Species[16] an environmental protection treaty, a trade regulating treaty, or something in between? Be that as it may, it is fair to admit that their sheer number makes it abundantly clear that IEL is predominantly shaped by

[12] ILC, 'Fragmentation of International Law: Difficulties Arising from the Diversification and Expansion of International Law: Report of the Study Group of the International Law Commission' (18 July 2006) UN Doc A/CN.4/L.702 [6, 11].

[13] On the numbers, lists and the challenges of cataloguing environmental agreements, see RB Mitchell et al, 'What we Know and Could Know About International Environmental Agreements' (2020) 20(1) Global Environmental Politics 103.

[14] *Case Concerning Pulp Mills on the River Uruguay* (*Argentina v Uruguay*) (Judgment) [2010] ICJ Rep 14.

[15] Convention on Biological Diversity (adopted 5 June 1992, entered into force 29 December 1993) 1760 UNTS 79.

[16] Convention on International Trade in Endangered Species of Wild Fauna and Flora (adopted 3 March 1973, entered into force 1 July 1975) 993 UNTS 243.

them. On top of that there are some treaties that, although they do not fall strictly under the rubric of IEL, have had an immense impact on the field like, most importantly, the UN Convention on the Law of the Sea (LOSC).[17] At the time of its adoption, it was the instrument with the most comprehensive environmental protection section that had ever appeared.[18]

There are also two other places, besides treaties, where the heavy influence of the written word on the formation and content of IEL shows. First, the soft law of the Stockholm and Rio Declarations.[19] It is undeniable that both Declarations shaped many aspects of IEL.[20] The Stockholm Declaration was the first document that attempted to provide for a complete account of the principles of international environmental law.[21] It is obvious that the Declaration is not binding. Yet, it is equally obvious, mainly from the language of the text,[22] that it aimed at setting the scene for further development of the principles into one or more legally binding documents. The Rio Declaration, concluded twenty years after Stockholm, showed that States had not, even at that time, reached a point where they could agree to a binding document on general IEL. Nonetheless, the precautionary principle, the principle of prevention and the principle of sustainable development were all proclaimed in these

[17] United Nations Convention on the Law of the Sea (adopted 10 December 1982, entered into force 16 November 1994) 1833 UNTS 3 (LOSC). On the environmental aspects of the Law of the Sea, see, among many others, J Harrison, *Saving the Oceans Through: The International Legal Framework for the Protection of the Marine Environment* (Oxford University Press 2017).

[18] This is also evident in the literature. See, for example, AE Boyle, 'Marine Pollution and the Law of the Sea Convention' (1985) 79(2) AJIL 347; JI Charney, 'The Marine Environment and the 1982 United Nations Convention on the Law of the Sea' (1994) 28(4) International Lawyer 879.

[19] Stockholm Declaration (n 1); UNGA, 'Rio Declaration on Environment and Development' (12 August 1992) UN Doc A/Conf.151/5/Rev.1.

[20] D Shelton, 'Stockholm Declaration (1972) and Rio Declaration (1992)' [2008] MPEPIL 1608 [21].

[21] See LB Sohn, 'The Stockholm Declaration on Human Environment' (1973) 14(3) HILJ 423.

[22] Principle 23 is a good example: 'Without prejudice to such criteria as may be agreed upon by the international community, or to standards which will have to be determined nationally, it will be essential in all cases to consider the systems of values prevailing in each country, and the extent of the applicability of standards which are valid for the most advanced countries but which may be inappropriate and of unwarranted social cost for the developing countries.' Stockholm Declaration (n 1) Principle 33. See also Stockholm Declaration (n 1) Principle 25.

documents.[23] Their role in the formation of both customary international environmental law and in shaping the content of many international environmental treaties cannot be overstated.

The second place where the influence of the written word on international environmental law is undeniable is the work of the International Law Commission (ILC) of the United Nations through the Articles on the Prevention of Transboundary Harm from Hazardous Activities and (ILC Prevention Articles) and the Principles on Allocation of Loss in the Case of Transboundary Harm from Hazardous Activities (ILC Allocation of Loss Principles).[24] While the ILC Allocation of Loss Principles represent a light prescriptive approach by generalizing the special rules on civil liability,[25] the ILC Prevention Articles mainly codify customary international environmental law.[26]

Both the declaratory instruments and the work of the ILC are not binding as such on States. They, nonetheless, exert an immense normative pull. The principles contained in the former have found their way in numerous ways in international environmental treaties while the latter, through the authoritative status of the ILC, have been relied upon by courts and States alike.[27] Parts of both sets of documents codify customary law, some have become customary law, no less because they have been included in these documents, and others still exist in the twilight of *lex ferenda*.

The second peculiarity of IEL is that it does not have a constituent binding international instrument that sets out the basic general rules.

[23] For a comprehensive account of the Rio Declaration, see J Viñuales (ed), *The Rio Declaration on Environment and Development: A Commentary* (Oxford University Press 2015).

[24] ILC, 'Articles on Prevention of Transboundary Harm from Hazardous Activities with Commentaries' [2001/II – Part Two] YBILC 144 (ILC Prevention Articles); ILC, 'Principles on the Allocation of Loss in the Case of Transboundary Harm Arising Out of Hazardous Activities, with Commentaries [2006/II – Part Two] YBILC 56.

[25] See AE Boyle, 'Globalizing Environmental Liability: The Interplay of National and International Law' (2005) 17(1) JEL 3, 16. Handl claims that most of the Principles represent progressive development of the law. See G Handl, 'International Accountability for Transboundary Environmental Harm Revisited: What Role for "State Liability"?' (2007) 37(2–3) EP&L 116, 122.

[26] I Plakokefalos, 'Prevention Obligations in International Environmental Law' (2012) 23(1) YBIEL 3.

[27] *Certain Activities Carried out by Nicaragua in the Border Area (Costa Rica v Nicaragua) and Construction of a Road in Costa Rica along the San Juan River (Nicaragua v Costa Rica)* (Judgment) [2015] ICJ Rep 665 [190]. See also *Responsibilities and Obligations of States Sponsoring Persons and Entities with Respect to Activities in the Area* (Advisory Opinion) [2011] ITLOS Rep 10 [116].

In the field of human rights there are major international conventions as well major regional conventions that share a common vocabulary and, in a way, contain the vast majority of human rights in fairly similar manner.[28] The LOSC also sets out the bulk of the rules that govern the oceans. In much the same way, the World Trade Organization (WTO) sets out the rules by which States conduct trade across the globe.[29] This is important because it means that, despite the vast number of IEL treaties, there is not a single place where one can look and identify the main rules that permeate the whole of IEL. This is reasonable. There are numerous components of the environment that merit separate, detailed attention.[30] At the same time, there are numerous environmentally harmful substances that also have to be regulated separately and in detail.[31] The level of detail required by most environmental regulation simply cannot be attained through a general instrument.

At the same time, it is submitted that an instrument containing the general principles of IEL and a host of generally accepted procedural, preventive rules that cut across all fields of environmental protection would be a welcome development. First, because it would crystallize relevant customary rules providing a basis for analysis and interpretation

[28] The European Convention on Human Rights and Fundamental Freedoms presents many similarities to the other regional human rights systems (Interamerican, African) as well as the International Covenant on Civil and Political Rights. A simple reading of the texts leads to that conclusion. Of course, there are differences among these instruments, but there are clear common threads. See A Huneus and M Rask Madsen, 'Between Universalism and Regional Law and Politics: A Comparative History of American, European, and African Human Rights Systems' (2018) 16(1) International Journal of Constitutional Law 136; C Haynes and M Killander, 'Universality and the Growth of Regional Systems' in D Shelton (ed) *The Oxford Handbook of International Human Rights Law* (Oxford University Press 2013) 670.

[29] Marrakesh Agreement Establishing the World Trade Organization (adopted 15 April 1994, entered into force 1 January 1995) 1867 UNTS 154.

[30] There are cross-cutting issues (such as climate change) that are influenced by every conceivable human activity but there are also specialized fields of IEL such as oil pollution (MARPOL) or the protection of migratory species. See Protocol of 1978 relating to the International Convention for the Prevention of Pollution from Ships, 1973 (adopted 17 February 1978, entered into force 2 October 1983) 1341 UNTS 3; Convention on the Protection of Migratory Species of Wild Animals (adopted 23 June 1979, entered into force 1 November 1983) 1651 UNTS 333.

[31] See, for example, Stockholm Convention on Persistent Organic Pollutants (adopted 22 May 2001, entered into force 17 May 2004) 2256 UNTS 119; Rotterdam Convention on the Prior Informed Consent Procedure for Certain Hazardous Chemicals and Pesticides in International Trade (adopted 10 September 1998, entered into force 24 February 2004) 2244 UNTS 337.

by courts and tribunals. This would bypass the process of affirming the existence of a customary rule and then going about defining its content.[32] Second, it would provide a starting point to courts and tribunals whose jurisdiction is limited to a single convention. The International Tribunal of the Law of the Sea (ITLOS) and the Arbitral Tribunals constituted under the LOSC, or the WTO panels, for instance, are mainly applying and interpreting the instruments that have conferred jurisdiction upon them. When they venture outside the confines of those instruments, they do so in order to interpret conventional rules by reference to other relevant instruments, under Article 31(3)(c) VCLT.[33] Despite their best efforts, these tribunals have both a built-in bias (since it is their job to apply the convention in question and not to apply IEL) and a constraint (since their jurisdiction is limited by the convention in question).

The number of IEL treaties, the complementing soft law instruments such as the Stockholm and Rio Declarations as well as the work of the ILC appear to cover most aspects of IEL regulation. It is probably, however, the lack of a general IEL treaty that lends IEL customary law its special significance. We are presented here with some sort of a paradox. The proliferation and sheer volume of IEL treaties apparently marginalize customary IEL, yet, at the same time, the lack of a general IEL treaty (let alone the lack of any specialized international court)[34] brings customary IEL squarely back into the picture. Therefore, if the question is 'how many customary international law rules exist that regulate international environmental law', the answer would be 'very few'. But if the question is tweaked and becomes 'how important are customary rules in international environmental law', the answer differs slightly.

4.3 Interpretation of Customary IEL

The starting point in this discussion is the issue of the applicable methods of interpretation of IEL. These methods should roughly correspond those enumerated in Articles 31–33 of the VCLT. Among these methods, some doubt remains as to the applicability of the 'object and purpose' of the

[32] P Merkouris (n 2).

[33] *The South China Sea Arbitration (Philippines v China)* (Award of 12 July 2016) PCA Case No 2013-19, 249 [956]; WTO Appellate Body Report, *United States – Import Prohibition of Certain Shrimp and Shrimp Products* (12 October 1998) WT/DS58/AB/R [131].

[34] The International Court of Justice introduced a Chamber on Environmental Matters in 1993. The Chamber was inactive since no cases were brought before it and the ICJ stopped holding elections for its Bench in 2006 effectively dismantling it.

rule, at least within the context of IEL.[35] It is submitted that it is extremely difficult, and possibly fruitless, to ascertain such an object and purpose to customary IEL. All the more so that most, if not all, IEL rules can be certainly read in multiple ways, pertaining to the protection of the environment within a given context: development, trade, the normal continuation of economic activity and the like. Therefore, most environmental rules can be seen as having contrasting objects and purposes.[36] This is the main reason why most environmental rules have by their inception an inherent constraint with regards to teleological interpretation as they yield to a number of considerations that have little to do with what could be assumed to be the object and purpose of an environmental rule, that is, simply the protection of the environment. The question that comes first is which are those rules with which international courts are faced. Bearing that in mind, two preliminary observations are in order.

First, most – if not all – IEL cases that have reached an international court or tribunal are one way or another connected to an international treaty. This may happen because the said court or tribunal is being set up by a treaty. The ITLOS, for instance, in the Advisory Opinion on the Deep Seabed analyzed the no-harm obligation in the context of the deep seabed as it appears in the LOSC.[37] It did not go about making far-reaching proclamations outside the scope of its jurisdiction. Similarly, the Arbitral Tribunal set up for the South China Sea dispute interpreted (in a very rigorous manner) the LOSC, at times looking also at other conventional instruments.[38] Yet, the fact remains that it was the LOSC that was the focus of the analysis. Second, customary IEL rules are, as often is the case with custom, rather vague and general in nature. This is not necessarily bad. On the contrary, it leaves plenty of room to the courts and tribunals to elaborate on the rule presenting it each time in its more up to date and fullest form.

[35] For the view that teleological interpretation is one of the most often used interpretative methods in customary international law, see P Merkouris, *Interpretation of Customary International Law: Of Methods and Limits* (Brill 2024) 27-9.

[36] For a forceful argument on the dilution of the identity of environmental norms, see Kysar (n 11).

[37] *Responsibilities and Obligations of States Sponsoring Persons and Entities with Respect to Activities in the Area* (n 27); See LOSC (n 17) art 139.

[38] *The South China Sea Arbitration* (n 33). This, of course, was deemed necessary in order to accurately interpret certain provisions of the LOSC regarding ecosystems and species protection.

In the cases where courts and tribunals have discussed customary IEL, the two customary obligations that feature prominently are the prohibition of transboundary environmental harm (or no-harm rule) and the obligation to conduct an environmental impact assessment (EIA). The no-harm rule is possibly the most basic obligation in IEL. The starting point for any discussion involving transboundary environmental harm is the content of the obligation of the state from whose jurisdiction or control the harm emanates.[39] The ILC managed to formulate the main aspects of the obligation in the Prevention Articles.[40]

With regard to the obligation to conduct EIA, as I have argued elsewhere,[41] it is an obligation of dual nature. On the one hand, it is a constitutive element of the broader no-harm obligation and, on the other hand, it is a free standing obligation of result The no-harm rule is an obligation of conduct and can be seen as containing a number of elements and the obligation to conduct an EIA is one of them.[42] On the other hand, the obligation to conduct an EIA is also an obligation of result generating its own content.[43] This is one way of looking, through a unifying concept, at the two obligations: the substantive obligation (no-harm) being analyzed in a series of procedural obligations, one of them being the obligation to conduct an EIA. Both rules are general in nature, yet not open ended, and they have evolved through time. This is evident both from the extensive discussions in the ILC, as well as the conclusion of numerous treaties that include either one or both rules. What is more, when it comes to the obligation to conduct an EIA, there is substantial state practice, as well as at least one dedicated treaty to the subject, namely the Espoo Convention.[44] It is, therefore, evident that when the courts have to apply either rule they have a variety of tools before them so as to proceed with the identification and elaboration of their content. The following section will look at the way the courts have approached these rules.

[39] F Fancioni and T Scovazzi (eds), *International Responsibility for Environmental Harm* (Kluwer 1991); P Okowa, 'Procedural Obligations in International Environmental Agreements'(1996) 67 BYBIL 275; Plakokefalos (n 26).

[40] ILC Prevention Articles (n 24) art 3.

[41] Plakokefalos (n 26).

[42] ibid 36.

[43] ibid 35.

[44] Convention on Environmental Impact Assessment in a Transboundary Context (adopted 25 February 1991, entered into force 10 September 1997) 1989 UNTS 309.

4.3.1 No-harm Obligation

This section explores the stance of international courts towards the customary rule of no-harm in IEL. The approach followed is a chronological one because in this way it is easier to follow the movement of the interpretative efforts of the jurisprudence. Ironically enough, the first proclamation on non-conventional IEL is to be found in the *Trail Smelter* case between the US and Canada regarding air pollution where the Arbitral Tribunal famously stated that

> no state has the right to use its territory or permit the use of its territory in such a manner as to cause injury by fumes in or to the territory of another or the properties or persons therein, when the case is of a serious consequence and the injury is established by clear and convincing evidence.[45]

The irony lies in the methodology of the Tribunal because it did not make that proclamation after reviewing the previous case law of international courts since such case law did not exist. The Tribunal made the point that it could not even draw an analogy with water pollution since there was no international case law on that issue either.[46] Therefore, it was forced to come up with a different solution since the applicable law on the case was international law, relevant rules of the law of the US, and the Tribunal was also directed to 'give consideration to the desire of the high contracting parties to reach a solution just to all parties concerned'.[47]

The Tribunal came up with the first iteration of the no-harm rule after reviewing the jurisprudence of the US Supreme Court on transboundary intra-state pollution. It used as a legal basis US law, and it declared that the same principles could be part of international law by analogy especially since there was no international rule contradicting them.[48] Moreover, the Tribunal, in the process of establishing the no-harm rule, also made explicit reference to the desire of the parties to reach a just solution. It appears that it took this to mean that it could go beyond existing international law offering an extra justification to its decision to draw an analogy between US and international law. Therefore, the Tribunal propounded the above dictum on the basis of the 'principles

[45] *Trail Smelter (United States, Canada)* (1941) III RIAA 1905, 1965.

[46] ibid 1963.

[47] This is stated in Article IV of the Convention for the Settlement of Difficulties Arising from Operation of Smelter at Trail BC; ibid 1908.

[48] ibid 1963–65.

of international law' as well as the law of the United States. It is not clear how the Tribunal uses the term 'principles' in the text. It could be that it wanted to denote that there is a general principle of law[49] or, more probably, it just used the term 'principle' interchangeably with the term 'rule'. The language in the pertinent paragraph indicates that it probably meant to give the term a normative value. The Tribunal refers to the 'right' of States, and it also refers to 'injury'. It, crucially, also includes the threshold of the application of the principle by stating that the consequences of the harm must be serious, and it also declares a standard of proof. While all this could be just the only wording the Tribunal had at its disposal, it most probably means that it viewed the principle as a legal rule. This becomes even clearer a few lines further down the text where the Tribunal holds that, on the basis of the dictum, it finds Canada responsible in international law.[50]

The crucial question is whether the Tribunal simply established the existence of the rule, or it also determined its content. It is obvious that the Tribunal did both, at least to some degree and with a twist. This is not a case where the judges look at the two elements of customary law, state practice and *opinio juris* and then decide whether a rule has come to existence. The Tribunal decided that a rule existed without looking at the two elements (they were not there) or even mentioning its nature, leaving it to be inferred from the wording of the decision. Then, it went on to shape its contours. Therefore, it did interpret the rule. Based on its reading of the jurisprudence of the US Supreme Court, it did set the threshold of application of the rule (serious consequence) and it did set the evidentiary standard required for the rule to be applied.

This is a striking dictum in that what can be seen as interpretation of the no-harm rule also serves as evidence that the Tribunal indeed meant to establish an international customary rule that does not come from international law as such. Rule identification and content determination, or rather interpretation, are intertwined in the dictum and still there is a way to distinguish them. For both identification and interpretation, though, there is no methodological consistency or clarity in the decision.

[49] In the standard sense of the term as used in the ICJ Statute. See Statute of the International Court of Justice (adopted 26 June 1945, entered into force 24 October 1945) 33 UNTS 993, art 38(1). Despite the fact that the Tribunal's decision predates the ICJ Statute, it is also clear that the concept itself predates it too. See Statute of the Permanent Court of International Justice (adopted 16 December 1920, entered into force 8 October 1921) 6 LNTS 389, art 38.

[50] *Trail Smelter* (n 45) 1965.

The identification of custom is unorthodox to say the least, and the interpretation also comes without any strong backing in practice, *opinio juris*, or other elements that could lead to evolutive or systemic interpretation. The Tribunal looked for an interpretative solution outside the confines of classic customary international law and therefore it worked its way through the analogy with US intrastate law. The award remains a testament to the efforts of the Tribunal to come up with a viable solution to a pressing problem while, at the same time, it brought the no-harm rule to life. And this is no small feat.

The general application of the rule was affirmed, albeit in a context outside IEL, by the ICJ in *Corfu Channel*.[51] It is submitted that it cannot be safely assumed that the ICJ had in mind the Trail Smelter judgment when formulating the dictum in *Corfu Channel*. In *Corfu Channel*, the ICJ held that every State has an 'obligation not to allow knowingly its territory to be used for acts contrary to the rights of other States'.[52] This is a less nuanced repetition of *Trail Smelter*. There are two points of contact between *Trail Smelter* and *Corfu Channel* dicta. First, it was clear in the *Trail Smelter* dictum that the rule can be breached through omission; and in *Corfu Channel*, the ICJ applied exactly this aspect of the rule since the harm was indeed caused by omission. Second, and more importantly, the rule in *Corfu Channel* becomes one of general application and is not confined to cases of injury by fumes. These points show that the ICJ did not move towards interpretation but that it simply generalized the *Trail Smelter* no-harm iteration. It also, importantly, did not adopt the extra elements of the *Trail Smelter* dictum, namely the requirement of seriousness and the evidentiary standard. This is not to say that there was any kind of judicial dialogue at play. It is merely a reading of the two cases with the benefit of hindsight. At the same time, the ICJ did include a criterion of knowledge that was not there in *Trail Smelter*. It is hard to see how this is an interpretative move at least not in the sense of refining the *Trail Smelter* dictum. The ICJ simply stated clearly what was implicit in *Trail Smelter* thereby deducing an obligation of notification. In *Trail Smelter*, the facts of the case did not leave any doubt as to the element of knowledge; therefore, it was only natural that the Tribunal would not linger on the issue. The operation in Trail was known to both parties and what was left to be determined was

[51] *Corfu Channel* (*United Kingdom v Albania*) (Merits) [1949] ICJ Rep 4.
[52] ibid 22.

responsibility and remedies. In *Corfu Channel*, the issue of knowledge was central to the facts and the ICJ gave more prominence to it.[53]

What seemed like a promising discussion regarding the no-harm rule in the 1940s became a non-issue in the following decades. When the issue resurfaced before the ICJ almost fifty years later in *Nuclear Weapons*, IEL had already exploded.[54] Both the Stockholm and Rio Declarations were adopted, the ILC had been working on the topic of injurious consequences arising out of acts not prohibited by international law for over a decade and most major environmental conventions were in place.[55]

Despite the developments in IEL, there was no actual environmental litigation before the ICJ or any other forum with general international law jurisdiction. It was only in 2010 in *Pulp Mills* that the ICJ had a chance to revisit the no-harm rule. In *Pulp Mills*, the ICJ took a surprising course that not only left the content of the rule opaque but also sparked some unneeded confusion. The dispute between Argentina and Uruguay concerned the possible environmental impact of the construction of pulp mills on the river Uruguay, as the river was a shared resource between the two States. The legal basis for the dispute was the Statute of the River Uruguay (CARU) that laid down the rules for the management of the river by the two parties before the Court. At the same time, however, the ICJ recognized that in order to interpret the obligations arising out of the Statute, it had to resort to general international law as well as subsequent agreements between the parties.[56] It was in this vein that the Court went on to discuss customary IEL.

The ICJ stated that 'that the principle of prevention, as a customary rule, has its origins in the due diligence that is required of a State in its territory'.[57] It then went on to cite *Corfu Channel* and *Nuclear Weapons* in support of this statement and it held that '[a] State is thus obliged to use all the means at its disposal in order to avoid activities which take place in its territory, or in any area under its jurisdiction, causing

[53] ibid 22–23.
[54] *Legality of the Threat or Use of Nuclear Weapons* (Advisory Opinion) [1996] ICJ Rep 226.
[55] See, for example, the Convention on Long-Range Transboundary Air Pollution (adopted 13 November 1979, entered into force 16 March 1983) 1302 UNTS 217; Vienna Convention on the Protection of the Ozone Layer (adopted 22 March 1985, entered into force 22 September 1988) 1513 UNTS 293; Convention on Biological Diversity (n 15); United Nations Framework Convention on Climate Change (adopted 7 May 1992, entered into force 21 March 1994) 1771 UNTS 107.
[56] *Pulp Mills* (n 14) [79].
[57] ibid [101].

significant damage to the environment of another State'.[58] To begin with, the wording of the no-harm obligation as it appears in *Pulp Mills* is different than the wording used in previous decisions. While the content remains the same, it is unnecessarily confusing. It is not clear why the Court referred to due diligence. Whether it did so because it considered due diligence a general obligation, rule, or principle is not clear. Due diligence speaks to the nature of an obligation denoting that it is an obligation of conduct and not of result.[59] It simply characterizes the obligation in question. In this instance, the no harm obligation is an obligation that requires due diligence on behalf of the State of origin of the activity. Second, the ICJ does not explain the relationship between the principle of prevention and due diligence. It could be that the Court really meant that there is a general obligation of due diligence, irrespective of the existence of a primary obligation like the no-harm rule in the context of international environmental law. It could be that the Court pointed to the dictum in *Corfu Channel* as establishing such a general principle. The fact that the Court cites *Corfu Channel* in the preceding sentence could point towards that direction. It is highly unlikely, however, that the Court would proceed to such an important statement without offering any support. Moreover, and just like in *Nuclear Weapons*, the ICJ did not make any use of the actual development and refinement of the customary obligation so as to interpret it in a new light. It could either decide that the rule has changed through state practice and *opinio juris*, it could interpret dynamically the rule and bring it up to modern standards, or it could look at the development of IEL as a whole and go for a systemic interpretation. The ICJ did not look at international practice, it did not take into account the work of the ILC, it did not look at relevant treaties or the work of their treaty bodies. It neither seemed to bother too much with the current understanding of environmental harm in science and technology.

[58] ibid.

[59] G Handl, 'Territorial Sovereignty and the Problem of Transnational Pollution' (1975) 69 AJIL 50, 59; R Pisillo Mazzeschi, *'Due Diligence' e Responsabilità Internazionale degli Stati* (Milano, Giuffrè 1989); PM Dupuy, 'Reviewing the Difficulties of Codification: on Ago's Classification of Obligations of Means and Obligations of Result in Relation to State Responsibility' (1999) 10 EJIL 371, 377; RP Barnidge, 'The Due Diligence Principle in International Law' (2006) 8 ICLR 81; S Besson, *Due Diligence in International Law* (Brill 2023). There is a growing discussion on whether due diligence is something more than an element of a primary obligation. See N McDonald, 'The Role of Due Diligence in International Law' (2019) 68(4) ICLQ 1041; R Mackenzie-Gray Scott, 'Due Diligence as a Secondary Rule of General International Law' (2021) 34 LJIL 343.

Nonetheless, the ICJ did follow the developments in IEL in one significant respect by introducing the threshold of 'significant harm'. The ILC in its Prevention Articles had already lowered the threshold from 'serious consequence' to 'significant harm' and it has not been seriously challenged before international courts. The ILC was clear that the threshold is that of 'significant harm'.[60] The ILC based its decision on the Brundtland Commission's Article 10, the Commission being a group of experts under the UN that produced the seminal 'Our Common Future' report.[61] The ILC went on to further define 'significant' as meaning '*something more than detectable but need not be at the level of "serious" or "substantial"*'.[62] The ILC makes a clear choice between the two thresholds. The Commentary to Article 2 acknowledges that the threshold of 'serious' is used both in *Trail Smelter* and in *Lake Lanoux*[63] arbitrations.[64] Both judgments were handed down decades before the ILC adopted the Articles on Prevention; and in between, IEL had developed in an explosive manner covering almost, if not all, areas of human activity and its connection to the environment. The ILC follows the development of the law towards a more progressive path.

The Court accepted the progress signalled by the ILC regarding the threshold of environmental harm, but it proceeded to introduce fresh confusion in the content of the no-harm rule. The ICJ cryptically stated that there is a 'functional link' between the substantive obligations of states (that presumably include the no-harm rule) and the procedural obligations of states (that include notification, EIA, the obligation to monitor the relevant activity, to consult and to cooperate, etc.).[65] The Court came to this conclusion interpreting the Statute of the River Uruguay and not a customary law obligation. Nonetheless, it is submitted that it is useful to look at the interpretation of the Statute and the distinction between substantive and procedural obligations therein as significant because the same distinction is reflected in the customary obligation of no-harm. There is the general substantive no-harm rule that prohibits States from using

[60] ILC Prevention Articles (n 24) 148–52. See Commentary to art 2(a) (referring to the risk of significant transboundary harm) and art 3 in particular.

[61] World Commission on Environment and Development, 'Our Common Future' (October 1987) <https://sustainabledevelopment.un.org/content/documents/5987our-common-future.pdf> (last accessed 1 June 2025).

[62] ILC Prevention Articles (n 24) 152 .

[63] *Lac Lanoux (Espagne, France)* (1957) XII UNRIAA 281.

[64] ILC Prevention Articles (n 24).

[65] *Pulp Mills* (n 14) [79].

their territory so as to cause harm to another State.[66] And then, there are procedural obligations that provide guidance to States as to the steps they must take to avoid causing such harm.[67]

The Court's dictum on the functional link between these two types of obligations is apparently promising in that it looks like it interprets the no-harm rule in a nuanced manner. However, it probably means, according to the judgment, that if the substantive obligation is not breached, a breach of a procedural obligation (in *Pulp Mills*, the obligation to notify)[68] is not important from the point of view of reparation. Indeed, the Court declared that the recognition of the breach in the judgment itself constitutes satisfaction. Yet the judgment does not explain in detail what this functional link is – a fact not lost on judges Al Khasawneh and Simma who criticized this lack of any explanation in their joint dissent.[69] The dissent also criticizes the view of the Court on the procedural obligations as unsatisfactory because it renders the procedural obligations essentially unimportant.[70] It is only natural that the 'functional link' statement has not been followed up in the case law that followed *Pulp Mills*. On the contrary, Judge Donoghue directly rejected it in her separate opinion in *Costa Rica/Nicaragua* stating that even '[i]f at a subsequent phase, the failure of a State to exercise due diligence in the implementation of a project causes significant transboundary harm, the primary norm that is breached remains one of due diligence, but the reparations due to the affected State must also address the material damage caused to the affected state' therefore it is not '[u]seful to draw distinctions between "procedural" and "substantive" obligations'.[71]

Pulp Mills was indeed a rare opportunity both from the standpoint of the substance of the case as well as from the standpoint of the evolution of the methodology of the ICJ in identifying and elaborating upon customary international law. The Court followed a path wherein it simply repeated its previous jurisprudence and declined to explain, at

66 Plakokefalos (n 26) 35–36.

67 ibid.

68 *Pulp Mills* (n 14) [111].

69 *Case Concerning Pulp Mills on the River Uruguay* (*Argentina v Uruguay*) (Judgment) (Joint Dissenting Opinion of Judges Al-Khasawneh and Simma) [2010] ICJ Rep 108 [25].

70 ibid [26]. '[T]he conclusion whereby non-compliance with the pertinent procedural obligations had no effect on compliance with the substantive obligations is a proposition that cannot be easily accepted.'

71 *Certain Activities Carried out by Nicaragua in the Border Area (Costa Rica v Nicaragua) and Construction of a Road in Costa Rica along the San Juan River (Nicaragua v Costa Rica)* (Judgment) (Separate Opinion of Judge Donoghue) [2015] ICJ Rep 782 [9].

the very least and even as *obiter*, what the functional link between procedure and substance is. This is even more frustrating if one takes into account the fact that Argentina claimed the breach of both substantive and procedural rules. When the ICJ went on to look at whether the mills had already caused harm to the river Uruguay it did so solely with reference to the Statute of the river as its legal basis.[72] It essentially dismissed all of Argentina's claims based on lack of proof of harm. The outcome of the decision is not unrelated to the lack of elaboration of the no-harm principle. A better enunciated rule could have been more useful in properly assessing the impact of the mills.[73]

The ICJ did not offer any more significant insights in its very brief mention of the no-harm rule in *Costa Rica/Nicaragua* where again it simply affirmed its existence.[74] It did not even look at the more elaborate definition of the rule and the insight to some of its content by the ITLOS in its Deep Seabed Advisory Opinion.[75] The ITLOS Special Chamber went on at some length in discussing the no-harm rule and it made a few interesting points along the way. First, it admitted that the content of due diligence is difficult to pin down.[76] Second, it gave an idea of the mechanics of the rule. The Chamber claimed that the 'obligation becomes stricter or more lenient depending on the activity'.[77] Despite not breaking new ground, the Chamber did interpret the no-harm

[72] In the process of interpreting the Statute, the ICJ relied on the 'Goals and Principles of Environmental Impact Assessment' of the United Nations Environment Programme (UNEP) and used as a reference tool the 'International Pollution Prevention and Control Reference Document on Best Available Techniques in the Pulp Industry' of the European Commission. *Pulp Mills* (n 14) [210, 225].

[73] It was not only the lack of elaboration of the no-harm rule that led to criticism of the judgment. The ICJ also declined to make use of experts in order to analyze the complex technical issues of the case. The Court literally stated that it 'will make its own determination of the facts', even though it acknowledged the complexity of these facts and the divergent evidence presented by the States. See *Pulp Mills* (n 14) [166–68]. Again, Simma and Al-Khasawneh raised the point in their dissent. See *Pulp Mills* (Joint Dissenting Opinion of Judges Al-Khasawneh and Simma) (n 69) [12].

[74] *Certain Activities Carried out by Nicaragua in the Border Area and Construction of a Road in Costa Rica along the San Juan River* (n 27) [104]. The Court merely added the obvious that the obligation applies to all types of activities and is not restricted to industrial activities only.

[75] For an analysis of the ITLOS Advisory Opinion on the issue of due diligence, see I Plakokefalos, 'Seabed Disputes Chamber of the International Tribunal for the Law of the Sea: Responsibilities and Obligations of States, Sponsoring Persons, and Entities, with Respect to Activities in the Area' (2012) 24(1) JEL 133.

[76] *Responsibilities and Obligations of States Sponsoring Persons and Entities with Respect to Activities in the Area* (n 27) [117].

[77] ibid.

obligation as one that does not remain constant in its application, but it must be applied differently depending on the circumstances. This is, according to the Chamber, how the nature of the obligation – that is, due diligence – affects the concrete application of the obligation. The ICJ did not engage with the Advisory Opinion and, like it had done in *Pulp Mills*, ignored the other developments in IEL. The only notable, and important, difference between *Pulp Mills* and *Costa Rica/Nicaragua* is that the ICJ dropped, without explanation, its idea of a functional link between procedural and substantive obligations, and that was a positive step.

What emerges from this picture is that the ICJ did not feel the need to expand upon, analyze, or identify the content of one of the cornerstones of IEL. Why the court made that choice is a matter of speculation. Especially when there is a rich customary as well as treaty background available to the ICJ. The outcome therefore can be described as regressive interpretation of the rule. This concept comes from the realm of human rights. The European Court of Human Rights (ECtHR) has since its early days treated the European Convention on Human Rights as a 'living instrument', that is, it interprets the Convention by adapting its content to the current political and social conditions.[78] In the following years, the ECtHR has interpreted the Convention following the 'living instrument' doctrine, but the interpretation has not been unidirectional towards the expansion of human rights. Research has convincingly shown that the ECtHR has also adopted a regressive interpretative approach overturning previous 'expansionist' decisions.[79] Methodologically speaking, there are significant differences between the two fields when it comes to studying the interpretation of the respective rules. The ECtHR has an impressive number of judgments that offer ample samples for qualitative and quantitative research.[80] The cases that involve IEL before the ICJ, or arbitral tribunals for that matter, are few and far between. Moreover, the ECtHR has the benefit of interpreting a Convention instead of customary international law; therefore, it has a more secure footing from the start. The ICJ, on the contrary, often identifies the customary IEL rule and interprets it at the same time.[81] The concept of regressive interpretation

[78] *Tyrer v United Kingdom* [CC] (25 April 1978) Application no 5856/72 [31]. For an updated and more contemporary assessment of evolutive interpretation under the Convention, see Sicilianos (n 8).

[79] Helfer and Voeten (n 9) 802–5, 817–19.

[80] ibid 817–19.

[81] See *Certain Activities Carried out by Nicaragua in the Border Area and Construction of a Road in Costa Rica along the San Juan River* (n 27) and the approach of the ICJ towards the obligation to conduct an EIA.

is used for what it actually is: a concept. It is not intended to serve as an analogy to human rights law or the human rights jurisprudence of the ECtHR. With few decisions and fewer dissenting or separate opinions, the concept is tested, for the most part, against settled doctrine.

With regressive interpretation in mind, the prehistory of IEL interpretation, traced back to *Trail Smelter*, offers some insights. The Arbitral Tribunal in *Trail Smelter* took very bold steps: it had to come up with analogies and essentially 'invent' a rule of international law that did not exist at the time. While it took time for IEL to develop and grapple with the difficulties of the no-harm rule, eventually the development did come about through the work of the ILC, through conventions that reflect the customary rule, as well as through elaborate doctrinal work. And then the ICJ started moving almost backwards in what can be seen as regressive interpretation. It did not interpret the rule in a way that captured the changes that had occurred in international law. It did not touch upon the threshold of the obligation; it did not offer insights regarding the nature of the rule (the declaration on the due diligence nature aside); and it certainly did not add anything to the rule. On the contrary, the ICJ added unnecessary confusion with the employment of the 'functional link' concept and the decoupling of the procedural obligations from the overall obligation to not cause transboundary harm. Overall, it seems that it regressed to something that falls behind the *Trail Smelter* dictum – let alone further developments in IEL – in terms of boldness and inventiveness.

4.3.2 The Obligation to Conduct an Environmental Impact Assessment

The situation regarding the treatment of the customary obligation to conduct an EIA is even more complex than that surrounding the no-harm rule. This section shows that the case law slowly, but surely, adopted an evolutive interpretation on two levels: first, on the level of the relevant legal framework (national/international) within which it must be conducted and, second, regarding the content of the obligation and the extent to which it can be accurately sketched by international courts.

The obligation to conduct an EIA features prominently in several IEL treaties, and it has become a rule of customary law.[82] EIA is the platform

[82] The Espoo Convention is the most comprehensive one. The obligation also appears in other treaties as well. LOSC (n 17) art 206; Convention on the Transboundary Effects of Industrial Accidents (adopted 17 March 1992, entered into force 19 April 2000) 2105 UNTS 457, art 4; Convention on Environmental Impact Assessment in a Transboundary Context (adopted

upon which states usually concentrate their disputes before international courts and tribunals.[83] Almost every environmental dispute that finds its way before a court has at least one of its aspects dedicated to EIA. What is more, the ITLOS has specifically instructed parties to disputes to cooperate in order to assess the risk of the activity[84] or to appoint experts to study the environmental impact of the activity.[85]

The beginning of the courts' involvement with the obligation to conduct an EIA was not promising. In *Gabčikovo/Nagymaros*, the ICJ had an opportunity to discuss EIA in detail. Despite the fact that the Court shied away from this discussion, it provided some insight as to how international environmental rules should be interpreted. The ICJ suggested that obligations geared towards monitoring transboundary risk are amenable to evolutive interpretation and that they cannot be treated as static norms.[86] This finding is important enough in and of itself and without any connection to the EIA or the no-harm rule. Yet, beside this dictum (better classified as obiter), the ICJ did not go any further. This attitude, even at the time of the *Gabčikovo/Nagymaros* judgment, is peculiar. It is not as if the parties to the dispute had not stressed the EIA, quite the contrary.[87] While the Espoo Convention lays down detailed conditions for the conduct of an EIA, the numerous treaties that contain the obligation do not go into such a detail. At the same time, the

25 February 1991, entered into force 10 September 1997) 1989 UNTS 309, art 2; UNEP, 'Goals and Principles of Environmental Impact Assessment' (1987) UNEP Resolution GC 14/25; Convention on Long-Range Transboundary Air Pollution (n 55) art 2.

83 *MOX Plant (Ireland v United Kingdom)* (Provisional Measures) [2001] ITLOS Rep 95; *Case Concerning the Gabčikovo Nagymaros Project (Hungary/Slovakia)* (Judgment) [1997] ICJ Rep 7; *Pulp Mills* (n 14); *Certain Activities Carried out by Nicaragua in the Border Area and Construction of a Road in Costa Rica along the San Juan River* (n 27).

84 *MOX Plant* (n 83) [89].

85 *Case Concerning Land Reclamation by Singapore in and around the Straits of Johor (Malaysia v Singapore)* (Provisional Measures) [2003] ITLOS Rep 10 [106].

86 *Case Concerning the Gabčikovo Nagymaros Project* (n 83) 140. Boyle states that these norms are not 'frozen in time'. See AE Boyle, 'The *Gabčikovo-Nagymaros* Case: Old Law in New Bottles' (1997) 8(1) YBIEL 13, 17.

87 The Memorial of Hungary is replete with references to the inadequacy of environmental impact assessment conducted for the project, and, most importantly, it expressly includes the lack of a substantive EIA in its reasons offered for the termination of the Convention with Slovakia. See *Case Concerning the Gabčikovo Nagymaros Project (Hungary/Slovakia)* (Memorial of the Republic of Hungary) [2 May 1994] Vol 1 [10.03]. For further arguments on the lack of proper EIA see [3.45–3.56, 5.06, 5.35 and 7.59–7.68]; *Case Concerning the Gabčikovo Nagymaros Project (Hungary/Slovakia)* (Memorial of the Slovak Republic) [2 May 1994] Vol 1 [1.17–1.19, 2.14].

ILC was not clear at all in its commentary to the Prevention Articles.[88] It follows that the snapshot the courts attempt to take of the obligation to conduct and EIA is of great importance as it informs the content of a ubiquitous obligation that seeks clarification.

The ICJ in *Pulp Mills* affirmed the customary nature of the obligation to conduct EIA coupled with an ongoing obligation to monitor the operation of the activity. After it set out the ground rule of customary law, the ICJ went on to discuss the obligation to conduct an EIA. The ICJ states that the CARU (the Statute of the River Uruguay) does not provide any content to the obligation.[89] It follows that up by stating that the scope and content of the obligation is not defined in general international law either.[90] This grossly inaccurate statement is the only way the ICJ can reach its conclusion that 'it is for each State to determine in its domestic legislation or in the authorization process for the project, the specific content of the environmental impact assessment'.[91] To be fair, this is the only time that *Pulp Mills* seems to follow the ILC in its assessment that each State determines the process and content of the EIA. But this is not entirely true. Indeed, the Commentary to Article 7 of the Prevention Articles of the ILC states that the specifics of what ought to be the content of the EIA are to be decided by the State that conducts the assessment.[92] This statement is however qualified further down in the Commentary. The ILC clarifies that the assessment must include the effects of the assessment. It goes on to add that the content of the assessment is dependent by the type of energy used for the activity, the activity's size, as well as its location.[93]

Therefore, the meaning of the *Pulp Mills* dictum on EIA merits closer attention. If the ICJ only meant that it is through domestic legislation that each State gives effect to its international customary obligation to conduct an EIA, then there is nothing further to discuss. This is true, yet it is also self-evident. If the ICJ meant just that, then it simply did not add anything new to the discussion. It is also true, however, that if national

[88] Art 7 of the ILC Articles on Prevention of Transboundary Harm requires from the State of origin to conduct a risk assessment prior to its authorization of a hazardous activity and as the comments to the Article make clear 'it does not specify what the content of the risk assessment should be'. See ILC Prevention Articles (n 24) 158.
[89] *Pulp Mills* (n 14) [205].
[90] ibid.
[91] ibid.
[92] ILC Prevention Articles (n 24) 157–58.
[93] ibid.

legislation is to indeed give effect to the international obligation, it cannot merely dictate the conduct of an EIA without any kind of prerequisites. If this was the reasoning of the ICJ behind this proclamation, then this is obviously unsatisfactory for two main reasons. First, the ICJ does not bother to look either to the ILC Articles or at the numerous international instruments that provide for an EIA and at the same time provide for a rudimentary framework. It is only natural that the technical details should be determined in the domestic legislation, but the overarching framework and broad directions could, relatively easily, be inferred from the ILC Articles, IEL conventions and practice. Second, the conduct of the EIA itself is highly complex. It can easily lead to disagreements between the State of origin and the potentially affected State meaning that a deadlock in the discussions is not unprecedented.[94] A clear framework could at least anticipate and address some of the most obvious obstacles in the process.

In *Nicaragua/Costa Rica*, the Court changed course in a spectacular way. It interpreted the obligation of an EIA in a rather open and progressive way, breaking away from *Pulp Mills*. It held that several factors are relevant in examining the proper adherence of the State to the obligation to conduct and EIA. The ICJ included the magnitude of the project, its context, the scale, location, as well as the geographical conditions.[95] This is clearly an interpretation of the obligation that incorporates elements found in environmental agreements, albeit without any such acknowledgement whatsoever. The Espoo Convention, being the most comprehensive international instrument regulating the conduct of EIA, offers significant guidance. Appendix II of the Convention sets out a number of criteria that determine the conduct of an EIA. The Appendix includes the size and the location of the activity as well as the nature and kind of damage that may occur. The ILC Commentary also adheres to these criteria.[96] They are very similar, practically identical to those propounded by the ICJ. In other words,

[94] The recently concluded Agreement under the United Nations Convention on the Law of the Sea on the Conservation and Sustainable Use of Marine Biological Diversity of Areas beyond National Jurisdiction (adopted 1 August 2023, not yet in force) currently available as UN Doc A/77/L.82 shows how important disagreements over EIA led to a convoluted drafting of the relevant Chapter.

[95] *Certain Activities Carried out by Nicaragua in the Border Area and Construction of a Road in Costa Rica along the San Juan River* (n 27) [155–56].

[96] It is not meant here that every international instrument that contains an EIA obligation is equally elaborate or includes the same criteria.

the Court caught up with the evolution of international environmental law in order to define the scope and content of the obligation. Whether the ICJ moved in that direction because it looked into relevant environmental law instruments, state practice, or other developments is not possible to know.

It is the lack of elaboration on behalf of the ICJ that leaves behind a question mark as to whether this can be classified as evolutive interpretation, or it is merely the application of the obligation to the facts of the case. On the one hand, the ICJ in *Nicaragua/Costa Rica* quoted (not with disapproval) the *Pulp Mills* dictum that the State determines the content of the EIA obligation in its domestic legislation. At the same time, the ICJ also looked at the fact that Costa Rica's domestic legislation provided for an emergency provision exempting the government from the obligation to conduct an EIA.[97] It determined that the emergency provisions could not trump the obligation of Costa Rica to carry out an EIA under international law.[98] This might be a hint of differentiation from *Pulp Mills*. Be that as it may, had the ICJ merely applied the *Pulp Mills* dictum as a definitive statement on the status as well as on the content of the obligation, it would have deferred any criteria on the content of the EIA to the relevant domestic legislation in question. The ICJ did something different. It interpreted the bare obligation as found in *Pulp Mills*. It gave flesh to its bones by interpreting it as containing specific criteria that the State of origin has to take into account when it transposes the international obligation to its domestic legal order. This, of course, is only one of the reasonable readings of the judgment, yet the most convincing. State practice, international agreements and the work of the ILC were all there when the ICJ decided *Pulp Mills*. It may be true that, rather than evolution, it seems more like catching up a few years later; the judgment is an example of expansive interpretation at least compared to the Court's past jurisprudence.

4.4 Conclusions

The first instance in international jurisprudence of identification and concurrent interpretation of an EIL norm was *Trail Smelter*. The Tribunal came up with the first definition and, concurrently, interpretation of the no-harm rule, and it definitely set the groundwork for what

[97] *Certain Activities Carried out by Nicaragua in the Border Area and Construction of a Road in Costa Rica along the San Juan River* (n 27) [157].

[98] ibid.

followed. It was then the turn of the ICJ to try its hand at the interpretation of IEL norms. The ICJ has taken a conservative approach in identifying the rules of customary IEL. Not only that, but it seems that the ICJ has been out of step with the state of development of IEL at the time it decided *Pulp Mills*, resorting to regressive interpretation. The Court failed to explain the content of the no-harm obligation and also declined to explain what the 'functional link' between substantive and procedural obligations is. Moreover, it seemed to hamper the effective application of the no-harm rule by disconnecting the breach of the obligation to notify from the substantive component of the obligation to not cause transboundary environmental harm. In *Nicaragua/Costa Rica*, the ICJ did not manage to shed further light on the content of the rule.

Regarding the obligation to conduct an EIA, the ICJ changed course from one case to the next. In *Pulp Mills*, the Court resorted again to regressive interpretation, falling behind the position of EIL on EIA at the time. The ICJ in *Costa Rica v Nicaragua/Nicaragua v Costa Rica* showed an imbalance in defining the threshold of the triggering of the obligation to conduct an EIA between the two proceedings. In *Costa Rica/Nicaragua*, the ICJ did not elaborate much on EIA. Nonetheless in *Nicaragua/Costa Rica* the Court did in fact develop the content of the obligation through evolutive interpretation. It caught up with, at least, the minimum content of the obligation as it appears in international texts and as it probably stands in state practice.

Overall, international courts and tribunals have interpreted IEL in expansive as well as restrictive ways. Sometimes they have even oscillated between the two. Starting from an expansive interpretation, as was the case in *Trail Smelter*, moving to regression in *Pulp Mills* and then correcting the course in *Nicaragua/Costa Rica*. Even though the lineage does not lie within the ambit of the jurisdiction of a single court, it is submitted that it is telling of the difficulties with which courts must grapple. Today, that IEL is not a novelty anymore, international courts will have the chance, and probably take it, to develop the content of customary IEL more freely and with a steadier hand.

PART II

Unity, Diversity, and Evolution of Interpretation of International Law across Actors

5

Interpretation of Customary International Law in an Institutional Context

CATHERINE BRÖLMANN

5.1 Introduction

As part of the research theme of interpretation of unwritten international law, this chapter zooms in on instances of interpretation of customary international law (CIL) within an institutional context. The involvement of such a 'context' – here used to refer primarily to the institutional environment of an international intergovernmental organization – has different facets, which so far have not been systematically examined. The aim of this chapter is to provide an overview of the ways in which institutional context may be connected to the interpretation of custom and to offer a hypothesis on interpretative approaches that may emerge therefrom.

Interpretation in (international) law is generally taken to refer to a 'process of assigning meaning to ... statements for the purposes of establishing rights, obligations, and other consequences relevant in a legal context'.[1] It is a commonplace that the interpretation of written international law is an elusive operation.[2] This holds both for interpretation performed as an explicit act, for instance, by a court, and for interpretation performed as a non-formal and often implicit act by legal actors and stakeholders involved. The interpretation of unwritten or customary international law is still a more complex exercise, which makes it a timely topic of study.[3] International organizations then are

[1] M Herdegen, 'Interpretation in International Law' (2020) MPEPIL 723 [1].

[2] cf the oft-quoted statement by the ILC that interpretation is 'to some extent an art, not an exact science' (ILC 'Draft Articles on the Law of Treaties with Commentaries' (4 May–19 July 1966) UN Doc A/CN.4/191, reproduced in [1966/II] YBILC 187, 218, Commentary to s 3 [5]).

[3] Some objections have been voiced to the interpretability of customary international law as it is unwritten – which could produce e.g. a Sorites paradox – but this chapter accepts the presumption of the TRICI-Law project that such interpretation is possible; see also B Etkin, 'The Changing Rivers of Customary International Law: The Interpretative

frequently the setting for interpretation of customary international law, even when the interpretation is not conceived as a formal or even explicit act.

The picture of custom interpretation in an institutional context is multifaceted. For one, it may be at issue where international custom is applied – and perhaps has been co-created – at general international level by an international organization. It may also be found when inside an organization's institutional order non-binding rules and norms are set (with resolutions of the UN General Assembly as a prominent example). Technically speaking, these rules may give rise to custom and ultimately become binding that way, to be subsequently interpreted when they are put to application, both by member states and by the organization and both inside and outside the organization's institutional sphere. In some cases, the organization's adoption of non-binding instruments such as 'resolutions', may as such amount to a form of interpretation, because of the resolution's (implicit) claim to be declaratory of existing custom.[4]

Interpretation of custom by courts and tribunals, even if these do have an institutional dimension, is in principle left out of the account in this chapter. Explicit acts of custom interpretation in a (semi-)judicial setting – eminently valuable for bringing concrete interpretative issues to a head – have already been examined comparatively extensively.[5] In order to capture also more implicit and fluid acts of interpretation, the present chapter focuses on (other) actors and institutional frameworks. This entails the use of a broad notion of 'interpretation', which essentially includes 'application'; this in recognition of the notoriously thin line between 'application' and 'interpretation'[6] (somewhat related to the dual meaning of 'interpretation' as CIL ascertainment and as CIL content determination),[7] as well as between 'interpretation' and 'modification' of

Process as Flux' (2022) 11(5) ESIL Reflections 1 <https://esil-sedi.eu/wp-content/uploads/2022/11/ESIL-Reflection-Basak-Etkin-FINAL.pdf> (last accessed 1 June 2025).

[4] As the ICJ said in the *Chagos* advisory opinion: 'although resolution 1514 (XV) is formally a recommendation, it . . . [had] declaratory character with regard to self-determination as a customary norm' (*Legal Consequences of the Separation of the Chagos Archipelago from Mauritius in 1965* (Advisory Opinion) [2019] ICJ Rep 95 [152]).

[5] See several in-depth analyses in P Merkouris, J Kammerhofer and N Arajärvi (eds), *The Theory, Practice, and Interpretation of Customary International Law* (Cambridge University Press 2022).

[6] G Nolte (ed), *Treaties and Subsequent Practice* (Oxford University Press 2013).

[7] P Merkouris, 'Interpreting the Customary Rules of Interpretation' (2017) 19 ICLR 126, 134–37; see also below n 45 and accompanying text.

rules.[8] It may be argued that such boundaries are still thinner for CIL than for written rules.

The chapter first addresses instances of organizations applying and interpreting customary international law on par with other international actors (Section 5.2), also considering the thorny subject of the contribution of organizations themselves to the formation of custom at international level (Section 5.3). Another main instance where 'institutional context' plays a role is when organizations or their member states apply and interpret unwritten international law within the institutional order (Section 5.4). A particular dynamic occurs when organizations produce within the institutional order acts of 'soft law', which plausibly in one way or another (co-)create customary international law, to be subsequently developed further through interpretation on the part of the organization and/or the member states (Section 5.5). The chapter then briefly considers the notion of 'customary institutional law' (Section 5.6) and proposes some considerations as to what interpretative trends may be surmised in relation to the institutional context (Section 5.7). It ends with concluding remarks (Section 5.8).

5.2 Organizations as Interpreters at International Level

One way in which an institutional context may be at play in interpretation is when international organizations as such apply and interpret general customary international law. A notable example is the domain of international human rights law (IHRL), with which the United Nations (UN) has engaged intensely over time, increasingly also with regard to its 'own' conduct. In the background, scholarly discussion continued to be animated by the question as to whether the UN, or any organization, could be considered bound by customary human rights law. The possibility of a customary basis for international human rights had been at issue already in the 1960s and 1970s and had culminated in an unsuccessful attempt in the context of General Comment 24 of the Human

[8] I Venzke, 'Authoritative interpretation' (2018) MPEPIL 3528 [46–50]; I Venzke, *How Interpretation Makes International Law: On Semantic Change and Normative Twists* (Oxford University Press 2012). The ILC also confirmed (though not condoned) this through Conclusion 7(3) and the commentary thereto in ILC, 'Draft Conclusions on Subsequent Agreements and Subsequent Practice in Relation to the Interpretation of Treaties, with Commentaries' (30 April–1 June and 2 July–10 August 2018) UN Doc A/73/10, reproduced in [2018/II – Part Two] YBILC 16, 52–55 [21–38].

Rights Committee[9] to list human rights in the Covenant with customary status.[10] In its 2007 judgment in the Diallo case, the ICJ confirmed that international human rights have assumed customary status.[11] Since the 2000s, rules of IHRL were essentially declared by the UN to be binding upon itself,[12] and thereby also came to be interpreted by the organization. The field of international humanitarian law (IHL) shows a similar development, as evidenced by the 1999 bulletin of the UN Secretary-General setting out 'fundamental principles and rules of international humanitarian law applicable to United Nations forces conducting operations under United Nations command and control'.[13]

At the same time, the view that international organizations as such could not generate legally relevant practice or *opinio juris* was widely shared, as appears in a general sense from the *travaux* of the 1986 Vienna Convention dating from the same period.[14] The 2018 ILC Conclusions on the identification of customary international law, addressed below, have echoes of this outlook. They suggest that a binding effect of custom on organizations would be incidental, since the symmetry envisaged in traditional international law – legal actors can only be bound by obligations to which they have consented or by law they have co-created – would be lacking.

Meanwhile, the debate has been spurred, especially by developments in the field of human rights, and the proposition that international organizations are fully bound by relevant customary international law has not

[9] HRC, 'General Comment No 24, Issues Relating to Reservations Made upon Ratification or Accession to the Covenant or the Optional Protocols thereto, or in Relation to Declarations under Article 41 of the Covenant' (11 November 1994) UN Doc CCPR/C/21/Rev.1/Add.6 [8].

[10] See W Schabas, *The Customary International Law of Human Rights* (Oxford University Press 2021) 9–39, tracing the development of the unwritten IHRL. The draft list of customary human rights based on a draft prepared by Rosalyn Higgins is described at ibid 31–32.

[11] *Ahmadou Sadio Diallo (Republic of Guinea v Democratic Republic of the Congo)* (Preliminary Objections) [2007] ICJ Rep 582 [39], as referred to also by N Quénivet, 'Binding the United Nations to Customary (Human Rights) Law' (2020) 17 IOLR 379.

[12] cf the account of Quénivet (n 11) 408.

[13] UN Secretariat, 'Secretary-General's Bulletin: Observance by United Nations Forces of International Humanitarian Law' (6 August 1999) UN Doc ST/SGB/1999/13 (note the deontic language: 'promulgates the following' and 'The present bulletin shall enter into force . . .' whereas the bulletin is not as such binding on the member states, nor even on the organization).

[14] C Brölmann, *The Institutional Veil in Public International Law* (Hart 2007) 197–244.

been controversial for at least two decades.[15] Still, while it is a well-received proposition, it is not always clear by what mechanism international organizations become bound by customary international law, including human rights law and humanitarian law.[16] According to one scholar 'jus cogens norms always bind IOs and ... general international law binds IOs as a default matter'.[17] Another author, after a careful examination of theoretical explanations of international organizations being bound by custom, and rejection of views that derive such bindingness in some way from the member states, opts for a constitutionalist (arguably 'public') view of international law, in which organizations are bound in their capacity of participants in the international order.[18]

Either way, it is clear that such binding effect cannot be accounted for in the voluntarist and symmetrist reasoning of classic international law, as appears from the next section, which addresses the limitations posed to international organizations as lawmaking actors. This must mean that the proposition rests at least partly on a public law conception of international law: only then does it make sense to admit new members to a 'legal community' on condition they accept the legal 'acquis' of that community. Such a public law conception in fact points to a view in which all customary international law – including branches that do not focus on the human individual in the way of IHRL and IHL – would be binding on international organizations.

5.3 The Contribution of Organizations to International Custom

Thus, international organizations acting in accordance with customary law that is (construed as) binding upon them is one way in which

[15] cf O de Schutter, 'Human Rights and the Rise of International Organisations: The Logic of Sliding Scales in the Law of International Responsibility' in J Wouters et al (eds), *Accountability for Human Rights Violations by International Organisations* (Intersentia 2010) 51, 56.

[16] N Blokker, 'International Organizations and Customary International Law: Is the International Law Commission Taking International Organizations Seriously?' (2017) 14 IOLR 1. Also the ICJ in *Interpretation of the Agreement of 25 March 1951 between the WHO and Egypt* (Advisory Opinion) [1980] ICJ Rep 73, answered this in the affirmative – although the function of the well-known paragraph 37 in the decision arguably is not immediately clear.

[17] K Daugirdas, 'How and Why International Law Binds International Organizations' (2016) 57 HILJ 325.

[18] Quénivet (n 11).

'institutional context' may be involved with the interpretation of custom. For a further understanding of such involvement, it is helpful also to consider the position of organizations from a reverse angle and look at the – fundamental – question of whether international organizations are able to produce custom or contribute to its formation. As mentioned above, the 2018 ILC Conclusions on the identification of customary international law suggest that contemporary international law and doctrine invariably accord a very modest role to international organizations as independent actors in the formation of customary international law.[19] This could seem remarkable, given that international organizations have an ever more prominent role in international legal life.

In the 2018 Conclusions, international organizations appear in two ways: as a platform for the (legal) acts of States and as an independent international-legal actor. Conclusion 4 ('Requirement of practice') para 2 is the only provision that refers to the practice of international organizations in their own right, as a possible contribution to 'the formation, or expression, of rules of customary international law'. This is most likely to occur, according to the commentary – with a clear (and restrictive) reference to 'regional (economic) integration organizations' such as the EU – when States have transferred competences to an international organization or 'conferred powers upon the international organization that are functionally equivalent to the powers exercised by States'.[20] The *opinio juris* of organizations is not mentioned, although the commentary states that para 2 of Conclusion 10 ('Forms of evidence of acceptance as law') is applicable *mutatis mutandis*.[21] More generally, the ILC commentary points to a key role for states – where it should be noted that the Reports of the Special Rapporteur in respect of organizations take a more nuanced approach, referring, for example, to 'operational activities' of

[19] cf C Brölmann, 'Capturing the Juridical Will of International Organisations' in S Droubi and J d'Aspremont (eds), *International Organizations and Non-State Actors in the Formation of Customary International Law* (Manchester University Press 2020) 42.

[20] ILC, 'Draft Conclusions on Identification of Customary International Law, with Commentaries' (30 April–1 June and 2 July–10 August 2018) UN Doc A/73/10, reproduced in [2018/II – Part Two] YBILC 91, 97 [5–6]; see also the chapter by J-B Merlin, 'The United Nations Secretariat and Custom' in S Droubi and J d'Aspremont (eds), *International Organizations, Non-State Actors and the Formation of Customary International Law* (Manchester University Press 2019) 261, retracing the discussions leading up to Conclusion 4(2); Quénivet (n 11) 414, holding that the ILC 'missed a tremendous opportunity'.

[21] ILC (n 20) 104, Commentary to Conclusion 10 [7].

organizations that may amount to 'relevant practice for purposes of formation and identification of customary international law'.[22]

Elsewhere I have proposed one explanatory factor for the limited role of organizations in the formation of custom. This is connected to the necessity in international law to ascribe to organizations a 'juridical will' – a term used as shorthand for the various subjective 'intentional states', such as 'intention', 'opinion', 'acquiescence', 'consent', that systems of law project onto legal participants in order to operationalize their legal agency.[23] International law seems to have (since the nineteenth century) no problem attributing such legally relevant 'psychological states' to a state but traditionally shows signs of hesitation when it comes to an international organization. This in turn can be linked to a functionalist, mechanistic view of organizations' legal personality, subservient to states as the original legal persons and prime political actors.[24] It is one reason why the ascertainment of an organization's *opinio juris*, or of an organization's distinct 'will' for the purpose of attributing a particular practice, can pose a challenge. It could certainly also stifle the position of organizations as interpreters of CIL at global level.

5.4 Interpretation of Custom inside the Institutional Framework

Another instance of interaction between custom interpretation and institutional context is found when customary rules are interpreted within the institutional framework of an organization. One example is the strong role in (customary) lawmaking processes by the UN High Commissioner for Refugees (UNHCR). It has been argued before that the slow development of treaty-based international refugee law has created a need for more informal 'soft law' standards to supplement the provisions found in the 1951 Convention.[25] Research shows how the UNHCR has filled that

[22] cf ILC 'Third Report on Identification of Customary International Law by Michael Wood, Special Rapporteur' (27 March 2015) UN Doc A/CN.4/682 [76–77] and references to extensive literature in support of an open approach to the role of IOs' practice beyond that of the Regional (economic) integration organization.

[23] Brölmann (n 19) 59.

[24] This argument is elaborated in C Brölmann, 'International Organizations and the Disaggregation of Consent' in S Besson (ed), *Consenting to International Law* (Cambridge University Press 2023) 115–34.

[25] A Corkery, 'The Contribution of the UNHCR Executive Committee to the Development of International Refugee Law' (2006) Aust ILJ 97.

gap, interpreting and to a limited extent shaping the obligation of non-refoulement.[26] This occurs especially through its Executive Committee, which annually adopts by consensus 'Conclusions on International Protection'. The conclusions are not binding upon states, but they are conceptualized (with an implicit interpretation-claim) as 'expressions of opinion which are broadly representative of the views of the international community'[27] and exercise a steady normative influence.[28] The UNHCR gives evidence of influence on refugee law in several respects, as is pointed out by Trevisanut,[29] and this is not just about interpretation of written rules. Non-refoulement, which became interlinked with the law of the sea, has long since been ascribed also customary status. This is expressed, for instance, in a UNHCR *amicus curiae* brief, in which the Agency addresses the geographical remit of the principle of non-refoulement and specifically its application at sea. The brief explicitly draws on 'the broader human right of refugees to seek asylum from persecution as set out in the Universal Declaration of Human Rights'.[30]

For one who adopts a legal lens, it is not always evident how to distinguish interpretation by the organization from that of the member states. That said, it is undisputed that inside an institutional framework both the organization and the individual member states may engage with rules of custom, sometimes simultaneously. Individual states' voting behaviour in the UN General Assembly, or inside the institutional framework, is a familiar element in the ICJ's reasoning on custom, as can be gleaned from the 1986 *Nicaragua* Judgment and the 1996 *Legality* Opinion.[31] Further deconstruction of an institutional procedure can be found in the 2011 dispute between the Former Yugoslav Republic of

[26] ibid.

[27] UNHCR, 'Executive Committee Documentation' (*UNHCR*, 2025) <www.unhcr.org/about-unhcr/governance-and-oversight/executive-committee/excom-plenary-sessions/executive-committee> (last accessed 1 June 2025).

[28] Corkery (n 25).

[29] S Trevisanut, 'The Contribution of UNHCR to Ocean Governance' in DJ Attard, M Fitzmaurice and A Ntovas (eds), *The IMLI Treatise on Global Ocean Governance*, vol 2 (Oxford University Press 2018) 243.

[30] 'UN High Commissioner for Refugees Responds to U.S. Supreme Court Decision in Sale *v* Haitian Centers Council' (1993) 32(4) ILM 1215, 1215, quoted by Trevisanut (n 29) 249.

[31] *Military and Paramilitary Activities in and against Nicaragua (Nicaragua v United States of America)* (Merits) [1986] ICJ Rep 14 [188, 204]; Legality of the Threat or Use of Nuclear Weapons (Advisory Opinion) [1996] ICJ Rep 226 [68–73].

Macedonia (FYROM) and Greece.[32] When at the 2008 NATO summit Greece blocked FYROM's bid to become a member of NATO, FYROM claimed that by putting in a negative vote, Greece had breached its obligations under Article 11 of the 1995 *Interim Accord* between Greece and FYROM. In order to examine possible legal responsibility on the part of Greece for its conduct within NATO, the International Court 'pierced' the institutional veil of the organization and found in favour of the claimant. Commentators spoke of 'the first time in which the ICJ so assertively identified the individual conduct of a State in the process of institutional decision-making.'[33]

Looking at states, it can moreover be difficult to distinguish between state (interpretative) acts 'inside' an international organization and those 'outside' of it. No doubt the – porous – boundary between the institutional order of an organization and the general international legal order is 'real' in a legal-doctrinal sense. This is borne out by straightforward examples such as Article 5 in the 1969 Vienna Convention on the Law of Treaties[34] (i.e. on how the law of treaties applies to treaties adopted within an institutional framework but 'without prejudice to any relevant rules of the organization') and Article 64 of the 2011 Draft Articles on the Responsibility of International Organizations[35] (on the 'rules of the organization', which as *lex specialis* would remain outside the scope of the Draft Articles). That said, especially with the (in the words of the ILC) 'holistic' exercise of interpretation, it can be unclear whether particular state conduct is part of – in legal terms – an institutional process or a global process. The distinction between the 'internal' institutional level and the general international level may be obfuscated all the more when these, in terms of membership, practically overlap, as in the case of an organization with universal membership such as the UN.

This is in addition to the above-mentioned fluidity of categories *within* the institutional framework, where it can be unclear whether an

[32] *Application of the Interim Accord of 13 September 1995 (the Former Yugoslav Republic of Macedonia v Greece)* (Judgment) [2011] ICJ Rep 644.

[33] AS Barros and C Ryngaert, 'The Position of Member States in (Autonomous) Institutional Decision-Making: Implications for the Establishment of Responsibility' (2014) 11 IOLR 53, 75.

[34] Vienna Convention on the Law of Treaties (adopted 22 May 1969, entered into force 27 January 1980) 1155 UNTS 331.

[35] ILC, 'Draft Articles on Responsibility of International Organizations' (26 April–3 June and 4 July–12 August 2011) UN Doc A/66/10, reproduced in [2011/II – Part Two] YBILC 46.

interpretative act must be attributed to the organization or to individual member state(s). In all cases, it seems logical to start from the 'constitutional limit' of organizations or, to put it differently, the principle of speciality,[36] to determine whether a particular organization as such is even suited to engage with a particular rule or norm. Otherwise, law and practice do not offer clear guidelines in respect of these fuzzy boundaries, which means that sometimes both the organization and the member states will be interpreting the same rule of custom. In a socio-legal vein, who can successfully claim to be the prime interpreting actor might depend on how they have negotiated authority. The shaping and solidifying of the customary 'human right to water', which has changed substance and scope several times over the past twenty years, may serve as an example. Apart from classic diplomatic work by states, such as by the international *watergezant* on behalf of the Netherlands,[37] the process has involved interpretation within the UN context by institutional bodies (examples are the 2002 General Comment 15 of the ICESCR Committee,[38] the 2008 Human Rights Council resolution on human rights and access to safe drinking water and sanitation,[39] and the (not unanimously adopted) 2010 UN General Assembly Resolution on the human right to water and sanitation)[40] and by states (examples are the 'acceptance speech' regarding the human right to water and sanitation by the Netherlands in Geneva in 2008[41] and individual abstentions by prominent states such as Canada when voting for the 2010 Resolution in the UN General Assembly).[42]

36 Which determines an organization's field of operation (*Legality of the Use by a State of Nuclear Weapons in Armed Conflict* (Advisory Opinion) [1996] ICJ Rep 66 [19, 25] (*WHO* opinion)).

37 cf the work of a thematic ambassador of the 'Water Envoy' appointed in 2015 by the Dutch government, available at <www.government.nl/topics/water-management/water envoy> (last accessed 1 June 2025).

38 CESCR, 'General Comment No 15: The Right to Water (Articles 11 and 12 of the Covenant)' (20 January 2003) UN Doc E/C.12/2002/11.

39 UNHRC, 'Res 7/22: Human Rights and Access to Safe Drinking Water and Sanitation' (28 March 2008) UN Doc A/HRC/RES/7/22.

40 UNGA, 'Res 64/292: The Human Right to Water and Sanitation' (28 July 2010) UN Doc A/RES/64/292.

41 The Foreign Minister of the Netherlands said on the 3rd of March, before the Human Rights Council, 'I am proud to announce here today that the Netherlands will join the group of countries who have recognised the right to water as a human right', as quoted in F Coomans, 'Erkenning van het recht op water als mensenrecht' (2009) 34(3) NJCM-B 249, 251.

42 UNGA, 'Resolutions and Decisions Adopted by the General Assembly During Its 64th Session' (25 December 2009–14 September 2010) UN Doc A/64/49 (Vol III), 45.

5.5 Normative Acts Produced within the Organization

The institutional context has an especially distinct role in case of the adoption, within an organization of a non-binding act (binding acts are left aside as they would call strictly speaking for the interpretation of *written* rules). Many 'soft law' acts will not give rise to custom, but some of them will. In the latter regard, a preliminary consideration is the classic requirement of a 'fundamentally norm-creating character',[43] to determine whether the normative and prescriptive content of the act is of a suitably general nature. The role of UNGA Resolutions in the formation of customary international law was hotly debated already in the 1970s.[44] The aforementioned ILC Conclusions on the identification of customary international law are a recent pronouncement in this delicate area of international law and doctrine. The Conclusions provide that 'a resolution adopted by an international organization ... may provide evidence for determining the existence *and content* of a rule of customary international law'.[45]

The relevance for custom interpretation is shown by certain UN General Assembly resolutions, which, as *instruments*, famously constitute 'soft law' and as normative substance are then recognized to have crystallized into customary international law. Now, how do non-binding, arguably CIL-creating resolutions of the UN General Assembly fare when it comes to interpretation – such as the 1960 Declaration on the Granting of Independence to Colonial Countries and Peoples[46] or the 1970 Declaration on Principles of International Law concerning Friendly Relations and Cooperation among States in accordance with the Charter of

[43] Introduced by the ICJ in the 1969 *North Sea Continental Shelf Cases (Federal Republic of Germany/Netherlands; Federal Republic of Germany/Denmark)* (Judgment) [1969] ICJ Rep 3 [72].

[44] SM Schwebel, 'The Effect of Resolutions of the UN General Assembly on Customary International Law' in (1979) 73 ASIL Proc 301; for a contemporary account of theoretical puzzles, see AI Baka, 'The Logic of Absence in Customary International Law: An Open-System Approach' in P Merkouris, J Kammerhofer and N Arajärvi (eds), *The Theory, Practice, and Interpretation of Customary International Law* (Cambridge University Press 2022) 63, 80 ff.

[45] ILC, 'Draft Conclusions on Identification of Customary International Law, with Commentaries' (30 April–1 June and 2 July–10 August 2018) UN Doc A/73/10, reproduced in [2018/II - Part Two] YBILC 91, 107, Conclusion 12(2) (emphasis added).

[46] UNGA Res 1514 (XV), 14 Dec 1960. See also F Cowell, 'Identifying Custom in Universal Periodic Review Recommendations' in P Merkouris, J Kammerhofer and N Arajärvi (eds), *The Theory, Practice, and Interpretation of Customary International Law* (Cambridge University Press 2022) 320, 321, on the re-citation of UNGA Resolutions.

the United Nations,[47] to name two classics? A solid answer to this question requires separate research. But there is no doubt that the resulting rules and norms are subject to some form of interpretation, be it a 'by proxy' textual interpretation (which is readily facilitated by the ample production of text in an institutional context – see below) or a 'logical interpretation'.[48] Neither is there any doubt that such interpretation can involve both organizations and states, as is apparent for instance in the *Chagos* Advisory Opinion when the ICJ in relation to the 'maximalist interpretation of self-determination'[49] based on resolution 1514 (XV) routinely refers to the considerations of both 'the General Assembly or any other organ of the United Nations' and of 'States [who] have consistently emphasized ... respect for the territorial integrity of a non-self-governing territory'.[50]

In relation to the interpretation of UN General Assembly resolutions, it is otherwise worthwhile to point to the powerful dynamic of contestation and confirmation, which is perhaps not found in regular international relations. This holds equally for other international organizations and their decision-making organs, especially when these are constituted by state representatives. The public records, public voting and tracing of numerical majorities and minorities make for a comparatively proceduralized and stylized process of custom formation and interpretation. This has, for instance, allowed us to follow the – in terms of normative content and customary legal status – hapless fate of the agenda of the 'New International Economic Order' that was importantly brought to the fore in the 1974 UNGA Resolution.[51] Also the development of the concept of Responsibility to Protect can be traced along a string of soft law instruments, from the 'launch' of the concept in 2001 by an external report commissioned by the UN Secretary-General (which left a small opening for the possibility of unilateral humanitarian intervention) to the 2005 UN 'Outcome Document' (in which the concept had been re-interpreted so as to align entirely with the collective security

[47] UNGA, 'Res 2625 (XXV) Declaration on Principles of International Law Concerning Friendly Relations and Co-operation among States in accordance with the Charter of the United Nations' (24 October 1970) UN Doc A/9082.

[48] P Merkouris, 'Interpreting Customary International Law: You'll Never Walk Alone' in P Merkouris, J Kammerhofer and N Arajärvi (eds), *The Theory, Practice, and Interpretation of Customary International Law* (Cambridge University Press 2022) 347.

[49] In the words of J Basu-Mellish, 'UN Resolution 1514: The Creation of a New Post-Colonial Sovereignty' (2023) 44 TWQ 1306, 1318.

[50] *Chagos Advisory Opinion* (n 4) [160].

[51] UNGA, 'Res 3201 (S-VI): Declaration on the Establishment of a New International Economic Order' (1 May 1974) UN Doc A/RES/S-6/3201; ME Salomon, 'From NIEO to Now and the Unfinishable Story of Economic Justice' (2013) 62 ICLQ 31.

system of the UN).[52] Already in the 1940s, a seminal piece was written on the (mostly legal) statements by the UN Secretary-General and their influence on international law.[53]

The 2015 UNGA Resolution promulgating the Sustainable Development Goals,[54] too, is well-placed to generate custom. The intricate process of application and interpretation[55] of the resolution will, interestingly, differ somewhat from classic examples because the normative framework is largely operationalized at the states' domestic level, through a complex system of indicators (themselves the subject of continuous discussion) and reporting on performance and implementation.

A final example to mention concerns the recommendations of the Universal Periodic Review organized by the Human Rights Council. Unlike the pronouncements and interpretative efforts of (semi-)judicial bodies, the Universal Periodic Review process is not based on a concrete complaint but on member states' reciprocal recommendations, involving in turn application and interpretation of human rights. As is set out in a fine analysis by Cowell, the '[r]ecommendations are numerous and wide ranging but, when aggregated, can demonstrate certain trends in relation to human rights protection'.[56]

It has been pointed out that customary international law as a *discourse* poses a foundational(ist) problem since its grounding is 'a past social reality' that 'can never be traced but can solely be presupposed'.[57] This question emerges also when custom is considered from an immanent, positive law-perspective. Here too, in a different guise, the interpretation of unwritten law is an exercise that rests on shaky ground, because no 'objective' text exists but only a proposed rule that is itself an

[52] ICISS, *The Responsibility to Protect: Report of the International Commission on Intervention and State Sovereignty* (International Development Research Centre 2001); UNGA, 'Res 60/1: 2005 World Summit Outcome' (16 September 2005) UN Doc A/RES/60/1.

[53] O Schachter, 'The Development of International Law Through the Legal Opinions of the United Nations Secretariat' (1948) 25 BYBIL 91.

[54] UNGA, 'Res 70/1: Transforming Our World: The 2030 Agenda for Sustainable Development' (25 September 2015) UN Doc A/RES/70/1.

[55] C Brölmann, 'Sustainable Development Goal 6 as a Game Changer for International Water Law' (2018) 7(5) ESIL Reflections 1 <https://esil-sedi.eu/wp-content/uploads/2018/08/ESIL-Reflection-Brolmann.pdf> (last accessed 1 June 2025).

[56] Cowell (n 46) 321.

[57] J d'Aspremont, 'The Custom-Making Moment in Customary International Law' in P Merkouris, J Kammerhofer and N Arajärvi (eds), *The Theory, Practice, and Interpretation of Customary International Law* (Cambridge University Press 2022) 29, 38.

interpretation – thus posing an interpretative challenge akin to that of infinite regress. While it may be true that in one way or another 'CIL is always shrouded in a "lexical garment"',[58] especially an environment which produces a considerable amount of written 'soft law' or 'informal law' – such as an international organization – may at some level bypass this infinite regress problem, as it creates text. Not only is it fair to say that some (non-binding) resolutions[59] *are* interpretations, especially where they claim to be declaratory of custom. It is also recognized that (written) re-statements of unwritten law (the Customary IHL Database of the ICRC is a prime example)[60] have a 'transformative' dimension.[61]

5.6 Customary Institutional Law

Focusing on substance, we see that the previous sections deal with 'general international customary law'. Next to this, a special category of 'institutional law' exists within the framework of every international organization. The domain of institutional law comprises both institutional acts with 'external' effect (that is, directed at the member states) and institutional acts with 'internal' effect (that is, directed at the administration and operation of the organization as such).[62] In principle, 'customary institutional law', either within a single organization or as some scholars would have it, shared by multiple organizations (thus amounting to the elusive 'common law of IOs'),[63] can come into existence through the same process of interpretation and application.

We frequently find application and interpretation of customary institutional law in the UN context. An example is the unwritten rules – in

[58] 'Since textual interpretation *stricto sensu* is not possible, what they [courts and tribunals] do is refer to documents which are allegedly reflective of CIL' (Merkouris (n 47) 353, 358, referring to, among others, F Müller, *Discours de la méthode juridique* (O Jouanjan tr, Presses Universitaires de France 1996)).

[59] But see criticism on the notion of resolution used by the ILC in R Deplano, 'Assessing the Role of Resolutions in the ILC Draft Conclusions on Identification of Customary International Law' (2017) 14 IOLR 227.

[60] Available at <https://ihl-databases.icrc.org/en/customary-ihl/v1> (last accessed 1 June 2025).

[61] W Werner, 'Custom as Rewritten Law: The Text and Paratext of Restatement Reports' (2020) 11(3) ESIL Reflections 1 <https://esil-sedi.eu/wp-content/uploads/2022/09/ESIL-Reflection-Wouter-Werner.pdf> (last accessed 1 June 2025).

[62] H Schermers and NM Blokker, *International Institutional Law* (6th edn, Martinus Nijhoff 2018).

[63] An advocate has been F Seyersted, *Common Law of International Organizations* (Brill 2008).

origin related to the UN Charter – concerning the voting procedure in the UN Security Council (UNSC), which were then applied and interpreted further by the Council in the 1950s when abstention from voting by a permanent member came to be interpreted in such a way that it did not amount to a negative vote and hence would not trigger the 'veto'.[64] Another example is the continuously developing body of customary institutional rules and legal classifications in regard of the phenomenon of 'peacekeeping' that famously has no basis in the UN Charter.[65] More recent re-interpretation of unwritten institutional rules is found with the UN General Assembly. Its practice of decision-making by consensus[66] dates to the 1960s and was itself for a long time based on UN institutional custom, unmentioned in the Rules of Procedure.[67] Interpretation and application of that unwritten rule then produced a new sub-category, the procedure entitled 'adoption without a vote'. In this case, the UNGA President asks the Assembly if it wishes to adopt a draft resolution or decision. If no objection is made, the president declares 'it is so decided.' But this decision, unlike a 'decision by consensus', is not followed by a proclamation that 'consensus has been reached' and, importantly, (according to current practice) states do not give public explanations of their position.[68] In recent years, this formula has come to be used for politically weighty resolutions.[69]

64 Charter of the United Nations (adopted 26 June 1945, entered into force 24 October 1945) 1 UNTS XVI, art 27(3) ('Decisions of the Security Council . . . shall be made by an affirmative vote of nine members including the concurring votes of the permanent members').

65 See a clear treatment of these developments and the different types of peace operations in S Chesterman, I Johnstone and DM Malone, *Law and Practice of the United Nations* (2nd edn, Oxford University Press 2016) 317 ff.

66 Consensus is reached when all member states agree on a text without taking a vote; states do not necessarily agree on every element of a draft document, and they can give an explanation of their position either before or after action is taken on the resolution. In the period 2000–2009, the General Assembly adopted 77 per cent of its 3,212 resolutions without a vote (UN Secretariat, *Repertory of Practice of United Nations Organs: Supplementary No 10 (2000–2009)*, vol 2, advanced version available at <https://legal.un.org/repertory/art18/english/rep_supp10_vol2_art18.pdf> (last accessed 1 June 2025) art 18, 8–9 [22]) as stated in R Higgins et al, *Oppenheim's International Law: United Nations* (Oxford University Press 2017) 363 ff.

67 Higgins et al (n 65) 363 ff.

68 No practice exists yet of states giving explanations in cases where they have accepted but do not agree to certain parts of the text – as there would be in case of decision-making by consensus.

69 E.g. UNGA, 'Standing Mandate for a General Assembly Debate When a Veto is Cast in the Security Council' (20 April 2022) UN Doc A/RES/76/262, adopted following mounting criticism on the Security Council's lack of action regarding the war in Ukraine.

5.7 Interpretative Trends

Can any interpretative trends be inferred from this cursory overview? Clearly, further research is needed for substantiated findings. It is, however, fair to mention that at first blush the examples recounted in this text, especially when these relate to interpretation within the institutional framework of an organization, suggest an alignment of the interpretative exercise with the 'objectives' of the organization. This would match a prime characteristic of treaty interpretation in an institutional context, as has been examined notably in relation to constitutive treaties.[70] Because of that match, and also because courts have been found to have recourse to rules of treaty interpretation when interpreting custom,[71] it is relevant briefly to consider interpretation of treaties in an institutional context.

In the 1996 *WHO* opinion, the International Court of Justice stated that 'the imperatives associated with the effective performance of [the organization's] functions as well as its own practice' deserved *'special attention' in the interpretation of constitutive treaties.*[72] How is this 'special attention' brought to bear? Traditionally, treaty interpretation accords considerable weight to the parties' consent as a basis for the treaty. Articles 31 and 32 of the VCLT thus emphasize a 'textual' approach, whether alone or in concert with an 'intentional' approach. A similar method may be gleaned from the ICJ's practice. Conversely, 'object and purpose' as an interpretative tool to establish the text's meaning receives less attention.[73]

In contrast, the interpretation of a constitutive treaty – which embodies the institutional context in that it grounds and sets out the structure of the organization – appears to have been generally inspired by the treaty's object and purpose or, put differently, by the principle of

[70] This section builds on C Brölmann, 'Specialized Rules of Treaty Interpretation: International Organizations' in DB Hollis (ed), *The Oxford Guide to Treaties* (2nd edn, Oxford University Press 2020) 524.

[71] M Fortuna, 'Different Strings of the Same Harp: Interpretation of Rules of Customary International Law, Their Identification and Treaty Interpretation' in P Merkouris, J Kammerhofer and N Arajärvi (eds), *The Theory, Practice, and Interpretation of Customary International Law* (Cambridge University Press 2022) 393, 407–13.

[72] *WHO* opinion (n 36) [74–75] (emphasis added).

[73] cf I Sinclair, *The Vienna Convention on the Law of Treaties* (2nd edn, Manchester University Press 1984) 131 ('there is also the risk that the placing of undue emphasis on the "object and purpose" of a treaty will encourage teleological methods of interpretation').

effectiveness in connection with the objective of the organization.[74] When it comes to organizations' (binding) secondary law, taken here as extended treaty law, the interpretative practice appears somewhat more restrained than the interpretation of constitutive instruments, likely due to 'the delegated character of secondary rules'.[75]

Overall, one trend in the interpretation of constitutive treaties that stands apart from standard practice is the 'teleological approach' to the text, similar to traditions of statutory interpretation in a domestic, constitutional context. Here, some terminological distinction is helpful: the familiar notion 'object and purpose' is used in Article 31 VCLT to elucidate a textual approach for discerning the 'ordinary meaning' to be given to a treaty's terms.[76] This is not quite the same as a 'teleological approach', which in its classic sense is a general interpretative approach, taking the treaty's objective as a guiding principle for an 'effective' interpretation of the text.[77] Both approaches play a role in the interpretation of constitutive treaties, but the teleological approach is most prominent. It is also the most relevant for the interpretation of custom because it is the least text-bound.

Why teleological treaty interpretation shows signs of prevalence in an institutional context is not entirely clear. One plausible factor is that organizations have a vertical dynamic, as was captured early on by the notion of 'centralization' used by Kelsen in relation to the United Nations.[78] Another factor may be that each organization represents a single epistemic community, or 'interpretive community', similar to a state domestic legal order governed by a single constitutional

[74] A Orakhelashvili, *The Interpretation of Acts and Rules in Public International Law* (Oxford University Press 2008) 394, 397.

[75] M Benzing, 'International Organizations or Institutions, Secondary Law' (2007) MPEPIL 508 [48], who states also that an additional principle suggests that legal acts of international organizations 'always have to be construed by reference to and in accordance with the constitutive instrument of the organization' and 'in conformity with general international law binding on the international organization' (ibid [47]); see also Orakhelashvili (n 73) 486–93.

[76] R Gardiner, *Treaty Interpretation* (2nd edn, Oxford University Press 2015) 211.

[77] E Bjorge, 'The Vienna Rules, Evolutionary Interpretation, and the Intentions of the Parties' in A Bianchi, D Peat and M Windsor (eds), *Interpretation in International Law* (Oxford University Press 2015) 189.

[78] H Kelsen, *The Law of the United Nations: A Critical Analysis of Its Fundamental Problems* (Stevens 1950) 329; he saw centralization as a precondition for the differentiation between the 'duties, rights and competences' of the organization and those of the member states.

instrument.[79] The existence of an interpretative community, reinforced by the 'sectoral constitutionalization' in an organization,[80] is a powerful influence – even if of course it is not a simple dynamic. Similar to different branches in public law professions (the legal advisor and the judge, to name two),[81] different organs within an organization are known to form distinctive interpretative communities: think of the 'three UNs'[82] or of the well-known contrast between the UN sector working on Peace and Security ('UN New York') and the UN sector involved in Human Rights work ('UN Geneva').

The hypothesis put forth in this chapter is that the institutional environment conducive to a teleological interpretation of treaty law also has this effect on the interpretation of customary international law.

5.8 Conclusions

The aim of this chapter is to provide a bird's-eye view of the scenarios in which custom interpretation is connected with an institutional context – a frequent occurrence. Insight into the specificities and intricacies of these scenarios is therefore an essential tool for our understanding of custom interpretation.

Institutional context can play a role in custom interpretation in two main ways: an international organization may engage in custom interpretation alongside states at the general international level. Secondly, custom may be interpreted by the organization or the member states *inside* the institutional framework – for instance, through deliberations or decisions of an organ. A striking phenomenon is the production of what this chapter has termed 'written custom': non-binding acts adopted by an organization, which give rise to custom that, in turn, is applied and interpreted within (and outside) the framework of the organization.

[79] See M Waibel, 'Interpretive Communities in International Law' in A Bianchi, D Peat and M Windsor (eds), *Interpretation in International Law* (Oxford University Press 2015) 147.

[80] G Çapar, 'The Paradox of Global Constitutionalism: Between Sectoral Integration and Legitimacy' (2024) 13(2) Global Constitutionalism 264, 271–73.

[81] A Zidar, 'Interpretation and the International Legal Profession – Between Duty and Aspiration' in A Bianchi, D Peat and M Windsor (eds), *Interpretation in International Law* (Oxford University Press 2015) 133.

[82] That is, Secretariat, Member States and NGOs; cf T Weiss et al, 'The 'Third' United Nations' (2009) 15 Global Governance 123.

A key proposition of this chapter is that the steady production of non-binding written instruments makes international organizations a dynamic normative environment with a thriving practice of – mostly implicit – custom interpretation. As argued, this interpretative practice is both relevant and understudied. Hence, the practice of custom interpretation in an institutional context deserves scholarly examination alongside the outstanding research that is focused on explicit efforts of custom interpretation carried out by courts, tribunals and semi-judicial bodies.

As this chapter sets out, the 'institutional context' has a number of complexities to be taken into account. Two may be reiterated here. First, the separate institutional sphere of an organization adds a layer of normativity and authority next to that of general international law. Therefore, it may happen that written rules created by the organization would have normative effect within the institutional framework but not per se in general international law (such as the Operational Policies and Procedures of the World Bank). Conversely, a rule of customary international law could be of uncontested validity but not automatically have normative force within the institutional framework.

Second, within the institutional framework, conduct of the organization may not be readily distinguishable from the conduct of member states. As confirmed in the ILC's work on custom identification, in some situations the question arises as to which entity actually is performing the interpretation. The answer may have implications for the authority and the embedding of the interpretative act. That said, international (institutional) law does not for now offer clear guidelines on this point – with the arguable exception of the 'principle of speciality'.

As for patterns of interpretation, the introductory overview in this chapter does not allow for solid conclusions. The examples do, however, suggest an orientation on the objective(s) of the organization and/or their expression in IO 'soft law' acts. In other words, they point to a predominantly teleological approach. This leads to another key proposition of this chapter, which is that the institutional context apparently conducive to a teleological interpretation of treaty law generally has the same effect when it comes to the interpretation of custom.

For the purpose of this chapter, 'institutional context' is defined as the institutional sphere of an international organization. However, we know that in relation to *treaty* interpretation the 'institutional effect' is also found in less formal and more fluid institutional arrangements, such as treaty regimes with a 'constitutional character' (possibly featuring a compliance mechanism or a mechanism for subsequent decisions by treaty parties).[83] Insofar as these regimes engage with custom, it is a reasonable expectation that the 'institutional effect' would work in the same way.

The current chapter takes the technical-legal dimension of 'institutional context' as a starting point, from the idea that this can contribute to the analytical clarity in a legal examination of custom interpretation. But more angles are possible. With the legal landscape becoming ever more dense, a focus on the politics of interpretation appears ever more important. As illustrated by the aforementioned process of interpretation of the 'responsibility to protect', the multilayered and proceduralized environment of an international organization such as the UN brings out the politics of interpretation much more clearly than a classic international law environment.

[83] Brölmann (n 24) 126.

6

Treaty Interpretation in the Fog of War

The Evolution of the ICRC's Methodology

ELLEN POLICINSKI

6.1 Introduction

International humanitarian law (IHL) is the body of law designed to apply in the most extreme circumstances and yet it is subject to the same public international law norms as other bodies of international law: its sources are those listed in Article 38 of the ICJ Statute; it is adjudicated by international and domestic tribunals; and, importantly for the purposes of this chapter, IHL treaties are subject to the same rules of interpretation embodied in the 1969 Vienna Convention on the Law of Treaties (VCLT).[1] This has been shown time and again by the practice of States[2]

[1] Vienna Convention on the Law of Treaties (adopted 23 May 1969, entered into force 27 January 1980) 1155 UNTS 331 (VCLT). The treaty interpretation rules enshrined in the VCLT are today generally recognized as being customary in nature. See *Award in Arbitration Regarding the Iron Rhine Railway Between the Kingdom of Belgium and the Kingdom of the Netherlands* (Decision of 24 May 2005) 27 RIAA 35, 62; *Territorial Dispute (Libyan Arab Jamahiriya v Chad)* (Judgment) [1994] ICJ Rep 6 [41]; *Kasikili/Sedudu Island (Botswana/Namibia)* (Judgment) [1999] ICJ Rep 1045 [18]; *Application of the Convention on the Prevention and Punishment of the Crime of Genocide (Bosnia and Herzegovina v Serbia and Montenegro)* (Judgment) [2007] ICJ Rep 43 [160]; *Question of the Delimitation of the Continental Shelf between Nicaragua and Colombia beyond 200 Nautical Miles from the Nicaraguan Coast (Nicaragua v Colombia)* (Preliminary Objections) [2016] ICJ Rep 100 [33]; ILC, 'Draft Conclusions on Subsequent Agreements and Subsequent Practice in Relation to the Interpretation of Treaties, with Commentaries' (30 April–1 June and 2 July–10 August 2018) UN Doc A/73/10, reproduced in [2018/II - Part Two] YBILC 16, 26 (Draft Conclusions on Subsequent Practice). See also R Gardiner, *Treaty Interpretation* (Oxford University Press 2008) 162–63; A Aust, *Modern Treaty Law and Practice* (3rd edn, Cambridge University Press 2013) 207.

[2] See e.g. Arrangement for the Transfer of Enemy Prisoners of War and Civilian Internees from the Custody of the British Forces to the Custody of the American Forces (31 January 1991) reproduced in P Rowe (ed), *The Gulf War 1990–91 in International and English Law* (Routledge 1993) Appendix I, 348–49; Memorandum of Understanding on the

and international bodies,[3] as well as in decisions of international tribunals.[4] It is also widely supported in the legal

Application of International Humanitarian Law between Croatia and the Socialist Federal Republic of Yugoslavia (27 November 1991) reproduced in M Mercier, *Crimes without Punishment: Humanitarian Action in Former Yugoslavia* (East Haven 1996) Appendix, Document IV, 196–98; Comprehensive Agreement on Respect for Human Rights and International Humanitarian Law between the Government of the Republic of the Philippines and the National Democratic Front of the Philippines (16 March 1998); Memorandum of Understanding between the Ministry of Defence of the Islamic Republic of Afghanistan and the Ministry of Defence of the Kingdom of Denmark concerning the Transfer of persons between the Danish Contingent of the International Security Assistance Force (ISAF) and Afghan authorities (8 June 2005, as amended on 1 May 2007); Arrangement for the Transfer of Detainees between the Government of Canada and the Government of the Islamic Republic of Afghanistan (3 May 2007); Arrangement between the Government of Canada and the Government of the United States of America concerning the Transfer of Persons between the Canadian Forces and the US Forces in Afghanistan (18 November 2011); Arrangement between the Government of the United Kingdom and the Government of the United States of America concerning US Support for the Transfer of UK-held Detainees from UK Detention to the Afghan Authorities (2 May 2013). See also the ICRC's study on customary international humanitarian law, which identified more than 160 rules based on a finding of State practice and *opinio juris*; ICRC, *Customary International Humanitarian Law* (Cambridge University Press 2005).

[3] See e.g. Supplemental Arrangement to the Status of Forces Agreement between the United Nations and the Government of the Republic of Mali concerning the Treatment of Individuals Detained and Handed over to the Government of Mali by the United Nations Multidimensional Integrated Stabilization Mission in Mali (MINUSMA) (signed and entered into force 1 July 2013) 2933 UNTS 25; UN Secretariat, 'Secretary-General's Bulletin: Observance by United Nations Forces of International Humanitarian Law' (6 August 1999) UN Doc ST/SGB/1999/13; ILC, 'Draft Articles on the Effects of Armed Conflicts on Treaties' (26 April–3 June and 4 July–12 August 2011) UN Doc A/66/10, reproduced in [2018/II - Part Two] YBILC 107, 112–16, esp arts 5, 7, 10; Agreement between the European Union and the Central African Republic Concerning Detailed Arrangements for the Transfer to the Central African Republic of Persons Detained by the European Union Military Operation (EUFOR RCA) in the Course of Carrying out its Mandate, and Concerning the Guarantees Applicable to such Persons [2014] OJ L251/3; Updated European Union Guidelines on Promoting Compliance with International Humanitarian Law (IHL) [2009] OJ C303/12.

[4] Notably, tribunals have been established specifically to address violations of international law, including IHL, following many modern armed conflicts. Examples include the International Criminal Tribunal for the former Yugoslavia, established in 1993; the International Criminal Tribunal for Rwanda, established in 1994; the Eritrea-Ethiopia Claims Commission, established in 2000; the Extraordinary Chambers in the Courts of Cambodia, in 2000; and the Special Court for Sierra Leone, established in 2000. In addition, the International Criminal Court, established by the Rome Statute in 1998, has jurisdiction over certain serious violations of the Geneva Conventions, and the International Court of Justice has also rendered decisions related to IHL, e.g. *Legal*

scholarship.[5] However, as this chapter will discuss, IHL treaties do have some specificities that affect how they are interpreted, one of which is that IHL has a 'guardian', the International Committee of the Red Cross (ICRC).

Before delving into how the rules of treaty interpretation apply to IHL treaties, this chapter will explore the ICRC's role as the guardian of IHL, which gives the organization unique insights into how this body of law, and in particular its core treaties, the Geneva Conventions and their Additional Protocols,[6] are interpreted and applied. It will then zoom in on the ICRC's legal Commentaries as one tool through which the

Consequences of the Construction of a Wall (Advisory Opinion) [2004] ICJ Rep 136; *Legality of the Threat or Use of Nuclear Weapons* (Advisory Opinion) [1996] ICJ Rep 226.

5 See e.g. ME O'Connell, 'Historical Development and Legal Basis' in D Fleck (ed), *The Handbook of International Humanitarian Law* (4th edn, Oxford University Press 2021) 1; M Sassòli, *International Humanitarian Law: Rules, Controversies and Solutions to Problems Arising in Warfare* (Edward Elgar 2019) 43 [4.1.8]; R Kolb and K del Mar, 'Treaties for Armed Conflict' in A Clapham and P Gaeta (eds), *The Oxford Handbook of International Law of Armed Conflict* (Oxford University Press 2014) 79; Y Ronen, '*Silent Enim Leges Inter Arma* – but Beware the Background Noise: Domestic Courts as Agents of Development of the Law on the Conduct of Hostilities' (2013) 26 LJIL 599; R Petit and N Jain, 'Preserving the Rule of Law in the Age of the "War on Terror": Lessons from the Experience of International Criminal Tribunals' (2008) 39 STLP 67; S Carvin, 'In Times of War the Law Is Not So Silent' (2008) 12(3) IJHR 471; CL Lim, '*Inter Arma Silent Leges*? Black Hole Theories of the Laws of War' in VV Ramraj (ed), *Emergencies and the Limits of Legality* (Cambridge University Press 2008) 385. But see NK Modirzadeh and DA Lewis, 'Humanitarian Values in a Counterterrorism Era' (2022) 103 IRRC 403; L Hajjar, 'The Counterterrorism War Paradigm versus International Humanitarian Law: The Legal Contradictions and Global Consequences of the US "War on Terror"' (2019) 44(4) LSI 922.

6 Geneva Convention (I) for the Amelioration of the Condition of the Wounded and Sick in Armed Forces in the Field (adopted 12 August 1949, entered into force 21 October 1950) 75 UNTS 31 (GCI); Geneva Convention (II) for the Amelioration of the Condition of Wounded, Sick and Shipwrecked Members of Armed Forces at Sea (adopted 12 August 1949, entered into force 21 October 1950) 75 UNTS 85 (GCII); Geneva Convention (III) relative to the Treatment of Prisoners of War (adopted 12 August 1949, entered into force 21 October 1950) 75 UNTS 135 (GCIII); Geneva Convention (IV) relative to the Protection of Civilians in Time of War (adopted 12 August 1949, entered into force 21 October 1950) 75 UNTS 287 (GCIV); Protocol Additional to the Geneva Conventions of 12 August 1949, and relating to the Protection of Victims of International Armed Conflicts (Protocol I) (adopted 8 June 1977, entered into force 7 December 1978) 1125 UNTS 3 (API); Protocol Additional to the Geneva Conventions of 12 August 1949, and relating to the Protection of Victims of Non-International Armed Conflicts (Protocol II) of 8 June 1977 (adopted 8 June 1977, entered into force 7 December 1978) 1125 UNTS 609 (APII); Protocol Additional to the Geneva Conventions of 12 August 1949, and relating to the Adoption of an Additional Distinctive Emblem (Protocol III) (adopted 8 December 2005, entered into force 14 January 2007) 2404 UNTS 261 (APIII).

organization has historically provided extensive guidance on interpreting the Geneva Conventions. Looking at the shifts in methodology behind these Commentaries over time gives important clues as to how IHL treaties have been interpreted over time. Although the Commentaries' interpretive methodology has evolved, it has done so apace with the evolution of the rules of treaty interpretation in general public international law – culminating in the adoption of the VCLT. The chapter will close by giving examples of how the VCLT methodology is used in the current project to update the ICRC Commentaries and examining some of the particularities of IHL treaties that impact how the VCLT rules are applied.

6.2 Born on the Battlefield: IHL and Its Guardian

In the words of International Law Commission (ILC) Special Rapporteur Georg Nolte, 'The role which ICRC assumes with regard to the Geneva Conventions for the protection of war victims and their Additional Protocols is a case apart.'[7] The ICRC has been involved in developing, codifying and clarifying IHL,[8] giving it unique insights that are invaluable in the related but distinct work of providing guidance on how to interpret those norms. The ICRC acts as the guardian of IHL in part because of their shared origins and history.[9] The ICRC's special role as guardian of IHL, most clearly laid out in the Statutes of the International Red Cross and Red Crescent Movement,[10] is also partially explained by its consistent response to humanitarian needs on the battlefield, which

[7] ILC, 'First Report on Subsequent Agreements and Subsequent Practice in relation to Treaty Interpretation' (19 March 2013) UN Doc A/CN.4/660, reproduced in [2013/II – Part One] YBILC 51 [141] (First Report Nolte).

[8] See K Lawand and I Robinson, 'Development of Treaties Limiting or Prohibiting the Use of Certain Weapons: The Role of the International Committee of the Red Cross' in R Geiß, A Zimmermann and S Haumer (eds), *Humanizing the Laws of War: The Red Cross and the Development of International Humanitarian Law* (Cambridge University Press 2017) 141.

[9] Y Sandoz, 'The International Committee of the Red Cross as Guardian of International Humanitarian Law' (*ICRC*, 1998) <www.icrc.org/en/article/guardian-international-humanitarian-law> (last accessed 1 June 2025).

[10] Statutes of the International Red Cross and Red Crescent Movement (adopted 31 October 1986, entered into force 8 November 1986, amended 21 June 2006), reproduced in ICRC and the International Federation of Red Cross and Red Crescent Societies, *Handbook of the International Red Cross and Red Crescent Movement* (14th edn, ICRC and the International Federation of Red Cross and Red Crescent Societies 2008) 519, art 5 <www.rcrc-resilience-southeastasia.org/wp-content/uploads/2017/12/Handbook-RCRC-Movement.pdf> (last accessed 1 June 2025).

serves as a foundation for its advocacy for better respect for legal protections and new protections where existing law is not sufficient.[11]

The ICRC undertakes 'to work for the faithful application of international humanitarian law applicable in armed conflicts . . . [and] to work for the understanding and dissemination of knowledge of international humanitarian law applicable in armed conflicts and to prepare any development thereof'.[12] Because of its role as guardian, the ICRC is an authority that States and scholars often turn to for guidance on how to interpret and apply IHL and an actor with which States actively engage on whether they agree or disagree with the its positions.[13] Indeed, the ICRC's history is so intertwined with the history of modern IHL and especially its core treaties, the Geneva Conventions and their Additional Protocols, that one might say the organization was "born" to play this role.

The birth of modern IHL and the birth of the ICRC are both commonly traced back to the battlefield at Solferino in 1859, where Swiss businessman Henry Dunant witnessed the battle and saw the townspeople of nearby Castiglione, in particular the women, organizing to collect and care for the wounded soldiers from both sides without distinction.[14] Dunant joined in their efforts along with several other

[11] G Abi-Saab, 'The Specificities of Humanitarian Law' in Christophe Swinarski (ed), *Studies and Essays on International Humanitarian Law and Red Cross Principles in Honour of Jean Pictet* (ICRC and Martinus Nijhoff 1984) 265, 279–80. See also Geiß, Zimmermann and Haumer (n 8) esp 242–44.

[12] Statutes of the International Red Cross and Red Crescent Movement (n 10) 519, arts 5 (2)(c), 5 (2)(g).

[13] M Zwanenburg, 'The "External Element" of the Obligation to Ensure Respect for the Geneva Conventions: A Matter of Treaty Interpretation' (2021) 97 ILS 621; MN Schmitt and S Watts, 'Common Article 1 and the Duty to "Ensure Respect"' (2020) 96 ILS 674; V Robson, 'The Common Approach to Article 1: The Scope of Each State's Obligation to Ensure Respect for the Geneva Conventions' (2020) 25(1) JCSL 101; E Stubbins Bates, 'Geneva Convention III Commentary: Unpacking the Potential of "Ensure Respect" in Common Article 1' (*Just Security*, 30 October 2020) <www.justsecurity.org/73166/geneva-convention-iii-commentary-unpacking-the-potential-of-ensure-respect-in-common-article-1> (last accessed 1 June 2025).

[14] H Dunant, *A Memory of Solferino* (first published 1862, ICRC 2016) 55, 58, 63 and 70. This is an inspiring origin story, but it's important to note that Henry Dunant was not the only one to have similar ideas, or even the first. By his own account, he took his inspiration from several prominent figures from history and from his own time. He lists Archbishop Charles Borromeo, Frederico Borromeo, Bishop Belzunce de Castel-Moron, John Howard, Sister Marthe of Besançon, Sister Barbe Schyner, Grand Duchess Helen Pawlowna of Russia, Florence Nightingale (ibid 118–19). See also D Palmieri, 'An Institution Standing the Test of Time? A Review of 150 Years of the History of the International Committee of the Red Cross' (2012) 94 IRRC 1273, 1276.

bystanders. He described the scene of the battle and the efforts to treat the wounded that followed in vivid detail in his 1862 book, *A Memory of Solferino*. He made two important proposals in the book: (1) that in every country societies be established – already in peacetime – for the assistance of wounded and sick soldiers (which was at the origin of the ICRC and the wider International Red Cross and Red Crescent Movement) and (2) that internationally agreed rules be laid out to protect the wounded and sick and those who cared for them (which was at the origin of the 1864 Geneva Convention, and its subsequent iterations).[15]

The ICRC, established in 1863, lobbied for the 1864 Geneva Convention and was present on the battlefield to observe how the law has been interpreted by States since its first application in the 1870–71 Franco-Prussian war.[16] Over time, its role in working to ensure respect for IHL was firmly established.[17] Because of the important work of the organization, the 1949 Geneva Conventions explicitly provided a role for the ICRC as a neutral intermediary and humanitarian actor, further cementing its special relationship with IHL.[18] These Conventions and their Additional Protocols are the core IHL treaties, but other treaties also contain IHL norms, for example, treaties regulating weapons.

Separate from its work in developing the law, the ICRC is uniquely placed to provide insights into how the law has been (and should be) interpreted and applied. It is constantly engaged in interpreting IHL. Indeed, the organization cannot fulfil its humanitarian mission without interpreting IHL treaties, which is 'at the heart of the ICRC's daily work'.[19]

[15] Dunant (n 14) 115, 126.

[16] Through the International Committee for Relief to the Wounded, based in Basel; Palmieri (n 14) 1277.

[17] See L Cameron, 'The ICRC in the First World War: Unwavering Belief in the Power of Law?' (2016) 97 IRRC 1099.

[18] See R Geiß and A Zimmermann, 'The International Committee of the Red Cross: A Unique Actor in the Field of International Humanitarian Law Creation and Progressive Development' in R Geiß, A Zimmermann and S Haumer (eds), *Humanizing the Laws of War: The Red Cross and the Development of International Humanitarian Law* (Cambridge University Press 2017) 222; R Heinsch, 'The International Committee of the Red Cross and the Geneva Conventions of 1949' in R Geiß, A Zimmermann and S Haumer (eds), *Humanizing the Laws of War: The Red Cross and the Development of International Humanitarian Law* (Cambridge University Press 2017) 55.

[19] J-M Henckaerts, 'Bringing the Commentaries on the Geneva Conventions and their Additional Protocols into the Twenty-First Century' (2012) 94 IRRC 1551, 1552; First Report Nolte (n 7) [141].

One way the ICRC does this is in providing guidance on how to best interpret and apply IHL norms.

The ICRC has produced numerous interpretive guides,[20] fact sheets,[21] articles[22] and other materials[23] designed to generate understanding and respect for the law, as well as facilitate its interpretation and application. It has published textbooks,[24] case books,[25] and a long-running academic journal (the *International Review of the Red Cross*)[26] and has produced online databases[27] and an application for smartphones.[28] Among this

[20] N Melzer, *Direct Participation in Hostilities* (ICRC 2009).

[21] See ICRC, '2013 Arms Trade Treaty' (*ICRC*, 21 April 2021) <www.icrc.org/sites/default/files/document/file_list/dp_consult_41_2013_arms_trade_treaty_web_0.pdf> (last accessed 1 June 2025); ICRC, 'National Committees for the Implementation of International Humanitarian Law' (*ICRC*, 21 May 2021) <www.icrc.org/sites/default/files/document/file_list/dp_consult_14_national_committees_for_the_implementation_of_ihl.pdf> (last accessed 1 June 2025); ICRC, 'Legal Review of New Weapons' (*ICRC*, 29 November 2021) <www.icrc.org/sites/default/files/document/file_list/dp_consult_12_legal_review_of_new_weapons.pdf> (last accessed 1 June 2025).

[22] See T Ferraro, 'The ICRC's Legal Position on the Notion of Armed Conflict Involving Foreign Intervention and on Determining the IHL Applicable to This Type of Conflict' (2016) 97 IRRC 1227; I Herbet and J Drevon, 'Engaging Armed Groups at the International Committee of the Red Cross: Challenges, Opportunities and COVID-19' (2020) 102 IRRC 1021; C Droege and E Giorgou, 'How International Humanitarian Law Develops' (2022) 104 IRRC 1798.

[23] See ICRC, 'Exploring Humanitarian Law (EHL)' (*ICRC*, 5 September 2023) <www.icrc.org/en/document/exploring-humanitarian-law-ehl-resource-pack> (last accessed 1 June 2025); ICRC, 'International Humanitarian Law and the Challenges of Contemporary Armed Conflicts: Recommitting to Protection in Armed Conflict on the 70th Anniversary of the Geneva Conventions' (*ICRC*, 22 November 2019) <www.icrc.org/en/document/icrc-report-ihl-and-challenges-contemporary-armed-conflicts> (last accessed 1 June 2025); ICRC, 'Gendered Impacts of Armed Conflict and Implications for the Application of International Humanitarian Law' (*ICRC*, 29 June 2022) <www.icrc.org/fr/publication/4634-gendered-impact-armed-conflict-and-ihl> (last accessed 1 June 2025).

[24] N Melzer and E Kuster (eds), *International Humanitarian Law: A Comprehensive Introduction* (ICRC 2022).

[25] M Sassòli, AA Bouvier and A Quintin, *How Does Law Protect in War? Cases, Documents and Teaching Materials on Contemporary Practice in International Humanitarian Law* (3rd edn, ICRC 2011).

[26] Available open access at <https://international-review.icrc.org> (last accessed 1 June 2025).

[27] The three databases ('Treaties, States Parties and Commentaries', 'Customary International Humanitarian Law' and 'National Practice') are available at <https://ihl-databases.icrc.org/en> (last accessed 1 June 2025).

[28] Available at <www.icrc.org/en/document/ihl-digital-app> (last accessed 1 June 2025).

wealth of IHL resources, treaty commentaries are the most exhaustive interpretive tools produced by the organization.

6.3 The ICRC Commentaries as Interpretive Tools

As IHL grew through the addition of new treaties, the ICRC produced legal commentaries explaining how each provision of those treaties should be interpreted and applied. The methodology behind these commentaries evolved apace with developments in general international law governing how treaties should be interpreted.[29]

6.3.1 The 1870 Commentary

The first ICRC Commentary was published in 1870, just a few years after the 1864 Geneva Convention.[30] It was the work of a single author, Gustave Moynier, who had been involved in the drafting of the 1864 Convention. This Commentary is based on the personal views of the author including on how the law should evolve, although it was generally framed as explaining the intent of the drafters in response to criticisms of the Convention following its first-ever application during the Franco-Prussian War.[31]

6.3.2 The 1908 Commentary

The Geneva Convention was revised in 1906, and at first the report of the drafting committee functioned as its Commentary.[32] Two years later, the ICRC endorsed a second Commentary on the 1906 Convention by the former Secretary General of the 1906 Diplomatic Conference, Swiss law professor Ernst Röthlisberger.[33] Similar to the 1870 Commentary, these were each the work of a single author presenting their views and framing

[29] For a detailed discussion on the history of ICRC Commentaries, see C Mohr and E Policinski, 'From the Gilded Age to the Digital Age: The Evolution of ICRC Legal Commentaries' (2022) 104 IRRC 1898.

[30] G Moynier, *Etude sur la Convention de Genève pour l'amélioration du sort des militaires blessés dans les armées en campagne: 1864 et 1869* (Librarie de J Cherbuliez 1870).

[31] ibid 63–64, 136–37, 177–82 and 191–93.

[32] Geneva Convention for the Amelioration of the Condition of the Wounded and Sick in Armies in the Field (adopted 6 July 1906, entered into force 9 August 1907) 11 LNTS 440; See ICRC, 'Le Comité international et la Conférence de 1906' (1906) 37 Bulletin 270.

[33] See ICRC, 'Prof Ernest Röthlisberger – La Nouvelle Convention de Genève' (1908) 39 Bulletin 254.

them as an explanation of the intent of the drafters. At this point, there was even less State practice to be taken into account than there had been when the 1870 Commentary to the 1864 Convention had been written, as these Conventions had not yet been applied at the time of writing the Commentary.

Although legal commentaries in general were becoming more common at this time, particularly in the German legal tradition, it was still unusual to have such detailed commentaries on international treaties.[34] Providing an in-depth examination of the drafters' intent was therefore a proactive choice made by the authors of these Commentaries in line with the contemporary trend to put a heavy emphasis on establishing the original intent of the drafters. As one tribunal put it in 1897, 'It is the meaning of the [individuals] who framed the treaty which we are to seek, rather than some possible meaning which can be forced upon isolated words or sentences.'[35]

6.3.3 The 1930 Commentaries

The next revision of the Geneva Convention protecting wounded and sick soldiers on the battlefield was in 1929, which also saw the addition of a new Geneva Convention designed to protect prisoners of war.[36] The 1930 Commentary on the revised Convention was drafted by ICRC member Paul Des Gouttes, who had taken part in the Diplomatic Conferences to draft the Convention and had in fact written the report of the 1929 Diplomatic Conference.[37] The Commentary on the revised Convention garnered additional weight thanks to the preface authored by then-ICRC president Max Huber, emphasizing that the institution was behind the Commentary. The ICRC also endorsed a Commentary on the new Convention relative to the Treatment of Prisoners of War, which was authored by a diplomat who had participated in the 1929 Conference.[38]

34 C Djeffal, 'Commentaries on the Law of Treaties: A Review Essay Reflecting on the Genre of Commentaries' (2013) 24 EJIL 1223.

35 First Award under the Convention between Costa Rica and Nicaragua of 8 April 1896 for the Demarcation of the Boundary between the two Republics (1897) 28 RIAA 215, 216.

36 Geneva Convention for the Amelioration of the Condition of the Wounded and Sick in Armies in the Field (adopted 27 July 1929, entered into force 19 June 1931) 118 LNTS 303; Geneva Convention relative to the Treatment of Prisoners of War (adopted 27 July 1929, entered into force 19 June 1931) 118 LNTS 343.

37 P Des Gouttes, *La Convention de Genève du 27 juillet 1929: commentaire* (ICRC 1930) Preface by M Huber, xviii.

38 G Werner, 'Un commentaire du Code des prisonniers de guerre' (1932) 159 Bulletin 199.

Each of these Commentaries were the work of a single author, but the weight given to the legal interpretations therein shifted over time. The earlier Commentaries relied largely on the author's role in the drafting of the treaty and partially from their respective reputations as prominent lawyers to being bolstered by the reputation of the ICRC as an institution, starting with the 1930 Commentaries. The emphasis remained on discovering the intent of the drafters, which around the same time Hersch Lauterpacht called 'the main task of interpretation'.[39]

6.3.4 The 1952–1960 Commentaries

The current iterations of the Geneva Conventions were drafted in 1949,[40] followed soon after by a corresponding set of Commentaries, published first in French and then in English translation between 1952 and 1960.[41] These Commentaries were the work of a team of principally ICRC staff under the direction of ICRC lawyer Jean Pictet,[42] which is why they are sometimes referred to as the 'Pictet Commentaries'. Today, Jean Pictet has quite an established reputation, in part due to these Commentaries. However, at the time he was a young lawyer who was much less well-known than the authors of previous Commentaries. These Commentaries were thus even more of an 'institutional' product, with the emblem of the red cross featuring prominently on their original covers. The

[39] H Lauterpacht, 'Restrictive Interpretation and the Principle of Effectiveness in the Interpretation of Treaties' (1949) 26 BYBIL 48, 55.

[40] GCI, GCII, GCIII and GCIV (n 6).

[41] JS Pictet (ed), *The Geneva Conventions of 12 August 1949: Commentary, Vol. I: Geneva Convention for the Amelioration of the Condition of the Wounded and Sick in Armed Forces in the Field* (ICRC 1952); JS Pictet (ed), *The Geneva Conventions of 12 August 1949: Commentary, Vol. II: Geneva Convention for the Amelioration of the Condition of Wounded, Sick and Shipwrecked Members of Armed Forces at Sea* (ICRC 1960); JS Pictet (ed), *The Geneva Conventions of 12 August 1949: Commentary, Vol. III: Geneva Convention relative to the Treatment of Prisoners of War* (ICRC 1960); JS Pictet (ed), *The Geneva Conventions of 12 August 1949: Commentary, Vol. IV: Geneva Convention relative to the Protection of Civilian Persons in Time of War* (ICRC 1958).

[42] The ICRC lawyers who worked on these Commentaries were Frédéric Siordet, Claude Pilloud, René-Jean Wilhelm, Jean-Pierre Schoenholzer, Oscar Uhler and Jean de Preux. The only external specialist on the team was Dutch naval captain and judge Major MW Mouton, to assist on the elaboration of the Commentary on the second Geneva Convention, relative to the protection of the wounded, sick and shipwrecked members of armed forces at sea. This perhaps demonstrates a certain reticence on behalf of IHL specialists regarding the complex area of the law of the sea, but also an openness to external input on an ICRC product (A CICR, minutes of meeting, working session (30 April 1953) available in the ICRC Archives).

Commentaries were drafted by a team of ICRC lawyers, some of whom had participated in the negotiations of the 1949 Conventions. There was still a reliance on their having been part of the treaty negotiations and therefore able to provide insights into the intent of the drafters.[43]

The methodology behind the Commentaries of the 1950s and 1960s was more developed than previous Commentaries, but as mentioned above they were still focused on explaining the intent of the drafters and still drew heavily from the inside knowledge of those authors who had participated in the negotiation process. However, these Commentaries relied to a greater extent on State practice prior to the negotiation of the Conventions, notably during the Second World War, during which the authors had been ICRC delegates and therefore had experienced for themselves how the previous Geneva (and Hague) Conventions were implemented in practice.

One reason for this more developed interpretive methodology is precisely because the Commentaries were drafted by a team, and therefore written guidelines needed to be agreed to ensure consistency. These methodological guidelines emphasized the importance of tying the analysis to the history of the Geneva Conventions, the events of the Second World War necessitating addition of new provisions or the revision of existing provisions and the records of the 1949 Diplomatic Conference and other preparatory works created from 1946 to 1948. They specified that 'although it [will be] a scientific work, the commentary must be clear and accessible to non-lawyers. The style, therefore, must be simple. It will be impersonal and if the author of the commentary has opinions to which he would like to give a more personal touch, he will mark them clearly in the margin.'[44] This differs from previous Commentaries, where the personal views of the authors were part and parcel of the interpretive guidance presented.

During this period, efforts to codify the rules of treaty interpretation (and thus make it more scientific) were underway, most importantly the ILC project that ultimately culminated in the 1969 VCLT.[45] In 1949, the

[43] Pictet, Siordet, Pillaud and Wilhelm had worked on the revision of the Conventions and followed the discussions of the 1949 Diplomatic Conference and the earlier expert meetings.

[44] *Schéma relatif à l'établissement des Commentaires des nouvelles Conventions de Genève.* A CICR, minutes of meetings, legal commission (14 September 1949) available in the ICRC Archives.

[45] See Gardiner (n 1) 51–73. Specifically looking at the evolution of international law commentaries as a medium for interpretation, see Djeffal (n 34) 1231–36.

UN Secretary General's Survey of International Law in Relation to the Work of Codification of the ILC listed the law of treaties as a topic ripe for codification.[46] Throughout the 1950s and 1960s, the ILC issued various reports proposing draft treaties, ultimately leading to the Vienna Conference on the Law of Treaties that took place in two sessions over 1968–69.[47] This culminated in the 1969 VCLT.[48] Some saw the interpretive rules contained in the VCLT as getting away from traditional interpretive approaches, which largely focused on determining the intent of the drafters.[49] However, others argued that the VCLT should rather be seen as requiring a more scientific way of determining that intent, one that allows for interpretations to evolve over time and therefore treaties to remain fit for purpose for longer.[50]

6.3.5 The 1987 Commentary

In the time between the VCLT's adoption in 1969 and its entry into force in 1980, IHL continued to develop and the ICRC continued to produce treaty Commentaries. In 1977, two Additional Protocols were concluded, one relating to international armed conflict and one to non-international armed conflict.[51] The Commentaries on the Additional Protocols, published in 1987, were drafted by a team of ICRC lawyers led by Claude Pilloud.[52] Most had been part of the ICRC delegation to the 1974–77 Diplomatic Conference and therefore based their observations on first-hand knowledge, although these Commentaries included many more

[46] UN Secretary-General, 'Survey of International Law in Relation to the Work of Codification of the International Law Commission' (10 February 1949) UN Doc A/CN.4/Rev.1, 51 ff. See also ME Villiger, *Commentary on the 1969 Vienna Convention on the Law of Treaties* (Martinus Nijhoff 2009) 28–38.

[47] Villiger (n 46) 35–38.

[48] VCLT (n 1).

[49] J-M Sorel and V Boré Eveno, 'Article 31' in O Corten and P Klein (eds), *The Vienna Convention on the Law of Treaties: A Commentary* (Oxford University Press 2011) 804.

[50] E Bjorge, 'The Vienna Rules, Evolutionary Interpretation, and the Intentions of the Parties' in A Bianchi, D Peat and M Windsor (eds), *Interpretation in International Law* (Oxford University Press 2018) 189, 203.

[51] API and APII (n 6).

[52] Jean Pictet served as the chairman the reading committee overseeing the project. The contributors included ICRC jurists Jean de Preux, Yves Sandoz, Bruno Zimmermann, Philippe Eberlin, Hans-Peter Gasser, Claude F Wenger, Philippe Eberlin and Sylvie-S Junod, the first woman to be part of a team drafting ICRC Commentaries. For detailed discussion, see Mohr and Policinski (n 29) 1906.

footnotes to the drafting history, State practice, case law and academic scholarship than previous Commentaries.

Looking at the Commentaries produced by the ICRC before 2011, it is tempting to identify individual elements that align with the interpretive norms reflected in the 1969 VCLT.[53] Indeed, the Commentary even relied on the VCLT – citing it seventy-eight times, principally on the permissibility of reservations. The VCLT was also relied upon in several instances to justify the interpretations presented.[54] The Commentary goes so far as to observe that the drafters of the Additional Protocols relied on the status of the VCLT as customary international law.[55] However the VCLT rules were not systematically used until the project to update the ICRC Commentaries that began in 2011. In this project, the methodology contained in Articles 31–33 of the VCLT would become the scaffolding upon which the ICRC's next Commentaries would be built.

Although these Commentaries did not yet adopt the VCLT's interpretive rules as a strict methodology, the foreword reveals a methodology that aims to ensure that the Commentaries were more than the personal opinions of their authors. Similar to the Commentaries drafted in the 1950s, the 1987 Commentaries were 'essentially concerned with explaining the provisions of the 1977 Protocols, primarily on the basis of the work of the Diplomatic Conference (CDDH) and other preparatory work. The authors were guided by existing international humanitarian law, general international law and legal literature.'[56] The authoritative weight of the Commentaries published between 1952 and 1960 as well as the 1987 Commentaries was reliant on the convincingness of their logic, the soundness of the underlying methodology and the reputation of the ICRC as an institution.[57] This meant necessarily that there was

[53] E.g. the 1870 Commentary referred to the 'esprit général' (general purpose) of the treaty, meaning its object and purpose. Moynier (n 30) 143. Similarly, the 1930 Commentary referred to 'the general purpose of the Convention must inform all of its application, even in the details'; Des Gouttes (n 37) 191. For more analysis, see Mohr and Policinski (n 29) 1909–10.

[54] For example, Y Sandoz et al (eds), *Commentary on the Additional Protocols of 8 June 1977 of the Geneva Conventions of 12 August 1949* (Martinus Nijhoff 1987) 58, 523, 541, 977, 1013–14 and 1035.

[55] ibid 1059–60.

[56] ibid xxv.

[57] On the sources of authority for ICRC materials, see L Mührel, *The Authority of the International Committee of the Red Cross: Determining What International Humanitarian Law Is* (Brill/Nijhoff, 2024) 31–32. Mührel finds that the marks perceived authority of the ICRC (and other non-State actors) come from the expertise and

more thought put into the methodology and less room for personal opinions.[58]

6.4 Applying the VCLT to the Geneva Conventions and Their Additional Protocols

In 2011, the ICRC began its project to update its Commentaries on the 1949 Geneva Conventions and their 1977 Additional Protocols, taking into account State practice and legal developments that have taken place in the decades since the Conventions were adopted to ensure the Commentaries are fit for purpose as an interpretive tool for practitioners in contemporary armed conflicts.[59]

There is a dedicated team of ICRC lawyers undertaking this project, authoring most of the commentaries on the articles of the Conventions and ensuring the overall coherence of the Commentaries. There are also

reputation of the author and their affiliated institution(s); the form, process, and methodology used for the work in question; and, lastly, tradition.

[58] Two shorter ICRC Commentaries published between 1987 and the launch of the project to update the ICRC Commentaries are worth mentioning here. When Annex I of the First Additional Protocol (containing the regulations for identification of various categories of persons and objects) was amended in 1993, the Commentary on it was amended as well, drafted by ICRC technical adviser Dominique Loye. D Loye, *Commentary on Annex I to Protocol Additional I to the Geneva Conventions of 1949: Regulations concerning identification, as amended on 30 November 1993* (ICRC 2002) <https://ihl-databases.icrc.org/en/ihl-treaties/api-amended-annex-i-1993> (last accessed 1 June 2025). Then the Third Additional Protocol was concluded in 2005. The Commentary was drafted by ICRC legal adviser Jean-François Quéguiner, who had been part of the ICRC delegation to the 2005 Diplomatic Conference. It was published in the *International Review of the Red Cross*. Each of these Commentaries is written by a single author on behalf of the ICRC.

[59] The three Commentaries that have been published at time of writing are: ICRC, *Commentary on the First Geneva Convention: Convention (I) for the Amelioration of the Condition of the Wounded and Sick in Armed Forces in the Field* (2nd edn, Cambridge University Press 2016) (Updated Commentary on GCI); ICRC, *Commentary on the Second Geneva Convention: Convention (II) for the Amelioration of the Condition of Wounded, Sick and Shipwrecked Members of Armed Forces at Sea* (2nd edn, Cambridge University Press 2017) (Updated Commentary on GCII); ICRC, *Commentary on the Third Geneva Convention: Convention (III) relative to the Treatment of Prisoners of War* (2nd edn, Cambridge University Press 2021) (Updated Commentary on GCIII). For details on the project and the rationale behind it, see J-M Henckaerts (n 18); L Lijnzaad and TK Githiora in S Longuet et al, 'Conference on the ICRC Updated Commentary on the First Geneva Convention: Capturing 60 Years of Practice', (2017–18) 56 MLLWR 1, 178, 211.

some external contributors invited to join the project,[60] as well as around fifty external peer reviewers from all over the world for each of the Commentaries and an editorial committee to provide guidance and support to the project team, made up of internal and external legal experts representing academics, judges and military practitioners.[61] This is a long way away from the Commentaries that were the work of a single author. The current way of working represents an openness to the views of diverse legal experts and a willingness to acknowledge alternate legal interpretations where there is no consensus.

The VCLT is relied upon as the basis for the interpretations presented in the updated Commentaries despite the fact that the VCLT was adopted twenty years after the conclusion of the 1949 Geneva Conventions, as 'an international instrument has to be interpreted and applied within the framework of the entire legal system prevailing at the time of the interpretation.'[62] Since the entry into force of the VCLT, the interpretive norms contained in Articles 31–33 have crystallized into customary international law.[63] It is therefore appropriate to rely on

[60] L Cameron et al, 'The Updated Commentary on the First Geneva Convention: A New Tool for Generating Respect for International Humanitarian Law' (2015) 97 IRRC 1212.

[61] The composition of the Editorial Committee has changed slightly for each Commentary published so far. For the Commentary on the First Geneva Convention, the Editorial Committee was made up of (in alphabetical order) Knut Dörmann, then-chief legal officer and head of the ICRC's legal division; Liesbeth Lijnzaad, a judge on the International Tribunal for the Law of the Sea; Marco Sassòli, professor at the University of Geneva, and Philippe Spoerri, the ICRC's then-Director of International Law and Cooperation. The Editorial Committee for the Commentary on the Second Geneva Convention was made up of Knut Dörmann, Liesbeth Lijnzaad, Marco Sassòli and Philippe Spoerri. The Editorial Committee for the Commentary on the Third Geneva Convention was Knut Dörmann, who at that time was the ICRC's head of delegation in Brussels; Cordula Droege, the ICRC's incoming chief legal officer and head of the legal division; Helen Durham, the ICRC's incoming Director of Law and Policy; Liesbeth Lijnzaad; Marco Sassòli; Philip Spoerri, who at that time was ICRC's head of delegation in New York; and Brigadier General Kenneth Watkin (ret.) a former judge advocate from the Canadian Armed Forces. For the forthcoming Commentary on the Fourth Geneva Convention, the Editorial Committee is Knut Dörmann; Cordula Droege; Liesbeth Lijnzaad; Nils Melzer, the incoming ICRC Director of Law, Diplomacy and Policy; Marco Sassòli; and Wing Commander Tim Wood, Chief Legal Adviser at Headquarters Joint Forces for New Zealand.

[62] *Legal Consequences for States of the Continued Presence of South Africa in Namibia (South West Africa) notwithstanding Security Council Resolution 276 (1970)* (Advisory Opinion) [1971] ICJ Rep 16 [53].

[63] See e.g. *Crime of Genocide* (n 1) [160]; *LaGrand (Germany v United States of America)* (Judgment) [2001] ICJ Rep 466 [101]; *Kasikili/Sedudu Island* (n 1) [18–20]; US Court of Appeals 2nd Cir, *Eahrlich v American Airlines* (2004) 360 F 3d 366, 373 fn 5; US Court of

Articles 31–33 of the VCLT as a reflection of customary international law that is applicable to the interpretation of IHL treaties.

The VCLT-based methodology being used to draft the ICRC's updated Commentaries on the 1949 Geneva Conventions and their 1977 Additional Protocols reflects the fact that IHL treaties must be interpreted according to the same rules as other treaties. While there has been some criticism of *how* the VCLT's treaty interpretation has been applied,[64] importantly there has not been any criticism of the use of that methodology, and the updated Commentaries have generally been well-received by the international legal community.[65] Although the updated Commentaries are not always explicit about each step in the interpretive process, the interpretive rules contained in the VCLT underlie the commentary on each article. The reliance on the VCLT represents a change from the methodology used in previous ICRC Commentaries, reflecting the evolution in the general international legal discourse rather than a change specific to IHL. It is also a means of establishing the reliability and authority of the interpretations contained in the Commentaries as based on an established means of treaty interpretation, rather than the personal opinions of their authors. Ultimately, the authority of these updated Commentaries stems from the diligent research on which it is based and faithful application of the rules on treaty interpretation methodology

Appeals 2nd Cir, *Chubb Son, Inc v Asiana Airlines* (2000) 214 F 3d 301; First Report Nolte (n 7) [8].

[64] See MW Meier, 'The Updated GCIII Commentary: A Flawed Methodology?' (*Lieber Institute – West Point*, 3 February 2021) <https://lieber.westpoint.edu/updated-gciii-commentary-flawed-methodology> (last accessed 1 June 2025); KJ Heller, 'First Thoughts from Academia on the Updated GCI Commentary' (*OpinioJuris*, 22 July 2016) <http://opiniojuris.org/2016/07/22/multi-blog-series-first-thoughts-on-the-updated-gci-commentary-from-academia> (last accessed 1 June 2025).

[65] See DM Amann, 'Commenting On the ICRC Geneva Commentaries' (*Diane Marie Amann*, 15 March 2016) <https://dianemarieamann.com/2016/03/15/commenting-on-the-icrc-geneva-commentaries-30-march-in-d-c/> (last accessed 1 June 2025); E Lapidor, 'New Developments in ICRC Commentaries to the POW Convention' (*Just Security*, 18 June 2020) <www.justsecurity.org/70863/pow-geneva-convention-commentary-highlights-of-new-developments/> (last accessed 1 June 2025); K Okimoto, 'The United Nations and the Third Geneva Convention' (*EJIL: Talk!*, 26 October 2020) <www.ejiltalk.org/the-united-nations-and-the-third-geneva-convention/> (last accessed 1 June 2025). The project to update the ICRC Commentaries was also the subject of the 22nd edition of the Bruges Colloquium, an annual workshop co-hosted by the ICRC and the College of Europe that brings together legal practitioners from around Europe. See the program here: <www.coe-icrc.eu/en/programme> (last accessed 1 June 2025).

found in the VCLT applied to each individual article in the 1949 Geneva Conventions and their 1977 Additional Protocols.

6.5 An Updated Interpretive Approach for the Updated Commentaries

The standard rules of treaty interpretation apply to IHL treaties as demonstrated through the following concrete examples from the ICRC's updated Commentaries of how IHL is interpreted today taken from the updated Commentary on the Third Geneva Convention, the most recently published in the series. This chapter will not endeavour to give an in-depth explanation of the VCLT's interpretive rules, which have been adequately expounded on elsewhere,[66] but rather will look at the particularities of applying these rules to IHL treaties as seen through the lens of the ICRC's updated Commentaries on the 1949 Geneva Conventions.

6.5.1 Good Faith and the Ordinary Meaning of the Text

The starting point is VCLT Article 31 (1), which provides that treaties must be 'interpreted in good faith in accordance with the ordinary meaning to be given to the terms of the treaty in their context and in the light of its object and purpose'. This step in the interpretive process is readily apparent throughout the updated Commentaries, notably through the reliance on dictionaries to provide the ordinary meaning of terms used in the text of the treaties.[67] To tease out an example that demonstrates this, we can look at paragraph 4 of Article 17 of the Third Convention, prohibiting physical or mental torture and 'any other form of coercion' to secure information from prisoners of war. The updated Commentary examines the ordinary meaning of 'coercion', defining 'coerce' as 'means to "persuade (an unwilling person) to do something by using force or threats"' and going on to clarify that 'the decisive factor in determining whether coercion has occurred or is occurring is whether

[66] See e.g. Gardiner (n 1). Specific to the ICRC's updated Commentaries, see Updated Commentary on GCIII (n 59) Introduction; J-M Henckaerts et al, 'ICRC Perspectives on the Interpretation of the Third Geneva Convention More Than Seventy Years after Its Adoption' in MN Schmitt and CJ Koschnitzky (eds) *Prisoners of War in Contemporary Conflict* (Oxford University Press 2023) 375–407.

[67] Updated Commentary on GCIII (n 59) [81].

the method used deprives or impairs the prisoner of the exercise of free will and autonomy'.[68]

Another example of where the ICRC's updated Commentaries on the Geneva Conventions have explicitly stated that they are relying on 'good faith' and 'ordinary meaning' aspects of Article 31 is found in Article 3 common to all four Geneva Conventions, which requires that parties to the conflict search for, collect and evacuate of the wounded and sick without delay after every engagement. Although there is no express requirement for a party to the conflict to carry out such search, collection and evacuation during an engagement, a good faith application to the rule may require it to do so where the possibility exists without great risk to its personnel.[69]

To give another example, in determining who is a civilian prisoner of war, the Detaining Power must apply the provisions of Article 4 (A)(4) and (5) 'in good faith and in line with the rationale behind the provisions in question'.[70]

The ordinary meaning of terms in the context of the treaty is also explicitly relied upon in the analysis in the updated Commentaries, for instance, the definition of 'convenience' is used to clarify the meaning of 'clean and hygienic conveniences' under Article 29 of the Third Convention.[71] Similarly, the definition of 'infirmary' clarifies that Article 30 refers to 'a place for the care of those who are ill or injured'.[72] In another example, the Commentary clarifies that the term 'military operations' in Article 75 of the Third Convention 'must be understood in the context of the provision', meaning that it is specific to military operations preventing the States from transporting letters, parcels and documents.[73]

6.5.2 *Context, Subsequent Agreements, Subsequent Practice and Other Relevant Rules of International Law*

For an example of how the context can inform the ordinary meaning of the text, we can look to the prohibition of murder found in common

[68] ibid [1824] (citations omitted).
[69] ibid [789–90].
[70] ibid [1046].
[71] ibid [2199].
[72] ibid [2228], citing *Concise Oxford English Dictionary* (12th edn, Oxford University Press 2011) 728.
[73] Updated Commentary on GCIII (n 59) [3315].

Article 3 to the four Geneva Conventions. Paragraph one of that article prohibits 'violence to life and person, in particular murder of all kinds, mutilation, cruel treatment at torture' in non-international armed conflict. The Commentary acknowledges that there are different possible interpretations on whether 'murder' in the sense of this provision includes killings that take place in the course of the conduct of hostilities.[74] It goes on to clarify that, in the ICRC's view,

> it follows from the context of the 1949 Geneva Conventions in which common Article 3 is placed, however, that it was not intended to govern the conduct of hostilities . . .. The primary concern of the Conventions is the protection of the victims of international armed conflicts in the power of a Party to the conflict, but not the regulation of the conduct of hostilities as such. The same should therefore apply for common Article 3, which was adopted to extend the essence of the Conventions to non-international armed conflicts.[75]

Under VCLT Article 31 (3)(a) and (b), subsequent agreements and subsequent practice of States party to a treaty is considered together with the context. This is sometimes referred to as the 'external' context of the treaty.[76] The universal character of the Geneva Conventions means that acceptance of such agreements and practice must be similarly 'universal'.[77] Not much can meet this high bar, although practice and agreements with less universal character may be considered as a supplementary means of interpretation under VCLT Article 32 (discussed below).

Under VCLT Article 31(3)(c), relevant rules of international law applicable in the relations between the parties are also considered as part of the 'external' context. There are numerous references to such rules in the updated Commentaries. To give just a few examples, the customary law norm prohibiting the arbitrary denial of humanitarian access is used to confirm the same obligation under Article 9 of the Third Convention.[78] In a similar vein, customary international law is used to clarify that combatants captured while engaged in espionage are not entitled to prisoner of war status under Article 4 of the Third

[74] ibid [575].
[75] ibid [576] (citations omitted).
[76] Sorel and Boré Eveno (n 49) 825.
[77] Or 'practically universal'. See *Loizidou v Turkey* (Preliminary Objections) (25 March 1995) Series A no 310 [79–80]. See also Draft Conclusions on Subsequent Practice (n 1) Conclusions 4 (1) and (2), 6 (1) and (2), 10.
[78] Updated Commentary on GCIII (n 59) [1357] fn 68.

Convention.[79] In another example, human rights norms serve as relevant rules of international law to clarify the judicial guarantees that must be provided under Article 129 of the Third Convention.[80] Lastly, the Universal Postal Convention clarifies what exemptions from charges apply to humanitarian relief shipments sent to prisoners of war and correspondence with prisoners of war under the Third Convention.[81]

6.5.3 Object and Purpose

The object and purpose of a treaty also informs the ordinary meaning of its text.[82] As the ICRC's updated Commentaries conclude, 'the balance between humanitarian considerations, on the one hand, and military necessity, on the other, is a hallmark of international humanitarian law'.[83] This informs how the object and purpose of each individual IHL treaty is identified,[84] which in turn informs how the ordinary meaning of individual provisions is determined where they are unclear. The object and purpose of the Third Convention is 'to ensure that prisoners of war are humanely treated at all times, while allowing belligerents to intern captured enemy combatants to prevent them from returning to the battlefield'.[85] This evidently embodies the balance between humanity and military necessity.

[79] ibid [988].
[80] ibid [5168].
[81] ibid [3282–90, 4873].
[82] VCLT (n 1) art 31. See also FG Jacobs, 'Varieties of Approach to Treaty Interpretation' (1969) 18(2) ICLQ 318, 319; ILC, 'Documents of the Second Part of the Seventeenth Session and of the Eighteenth Session Including the Reports of the Commission to the General Assembly' (19 July 1966) UN Doc A/CN.4/SER.A/1966/Add.1; R Gardiner, *Treaty Interpretation* (2nd edn, Oxford University Press 2015) 215–16; A Aust, *Modern Treaty Law and Practice* (3rd edn, Cambridge University Press 2013) 205.
[83] Updated Commentary on GCIII (n 59) Introduction, [91]. See also *Corfu Channel (United Kingdom v Albania)* (Merits) [1949] ICJ Rep 4, 22.
[84] The object and purpose of each Geneva Convention is laid out in the introduction of the corresponding Commentary. For details on the object and purpose of the Third Convention, see L Lijnzaad, 'Swimming into Deep Water: Article 91(3) of the Third Geneva Convention and the Successful Escape of Prisoners of War by Sea' in S Marquardt and S Blockmans (eds), *The European Union's Contribution to International Peace and Security: Liber Amicorum in honour of Gert-Jan van Hegelsom* (Brill 2023) 310. For details on how the object and purpose of the Fourth Geneva Convention was identified, see K Mačák and E Policinski, 'In Pursuit of a Treaty's Soul: A Study of the Object and Purpose of the Fourth Geneva Convention' (2024) 73 ICLQ 385.
[85] Updated Commentary on GCIII (n 59) [89].

An example where the object and purpose of the Third Convention informs the interpretation of the text is found in the Commentary on Article 92, which governs the recapture of prisoners of war after an unsuccessful escape attempt. According to paragraph one, 'a prisoner of war who attempts to escape and is recaptured before having made good on his escape in the sense of Article 91 shall be liable only to a disciplinary punishment in respect of this act, even if it is a repeated offence'. According to a strict reading of the text, this would appear to apply only to attempted escapees who evade the custody of the Detaining Power and not, for example, to a prisoner of war who was stopped by guards before leaving the camp. However, as the Commentary points out, 'such an interpretation would lead to an unreasonable result (which also runs counter to the spirit of the Convention) and must be rejected'.[86] The object and purpose thus clarifies the ordinary meaning of the provision.

6.5.4 *Supplementary Means of Interpretation*

Article 32 of the VCLT refers to supplementary means of interpretation that can confirm or clarify the interpretation of treaty provisions after having applied the general rule in Article 31. These include the treaty's preparatory work, State practice that does not fall under Article 31,[87] the circumstances of the treaty's conclusion, judicial decisions and scholarly literature.[88] The drafting history of the 1949 Geneva Conventions is a particularly important supplementary means of interpretation used in the updated ICRC Commentaries. In addition, the majority of State practice featured in the updated Commentaries is subsequent practice in the sense of Article 32, meaning it is subsequent practice of some States rather than practice of all States party to the Conventions.[89]

This type of practice is used by the Commentaries to clarify that there is an exception to the obligation to repatriate prisoners of war at the close of hostilities under Article 118 of the Third Convention where a prisoner refuses repatriation for fear of violation of their fundamental

[86] ibid [3819].

[87] Draft Conclusions on Subsequent Practice (n 1) Conclusions 4 (3), 6 (3), 7.

[88] Y Le Bouthillier, 'Article 32' in O Corten and P Klein (eds), *The Vienna Convention on the Law of Treaties: A Commentary* (Oxford University Press 2011) 841, 861–62.

[89] J-M Henckaerts and E Pothelet, 'The Interpretation of IHL Treaties: Subsequent Practice and Other Salient Issues' in H Krieger and J Püschmann (eds), *Law-Making and Legitimacy in International Humanitarian Law* (Edward Elgar 2021) 150, 162–68.

rights.[90] It is also used to confirm that under Article 120 of the Third Convention the Detaining Power is 'to ensure the actual burial or cremation of the dead'.[91]

The decades between the conclusion of the treaties in question and the updated Commentaries have allowed time for States to put them into practice, giving the drafters more information to work with than their predecessors. State practice is cited throughout the Commentaries, but there are some examples that clearly show how this element operates to inform the way the provisions are interpreted. For example, the text of Article 30 of the Third Convention governing the medical attention prisoners of war are entitled to provides in paragraph one that 'every camp shall have an adequate infirmary where prisoners of war may have the attention they require'. The Commentary clarifies that 'mental health care is generally included in the health services required for prisoners of war; in this regard, some recent State practice (confirmed by ICRC observations) requires that on-site medical personnel have some experience in mental health, while in other contexts mental health services were provided through regular visits by specialists'.[92] Another example where an interpretation explicitly relies on State practice to modify the ordinary meaning of a provision is the exception to the obligation to repatriate prisoners of war after the cessation of active hostilities under Article 118 of the Third Convention. State practice and the principle of non-refoulement under international law support the interpretation that 'while there is no explicit exception in Article 118, the obligation to repatriate must be understood as subject to an exception where the prisoners face a real risk of violation of fundamental rights by their own country'.[93]

6.5.5 *Equally Authentic Languages*

VCLT Article 33 provides that where there are authentic versions of a treaty in two or more languages, they are equally authentic unless otherwise agreed by the parties. For the four Geneva Conventions, this means that the English and French versions have equal weight, and one can be used to shed light on the meaning of the other. This could be a more complex analysis for the 1977 Additional Protocols, since they were

[90] Updated Commentary on GCIII (n 59) [4469].
[91] ibid [1672] (citations omitted).
[92] ibid [2229].
[93] ibid [4469].

drafted in the six official UN languages and they are all equally authentic.[94]

An example of how this operates in practice is seen with regard to Article 13 of the Third Geneva Convention, the first sentence of which requires that 'Prisoners of war must at all times be humanely treated.' In the updated Commentary on this article, the ordinary meaning of the word 'humane' is given as 'compassionate or benevolent', before looking to the equally authentic French text, in which the relevant term is slightly different, although not inconsistent: 'traitées avec humanité'. Since both versions are equally authoritative, the text thus requires that 'persons protected under Article 13 be "treated with humanity"'.[95]

Another example is found in Article 3 common to all four Geneva Conventions, where the French 'les personnes qui ne participant pas *directement* aux hostilités' is used ('persons taking no *active* part in hostilities' in the English text) to clarify that the reference to 'active' participation in hostilities is a reference to the concept of direct participation in hostilities (as it is phrased in API and APII).[96] The French 'directement' makes it clear that 'direct participation in hostilities' has the same meaning as 'active participation in hostilities'. Similarly, the French text of Article 32 of the Third Convention clarifies what is meant by the requirement that medical personnel who are retained to perform medical functions must do so on behalf of prisoners 'dependent on the same Power.' The French text states that medical functions must be in the interest of prisoners of war 'dépendent de la même Puissance *qu'eux-mêmes*', clarifying that medical personnel exercise their functions on behalf of prisoners of war belonging to the same Power as themselves.[97]

6.5.6 Particularities

There are two particularities of IHL as a body of law worth mentioning since they impact how the VCLT's interpretive rules are applied: first, the *erga omnes* character of IHL obligations and, second, the principles of humanity and military necessity that underlie IHL as a body of law. Only this second particularity is unique to IHL as a body of law, and similar

[94] The six official UN languages are (in alphabetical order): Arabic, Chinese, English, French, Russian and Spanish. See UN, 'Official Languages' (*UN*, 2025) <www.un.org/en/our-work/official-languages> (last accessed 1 June 2025).
[95] Updated Commentary on GCIII (n 59) [1573].
[96] ibid [559] fn 265.
[97] ibid [2312].

underlying principles presumably impact the interpretation of other multilateral, norm-setting treaties, such as human rights treaties. Neither of these particularities make IHL subject to special rules of interpretation, although they may impact how IHL treaties are interpreted when the rules of interpretation are applied.

The *erga omnes* character of IHL treaties means that all States have an interest in upholding IHL and thus that all States' practice is relevant in interpreting IHL treaties.[98] It also means that no State (no matter how bellicose) can claim that its practice should have more weight than that of other States. Under Common Article 1 of the 1949 Geneva Conventions, States must not only apply the provisions, but they must also do everything reasonably in their power to ensure respect for the provisions by others, demonstrating the *erga omnes* nature of the obligations created by these core IHL treaties.[99]

Particular to IHL is the underlying balance between military necessity and considerations of humanity. These two overarching principles form the basis for IHL, underlying all IHL treaties, as well as customary IHL norms.[100] Military necessity is 'the necessity for measures which are essential to attain the goals of war, and which are lawful in accordance with the laws and customs of war'.[101] In other words, it permits the use of force only insofar as it is required to achieve the legitimate aim of an armed conflict (partial or total submission of the enemy with the

[98] *Wall* (n 4) [157]; *Prosecutor v Kupreškić et al* (Trial Chamber Judgment) IT-95-16-T (14 January 2000) [519]; Updated Commentary on GCI (n 59) [71, 119, 177]; Updated Commentary on GCII (n 59) [92, 141, 199]; Updated Commentary on GCIII (n 59) [152, 210]; Abi-Saab (n 11) 271; Pictet (n 40) 17–18 ('it is not merely an engagement concluded on a basis of reciprocity, binding each party to the contract only in so far as the other party observes its obligations. It is rather a series of unilateral engagements solemnly contracted before the world as represented by the other Contracting Parties').

[99] Updated Commentary on GCIII (n 59) [152–53]; Pictet (n 41) 18. See *Military and Paramilitary Activities in and against Nicaragua (Nicaragua v United States of America)* (Merits) [1986] ICJ Rep 14 [220]; ICRC, *Customary* (n 2) Vol I, Rule 144, 509–13. See also Zwanenburg (n 13); Stubbins Bates (n 13); L Hill-Cawthorne, 'Common Article 1 of the Geneva Conventions and the Method of Treaty Interpretation' (2023) 72 ICLQ 869. But see Schmitt and Watts (n 13); Robson (n 13).

[100] A Clapham, *War* (Oxford University Press 2021) 264; A Quintin, *The Nature of International Humanitarian Law: A Permissive or Restrictive Regime?* (Elgar 2020) 16, 257.

[101] Sandoz et al (n 54) 393. See also Instructions for the Government of Armies of the United States in the Field (Lieber Code) (24 April 1863) <https://ihl-databases.icrc.org/en/ihl-treaties/liebercode-1863> arts 14–16 (last accessed 1 June 2025); WG Downey, 'Law of War and Military Necessity' (1953) 47 AJIL 251, 254; A Ghazali Abu Hassan, 'Military Necessity and the Restriction on Methods and Means of Warfare' (2006) 2 JIS 23, 26; S Zgaga, 'Military Necessity in International Criminal Law' (2012) 17 Review of Comparative Law 109, 111.

minimum use of time and resources).[102] The principle of humanity guards against the unlimited resort to total war by requiring that human life, health and dignity be respected in the conduct of hostilities.[103] It 'protects combatants from unnecessary suffering, and individuals who are no longer, or never were, active participants in hostilities by mandating that they be treated humanely at all times'.[104] Rather than being opposed, these two principles act together to 'reduce the sum total of permissible military action from that which humanitarian law does not expressly prohibit to that which is actually necessary for the accomplishment of a legitimate military purpose in the prevailing circumstances'.[105]

The balance between military necessity and humanity underlies all IHL norms, including those contained in the Third Convention. For example, Article 109 of the Third Geneva Convention, regarding the repatriation of prisoners of war, 'explicitly embodies the balance that Parties to a conflict need to seek between military necessity and humanity in their decision to intern prisoners of war', therefore prisoners of war must be repatriated when there is no longer a military necessity for interning them.[106] As noted above, this balance also impacts the identification of the object and purpose of the treaty.

6.6 Conclusion

Since the first ICRC Commentary in 1870, the ICRC's Commentaries on the core IHL treaties are an important demonstration of how IHL treaties should be interpreted in light of the contemporary legal framework. The fact that these Commentaries have consistently been based on the

[102] ICRC, *International Humanitarian Law: Answers to Your Questions* (ICRC 2023) 6.

[103] See Sandoz et al (n 54) 392–93, paras 1388–89; ICRC (n 102) 6. Kolb and Del Mar argue that under the Geneva Conventions, the principle of humanity took on increasing weight in IHL interpretation, 'amplifying' the protections contained in IHL norms. 'Thus, the interpretation of IHL provisions progressively became more liberal and more expansive. HRL equally pushed in that direction.' According to their view, before the 1949 Geneva Conventions, IHL was principally viewed as a set of norms limiting permissible means and methods of warfare, and norm-setting provisions such as the Martens Clause were interpreted as aspirational rather than as binding legal norms. In other words, they were 'not yet taken seriously'. Kolb and Del Mar (n 5) 79–80.

[104] GS Corn, 'Principle of Humanity' (2013) MPEPIL 1810.

[105] Updated Commentary on GCIII (n 59) [497] fn 181. See also F Bouchet-Saulnier, *The Practical Guide to Humanitarian Law* (3rd edn, Rowman and Littlefield 2014) 396 ('any violence or destruction that is not justified by military necessity is prohibited by the law of armed conflict'); E David, *Principes du droit des conflits armés* (4th edn, Bruylant 2008) 106–14.

[106] Updated Commentary on GCIII (n 59) [4293].

interpretive methodology common to all bodies of public international law is decisive proof that IHL is subject to the same interpretive rules as other bodies of law.

As the general international law discourse on treaty interpretation has become more sophisticated, so has the methodology behind the ICRC's legal commentaries, reflecting the organization's understanding of how international humanitarian law treaties are interpreted. Early ICRC Commentaries were presented as the work of a single author expounding on their (actually, his) opinion on how the law should be interpreted and applied, relying on their presence during the negotiations of the treaty in question.

The weight of these Commentaries was expected to come from the reputation of the author, many of whom incorporated their personal views into the text. As time went on, presenting such personal opinions became frowned upon and starting with the 1930 Commentaries the reader gets the sense that the interpretive guidance being provided is focused on the *lex lata*, rather than the *lex feranda* in the eyes of the author.

As the international legal community began to approach treaty interpretation with more scientific rigour so did the ICRC. Beginning in the 1950s, teams of legal scholars worked together to present a view of the law informed not only by the negotiations but also the humanitarian needs caused by armed conflict driving the drafters to the negotiating table. In the 1980s even more emphasis was put on convincing readers of the soundness of the interpretations presented through logic, rather than dazzling them with the reputation of the authors.

The current project to update the ICRC Commentaries on the 1949 Geneva Conventions and their 1977 Additional Protocols is using the methodology found in the interpretive rules of the VCLT. Although there are some aspects of IHL that may affect how these rules are applied, it is nevertheless undeniable that they do apply. Furthermore, it is likely that norm-setting multilateral treaties from other bodies of international law would have similar particularities.

Today, the updated Commentaries rely on the practice implementing the 1949 Geneva Conventions and their Additional Protocols, rather than practice that occurred before their conclusion. In contrast to early Commentaries, the updated Commentaries rely on extensive research and the scientific rigour of the methodology to gain the confidence of readers.

At the same time, the updated Commentaries are open to a diversity of views, indicating where there are diverging views and where the ICRC is presenting its own position in the interest of transparency. The involvement of jurists from outside the organization in the drafting process (as authors, peer reviewers and members of the Editorial Committee overseeing the work) indicates a strong desire to produce a practical tool for interpretation of the core IHL treaties that is accepted by practitioners and academics alike.

7

The Sui Generis Interpretative Practices of International Human Rights Bodies

'Thrown for a Loop' or 'Thrown into the Crucible'?

MARLIES HESSELMAN

7.1 Introduction

International human rights supervisory bodies often engage in human rights treaty interpretation when fulfilling their human rights monitoring tasks. Such tasks include considering individual and inter-State complaints, periodic State reports or adopting General Comments. When engaging in interpretation, such bodies may follow certain 'methods' of human rights treaty interpretation – including as (loosely) derived from Articles 31–32 of the Vienna Convention on the Law of Treaties (VCLT) or not.[1] In nearly all cases, however, bodies will refer to previous interpretative practices generated by themselves or by other bodies and accord to such interpretative practice considerable, great or even 'authoritative' weight.

This chapter examines the formal legal role of different 'interpretative monitoring practices' of international human rights bodies within the wider 'practice of international human rights treaty interpretation'. With

[1] See M Fitzmaurice, 'Interpretation of Human Rights Treaties' in D Shelton (ed), *The Oxford Handbook of International Human Rights Law* (Oxford University Press 2013) 739, 757–60; M Scheinin, 'The Art and Science of Interpretation in Human Rights Law' in B Andreassen, HO Sano and S McInerney-Lankford (eds), *Research Methods in Human Rights: A Handbook* (Edward Elgar 2017) 17; J Christoffersen, 'Impact on General Principles of Treaty Interpretation' in MT Kamminga and M Scheinin (eds), *The Impact of Human Rights Law on General International Law* (Oxford University Press 2009) 37; B Schlütter, 'Aspects of Human Rights Interpretation by the UN Treaty Bodies' in H Keller and G Ulfstein (eds), *UN Human Rights Treaty Bodies: Law and Legitimacy* (Cambridge University Press 2012) 261; K Mechlem, 'Treaty Bodies and the Interpretation of Human Rights' (2009) 42 Vanderbilt Journal of Transnational Law 905.

'practice of human rights treaty interpretation' this chapter refers to the ongoing day-to-day efforts of independent international human rights supervisory bodies to provide meaning to human rights treaties under their supervision, often in response specific questions, situations or contexts. With the 'interpretative practices' of supervisory bodies, this chapter refers to the sizeable and diverse body of interpretative materials that are generated by such bodies through their diverse monitoring activities, and which is often attributed some 'interpretative value'. Key examples of such interpretative practices include the statements made by United Nations (UN) human rights treaty monitoring bodies (UNTBs) in their Views, General Comments or Concluding Observations; or the contributions made by UN Special Procedures of the Human Rights Council through their voluminous body of (thematic) reports or communications. The chapter is premised on the understanding that the different ways in which international human rights bodies are called upon to engage in the development of the content of the treaties, and the wide variety and diversity of interpretative practice that results from this, is arguably unlike any other field of law. The breadth and variety of interpretative practices is rather unique, forming an amorphous body of guidance that is collectively shaping the (evolving) content of the legal framework. This chapter posits that the unique nature of these interpretative practices, both when taken individually and together, is perhaps not fully understood yet as a matter of international law.

By narrowing in on the role(s) of these practices in treaty interpretation, this chapter specifically responds to two recent studies of the United Nations International Law Commission (ILC) that aimed to elucidate the legal value of various 'pronouncements of (human rights) expert bodies'. First, it recently discussed the 'interpretative practices' of human rights bodies as a possible form of 'subsequent practice' for treaty interpretation in the sense of Articles 31–32 VCLT.[2] Secondly, it currently considers them as 'subsidiary means for the determination of rules of international law' in the sense of Article 38 ICJ Statute. The chapter will incorporate and reflect on these studies and additionally considers several recent judgments of the International Court of Justice that

[2] ILC, 'Draft Conclusions on Subsequent Agreements and Subsequent Practice in Relation to the Interpretation of Treaties, with Commentaries' (30 April–1 June and 2 July–10 August 2018) UN Doc A/73/10, reproduced in [2018/II - Part Two] YBILC 16 [107]. Referring to 'relevant factual and normative assessments by expert treaty bodies' (ILC Draft Conclusions 2018).

embraced or rejected the use of interpretative practices by UNTBs and UN Special Procedures. Taking into account the ongoing debates in literature as well, it seems that scholarly and practioner's opinions on the exact legal value or weight to be accorded to human rights bodies' practices still differ considerably. In several respects, it even seems that they may possess some type of sui generis interpretative value, which is unique to human rights law and that is perhaps not yet well captured to date.

The main aim of this chapter then, is to analyze some of the different positions or approaches taken to date in literature (Section 7.1); by the ILC (Section 7.2); by the ICJ (Section 7.3) and to draw some conclusions as to the formal legal bases or conditions under which various practices could or should be taken into account in practices of human rights treaty interpretation. When or under which conditions may these practices be 'thrown into the crucible' of human rights treaty interpretation as part of a so-called single combined operation of treaty interpretation, along with other means to arrive at a 'legally relevant' interpretation?[3] The '*crucible*' metaphor was notoriously introduced by the ILC in 1966 to highlight that a range of means of interpretation might be available and engaged for treaty interpretation and that the weight to be accorded to them may depend on the specific treaty (provision) and the interpreter involved.[4] In international human rights law, key interpretative means available will typically at least include: 'the *ordinary meaning* to be given to the terms of the treaty *in their context* and in the light of its *object and purpose*', as well as the principle of '*good faith*' interpretation.[5] However, by now, it certainly also includes the vast and ubiquitous interpretative monitoring practices of a range of monitoring bodies that together incrementally develop the content of treaty norms over time. This chapter considers specifically which formal role the interpretative practices of the UNTBs

[3] ME Villiger, 'The Rules on Interpretation: Misgivings, Misunderstandings, Miscarriage? The "Crucible" Intended by the International Law Commission' in E Cannizzaro (ed), *The Law of Treaties Beyond the Vienna Convention* (Oxford University Press 2011) 105; See also ILC Draft Conclusions 2018 (n 2) Conclusion 2(5): 'The interpretation of a treaty consists of a single combined operation, which places appropriate emphasis on the various means of interpretation indicated, respectively, in articles 31 and 32'. The ILC hereby affirms that the 'single combined operation' includes both arts 31 and 32 VCLT as appropriate.

[4] Villiger (n 3); ILC Draft Conclusions 2018 (n 2) 22.

[5] Vienna Convention on the Law of Treaties (adopted 23 May 1969, entered into force 27 January 1980) 1155 UNTS 331, art 31(1) (VCLT).

and UN Special Procedures of the Human Rights Council could play and also points out that several criteria may be emerging that can help interpreters to determine how to weigh or take into account this body of interpretative guidance as part of the 'single combined operation' of treaty interpretation supported by the ILC.

Finally, as noted, the chapter specifically suggests that there may be a unique and still somewhat undefined quality to this body of interpretative work, which deserves to be better fleshed out and studied. Specifically, it posits that the interpretative practice generated by UN bodies might occupy some sui generis position as a means of interpretation, either within, or beyond the context of the VCLT or ICJ Statute. The ILC seems to be trying to articulate this special position through its currently ongoing study on the 'subsidiary means for the determination of rules of international law', but it is too early to tell at the time of writing whether the ILC's conclusions will indeed offer conclusive guidance. This chapter will certainly offer some opinions of its own.

7.2 The Interpretative Practices of International Human Rights Bodies according to Literature

This section introduces and unpacks the different types of interpretative practices of independent UN human rights supervisory bodies, with emphasis on UNTBs and the independent UN Special Rapporteurs of the Human Rights Council. Special emphasis is placed on the 'formal' legal arguments that are presented by authors in relation to the legal value and weight to be attached to these practices, for example, by situating them in the context of Articles 31–32 VCLT or Article 38 ICJ Statute, or otherwise. It is noted that the interpretative value of different types of UNTBs monitoring practices has been rather well discussed in literature, although, seemingly, without any consensus on the formal role or position of these practices. Especially the formal role and place of Concluding Observations remains debated. In respect of the UN Special Procedures, it is increasingly recognized that also these bodies by now have engaged in 'significant law-making and jurisprudential activities that are worthy of note and of systematization'.[6] These points will be further analyzed in this section.

[6] B Ramcharan, *The Protection Role and Jurisprudence of the United Nations Human Rights Council* (Brill Nijhoff 2022) 169; A Nolan, R Freedman and T Murphy (eds), *The United Nations Special Procedures System* (Brill Nijhoff 2017); E Domínguez Redondo, 'Human

7.2.1 *Interpretative Practices of the UN Human Rights Treaty Bodies*

Firstly, UNTBs typically consist of fifteen or more independently appointed experts working together on monitoring the implementation of a specific human rights treaty by States Parties. It is generally accepted that in order to fulfil their monitoring tasks adequately, UNTBs inevitably engage in acts of interpretation. For, it is impossible to assess or offer guidance on the implementation of vaguely worded treaty provisions otherwise.[7] The most important monitoring activities generating interpretative practices are UNTBs' adoption of General Comments and Views and Concluding Observations following State reporting procedures.

7.2.1.1 General Comments

General Comments are often seen as offering some of the most important or 'authoritative' interpretative guidance to States parties, because their sole aim is to clarify the scope of rights and obligations following from treaty provisions. General Comments do this, in large part, by 'synthesizing' or 'settling' a wider body of interpretative practices generated by the monitoring activities of UNTBs, for example, in Views or Concluding Observations.[8]

General Comments are typically sizeable documents adopted by consensus by the full UNTB, involving several rounds of careful drafting and

Rights Through the Backdoor: The Contribution of Special Procedures to the Normative Coherence and Contradictions of International Human Rights Law' in C Buckley, A Donald and P Leach (eds), *Towards Convergence in Human Rights Law: Approaches of Regional and International Systems* (Brill Nijhoff 2016) 543–66; C Golay, C Mahon and I Cismas, 'The Impact of the UN Special Procedures on the Development and Implementation of Economic, Social and Cultural Rights' (2011) 15 IJHR 299, 303–4; E Domínguez Redondo, 'Rethinking the Legal Foundations of Control in International Human Rights Law: the Case of Special Procedures' (2011) 29(3) NQHR 261.

7 See e.g. M Scheinin, 'The Human Rights Committee's Pronouncements on the Right to an Effective Remedy – an Illustration of the Legal Nature of the Committee's Work under the Optional Protocol' in N Ando (ed), *Towards Implementing Universal Human Rights: Festschrift for the Twenty-Fifth Anniversary of the Human Rights Committee* (Brill Nijhoff 2004) 106. '[T]here is no comparable alternative international authority entrusted with the regular task of issuing legal interpretations of Covenant obligations.' See also M O'Flaherty, 'The Concluding Observations of the United Nations Human Rights Treaty Bodies' (2006) 27 HRLR 27, 33–34, also referring to a similar position by Norway.

8 D Shelton, 'The Legal Status of Normative Pronouncements of Human Rights Treaty Bodies' in H Hestermeyer et al (eds), *Coexistence, Cooperation and Solidarity: Liber Amicorum Rüdiger Wolfrum* (Brill 2012) 553, 563–65.

consultations with States parties and other stakeholders.[9] Due to their robust aims and procedures, and because they are adopted by the 'independent bodies especially established' by States to monitor treaty implementation, General Comments tend to be referred to as 'extremely useful jurisprudential tools' and 'enormously important as global jurisprudential resources', which carry a 'strong persuasive force' as official or 'authoritative interpretations of legally binding documents'.[10]

A number of scholars argue that the principle of 'good faith' interpretation in Article 31(1) VCLT would oblige interpreters of human rights treaties to seriously 'take into account' the General Comments of UNTBs – along with possible other non-binding interpretative guidance of UNTBs, for example, in Views or Concluding Observations.[11] The principle of 'good faith' in Article 31(1) VCLT is thereby a first 'formal' legal ground for throwing these practices into the 'crucible' of human rights treaty interpretation.[12] Several scholars even go so far as to suggest that UNTBs' interpretations come with 'a presumption of correctness': States or other actors would have to carefully justify why they would *not* follow the non-binding interpretative guidance developed by a UNTB on a given point.[13] Interpretations should generally be respected and explicit deviations must be well justified, again in good faith. Relevant

[9] See H Keller and L Grover, 'General Comments of the Human Rights Committee and their Legitimacy' in H Keller and G Ulfstein (eds), *UN Human Rights Bodies: Law and Legitimacy* (Oxford University Press 2012) 118, 128, 132–33; Shelton (n 8) 562.

[10] S Joseph and J Kyriakakis, 'The United Nations and Human Rights' in S Joseph and A McBeth (eds), *Research Handbook on International Human Rights Law* (Edward Elgar 2010) 21.

[11] See Shelton (n 8) 569–70; W Kälin, 'Examination of State Reports' in H Keller and G Ulfstein (eds), *UN Human Rights Treaty Bodies: Law and Legitimacy* (Cambridge University Press 2012) 32; Scheinin (n 1) 33; Schlütter (n 1) 286–87; R van Alebeek and A Nollkaemper , 'The Legal Status of Decisions by Human Rights Treaty Bodies in National Law' in H Keller and G Ulfstein (eds), *UN Human Rights Treaties Bodies: Law and Legitimacy* (Cambridge University Press 2012) 356, 384–87; G Ulfstein, 'Individual Complaints' in H Keller and G Ulfstein (eds), *UN Human Rights Treaty Bodies: Law and Legitimacy* (Oxford University Press 2012) 73, 92–100; D Moeckli, 'Interpretation of the ICESCR: Between Morality and State Consent' in D Moeckli, H Keller and C Heri (eds), *The Human Rights Covenants at 50: Their Past, Present and Future* (Oxford University Press 2018) 51.

[12] E.g. Kälin (n 11); ILC, 'Fourth Report on Subsequent Agreement and Subsequent Practice in Relation to the Interpretation of Treaties, by Georg Nolte, Special Rapporteur' (7 March 2016) UN Doc A/CN.4/694 [52].

[13] Keller and Grover (n 9); Schlütter (n 1); Moeckli (n 11) 50, 68–71; D McGrogan, 'On the Interpretation of Human Rights Treaties and Subsequent Practice' (2014) 32(4) NQHR 352, 363, 374–76; D Azaria, 'The Legal Significance of Expert Treaty Bodies

justifications for deviating from UNTBs' interpretations could include concerns about the quality of evidence, legal reasoning or justifications provided by bodies to arrive at certain progressive or conservative treaty interpretation.[14] Alternatively, UNTBs' interpretative practices might plainly be consulted to help generally determine 'the ordinary meaning of the terms in their context and in light of the object and purpose of the treaty', including possibly with emphasis on the object and purpose of the treaty[15] Sections 7.4 and 7.5 address these points in some further detail.

General Comments are also positioned in literature as possibly relevant 'subsequent interpretative practices' under Articles 31(3)b and 32 VCLT, or as 'teachings of highly qualified publicists' or 'judicial decisions' in the sense of Article 38 ICJ Statute.[16] Each of these positions is further highlighted in Section 7.3, but UN ILC Rapporteur George Nolte noted on this point that Views share 'certain elements in common with court decisions', whereas General Comments are more akin to 'teachings due to their general nature' or might also 'display features of jurisprudence or a settled case law'.[17]

Whether General Comments would qualify as relevant 'subsequent practice' under Articles 31(3)b or Article 32 VCLT or fit in as subsidiary means under Article 38 ICJ Statute bears some legal relevance.[18] For, Article 38(1)d ICJ Statute states that the means listed in this provision '*shall*' be applied by the ICJ.[19] The means listed in Article 31 VCLT also '*shall*' be taken into account for treaty interpretation, but those listed in Article 32 VCLT '*may*' be taken into account. Typically, only *after* the application of Article 31 VCLT still left the meaning unclear or ambiguous or in need of confirmation. Villiger opines that it would be 'difficult to imagine situations where the means of Article 32 may not be

Pronouncements for the Purpose of the Interpretation of Treaties' (2020) 22(1) ICLR 46, referring to ILC (n 12) [55]; O'Flaherty (n 7) 34.

14 See O Dörr, 'Article 32' in O Dörr and K Schmalenbach (eds), *Vienna Convention on the Law of Treaties* (2nd edn, Oxford University Press 2018) 627; see also Mechlem (n 1).

15 ILC Draft Conclusions 2018 (n 2) 115–16.

16 See M Andenas and JR Leiss, 'The Systemic Relevance of "Judicial Decisions" in Article 38 of the ICJ Statute' (2017) 77 ZaöRV 907; Scheinin (n 1) 27–30; Van Alebeek and Nollkaemper (n 11) 408–10; Shelton (n 8) 568–69, 572, 574; Joseph and Kyriakakis (n 10) 2; Ulfstein (n 11) 96–97. See also ILC Draft Conclusions 2018 (n 2) 115–16.

17 ILC Draft Conclusions 2018 (n 2) [63].

18 ibid, referring to I Sinclair, *The Vienna Convention on the Law of Treaties* (2nd edn, Manchester University Press 1984) 138. See also ILC (n 12) [52–55].

19 See Andenas and Leiss (n 16) 944 for some discussion, also noting that it seems somewhat awkward to consider the use of teachings mandatory for the ICJ.

employed';[20] whilst Dörr considers that 'it basically depends on the assessment of the interpreter' whether certain materials 'can reasonably be thought to assist in establishing the meaning of the treaty under consideration, and if it does, there are scarcely any clear limits to taking it into account under Article 32'.[21] To complicate matters further: the ILC is currently studying the possible interaction or overlap between means covered by Article 38 ICJ Statute and the VCLT.

All in all, the interpretative value of non-binding General Comments seems generally affirmed, but scholarly positions on their formal legal status within the context of the VCLT, ICJ Statute or otherwise differ considerably. Section 7.5 will reflect somewhat further on the question whether the exact formal qualification within the VCLT or ICJ Statute matters all too much.

7.2.1.2 Views

The non-binding Views adopted by the 'quasi-judicial' UNTBs are also generally seen as possessing strong interpretative legal value, although their exact legal status or place within the practice of human rights treaty interpretation is ambiguous too. Since Views are adopted to conclude on individual or Inter-State complaints procedures, they benefit from closely resembling the traditional category of 'judicial decisions' listed in Article 38(1)d ICJ Statute. It has also been argued that Views could be seen as relevant 'subsequent interpretative practice' that can enter into play based on Article 32 VCLT (see further Section 7.3).

Specifically, scholarship has supported the 'judgment-like quality' of Views, noting they are adopted in a 'judicious spirit' according to similar procedures normally followed by human rights courts for binding judicial decisions.[22] Andenas and Leiss further argue that the term 'judicial decisions' in Article 38 ICJ Statute (by now) should be understood broadly, that is, to include various 'quasi-judicial' monitoring outputs such as Views and General Comments.[23] Sections 7.3 and 7.4 show that the ILC may be inclined to follow this view in its new study and that the

20 ME Villiger, *Commentary on the 1969 Vienna Convention on the Law of Treaties* (Brill 2009) 447.

21 Dörr (n 14) 627.

22 E.g. Shelton (n 8) 567–69, also referring to HRCttee, 'General Comment No 33: Obligations of States Parties under the Optional Protocol to ICCPR' (5 November 2008) UN Doc CCPR/C/GC/33 [11–13]; Mechlem (n 1) 926; Schlütter (n 1) 266–67; Ulfstein (n 11) 92–93.

23 Andenas and Leiss (n 16) 952–53.

ICJ has referred to both Views and General Comments as constituting the 'case-law' or 'jurisprudence' of the Human Rights Committee.[24]

Arguably, very few scholars would by now reject the formal legal interpretative value of Views of UNTBs, even if the exact legal basis for taking them into account is not entirely settled. The ILC study on Article 38 ICJ Statute will likely clarify their status as forming part of the category of 'judicial decisions' specifically.

7.2.1.3 Concluding Observations

Literature is most divided about the legal interpretative value of *Concluding Observations*, despite these interpretative practices constituting the most voluminous body of UNTBs' day-to-day 'jurisgenerative' monitoring practice.[25] Some argue that Concluding Observation's interpretative role and 'jurisprudential impact is marginal and exceptional' at first glance, even though both governments and NGOs accord great *de facto* legal importance to them.[26] Others are more optimistic, noting that they are 'the single most important activity of human rights treaty bodies' and despite their non-binding status, 'have considerable authority in so far they pronounce on violations and otherwise offer interpretations of how uphold treaty provisions'.[27] Shelton argues that concluding observations may represent 'the consensus of the Committee on how provisions in the treaty should be interpreted and applied'.[28] According to her, Concluding Observations may include legal determinations on whether certain situations comply with the treaty, and as such they can carry general interpretative significance for all parties, especially if they are precisely drafted and reasoned.[29] Unfortunately, the latter is not always

[24] The ILA also concluded that by then Views and General Comments were most often cited, though not necessarily with express reference to Article 38 ICJ Statute; ILA, 'Final Report on the Impact of Findings of the United Nations Human Rights Treaty Bodies of the Committee on International Human Rights Law and Practice' (Berlin Conference 2004) [175–76]; see also see discussion in ILC (n 12) 49–52.

[25] Keller and Grover (n 9) 166.

[26] Mechlem (n 1) 922, 924.

[27] O'Flaherty (n 7) 27, 36, 51; McGrogan (n 13) 364–65, or Kälin (n 11) 31. In case certain interpretations 'of the convention in question are consistently reiterated in Concluding Observations, they may even acquire soft law quality', referring to O'Flaherty.

[28] Shelton (n 8) 565–66.

[29] Shelton (n 8) 566. See also J Krommendijk, *The Domestic Impact and Effectiveness of the Process of State Reporting under UN Human Rights Treaties in the Netherlands, New Zealand and Finland: Paper Pushing or Policy Prompting?* (Intersentia 2014) 9, 17–18.

the case, although the prescriptive quality and thus the interpretative value of Concluding Observations seems to have improved over time.[30]

Formally, Concluding Observations are probably best seen as a 'supplementary means' of treaty interpretation under Article 32. As a single statement, a concluding observation is typically only a short statement issued against a single State; it is not (yet) a General Comment that reflects a more 'settled position on a question of interpretation' for the benefit of all States Parties.[31] At the same time, General Comments are often based on a large and consistent body of Concluding Observations issued in response to matters raised by governments and civil society during State reporting procedures over a period of time. This author strongly supports the argument that a *series of Concluding Observations*, that is, reaffirming certain specific interpretations of a treaty over time, can carry considerable interpretive value, especially when seen in conjunction with reactions by States.[32] In addition, one or a few Concluding Observations could arguably indicate a new direction of interpretation, especially when sufficiently precisely formulated.[33]

Finally, Creamer and Simmons recently found, based on an extensive study of European and Inter-American human rights court judgments, that these regional courts 'frequently' refer to *all three types* of UNTB interpretative practices when interpreting their own treaties (i.e. Views, Concluding Observations and General Comments). Concluding Observations are most commonly cited, whilst Views and General Comments have enjoyed more attention over time.[34] They additionally note that UNTBs' interpretations are seldom a definitive factor in developing new interpretations of European or Inter-American treaties. They are used to support a wider practice of interpretation, including by 'confirming' interpretations or affirming 'consistency' of interpretation.[35]

[30] Shelton (n 8) 566.

[31] ibid 564.

[32] See for this argument generally O'Flaherty (n 7). See also ILC (n 12) [56]; Keller and Grover (n 9) 145, 151–54; Kälin (n 11) 31; M Hesselman, 'Human Rights and Access to Modern Energy Services' (PhD thesis, University of Groningen 2023) 16, 21, 35–36.

[33] Hesselman (n 32) 29.

[34] CD Creamer and BA Simmons, 'The Proof Is in the Process: Self-Reporting under International Human Rights Treaties (2020) 114 AJIL 1, 40–43. See also A Mowbray, 'The European Court of Human Rights' Recourse to External Legal Materials When Interpreting and Applying the Right to Private Life' in C Buckley, A Donald and P Leach (eds), *Towards Convergence in Human Rights Law: Approaches of Regional and International Systems* (Brill Nijhoff 2016) 131.

[35] ibid.

Dissenting and separate opinions of regional human rights judges especially 'heavily' draw on all three types of interpretative practices 'to establish applicable international law standards and to help clarify the legal reasoning in the majority judgment'.[36]

All in all, human rights scholarship strongly supports the legal interpretative value of different UNTBs monitoring practices, even if some unclarity remains about their exact formal legal status or role within the wider context of international law or international human rights law as a sub-branch. In fact, a final option has not been sufficiently mentioned yet, which is that due to the special nature and role of international human rights treaties, and their independent supervisory bodies, as well as in light of the old (perhaps outdated) texts of the VCLT (1969) and ICJ Statute (1945), the wealth of interpretative practice of human rights bodies developed since then may not fit these old frameworks well. We will explore the contributions to this debate by the ILC and ICJ recently in the following sections, noting that the ILC especially is seeking to provide a thorough evolutive update of Article 38 ICJ Statute in light of the wealth of legal developments found across different fields of public international law since 1945. Another important question to be unpacked after all these considerations is whether all interpretative practices of UNTBs carry equal interpretative value or weight. Instead, should one or more be seen as '*primus inter pares*' – for example, General Comments or Views? If so, how to accord weight to specific practices?

7.2.2 *Interpretative Practices of the UN Special Procedures of the Human Rights Council*

The UN Special Procedures of the Human Rights Council are typically appointed as single independent experts working on a specific human rights issue or country over a longer period of time. They derive their monitoring mandates from the UN Charter and their contributions to interpretation of specific human rights treaties seem even more under-theorized than UNTBs practices. Recently, some scholarly work has turned its attention to their contributions more firmly,[37] but ILC seems to overlook their interpretative work entirely in its studies on the VCLT

[36] Creamer and Simmons (n 34) 42; dissenting and separate opinions of ICJ judges discussed in Section 7.3.2 show a similar a development.

[37] See supra (n 22).

and ICJ Statute. The ICJ has referred to Special Procedures' work on occasion.

The most important monitoring practices of Special Procedures generating interpretative statements include: annual thematic reports to the Human Rights Council and UN General Assembly, the (joint) communications of Special Procedures to States and other relevant stakeholders about complaints on human rights abuses, country mission reports and the adoption of general guidelines or principles on thematic issues.[38] There is evidence that the work of UN Special Procedures is regularly consulted by international and regional human rights treaty supervisory bodies when applying their treaties, both in relation to the establishment of facts and the application and interpretation of human rights in the context of relevant facts.[39] In fact, according to Domínquez Redondo, the work of UN Special Procedures in terms of (authoritatively) clarifying the scope of existing norms in response to new issues or contributing to the creation and consolidation of (new) international human rights standards is 'one of their least contested activities' by now.[40]

An important first question for evaluating Special Procedures' contributions to treaty interpretation is how these bodies are relevant to the interpretation of the nine core UN human rights treaties supervised by UNTBs. At least institutionally, these UN Charter-based bodies are further removed from such treaties than the 'specially established' UNTBs.[41] This question was resolved through the adoption of UN HRC Resolution 5/1 on Institution Building (2006), which established the new UN Human Rights Council to succeed the Commission on Human Rights, along with UN HRC Resolution 5/2 on the Code of

[38] See M Limon and T Piccone, *Human Rights Special Procedures: Determinants of Influence* (Foreign Policy at Brookings 2014).

[39] Andenas and Leiss (n 16) 957; *Legal Consequences of the Construction of a Wall* (Advisory Opinion) [2004] ICJ Rep 136 [133–34]. See also e.g. recently UN Special Procedures' thematic reports in *Standard Verlagsgesellschaft mbH v Austria (no 3)* [CC] (21 December 2021) Application no 39378/15 [41, 46–48, 74] on freedom of expression; *MS v Croatia* [CC] (2 February 2015) Application no 75450/12 [49, 105] on issues of abusive practices in health-care settings.

[40] Domínguez Redondo 'Human Rights . . .' (n 6) 565–66.

[41] See e.g. Domínguez Redondo 'Rethinking . . .' (n 6) 287; N Bernaz, 'Reforming the UN Human Rights Protection Procedures: A Legal Perspective on the Establishment of the Universal Periodic Review Mechanism' in K Boyle (ed), *New Institutions for Human Rights Protection* (Oxford University Press 2009) 75, 79–81.

Conduct for the Special Procedures and their own Manual.[42] Accordingly, all Special Procedures mandate holders shall establish facts based on objective, reliable and credible sources of information, including any information provided by States, and *evaluate such information* 'in the light of internationally recognized human rights standards relevant to their mandate, and of *international conventions to which the State concerned is party*'.[43] This clearly affirms their mandates in relation to UN human rights treaty monitoring.[44] Various scholars also note the valuable contributions made by UN Special Procedures over time, including to 'defining the normative content of economic, social and cultural rights and the correlative States' obligations, as well as to the development of interpretative instruments'.[45] Examples of guidelines or principles that are widely regarded as key standard-setting documents in international human rights law, with far-ranging legal impacts, include the *UN Guiding Principles on Internal Displacement* or *UN Guiding Principles on Business and Human Rights.*[46]

The adoption of *Annual Thematic Reports* is one of the most comprehensive ways in which UN Special Procedures contribute to the clarification of human rights norms. Their thematic reports tend to be sizeable and dense resources on specific 'legal aspects' that are highly 'informative' for the purposes of understanding the content of specific human rights in relation to specific issues.[47] Thematic reports may synthesize relevant previous (international) interpretative practices or (national)

[42] See e.g. Domínguez Redondo 'Human Rights . . .' (n 6); Domínguez Redondo 'Rethinking . . .' (n 6).

[43] HRC, 'Res 5/2: Code of Conduct for Special Procedures Mandate Holders of the Human Rights Council' (8 June 2007) UN Doc A/HRC/RES/5/2 art 6.

[44] Domínguez Redondo 'Rethinking . . .' (n 6) 287.

[45] Golay, Mahon and Cismas (n 6) 312; Andenas and Leiss (n 16) 957; Domínguez Redondo 'Rethinking . . .' (n 6) 287; S Shah and S Sivakumaran, 'The Use of International Human Rights Law in the Universal Periodic Review' (2021) 21 HRLR 301; W Kälin, 'Human Rights Treaties within the UPR Process: Opportunities and Limits of Intergovernmental Monitoring of Human Rights' (2017) 60 JYBIL 243, 256; OC Okafor, 'The Future of the Human Rights Council: Insights at the Inter-Luminated Juncture of Thought and Experience' (2021) 23 MPYBUNL 40, 43. See also generally the contributions in Nolan, Freedman and Murphy (n 6).

[46] Limon and Piccone (n 38) 15–16; Golay, Mahon and Cismas (n 6) 303–4;

[47] J Hohmann, 'Principle, Policy and Practice: The Role of the UN Special Rapporteurs on the Right to Adequate Housing in the Development of the Right to Housing in International Law' in A Nolan, R Freedman and T Murphy (eds), *The United Nations Special Procedures System* (Brill Nijhoff 2017) 275.

state practices but also offer novel interpretations.[48] In some cases, mandates are specifically charged to progressively develop the content of certain rights, for example, the right to water. Occasionally, reports will develop new sets of guidelines or principles. The Special Procedures Manual requires reports to be based on 'thorough research' and encourages 'replies to questionnaires or other requests for information transmitted to governments, United Nations agencies, NGOs, treaty bodies, regional organizations, other experts, or partners'.[49] This also ensures the interaction with States and the incorporation of States' views on how the norm should be interpreted.

Another important means through which UN Special Procedures endorse or provide interpretations of human right treaty norms are their (joint) '*communications*' issued in response to credible complaints about human rights abuses from the public. This activity tends to be somewhat overlooked in human rights literature, potentially because this body of work was not well publicized in accessible databases until recently. However, the Special Procedures communications database, launched on the website of the Office of the High Commissioner on Human Rights (OHCHR) in 2017, indicates that over 8,600 communications were issued to States and other actors, since 2010 alone.[50]

Communications are typically issued as a 'letter of allegation' (AL) or an 'urgent appeal' (UA) to States or other actors accused of human rights violations based on credible and detailed information from victims or civil society organizations. A communication may be issued individually or jointly by Special Procedures, depending on the type of expertise needed to respond to the complaint adequately. The communication will set out alleged facts, explain which legal frameworks are applicable to the situation and how (e.g. treaty provisions, General Comments, soft law standards) and formulate a range of questions to respondents about how human rights were guaranteed (or not). These questions also offer guidance about what may be required of States or others to implement

48 D Desierto and CE Gillespie, 'Evolutive Interpretation and Subsequent Practice: Interpretative Communities and Processes in the Optional Protocol to the ICESCR' (2013) 73 ZaöRV 574.

49 OHCHR, 'Manual of Operations of the Special Procedures of the Human Rights Council' (11 August 2008) 76 <https://www.ohchr.org/sites/default/files/Documents/HRBodies/SP/Manual_Operations2008.pdf > (last accessed 1 June 2025).

50 See OHCHR, 'Communication Report and Search' (*OHCHR*, 2025) <https://spcommreports.ohchr.org/> (last accessed 1 June 2025).

certain treaty norms.[51] Communications may also 'ask that the violations are prevented, stopped, investigated, or that remedial action is taken'.[52]

All in all, the interpretative value of these communications can thus be rather high, as they include legal statements on whether certain situations comply with treaty norms or not. Respondents are also invited to reply to the allegations, which may or may not occur; their replies are sent to the Human Rights Council and put on public record. In quite a few cases, States do not seem to respond, and the procedure ends with questions unanswered. According to the Office of the High Commissioner for Human Rights (OHCHR) website, 'the complaints procedure of the Special Procedures is not a quasi-judicial procedure, and the Special Procedures do not have power or authority to enforce their views or recommendations.'[53] The latter, of course, counts for most human rights supervisory bodies in international law.

In terms of legally characterizing the interpretative statements of UN Special Procedures, it is likely that most of them count as 'supplementary' or 'subsidiary' means for determining the content of human rights treaties in the sense of Article 32 VCLT or Article 38(1)d ICJ Statute. Similar to the work of UNTBs, an argument can be made that a 'good faith' interpretation of human rights treaties requires interpreters to take into account the available interpretative guidance of UN Special Procedures on a specific treaty norm. An argument could further be made that especially the thematic reports of Special Procedures could be seen as works of 'highly qualified publicists': rapporteurs are often eminent human rights experts and scholars, and their reports tend to be the size of journal articles and well researched.[54] Some Special Procedure mandates also exist as entire Working Groups, and the communications of Special Procedures are often issued by several of 'eminent' experts jointly.[55] This could reinforce their interpretative value as the joint opinions of a group of highly qualified experts. Of some interest is whether communications of Special Procedures could be viewed as 'judicial decisions' in the sense of Article 38 ICJ Statute, which the court 'shall apply'. There is limited discussion on this point in the literature or in the work of the ILC or ICJ, so far (see further Sections 7.3 and 7.4).

51 OHCHR, 'Special Procedures of the Human Rights Council: What Are Communications? (*OHCHR*, 2025) <https://www.ohchr.org/en/special-procedures-human-rights-council/what-are-communications> (last accessed 1 June 2025).

52 ibid.

53 ibid.

54 See e.g. Andenas and Leiss (n 16) 943–44.

55 Hesselman (n 32).

Preliminary research of the case-law of the European Court of Human Rights (ECtHR) suggests that communications are consulted by this Court – alongside country reports, thematic reports and standard setting documents.[56] In fact, the ECtHR even expressly considered that the communications of the UN Working Group on Arbitrary Detention (WGAD) constitute 'a procedure of international investigation or settlement within the meaning of Article 35(1) ECHR', sharing 'many similarities to that before the United Nations Human Rights Committee' and 'akin, from both a procedural perspective and in terms of its potential impact, to the individual application provided for by Article 34 of the Convention'.[57] The communications procedure of the WGAD is slightly more formalized than those of other Special Procedures,[58] so it may not be possible to generalize this conclusion for all UN Special Procedure communications. However, these considerations deserve attention by the ILC in its ongoing study on the nature and scope of 'subsidiary means' under Article 38 ICJ Statute.

In conclusion, scholarship is highly supportive of the fact that the work of the UN Special Procedures can and has made valuable contributions to the interpretation of international human rights treaty norms, even if their work may not share the same 'quasi-judicial' characteristics as that of UNTBs. The chapter now turns to recent views on the value of these interpretative practices by the ILC and ICJ, respectively, including some further reflections on the legal grounds and/or conditions they are ascribed 'great weight' in interpretation.

7.3 Interpretative Practices of International Human Rights Bodies according to the ILC

The ILC has recently been studying the formal legal interpretative value of UN human rights bodies' monitoring practices in two separate studies. Firstly, between 2008 and 2018 it considered the meaning of 'subsequent

[56] E.g. consider *Valentin Câmpeanu v Romania* [GC] (7 July 2014) Application no 47848/08 [78].

[57] *Peraldi v France* [CC] (7 April 2009) Application no 2096/05; *Gürdeniz v Turkey* [CC] (18 March 2014) Application no 59715/10.

[58] See e.g. HRC, 'Opinions adopted by the Working Group on Arbitrary Detention at its Ninety-second Session' (*OHCHR*, 15–19 November 2021) <https://www.ohchr.org/en/special-procedures/wg-arbitrary-detention/opinions-adopted-working-group-arbitrary-detention/opinions-adopted-working-group-arbitrary-detention-its-92nd-session> (last accessed 1 June 2025); HRC, 'Opinion No 83/2021 concerning Ahmed Samir Santawy (Egypt)' (28 January 2022) UN Doc A/HRC/WGAD/2021/83.

agreements and practice' under Articles 31 and 32 VCLT.[59] Secondly, since 2022 it studies 'subsidiary means for the determination of rules of international law' under Article 38 of the ICJ Statute. So far, both studies focus mostly on the work of UNTBs, as State-created (independent) expert bodies especially established to monitor a treaty.[60] The ILC seems to readily accept that Views, General Comments and Concluding Observations 'often, explicitly or implicitly, interpret the treaty' and therefore all deserve consideration.[61] However, its first study did not consider the work of the UN Special Procedures at all; and a preparatory memorandum for the study on Article 38 prepared by the ILC Secretariat only briefly notes that the work of UN Special Procedures is occasionally referred to by some judicial bodies, for example, when interpreting the term 'torture'.[62] It is still unclear whether the study on Article 38 ICJ Statute will embrace Views, General Comments and Concluding Observations in equal measure – or perhaps focus on the former two – and will come to include the work of UN Special Procdures. This chapter argues that their work should be part of the study.

The following paragraphs show and discuss how the ILC has obviously been struggling to qualify the legal value of various interpretative monitoring practices of human rights expert bodies in the practice of human rights treaty interpretation. In part, this struggle is caused by the general unclarity on the use of their work in legal practice and literature.

7.3.1 'Subsequent Practice' in Light of Articles 31–32 VCLT?

According to Article 31(3)b VCLT, acts of treaty interpretation shall take into account relevant existing 'subsequent practice in the application of the treaty *which establishes the agreement of the parties regarding its interpretation*'. Obviously, the practices generated by UNTBs or UN

[59] ILC, 'Analytical Guide to the Work of the International Law Commission: Subsequent Agreement and Subsequent Practice in Relation to Interpretation of Treaties' (*ILC*, 5 July 2024) <https://legal.un.org/ilc/guide/1_11.shtml> (last accessed 1 June 2025).

[60] ILC Draft Conclusions 2018 (n 2) 106–7: The draft conclusions on subsequent practice do not preclude that 'the substance of the present draft conclusion may apply, *mutatis mutandis*, to pronouncements of independent expert bodies that are organs of international organizations', referring explicitly to the WAGD as an example.

[61] ibid 109.

[62] ILC Secretariat, 'Memorandum prepared by the Secretariat: Subsidiary Means for the Determination of Rules of International Law' (17 January 2024) UN Doc A/CN.4/765 [356].

Special Procedures do not, strictly speaking, 'establish the agreement of the parties'.[63] At most, General Comments and thematic reports of UN Special Procedures might be based on or reflect such practices. In both cases, input from States may be actively invited.

According to the ILC, pronouncements of UNTBs cannot generally be understood as constituting 'subsequent practice' under the VCLT; instead, they '*may give rise to, or refer to*, a subsequent agreement or subsequent practice by parties in Article 31, paragraph 3, or subsequent practice under article 32'.[64] More specifically, a pronouncement may 'give rise to' States' practices when parties react to the pronouncement in some form or other; in this scenario, a General Comment, View or Concluding Observation may act as a 'catalyst for the subsequent practice of States parties'.[65] Alternatively, pronouncements may 'refer' to subsequent practice of States when a certain practice and/or a possible agreement of the parties has 'developed before the pronouncement' and the body indicates that practice or agreement.[66] The ILC explicitly clarifies that parties' silence cannot be 'presumed to constitute subsequent practice under article 31, paragraph 3 (b)': for 'it cannot usually be expected that States parties take a position with respect to every pronouncement by an expert treaty body', especially when they are 'addressed to another State or to all States generally'.[67] It is unclear whether their 'silence' could be a form of practice to be taken into account more loosely for purposes of interpretation under Article 32; a point that is debated in literature as well.[68] Moeckli argues that a relevant interpretative practice of UNTBs would have to be 'actively shared by at least some States parties and acquiesced in by the others'; whereas Ssenjonyo opines that the lack of (negative) responses to CESCR General Comments would indicate a 'wide acceptance' of them.[69] The ILC does not offer concrete examples of how Views, Concluding Observations or General Comments might

[63] For example, Moeckli notes that the General Comment process might reflect an exercise of consensus building amongst States and the Committee. Moeckli (n 11) 64, 69–71. See also Shelton (2009) 563–64; Mechlem (n 1) 920; M Ssenjonyo, 'Reflections on State Obligations with Respect to Economic, Social and Cultural Rights in International Human Rights Law' (2011) 25 IJHR 969, 975. Treaty bodies set out 'interpretive positions around which state practice may unite'.

[64] ILC Draft Conclusions 2018 (n 2) Draft Conclusion 13(3), 116.

[65] ibid 113.

[66] ibid 112–13.

[67] ibid.

[68] See e.g. Hesselman (n 32).

[69] Moeckli (n 11) 64, 69–71; Ssenjonyo (n 63).

'refer' to a State practice or agreement, so it is not easy to determine under what conditions certain interpretative statements could be considered to genuinely reflect or refer to a pre-existing practice or agreement.

All in all, it is thus uncertain under which circumstances a General Comment, Thematic Report or Communication might meet the (seemingly) strict threshold of the ILC's definition of a relevant 'subsequent practice' under Articles 31 and 32 VCLT. Indeed, the ILC is even somewhat unclear about whether UNTBs statements might be seen as relevant 'subsequent practice' under Article 32 VCLT. The ILC takes a rather 'State-centric' interpretation of the concept of 'subsequent practice', although States are only mentioned in Article 31 VCLT but not Article 32 VCLT. In 2004, the International Law Association's Committee on Human Rights Law and Practice noted on this point that a less 'traditional' State-oriented reading of the VCLT would support a broader understanding of the notion 'subsequent practice'. Especially in light of the *special nature* of human rights treaties – which involve 'third-party beneficiaries and an independent monitoring mechanism' – the 'considered views' of UNTBs adopted while performing 'the functions conferred on them by the States parties' could be seen as 'subsequent' interpretative practice under Article 31(3)b.[70] The ILC does not seem to follow this more liberal reasoning.

Evidently struggling to explain how UNTB's interpretative statements might be relevant to treaty interpretation nonetheless,[71] the ILC finally concluded that this particular study is 'without prejudice to the contribution' such statements might 'make to the interpretation of the treaties' otherwise, for example, 'under their mandates'.[72] It acknowledged several other options mentioned in literature and practice, including as another type of 'supplementary means' under Article 32 VCLT or based on Article 38 ICJ Statute. The latter is under debate by the ILC.

7.3.2 *'Subsidiary Means' in Light of Article 38 ICJ Statute?*

Article 38 ICJ Statute states that the ICJ 'shall apply' as 'subsidiary means for the determination of rules of law' so-called 'judicial decisions' and 'teachings of highly qualified publicists of the various nations'. The ILC

[70] ILA (n 24) 6.
[71] ILC Draft Conclusions 2018 (n 2) 115.
[72] ibid, Conclusion 13(1)–(3).

Drafting Committee clarifies that these subsidiary means are not a source of international law in themselves; they are 'mainly resorted to when identifying, interpreting and applying the rules of international law derived from the [primary] sources of international law', including treaty law and customary law.[73] This obviously affirms an 'interpretive function' for these means and thereby suggests a potential overlap with the means listed in the VCLT, which still needs to be further defined and settled.[74]

According to ILC Rapporteur Mr Jalloh, there is 'broad support' amongst ILC members to include the 'decisions of international human rights treaty bodies' within the scope of this study, either 'as judicial decisions or under a separate category'.[75] The ILC Secretariat's background memorandums also includes an extensive analysis of the manner in which human rights treaty bodies have used their own and other bodies' interpretative practices to date.[76] It seems generally supported that the Views of UNTBs (as 'quasi-judicial bodies') fall in the category of 'decisions of courts and tribunals'.[77] Indeed, at first sight, the ILC Drafting Committee may be aiming to considerably reframe the notion of 'judicial decisions', accounting for the wide variety of 'decisions' made by modern monitoring bodies. The conclusions provisionally adopted on Article 38 ICJ Statute read that:

> Subsidiary means for the determination of rules of international law include:
>
> (a) decisions of courts and tribunals;
> (b) teachings;
> (c) any other means generally used to assist in determining rules of international law[78]

[73] ILC, 'Second Report on Subsidiary Means for the Determination of Rules of International Law by Special Rapporteur Charles Chernor Jalloh' (30 January 2024) UN Doc A/CN.4/769 [8, 41, 63, 124–26].

[74] ILC, 'Third Report on Subsidiary Means for the Determination of Rules of International Law by Special Rapporteur Charles Chernor Jalloh' (29 January 2025) UN Doc A/CN.4/781 [311, 322 et seq].

[75] ILC, 'Report of the International Law Commission, Seventy-fourth Session' (24 April–2 June and 3 July–4 August 2023) UN Doc A/78/10, 88, [116].

[76] ILC Secretariat (n 62).

[77] ILC Report Seventy-fourth Session (n 75) 82; ILC (n 73) [161]; ILC Secretariat (n 62) [597].

[78] ILC, 'Titles and Texts of Draft Conclusions 1 to 3 Provisionally Adopted by the Drafting Committee on the Topic of Subsidiary Means for the Determination of Rules of International Law' (2 June 2023) UN Doc A/CN.4/L.985, Draft Conclusion 1.

The most recent report by rapporteur Jalloh of January 2025, shows that some states, including China, have pushed back on including decisions of human rights bodies as subsidiary means generally, or characterizing them as judicial or quasi-judicial decisions specifically.[79] Yet, after hearing the various contradictory opinions of States, Rapporteur Jalloh maintains his view that decisions of UNTBs fall under the notion of decision.[80] In addition, he added some further clarifications, such as that the work of 'State-created' expert bodies, like UNTBs, should generally be seen as 'separate from teachings'.[81] At the same time, in a separate section devoted to UNTBs' work, he also notes that General Comments may actually possess a 'dual character' between teachings and decisions, and as such they are not 'necessarily in one category'.[82] Concluding Observations are not really discussed, but he notes that the range of activities of UNTBs varies and that the functions and characterization of the different outputs generated therefore may also differ.[83] No clear conclusions are presented about where each type of interpretative practice fits. As previously noted, the work of UN Special Procedures seems entirely ignored. The currently proposed draft conclusion on expert bodies plainly reads that 'a pronouncement of an expert body may serve as a subsidiary means for the determination of the existence and content of rules of international law'; this is 'without prejudice to their use for other purposes'.[84]

Finally, the last category, 'other means', is of course of particular interest too. I suggests the ILC may be after a thorough update of the categories of subsidiary means that 'shall be applied' to understand or interpret the scope and content of international law.[85] Recognizing that the list of sources in Article 38 ICJ Statute is 'not necessarily exhaustive', the ILC Rapporteur even suggests that certain subsidiary means could 'serve as an independent basis for rights and obligations for the subjects of international law' and function as means for 'interpreting or complementing the rules of international law, including addressing lacunae in

[79] ILC (n 74) [57].
[80] ibid [149–50].
[81] ibid [126].
[82] ibid [145–52, 161–62].
[83] ibid [147–48].
[84] ibid [162].
[85] ILC (n 73) [84]; ILC, 'First Report on Subsidiary Means for the Determination of Rules of International Law by Charles Chernor Jalloh, Special Rapporteur' (13 February 2023) UN Doc A/CN.4/760 [351–74].

the law or advancing the coherence or the systemic nature of international law as a legal system'.[86] It refers here explicitly to 'judicial decisions' and 'decisions of expert bodies' but notes that this aspect needs to be further studied and that courts also refer to each other's interpretative practices to fill gaps or ensure consistency interpretations.[87] These comments have led to a range of critical comments by States, which the rapporteur is now working through, although he seems to favour a broader understanding of the 'auxiliary' use of subsidiary means.[88] This includes an understanding – informed by the drafting history of Article 38 ICJ Statute and 'reality of international legal practice' – that certain subsidiary means may help to 'mould, shape or even develop international law'.[89]

It will be of great interest to the field of international human rights law to see how the various 'subsidiary means' will be defined over the coming years. They clearly might come to include different types of statements of UNTBs.[90] This author argues that in light of the discussions in Section 7.2.2, it would be highly appropriate to consider the work of UN Special Procedures of the Human Rights Council too.

Importantly, it is of interest that the ILC so far suggests that 'pronouncements' of expert bodies *may fit into a variety of categories* under Article 38 ICJ Statute, and that their interpretative practices may hold some still undefined sui generis position as a means of interpretation or source of obligations in human rights law.

7.4 Interpretative Practices of Human Rights Bodies according to the ICJ

Finally, the ICJ has perhaps struggled most with according a certain legal interpretative value to UN human rights monitoring bodies' work and formally clarifying their legal status. A first important observation is that the ICJ actually takes various types of interpretative practices of international monitoring bodies 'into account' when interpreting specific human right treaties. It emphasizes General Comments and Views of

[86] ILC (n 73) [82–88, 119–25, 145–47] especially [124–25].
[87] ibid [6, 62–63, 84, 99–103, 125, 225].
[88] ILC (n 74) [329]. The rapporteur notes he finds himself in a 'difficult position' due to the rather diverging views of States on the functions of subsidiary means.
[89] ibid [42, 313, 326, 329].
[90] ILC (n 73) [25–26]; ILC (n 85) [362]; ILC (n 75) 88 [116].

UNTBs but also refers to Concluding Observations or findings of UN Special Rapporteurs. The ICJ has argued that while it is not legally obliged to follow the interpretations offered by 'other' supervisory bodies, it 'must take due account' of the legal interpretations offered by 'independent bodies which have been specifically created' to monitor the application of specific treaties, and 'it should ascribe great weight' to them.[91]

Thus, in the *Wall Opinion* (2004), the ICJ considered the content of General Comments, Views and Concluding Observations equally, without clearly distinguishing which may be more or most important or 'authoritative'.[92] In *Ahmadou Diallo* (2010) it noted that the Human Rights Committee 'built up a considerable body of interpretative case law', referring both to its Views and General Comments.[93]

However, the ICJ notoriously does not explicitly clarify on which legal grounds it takes into account or ascribes great weight to various interpretive practices.[94] In *Ahmadou Diallo*, the ICJ has been most explicit about its reasons, notably: 'the point' of consulting the practice of the Human Rights Committee is to 'achieve the necessary clarity and essential consistency of international law, as well as legal security'.[95] It argued that both 'individuals with guaranteed rights' and States parties are 'entitled' to this.[96] According to some, this shows support for a 'systemic argument' regarding the importance of promoting 'legal certainty' or 'unity of law'.[97] This point is also highlighted in ILC Rapporteur Jalloh's latest report, addressing the role of subsidiary means in striving for unity of legal interpretations.[98]

[91] Azaria (n 13) 40; J Crawford and A Keene, 'Interpretation of the Human Rights Treaties by the International Court of Justice' (2019) 24 IJHR 935, 940–42; *Legal Consequences of the Construction of a Wall* (n 39) 136 [109–12]; In *Ahmadou Sadio Diallo*, the ICJ consulted the 'jurisprudence' of the HRCtee and of regional bodies to corroborate interpretations, i.e. viewing the former as 'established by the Covenant to ensure compliance with that instrument by the States parties'; *Ahmadou Sadio Diallo* (*Republic of Guinea v Democratic Republic of the Congo*) (Merits) [2010] ICJ Rep 639 [66–67].

[92] *Legal Consequences of the Construction of a Wall* (n 39) 136; [109–12]; Azaria (n 13) 39–40; L Crema, 'The Interpretative Work of Treaty Bodies: How They Look at Evolutionary Interpretation and How Other Courts Look at Them' in G Abi-Saab et al (eds), *Evolutionary Interpretation and International Law* (Hart 2019) 84; Crawford and Keene (n 91) 941.

[93] *Ahmadou Sadio Diallo* (n 91) 66.

[94] Azaria (n 13) 39–40.

[95] ibid.

[96] ibid.

[97] G Ulfstein, 'Who is the Final Interpreter in Human Rights: the ICJ v CERD?' (EJILTalk, 22 February 2021) <https://www.ejiltalk.org/who-is-the-final-interpreter-in-human-rights-the-icj-v-cerd/> (last accessed 1 June 2025).

[98] ILC (n 74) [211 et seq] especially [264 et seq].

Problematically, the weight attached to interpretations of UNTBs and Special Procedures by the ICJ differs considerably from case to case, often without much explanation.[99] This reflects poorly on the quality and interpretative legal value of ICJ case-law in this respect. For instance, in its two *Advisory Opinions on Israel* (2004 and 2024), the ICJ widely refers to a range of interpretative practices of UN bodies to find violations of international human rights law; whilst in the *Chagos Advisory Opinion* (2019), it only tangentially cites Concluding Observations of the Human Rights Committee to the UK, that is, as part of a wider pattern of argumentation or factual context.[100] In the *Policies and Practices of Israel*-opinion (2024), the ICJ even seems to go as far as largely substituting its own assessments of violations of treaty obligations for findings by different UNTBs. In this advisory opinion, it cites several CERD Concluding Observations to Israel to affirm that the CERD applies extraterritoriality to occupied territories, which are seen as 'territories under jurisdiction',[101] as well as several Concluding Observations of the CERD Committee and Human Rights Committee to support 'the view that Israel's residence permit policy is inconsistent with its obligations under CERD and the ICCPR', resulting 'in the differential treatment of Palestinians in relation to their right to reside in East Jerusalem'.[102] Similarly, it cites several CERD and ICESCR Concluding Observations to support that the residence permit policy violates the 'right to family life, as guaranteed under Article 10 of the ICESCR and Article 17 of the ICCPR'.[103]

On the contrary, in two recent contentious cases on CERD, *Qatar v. United Arab Emirates* (2021) and *Ukraine v. Russia* (2022), the ICJ took rather evasive stances and deviated from interpretations of the CERD Committee without any meaningful justification or engagement with its actual pronouncement. This was heavily critiqued by several judges and in literature.[104]

[99] See also Hesselman (n 32) 28.

[100] *Legal Consequences of the Separation of the Chagos Archipelago from Mauritius in 1965* (Advisory Opinion) [2019] ICJ Rep 95 [123, 126].

[101] *Legal Consequences arising from the Policies and Practices of Israel in the Occupied Palestinian Territory, including East Jerusalem* (Advisory Opinion of 19 July 2024) [101] <https://www.icj-cij.org/case/186/advisory-opinions> (last accessed 1 June 2025).

[102] ibid [194].

[103] ibid [195].

[104] Ulfstein (n 97); K Pan, 'Difference Between the ICJ and the CERD Committee: A Comment on the *Application of the International Convention on the Elimination of All Forms of Racial Discrimination (Qatar v United Arab Emirates)* Case' (2022) 21 Chinese JIL 195; WT Worster, 'The Divergence Between the ICJ and the Committee on the Elimination of Racial Discrimination regarding Nationality-Based Discrimination' 26(13) ASIL Insights 1

In *Qatar v. United Arab Emirates*, the ICJ at least still paid lip service to the idea of 'ascribing great weight' to the interpretations of CERD, but it ultimately only indicated that it 'carefully considered' the CERD interpretations but arrived at its own interpretations.[105] There was little discussion of why it dismissed them. More generally, the interpretative approach of the ICJ in this judgment is somewhat bewildering. For the ICJ seems to deliberately place its consideration of CERD practice outside the VCLT framework. The judgment is structured in such a way that the interpretation of Article 1 CERD takes place through a fairly elaborate consideration of the three elements in Article 31 VCLT (i.e. ordinary meaning, context, object and purpose), followed by a fairly reluctant recourse to the *travaux preparatoires* of CERD as a 'subsidiary means of interpretation' under Article 32 VCLT. Only then, the work of CERD is 'considered'. According to the ICJ:

> the Court will interpret CERD [. . .] by applying the rules on treaty interpretation enshrined in Articles 31 and 32 of the Vienna Convention on the Law of Treaties. [. . .] The Court will interpret the term "national origin" by reference, *first*, to the elements set out in Article 31 of the Vienna Convention [. . .] which states the general rule of treaty interpretation. *Only then* will the Court turn to the supplementary means of interpretation provided for in Article 32 in order to confirm the meaning resulting from that process, or to remove ambiguity or obscurity, or to avoid a manifestly absurd or unreasonable result. The Court *will also examine* the practice of the CERD Committee and of regional human rights courts.[106]

(*ASIL Insights*, 22 November 2022) <https://www.asil.org/insights/volume/26/issue/13> (last accessed 1 June 2025); G García Escobar, 'ICJ's Judgment in Ukraine v Russia regarding CERD's Scope of Racial Discrimination: ICJ's Approach to CERD Committee's Views' (*EJILTalk!*, 29 February 2024) <https://www.ejiltalk.org/icjs-judgment-in-ukraine-v-russia-regarding-cerds-scope-of-racial-discrimination-icjs-approach-to-cerd-committees-views/> (last accessed 1 June 2025).

105 *Application of the International Convention on the Elimination of All Forms of Racial Discrimination* (*Qatar v United Arab Emirates*) (Preliminary Objections) [2021] ICJ Rep 71 [100–101].

106 ibid [75–77] (emphasis added); ILC (n 74) [390–92]. ILC Rapporteur Jalloh also notes the curious position of the CERD practice, but somewhat more optimistically concludes that the ICJ must have seen them as additional supplementary means in the sense of art 32 VCLT. This author is unsure whether this argument can be sustained and argues, instead, that the invocation seems to take place in another, still undefined way. One option is that the interpretative practice of CERD is viewed as a 'subsidiary means' in the sense of art 38 ICJ Statute, or in some sui generis manner. The author does agree with Rapporteur Jalloh that in this particular case, the ICJ does not seem to use the practice as a 'primary interpretative tool'.

Several ICJ judges critiqued this approach. For example, Judge Robinson saw no reason 'why the Court should not attach great weight to the recommendations of the CERD Committee (which is properly seen as the guardian of the Convention), if they are not in conflict with international human rights law or general international law'.[107] Doing so would 'promote the achievement of the clarity, consistency and legal security' aspired to by the Court in *Ahmadou Diallo*.[108] He regrets that the majority did not follow the CERD Committee's recommendation, nor offer 'any explanation for not following it'.[109] Judge Bhandari similarly notes that the majority seems to break with the ICJ's previous jurisprudence of 'ascribing great weight' to the interpretative practice of monitoring bodies and 'provides no compelling reason as to why it has chosen to depart from the reasoning' of the CERD Committee or failed to attach great weight to it.[110] In defence of CERD's interpretative practice, Judge Bhandari addresses the functioning and work of the Committee in detail. This includes its 'primary function' of analyzing and commenting on State reports and its related practice of 'establishing certain rules in dialogue' with the parties, as well as its 'judicial' approach to matters.[111] He also calls this committee a 'guardian of the convention'.[112]

Unfortunately, none of the judges point to a clear legal ground for 'ascribing great weight' to CERD practice – except for Judge Bhandari. He considers that the independent Committee Members 'fall into the category of the "most highly qualified publicists" in this field',[113] thus invoking the notion of 'teachings of highly qualified publicists' under Article 38 of the ICJ Statute.

Significantly, several judges noted that the ICJ appears to have misrepresented the legal argument that Qatar presented about (indirect) discrimination and potentially also the CERD Committee's line of reasoning

[107] *Application of the International Convention on the Elimination of All Forms of Racial Discrimination (Qatar v United Arab Emirates)* (Preliminary Objections) (Dissenting Opinion of Judge Robinson) [2021] ICJ Rep 146 [13].
[108] ibid.
[109] ibid.
[110] *Application of the International Convention on the Elimination of All Forms of Racial Discrimination (Qatar v United Arab Emirates)* (Preliminary Objections) (Dissenting Opinion of Judge Bhandari) [2021] ICJ Rep 133 [21, 23–24].
[111] ibid [22].
[112] ibid [21].
[113] ibid [22].

on indirect discrimination to date.[114] In this sense, it is vital to ensure that the ICJ, as a general court of law, has a sound understanding of the Convention that it is interpreting, including the (nuanced) interpretative practices developed by a dedicated expert body over a long period of time. The CERD Committee interprets its treaty through day-to-day practice of regularly and consistently engaging with the Convention, its States parties, beneficiaries and the various situations put before it. This seems to be the main message of Judge Bhandari too: the ICJ must tread with caution in providing (one-off) interpretations of human rights treaties, that other bodies have devoted a lifetime of practice to. There may be many interpretative nuances that are missed. Indeed, other judges called out the largely 'theoretical' and abstract definitional exercise of the ICJ in *Qatar v. UAE.*[115] An important question is then whether the ICJ has engaged in 'good faith' interpretation under Article 31 VCLT by dismissing the work of the CERD Committee as it did. At a minimum, the ICJ and the parties should have engaged with the substance of arguments or interpretations made by the committee, but they did not.

Finally, in *Ukraine v. Russia* (2024), similar concerns of misunderstanding of parties' arguments played a role, with this judgment largely ignoring available interpretative guidance of UN bodies invoked by Ukraine, including from the CERD Committee.[116] Throughout this judgment, CERD pronouncements are mostly referred to by the ICJ in relation to issues of fact – thereby avoiding statements on their legal interpretative value. This was again critiqued by some judges and in academic debate; the outcome of this case could have been swayed in another direction had the ICJ followed the concept of (intersectional) indirect discrimination set out by CERD in its General Recommendations more closely.[117]

[114] See *Application of the International Convention on the Elimination of All Forms of Racial Discrimination (Qatar v United Arab Emirates)* (Preliminary Objections) (Dissenting Opinion Judge Sebutinde) [2021] ICJ Rep 117 [20–22]; *Application of the International Convention on the Elimination of All Forms of Racial Discrimination (Qatar v United Arab Emirates)* (Preliminary Objections) (Declaration of President Yusuf) [2021] ICJ Rep 111 [2–11, 13].

[115] *Application of the International Convention on the Elimination of All Forms of Racial Discrimination* (Dissenting Opinion Judge Sebutinde) (n 114) [20, 22].

[116] *Application of the International Convention for the Suppression of the Financing of Terrorism and of the International Convention on the Elimination of All Forms of Racial Discrimination (Ukraine v Russian Federation)* (Judgment) [2024] ICJ Rep 78 [172, 182–83, 231, 277, 283, 333–34].

[117] See e.g. Escobar (n 104).

Dissenting judges agreed that the General Comments of the CERD Committee – which Judge Charlesworth calls 'the independent body established specifically to supervise the interpretation and application of CERD' – provide relevant requirements for assessing indirect discrimination; and the same counts for the interpretative practices of other treaty bodies and courts that supervise *'comparable' non-discrimination provisions*, for example, Human Rights Committee, the ICESCR Committee, the CEDAW Committee and European and Inter-American Court of Human Rights.[118] This suggests that these judges support a 'systemic approach' to the interpretation of similar treaty terms. Indeed, Judge Iwasawa explicitly favours an interpretation that 'is consistent with the notion of indirect discrimination adopted by other international human rights courts and treaty bodies'.[119] He supports taking into account interpretative practices related to 'analogous non-discrimination provisions' in search of 'similar interpretations',[120] rather than relying solely on the ICJ's own judgment in the matter. Iwasawa thus favours searching for 'unity' in the interpretation of similar terms, even across a wider range of treaties than the one under review.

Escobar has recently suggested that the ICJ's dismissal of UNTBs interpretations could stem from the (occasional) criticism that expert bodies' interpretations may be too bold or lack 'rigorous legal and methodological' analysis or justifications.[121] Yet, omitting any meaningful engagement with the pronouncements of UNTBs, either by dismissing them without reason or, instead, referring to them plainly as evidence of certain violations, will not help to move such critiques forward. It only aggravates them. In addition, it is worthwhile to note that ICJ judgments

[118] See *Application of the International Convention for the Suppression of the Financing of Terrorism and of the International Convention on the Elimination of All Forms of Racial Discrimination* (*Ukraine v Russian Federation*) (Judgment) (Separate Opinion Judge Iwasawa) [2024] ICJ Rep 261 [8–17]; *Application of the International Convention for the Suppression of the Financing of Terrorism and of the International Convention on the Elimination of All Forms of Racial Discrimination* (*Ukraine v Russian Federation*) (Judgment) (Separate Opinion Judge Charlesworth) [2024] ICJ Rep 270 [24–25]; *Application of the International Convention for the Suppression of the Financing of Terrorism and of the International Convention on the Elimination of All Forms of Racial Discrimination* (*Ukraine v Russian Federation*) (Judgment) (Separate Opinion ad hoc Judge Pocar) [2024] ICJ Rep 289 [22–24].

[119] *Application of the International Convention for the Suppression of the Financing of Terrorism and of the International Convention on the Elimination of All Forms of Racial Discrimination* (Separate Opinion Judge Iwasawa) (n 118) [18].

[120] ibid [8].

[121] Escobar (n 104).

may base its interpretation of a specific provision only on the arguments of a small number of concerned parties; UN expert bodies typically arrive at their interpretations through much more extensive and prolonged engagement or 'dialogue' with a range of different parties, including those benefitting from treaty norms. This author argues that deriving from the rather unique nature of the monitoring work of UN expert bodies, also a more nuanced sui generis position could be carved out for them. This argument is further elaborated below.

7.5 'Thrown for a Loop' or 'Thrown into the Crucible? Reflections on the Legal Value of Various Interpretative Practices

The preceding analysis clearly shows a rather mixed assessment of the 'formal' legal value or weight to be accorded to the interpretative practices of UN human rights monitoring bodies in international law. Whilst there seems to be a broad agreement that 'specially mandated' expert bodies play an important role in treaty interpretation, the exact legal ground(s) for 'taking into account', 'ascribing great weight' or using them otherwise ('in good faith') still remains somewhat shrouded in legal mystery.

The growth and ubiquity of these interpretative practices after the adoption of the VCLT (1969) and ICJ Statute (1948) means that it has become imperative to consider on which basis, or under which conditions, such interpretations should or must play any authoritative, supplementary, subsidiary, auxiliary or other type of role in providing interpretations of treaties. How might they assist with determining the (ordinary) meaning of treaty terms 'in their context and in light of the object and purpose of the treaty', over time?[122] In the words of ILC Rapporteur Jalloh, the question whether the various practices serve a role as 'subsidiary means' in the sense of Article 38 ICJ Statute is 'ripe for discussion'.[123]

As evident from the analysis above, the monitoring practices of different bodies have been variously framed as potentially entering into play under Articles 31 and 32 VCLT (e.g. good faith interpretation, supplementary means or for even systemic interpretation by referring to practices of other bodies interpreting similar norms) or Article 38 ICJ Statute

122 ILC Draft Conclusions 2018 (n 2) [115–16].
123 ILC (n 74) [146].

(judicial decisions, teachings or other). They have also been used or ignored without much clarification at all by the ICJ, and there are some indications that they occupy some special sui generis position, either outside the VCLT or within Article 38 ICJ Statute, which is not yet fully articulated to date. Of importance in this respect could be the special way in which interpretative practices of UN human rights bodies come about 'in dialogue with the parties' and other beneficiaries over a long period of time and through a variety of monitoring activities.[124]

This chapter has not analyzed how international and/or regional human rights bodies *themselves* have engaged with their own and others' interpretative practices in any detail. However, it is doubtful that an unambiguous picture would emerge from such study.[125] At present, the ILC seems to be the body mostly clearly and structurally considering their legal value/status/weight. Yet the ILC also admits it has been somewhat limited by the specific topics through which these practices are studied so far. This author is of the opinion that, ultimately, the *exact legal status or place* of these interpretative practices within the VCLT, Article 38 ICJ Statute or otherwise, may *not* be the most vital legal question. Instead, this author wants to draw attention to a somewhat more pragmatic line of reasoning that may help to decide *which* and *how* certain practices might be 'thrown into the crucible' of treaty interpretation, as well as weighted as part of a larger 'single combined operation' of treaty interpretation. For, even if it *were* possible to establish exactly which interpretative practices may or must be taken into account, there may still be *additional questions* about the overall or specific usefulness of *any specific set* of Views, General Comments, Concluding Observations, reports etc. In particular, it has been suggested that the interpretative value of specific interpretative statements by UNTBs and Special Procedures may depend on a number of additional factors, which have also been recognized by the ILC and may need to be considered on a case-by-case basis.[126]

The ILC recently has begun to formulate several criteria that interpreters may use to pick, weigh and/or emphasize different available means of interpretation. Specifically, it affirmed that the 'means of interpretation' listed in Articles 31 and 32 VCLT may be differently emphasized by

[124] *Application of the International Convention on the Elimination of All Forms of Racial Discrimination* (Dissenting Opinion of Judge Bhandari) (n 110) [22].

[125] See e.g. ILA (n 24).

[126] Hesselman (n 32) 29; ILC Draft Conclusions 2018 (n 2) 70; generally, Azaria (n 13).

interpreters 'depending on the treaty or treaty provisions concerned', including the 'character of the treaty or provision'.[127] The weight to be accorded to different available means of interpretation under Article 31 and 32 VCLT collectively, may depend, inter alia, on the clarity and specificity of a practice (e.g. 'sufficiently concrete') or on 'whether and how it is repeated' (unmindful, with intention, frequency, uniformity).[128] These criteria are not intended to be exhaustive,[129] and the ILC previously mentioned cogency and consistency amongst means found their direct relevance to the treaty term or the number of parties involved in the evolution of particular means.[130]

Recently, the ILC's study on Article 38 ICJ Statute similarly suggested in Draft Conclusion 3 that:

> When assessing the weight of subsidiary means for the determination of rules of international law, regard should be had to, *inter alia:*
>
> (a) their degree of representativeness;
> (b) the quality of the reasoning;
> (c) the expertise of those involved;
> (d) the level of agreement among those involved;
> (e) the reception by States and other entities;
> (f) where applicable, the mandate conferred on the body.[131]

The present author recently proposed a range of possible criteria relevant to human rights supervisory bodies' practice specifically based on an extensive analysis of positions in human rights literature, practice and in ILC studies, to date.[132] Those criteria include, inter alia:

- a human rights expert body's use of specific, obligatory, recommendatory, urgent, strong/weak, precise/vague language in its Views, General Comments, Concluding Observations, Reports, Communications etc (e.g. shall, should, may, must; articulating clear courses of action, violations or prohibitions);
- the proximity of a specific statement to an actual piece of treaty text (e.g. does the interpretation intend to offer a clear interpretation of a specific term, e.g. the meaning of torture);

[127] ILC Draft Conclusions 2018 (n 2) 22.
[128] ibid, Draft Conclusion 9.
[129] ibid 71.
[130] See e.g. ILC Draft Conclusions 2018 (n 2) 70; ILC (n 12) 55–56; Villiger (n 20) 446.
[131] ILC (n 78).
[132] Hesselman (n 32) 29–32.

- has the interpretation been (meaningfully) repeated over time (e.g. by the same or by different bodies; has it become a settled interpretation? have any States opposed or supported it; if so, how many and which, on which grounds?);
- what is the procedural quality of the adoption of the statement, e.g. has a certain interpretation been adopted after considerable deliberation, dialogue or consultation, amongst variety or number of different actors and/or after hearing and entertaining different possible legal interpretations, with reference to any specific method of interpretation supported by the VCLT or otherwise?[133]

All of these criteria may need to be fleshed out further over time, but it is argued here that such criteria might ultimately be more 'legally relevant' to efforts of treaty interpretation than any 'formal' legal placing within the context of the VCLT, ICJ Statute or otherwise.[134] Especially when it comes to the diverse body of interpretative practices of UNTBs and UN Special Procedures, with its variegated qualities, functions and characteristics, such more refined criteria may be of considerable use.

Finally, the analysis presented in this chapter expressly leaves open the possibility that the interpretative practices of UN human rights expert bodies – as day-to-day 'guardians' of major multilateral human rights treaties regulating relations between many States and many individuals – indeed occupy somewhat of a sui generis position in international law. For, although human rights monitoring bodies are occasionally admonished for not following any clear methods of interpretation or for not closely adhering to the VCLT, there may in fact be something unique about the (incremental) modes of monitoring and interpretation of these treaties through a wide variety of monitoring activity. As stated several times, human rights treaty interpretation takes place across a wide range of bodies, typically through sustained dialogues with States parties, NGO and victims. Moreover, not yet discussed, human rights treaty interpretation also typically involves capturing the ever-evolving societal notions regarding human rights protection (i.e. the methods of 'evolutive' or 'systemic' interpretation in human rights practice, their places within the VCLT and the ways in which different practices could enter into play there as well, which were not even properly discussed in the chapter so far).[135]

133 ibid 32.
134 ibid.
135 It is also beyond this chapter to discuss this in detail; see for further discussion Hesselman (n 32) 244–50.

All in all, it may be argued that at present, there is no comparably complex, expansive, diverse and intertwined system of expert-based monitoring available in any other field of public international law; vice-versa, the international human rights law system does not benefit from any systems of State-led development of treaty interpretations, for example, through regular meetings of and decisions by Conferences of Parties.

The efforts of the ILC to uncover the special legal value of the interpretative monitoring practices of UN bodies should therefore be applauded. More generally, the efforts of the ICJ and other bodies to meaningfully and in good faith engage in interpretations of human rights treaties through the VCLT, with 'great' or 'careful' attention to the various available expert pronouncements, can be improved.

7.6 Conclusion

Rather than remaining 'thrown for a loop' about the potential legal value(s) of interpretative monitoring practices of different UN human rights bodies in the practice of human rights treaty interpretation, this chapter suggests leaving some of the formalistic discussions behind somewhat and taking a 'leap of (good) faith'. It is vital to acknowledge the unique and large volumes of interpretative practices generated by UNTBs and UN Special Procedures. As attested by many, these contributions deserve to be seriously 'taken into account', 'carefully considered', 'ascribed great weight' or appraised 'in good faith' when trying to understand the meaning of any specific human rights treaty norm. The basis for doing so may ultimately not (only) be found in a formal interpretation of Articles 31–32 VCLT, Article 38 ICJ Statute or even, strictly speaking, the mandates of specific bodies. This chapter has shown that there could be many different reasons to take practices into account, as well as possibly reasons to take them into account less so.

The International Law Commission is currently firmly taking the lead on studying the legal value(s) to be accorded to a range of legal practices and materials in international law. Amongst them are the various interpretative practices of UN human rights expert bodies, with a focus on the UNTBs. The lack of attention to the work of UN Special Procedures of the Human Rights Council, as another type of State-appointed independent expert, is a major omission.

Interestingly, even since 1966, the ILC has been suggesting that interpretation is to some extent 'an art, not an exact science'.[136] In particular, there may be various factors or criteria that could be relevant to determining which elements/means can or must be 'thrown into the crucible' of treaty interpretation and how they may interact or be weighted as part of a 'single combined operation' to find the 'legally relevant' interpretation. There is no doubt that the interpretative practices of UN monitoring bodies bear legal relevance to the practice of human rights treaty interpretation. However, whether and how specific interpretative practices might be engaged in any specific act of interpretation, or 'thrown into any specific crucible', will depend on the specific treaty (provision) concerned; the breadth, depth and quality of interpretative practice available; and perhaps even on the interpreter.[137]

The ILC so far suggests that a range of criteria could be relevant to engaging and/or weighing certain available means of interpretation.[138] Such criteria might include the extent to which certain interpretations came about through a specific formal method or means of interpretation, for example, under the VCLT or ICJ Statute, but more likely, also how well a certain interpretative practice reflects a specific consensus on a certain interpretation by States and others, for example, including beneficiaries of human rights treaties, other supervisory bodies working with similar norms or highly qualified publicists, etc; The author recently proposed a range of criteria that may be relevant to the human rights context specifically (see Section 7.5).[139]

This chapter suggests that leaving some of the more formalistic approaches under Articles 31–32 VCLT or Article 38 ICJ Statute behind us, in favour of a set of substantive and procedural criteria for engaging and weighting different interpretative means available, could offer a (more) meaningful way forward for human rights interpretation. In the end, the *form* of the interpretative practices by expert bodies (General Comments, Views, Concluding Observations, communications, Thematic Reports) may only be a starting point; the quality and usefulness of the interpretative practice in a given setting may still need to be

[136] ILC 'Draft Articles on the Law of Treaties with Commentaries' (4 May–19 July 1966) UN Doc A/CN.4/191, reproduced in [1966/II] YBILC 187, 223.

[137] ILC Draft Conclusions 2018 (n 2) 22. Different interpreters may differently emphasize various means of interpretation 'depending on the treaty or treaty provisions concerned'.

[138] ibid 21–22; ILC (n 12) [55].

[139] See Hesselman (n 32) 29–31.

assessed on a case-by-case basis.[140] In this sense, the interpretative practices of UN human rights bodies might even occupy some sui generis nature in public international law compared to other regimes: international human rights law uniquely takes shape through, and might be best interpretated based on, the large and amorphous body of continuous and simultaneously occurring (incremental) interpretative practice(s) generated by a variety of repeated supervisory activities of expert bodies, with the inputs from a large range of relevant interpretative actors. The full breadth of this practice may then, in theory, be 'thrown into the crucible', but an interpreter should (be able to) justify in good faith with which interpretative means it has (not) engaged, why and how. Section 7.5 proposed a number of criteria to guide this justificatory process. Additional guidance on weighting various means of interpretation, amongst a larger set of means, may become available from the ILC over the next few years through its study on Article 38, but arguably such guidance has to be made practicable for the unique context of human rights law specifically. Ideally the ILC incorporates the work of UN Special Procedures into its consideration of human rights expert bodies' contributions as well.

[140] ibid.

8

Co-developing a Transformative Interpretation of International Law on the Protection of the Marine Environment and Human Rights

A Reflection on the Experience of the One Ocean Hub

ELISA MORGERA

8.1 Introduction

This is a self-reflective essay that aims to discuss the contributions of non-judicial actors,[1] ranging from United Nations' (UN) bodies to academic researchers in legal, natural and social sciences, as well as non-governmental organizations (NGOs) and human rights holders, to treaty interpretation as a matter of research design of an inter- and transdisciplinary project – the One Ocean Hub,[2] which the author led. The reflection allows to shed light on the role of diverse actors and experts to co-develop a mutually supportive interpretation of international environmental law, the law of the sea and international human rights law that contributes to enhance, and potentially transform, the protection of the marine environment and of the human rights dependent on a healthy ocean.

As discussed in other chapters of this edited volume, 'the law and practice in specific fields of international law has reached an unprecedented level of sophistication',[3] and this in itself has been a barrier to

[1] Norm entrepreneurs comprising scholars, NGOs, advocacy networks and international bureaucrats. See I Venzke, *How Interpretation Makes International Law: On Semantic Change and Normative Twists* (Oxford University Press 2012) 64–67 and 69–71.

[2] The One Ocean Hub was a collaborative research for sustainable development project funded by UK Research and Innovation (UKRI) through the Global Challenges Research Fund (GCRF) (Grant Ref: NE/S008950/1) from 2019–2025. GCRF aimed at delivering the UK AID strategy and puts UK-led research at the heart of efforts to tackle the United Nations Sustainable Development Goals.

[3] See Chapter 1 to this volume.

connecting efforts to address the intertwined challenges of the protection of the marine environment and the protection of human rights.[4] The inter-linkages among these challenges have become increasingly clear in non-legal research, notably in marine and social sciences research,[5] as well as in the actions of researcher-activists working in solidarity with human rights holders.[6] As part of a broader effort of mapping out the current trends in the study of the process of interpretation in international law, this chapter therefore reflects on the increasing need to interpret in an evolutive and mutually supportive manner the rules of international environmental law, the law of the sea and international human rights law. Such evolutive and mutually supportive interpretation is based on new knowledge integrating local experiences of lack of sustainability and other injustices, interdisciplinary scientific evidence and Indigenous and local knowledge systems shedding light on the interdependence of diverse international treaty objectives. This appears necessary with a view to enhancing equity and effectiveness in the realization of the objectives of relevant treaties[7] and potentially contribute to transforming current governance into more inclusive, sustainable and fair practices at different levels.

To that end, the chapter reflects on the efforts of different UN and other international bodies that provide advisory services to States on how to implement international law,[8] researcher-activists that seek to respond to pressing socio-cultural and environmental injustices at the local and national levels by relying on international law, as well as civil society and human rights holders working with them. The chapter focuses in particular on how these actors are increasingly working together to

[4] B Erinosho et al, 'Transformative Governance for Ocean Biodiversity' in IJ Visseren-Hamakers and M Kok (eds), *Transforming Biodiversity Governance* (Cambridge University Press 2022) 313–38.

[5] M Lombard et al, 'Principles for Transformative Ocean Governance' (2023) Nature Sustainability 1587.

[6] T Pereira and K Erwin, 'Surfacing Solidarity Praxis in Transdisciplinary Research for Blue Justice' (2023) 19 Ecosystems and People 2260502; D McGarry, 'When Ancestors Are Included in Ocean and Decision-making' in T Shefer et al (eds), *Hydrofeminist Thinking with Oceans: Political and Scholarly Possibilities* (Routledge 2024) 15.

[7] E Morgera and M Lennan, 'Ensuring Mutual Supportiveness of the Paris Agreement with other Multilateral Environmental Agreements: A Focus on Ocean-Based Climate Action' in A Zahar (ed), *Research Handbook on the Law of the Paris Agreement* (Edward Elgar 2024) 362; and E Morgera, 'The Progressive Development of International Biodiversity Law: From Nature Conservation to the Biodiversity–Human Rights–Ocean-Climate Nexus' in J Ebbeson and D Langlet (eds), *Fifty Years of International Environmental Law: Developments Since the 1972 Stockholm Conference* (Cambridge University Press 2026).

[8] An earlier reflection can be found in E Morgera, 'Global Environmental Law and the Comparative Legal Method(s)' (2015) RECIEL 254.

co-develop mutually supportive interpretations based on local-level experiences of lack of sustainability and of intergenerational injustices, interdisciplinary scientific evidence and Indigenous and local knowledge systems, in order to influence public authorities towards transforming environmental governance into more inclusive, sustainable and fair approaches. The chapter will take as a specific case study for analyzing this trend the One Ocean Hub research programme, which involved all the above-mentioned actors in activities related to the growing international recognition of human rights dependent on a healthy ocean[9] on the basis of mutually supportive interpretations of the international law on the marine environment, international biodiversity law, international climate change law and international human rights law. The chapter will first introduce the concepts of mutual supportiveness under the international law of treaty interpretation, together with the need for self-reflection by international law scholars and the role of collective approaches to interpretation as co-development. The One Ocean Hub will then be introduced as a case study of an inter- and transdisciplinary research programme that was designed on the basis of a mutually supportive interpretation, and the role of international law research as part of inter- and trans-disciplinarity. The chapter will then reflect on the distinctive role of a variety of non-judicial actors in co-developing mutually supportive interpretations of international law on the protection of the marine environment and human rights. Attention will focus on specific examples related to the recognition of 'ocean defenders' as environmental human rights defenders. The chapter will conclude with a reflection on how co-development of mutually supportive interpretations can also be institutionalized under treaty law, as a participatory monitoring, evaluation and learning approach embedded in treaty bodies devoted to the review of implementation and/or to technical and scientific advice.

8.2 Mutually Supportive Interpretations of International Law and the Need for Collective Approaches to Self-reflection

Mutual supportiveness is an emerging principle of international law[10] that builds upon the customary rule of treaty interpretation of systemic

[9] N Bennett et al, 'Ocean Defenders and Human Rights' (2023) 9 Frontiers in Marine Science 1; N Bennett et al, 'Environmental (In)Justice in the Anthropocene Ocean' (2022) 147 Marine Policy 105383.

[10] R Pavoni, 'Mutual Supportiveness as a Principle of Interpretation and Law-Making: A Watershed for the WTO-and-Competing-Regimes Debate?' (2010) 21 EJIL 649; L Boisson de Chazournes and MM Mbengue, 'A "Footnote as a Principle". Mutual Supportiveness in an Era of Fragmentation' in P Holger et al (eds), *Coexistence,*

integration, as enshrined in the Vienna Convention on the Law of Treaties – the need to take into account, 'any relevant rules of international law applicable in the relationships between the parties'.[11] Both mutual supportiveness and systemtic integration seek to find a reasonable way to apply different international instruments with minimal disturbance to the operation of the whole international legal system,[12] with a view to preserving the unity of the international legal order.[13] In this sense, both also support the principle of good faith, which in its own right supports 'cross-fertilization and coherence of international legal system'[14] through treaty interpretation.[15]

Systemic integration, however, strictly speaking, applies only to treaties and other binding sources of international law, and there have been debates about whether it only applies to treaties among the same parties.[16] Due to these uncertainties, international law scholars have turned their attention to mutual supportiveness, which privileges an interpretative solution that also draws on decisions of treaty bodies[17] and other forms of normative interactions among different international regimes.[18] Drawing on such multitude of international legal materials,

Cooperation and Solidarity – Liber Amicorum Rüdiger Wolfrum (Martinus Nijhoff 2011) 1615.

11 Vienna Convention on the Law of Treaties (adopted 23 May 1969, entered into force 27 January 1980) 1155 UNTS 331, art 31(3)(c) (VCLT).

12 ILC 'Fragmentation of International Law: Difficulties Arising from the Diversification and Expansion of International Law: Report of the Study Group of the International Law Commission' (13 April 2006) UN Doc A/CN.4/L.682 [410].

13 R Wolfrum, 'General International Law (Principles, Rules and Standards)' [2012] MPEPIL 1408 [63]; PM Dupuy, 'L' unité de l' ordre juridique international' (2003) 297 RdC 9.

14 Wolfrum (n 13).

15 See UNGA, 'Declaration on Principles of International Law concerning Friendly Relations and Co-operation among States in accordance with the Charter of the United Nations' (24 October 1970) UN Doc A/RES/25/2625 and VCLT (n 11) arts 26 and 31. For an overview, see generally M Kotzur, 'Good Faith (Bona Fide)' [2009] MPEPIL 1412.

16 E.g. C McLachlan, 'The Principle of Systemic Integration and Article 31(3)(c) of the Vienna Convention' (2005) 54 ICLQ 279.

17 ILC (n 12) [493].

18 For instance, the adoption of soft law under international organizations to support harmonious interpretation of multiple international treaties. Two examples that are particularly relevant for this chapter are is the FAO, 'Voluntary Guidelines for Securing Sustainable Small-scale Fisheries in the Context of Food Security and Poverty Eradication' (adopted at the 31st Session of the Committee on Fisheries, 9–13 June 2014) <https://openknowledge.fao.org/server/api/core/bitstreams/edfffbfc-81e5-4208-a36f-334ff81ac10f/content> (last accessed 1 June 2025) and the UN HRC, 'United Nations Declaration on the Rights of Peasants and Other People Working in Rural Areas' (8 October 2018) UN Doc A/HRC/

mutual supportiveness requires, at the interpretative level, that states disqualify solutions to tensions between competing regimes involving the subordination of one regime to the other.[19] Mutual supportiveness is enshrined in specific multilateral environmental treaties[20] and is understood as a corollary of the principle sustainable development,[21] which is often part of the object and purpose of international environmental law treaties.[22]

In particular, mutual supportiveness contributes to clarify the legal content of fairness and equity, which are seen as a reflection of both sustainable development and of the general principle of good faith.[23] Fairness is usually contained in open-ended treaty provisions in international environmental law and the law of the sea, so these provisions can be filled with content by establishing a linkage with different international legal sub-systems through mutual supportiveness.[24] As I have argued in earlier work, in the specific case of human rights and the environment, these developments can be understood as evolutive interpretation of the object and purpose of relevant treaties (sustainable development, equity) in the light of emerging (natural and social) scientific evidence that human rights are dependent on healthy ecosystems.[25] This interpretation in turn contributes to teleological clarity and effectiveness[26] based on the realization that the respective objectives of

RES/39/12. For a discussion, see E Morgera and J Nakamura, 'Shedding a Light on the Human Rights of Small-scale Fisherfolk: Complementarities and Contrasts between the UN Declaration on Peasants' Rights and the Small-Scale Fisheries Guidelines' in M Alabrese et al (eds), *Commentary on the Declaration on the Rights of Peasants* (Routledge 2022) 62.

19 Pavoni (n 10), particularly at 661–69.

20 Nagoya Protocol on Access to Genetic Resources and the Fair and Equitable Sharing of Benefits Arising from Their Utilization (adopted 29 October 2010, entered into force 12 October 2014) 3008 UNTS 3, art 4(3) and in the preamble of other environmental treaties. See Boisson de Chazournes and Mbengue (n 10) 1625–30; E Morgera, E Tsioumani and M Buck, *Unraveling the Nagoya Protocol: A Commentary of the Protocol on Access and Benefit-Sharing to the Convention on Biological Diversity* (Martinus Nijhoff 2014) 84–109.

21 Morgera, Tsioumani and Buck (n 20) 661–62.

22 E.g. V Barral, 'National Sovereignty over Natural Resources: Environmental Challenges and Sustainable Development' in E Morgera and K Kulovesi (eds), *Research Handbook on Natural Resources and International Law* (Edward Elgar 2016) 3.

23 See generally R Kolb, *Good Faith in International Law* (Hart 2017).

24 F Francioni, 'Equity' [2020] MPEPIL 1399.

25 E Morgera, 'The Need for an International Legal Concept of Fair and Equitable Benefit-sharing' (2016) 27 EJIL 353.

26 ILC (n 12) [414]. This was first discussed by E Morgera, S Switzer and E Tsioumani, 'Study into Criteria to Identify a Specialized International Access and Benefit-sharing

different treaties are interdependent for their realization[27] and therefore increased cooperation is needed across these regimes to that end.[28] Such interpretative directions have been adopted explicitly by a variety of global and regional human rights courts[29] and non-judicial bodies[30] in light of human rights and environmental treaties, such as the Convention on Biological Diversity (CBD), as well as in the light of decisions adopted under the CBD.[31]

As I came to realize in my individual and collective international law research aimed at developing mutually supportive interpretations,[32] however, self-reflexivity needs to be a part of a heightened awareness with regard to unconscious and conscious power and influence[33] on

Instrument, and a Possible Process for Its Recognition' (29 May 2018) UN Doc CBD/SBI/2/INF/17.

[27] E Morgera, 'Dawn of a New Day? The Evolving Relationship between the Convention on Biological Diversity and International Human Rights Law' (2018) 54 Wake Forest Law Review 691.

[28] E Franckx, 'The Protection of Biodiversity and Fisheries Management: Issues Raised by the Relationship between CITES and LOSC' in D Freestone, R Barnes and D Ong (eds), *The Law of the Sea: Progress and Prospects* (Oxford University Press 2006) 210, 231–32 (albeit focused on *lex posterior* rather than *lex specialis*).

[29] E Morgera, 'Under the Radar: The Role of Fair and Equitable Benefit-sharing in Protecting and Realizing Human Rights connected to Natural Resources' (2019) 23 IJHR 1098; *Case of the Saramaka People v Suriname* (Preliminary Objections, Merits, Reparations and Costs) IACtHR, Series C No 172 (28 November 2007); *Case of the Saramaka People v Suriname* (Interpretation of the Judgment on Preliminary Objections, Merits, Reparations and Costs) IACtHR, Series C No 185 (12 August 2008); *Centre For Minority Rights Development and Another v Kenya* (25 November 2009) [2009] ACHPR 102, Communication no 276/2003.

[30] UNGA, 'Report of the Special Rapporteur on the Issue of Human Rights Obligations relating to the Enjoyment of a Safe, Clean, Healthy and Sustainable Environment' (24 January 2018) UN Doc A/HRC/37/59, Section on 'Framework Principles on Human Rights and the Environment', referring to fair and equitable benefit-sharing from the use of genetic resources under Framework Principle 15 (particularly [53]) (Framework Principles on Human Rights and the Environment).

[31] *Case of the Kaliña and Lokono Peoples v Suriname* (Merits, Reparations and Costs) IACtHR, Series C No 309 (25 November 2015).

[32] E Morgera, *Fair and Equitable Benefit-sharing in International Law* (Oxford University Press 2024).

[33] N Walker, 'The Gap between Global Law and Global Justice: A Preliminary Analysis' in N Rougham and A Halpin (eds), *In Pursuit of Pluralist Jurisprudence* (Cambridge University Press 2017) 216. See also M Koskenniemi, 'Between Commitment and Cynicism: Outline for a Theory of International Law as Practice' in *Collection of Essays by Legal Advisers of States, Legal Advisers of International Organizatios and Practitioners in the Field of International Law* (United Nations 1999) 495; J d'Aspremont, 'Three International Lawyers in a Hall of Mirrors' (2019) 32 LJIL 367.

international law[34] and national, ideological and structural biases[35] and blind spots.[36] International law scholarship had already underscored that scholars do not explicitly interrogate whether their interpretative efforts are inclusive or exclusive of marginalized voices.[37] As a result, I have been increasingly interested in the concept explored in the social sciences of self-reflexivity, which includes 'the explicit articulation of values, assumptions and normative orientations; and renewed attention to asymmetries in power'[38] in considering how we see our 'scientific practice, our engagement with other agents within the process of research, how values are reflected in the work we do, and how we sense that research leads to social and political change and transformation'.[39]

In this reflection, I have developed a proposition that a self-reflective interpretative approach to mutual supportive interpretations requires a collective effort among legal scholars[40] to help one other to identify respective blind spots and biases.[41] Based on a distinction proposed by Neil Walker, I have argued that 'pragmatist', 'idealist' and 'radically critical' legal scholars[42] should work together and constructively challenge one another with their respective insights on other scholars' limitations. Critical legal scholars can support other lawyers with their 'systematic attempt to include both the dimension of power and a theory of domination, and the relentless questioning of the "dark sides" of

[34] See also different traditions in different legal cultures about the role of international law scholars. A Roberts, *Is International Law International?* (Oxford University Press 2017).

[35] R Collins and A Bohm, 'International Law as Professional Practice: Crafting the Autonomy of International Law' in J d'Aspremont et al (eds), *International Law as a Profession* (Cambridge University Press 2017) 67, 91; A Peters, 'International Legal Scholarship under Challenge' in J d'Aspremont et al (eds), *International Law as a Profession* (Cambridge University Press 2017) 117, 124–25; G Hernandez, 'The Responsibility of the International Legal Academic: Situating the Grammarian within the "Invisible College"' in J d'Aspremont et al (eds), *International Law as a Profession* (Cambridge University Press 2017) 160, 186–88.

[36] Biases were underscored as a key finding arising from examining international law as a profession. J d'Aspremont et al, 'Introduction' in J d'Aspremont et al (eds), *International Law as a Profession* (Cambridge University Press 2017) 1.

[37] K Kulovesi, M Mehling and E Morgera, 'Global Environmental Law: Context and Theory, Challenge and Promise' (2019) 8 TEL 405.

[38] L Temper, D McGarry and L Weber, 'From Academic to Political Rigour: Insights from the "Tarot" of Transgressive Research' (2019) 164 Ecological Economics 106379.

[39] ibid.

[40] Kulovesi, Mehling and Morgera (n 37) 431–34.

[41] Roberts (n 34) xxii, 16, 25–26.

[42] Walker (n 33).

apparently emancipatory and progressive agendas' in law.[43] In turn, pragmatic lawyers can support critical lawyers in fully taking into account the actual nuances in the law and support idealist lawyers in anchoring their arguments in existing details of the law or actual workings of it. For their part, idealist lawyers can support both critical and pragmatic legal scholars to move beyond a negative critique or technicist analysis of the law, towards the development of a constructive proposition that can systematically consider the dark sides of law and accurately assess opportunities and constraints in its detailed workings.

What I explored more in my current collaborative research is the contribution of an even broader conversation with other epistemic communities, such as environmental justice scholars[44] and transdisciplinary researchers exploring the points of contact between different knowledge systems, including natural and social sciences, Indigenous and local knowledge systems and other forms of knowing. Such conversation can feed into the co-developing of mutually supportive interpretations of international law that respond to the needs, insights and life experiences of those most vulnerable to environmental degradation, while taking into account historic, systemic and cross-scalar injustices and carefully surfacing blind spots among all co-researchers, as discussed below.

8.3 The One Ocean Hub as an Example of Research Design Inspired by Mutually Supportive Interpretation

The One Ocean Hub (2019–25) was an inter- and transdisciplinary ocean research collaboration aiming to support fair and inclusive decision-making for a healthy ocean whereby people and the planet flourish. The Hub sought, from the outset, to integrate marine and social sciences, and the arts, as well as Indigenous and local knowledge systems and other forms of knowing, by relying on mutually supportive interpretations of international law on human rights and the marine environment. Such mutually supportive interpretation acted as a connecting frame across academic disciplines and diverse knowledge systems and as a platform for influencing ocean governance across temporal and

[43] U Mattei, 'Comparative Law and Critical Legal Studies' in M Reimann and R Zimmermann (eds), *The Oxford Handbook of Comparative Law* (Oxford University Press 2006) 815, 835.

[44] For an attempt, see E Morgera, 'Justice, Equity and Benefit-Sharing under the Nagoya Protocol to the Convention on Biological Diversity' (2015) IYBIL 113.

geographical scales. The attention to different scales implies attention both to historical and current sources of injustices, including intergenerational trauma and colonial legacies, as well as to influences across different geographical scales, including local-to-global or global-to-local dynamics and Global North/South dynamics.

As an inter- and transdisciplinary ocean research[45] collaboration that was specifically mandated by its funder to achieve long-lasting, sustainable development impacts,[46] the One Ocean Hub had the ambition to serve as a prototype for transformative ocean governance at different scales. Interdisciplinarity refers to efforts to integrate research efforts across different academic disciplines: the intention and challenge here is to move beyond multi-disciplinarity, where different academic disciplines proceed in parallel, and their separate findings are then brought together (juxtaposed) at the end. Instead, interdisciplinarity entails that the basic assumptions, key concepts and prior findings of various disciplines interrogate and challenge one another at the outset of the project, with a view to identifying respective blind spots and biases, eventually leading to the co-identification of research questions, which will then be pursued by various constellations of mixed approaches and findings from different disciplines. At that point, it is still possible and helpful to undertake also disciplinary research (including intra-disciplinary research, such as across different areas of legal scholarship) as long as the research questions are clearly anchored in and informed by the overall interdisciplinary research approach of the project and there are iterative ways to keep interrogating disciplinary research from the perspective of the other disciplines. In addition, transdisciplinarity refers to the effort to co-develop research across academic disciplines and diverse knowledge systems, such as Indigenous science and local knowledge, and the lived experiences and distinctive insights of other human rights holders, such as women and children.

[45] M Strand et al, 'Transdisciplinarity in Transformative Ocean Governance Research – Reflections of Early Career Researchers' (2022) 79 ICES Journal of Marine Science 2163; J Hills and P Maharaj, 'Designing Transdisciplinarity for Transformative Ocean Governance' (2023) 10 Frontiers in Marine Sciences 1.

[46] The premise of the funding source was quite innovative in setting out that researchers were expected to take stock of the limitations of previous development cooperation approaches and engage explicitly in conversations on fairness in research collaborations with partners in the Global South. UKRI, 'GCRF Global Interdisciplinary Research Hubs' (*UK Research and Innovation*, 13 March 2023) <https://www.ukri.org/publications/gcrf-global-interdisciplinary-research-hubs/> (last accessed 1 June 2025).

The Hub brought together ocean-dependent people, decision-makers, and civil society in Ghana, Namibia and South Africa, and academic researchers from these countries, the UK and the two regional universities in the Caribbean and South Pacific. In addition, the Hub included legal officers from UN bodies: the UN Environment Programme, the UN Division on Ocean Affairs and the Law of the Sea, the UN Development Programme, the Food and Agriculture Organization of the UN and the Convention on Biological Diversity.[47] Over time, the One Ocean Hub also worked closely with the Office of the High Commissioner for Human Rights and several UN Special Rapporteurs, particularly on Environment and Human Rights, Climate Change and the Right to Food. The Hub, therefore, was conceived as an ambitious attempt to co-develop knowledge across disciplines in different sectors and at different scales (global-local) to address multiple challenges to ocean health that undermine multiple Sustainable Development Goals (SDGs), while developing capacities and approaches to value, and learn from, different knowledge systems and voices at different scales. This was considered necessary to respond more holistically to the cumulative challenges facing marine ecosystems and undermining their multiple contributions to sustainable development.

The Hub research design, and model for research partnerships with all these diverse actors, was framed by international law scholarship and included explicit commitments to contribute to the mutually supportive and evolutive interpretation of international environmental law, the law of the sea and international human rights law in the light of co-produced knowledge on local experiences of lack of sustainability and injustices, interdisciplinary scientific evidence and Indigenous science and local knowledge systems. Specifically, the Hub aimed to develop a mutually supportive interpretation of the ecosystem-based approach under international environmental law and the human rights–based approaches for enhancing the effectiveness and fairness of the implementation of the law of the sea. This was with a view to supporting the implementation of the law of the sea to address multiple and cumulative threats: ocean plastics; ownership, tenure, stewardship and benefit-sharing of ocean space and resources; sustainable renewables and tourism development; climate change responses and disaster risk reduction. To that end, the One Ocean Hub was conceived as the first attempt to test the potential of

[47] One Ocean Hub, 'About Us' (*One Ocean Hub*, 2024) <https://oneoceanhub.org/> (last accessed 1 June 2025).

the Framework Principles on Human Rights and the Environment developed by the UN Special Rapporteur on Human Rights and the Environment, John Knox,[48] to guide the development of coherent, pro-poor, gender-sensitive, climate-proofed and transparent frameworks for ocean management across these sectors.

The Hub took as interdisciplinary research questions to what extent international law on the marine environment is a governance problem, why this is the case and who (among humans and across the marine environment) is most affected by it.[49] Those interdisciplinary research questions were, in turn, meant to allow the Hub to test the extent to which international law can overcome its perceived limits to address intractable challenges through creative reading of existing legal instruments and legal forecasting,[50] based on the understanding arising from the social and marine sciences research, as well as diverse knowledge systems. For instance, what is the potential of legal processes on public consultations, from the local to the international level, to truly take into account the lived experiences, needs, aspirations, distinct knowledge systems and human rights of Indigenous peoples and other ocean-dependent communities, as well as rural women and children, as they are developed and run in ways that are inherently limiting and disempowering.[51]

The underlying intuition was that the way science and evidence are produced to support future decision-making on the ocean (but also other areas of the global and national sustainable development agendas) is where one needs to ensure genuine co-development by different knowledge holders. Without a co-developed integrated evidence base, it is much harder for ocean decision-makers to consider and understand the perspectives of those that are usually not represented in scientific

[48] Framework Principles on Human Rights and the Environment (n 30).

[49] D Wilson, 'European Colonisation, Law, and Indigenous Marine Dispossession: Historical Perspectives on the Construction and Entrenchment of Unequal Marine Governance' (2021) 20 Maritime Studies 387; A Christoffels-DuPlessis et al, 'Navigating a Sea of Laws: The Quests of Small-scale Fishing Communities in Ghana and South Africa for Protecting their Customary Rights' in R Bosewell, D O' Kane and J Hills (eds), *The Palgrave Handbook of Blue Heritage* (Palgrave 2022) 325.

[50] N Walker, *Intimations of Global Law* (Cambridge University Press 2014); Kulovesi, Mehling and Morgera (n 37) 434.

[51] D Lupin Townsend, 'Silencing, Consultation and Indigenous Descriptions of the World' (2019) 10 JHRE 193; D Lupin and L Townsend, 'The Right to Consultation Is a Right to Be Heard' in D Lupin (ed), *A Research Agenda for Human Rights and the Environment* (Edward Elgar 2023) 103.

knowledge production, and therefore to give due consideration to their insights on ocean health and human well-being. In other words, without the inclusion of human rights holders and diverse knowledge holders in the production of evidence base, the opportunities to protect their human rights in decision-making are drastically reduced. On the other hand, relying on the recognition in international law of the interdependence of a healthy environment (including a healthy ocean) and basic human needs (protected as human rights)[52] – as a matter of international law interpretation and research design – served to underscore the need for researchers to engage in inter- and transdisciplinary practices. In turn, integrated evidence from inter- and transdisciplinary research supports decision-makers to prioritize and take action on, as a matter of international law, key findings from the marine and social sciences that aligned in showing how to protect the marine environment with clear benefits for the protection of basic human needs. As part of this process, international law scholarship, particularly focused on treaty interpretation, contributed to build the capacity of different sectors of society (small-scale fishers, Indigenous Peoples, rural women, children, and researchers themselves) to demand legal protection for the ocean and their ocean-dependent human rights and to clarify the corresponding duties of public authorities.[53]

The ultimate assumption of the One Ocean Hub was that the interpretation of international law, in a dialogue with marine and social sciences research co-developed with diverse knowledge holders and human rights holders, could contribute to transformation[54] – the shift

[52] UNGA, 'Res 76/300: The Human Right to a Clean, Healthy and Sustainable Environment' (1 August 2022) UN Doc A/RES/76/300; HRC, 'Report of the UN Special Rapporteur (J Knox) on the Issue of Human Rights Obligations relating to the Enjoyment of a Safe, Clean, Healthy and Sustainable Environment' (19 January 2017) UN Doc A/HRC/34/49.

[53] E Webster and E Morgera, 'Transformative Capacity Building around a Right to Healthy Environment: What Role for Dignity as a Human Rights Value?' (2021) 9 Griffith Journal of Law and Human Dignity 55.

[54] UN Ocean Conference, 'Our Ocean, our Future, our Responsibility: Draft Declaration' (17 June 2022) UN Doc A/Conf.230/2022/12; UNGA, 'Transforming our World: the 2030 Agenda for Sustainable Development' (21 October 2015) UN Doc A/RES/70/1; IPCC, 'Special Report on the Impacts of Global Warming of 1.5°C above Pre-industrial Levels and Related Global Greenhouse Gas Emission Pathways, in the Context of Strengthening the Global Response to the Threat of Climate Change, Sustainable Development, and Efforts to Eradicate Poverty' (2018) <https://www.ipcc.ch/site/assets/uploads/sites/2/2022/06/SR15_Full_Report_HR.pdf> (last accessed 1 June 2025); IPBES, 'Global Assessment Report of the Intergovernmental Science-Policy Platform on

away 'from the technocratic and regulatory fix of environmental problems to more fundamental and transformative changes in social-political processes and economic relations'[55] – in ocean governance at different scales.[56] Here the overarching research question was how to interpret – to the full extent of their potential – provisions in international environmental law, the law of the sea and international human rights law[57] to identify 'solutions that also have sustainable impacts at other scales and in other sectors' and 'empower those whose interests are currently not being met and represent transformative sustainability values'.[58]

To close the circle, transformation is understood to require *transdisciplinary* governance – the recognition of different knowledge systems and the inclusion of underrepresented types of knowledge in decision-making processes.[59] International environmental law, to some extent, and international human rights law already recognize the need to recognize and integrate Indigenous and local knowledge,[60] but much remains to be clarified about how to genuinely and respectfully do so, while preventing a shifting of the burden of response onto the vulnerable and addressing issues of power and legitimacy.[61] These were further research questions that shaped the design and practices of the One Ocean Hub and shed light on the topicality of interpretation across international environmental law, the law of the sea and international human rights law to support transdisciplinarity as an essential precondition for transformation.

Biodiversity and Ecosystem Services' (2019) <https://www.ipbes.net/global-assessment> (last accessed 1 June 2025); CBD, 'Decision XV/4: Kunming-Montreal Global Biodiversity Framework' (19 December 2022) UN Doc CBD/COP/DEC/15/4.

55 I Visseren-Hamakers and M Kok, 'Introduction' in I Visseren-Hamakers and M Kok (eds), *Transforming Biodiversity Governance* (Cambridge University Press 2022) 3.

56 Erinosho et al (n 4) 331.

57 E Morgera et al, 'Legal Note: The Request for an Advisory Opinion from the International Court of Justice on the Obligations of States in Respect of Climate Change' (*One Ocean Hub*, 22 March 2024) <https://oneoceanhub.org/publications/legal-note-the-request-for-an-advisory-opinion-from-the-international-court-of-justice-on-the-obligations-of-states-inrespect-of-climate-change/> (last accessed 1 June 2025).

58 Visseren-Hamakers and Kok (n 55) 10–11.

59 ibid.

60 E.g. Convention on Biological Diversity (adopted 5 June 1992, entered into force 29 December 1993) 1760 UNTS 79 art 8(j) and 10(c) (CBD); Paris Agreement (adopted 12 December 2015, entered into force 4 November 2016) 3156 UNTS 79, art 7(5); Agreement under the United Nations Convention on the Law of the Sea on the Conservation and Sustainable Use of Marine Biological Diversity of Areas beyond National Jurisdiction (adopted 19 June 2023, not yet in force) UN Doc A/CONF.232/2023/4, art. 5(i) (BBNJ Agreement).

61 Erinosho et al (n 4) 328.

Transdisciplinarity, as mentioned above, requires engaging with and recognizing the value of non-academic experts, and from an interpretation perspective, this specifically requires engaging with understandings of the law and its underpinnings from legal professionals outside academia (such as UN officers, or lawyers working in NGOs) as well as with Indigenous peoples and local community representatives or children. These were the non-judicial actors that, together with legal scholars, contributed to the co-development of mutually supportive interpretations under the One Ocean Hub.

8.4 The Role of Non-judicial Actors

There is already a significant body of literature on the practices and importance of interpretation 'from below' in international human rights law,[62] in particular with a view to overcoming colonial legacies and preventing cultural impositions. These interpretative debates, however, remain limited in international environmental law and even more so in the law of the sea. It has thus been the area of cross-fertilization between international environmental law and international human rights law that initially created a space for shared scholarship on the importance of interpretation from below, notably with a focus on Indigenous Peoples' human rights.[63]

On the one hand, these mutually supportive interpretation efforts serve to identify and address blind spots and limitations in the State-centric international environmental law, notably with regard to indeterminate environmental obligations with a very wide margin of discretion and an apparent lack of procedural guarantees.[64] A paradigmatic example is that of obligations to carry out environmental impact assessments, which can be found in general international law,[65] as well as international biodiversity law[66] and

[62] J Ilfe, *Human Rights from Below* (Cambridge University Press 2012); L Cotula and E Webster, 'COVID-19 and the Sites of Rights Resilience' (*University of Strathclyde Law School Blog*, 2020) <https://www.strath.ac.uk/humanities/lawschool/blog/covid-19andthesitesofrightsresilience/> (last accessed 1 June 2025).

[63] Morgera (n 27) 106–18.

[64] ibid 102.

[65] *Case Concerning Pulp Mills on the River Uruguay* (*Argentina v Uruguay*) (Judgment) [2010] ICJ Rep 14 [204].

[66] CBD (n 60) art 14; N Craik, 'Environmental Impact Assessment' in E Morgera and J Razzaque (eds), *Encyclopedia of Environmental Law: Biodiversity and Nature Protection Law* (Edward Elgar 2017) 431.

the law of the sea.[67] These obligations have been considered so general by the International Court of Justice that the precise content and process of an environmental impact assessment (EIA) was considered a matter left to the State's discretion.[68] The ICJ, however, in reaching this conclusion, did not consider that the 196 CBD Parties had already clarified, by consensus, the content and process of an EIA to a significant degree.[69] In addition, in a separate decision, the International Court of Justice (ICJ) had interpreted the wording of the applicable CBD provision on EIA as not even giving rise to a legally binding obligation, because of the vagueness of its formulation.[70] Instead, in my previous legal research, I had contended that the CBD wording[71] only opens up a margin of discretion for different parties to decide how (not whether) to implement such duty.[72] This margin of discretion is further limited by the joint reading of States' obligations to prevent negative impacts on the marine environment under their

[67] United Nations Convention on the Law of the Sea (adopted 10 December 1982, entered into force 16 November 1994) 1833 UNTS 3 art 206 (UNCLOS).

[68] *Pulp Mills on the River Uruguay* (n 65) [205].

[69] CBD, 'Decision VIII/28: Voluntary Guidelines on Biodiversity-Inclusive Impact Assessment' (9 January 2006) UN Doc UNEP/CBD/COP/8/27/Add.2; CBD, 'Decision XI/18: Marine and Coastal Biodiversity: Sustainable Fisheries and Addressing Adverse Impacts of Human Activities, Voluntary Guidelines for Environmental Assessment, and Marine Spatial Planning' (5 December 2012) UN Doc UNEP/CBD/COP/DEC/XI/18, 7–8 'Section B. Voluntary Guidelines for the Consideration of Biodiversity in Environmental Impact Assessments and Strategic Environmental Assessments in Marine and Coastal Areas'; CBD, 'Decision VII/16: Article 8(j) and Related Provisions' (13 April 2004) UN Doc UNEP/CBD/COP/DEC/VII/16, 10 ff 'Section F: Akwé Kon – Voluntary Guidelines for the Conduct of Cultural, Environmental and Social Impact Assessment regarding Developments Proposed to Take Place on, or which are Likely to Impact on, Sacred Sites and on Lands and Waters Traditionally Occupied or Used by Indigenous and Local Communities'.

[70] *Certain Activities Carried Out by Nicaragua in the Border Area (Costa Rica v Nicaragua) and Construction of a Road in Costa Rica along the San Juan River (Nicaragua v Costa Rica)* (Judgment) [2015] ICJ Rep 665 [164].

[71] The obligation contained in CBD art 14 ('shall') is qualified by the words 'as far as possible and as appropriate' – a qualification common in other international biodiversity-related conventions. The High Court of Australia in High Court of Australia, *Commonwealth v Tasmania* (1983) HCA 21 – 158 CLR 1 [24] looked at similarly qualified language in arts 4 and 5 of the Word Heritage Convention.

[72] E Morgera, 'Biodiversity as a Human Right and its Implications for the EU's External Action' (*European Parliament*, 2020) <https://www.europarl.europa.eu/RegData/etudes/STUD/2020/603491/EXPO_STU(2020)603491_EN.pdf> (last accessed 1 June 2025); See also S Maljean-Dubois and E Morgera, 'International Biodiversity Litigation: The Increasing Emphasis on Biodiversity Law before International Courts and Tribunals' in G Futhazar, S Maljean-Dubois and J Razzaque (eds), *Biodiversity Litigation* (Oxford University Press 2022) 331.

jurisdiction, pursuant to the law of the sea[73] and on human rights arising from biodiversity degradation under international biodiversity law and international human rights law.[74] Hub research expanded this argument, by showing how diffuse environmental harm and degradation of nature's benefits to human well-being (which could be considered foreseeable negative impacts on human rights), as well as historical evidence on marginalization from decision-making and current disregard for cultural rights linked to the effective protection of the marine environment, were routinely left out of EIAs.[75] A mutually supportive interpretation of international biodiversity law, the law of the sea and international human rights law, therefore, served to identify some minimum content for the EIA obligation, which allowed to take into account the findings from the marine sciences about environmental blind spots in current EIA practices, as well as social sciences findings about negative impacts on human rights.[76] This interpretation finds resonance in the 2023 Agreement on the Conservation and Sustainable Use of Marine Biological Diversity of Areas beyond National Jurisdiction, which requires States to carry out EIAs[77] in order to duly consider 'consequences of climate change, ocean acidification and related impacts',[78] as well as 'economic, social, cultural and human health impacts'.[79] This is therefore an example in which mutually supportive interpretations contribute to the evolutive and effective interpretation of the law of the sea, by providing more normative detail to generic terms, with a view to better achieving interdependent treaty objectives in the light of new (natural and social) scientific evidence, local intergenerational

[73] See UNCLOS (n 67) art 206 and the other general provisions under Part XII UNCLOS on the protection and preservation of the marine environment. See also other international law instruments including, amongst others, UNFSA.

[74] For a summary of relevant international legal bases, see Framework Principles on Human Rights and the Environment (n 30) Principles 8 and 15.

[75] McGarry (n 6).

[76] J Nakamura, D Diz and E Morgera, 'International Legal Requirements for Environmental and Socio-cultural Assessments for Large-scale Industrial Fisheries' (2022) 31 RECIEL 336.

[77] BBNJ Agreement (n 60) art 28.

[78] ibid, art 1(6). The obligation to assess the 'cumulative impact' is expressly envisaged in the provision regarding, e.g., the scoping of EIAs, namely art 31(1)(b) BBNJ Agreement. This has further implications with respect to the protection of human rights. E Morgera et al, 'Addressing the Ocean-Climate Nexus in the BBNJ Agreement: Strategic Environmental Assessments, Human Rights and Equity in Ocean Science' (2023) 38 IJMCL 447.

[79] BBNJ Agreement (n 60) art 31(1)(b) as part of the broad notion of 'cumulative impacts' within the meaning of art 1(6) of the BBNJ Agreement.

experiences of lack of sustainability and injustices, and Indigenous Peoples' and local knowledge systems.

Such a mutually supportive interpretation is innovative because while human rights and the environment has been a well-established area of international law scholarship since the 1990s,[80] it has mainly focused on land-based issues and more recently on climate change.[81] Instead, little attention has been paid until very recently to human rights issues related to the protection of the marine environment, in particular of marine areas beyond national jurisdiction.[82] The case of the human rights dimensions of deep-seabed mining are quite instructive in this respect: international law scholarship started raising these questions only in 2019 from an Indigenous Peoples' human rights perspective,[83] and in 2022 from a general human rights perspective,[84] with the UN Human Rights Office issuing a note in 2023.[85] These interpretative developments can be explained on the basis of the emerging marine biodiversity evidence on the irreversible environmental impacts of deep-seabed

[80] E.g. AE Boyle and MR Anderson (eds), *Human Rights Approaches to Environmental Protection* (Oxford University Press 1996).

[81] E.g. AE Boyle, 'Climate Change, The Paris Agreement and Human Rights' (2018) 67 ICLQ 759.

[82] E Morgera, 'The Relevance of the Human Right to Science for the Conservation and Sustainable Use of Marine Biodiversity of Areas Beyond National Jurisdiction: A New Legally Binding Instrument to Support Co-Production of Ocean Knowledge across Scales' in V de Lucia, A Oude Elferink and L Ngoc Nguyen (eds), *International Law and Marine Areas beyond National Jurisdiction: Reflections on Justice, Space, Knowledge and Power* (Brill 2022) 242; R Albar, 'Common Heritage of Mankind at the Expense of Indigenous People's Rights? BBNJ Treaty and Beyond' (*HHRJ*, 25 October 2023) <https://journals.law.harvard.edu/hrj/2023/10/common-heritage-of-mankind-at-the-expense-of-indigenous-peoples-rights-bbnj-treaty-and-beyond/> (last accessed 1 June 2025).

[83] J Aguon and J Hunter, 'Second Wave Due Diligence: The Case for Incorporating Free, Prior, and Informed Consent into the Deep-Sea Mining Regulatory Regime' (2019) 38 Stanford EnvtlLJ 3. See also 'International Laws Public and Private in Memory of Karen Knop' Symposium, available in AJIL-Unbound <https://www.cambridge.org/core/journals/american-journal-of-international-law/ajil-unbound-by-symposium/international-laws-public-and-private-in-memory-of-karen-knop> (last accessed 1 June 2025).

[84] G Hamley, 'The Implications of Seabed Mining in the Area for the Human Right to Health' (2022) 31 RECIEL 389; E Morgera and H Lily, 'Public Participation at the International Seabed Authority: An International Human Rights Law Analysis' (2022) 31 RECIEL 374.

[85] OHCHR, 'Key Human Rights Considerations on the Impact of Seabed Mining' (2023) <https://www.ohchr.org/sites/default/files/documents/issues/climatechange/information-materials/ohchr-seabed-mining-10-july.pdf> (last accessed 1 June 2025).

mining[86] and social science research and Indigenous knowledge[87] on the importance of the deep seabed for humankind.

As part of this ongoing process of cross-fertilization with these areas of international law, the One Ocean Hub researchers partnered with different UN bodies, whose mandates focused on human rights, the environment and the ocean, respectively. The partnership meant discussing research questions with UN officers to make sure that research findings could contribute to ongoing international negotiations or UN-led legal advisory and capacity-building initiatives to support the implementation of international law and guidelines at the national level. Interestingly, through these conversations, it also became clear which international law interpretation questions were identified but could not be investigated by UN officers themselves, either for lack of research time and resources, or for the risk of appearing to overstep their mandate. For instance, fully understanding the extent of the human rights–based approach to small-scale fisheries, particularly in as far as it related also to cultural rights and intangible ocean cultural heritage, required a new joint effort between Hub researchers, the Food and Agriculture Organization (FAO) and the Office of the High Commissioner for Human Rights (OHCHR), with the two UN bodies collaborating for the first time on that topic.[88] In particular, social sciences and art-based participatory research in South Africa served to shed a light on the lack of understanding and consideration of intangible cultural and spiritual connection of certain Indigenous Peoples with the seabed. This in turn led to a disregard for their procedural rights in decision-making processes on offshore oil and gas exploration that would negatively impact also on their fishing activities and human right to food.[89] These considerations, in addition, revealed the need to consider and protect the human rights of fishers also in the context of the conservation and management of marine areas beyond national jurisdiction, including from a climate change

[86] E.g. E Simon-Lledó et al, 'Biological Effects 26 Years after Simulated Deep-Sea Mining' (2019) 9 Scientific Reports 8040.

[87] M Mtombheni et al, 'Deep Sea Decisions can Consider Indigenous Knowledge' (*360 Info*, 2023) <https://360info.org/deep-sea-decisions-can-consider-indigenous-knowledge/> (last accessed 1 June 2025).

[88] FAO, One Ocean Hub and Office of the High Commissioner for Human Rights, 'Policy Brief: Applying Coherently the Human Rights-based Approach to Small-scale Fisheries for Achieving Multiple Sustainable Development Goals' (2023) <https://www.fao.org/3/cc3251en/cc3251en.pdf> (last accessed 1 June 2025).

[89] McGarry (n 6).

perspective.[90] Conversely, it was difficult for FAO to integrate human rights considerations in its role as one of the relevant UN agencies involved in the development and implementation of the WTO Fisheries Subsidies Agreement.[91] So, an independent academic reflection on the need to interpret that Agreement and shape its implementation in accordance with the protection of human rights, including the human rights of small-scale fishers, was necessary. Such academic reflection allowed to carefully identify the role of FAO in supporting the human rights–based approach as part of its capacity-building mandate vis-à-vis States,[92] as opposed to a monitoring approach that would appear more appropriate for international human rights treaty bodies.

The collaboration between international law scholars and marine scientists under the One Ocean Hub was also distinctly instructive in supporting a mutually supportive interpretation between international biodiversity law, the law of the sea and international human rights law. Fisheries sciences experts were developing an evidence base of collapsing fisheries, and tools for the government to manage enhanced risks for the conservation and sustainable use of marine biodiversity due to other pressures, exacerbated by climate change. In addition, deep-sea biodiversity scientists clarified the current state of knowledge of the state and functioning of life in the depths of the marine environment, as well as the limitations of such knowledge that provide grounds for precautionary approach. Finally, ecosystem services research provided the essential bridging evidence between the knowledge of the functions of marine life and its complexes and benefits to human well-being (nutrition, health, cultural and spiritual well-being, purification of water and air, and resilience to climate change)[93]. In other words, ecosystem services research explained how and to what extent a healthy ocean contributes to the protection of a variety of human rights. At the same time, collaboration

[90] J Nakamura et al, 'International Legal Responses for Protecting Fishers' Fundamental Rights Impacted by a Changing Ocean' (2023) 38 IJMCL 516.

[91] S Switzer, E Morgera and E Webster, 'Casting the Net Wider? The Transformative Potential of Integrating Human Rights into the Implementation of the WTO Agreement on Fisheries Subsidies' (2022) 31 RECIEL 360.

[92] One Ocean Hub, 'Policy Brief: The Implementation of the WTO Fisheries Subsidies Agreement should Support the Human Rights of Small-Scale Fisheries' (2023) <https://oneoceanhub.org/wp-content/uploads/2023/10/Policy-Brief-WTO-Fisheries-Subsidies_26.10.23.pdf> (last accessed 1 June 2025).

[93] Millenium Ecosystem Assessment, 'Living Beyond Our Means: Natural Assets and Human Wellbeing' (2005) <https://documents1.worldbank.org/curated/en/366241468134713390/pdf/453520WP0BOX0334087B01PUBLIC1.pdf> (last accessed 1 June 2025).

between international law scholars and marine scientists allowed to identify blind spots in the production of natural science evidence in terms of assumptions about undifferentiated human needs and vulnerabilities, as well as the limited capacity to integrate cultural rights or diverse knowledge systems within current methods for assessing, mapping and modelling impacts and responses for the protection of the marine environment.[94]

Marine science experts were quite familiar with international environmental law concepts related to precaution and the ecosystem approach but were generally unaware of the connections between these concepts and international human rights law.[95] In effect, the interpretative efforts of the 196 Parties to the CBD had already clarified that the ecosystem approach entails understanding and factoring in societal choices, rights and interests of Indigenous Peoples and local communities, along with intrinsic as well as tangible and intangible values attached to biodiversity, ultimately leading to a balance between local interests and the wider public interest. It also entails ensuring appropriate representation of community interests in the decision-making process.[96] Instead, marine scientists generally saw their role as carrying out technical stakeholder consultations for the purposes of gaining social traction of their findings, while for their part they felt an obligation to treat all groups (be they large-scale business as opposed to subsistence fishers) equally despite power imbalances and differentiated vulnerabilities to environmental impacts. As a result, their evidence base and tools for decision-making would not support decision-makers to fulfil their international human rights obligations in the context of the protection of the marine environment. This is because such evidence did not include disaggregated data analysis, consideration of differentiated impacts on different sectors of society and an effort to prioritize the needs of the most vulnerable as part of ensuring environmental sustainability of ocean use or marine conservation.

The collaboration between international law scholars and social scientists, notably experts in educational sociology, ethnographic sociology,

[94] K Erwin et al, '*Lalela uLwandle*: An Experiment in Plural Governance Discussions' in R Bosewell, D O' Kane and J Hills (eds), *The Palgrave Handbook of Blue Heritage* (Palgrave 2022) 383.

[95] HRC (n 52); E Morgera, 'The Ecosystem Approach and the Precautionary Principle' in E Morgera and J Razzaque (eds), *Encyclopedia of Environmental Law: Biodiversity and Nature Protection Law* (Edward Elgar 2017) 70.

[96] CBD, 'Decision VII/11: Ecosystem Approach' (13 April 2004) UN Doc UNEP/CBD/COP/DEC/VII/11 [9, 11].

anthropology, human geography, history and political ecology, as well as art-based participatory research approaches, was crucial to understand lived experiences, living memories, the existence of distinctive knowledge systems[97] and the differentiated impacts of the degradation of ocean health and the modalities and impacts of exclusionary ocean research and governance practices on human rights holders. In other words, it allowed all researchers to realize where their own assumptions and the scope of their work had prevented consideration of relevant human rights and how to ensure the protection of persons against negative consequences of their scientific research or its applications on the environment.[98] Further, earlier social sciences research on ocean-dependent communities, small-scale fisheries, environmental justice issues and exclusion in decision-making also revealed itself essential to ground the design and planning of transdisciplimary research, with a view to ensuring contextualization and avoiding 'parachute science'.[99] It also served to build or enhance the understanding and capacity of other researchers, from law and the marine sciences, to relate their own work to the local context and identify potential areas of interdisciplinary collaboration across the team. This allowed researchers to ensure that priorities for scientific research should focus on key issues for the most vulnerable and strive towards scientific progress that is critical to the enjoyment of the human right to health and other economic, social and cultural rights.[100] These approaches were then essential to engage in a respectful way and ensure mutual learning and knowledge co-development with human rights holders themselves, without creating new exclusion or injustices in the context of other research under the One Ocean Hub.[101]

[97] McGarry (n 92); McGarry (n 6); Mtombheni et al (n 87).

[98] This is one dimension of the human right to science: UNGA, 'Report of the Special Rapporteur in the Field of Cultural Rights, Farida Shaheed: the Right to Enjoy the Benefits of Scientific Progress and its Applications' (14 May 2012) UN Doc A/HRC/20/26.

[99] C Watson, 'Parachute Science Falls to Earth' (*Nature Index*, 13 April 2021) <https://www.nature.com/nature-index/news/parachute-science-falls-to-earth> (last accessed 1 June 2025).

[100] These are dimensions of the human right to science. UNGA (n 98); UN Committee on Economic, Social and Cultural Rights, 'General Comment No 25 (2020) on Science and Economic, Social and Cultural Rights (Article 15(1)(b), (2), (3) and (4) of the International Covenant on Economic, Social and Cultural Rights' (30 April 2020) UN Doc E/C.12/GC/25.

[101] Pereira and Erwin (n 6).

In particular, environmental justice scholarship from the Global South[102] provides a plural and contextually located approach to contrast Western ways of thinking and doing,[103] which are underlined by a perception that humans and other species of plants and animals are distinct and separate, on a universal scale.[104] This area of scholarship unveils how today's environmental injustices are profoundly shaped by persistent colonial legacies[105] and intertwined global and local power imbalances arising from competing economic interests, exploitative processes and inequality, which are increasing embodied in growing demand for marine resources, globally and nationally.[106] Environmental justice scholarship from the Global South also critically reflects on how 'these dominant frameworks frequently draw on science as the only legitimate form of knowledge for understanding our natural environments and developing related policies and regulations. This can inadvertently delegitimize and exclude other ways of knowing and living with the natural world, such as Indigenous science and local knowledge.'[107] The dialogue with environmental justice scholars from the Global South, including their praxis as researchers and human rights advocates working in solidarity with human rights holders, supported imaginative thinking on alleviating planetary harms and socio-cultural and economic injustices[108] and fed into interpretative efforts at the intersection of international environmental law, international human rights law and the law of the sea.

In particular, social sciences and art-based participatory research in South Africa served to shed a light on the lack of understanding and consideration

102 The remainder of the paragraph builds on D McGarry, K Erwin and E Morgera, 'What Is Environmental Justice: Understandings from the Global South' (*One Ocean Hub*, 2023) <https://oneoceanhub.org/publications/infosheet-what-is-environmental-justice-understandings-from-the-global-south/> (last accessed 1 June 2025).

103 L Álvarez and B Coolsaet, 'Decolonizing Environmental Justice Studies: A Latin American Perspective' (2020) 31 Capitalism Nature Socialism 50.

104 T Morton, *Ecology without Nature: Rethinking Environmental Aesthetics* (Harvard University Press 2009).

105 A Arowolo and O Lalude, '"Their Color Is a Diabolic Die," Colonialism and the State of Environmental Justice in Africa' (2022) 4 Society & Sustainability 1.

106 N Bennett et al, 'Blue Growth and Blue Justice: Ten Risks and Solutions for the Ocean Economy' (2021) 125 Marine Policy 104387; N Bennett et al, 'Towards a Sustainable and Equitable Blue Economy' (2019) Nature Sustainability 991; HJ Niner et al, 'Issues of Context, Capacity and Scale: Essential Conditions and Missing Links for a Sustainable Blue Economy' (2022) 130 Environmental Science and Policy 25.

107 McGarry, Erwin and Morgera (n 102).

108 N Singh, 'Environmental Justice, Degrowth and Post-Capitalist Futures' (2019) 163 Ecological Economics 138.

of intangible cultural and spiritual connection of certain Indigenous peoples with the seabed. This in turn led to a disregard for their procedural rights in decision-making processes on offshore oil and gas exploration that would negatively impact also on their fishing activities and human right to food. These approaches place the experiences, needs, knowledge and human rights of local actors at the outset as a way to interrogate different meanings of international law, to identify how to best respond to local understandings of sustainability and justice, as well as be aligned with the natural sciences evidence and, on that basis, assess whether national law was in compliance with the underlying international treaties.[109]

Over time, this approach allowed the Hub to contribute to the development of new international interpretative guidance on the human rights of the child and a healthy environment,[110] as well as integrate such interpretation in ongoing research efforts.[111] Hub interdisciplinary research on the importance of marine biodiversity for children's human rights, including their right to development and culture,[112] as well as on the importance of a healthy ocean for climate change mitigation and adaptation[113] and insights arising from partnerships with children rights

[109] This was embedded in the design suggested by Taryn Pereira and Kira Erwin for a joint FAO-One Ocean Hub regional workshop on the national implementation of the SSF Guidelines in 2021. S Febrica, 'The Food and Agriculture Organization and the One Ocea Hub Co-organized a Workshop on Sustainable Small-Scale Fisheries Law' (*One Ocean Hub*, 28 April 2021) <https://oneoceanhub.org/1939-2/> (last accessed 1 June 2025).

[110] Committee on the Rights of the Child, 'General Comment No 26 on Children's Rights and the Environment with a Special Focus on Climate Change' (22 August 2023) UN Doc CRC/C/GC/26.

[111] E Morgera and S Shields, 'Policy Brief: Integrating the General Comment 26 on Children's Rights and a Healthy Environment in the Implementation of the FAO Guidelines on Small-scale Fisheries' (*One Ocean Hub*, 5 February 2024) <https://oneoceanhub.org/wp-content/uploads/2024/02/Policy-Brief-integrating-the-general-comment.FAO-Guidelines-on-Small-scale-Fisheries_12.02.24_1.pdf> (last accessed 1 June 2025); E Morgera and S Shields, 'Policy Brief: Integrating the General Comment 26 on Children's Rights and a Healthy Environment in the Implementation of the Global Biodiversity Framework' (*One Ocean Hub*, 5 February 2024) <https://oneoceanhub.org/wp-content/uploads/2024/02/Policy-Brief-integrating-the-General-Comment-26-on-Childrens-Rights-.12.02.24_2-.pdf> (last accessed 1 June 2025).

[112] M Strand et al, 'Protecting Children's Rights to Development and Culture by Re-imagining "Ocean Literacies"' (2023) 31 International Journal of Children's Rights 941.

[113] E Morgera et al, 'Ocean-based Climate Action and Human Rights Implications under the International Climate Change Regime' (2023) 38 IJMCL 411; E Morgera and M Lennan, 'Strengthening Intergenerational Equity at the Ocean-Climate Nexus: Reflections on the UNCRC General Comment No 26' (2022) 52 EP&L 445.

organizations at the ocean-climate nexus,[114] were shared in various ways during the development of the 2023 UN General Comment on Children's Human Rights and the Environment, with a focus on Climate Change.[115] As a result, the General Comment clarifies that children's human right to a healthy environment includes obligations for States to take 'immediate action' to 'conserve, protect and restore biodiversity', 'prevent marine pollution, by banning the direct or indirect introduction of substances into the marine environment that are hazardous to children's health and marine ecosystems' and ' transform industrial fisheries to produce healthy and sustainable food aimed at preventing malnutrition and promoting children's growth and development'.[116] This guidance, therefore, enshrines a mutually supportive and evolutive interpretation of international human rights law, international biodiversity law, international climate change law and the law of the sea,[117] on the basis of new (natural and social) scientific evidence of the interdependence of their respective objectives as reflected in children's own understandings. Such a holistic interpretation of children's human right to a healthy environment has then supported further interpretative work by the One Ocean Hub, as part of international civil society networks advocating for the respect of children's human rights in the international climate change regime. This co-development led to the integration of interpretative arguments prioritizing ocean-based and other nature-based solutions to climate change,[118] as opposed to unproven and dangerous

[114] S Shields et al, 'Children's Human Right to Be Heard at the Ocean-Climate Nexus' (2023) 38 IJMCL 545.

[115] Initial written submissions; participation in thematic consultations, including co-leading a thematic consultation on biodiversity; and comments on the zero draft of the General Comment. See reflection and evidence in E Morgera and S Shields, 'UN Guidance on Children's Human Right to a Healthy Environment Calls for Protecting Marine Ecosystems, Transforming Industrial Fisheries, and Preventing Marine Pollution' (*One Ocean Hub*, 29 August 2023) <https://oneoceanhub.org/un-guidance-on-childrens-human-right-to-a-healthy-environment-calls-for-protecting-marine-ecosystems-transforming-industrial-fisheries-and-preventing-marine-pollution/> (last accessed 1 June 2025); E Morgera et al, 'The Ocean Is Included in the Zero Draft of the UN General Comment on Children's Rights to a Healthy Environment' (*One Ocean Hub*, 6 December 2022) <https://oneoceanhub.org/the-ocean-is-included-in-the-zero-draft-of-the-un-general-comment-on-childrens-rights-to-a-healthy-environment/>.

[116] Committee on the Rights of the Child (n 110) [65(c)–(f)].

[117] E Morgera, 'Re-imagining the Future of International Environmental Law through Children's Human Rights' (2023) 53 EP&L 307.

[118] Inputs of the Human Rights and Climate Change Working Group for CAN paper on nationally determined contributions guidelines (April 2024); One Ocean Hub,

technologies to mitigate climate change.[119] These contributions were in addition to interpretative arguments focused on enhanced social protection for children in the face of the negative impacts of climate change. These are further examples of mutually supportive interpretations based on international biodiversity law and international human rights law that underpin an evolutive interpretation of international law of the sea and international climate change law based on a new understanding of the interdependence of their respective objectives in the light of local experiences of lack of sustainability and injustices, interdisciplinary scientific evidence and Indigenous science and local knowledge systems.

8.5 Aligning Interpretative Efforts: The Case of Ocean Defenders

This section now delves into a particular area of co-development of a mutually supportive interpretation that emerged from the interactions among the non-judicial actors involved in the One Ocean Hub: the concept of 'ocean defenders' as part of environmental human rights defenders. Environmental human rights defenders were defined by former UN Special Rapporteur on Human Rights Defenders Michel Forst, as the individuals and communities that raise awareness about the negative impacts on human rights of unsustainable decisions on the environment.[120] Environmental human rights defenders are increasingly the object of (often lethal) attacks by governments or private actors, as well as harassment, denigration or side-lining.[121] They are recognized

'Contributing Views on Future Work of the Just Transition Work Programme of the UN Climate Change Convention and the 2024 Bonn Ocean-Climate Dialogue' (*One Ocean Hub*, 28 March 2024) <https://oneoceanhub.org/contributing-views-on-future-work-of-the-just-transition-work-programme-of-the-un-climate-change-convention-and-the-2024-bonn-ocean-climate-dialogue/> (last accessed 1 June 2025); Children's Environmental Rights Initiative, 'Centring Child Rights at COP28: Asks of UNFCCC Party Negotiators' (*Children's Environmental Right Initiative*, 2023) <https://ceri-coalition.org/wp-content/uploads/2023/11/CERI-Policy-Brief_Centring-Child-Rights-at-COP28.pdf> (last accessed 1 June 2025).

119 HRC Advisory Committee, 'Impact of New Technologies Intended for Climate Protection on the Enjoyment of Human Rights' (10 August 2023) UN Doc A/HRC/54/47.

120 ibid; see also HRC (n 52) [31–32, 68]; see also UNGA (n 30), Framework Principle 4.

121 Global Witness, 'Defending Tomorrow: The Climate Crisis and Threats Against Land and Environmental Defenders' (*Global Witness*, 29 July 2020) <https://www.globalwitness.org/en/campaigns/environmental-activists/defending-tomorrow> (last accessed 1 June 2025).

and studied as agents of change,[122] including for their role in preventing unsustainable and unjust uses of the environment that may lead to conflict.[123]

Environmental human rights defenders are entitled to all the rights and protections set out in the 1998 UN Declaration on the Right and Responsibility of Individuals, Groups and Organs of Society to Promote and Protect Universally Recognized Human Rights and Fundamental Freedoms (Declaration on Human Rights Defenders).[124] To respect defenders' human rights, States must ensure a safe and enabling environment for them to operate free from threats, harassment, intimidation and violence, including by providing appropriate training for security officials. Protection further entails publicly recognizing the contributions of defenders to society and ensuring that their work is not stigmatized.[125] Heightened levels of protection are needed for child defenders.[126]

As for other areas of cross-fertilization between international human rights law and international environmental law, however, international interpretative guidance on environmental human rights defenders has mainly focused on land-based issues, and in fact there are often references to 'land and environment human rights defenders'.[127] As a result,

[122] A Nah et al, 'A Research Agenda for the Protection of Human Rights Defenders' (2013) 5 JHRP 522.

[123] A Scheidel et al, 'Environmental Conflicts and Defenders: A Global Overview' (2020) 63 Global Environmental Change 102104.

[124] See also regional developments, such as Regional Agreement on Access to Information, Public Participation and Justice in Environmental Matters in Latin America and the Caribbean (adopted 4 March 2018, entered into force 22 April 2021) 3388 UNTS 195 (Escazú Agreement) art 9; UNECE, 'Decision VII/9 on a Rapid Response Mechanism to Deal with Cases Related to Article 3(8) of the Convention on Access to Information, Public Participation in Decision-making and Access to Justice in Environmental Matters' (18–20 October 2021) UN Doc ECE/MP.PP/2021/CRP.8.

[125] UNGA, 'Human Rights Defenders – Report of the Special Rapporteur (Margaret Sekaggya) on the Situation of Human Rights Defenders' (28 July 2011) UN Doc A/66/203; UNGA, 'Situation of Human Rights Defenders – Report of the Special Rapporteur (Michel Forst) on the Situation of Human Rights Defenders' (3 August 2016) UN Doc A/71/281.

[126] Committee on the Rights of the Child (n 110) [17]; L Lundy, *The Rights of Child Human Rights Defenders: Implementation Guide* (Child Rights Connect 2020).

[127] UNEP, 'Guidance Note for United Nations Resident Coordinators & Country Teams: Supporting Governments to better Respect, Promote and Protect Environmental Human Rights Defenders' (*UNEP*, November 2023) <https://www.unep.org/resources/policy-and-strategy/united-nations-guidance-note-environmental-human-rights-defenders> (last accessed 1 June 2025).

the specific challenges faced by ocean defenders[128] have not yet been specifically included in these interpretative efforts, which have very practical implications in terms of ensuring the prompt release of financial, legal and security support from UN country offices to defenders at risk. Nevertheless, One Ocean Hub researchers from an international law and social sciences background have contributed to UN consultations on this issue[129] and are collaborating with researchers and activists around the world to increase the documentation and understanding of the work and risks of ocean defenders.[130] They are also raising awareness among conservation organizations and marine scientists[131] about the significance of scientific evidence on environmental vulnerabilities and specific needs for environmental protection with demands for environmental protection of ocean defenders. These demands are based on their interconnected human rights to livelihoods, health and culture, and to a healthy ocean. In other words, innovative solidarity practices emerged

[128] Bennett et al (n 9); S Shields and E Morgera, 'Policy Brief: What Child Environmental Human Rights Defenders Need to Know to Defend and Protect a Healthy Ocean' (*One Ocean Hub*, 12 December 2023) <https://oneoceanhub.org/wp-content/uploads/2023/12/Policy-Brief-What-child-environmental-human-rights-defenders-need-to-know.12.12.23.pdf> (last accessed 1 June 2025).

[129] E Morgera, 'Contributing to the 2025 UN Call for Action on Human Rights with a Focus on Ocean Defenders' (*One Ocean Hub*, 23 October 2023) <https://oneoceanhub.org/contributing-to-the-un-call-for-action-on-human-rights-with-a-focus-on-ocean-defenders/> (last accessed 1 June 2025); E Morgera, 'Calling Attention to Children Ocean Defenders' (*One Ocean Hub*, 12 December 2023) <https://oneoceanhub.org/calling-attention-to-children-ocean-defenders/> (last accessed 1 June 2025); S Febrica, 'One Ocean Hub Highlights Role and Needs of Small-scale Fishers at UN Consultations on Environmental Human Rights Defenders' (*One Ocean Hub*, 28 May 2021) <https://oneoceanhub.org/one-ocean-hub-highlights-role-and-needs-of-small-scale-fishers-at-un-consultations-on-environmental-human-rights-defenders/> (last accessed 1 June 2025).

[130] S Febrica, 'Key Messages from the UNEP Winter/Summer School on Human Rights "From Oceans to Taps" (Part: 2) Children, Ocean Defenders, and Plastics' (*One Ocean Hub*, 30 August 2022) <https://oneoceanhub.org/key-messages-from-the-unep-winter-summer-school-on-human-rights-from-oceans-to-taps-part-2-children-ocean-defenders-and-plastics/> (last accessed 1 June 2025); The Ocean Defenders Project, 'Ocean Defenders at the Forefront of Efforts to Protect the Oceans Against Threats to the Marine Environment and Human Rights' (*The Ocean Defenders Project*, 2023) <https://oceandefendersproject.org> (last accessed 1 June 2025); see in particular, T Pereira, 'Ocean-defending Small-scale Fishers in South Africa say NO to Seismic Surveys' (*The Ocean Defenders Project*, 2023) <https://oceandefendersproject.org/case-study/no-to-seismic-surveys/> (last accessed 1 June 2025).

[131] T Pereira, 'Spotlighting Ocean Defenders and the Responsibilities of Marine Conservation Organizations' (*One Ocean Hub*, 12 December 2023) <https://oneoceanhub.org/spotlighting-ocean-defenders-and-the-responsibilities-of-marine-conservation-organizations/> (last accessed 1 June 2025).

in connecting different bodies of evidence (from within and outside academia), whereby natural science evidence aligned with ocean defenders' priorities in terms of environmental protection, and therefore also backing the protection of ocean-dependent human rights. In this case too, mutually supportive interpretations based on international biodiversity law and international law of the sea underpin an evolutive interpretation of international human rights law based on a novel understanding of the interdependence of their respective objects and purposes.

These inter- and transdisciplinary bases for mutually supportive interpretation have also been brought together into submissions to the three international tribunals requested to issue an advisory opinion on States' climate change obligations – the International Tribunal for the Law of the Sea,[132] the ICJ[133] and the Inter-American Court of Human Rights.[134] In all these submissions, mutually supportive interpretations drawing on the Hub's inter- and transdisciplinary research emphasized the need to understand States' obligations under the international climate change regime also in the light of the law of the sea, international biodiversity law and international human rights law, because of what biodiversity science shows about the role of the ocean in the global climate regulation, which is still overlooked[135] under the international climate change regime[136] and the social science evidence and views of ocean defenders,

[132] *Request for an Advisory Opinion Submitted by the Commission of Small Island States on Climate Change and International Law* (Advisory Opinion) 21 May 2024 <https://www.itlos.org/fileadmin/itlos/documents/cases/31/Advisory_Opinion/C31_Adv_Op_21.05.2024_corr.pdf> (last accessed 1 June 2025). In this case, the One Ocean Hub's independent submission was not considered an official part of the file but was published on the ITLOS website and considered by judges. See E Morgera, 'Written Statement of the One Ocean Hub to the International Tribunal for the Law of the Sea' (Statement not submitted Pursuant to Article 138(3) and 133(3) of the Rules of the Tribunal) (*One Ocean Hub*, 2023) <https://www.itlos.org/fileadmin/itlos/documents/cases/31/written_statements/4/C31-WS-4-10-OOH.pdf> (last accessed 1 June 2025).

[133] *Obligations of States in Respect of Climate Change* (Request for Advisory Opinion) General List No 187 (29 March 2023).

[134] *Request for an Advisory Opinion on the Climate Emergency and Human Rights submitted to the Inter-American Court of Human Rights by the Republic of Colombia and the Republic of Chile*, OC-32 (9 January 2023).

[135] Despite the 2022 recognition of the need to address ocean-based climate action under the Paris Agreement. UNFCCC, 'Glasgow Climate Pact' (13 November 2021) Decision 1/CMA.3. See initial discussion in M Lennan and E Morgera, 'The Glasgow Climate Conference (COP26)' (2022) 37 IJMCL 137.

[136] Morgera et al (n 113).

including child and young ocean defenders.[137] These submissions then included new interpretative arguments that State obligations across the treaties related to climate change, the sea, biodiversity and human rights imply a due diligence obligation to ensure the meaningful participation of ocean defenders in the design, implementation, financing, monitoring and review of climate, biodiversity and ocean policies, plans and actions, including 'just transition' or 'blue economy' policies, plans and actions, as well as marine protected areas and other marine conversation measures.[138] This was accompanied by another interpretative argument about the need for States, as part of their human rights obligations related to climate change, to protect ocean defenders that protest against deep-seabed mining.[139] The latter argument found support in statements made by the UN Special Rapporteur on Toxics and Human Rights and the Aarhus Convention Special Rapporteur on Defenders in March 2024 to the States members of the International Seabed Authority.[140]

8.6 Institutionalizing Treaty Interpretation Co-development under Existing Treaty Structures

There are opportunities as part of the implementation of treaties to advance these interpretations and in fact embed similar processes of interpretation co-development with ocean defenders as well as a range of diverse experts and knowledge holders, by re-imagining the composition and approaches of treaty-based implementation review bodies and/or technical and scientific advice committees.

137 One Ocean Hub, 'Children and Young Peoples' Human Rights to a Healthy Ocean' (*Youtube*, 12 November 2021) <https://www.youtube.com/watch?v=TVoF8hmSpEE&t=414s> (last accessed 1 June 2025); S Álvarez Peña et al, 'Youths Call for a Deep-Sea Mining Moratorium' (*Youth Policy Advisory Council of the Sustainable Ocean Alliance*, 22 September 2022).

138 A Malinde Lancaster et al, 'Joint Submission to the Inter-American Court of Human Rights' (*One Ocean Hub*, 18 December 2023) <https://oneoceanhub.org/wp-content/uploads/2024/02/Alana_Lancaster_Final-Updated-Joint-Submission-To-The-Inter-American-Court-Amicii-Of-The-FoL-OOH-RenewTT-GNHRE-Caribbean-ILA-Caribbean_12.02.24.pdf> (last accessed 1 June 2025).

139 ibid [62–63].

140 M Forst, 'Statement in Support of Ocean Defenders and Protest at Sea' (*Youtube*, 19 March 2024) <https://www.youtube.com/watch?v=AFCnFydWvic> (last accessed 1 June 2025); UN Human Rights – Meetings and Trainings, 'Special Rapporteur on Toxics and Human Rights, Mr Marcos Orellana' (*Youtube*, 19 March 2024) <https://www.youtube.com/watch?v=ZR5UZcQY6YM> (last accessed 1 June 2025).

Participatory governance and iterative learning from treaty implementation have already been considered in the literature on international environmental law as essential pre-conditions to ensure the effectiveness of certain treaty regimes because of the complexity of the subject matter and the need to understand different experiences of equity, as well as potential impacts across the biodiversity research, innovation and governance landscape.[141] Such an approach would be a departure from current practices focusing only on technical expertise and natural sciences background in subsidiary treaty bodies. Instead, the membership of these bodies could include experts from different communities of practices in the Global North and the Global South (scientists from different geographies and disciplines), notably with social scientists, Indigenous Peoples and local knowledge holders.[142] The role of social sciences experts would be essential to support the overcoming of stereotypes about the relevance and capacity of diverse knowledge holders to meaningfully contribute to international processes.[143]

This is also true for the genuine inclusion of children's voices in these processes,[144] which is something to which the whole UN Systems is committed to.[145] Along similar lines, UN General Comment No 26 also clarified that

> At the international level, States, intergovernmental organizations and international non-governmental organizations should facilitate the involvement of children's associations and child-led organizations or groups in environmental decision-making processes. States should ensure that their obligations concerning children's right to be heard are incorporated into international environmental decision-making processes, including in negotiations and the implementation of instruments of international environmental law. Efforts to enhance youth participation

[141] Morgera (n 32); S Leonelli and H Williamson, 'Introduction: Towards Responsible Plant Data Linkage' in H Williamson and S Leonelli (eds), *Towards Responsible Plant Data Linkage* (Springer, 2023) 1.

[142] The BBNJ Agreement includes some innovative provisions in terms of integrating Indigenous science and local knowledge in treaty bodies. BBNJ Agreement (n 60) arts 7, 13, 19, 21, 24, 26, 31–32, 35, 37, 41; see also Morgera et al (n 78).

[143] Lupin and Townsend, 'The Right to Consultation Is a Right to Be Heard' (n 51) 103, albeit referring to adult human rights-holders.

[144] Shields et al (n 114).

[145] UN, 'Step Up: A Joint Commitment by Heads of United Nations Entities to Promote the Right to a Healthy Environment of Children and their Participation in Climate Justice Decision-making at all Levels' (June 2021) <https://wedocs.unep.org/handle/20.500.11822/41648> (last accessed 1 June 2025).

in environmental decision-making processes should be inclusive of children.[146]

Methodologies developed by children's rights experts could be adapted to international treaty bodies,[147] with the benefit that these methodologies could also support transformative legal interpretation among adults,[148] as they rely on fun, play and arts[149] to challenge vested interests, power asymmetries and tendencies towards short-term decision-making.[150]

Thus re-conceived, these treaty-based review and advisory processes could support iterative interpretations of treaties in the light of changing scientific practices, scientific understandings of the status of the marine environment and the flow of its benefits to humankind, as well as evolving understanding of environmental sustainability and equity in the life experiences of ocean defenders. These treaty bodies could therefore integrate the insights from inter- and transdisciplinary dialogue into co-developed iterative interpretations of a treaty, which in turn would shape funding modalities, taking into account the range of needs of relevant human rights holders and setting research priorities to further support collaboration with diverse knowledge holders at national and local levels. They could also generally look at questions of efficacy together with questions of equity, with a view to suggesting clarifications in interpretation for the consideration by the governing body of the treaty. Given the need for systemic interpretation and joined-up implementation of treaties in the areas of climate change, biodiversity, the ocean and human rights, these subsidiary bodies could also maximize opportunities for regime interaction and cross-regime learning.[151]

146 ibid [28].

147 Shields et al (n 114) 14.

148 D McGarry, *Empathy in the Time of Ecological Apartheid: A Social Sculpture Practice-led Inquiry into Developing Pedagogies for Ecological Citizenship* (PhD Thesis, Rhodes University, South Africa 2014); C Wyborn et al, 'Imagining Transformative Biodiversity Futures' (2020) 3 Nature Sustainability 670.

149 LHV Wright, K Tisdall and N Moore, 'Taking Emotions Seriously: Fun and Pride in Participatory Research' (2021) 41 Emotion, Space and Society 100836; M Rosen, *Book of Play* (Profile Books 2020).

150 Shields et al (n 114) 560.

151 Morgera, Switzer, and Tsioumani (n 26); Morgera et al (n 78) 473–76. Developments in this direction can be found in BBNJ Agreement (n 60) arts 15(5), 22(3), 24(2), 26(2), 29 (2)–(3), 47(6)(c), 50(4)(d), 51(4), 55(4).

8.7 Conclusions

The triple planetary crisis (climate change, biodiversity loss and toxic pollution) and its multiple impacts on human well-being increasingly require evolutive and systemic[152] interpretation of State obligations across international environmental law, the law of the sea and international human rights law. Collective interpretative practices by non-judicial actors can support an understanding of how international law can effectively respond to these challenges, on the basis of the lived experiences of the most vulnerable human rights holders, across scales. This chapter calls attention towards inter- and transdisciplinary research projects as potentially fertile and flexible spaces for UN and other international bodies that provide advisory services to States on how to implement international law to co-identify critical legal questions and co-develop evolutive interpretative solutions with researchers in law, natural and social sciences and the arts, based on local-level experiences of lack of sustainability and injustices, interdisciplinary scientific evidence, Indigenous science and other knowledge systems.

These interpretative efforts can support national public authorities in ensuring the effectiveness of their treaties[153] and in shifting towards the transformation of environmental governance into more inclusive, sustainable and fair approaches that also contribute to the protection of human rights. Equally, they can support multilateral cooperation, and possibly be institutionalized under treaty law, as part of treaty bodies focusing on implementation review and on technical and scientific advice.

The importance of these interpretative collaboration efforts cannot be overestimated, as a form of transdisciplinary governance that can lead to the transformation needed to effectively tackle the triple planetary crisis – a systemic change across sectors and scales that 'empower those whose interests are currently not being met and represent transformative sustainability values',[154] such as ocean defenders.

[152] E Bjorge, *The Evolutionary Interpretation of Treaties* (Oxford University Press 2014) 50.

[153] On the importance of evolutive interpretation for effectiveness: Bjorge (n 152) 8, 190; *Award in Arbitration Regarding the Iron Rhine Railway Between the Kingdom of Belgium and the Kingdom of the Netherlands* (Decision of 24 May 2005) 27 RIAA 35, 49, 64. Note also reflections on whether international legal scholars take a 'back seat' in the 'effectivity' of international law: J d'Aspremont, *Epistemic Forces in International Law* (Edward Elgar 2015) 169–74.

[154] Visseren-Hamakers and Kok (n 55) 10–11.

PART III

Unity, Diversity, and Evolution of Interpretation across Subject Matters of International Law

9

Application of the General Rule of Interpretation by the WTO Dispute Settlement System

GABRIELLE MARCEAU, MARIA GEORGE, AND VISHAKHA RAJ*

9.1 Introduction

This edited volume reviews how different tribunals and legal systems have used public international law (PIL) principles of interpretation. The World Trade Organization (WTO) Dispute Settlement System (DSS) is governed both by general and specific rules of interpretation. Firstly, Article 3.2 of the DSU provides that the WTO provisions should be interpreted using customary rules of interpretation in PIL. Panels and the Appellate Body (AB) have applied the traditional tools of interpretation (including Articles 31–33 of the Vienna Convention on the Law of Treaties) against the backdrop of the WTO's unique framework of agreements. Secondly, and more specifically, the Dispute Settlement Understanding (DSU) and the Marrakesh Agreement Establishing the World Trade Organization (WTO Agreement) refer explicitly to the need to consider the historical background of the WTO and its General Agreement on Tariffs and Trade (GATT) practices and decisions. For example, in Article 3.1 of the DSU, WTO Members affirm their adherence to the principles of management of disputes under Articles XXII and XXIII of the GATT 1947. Also, Article XVI of the WTO Agreement requires that the functioning of the WTO (including its dispute settlement system) be guided by the decisions, procedures, and customary practices of the GATT 1947.[1] The

* The analysis in the chapter is based on the state of WTO jurisprudence in 2023–2024. We thank Anand Nandakumar, Jenya Grigorova and Leon Seidl for their comments on earlier drafts. The opinions expressed in this chapter are those of the authors. They do not represent the positions or opinions of the WTO or its Members and are without prejudice to Members' rights and obligations under the WTO. Any errors are attributable to the authors.

[1] Marrakesh Agreement Establishing the World Trade Organization (concluded 15 April 1994, entered into force, 1 January 1995) 1867 UNTS 154, art XIV.1 (Marrakesh Agreement).

decisions, customary practices, and procedures of the contracting parties thus continue to remain relevant and have a guiding role.

A unique feature of the WTO treaty is that it comprises several agreements all of which bind WTO Members simultaneously and cumulatively (referred to as the 'WTO covered agreements') – this principle is known as the *single undertaking* – a concept that has both political and legal meanings and implications. To understand the complexity of implementing the WTO covered agreements as a Single Undertaking, it must be recalled that they were not negotiated in one coordinated effort, rather, in fifteen different working groups for each covered agreement's text.[2] Towards the very end of the Uruguay Round, these texts were brought together and annexed to the WTO Agreement to form the Single Undertaking.[3] In a way, each covered agreement is like a small treaty: each agreement has their own Preamble and their own object and purpose.

To maintain coherence and reduce conflict within this Single Undertaking, the WTO DSS has engaged in horizontal cross-fertilisation of jurisprudence across agreements. Exactly how panels and the AB identify the ordinary meaning of provisions in their context and in light of the object and purpose of the WTO treaty will be the subject of the following discussion, noting first the nature of the WTO Single Undertaking in more detail. This chapter seeks to first trace the legal implications of the Single Undertaking on interpretations of provisions of the WTO covered agreements and thereafter elaborates on the manner in which the WTO DSS has employed the general rules of interpretation as per Articles 31, 32, and 33 of the Vienna Convention on the Law of Treaties (VCLT).

9.2 Single Undertaking

As explained earlier, although fifteen different working groups negotiated and finalised the text of each corresponding agreement,[4] it was agreed that no reservations would be possible[5] and that all WTO Members were

[2] G Marceau and JP Trachtman, 'A Map of the World Trade Organization Law of Domestic Regulation of Goods: The Technical Barriers to Trade Agreement, the Sanitary and Phytosanitary Measures Agreement, and the General Agreement on Tariffs and Trade' (2014) 48(2) JWT 351, 352–53.

[3] ibid; Marrakesh Agreement (n 1) art II.

[4] Marceau and Trachtman (n 2) 352–53.

[5] Marrakesh Agreement (n 1) art XVI:5.

bound by all provisions of all covered agreements.[6] Thus, all covered agreements created obligations on Members, but there was no formal discussion or express indication on the hierarchy of WTO norms under the covered agreements and how the obligations created by each of these would interact.[7] This understanding of the WTO covered agreements as a Single Undertaking has significant implications on the interpretation of the provisions of these agreements, and in this section two aspects are explored: *first*, the cumulative and simultaneous application of all the provisions of the WTO covered agreements becomes an expression of the principle of *effectiveness*; and, *secondly*, the principle of Single Undertaking impacts the manner in which conflicts are defined under WTO Agreements and the manner in which they are resolved through treaty interpretation.

9.2.1 Cumulative and Simultaneous Application of All WTO Provisions

To briefly recount the jurisprudence of the WTO DSS relating to the implications of the WTO covered agreements forming a Single Undertaking, the Panel Report in *Indonesia – Autos* is a useful starting point. Indonesia was challenged for maintaining some local content requirements in its taxes, contrary to the Trade Related Investment Measures (TRIMS) and Subsidies and Countervailing Measures (SCM) Agreements. Indonesia invoked the right to maintain local content prohibitions during three years of transition under TRIMS without any specific notification. The Panel, however, concluded that because WTO Members must comply with all WTO provisions cumulatively and simultaneously, Indonesia was also obliged to comply with the provisions of the SCM Agreement, which allowed for transitional local content requirements only if they were fully notified to the WTO. Since Indonesia did not notify the WTO of its measures, Indonesia was considered to have violated the local content requirements of the SCM and the GATT Article III:4.

Later on, the AB in *Korea – Dairy*[8] reiterated the cumulative and simultaneous application of the WTO Single Undertaking. This dispute dealt with

6 Marrakesh Agreement (n 1) art II:2.

7 Note that the expression Single Undertaking also means that the negotiations are not completed until the negotiation of each and all agreements. This is often referred to as the political Single Undertaking.

8 WTO Appellate Body Report, *Korea – Definitive Safeguard Measure on Imports of Dairy Products* (14 December 1999) WT/DS98/AB/R [74–75] (*Korea – Dairy*); Marceau and Trachtman (n 2) 418–19.

the relationship between Article XIX of the GATT and the Agreement on Safeguards. The AB, confirming the decision of the panel, concluded that because of the WTO Single Undertaking, the provisions of the GATT and those of the Agreement on Safeguards must apply cumulatively and simultaneously. The AB recalled the following statement of the Panel:

> It is now well established that the WTO Agreement is a 'Single Undertaking' and therefore all WTO obligations are generally cumulative, and Members must comply with all of them simultaneously.[9]

Given that provisions of different covered agreements may have different, sometimes overlapping and even conflicting scopes, the AB concluded that the provisions of the WTO covered agreements must be interpreted harmoniously and the *treaty* should be read as a whole. As noted by the AB, this is a necessary implication of the *principle of effectiveness*, which, in the case of WTO covered agreements, relates to the provisions of the Single Undertaking cumulatively and simultaneously. The AB states that:

> In light of the interpretive principle of effectiveness, it is the duty of any treaty interpreter to 'read all applicable provisions of a treaty in a way that gives meaning to all of them, harmoniously.' An important corollary of this principle is that a treaty should be interpreted as a whole, and, in particular, its sections and parts should be read as a whole . . .. Article II:2 of the WTO Agreement expressly manifests the intention of the Uruguay Round negotiators that the provisions of the WTO Agreement and the Multilateral Trade Agreements included in its Annexes 1, 2 and 3 must be read as a whole.[10]

Indeed, the principle of the Single Undertaking has become a general principle of interpretation for the relationship between WTO covered agreements and provisions. The implication being that annexed agreements need to be viewed as a whole and interpreted *harmoniously, cumulatively, and simultaneously as a single treaty.*

Other instances in which two provisions from different agreements have been given cumulative and simultaneous effect include GATT and GATS provisions in the decisions of *EC – Bananas III* and *Canada – Periodicals*,[240] GATT Article III and Article XIII of the Agreement on Safeguards in *US – Line Pipe*,[242] Agreement on Agriculture and the SCM Agreement in *US – Upland Cotton*,[11] Article XIX of the GATT and the

[9] *Korea – Dairy* (n 8) [74].

[10] ibid [81] (references omitted).

[11] WTO Appellate Body Report, *United States – Subsidies on Upland Cotton* (3 March 2005) WT/DS267/AB/R [549] (*US – Upland Cotton*).

Agreement on Safeguards in *Argentina – Footwear (EC)*,[12] and the GATT and Article XIII of the Agreement on Agriculture. The principle of effectiveness has been used by the AB to harmoniously apply different provisions of the WTO covered agreements.

A corollary to the application of the principle of effectiveness in the context of the WTO Single Undertaking is that no provision of the treaty should be made a 'nullity'.[13] The AB in *US – Gasoline* found that the principle of effectiveness went hand in hand with the general rule of interpretation under the VCLT. This finding was made in the context of the GATT where the AB held that Article XX (an exception to GATT obligations such as national treatment) does not call for the application of the same standards as Article III of the GATT (dealing with national treatment). The AB cautioned against reading WTO covered agreements in such a manner that would reduce paragraphs or clauses of a treaty to redundancy or inutility.[14] They referred principally to the general rule of interpretation in Article 31(1) of the VCLT and noted that the Panel Report failed to take adequate account of the words actually used by Article XX in its several paragraphs. This approach has been followed in *Brazil – Desiccated Coconut*, where it was held that Article VI of the GATT could not be interpreted in a manner that nullifies transitional rights of developing countries under the SCM Agreement.[15] Similarly, in *Turkey – Textiles*, it was held that the right to enter into regional trade agreements (RTAs) under Article XXIV of the GATT could not be made a nullity through the interpretation of other GATT provisions.[16]

9.2.2 Narrow Definition of Conflicts and Harmonious Interpretation

The principle of Single Undertaking also influences how potential conflicts *inter se* between WTO covered agreements are viewed. The guiding rule here is that there is a presumption against conflicts within the WTO Single Undertaking. This section explores how the WTO DSS

[12] WTO Appellate Body Report, *Argentina – Safeguard Measures on Imports of Footwear* (14 December 1999) WT/DS121/AB/R [89] (*Argentina – Footwear (EC)*).

[13] *Korea – Dairy* (n 8) [74].

[14] WTO Appellate Body Report, *United States – Standards for Reformulated and Conventional Gasoline* (29 April 1996) WT/DS2/AB/R, 23 (*US – Gasoline*).

[15] WTO Appellate Body Report, *Brazil – Measures Affecting Desiccated Coconut* (21 February 1997) WT/DS22/AB/R, 17 (*Brazil – Desiccated Coconut*).

[16] WTO Panel Report, *Turkey – Restrictions on Imports of Textiles and Clothing Products* (31 May 1999) WT/DS34/R [9.96, 9.103] (*Turkey – Textiles*).

has been influenced by the principle of Single Undertaking when resolving conflicts, by *firstly*, adopting a narrow definition of conflict while interpreting WTO covered agreements, and *secondly*, the manner in which they are resolved through treaty interpretation.

The General Interpretative Note to Annex 1A to the WTO Agreement (the 'General Interpretative Note') provides that:

> [i]n the event of conflict between a provision of the General Agreement on Tariffs and Trade 1994 and a provision of another agreement in Annex 1A to the Agreement establishing the World Trade Organization (referred to in the agreements in Annex 1A as the 'WTO Agreement'), the provision of the other agreement shall prevail to the extent of the conflict.

The other agreements in Annex 1A include, *inter alia*, the Agreement on Sanitary and Phytosanitary Measures and the Agreement on Technical Barriers to Trade. Thus, the latter Agreements prevail over the more general GATT in the event of conflict. However, the manner in which potential conflicts have been resolved by the WTO DSS is more nuanced than a straightforward application of the General Interpretative note and warrants further examination.

Before proceeding to examine the WTO DSS jurisprudence on this, it is also necessary to recount the practice under general international law. In general international law, 'conflict'[17] is a rather specific and narrow concept. One possible definition is as stated below:

> [T]echnically speaking, there is a conflict when two (or more) treaty instruments contain obligations which cannot be complied with simultaneously .... Not every such divergence constitutes a conflict, however .... Incompatibility of contents is an essential condition of conflict.[18]

[17] For a thorough discussion on the concept of conflict, see J Pauwelyn, *Conflict of Norms in Public International Law: How WTO Law Relates to Other Rules of International Law* (Cambridge University Press 2009); G Marceau, 'Conflicts of Norms and Conflicts of Jurisdictions: The Relationship Between the WTO Agreement and MEAs and Other Treaties' (2001) 35(6) JWT 1081; G Marceau and A Gonzalez-Calatayud, 'The Relationship between Dispute Settlement Mechanisms of Multilateral Environment Agreements (MEAs) and those of the WTO' (2002) 11(3) RECIEL 275; G Marceau, 'WTO Dispute Settlement and Human Rights' (2002) 13(4) EJIL 753.

[18] WTO Panel Report, *Indonesia – Certain Measures Affecting the Automobile Industry* WT/DS54/R, WT/DS55/R, WT/DS59/R, WT/DS64/R (2 July 1998) [5.344] (*Indonesia – Autos*). See also W Jenks, 'The Conflict of Law-Making Treaties' (1953) 29 BYBIL 401. For in such a case, it is possible for a state that is a signatory of both treaties to comply with both treaties at the same time. The presumption against conflict is especially reinforced in cases where separate agreements are concluded between the same parties,

Now, coming to the WTO context, a narrow definition of conflict was adopted by the Panel in *EC – Bananas III*. The Panel found that any conflict between WTO obligations that would warrant one obligation prevailing over another only refers to instances in which there are *mutually exclusive obligations or when a rule in one agreement prohibits what is explicitly permitted by a rule in another agreement.*[19] This approach was confirmed by the AB in *Guatemala – Cement*,[20] where it held that the mere existence of provisions addressing the same issue would not warrant a finding that one provision prevails over the other. In this dispute, the panel had found that Article 17.3 of the Anti-dumping Agreement (ADA), which provided for consultations, replaced the rules and procedures of the DSU. The AB found that this interpretation was incorrect as there was no conflict between the provisions of the ADA and the DSU, as consultations under the DSU and the ADA were not mutually exclusive.[21]

Subsequently, in *US – Hot Rolled Steel from Japan*, the AB supported again a narrow definition of 'conflict' and stated that 'there is no conflict between Article 17.6(i) of the ADA and Article 11 of the DSU'[22] and 'we see Article 17.6(ii) as supplementing, rather than replacing, the DSU,

since it can be presumed that they are meant to be consistent with each other, failing any evidence to the contrary. See also EW Vierdag, 'The Time of the "Conclusion" of a Multilateral Treaty: Article 30 of the Vienna Convention on the Law of Treaties and Related Provisions' (1988) 64 BYBIL 100; R Jennings and A Watts (eds), *Oppenheim's International Law* (9th edn, Oxford University Press 1992) vol 1, parts 2–4, 1280; G Fitzmaurice, 'The Law and Procedure of the International Court of Justice 1951–1954: Treaty Interpretation and Other Treaty Points' (1957) 33 BYBIL 211, 237; I Sinclair, *The Vienna Convention on the Law of Treaties* (2nd edn, Manchester University Press 1984) 97.

19 G Marceau, 'Balance and Coherence by the WTO Appellate Body: Who Could Do It Better?' in G Sacerdoti, A Yanovich, J Bohannes (eds), *The WTO at Ten – The Contribution of the Dispute Settlement System* (World Trade Organization 2006) 326; WTO Panel Report, *European Communities – Regime for the Importation, Sale, and Distribution of Bananas, Complaint by Guatemala and Honduras* (22 May 1997) WT/DS27/R/GTM, WT/DS27/R/HND [7.159–7.169] (*EC – Bananas III (Guatemala and Honduras)*).

20 WTO Appellate Body Report, *Guatemala – Anti-Dumping Investigation regarding Portland Cement from Mexico* (2 November 1998) WT/DS60/AB/R (*Guatemala – Cement I*); *Indonesia – Autos* (n 18) [14.29–14.36, 14.97–14.99].

21 *Guatemala – Cement I* (n 20) [67].

22 WTO Appellate Body Report, *United States – Antidumping Measures on Certain Hot-Rolled Steel Products from Japan* (24 July 2001) WT/DS184/AB/R [55] (*US – Hot-Rolled Steel*).

and Article 11 in particular'.[23] The strict conflict approach was also followed by the *Indonesia – Autos* Panel, which referred to the definition of conflict in general public international law and noted that the incompatibility of treaty provisions is essential to a finding of conflict, divergence alone is not sufficient.[24]

In *US – Upland Cotton*, the AB expanded the definition of conflict by providing three instances in which the Agreement on Agriculture would prevail over the SCM Agreement. These included an explicit carveout from the SCM Agreement, a situation wherein a Member could not comply with obligations under both agreements simultaneously and when the Agreement on Agriculture expressly authorised a measure prohibited under the SCM Agreement.[25] The AB recalled that all covered agreements form a part of the Single Undertaking and that Members are bound by all obligations contained therein. It was thus the duty of the adjudicator to *read all applicable provisions harmoniously* so as to give effect to all of them. The AB held that the application of Article 3.1(b) of the SCM Agreement could not be excluded for the purpose of domestic support subsidies in the Agreement on Agriculture as nothing to this effect was stated in the latter.[26]

Therefore, the WTO DSS is seen to have avoided the necessity of finding a conflict between the provisions of various covered agreements under the Single Undertaking, by adopting a narrow definition of conflict. This implied a *harmonious construction* of two provisions, instead of applying the principle of conflict resolution captured in General Interpretative Note to Annex 1A.

The General Interpretative Note to Annex IA of the WTO Agreement can be considered an expression of the *lex specialis derogat legi generali* principle. It posits that special law derogates from general law. This legal maxim does not appear in the VCLT but has been referred to in decisions of the International Court of Justice, learned commentators, and decisions of WTO DSS.[27] The rule of *lex specialis* helps deal with situations in which there is a general rule and a special rule, both of

[23] ibid [62].

[24] *Indonesia – Autos* (n 18) [649]. For further discussion on the conflicts within the WTO and conflicts between WTO provisions and provisions of treaties or customs, see Marceau 'The WTO Dispute Settlement . . .' (n 17); Pauwelyn (n 17).

[25] *US – Upland Cotton* (n 11) [532].

[26] ibid [546, 549–50].

[27] *Indonesia – Certain Measures Affecting the Automobile Industry* (n 18); Fitzmaurice (n 18).

which cannot be read harmoniously.[28] In such a situation, the special rule would prevail. However, the implications of *lex specialis* are still subject to discussion: the special rule could supersede or cancel out the general rule; or *lex specialis* could be used as a principle of interpretation that does not allow for the general rule to be superseded, rather, the specific provision is taken out of the scope of the general rule.[29]

The use of the principle by Panel and AB decisions are informative of its use as a principle of interpretation.[30] In *EC – Bananas III*, the AB Report demonstrated how the relative specificity of an agreement can be used to resolve a situation of conflict. Whenever GATT and another agreement in Annex 1A to the WTO Agreement appear to apply to a measure, the measure should be examined on the basis of the agreement that 'deals specifically, and in detail', with measures of that kind.[31]

Therefore, as may be seen from the above section, the principle of Single Undertaking impacts the manner in which conflicts are defined under WTO Agreements and the manner in which they are resolved through treaty interpretation.

The next section examines the application of customary rules of interpretation by WTO DSS in more detail.

9.3 Application of Customary Rules of Interpretation under VCLT – Article 31

The discussion focuses on Article 31 of the VCLT, which requires treaty terms to be interpreted in their context and in light of the object and purpose of the treaty. The AB, very early in *US – Gasoline*, recognised that the general rule of interpretation under Article 31 of the VCLT has attained the status of customary international law.[32] The uniqueness of the WTO framework and the implications of the Single Undertaking

[28] Fitzmaurice (n 18).

[29] ibid.

[30] WTO Panel Report, *United States – Anti-Dumping Act of 1916, Complaint by Japan* (29 May 2005) WT/DS162/R (*US – 1916 Act (Japan)*), as upheld by WTO Appellate Body Report, *United States – Anti-Dumping Act of 1916* (28 August 2000) WT/DS136/AB/R, WT/DS162/AB/R [675] (*US – 1916 Act*), citing *EC – Bananas III* (n 19) [204]. But see R Howse and PC Mavroidis, 'Europe's Evolving Regulatory Strategy for GMOs – the Issue of Consistency with WTO Law: of Kine and Brine' (2000) 24 Fordham IntlLJ 317, 322–23 (suggesting that *lex specialis* is not part of customary international law).

[31] *EC – Bananas III* (n 19) [155] [204].

[32] *US – Gasoline* (n 14) 17.

discussed above also inform the application of Article 31 of the VCLT to WTO covered agreements. Panels and the AB have had to move across WTO covered agreements in search of context and object and purpose of provisions, as the covered agreements are a 'Single Undertaking' and interpreted as one treaty. Accordingly, the practice of WTO dispute settlement has been to use Article 31 to facilitate cross-fertilisation across agreements and increase coherence within the Single Undertaking.

Article 3.2 of the DSU requires the WTO DSS to clarify existing provisions of covered agreements in accordance with 'customary rules of interpretation under public international law'.[33] Rules of treaty interpretation thus play a significant role in the WTO system as adjudicators have been given the task of clarifying the rights and obligations of WTO Members without adding to them or diminishing them.

All Members seem to agree that customary rules of treaty interpretation refer to rules in the VCLT, namely, those contained in Articles 31–33. Accordingly, this section examines the application of the general rule of interpretation.

The general rule of interpretation contained in Article 31(1) of the VCLT posits that:

> [a] treaty shall be interpreted in good faith in accordance with the ordinary meaning to be given to the terms of the treaty in their context and in the light of its object and purpose.

In its first decision, the AB held that the GATT cannot be read in clinical isolation and will have to be interpreted by applying the customary rules of interpretation.[34] This decision explicitly identified Article 31 of the VCLT as a customary rule of treaty interpretation and thus applicable when interpreting the GATT and other covered agreements.[35] The crux of the interpretative exercise involves *three interrelated elements*. The ordinary meaning of a treaty term is discerned using dictionaries and the grammatical construction of the provision, while taking into account the context in which a treaty term is placed and its object and purpose.

[33] Understanding of the Rules and Procedures Governing the Settlement of Disputes (adopted 15 April 1994, entered into force 1 January 1995) 1869 UNTS 401, art 3.2 (DSU).

[34] *US - Gasoline* (n 14) 17.

[35] ibid.

This exercise is not carried out in distinct steps but is done holistically by the interpreter with each element influencing the other.[36]

9.3.1 Good Faith

Good faith is a recognised general principle of law, a principle of interpretation and it is also explicitly mentioned in the DSU.[37] The principle of good faith informs the application of Article 31(1) of the VCLT and the use of a treaty term's context and relevant object and purpose discussed above.[38] The AB has recognised this role of good faith in the application of treaties and at times combined it with the principle of *abus de droit*.[39] In *US – Shrimp*, for instance, the AB held that the Chapeau of Article XX of the GATT, which requires Members to apply measures that derogate from GATT obligations in a manner that is not arbitrary or a disguised restriction on trade, was an expression of good faith.

The chapeau of Article XX is, in fact, but one expression of the principle of good faith. This principle, at once a general principle of law and a general principle of international law, controls the exercise of rights by states. One application of this general principle, the application widely known as the doctrine of *abus de droit*, prohibits the abusive exercise of a state's rights and enjoins that whenever the assertion of a right 'impinges on the field covered by [a] treaty obligation, it must be exercised bona fide, that is to say, reasonably'. An abusive exercise by a Member of its own treaty right thus results in a breach of the treaty rights of the other Members, as well as, a violation of the treaty obligation of the Member so acting. Having said this, our task here is to interpret the language of the chapeau, seeking additional interpretative guidance, as appropriate, from the general principles of international law.[40] Good

[36] WTO Appellate Body Report, *United States – Measures Affecting the Production and Sale of Clove Cigarettes* (4 April 2012) WT/DS406/AB/R [273] (*US – Clove Cigarettes*).

[37] See DSU (n 33) arts 3–4; R Gardiner, *Treaty Interpretation* (2nd edn, Oxford University Press 2015) 167–68.

[38] Gardiner (n 37) 167–68.

[39] WTO, 'Analytical Index – Annex 2: Dispute Settlement Understanding, Article 3' (WTO, 2023) 10 <https://www.wto.org/english/res_e/publications_e/ai17_e/dsu_art3_jur.pdf> (last accessed 1 June 2025) (Analytical Index).

[40] WTO Appellate Body Report, *United States – Import Prohibition of Certain Shrimp and Shrimp Products* (12 October 1998) WT/DS58/AB/R [158] (*US – Shrimp*) (references omitted).

faith interpretation of treaty obligations became one of the central issues in *Russia – Traffic in Transit* wherein the Panel found that the discretion of a Member to designate particular concerns as an 'essential security interest' was limited by their obligation to interpret and apply the security exception in good faith.[41]

9.3.2 *Ordinary Meaning and the Use of Dictionaries*

In *EC – Asbestos*, the AB referred to a dictionary, as a starting point for determining the meaning of the word 'like', which appears in Article III.4 of the GATT. The AB was, however, quick to note that questions regarding what product characteristics were important to assess likeness could not be answered by simply looking at the dictionary meaning.[42] The adjudicator also had to make a judgment with regard to the degree of likeness required under Article III and to the perspective from which this likeness was to be ascertained (consumers or producers).[43] To answer these questions, the AB turned to the context of Article III.4, thus applying the general rule of interpretation.

There are rare occasions in which the AB has considered the dictionary meaning, or definition, to be conclusive or sufficient in interpreting a term.[44] In *Brazil – Aircraft (Article 21.5 – Canada)*, the AB referred to the ordinary meaning of the term 'withdraw' under Article 4.7 of the SCM Agreement on whether Brazil had complied with the recommendation of the DSB to withdraw the subsidy in question. The AB referred to the Oxford Concise Dictionary and Black's Law Dictionary, concluding that the ordinary meaning of withdraw was the 'removal' or 'taking away' of a subsidy. However, it may be possible that the AB relied on contextual elements without mentioning them in the Report to arrive at the ordinary meaning in this case.[45]

[41] WTO Panel Report, *Russia – Measures Concerning Traffic in Transit* (5 April 2019) WT/DS512/R [7.132] (*Russia – Traffic in Transit*).

[42] WTO Appellate Body Report, *European Communities – Measures Affecting Asbestos and Products Containing Asbestos* (12 March 2001) WT/DS135/AB/R [92-3] (*EC – Asbestos*); WTO Appellate Body Report, *China – Measures Affecting Trading Rights and Distributing Services for Certain Publications and Audiovisual Entertainment Products* (21 December 2009) WT/DS363/AB/R [348] (*China – Publications and Audiovisual Products*).

[43] ibid.

[44] I Van Damme, *Treaty Interpretation by the WTO Appellate Body* (Oxford University Press 2009) 223.

[45] ibid.

9.3.3 *Context*

9.3.3.1 Immediate Context – within the Covered Agreement

The search for context by WTO panels and the AB is not restricted to the covered agreement in which a relevant provision is found. Recalling that obligations of the Single Undertaking fall simultaneously and cumulatively on Members, this discussion examines how panels and the AB have identified context in the Single Undertaking framework.

The AB has considered the provisions within the immediate vicinity of a treaty term as its context. In *US – Shrimp*, for instance, the AB faulted a panel's findings because they did not reflect the *immediate* context of sub-paragraph (g) of Article XX, which was the Chapeau of Article XX. In *US – Clove Cigarettes*, AB used the context provided by Article 2.2 of the Technical Barriers to Trade (TBT) Agreement to find that not all obstacles to international trade are prohibited under Article 2.1. In other instances, panels and the AB have moved across WTO covered agreements when searching for the context and object and purpose required to interpret a provision. The AB used this approach when it had the occasion to examine the meaning of the term 'like' in Article III.4 of GATT for the first time.[46] In interpreting the term, the AB held that 'like' under GATT may not have the identical meaning as the same term used in other covered agreements. But these covered agreements would nonetheless be relevant *context* in interpreting the term under Article III.4 of the GATT. This is further elaborated below.

9.3.3.2 Context across WTO Covered Agreements

The search for context by the WTO adjudicators is indicative of a holistic approach to interpreting the Single Undertaking recognising the need to maintain coherence between the obligations of the various covered agreements. As mentioned above, the AB has noted that the term *like products* was used in several WTO covered agreements such as the GATT, the SCM Agreement, the ADA, the Agreement on Safeguards, etc. Likeness was thus a key concept used across WTO disciplines. In some agreements, the meaning attributable to the term was specific and expressed in clear terms in the agreement. For instance, Article 2.6 of the ADA states that the term 'like product' should be interpreted to mean identical products throughout the Agreement and in the event that

[46] *EC – Asbestos* (n 42) [88].

such product does not exist, like products would be those products that are not alike in all respects but still have characteristics that closely resemble each other. However, in most covered agreements, no such specific definition exists. Accordingly, the AB held that the term 'like products' should be interpreted in light of the context and the object and purpose of the provision in which it is found and the object and purpose of the relevant covered agreement. *This means that the same term may have different scope, different components across different agreements.*[47]

The AB decision in *US – Clove Cigarettes* is a valuable illustration of how *context* is found within the relevant covered agreement and other WTO covered agreements. In this dispute, the operation of the WTO covered agreements as a single treaty and their collective relevance in the interpretation of treaty provisions was noted by the AB. It recalled its decision in *EC – Asbestos*, which identified the *context* of a provision as the terms within the covered agreement in question and similar terms in other covered agreements.[48]

The AB used Article III.4 of the GATT and its jurisprudence as *context* for interpreting the meaning of 'like' products under Article 2.1 of the TBT and identifying the balance between rights and obligations contained within the article. The US had appealed the panel's finding that clove and menthol cigarettes were like products. The US argued that clove and menthol cigarettes are not like products because clove cigarettes were disproportionally smoked by young smokers whereas menthol cigarettes are smoked evenly by both young and adult smokers.[49] The US submissions thus emphasised that not all consumers were willing to substitute clove and menthol cigarettes to the same degree (youth, for instance, had a stronger preference for clove cigarettes). The AB found that it was not necessary to show that a product was substitutable for all consumers in order to establish that they were alike.

In reaching its conclusion on likeness, the AB referred to its decision in *Philippines – Distilled Spirits*,[50] which discussed the second sentence of Article III.2 where like products are defined as products that are directly

[47] ibid [89].
[48] *US – Clove Cigarettes* (n 36) fn 275.
[49] ibid [140].
[50] ibid [141–42]; WTO Appellate Body Report, *Philippines – Taxes on Distilled Spirits* (21 December 2011) WT/DS396/AB/R, WT/DS403/AB/R [149] (*Philippines – Distilled Spirits*).

competitive or substitutable. The AB held that the interpretation of like products under Article III.2 would be relevant for the purpose of Article III.4 of the GATT and Article 2.1 of the TBT Agreement because a competitive relationship between products is determinative of likeness in each of these provisions. Though young smokers preferred clove cigarettes, for those who were starting to smoke, menthol and clove cigarettes were preferred as they both masked the otherwise harsh taste of tobacco. For the AB, the interchangeability of these cigarettes among young smokers was sufficient to establish their likeness for the purpose of Article 2.1.[51]

After examining the meaning of likeness under Article 2.1 of the TBT Agreement and its application to clove and menthol cigarettes, the AB turned to the interpretation of Article 2.2 of the TBT and its interaction with Article 2.1. Specifically, the AB sought to understand the extent to which Article 2.1 permitted discrimination for the purpose of achieving legitimate regulatory objectives. Article 2.2 requires that technical regulations be put in place by Members only to achieve legitimate objectives, that they are not applied in a manner so as to cause arbitrary discrimination, and any regulations should not be more trade restrictive than necessary to achieve the objective of the regulation. The AB used Article 2.2 as context for Article 2.1, which allowed it to interpret the latter as not prohibiting all technical regulations that are obstacles to international trade. The AB used the principle of effectiveness and found that a strict reading to Article 2.1, which prevented all differentiation between like imported and domestic products, would amount to depriving Article 2.2 of the TBT Agreement of its *effet utile*.[52] Article 2.2, which provides the *context* for Article 2.1, suggests that obstacles to international trade would be permitted insofar as they are not found to be 'unnecessary'. Therefore, if any prohibition on international trade was sufficient to establish a violation of Article 2.1, it would deprive Article 2.2 of its *effet utile*.

In order to interpret whether the US regulations banning clove cigarettes conferred less favourable treatment to products of foreign origin under Article 2.1 of the TBT Agreement, the parties and the AB found it useful to turn to Article III.4 of the GATT. On the issue of regulatory distinctions, the AB referred to *EC – Asbestos*, which held that regulatory distinctions that afford protection to domestic production would accord

[51] *US – Clove Cigarettes* (n 36) [143–44].
[52] ibid [171].

treatment less favourable to like imported products.[53] The requirement to accord treatment no less favourable was interpreted broadly under the GATT, and the AB followed this position for Article 2.1 of the TBT Agreement as well. However, it found the need to temper this requirement because of the specific context of the TBT Agreement, especially as evident from the Preamble of the agreement.

Therefore, context as a tool of interpretation by the WTO DSS has seen the employment of provisions that are both within the Agreement in question, as well as other Agreements that are part of the WTO covered agreements. This is a direct consequence of the principle of Single Undertaking.

9.3.3.3 Preambular Language as Context

Preambular language has been an important source of context in several decisions of the AB.[54] Of note is the decision in *US – Shrimp*, which used preambular language to give a contemporaneous interpretation of Article XX of the GATT. As mentioned above, Article XX is the exceptions clause of the GATT and allows Members to derogate from their market access and other obligations of the GATT to meet certain policy objectives. Any measures enacted under Article XX must not be applied in an arbitrary or discriminatory manner or be a disguised restriction to trade. The policy objectives for which Article XX may be invoked are provided in the text of the provision. These objectives include the protection of public morals; human, plant, and animal life and health; conservation of gold and silver reserves; and measures relating to prison labour. The dispute in *US – Shrimp* concerned Article XX(g), which refers to measures relating to the conservation of exhaustible natural resources if such measures are in conjunction with domestic production and consumption.

The United States had invoked this exception to defend a measure that banned the import of shrimp that was caught without using Turtle Excluder Devices (TEDs). TEDs were designed to allow turtles to swim out of shrimp nets instead of getting caught in them and suffering from injury or suffocating. One of the arguments of the complaining parties (India, Pakistan, and Thailand) was that exhaustible natural resources referred to non-living, non-renewable natural resources. Their

[53] ibid [178].

[54] See Vienna Convention on the Law of Treaties (adopted 23 May 1969, entered into force 27 January 1980) 1155 UNTS 331, art 31(2) mentioning the Preamble as an example of context.

interpretation of Article XX(g) was based on arguments made by delegations when the provision was being negotiated. The complaining parties posited that exhaustible natural resources referred to substances such as minerals and other non-biological natural resources.[55] The AB was not persuaded by this reasoning and referred to the text and context of Article XX(g) to determine its meaning.

The AB noted that half a century had passed between the drafting of Article XX(g) and the dispute. During the Uruguay round that established the WTO, there was a chance to modify Article XX(g) but this did not occur. However, the WTO Agreement was adopted in this round along with its Preamble that referred to the objective of sustainable development.[56] The use of the phrase sustainable development in the Preamble of the WTO Agreement prompted the AB to interpret Article XX(g) in a more *fluid and contemporaneous manner*. The meaning of exhaustible natural resources would not remain static and tied to the understanding of the term fifty years ago. The United Nations Convention of the Law of the Sea (UNCLOS), for instance, defines natural resources as both living and non-living. Taking a cue from the international community, which acknowledges the need to protect living natural resources and the recognition of the objective of sustainable development, the AB held that turtles were exhaustible natural resources, the protection of which would be a legitimate policy objective under Article XX(g).

> As this preambular language reflects the intentions of negotiators of the WTO Agreement, we believe it must add colour, texture and shading to our interpretation of the agreements annexed to the WTO Agreement, in this case, the GATT 1994.[57]

Once identified, the context of a provision has been used to breathe life into it and inform new interpretations of it. In *US – Shrimp*, the value of the WTO Agreement's preambular language guided the interpretive efforts of the AB helping it arrive at a contemporaneous meaning for Article XX(g).

Turning once again to *US – Clove Cigarettes*, the dispute serves as another example of the use of Preambular language as context. The sixth recital of the Preamble of the TBT Agreement recognises that Members

[55] *US – Shrimp* (n 40) [127].
[56] ibid [129].
[57] ibid [153].

should not be prevented from taking measures that are necessary to prevent deceptive practices; protect animal, plant, and human life or health; and decide the appropriate levels of protection it wants to afford to each of these concerns. The prohibition contained under Article 2.1 thus needs to be balanced with Members' right to regulate as enshrined in the Preamble and under Article 2.2. The AB noted that unlike the GATT, which explicitly allows for derogations from Article III (and other Articles of the GATT) through Article XX, the TBT Agreement does not contain a provision containing exceptions. Nonetheless, the AB found that the balance struck by the TBT Agreement between trade liberalisation and Members' right to regulate, found in Article 2.1 itself, was not principally different from the balance struck by the GATT through the introduction of Article XX.[58] AB decisions in *US – COOL*[59] and *US – Tuna II (Mexico)*[60] also follow this approach and used Article III.4 of GATT as relevant context for interpreting Article 2.1 of TBT.

9.3.4 *Object and Purpose of Covered Agreements and/or Specific Provisions*

The object and purpose of a treaty refers to the teleology or the mission of a treaty.[61] The concept itself is an evolving one and can only be defined in general terms if one is not referring to a specific treaty.[62] The phrase 'object and purpose' under Article 31 of the VCLT is understood as referring to the object and purpose of the treaty as a whole and not to individual provisions of a treaty.[63] Panels and the AB have often used the object and purpose of a provision in addition to the treaty to shed light on the ordinary meaning of a provision.[64]

58 *US – Clove Cigarettes* (n 36) [109].

59 WTO Appellate Body Report, *United States – Certain Countries of Origin Labelling (COOL) Requirements* (29 June 2012) WT/DS384/AB/R, WT/DS386/AB/R [269] (*US – COOL*).

60 WTO Appellate Body Report, *United States – Measures Concerning the Importation, Marketing and Sale of Tuna and Tuna Products* (16 May 2012) WT/DS381/AB/R [214-5] (*US – Tuna II (Mexico)*).

61 Van Damme (n 44) 257.

62 ibid.

63 Gardiner (n 37) 213, 220–21; Van Damme (n 44) 258.

64 WTO Appellate Body Report, *European Communities – Customs Classification of Frozen Boneless Chicken Cuts* (12 September 2005) WT/DS269/AB/R, WT/DS286/AB/R [238] (*EC – Chicken Cuts*).

When deciding what the phrase 'based on' under Article 5.1 of the Agreement on the Application of Sanitary and Phytosanitary Measures (SPS Agreement) meant, the AB referred in *EC – Hormones* to *the object and purpose of the provision* to find that the phrase required an objective relationship between sanitary and phytosanitary measures (SPS measures) and the risk assessment of the persisting situation.[65]

> We believe that 'based on' is appropriately taken to refer to a certain objective relationship between two elements, that is to say, to an objective situation that persists and is observable between an SPS measure and a risk assessment. Such a reference is certainly embraced in the ordinary meaning of the words 'based on' and, when considered in context and in the light of the object and purpose of Article 5.1 of the SPS Agreement, may be seen to be more appropriate than 'taking into account'.[66]

In *EC – Hormones*, the AB held that while the European Communities had a right to establish a higher level of protection, it was bound to comply with the requirements of Article 5.1 of the SPS Agreement such as taking into account risk assessment techniques developed by relevant international organisations.[67] In arriving at this conclusion, the AB referred to the *object and purpose* of the SPS Agreement as a whole and of Article 3 in particular. Article 3.1 of the SPS Agreement requires Members to base their SPS measures on international standards, guidelines, and recommendations. The thrust of this paragraph under Article 3 is to promote harmonisation. If Members decide to take SPS measures that conform to international standards (thus implying a closer link than measures that are 'based on' international standards as under Article 3.1), they benefit from a rebuttable presumption that these measures conform to the SPS Agreement. Under Article 3.3 of the SPS Agreement, Members have the right to introduce measures that achieve a higher level of sanitary and phytosanitary protection than what would be achieved by measures based on international standards.

With respect to object and purpose of the provision, the *object and purpose of* Article 3 was identified as promoting the harmonisation of SPS measures while recognising and safeguarding Members' right to

[65] WTO Appellate Body Report, *European Communities – Measures Concerning Meat and Meat Products* (16 January 1998) WT/DS26/AB/R, WT/DS48/AB/R [177] (*EC – Hormones*).

[66] ibid [189].

[67] ibid [176].

regulate and protect the life and health of their people.[68] The SPS Agreement attempted to strike a balance between the promotion of international trade and the protection of the life and health of human beings. Considering this, Article 5.1 was an important countervailing force to Article 3. The two had to be read in conjunction with each other.[69]

One implication of the teleological approach in the context of the WTO covered agreements is that the object and purpose of ostensibly similar provisions allows for their varied interpretation and application. The ordinary meaning of a provision requires an examination of the provision's context and object and purpose, and this extends to exceptions as well. In *US-Shrimp*, the panel report had found that the WTO Agreement emphasises multilateralism[70] and used this to hold that Article XX of the GATT, when read in light of the *context* and *object and purpose* of the GATT and the WTO Agreement, would not accommodate unilateral measures.[71] The AB found that the panel had erred in arriving at this conclusion. The panel's error was attributed to its interpretative approach and incomplete identification of the relevant object and purpose. For the AB, the panel had improperly ignored *the object and purpose of the Chapeau of Article XX* during its interpretative exercise. The AB took issue with the panel's exclusive focus on the object and purpose of the GATT as a whole and the WTO Agreement. The panel found that the object and purpose of the Chapeau of Article XX was the prevention of abuse of exceptions under Article XX. This, however, did not result in an *a priori* prohibition of unilateral measures.[72] To the contrary, the AB found that unilateral measures fell within the scope of the sub-paragraphs of Article XX as long as they could be linked to the policy objectives and meet the requirements of the Chapeau

[68] ibid [177].

[69] ibid.

[70] WTO Panel Report, *United States – Import Prohibition of Certain Shrimp and Shrimp Products* (15 May 1998) WT/DS58/R [7.43, 7.45, 7.60] (*US – Shrimp*)

[71] ibid.

[72] See also WTO Panel Report, *United States – Origin Marking Requirement* (21 December 2022) WT/DS597/R [7.142, 7.150] (*US – Origin Marking (Hong Kong, China)*). The panel identified the security and predictability of the multilateral trading system as one aspect of the object and purpose of the GATT 1994 and the WTO covered agreements more generally. This identification of object and purpose was used to conclude that sub-paragraph (b) of Article XXI of the GATT is not self-judging and subject to the Panel's review.

of Article XX.[73] Similarly, in *US – Gasoline*, the AB had held that though Article XX of the GATT conferred a legal right, to be exercised in a manner that did not frustrate legal obligations of a Member under the WTO Agreement.[74]

9.3.4.1 Interpretation of Justifications – Use of Object and Purpose and Rebalancing Burden of Proof

In the context of exceptions, the burden of proof falls on the defendant to justify their invocation of the exception once the complaining party has fulfilled the burden of showing the violation of the general rule.[75] Under Article XX of the GATT, for instance, it is for the responding party invoking the exception to show that the design of the measure falls under one of the sub-paragraphs of Article XX and that it passes the Chapeau test. There are some types of exceptions that offer a contrasting example, where the burden of proof is rebalanced and shifted towards the complaining party. This is not to say that the defending party no longer has the burden of justifying the invocation of a defence; but in the cases discussed below, the AB has required the complainant to do more before the burden of proof falls on the defendant.

In *EC – Hormones*, the AB found that Article 3 of the SPS agreement and its sub-paragraphs, though characterised as an exception, were qualitatively different from Article XX of the GATT.[76] The AB held that Article 3.3 of the SPS Agreement conferred an autonomous right on Members to adopt their own levels of protection or measures that achieve a level of protection that goes beyond international standards. It was emphasised that characterising a provision as an exception would *not automatically warrant a stricter or narrower interpretation of that provision*. The interpretation of an exception would also require an adjudicator to arrive at its ordinary meaning in light of its context and the object and purpose of the treaty.[77] A similar interpretation was adopted with reference to the interaction between Article 2.2 and Article 5.7 of the SPS Agreement.[78]

[73] *US – Shrimp* (n 40) [121].
[74] *US – Gasoline* (n 14) 22.
[75] ibid 16.
[76] *EC – Hormones* (n 65) [104].
[77] ibid.
[78] WTO Appellate Body Report, *Japan – Measures Affecting Agricultural Products* (22 February 1999) WT/DS76/AB/R [80] (*Japan – Agricultural Products II*); WTO Panel Report, *European Communities – Measures Affecting the Approval and Marketing of*

Subsequently, in *EC – Sardines*, the AB found that its decision in *EC – Hormones*, which clarified the burden of proof under arts 3.1 and 3.3 of the SPS Agreement, would be relevant to a case involving Article 2.4 of the TBT Agreement as well. Though the provisions at issue in *EC – Hormones* and *EC – Sardines* were found in different covered agreements (SPS and TBT, respectively), the AB in *EC – Sardines* used the conceptual similarity of these provisions to maintain a consistent approach to their interpretation.[79] Article 2.4 of the TBT Agreement requires Members to base their technical regulations on international standards except when these standards would be ineffective or inefficient for the fulfilment of the objective pursued by the Member. The AB in *EC – Sardines* used Articles 3.1 and 3.3 as context, holding that like those articles under the SPS Agreement, Members' ability to deviate from international standards as a basis for measures under Article 2.4 of the TBT Agreement was not an exception. Rather, it was a right given to Members, and a complaining party would bear the burden of showing that international standards are in fact inappropriate for fulfilling the objective of the responding Member.[80] Accordingly, it was for the complainant to show that a technical regulation is not based on an international standard and that international standards are adequate to fulfil the legitimate objectives of the responding member.[81]

The AB referred to its jurisprudence on Article XX of the GATT while interpreting Article XIV of the GATS in *US – Gambling*. Article XIV is analogous to Article XX and follows a similar structure (enumeration of policy objectives in sub-paragraph with an overarching requirement for measures not to be discriminatory or operate as a disguised restriction to trade in the Chapeau). The GATS, concluded in 1994, is a more recent agreement compared to the GATT. However, the AB used a consistent interpretive approach to both agreements. In *US – Gambling*, the AB reiterated that the exceptions provision under Articles XX and XIV gave Members the right to set their own desired level of protection with relation to the policy objectives enumerated in the exceptions. While the responding Member had to demonstrate the necessity of the measure, it was for the complaining party to demonstrate the existence of alternative measures, if

Biotech Products (29 September 2006) WT/DS291/R, WT/DS292/R, WT/DS293/R [7.2969] (*EC – Approval and Marketing of Biotech Products*).

79 WTO Appellate Body Report, *European Communities – Trade Description of Sardines* (26 September 2002) WT/DS231/AB/R [275] (*EC – Sardines*).

80 ibid.

81 ibid.

any. These measures proposed by the complaining party would be considered alternatives only if they were equally feasible for the responding member, did not impose an undue burden, and achieved the level of protection set by the responding Member. The treatment of exceptions under the GATS and the GATT is a valuable example of cross-fertilisation between agreements and the AB's attempt to maintain internal coherence.

The Enabling Clause and special and differential treatment provisions are also examples of how exceptions are treated differently depending on their object and purpose. The Enabling Clause allows developed country Members to give enhanced market access to products from developing country Members. It is thus an exception to Article I.1 of GATT that requires that Members accord to all Members, immediately and unconditionally, the same level of treatment without favouring one Member over others. Despite being characterised as an exception, the general rule for allocation of burden of proof used for exceptions does not strictly apply to the Enabling Clause. In *EC – Tariff Preferences*, the AB noted the special and fundamental nature of the Enabling Clause to the WTO DSS. Pursuant to its important role, the AB held that a complaining party had to do more than simply allege inconsistency of a measure with Article I.1 of GATT, it has also to explain why the challenged measure is also inconsistent with the provisions of the Enabling Clause.[82] Specifically, a complaining Member alleging a violation of the Enabling Clause would have to explain which conditions of the Enabling Clause were not met by the provider of the special and differential treatment. It is only upon such identification that the burden of proof would switch to the defending party.

> In the light of the extensive requirements set forth in the Enabling Clause . . . a complaining party cannot, in good faith, ignore those provisions and must, in its request for the establishment of a panel, identify them and thereby 'notif[y] the parties and third parties of the nature of [its] case'. For the failure of such a complaining party to raise the relevant provisions of the Enabling Clause would place an unwarranted burden on the responding party.[83]

The AB adopted a similar line of reasoning when interpreting Article 27.4 of the SPS Agreement in *Brazil – Aircraft*. Article 27 is a special and

[82] WTO Appellate Body Report, *European Communities – Conditions for Granting of Tariff Preferences to Developing Countries* (7 April 2004) WT/DS246/AB/R [106, 113–14] (*EC – Tariff Preferences*).

[83] ibid [113].

differential treatment provision under the SCM Agreement and allows developing country Members to maintain export subsidies that are required for their development needs. Article 27.4 contains certain conditions that developing country Members need to fulfil in order to avail of the special and differential treatment under Article 27; for instance, developing country Members need to phase out export subsidies in a progressive manner and not increase their level of export subsidies. The AB found that the conditions under Article 27.4 are 'positive obligations' and not 'affirmative defences'.[84] Accordingly, the burden of proof falls on the complaining party to demonstrate that any of the conditions set out in Article 27.4 have not been complied with by a developing country Member.[85]

Therefore, as may be seen from the above cases, the interpretation of a provision as a positive right, as opposed to an affirmative defence, determines the burden of proof applicable in a present case.

9.3.5 Agreement at the Time of Conclusion of the Treaty – Article 31(2) of the VCLT

Article 31(2) of the VCLT elaborates on two sources of 'context' for the purposes of interpretation of a treaty. It refers to any agreement relating to the treaty that was made between all the parties in connection with the conclusion of the treaty and any instrument made by one or more parties in connection with the conclusion of the treaty and accepted by other parties as an instrument related to the treaty. In *EC – Computer Equipment*, the AB noted that the Panel erred in not considering the International Convention on the Harmonized Commodity Description and Coding System, and its Explanatory Notes, in interpreting the terms of Schedule LXXX. Although they did not explicitly refer to these as falling within the scope of Article 31(2), they do note that the EC and the United States were parties to the Harmonized System during the Uruguay Rounds implying that this could be within the scope of agreement at the time of conclusion of the treaty.[86]

84 WTO Appellate Body Report, *Brazil – Export Financing Programme for Aircraft* (2 August 1999) WT/DS46/AB/R [140] (*Brazil – Aircraft*).

85 ibid [141].

86 WTO Appellate Body Report, *European Communities – Customs Classification of Certain Computer Equipment* (5 June 1998) WT/DS62/AB/R, WT/DS67/AB/R, WT/DS68/AB/R [89] (*EC – Computer Equipment*).

As noted by the AB in *China – Auto Parts*, this context is *relevant* for a treaty interpreter to the extent that it may shed light on the interpretative issue to be resolved. It is not just sufficient that the agreement or instrument fall within the scope of Article 31(2). The AB narrows the scope of Article 31(2) further by stating that the agreement or instrument must have some pertinence to the language being interpreted that renders it capable of helping the interpreter determine the meaning of such language. In *China – Auto Parts*, while it was accepted that the Harmonized System is apt to shed light on the meaning of terms used in the WTO Members' Schedule of Concessions, it was stated that it does not automatically imply that it is also context *relevant* for the interpretative question faced by the Panel.[87] The interpretative task of the Panel was the assessment of the respective scope of application of 'ordinary customs duties' in the first sentence of Article II:1(b) and 'internal charges' in Article III:2 of the GATT. Therefore, the Harmonized System was not considered context *relevant* for such interpretative exercise.

In *EC – Chicken Cuts*, the AB noted that the Harmonized System would be such relevant context for the interpretation of the EC Schedule. The interpretative task was of the term 'salted' in heading 02.10 of the EC Schedule. The broader context includes the other headings in Chapter 2 of the EC Schedule, other WTO Member Schedules, as well as the Harmonized System, although not formally a part of the WTO Agreement.[88]

On the substantive requirements under Article 31(2), the AB in *US – Gambling* found that the W/120 and the 1993 Scheduling Guidelines did not constitute sufficient context for the interpretation of the United States' GATS Schedule. It was noted that the parties in the negotiations had not accepted them as agreements or instruments related to the treaty. The AB has also excluded from the scope of Article 31(2), jurisprudence of the WTO DSS,[89] and the Tokyo Round Subsidies Code, which was a predecessor agreement.[90]

87 WTO Appellate Body Report, *China – Measures Affecting Imports of Automobile Parts*, (15 December 2008) WT/DS339/AB/R, WT/DS340/AB/R, WT/DS342/AB/R [151] (*China – Auto Parts*).

88 *EC – Chicken Cuts* (n 64) [193, 195].

89 WTO Appellate Body Report, *United States – Definitive Anti-Dumping and Countervailing Duties on Certain Products from China* (11 March 2011) WT/DS379/AB/R [325] (*US – Anti-Dumping and Countervailing Duties (China)*).

90 ibid [579].

9.3.6 Subsequent Agreement, Subsequent Practice, and Relevant Rules of International Law – Article 31(3) of the VCLT

9.3.6.1 Subsequent Agreement Regarding Interpretation or Application of its Provisions

Article IX:2 of the WTO Agreement sets out specific requirements for decisions that may be taken by the Ministerial Conference or the General Council to adopt interpretations of provisions of the WTO covered agreements. However, these are exclusively intended to clarify the meaning of existing provisions and should not be used to undermine the amendment provisions under Article X. The AB in *EC – Bananas III* has noted that a multilateral interpretation pursuant to Article IX:2 is akin to a subsequent agreement recognised under Article 31(3)(a) of the VCLT on the interpretation of the concerned agreements.[91] However, the AB in *US – Clove Cigarettes* emphasised that Article IX:2 of the WTO Agreement, and Article 31(3)(a) of the VCLT have different functions and have different legal effects.[92] In order to fall within the scope of Article 31(3)(a), it is necessary to look at the *substance*, rather than the form of the agreement. Therefore, the AB found that a decision adopted by Members at the Doha Ministerial Conference may constitute a 'subsequent agreement' on the interpretation of the term 'reasonable interval' in Article 2.12 of the TBT Agreement, under Article 31 (3)(a) of the VCLT.[93] The AB in *US – Tuna II* held that the TBT Committee Decision on international standards is a 'subsequent agreement' for the purpose of Article 31(3)(a) since it was adopted subsequent to the conclusion of the TBT Agreement by consensus and with the objective of clarifying the application of the TBT Agreement.[94]

[91] WTO Appellate Body Report, *European Communities – Regime for the Importation, Sale and Distribution of Bananas – Second Recourse to Article 21.5 of the DSU by Ecuador* (26 November 2008) WT/DS27/AB/RW2/ECU [390] (*EC – Bananas III (Article 21.5 – Ecuador II)*); WTO Appellate Body Report, *European Communities – Regime for the Importation, Sale and Distribution of Bananas – Recourse to Article 21.5 of the DSU by United States* (26 November 2008) WT/DS27/AB/RW/USA [390] (*EC – Bananas III (Article 21.5 – US)*).

[92] *US – Clove Cigarettes* (n 36) [257–58].

[93] ibid [268].

[94] *US – Tuna II (Mexico)* (n 60) [371–72].

9.3.6.2 Subsequent Practice Establishing Agreement Regarding Its Interpretation

In establishing 'practice' within the meaning of Article 31(3)(b) of the VCLT, the AB in *US – Gambling* identified two necessary elements: (i) that there must be a common, consistent, discernible pattern of acts or pronouncements; and (ii) those acts or pronouncements must imply agreement on the interpretation of the relevant provision. In the said case, speaking of the 2001 Guidelines adopted by the Council for Trade in Services, it was concluded that this could not constitute subsequent practice for the interpretation of the GATS as this was in the context of negotiation of *future* commitments. Therefore, such Guidelines could not constitute an agreement regarding Members' interpretation of *existing* commitments.[95]

Now, coming to the question of how many parties need to undertake a 'practice' to satisfy the threshold of Article 31(3)(b), the AB in *EC – Chicken Cuts* provides guidance. While clarifying that it would be possible to establish a common intention of all the parties, even if the practice has not been undertaken by *all* the parties, the AB was interpreting the tariff commitments in the WTO Schedule of the European Communities. However, the AB disagreed with the Panel that the practice of one Member alone could establish subsequent practice as per Article 31(3)(b). There was a need to establish an agreement of all the Members, even those that had not engaged in the said practice. The mere lack of reaction or protest to a practice by one Member, although sufficient in some cases, cannot in all cases be sufficient to establish agreement with the interpretation of the Member.[96]

It is also necessary to recall the caution advocated by the AB in *Japan – Alcoholic Beverages II* in relying on 'subsequent practice' for purposes of interpretation, stating that it must not lead to interference with the 'exclusive authority' of the Ministerial Conference and the General Council to adopt interpretations of WTO covered agreements that are binding on all Members as per Article IX:2 of the WTO Agreement.[97]

[95] WTO Appellate Body Report, *United States – Measures Affecting the Cross-Border Supply of Gambling and Betting Services* (7 April 2005) WT/DS285/AB/R [192–93] (*US – Gambling*).

[96] *EC – Chicken Cuts* (n 64) [272].

[97] WTO Appellate Body Report, *Japan – Taxes on Alcoholic Beverages* (4 October 1996) WT/DS8/AB/R, WT/DS10/AB/R, WT/DS11/AB/R, 13–14 (*Japan – Alcoholic Beverages II*).

9.3.6.3 Relevant Rules of International Law Applicable in the Relations Between the Parties

There are three elements to be established in order to fall within the scope of Article 31(3)(c) of the VCLT: the principle must be a 'rule of international law', the rule must be 'relevant', and lastly, such rule must be applicable in the relations between the parties. Regarding the first two of these criteria, the AB in *US – Anti Dumping and Countervailing Duties* elaborated that:

> First, the reference to 'rules of international law' corresponds to the sources of international law in Article 38(1) of the Statute of the International Court of Justice and thus includes customary rules of international law as well as general principles of law. Second, in order to be relevant, such rules must concern the same subject matter as the treaty terms being interpreted.[98]

Now, coming to the final element of Article 31(3)(c), *the parties to which the rule is relevant*, there is still uncertainty as to the threshold to be satisfied. This becomes important as the relevant rule can be a rule of customary international law, that is generally applicable to all parties, or a treaty rule, that may be applicable only to certain parties. The question that arises is whether the term 'the parties' refers to the parties to a present dispute, or whether it means parties to the WTO Agreement as a whole.

The European Communities in *EC – Biotech* argued that the WTO covered agreements must be interpreted and applied by reference to relevant rules of international law arising outside the WTO context, as reflected in international agreements and declarations. They argued that the 1992 Convention on Biological Diversity and the 2000 Cartagena Protocol on Biosafety to the Convention on Biological Diversity fall within the scope of Article 31(3)(c) of the VCLT for the purposes of interpretation of the SPS Agreement, TBT Agreement, and GATT 1994. The Panel makes the following observations about the threshold requirements under Article 31(3)(c):

> Furthermore, and importantly, Article 31(3)(c) indicates that it is only those rules of international law which are 'applicable in the relations between the parties' that are to be taken into account in interpreting a treaty. This limitation gives rise to the question of what is meant by the term 'the parties'. In considering this issue, we note that Article 31(3)(c)

[98] *US – Anti-Dumping and Countervailing Duties (China)* (n 90) [308].

> does not refer to 'one or more parties'. Nor does it refer to 'the parties to a dispute'. We further note that Article 2.1(g) of the Vienna Convention defines the meaning of the term 'party' for the purposes of the Vienna Convention. Thus, 'party' means 'a State which has consented to be bound by the treaty and for which the treaty is in force'. It may be inferred from these elements that the rules of international law applicable in the relations between 'the parties' are the rules of international law applicable in the relations between the States which have consented to be bound by the treaty which is being interpreted, and for which that treaty is in force. This understanding of the term 'the parties' leads logically to the view that the rules of international law to be taken into account in interpreting the WTO agreements at issue in this dispute are those which are applicable in the relations between the WTO Members.[99]

The Panel therefore concluded in favour of a narrow interpretation of this clause[100] because all WTO Members, including some parties to the dispute, were not parties to the Convention on Biological Diversity and the Biosafety Protocol. However, given that even the more liberal requirement was not satisfied, as the disputing parties were not all parties to the Convention on Biological Diversity and the Biosafety Protocol, the Panel in effect refused to consider if the term 'the parties' in Article 31(3)(c) of the VCLT was a reference to *all the* parties to treaties.

Later, the AB in *EC – Aircrafts* noted that in a multilateral context like the WTO, a balance is required to be struck between the individual WTO Member's international obligations and ensuring a harmonious approach to interpretation of WTO law among all WTO Members.[101] This AB report suggests a move away from a purely conservative approach. However, in this case, the AB did not proceed to settle this issue as the second requirement under Article 31(3)(c) relating to relevance of the rule was not satisfied. Therefore, the AB has yet to conclusively pronounce on this issue, and it is presently under consideration by the ILC study group on fragmentation of international law and stands unresolved.[102]

At this juncture, it is also necessary to explain a peculiarity of the WTO DSS with respect to *application* of rules and *interpretation* of rules. This is particularly important in the context of understanding the

[99] *EC – Approval and Marketing of Biotech Products* (n 78) [7.68].

[100] ibid.

[101] WTO Appellate Body Report, *European Communities and Certain Member States – Measures Affecting Trade in Large Civil Aircraft* (18 May 2011) WT/DS316/AB/R [845] (*EC and Certain Member States – Large Civil Aircraft*).

[102] Gardiner (n 37) 317.

relationship between WTO covered agreements and general international law. The mandate of the WTO DSS, through Panels and the AB, is to determine whether the provision of WTO covered agreements[103] have been violated. The provisions of the DSU governing the terms of reference to Panels,[104] on function of Panels,[105] and recommendations of Panels and AB[106] limit in various ways the applicable law before the WTO DSS. In all these instances, the applicable law is restricted to WTO covered agreements, and the WTO DSS can only apply these WTO rules in any given dispute.[107] However, this restriction does not imply clinical isolation of the WTO rules from the rest of international law.[108] This restriction is precisely what makes Article 31(3)(c) of the VCLT an important tool in the interpretation of WTO covered agreements: It is an entry point for the relationship between WTO rules and public international law and a mechanism to promote coherence in international law. This makes the scope of Article 31(3)(c) and the interpretation of the term 'the parties' a critical determinant in allowing Panels and the AB to use non-WTO rules. If a strict and narrow interpretation of this term is adopted, to mean *all* WTO Members, this detracts from allowing Members to comply cumulatively and simultaneously with all their international obligations.

In this regard, an important consideration to be kept in mind with respect to the WTO Agreement is that the membership includes customs territories having full autonomy of its trade policies. However, other treaties do not include such actors within the scope of their membership. If a narrow interpretative approach is adopted to determine the scope of 'parties' in Article 31(3)(c) as meaning *all the parties* to the treaty, it would restrict the possibility of taking into account various other

[103] As listed in Appendix 1 of the DSU.

[104] DSU (n 33) art 7.

[105] ibid, art 11.

[106] ibid, art 19.

[107] For an opposing view see L Bartels, 'Applicable Law in WTO Dispute Settlement Proceedings' (2001) 35(3) JWT 499; J Pauwelyn, 'How to Win a WTO Dispute Based on Non-WTO Law? Questions of Jurisdiction and Merits' in S Griller (ed), *At the Crossroads: The World Trading System and the Doha Round* (Springer 2008) 1. For a more general discussion, see G Marceau and A Tomazos, 'Comments on Joost Pauwelyn's Paper: 'How to Win a WTO Dispute Based on Non-WTO Law?' in S Griller (ed), *At the Crossroads: The World Trading System and the Doha Round* (Springer 2008) 54.

[108] See G Marceau, 'A Call for Coherence in International Law: Praises for the Prohibition Against "Clinical Isolation" WTO Dispute Settlement' (1999) 33(5) JWT 87.

international agreements that may be relevant for the interpretative exercise and to promote coherence.

9.4 Supplementary Means of Interpretation and Treaties Authenticated in Multiple Languages

Articles 32 and 33 of the VCLT are considered customary international law along with Article 31, which has been the subject of discussion thus far.[109] When there are any gaps or ambiguity that persist regarding the meaning of a treaty term after the application of Article 31, the VCLT provides for further rules of interpretation under Articles 32 and 33. Recourse to supplementary means of interpretation under Article 32 can be used to confirm the meaning resulting from the application of Article 31 or to clarify it. Supplementary means of interpretation can be used when the meaning of a treaty term after the application of Article 31 is ambiguous or obscure or leads to a result that is manifestly absurd or unreasonable.[110] Article 33 of the VCLT is pertinent in the context of the WTO as the texts of the covered agreements have been authenticated in three languages – English, French, and Spanish. According to Article 33 of the VCLT, the texts in each of these languages would be authoritative.

9.4.1 Article 32 – Supplementary Means of Interpretation

The VCLT mentions preparatory work and circumstances under which the treaty was concluded as supplementary means of interpretation. The AB has emphasised that Article 32 does not provide an exhaustive list and that an interpreter retains flexibility when considering sources that may shed light on the common intention of parties.[111] In *EC – IT*

[109] WTO Appellate Body Report, *United States – Countervailing Duties on Certain Corrosion-Resistant Carbon Flat Steel Products from Germany* (28 November 2002) WT/DS213/AB/R [61–62] (*US – Carbon Steel*); WTO Appellate Body Report, *Chile – Price Band System and Safeguard Measures Relating to Certain Agricultural Products* (23 September 2002) WT/DS207/AB/R 271 (*Chile – Price Band System*); WTO Appellate Body Report, *United States – Final Countervailing Duty Determination with Respect to Certain Softwood Lumber from Canada* (19 January 2004) WT/DS257/AB/R [59] and fn 50 (*US – Softwood Lumber IV*).

[110] VCLT (n 54) art 32.

[111] *EC – Chicken Cuts* (n 64) [95].

Products, the panel held that HS2007 (Harmonized System)[112] could be a supplementary means of interpretation though it was concluded after the covered agreements and does not constitute preparatory work.[113] The panel noted that HS Codes are subject to evolution and if a current HS Code reflects the intention of parties at the time of concluding the treaty, it would serve as a supplementary means of interpretation.[114] The panel ultimately did not rely on HS2007 in this dispute as it found that the updated HS code did not reflect the common intention of parties when the treaty was concluded.

Supplementary means of interpretation have been used on several other occasions to confirm the meaning of treaty terms. In *Canada – Dairy* and *US – Gambling*, the AB used supplementary means to clarify the meaning of entries in the goods and services schedules of Canada and the US, respectively. The supplementary means used in *Canada – Dairy* were the circumstances surrounding the conclusion of the treaty, namely negotiations between Canada and the US on reciprocal market access. Scheduling Guidelines were used as a supplementary means in *US – Gambling*.[115] In the context of preparatory work, the AB has been cautious while giving weight to the negotiating history of a provision because there is no official record of negotiations for the WTO.[116]

When considering circumstances of the conclusion of a treaty as a supplemental means of interpretation, the value of unilateral practices of Members has often come up.[117] With respect to practices relating to tariff classifications, the AB has held that the practice of one Member would have limited value but would not be wholly irrelevant. In *EC – Computers*, the AB found that the panel had erred by not considering

[112] The Harmonised System is an international nomenclature developed by the World Customs Organization; WTO, 'Glossary' (*WTO*, 2023) <https://www.wto.org/english/thewto_e/glossary_e/glossary_e.htm> (last accessed 1 June 2025).

[113] WTO Panel Report, *European Communities and its member States – Tariff Treatment of Certain Information Technology Products* (16 August 2010) WT/DS375/R, WT/DS376/R, WT/DS377/R [7.694] (*EC – IT Products*).

[114] ibid [7.695].

[115] See e.g. WTO Panel Report, *China – Measures Affecting the Protection and Enforcement of Intellectual Property Rights* (26 January 2009) WT/DS362/R [7.260] (*China – Intellectual Property Rights*); WTO Appellate Body Report, *Canada – Certain Measures Concerning Periodicals* (30 June 1997) WT/DS31/AB/R, 33–34 (*Canada – Periodicals*).

[116] WTO Appellate Body Report, *India – Quantitative Restrictions on Imports of Agricultural, Textile, and Industrial Products* (23 August 1999) WT/DS90/AB/R, 94 (*India – Quantitative Restrictions*).

[117] Analytical Index (n 39) [88–90].

the tariff classification practice of the US.[118] In *EC – Chicken Cuts*, the AB broadened the scope of things that could be considered 'circumstances of the conclusion' of a treaty to include consistent classification practice of customs authorities, legislations' and judgemnts of domestic courts.[119] Dispute settlement reports have consulted a variety of sources under Article 32 of the VCLT. However, panels and the AB have been cautious when discerning a common interest from the negotiating history of the WTO as there is no official record.[120]

9.4.2 *Article 33 – Treaties Authenticated in Two or More Languages*

The last paragraph of the WTO Agreement unequivocally states that the English, French, and Spanish language versions of the treaty are authentic. When a treaty is authentic in more than one language, the presumption is that the provisions of all treaty texts have the same meaning and reflect the common intention of parties.[121] The Spanish and French versions of the GATT were used by the AB to explain the meaning of 'like' products under Article III:4,[122] when deciding between two meanings that could be ascribed to the preposition 'under' in Article X:2 of the GATT. Specifically, the AB was examining whether 'under' qualified the phrase 'rate of duty'. After referring to the French and Spanish versions, which used the phrase 'en vertu de' and 'en virtud de' (which translates in English as 'by virtue of'), the AB concluded that 'under' could not qualify the phrase 'rate of duty' as this would not be a possible construction in the Spanish and French versions.[123] The AB thus opted for an interpretation that was reconcilable with the other two versions.[124] The Panel in *United States – Origin Marking (Hong Kong, China)* refered to the texts in all three authenticated languages to find that not every tension or difference in international relations is an

[118] *EC – Computer Equipment* (n 86) [93–95].

[119] *EC – Chicken Cuts* (n 64) [287–309].

[120] See WTO Panel Report, *India – Export Related Measures* (31 October 2019) WT/DS541/R (*India – Export Related Measures*); Analytical Index (n 39) [84].

[121] WTO Panel Report, *Dominican Republic – Safeguard Measures on Imports of Polypropylene Bags and Tubular Fabric* (31 January 2012) WT/DS415/R, WT/DS416/R, WT/DS417/R, WT/DS418/R [7.433] (*Dominican Republic – Safeguard Measures*).

[122] *EC – Asbestos* (n 42) [91].

[123] *US – Anti-Dumping and Countervailing Duties (China)* (n 90) [4.76-4.77].

[124] ibid. See also Analytical Index (n 39) [98].

'emergency in international relations'. The situation has to represent a breakdown or near breakdown of international relations.[125]

Despite the covered agreements being authentic in three languages, Members will often designate only one or two of these languages as authentic for the purpose of their Schedules. Argentina's Schedule for specific commitments in Services is authentic only in Spanish.[126] Similarly, the Schedule of Concessions for goods of Canada was authenticated only in English and French at the conclusion of the Uruguay Round.[127] The latest version of the Schedule, however, is authentic only in English.[128] Following this practice, the Accession Protocol of Russia explicitly states that the protocol itself is authentic in the three official languages; however, the Schedule annexed is authentic only in English.[129]

One should also note that the negotiations during the Uruguay Rounds took place in English and the agreements were translated into French and Spanish before being authenticated. Thus, there is no formal hierarchy of languages in the WTO, and one may say that the WTO Agreement prohibits such a hierarchy. However, the question of whether, in practice, the authentic texts operate with a hierarchy is one worth exploring. Van Damme, for instance, posits that the AB has often failed to respond to Members contentions that are based on comparisons between texts of converted agreements in the three languages.[130] It would be interesting to see how claims made by a WTO Member relying on the French or Spanish text as the primary treaty text would be interpreted in light of the English text, before a WTO DSS body.

9.5 Other Principles Applicable to Treaty Interpretation in the WTO Context

While the VCLT codified some of the relevant customary rules of treaty interpretation, they are not exhaustive. There are several uncodified

[125] *United States – Origin Marking (Hong Kong, China)* (n 72) [7.289].

[126] WTO, 'Argentina, Schedule of Specific Commitments – Supplement I' (7 May 1997) GATS/SC/4/Suppl.1/Rev.1.

[127] WTO, 'Canada, Certification of Modifications and Rectifications of Schedule V' (16 December 1994) WT/LET/536.

[128] WTO, 'Canada, Schedule V' (12 May 2020) WT/LET/1469.

[129] WTO, 'Accession of the Russian Federation, Decision of 16 December 2011' (16 December 2011) WT/MIN(11)/24; WTO, 'Summary Record of the Third Meeting' (20 April 2012) WT/MIN(11)/SR/3.

[130] Van Damme (n 44) 333.

principles of treaty interpretation that Panels and the AB have resorted to. The AB in *US – Gasoline* held that the principle of effectiveness is one of the corollaries of the general rule of interpretation under the VCLT. An interpreter should, in light of good faith and the object and purpose of the treaty,[131] give meaning and effect to all the terms of the treaty[132] harmoniously.[133] The principle of evolutionary interpretation was used by the AB in *US – Shrimp* while holding that the term 'natural resources' in Article XX(g) of the GATT is not static and should be interpreted in light of 'contemporary concerns of the community of nations'.[134] In factual situations where two laws apply simultaneously, Panels and the AB have used the *lex specialis* doctrine to apply the one that applies specifically to the factual situation over the general one.[135]

9.6 Interpretation v. Application

Panels under the WTO DSS are, under their terms of reference, restricted from applying any legal instrument other than the covered agreements in examining a dispute referred to them.[136] Pursuant to Article 19 of the DSU, a Panel or AB can only make a finding and recommendations on the challenged measure's alleged inconsistency with a covered agreement.[137] No finding or recommendation can be made with respect to any legal instrument that is not a covered agreement.[138]

In *Peru – Agricultural Products*, the AB held that Members cannot enter into an agreement to maintain WTO-inconsistent measures. While Peru relied on Article 41 of the VCLT (agreements to modify multilateral treaties between certain of the parties only) to justify such WTO-inconsistent measures, the AB held that specific provisions on

131 ILC 'Draft Articles on the Law of Treaties with Commentaries' (4 May–19 July 1966) UN Doc A/CN.4/191, reproduced in [1966/II] YBILC 187, 219.

132 *US – Gambling* (n 95).

133 *Korea – Dairy* (n 8) [81].

134 *US – Shrimp* (n 40) [129–30].

135 *EC – Bananas III* (n 19) [204]; *US – 1916 Act* (n 30) [32]; WTO Panel Report, *United States – Measures Relating to Shrimp from Thailand* (29 February 2008) WT/DS343/R [7.159-7.160] (*US – Shrimp (Thailand)*).

136 DSU (n 33) art 7.1.

137 ibid, art 19.1.

138 WTO Appellate Body Report, *Mexico – Tax Measures on Soft Drinks and Other Beverages* (6 March 2006) WT/DS308/AB/R [78] (*Mexico – Taxes on Soft Drinks*).

amendments, waivers, or exceptions for RTAs under the WTO covered agreements would prevail over the general provision in the VCLT.[139]

However, this does not mean that non-WTO covered agreements have no role to play in WTO dispute settlement process. As stated by the AB in *US – Gasoline*, WTO covered agreements should not be interpreted in clinical isolation. As discussed herein above, the customary rules of interpretation may cause the interpretation of WTO provisions to be altered and influenced by other international rights and obligations. Article 31(3)(c) of the VCLT can be particularly important in this regard.[140]

9.7 Conclusion

The WTO dispute settlement system, through panels and the AB, has used the tools and principles of treaty interpretation to maintain an internal coherence between the various WTO covered agreements. The peculiarities of the WTO rules must be kept in mind while understanding the manner in which the WTO DSS employs customary rules of interpretation, specifically relating to the principle of the Single Undertaking.

The process of horizontal cross-fertilisation between agreements during the interpretative exercise has contributed to reducing conflict in the interpretation of similar provisions. By prioritising the principle of effective interpretation, the AB has ensured that Members' rights continue to be recognised in contemporaneous circumstances which may not have been foreseen by GATT negotiators (for instance, the interpretation of exhaustible natural resources in *US – Shrimp*). That context is found across various provisions of the WTO covered agreements and in the immediate surrounding words of the treaty term in question and this has allowed dispute settlement reports to maintain consistency without compromising on the specific purpose of provisions in different WTO covered agreements. For instance, when deciding on issues relating to burden of proof for provisions framed as exceptions, the AB used the context and object and purpose of these provisions to identify how burden of proof should be allocated. Likewise, in *EC – Tariff Preferences*, the AB found the Enabling Clause was an exception but one of a different shade given its objective to encourage non-most-

[139] WTO Appellate Body Report, *Peru – Additional Duty on Imports of Certain Agricultural Products* (20 July 2015) WT/DS457/AB/R [5.110-5.119] (*Peru – Agricultural Products*).

[140] Marceau and Tomazos (n 35) 54.

favored-nation (non-MFN) treatment for developing countries by developed countries. The use of the customary rules of interpretation has thus facilitated the coherent application of WTO covered agreements, which have myriad rules but no formal normative hierarchy that informs their application. Further, they hold the potential, through provisions like Article 31(3)(c) of the VCLT, to avoid clinical isolation of the WTO rules and promote coherence between WTO rules and international law.

10

Methods of Interpretation of International Investment Law

The Use of the Object and Purpose of Investment Treaties in Interpreting Territoriality

THOMAS NEKTARIOS PAPANASTASIOU

10.1 Introduction

This chapter aims to analyze the interpretation of the territoriality requirement under international investment treaties and explore the application of customary international law and the Vienna Convention on the Law of Treaties (VCLT), in particular Article 31, in international investment arbitration. It focuses on whether and to what extent special rules and methods pertaining to the process of interpretation have emerged in the field of international investment law.[1] International investment treaties, as a rule, extend protection only to assets that qualify as 'investments'. Similarly, the foreign private party's right to initiate dispute resolution against the host State under a treaty or investment law extends only to disputes arising out of that party's investments.[2]

[1] This chapter was presented in the conference 'The Practice of Interpretation in International Law: Unity, Diversity, and Evolution' that took place in the Hotel des Indes, The Hague, on 1–2 December 2022 organized under the TRICI-Law Project and the Department of Transboundary Legal Studies of the University of Groningen. The information and case-law referred to in this article were those available up until the time of organization of the conference.

[2] Investment is 'every kind of asset owned or controlled, directly or indirectly, by an investor'. OECD, 'The Multilateral Agreement on Investment: Draft Consolidated Text' (22 April 1998) OECD Doc DAFFE/MAI(98)7/Rev1, art II (2). Economists and legal commentators, meanwhile, more often describe investment as a phenomenon, a process, or an action. According to Sornarajah, '[f]oreign investment involves the transfer of tangible or intangible assets from one country into another for the purpose of use in that country to generate wealth under the total or partial control of the owner of the assets'.

The reason for this limitation is the perception among both less-developed and industrialized States that private investment is a catalyst for development and prosperity.[3] International investment treaties, including the Washington Convention and bilateral investment treaties (BITs),[4] constitute a conscious, and potentially politically costly, derogation of State sovereignty.[5] The State's sacrifice of freedom of action is done for a particular purpose, and that purpose closely defines the scope of operation of international investment treaties. The primary motivation for both developing and developed States to enter into these agreements is, in the words of the Washington Convention preamble, 'the need for international cooperation for economic development, and the role of private international investment therein', along with the need to create an international dispute resolution mechanism that can effectively protect foreign investments.[6] Thus, there is a recognition that a certain

M Sornarajah, *The International Law on Foreign Investment* (3rd edn, Cambridge University Press 2010) 8.

[3] On the importance of foreign investment to industrialized countries, see W Sholz, 'International Regulation of Foreign Direct Investment' (1998) 31 Cornell IntlLJ 485, 486. On the role of investment in Third World development, see World Bank, 'Development Issues: Presentations to the 41st Meeting of the Development Committee, 1991' (*World Bank*, 1991) 39 (Section on: The Role of Foreign Direct Investment in Development) <https://documents1.worldbank.org/curated/en/301731468765567295/pdf/multi-page.pdf> (last accessed 1 June 2025); I Shihata, *Legal Treatment of Foreign Investment: The World Bank Guidelines* (Brill 1993) 11; TW Wälde, 'Investment Arbitration under the Energy Charter Treaty' (1996) 12(4) Arbitration International 429, 430–31. The ostensible benefits of foreign direct investment (FDI) include wage increases, reduced unemployment, increased demand for local goods, inflow of foreign capital, opening of markets, improved balance of payments, transfer of industrial skills and knowledge, transfer of management skills, increased tax revenues and improved infrastructure. TG Telford and HA Ures, 'The Role of Incentives in Foreign Direct Investment' (2001) 23(4) Loyola International and Comparative Law Review 605, 615–16.

[4] Both bilateral and multilateral investment agreements are treaties within the meaning of art 1(1)(a) of the Vienna Convention on the Law of Treaties; Vienna Convention on the Law of Treaties (adopted 23 May 1969, entered into force 23 January 1980) 1155 UNTS 331 (VCLT).

[5] For the United States, investor-state arbitration 'requires the federal government's liability to be decided not by judges appointed by the President with the advice and consent of the Senate, but by a panel of international arbitrators'; B Legum, 'Federalism, NAFTA Chapter Eleven and the Jay Treaty of 1794' (2001) 95 ASIL Proc 202. From a Mexican point of view on the extent of derogation from state sovereignty as a result of international investment treaties and the consequent political cost, see B Sepulveda Amor, 'The NAFTA and the Claims of Mexican Jurisdiction' (1997) 19 Houston JIntlL 565, 586–91.

[6] Convention on the Settlement of Investment Disputes between States and Nationals of Other States (adopted 18 March 1965, entered into force 14 October 1966) 575 UNTS 159, Preamble (Washington Convention). For an illuminating and convincing economic

category of cross-border economic action, called 'foreign investment', helps expand welfare around the globe.[7] In addition, the majority of BITs indicate in the preamble their purpose to protect investments. The corollary is that other kinds of activities are not considered to have the same effect: short-term capital flows, particularly those involving speculation in debt or currency, are widely seen by host States as sources of monetary or economic instability, rather than stability and prosperity.[8] The derogation of State sovereignty necessary for a direct investor-State dispute resolution system is therefore generally viewed to be worth undertaking to the extent that it helps a developing country compete to attract 'good' asset flows, designated as 'investments'.[9]

However, one of the most challenging issues in international investment treaties is defining what qualifies as an 'investment'. This definition is crucial because it determines whether a foreign investor can initiate dispute resolution under a treaty or contract and whether the arbitral tribunal has jurisdiction *ratione materiae*.[10] Treaties signed before the 1990s often provided a relatively restricted definition of 'investment', sometimes expressly linking the concept to 'capital' or requiring that a local business enterprise be established to qualify for protection.[11] Other

analysis of developing countries' motivation in signing bilateral investment treaties, see AT Guzman, 'Why LDCs Sign Treaties That Hurt Them: Explaining the Popularity of Bilateral Investment Treaties' (1998) 38 VJIL 639. See also C Salgado Levy, 'Drafting and Interpreting International Investment Agreements from a Sustainable Development Perspective' (2015) 3(1) GroJIL 59, 67–68.

[7] TW Wälde and T Weiler, 'Investment Arbitration under the Energy Charter Treaty in the Light of New NAFTA Precedents: Towards a Global Code of Conduct for Economic Regulation?' in G Kaufmann-Kohler and B Stucki (eds), *Investment Treaties and Arbitration* (Swiss Arbitration Association 2002) 159, 160–62.

[8] A Lemaire, 'Le nouveau visage de l' arbitrage entre État et investisseur étranger: le chapitre 11 de l' ALENA' [2001] Revue de l'arbitrage 43, 59.

[9] Despite the overall benefits introducing the Investor-State dispute resolution regime, it is still unclear whether such a regime has supported host States to attract foreign investments. See J Webb Yackee, 'Do Bilateral Investment Treaties Promote Foreign Direct Investment? Some Hints from Alternative Evidence' (2010) 51 VJIL 397; UNCTAD, 'The Impact of International Investment Agreements on Foreign Direct Investment: An Overview of Empirical Studies 1998–2004' (IAA Issues Note – Working Draft 2014).

[10] About investment definition and what is protected by international investment treaties, see N Rubins QC, TN Papanastasiou and NS Kinsella, *International Investment, Political Risk, and Dispute Resolution. A Practitioner's Guide* (2nd edn, Oxford University Press 2020) 333–54.

[11] World Bank, 'Legal Framework for the Treatment of Foreign Investment: Survey of Existing Instruments – Vol 1' (Progress Report And Background Studies 24, World

BITs based on developed countries models[12] provided a broader and a more descriptive definition of investments including new forms of investments based on a non-exhaustive list of assets.[13]

The vast majority of international investment treaties include a specific wording in defining the term 'investment' or 'covered investment', requiring the investment to be made 'in the territory' of the host State. A typical example of a Treaty defining 'investment' is Article 1(2)(a) of the Colombia-UK BIT (2010) according to which 'Investments means every kind of economic asset, owned or controlled directly or indirectly, by investors of a Contracting Party *in the territory* of the other Contracting Party, in accordance with the law of the later.'[14] According to this condition, that the investment shall be made 'in the territory of the host State', it is evident that *ratione materiae* jurisdiction relies upon a territorial requirement. Arbitral tribunals follow specific rules and methods of interpretation in determining the territoriality requirement of investments in international investment arbitration.

On many occasions, arbitral investment tribunals have adopted interpretative approaches that prioritize the object and purpose of investment treaties – typically the promotion and protection of foreign investment – over other interpretative elements outlined in Articles 31 to 33 of VCLT.[15] The object and purpose of an international investment treaty

Bank 1992) <https://documents1.worldbank.org/curated/en/790571468782168106/pdf/multi-page.pdf> (last accessed 1 June 2025).

12 UNCTAD, 'International Investment Agreements: Flexibility for Development' [2000] UNCTAD Series on Issues in International Investment Agreements UNCTAD/ITE/IIT/18, 70.

13 Such list of assets consists of real estate and other direct property rights, shareholdings and other forms of participation in local companies, claims to payment or performance, intellectual property and other intangibles and concession or other similar types of agreements; CH Schreuerand et al, *The ICSID Convention: A Commentary* (2nd edn, Cambridge University Press 2010) 129. The US Model for Free Trade Agreements includes in its broad list of 'covered' investments various debt instruments, futures, options and other derivatives as well as concession, project financing or other similar contracts. See, for example, Singapore-United States, Free Trade Agreement (FTA) (adopted 6 May 2003, entered into force 1 January 2004) art 15.1(13) <https://www.ustr.gov/sites/default/files/uploads/agreements/fta/singapore/asset_upload_file708_4036.pdf> (last accessed 1 June 2025).

14 Colombia-United Kingdom, Bilateral Agreement for the Promotion and Protection of Investments (adopted 17 March 2010, entered into force 10 October 2014) (emphasis added) <https://investmentpolicy.unctad.org/international-investment-agreements/treaty-files/3253/download> (last accessed 1 June 2025).

15 VCLT (n 4); See CH Schreuer, 'Diversity and Harmonization of Treaty Interpretation in Investment Arbitration' in M Fitzmaurice, O Elias and P Merkouris (eds), *Treaty*

is usually referred to in the preamble of the treaty, which has a different wording and style than the main text of the treaty. This chapter explores how arbitral tribunals use the object and purpose of international investment treaties in interpreting territoriality, according to the rule of interpretation set forth in Article 31 of the VCLT. However, as it will be shown, the use of the object and purpose of a treaty shall not be used in a way to extend the obligations of the respondent State by overriding the text of the treaty.[16]

Arbitral tribunals tend to interpret the treaty's scope *ratione loci and ratione materiae* more broadly, requiring the territorial application of international investment treaties as compatible with the object and purpose of the treaties. Arbitral tribunals, in these instances, seem to lean towards *pro investore* interpretative constructions by prioritizing teleological interpretation and the principle of effectiveness, sometimes over other interpretative elements, including that of the principle of systemic integration. They do so, by resorting to specific objectives such as the protection and promotion of foreign investments, and the economic development of the States, considering them as the main purpose of international investment treaties.

As will be analyzed in Section 10.2, such methods may apply to economic services performed outside the national jurisdiction of host States. In more detail, the economic dimension of the territorial requirement may differ according to the interpretative approach taken by investment tribunals. Section 10.2.1 will focus on the 'economic benefit" approach. Section 10.2.2 will supplement this analysis by examining the 'economic unity of the investment' approach.

Interpretation and the Vienna Convention on the Law of Treaties: 30 Years On (Brill/Nijhoff 2010) 129.

[16] As emphasized in the *Ambiente* Dissenting Opinion: 'It is evident that reading away Article 25's investment requirement is at odds with the treaty interpretation rules of the VCLT which are based on the principle that the text must be presumed to be the authentic expression of the intention of the parties and which incorporate also the principle of "effective interpretation" *(effet utile)* under the control of good faith and the object and purpose of the treaty subject to the interpretation. As explained by Professor Abi-Saab in his dissenting opinion in 2011 *Abaclat* decision, the term "investment" in art 25(1) "whilst flexible enough is not infinitely elastic" it has a "hard-core", which should be identified looking into the general context of the ICSID Convention and the circumstances surrounding its elaboration as well as to its object and purpose'; *Ambiente Ufficio SPA and others v the Argentine Republic* (Dissenting Opinion of Santiago Torres Bernárdez to Decision on Jurisdiction and Admissibility of 2 May 2013) ICSID Case No ARB/08/9 [203].

Section 10.3 will then argue that the interpretative methods employed by investment tribunals that give preference to teleological and effectiveness interpretative constructions, and which prioritize the protection of the investor (*pro investore* interpretation), may also apply to foreign investments established in the territory of another state where the host State exercises effective control but does not have sovereign rights. In more detail, this chapter will delve into the extraterritorial application of BITs in situations where these investments are located in occupied areas, such as recent arbitration cases that are related to Russia's illegal annexation of Crimea (Section 10.3.1). While the primary focus remains on the investment law implications, it is important to acknowledge that the scenarios under discussion also engage broader and complex questions of sovereignty, territorial status and the legality of competing claims. Although these issues fall outside the core scope of the present analysis, their relevance cannot be overlooked, and they are therefore briefly addressed at appropriate points in the chapter to provide necessary context.

10.2 The Territorial Nexus between the Investment and the Host State (*ratione materiae*): The Economic Dimension of the Territorial Requirement

The notion of investment and its definition has yet to become a serious barrier to jurisdiction in investor-State arbitration.[17] Nevertheless, respondent States have raised the issue as a jurisdictional objection in a large number of ICSID cases. Tribunals have tended to approach each such objection largely on its own merits and with regard to the circumstances of the case at hand.[18]

According to the majority of international investment treaties, the territorial requirement of investment is considered as a jurisdictional condition. Only investments made 'in the territory' of the host State can be a 'protected investment'. The territoriality requirement plays a central role in determining the scope of application *ratione materiae* of

[17] GR Delaume, 'Consent to ICSID Arbitration' in JJ Norton, M Footer and M Andenas (eds), *The Changing World of International Law in the Twenty-First Century: A Tribute to the Late Kenneth R. Simmonds* (Kluwer Law International 1998) 155, 155–74.

[18] Generally, tribunals interpret 'investment' liberally; *Fedax NV v Republic of Venezuela* (Decision on Objections to Jurisdiction on 11 July 1997) ICSID Case No ARB/96/3; *Fedax NV v The Republic of Venezuela* (Award of 9 March 1998) ICSID Case No ARB/96/3.

BITs, as it links the protection afforded by the treaty to investments made within the territory of the host State.[19] While the ICSID Convention does not explicitly define the territorial requirement, it implicitly incorporates this notion through its reference to a 'dispute arising directly out of an investment' under Article 25. In practice, ICSID tribunals often rely on the territorial scope defined in the underlying BIT or investment contract to assess whether the dispute falls within their jurisdiction.[20] Thus, arbitral tribunals have jurisdiction *ratione materiae* to adjudicate a case only when the investment at stake is located in the territory of the host State.[21] However, unlike tangible assets that have physical presence and it is easy to identify the investment (e.g. immovable property), it is difficult to determine whether non tangible assets, such as contractual rights, financial transactions and economic activities performed outside of the host State, are 'located' in the territory of the host State. Those assets have an immaterial nature as they lack a physical location.

In general, as a jurisdictional condition for the arbitral system of dispute resolution, 'the conception of an investment at the jurisdictional stage can only serve the object and purpose of the treaty if it is conducive

[19] In the majority of BITs, the territorial requirement is included in the definition of investment clauses. For example, see the Agreement Concerning the Encouragement and Mutual Protection of Investments between Russia and Ukraine (adopted 27 November 1998, entered into force 27 January 2000) art 1(1) <https://investmentpolicy.unctad.org/international-investment-agreements/treaty-files/2233/download> (last accessed 1 June 2025), 'For the purposes of this Agreement: 1. "*Investments*" shall denote all kinds of property and intellectual values, which are put in by the investor of one Contracting Party *on the territory* of the other Contracting Party in conformity with the latter's legislation, and in particular: a) movable and immovable property and any other rights of property therein; b) monetary funds and also securities, liabilities, deposits and other forms of participation; c) rights to objects of intellectual property, including authors' copyrights and related rights, trade marks, the rights to inventions, industrial samples, models and also technological processes and know-how; d) rights to perform commercial activity, including rights to prospecting, development and exploitation of natural resources. No alteration of the type of investments, which the funds are put in, shall affect their nature as investments, unless such alteration is contrary to the laws of a Contracting Party on *whose territory the investments were made*' (emphasis added).

[20] The Tribunals underline that both the BIT and the ICSID Convention require a territorial link between the investment and the host State. See *Sociedad General de Aguas de Barcelona SA (Agbar) v Argentine Republic* (Decision on Jurisdiction of 2 May 2006) ICSID Case No ARB/03/17 [65].

[21] A Reinisch, 'Investment Disputes and their Boundaries' in Société Française pour le Droit International (ed), *Droit des* Frontières *Internationales: The Law of International Borders* (Pedone 2016) 207, 208–10.

to a relatively high degree of legal certainty'.[22] One of the necessary elements in determining the investment concept is the territorial connection with the host State. In addition, considering the notion of territory, international investment treaties often implicitly or explicitly tie the concept of territory to the sovereign power of the host State. Sovereign power refers to the State's capacity to govern and exercise authority over its territory and people. This includes creating and enforcing laws, regulating economic activities and upholding public order. The exercise of enforcement jurisdiction is particularly significant as it denotes not only a State's legal authority but also its actual ability to apply and enforce its laws within a given territory.[23] Actually, the territorial link between an investment and the host State and the extent of sovereign power of contracting states to enforce their laws are at the heart of international investment law.[24] Otherwise, arbitral tribunals cannot accept that the alleged violations fall within the jurisdiction of the host State. Therefore, no international responsibility can be attributed to the host State if it has no jurisdiction and sovereign power over the investment or the investor. Thus, the essential rule of international investment law that contracting States must avoid any arbitrary behaviour towards foreign investments in their territory (the so called 'political' or 'sovereign' risk)[25] is combined with their obligation to enforce their national laws 'consistently' along

[22] Z Douglas, 'Property, Investment, and the Scope of Investment Protection Obligations' in Z Douglas, J Pauwelyn and JE Viñuales (eds), *The Foundations of International Investment Law: Bringing Theory into Practice* (Oxford University Press 2014) 362, 372.

[23] For example, art 1(6) of Italy-Turkey BIT refers that the term 'territory' designates: 'the land within the land boundaries and the territorial waters of each contracting Party as well as the exclusive economic zone and the continental shelf that extends outside the limits of the territorial waters of each of the Contracting Parties over which they have or could have jurisdiction or sovereign rights'. See Agreement Concerning Reciprocal Promotion and Protection of Investments between Turkey and Italy (adopted 22 March 1995, entered into force 2 March 2004) <https://edit.wti.org/document/show/4cf0850e-3460-4238-9b9c-f9391198a4fc> (last accessed 1 June 2025). See also CR Zheng, 'The Territoriality Requirement in Investment Treaties: A Constraint on Jurisdictional Expansionism' (2016) 34 SingLR 139, 147.

[24] A Tancredi, 'Some Thoughts on Deterritorialization and Effectiveness in International Law' in A di Stefano (ed), *A Lackland Law? Territory, Effectiveness and Jurisdiction in International and European Law* (Giappichelli 2015) 52.

[25] For an analysis of the role of international investment law in mitigating political risk, see TN Papanastasiou, *The Legal Protection of Foreign Investments Against Political Risk: Japanese Business in The Asian Energy Sector* (Quid Pro 2015).

with their responsibility to protect investments.[26] In fact, the host State's obligation to protect investments located in its territory is the primary objective of all international investment treaties, along with the economic development of the host State and the enhancement of economic cooperation between the contracting States. Host States are not required to protect investments located outside their territory, unless a territorial link is established.[27]

Where contractual rights or intangible 'assets' constitute an investment, there is still a need for that investment to qualify for a territorial link with the host State. Therefore, it is a requirement of international law that the territorial jurisdiction of the host State is necessary even for non-tangible investments, to enforce its laws in accordance with its general obligation to protect the investment.

For this reason, this section seeks to identify methods of interpreting territoriality applied by arbitral tribunals in determining their jurisdiction for cases involving financial transactions or other economic activities.[28]

To interpret territoriality according to customary law as enshrined in Article 31 VCLT, there are several criteria applied by arbitral tribunals in order to satisfy the condition of the BITs on the definition of protected investment. Taking into consideration these criteria, there are two approaches used in arbitral practice: (i) the subjective approach to the 'economic utility of the investment for the host State', the so called 'economic benefit test'; and (ii) the integrated aspect of the investment, the so called 'economic unity of the investment' test.[29]

[26] According to Douglas, this is actually the raison d' être of an investment treaty and the international investment law: 'the whole architecture of an investment treaty rests upon the imposition of constraints upon the exercise of territorial jurisdiction by the contracting States parties'. Douglas (n 22) 372–73.

[27] Either by actual proof for the locus of a tangible asset or by the host State's private international law for an intangible asset. With regard to private international law, the territorial link is determined by factors such as choice of law, choice of forum, the situs of financial damage etc; Douglas (n 22) 373–86. There are also many international investment treaties that incorporate private international law rules when they provide that arbitral tribunals decide on the basis of the contracting party's laws *as well as its rules on the conflict of laws*. See Agreement on the Promotion and Protection of Investments between Argentina and Italy (adopted 22 May 1990, entered into force 14 October 1993) art 8(7) <https://edit.wti.org/document/show/5b96aa7a-a6d0-4fa5-be70-660428ddcb86> (last accessed 1 June 2025).

[28] In other words, to assess the localization of financial investments fulfilling the requirement of territorial jurisdiction.

[29] These approaches are identified in A Pecoraro, 'Law of the Sea and Investment Protection in Deep Seabed Mining' (2020) 19 MJIL 530, 530–71; see also C Kleiner and F Costamagna, 'Territoriality in Investment Arbitration: The Case of Financial Instruments' (2018) 9 JIDS 315, 315–38.

10.2.1 The 'Economic Benefit' Test

The 'economic benefit' test or approach was taken by arbitral tribunals in cases related to various financial instruments issued by the host State, such as promissory notes,[30] bonds,[31] hedging agreements,[32] loans[33] and others. According to these cases, arbitral tribunals interpreted the territorial requirement by using economic characteristics of the investment, such as whether there is any economic contribution to the host State, which is an assertion made simply favouring an interpretation that gives full effect to the rights of investors. For example, the arbitral tribunal in *Abaclat* adopted a functional (economic) interpretation of the investment's territorial-link requirement for the financial assets at stake to be considered as 'covered investments' under the Italy-Argentina BIT:

> With regard to investments of a purely financial nature, the relevant criteria should be where and/or for the benefit of whom the funds are ultimately used, and not the place where the funds were paid out or transferred. Thus, the relevant question is where the invested funds ultimately made available to the Host State [sic] and did they support the latter's economic development . . . it was used by Argentina to manage its finances, and as such must be considered to have contributed to Argentina's economic development and thus to have been made in Argentina.[34]

For some types of investment like financial instruments and transactions taken outside the host State, arbitral tribunals considered that physical

[30] *Fedax, NV v Republic of Venezuela* (n 18).

[31] Cases related to the 2001 Argentinean sovereign debt restructuring and the following request for arbitration by creditors that gave rise to various decisions by arbitral tribunals. For example, *Abaclat and others (formerly Giovanna A Beccara and others) v the Argentine Republic* (Decision on Jurisdiction and Admissibility of 4 August 2011) ICSID Case No ARB/07/5; *Ambiente Ufficio SPA and others v the Argentine Republic* (Decision on Jurisdiction and Admissibility of 8 February 2013) ICSID Case No ARB/08/9; *Giovanni Alemanni and others v the Argentine Republic* (Decision on Jurisdiction and Admissibility of 17 November 2014) ICSID Case No ARB/07/8.

[32] *Deutsche Bank AG v Democratic Socialist Republic of Sri Lanka* (Award of 31 October 2012) ICSID Case No ARB/09/2.

[33] *Ceskoslovenska Obchodni Banka, as v the Slovak Republic* (Decision of the Tribunal on Objections to Jurisdiction of 24 May 1999) ICSID Case No ARB/97/4.

[34] *Abaclat and others (formerly Giovanna A Beccara and others) v the Argentine Republic*, (n 31) [374]. According to the *Ambiente Ufficio* case, 'in order to identify in which State's territory an investment was made, one has to determine first which State benefits from this investment . . .. Accordingly, to assess where the investment was made, the criterion must be to whose economic development an investment contributed'. *Ambiente Ufficio SPA and others v the Argentine Republic* (n 31) [499].

presence of an investment should not be a decisive factor, because the relevant criteria cannot be the same as those applying to an investment with a tangible nature. An important factor for the territorial requirement of investments with a purely financial nature should be whether such financial transactions were made available and utilized for the economic benefit of the host State.[35]

Such an interpretative approach of the territorial requirement based on the economic benefit condition is problematic. In fact, by replacing the required territorial link between the investment and the host State with the condition of the host State's economic benefit, it creates different results than the textual meaning of the investment treaties' provisions.[36] According to arbitral tribunals, the 'economic benefit' test replaces the requirement that an investment be 'made in the territory of the host State' by a subjective criterion, that an investment be made for the 'benefit of the host State'. In this vein, there is neither a need to localize financial instruments nor to demonstrate whether financial entitlements are associated with a specific investment project located in the host State, therefore invalidating territoriality as a jurisdictional requirement in international investment arbitration. Finally, concerning the application of the benefit test to sovereign debt instruments like the bond cases in Argentina, apart from the difficulty to prove that the host State is the ultimate beneficiary of financial entitlements on the secondary market,[37] it is quite unclear how to establish the required connection of the funds generated by the purchase of such instruments for the benefit or economic development of the host State.[38] Otherwise, if arbitral tribunals

[35] In the *Fedax v Venezuela* award, the arbitral tribunal emphasized that: 'The important question is whether the funds made available are utilized by the beneficiary of the credit, as in the case of the Republic of Venezuela, so as to finance its various governmental needs'; *Fedax, NV v Republic of Venezuela* (n 18) [48]; *Abaclat and others (formerly Giovanna A. Beccara and others) v the Argentine Republic* (n 31) [374]; *Ambiente Ufficio SPA and others v the Argentine Republic* (n 31) [504]; see also *Deutsche Bank AG v Democratic Socialist Republic of Sri Lanka* (n 32) [292].

[36] Such approach 'clearly goes against the ordinary meaning of the words included in the treaty'; A Arcuri and F Violi, 'Reconfiguring Territoriality in International Economic Law' (2017) 47 NYBIL 175, 202–4. Additionally, it 'converts the objective condition attached to the localization in the territory of the host State into a subjective criterion'. Kleiner and Costamagna (n 29) 315–23.

[37] It cannot be shown how the host State can gain any benefit from financial transactions that take place in the secondary market (where funds go from the bondholders to intermediaries).

[38] In some cases, the arbitral tribunal did not even justify that there was an actual benefit to the economic development of the host State but merely proved that there was an

assume that any financial instrument that can benefit the host State can satisfy the concept of 'investment' or 'protected investment' through such a 'functional' interpretation of the territoriality requirement, then there is no substantial difference between foreign direct investments and portfolio investments or simple cross-border payments.[39] Therefore, such a broad and loose interpretation of territoriality leads to a subjective and absurd result that is contrary to the textual interpretation of the territorial clause contained in most international investment treaties.

10.2.2 The 'Economic Unity of the Investment' Test

In order to fulfil the territorial requirement of investment and establish the *ratione materiae* jurisdiction of arbitral tribunals, it is important to justify a connection between the financial operation and the territory of the host State. Such territorial nexus cannot be circumvented by a loose and exaggerated interpretation of the territorial requirement contained in most international investment treaties, transforming the territorial into an economic or functional element.[40] Judge Abi-Saab in his Dissenting Opinion in *Abaclat* criticized the opinion of the majority in defining investment and emphasized that the ordinary meaning of the investment made in the territory of the other Party could not be clearer, 'except by tracing it to a specific project, enterprise or activity in that territory that corresponds to the economic meaning of investment in article 25 of the ICSID Convention'.[41] As the tribunal held in *SGS v Philippines*, '[i]n

intention to benefit the host State. See *Deutsche Bank AG v Democratic Socialist Republic of Sri Lanka* (n 32) [286–87].

39 Douglas (n 22) 384–85. Actually, concerning the problem of including financial instruments in the notion of investment is not a problem of the intangible character or other characteristics of these instruments; 'it is rather related to the remoteness of these products from the economic activity, project or enterprises which materialize the investment within the territory of the host State'. See Arcuri and Violi (n 36) 175–215.

40 Pecoraro (n 29) 530–71. See also Kleiner and Costamagna (n 29) 315–38. See the dissenting opinion in *Abaclat*: 'This requisite territorial link is clearly absent in the present case. The alleged investment, the security entitlements, are not located in Argentina by applying either the legal or the material criteria for determining such location'; *Abaclat and others v the Argentine Republic* (Dissenting Opinion of Georges Abi-Saab to Decision on Jurisdiction and Admissibility of 28 October 2011) ICSID Case No ARB/07/5 [77]; see also *Ambiente Ufficio SPA and others v the Argentine Republic* (Dissenting Opinion of Santiago Torres Bernárdez to Decision on Jurisdiction and Admissibility of 2 May 2013) (n 16) [243–46, 299].

41 *Abaclat and others v the Argentine Republic* (Dissenting Opinion of Georges Abi-Saab to Decision on Jurisdiction and Admissibility of 28 October 2011) (n 40) [95].

accordance with normal principles of treaty interpretation, investments made outside the territory of the Respondent State, however beneficial to it, would not be covered by the BIT'.[42]

Alternatively, arbitral tribunals have developed through their case-law a method of interpreting territoriality based on the 'economic unity of the investment'.[43] Such an approach is different to the 'economic benefit' concept as it does not circumvent the textual interpretation of territorial clauses but can still be adopted in investments with a non-physical nature or operations performed outside the host State. The 'economic unity of the investment' test examines whether each activity is a 'substantial and non-severable aspect of the overall service' that is provided in the territory of the host State.[44] According to this approach, if an activity or a financial transaction is carried outside the host State, and is verified as an integral part of the overall operation (the investment), or can be traced to a specific project that is localized in the territory of the host State, then this activity can qualify as a protected investment in the territory of that State.[45]

This approach, known as the 'economic unity of the investment' doctrine, assesses whether or not separate activities can be regarded as part of an overall operation that needs to be performed in the territory of the host State.[46] For example, in *SGS v Philippines*, the activity at stake performed outside the Philippines was related to the provision of

[42] *SGS Société Générale de Surveillance SA v Republic of the Philippines* (Decision of the Tribunal on Objections to Jurisdiction of 29 January 2004) ICSID Case No ARB/02/6 [99]. See also *Deutsche Bank AG v Democratic Socialist Republic of Sri Lanka* (n 32) [292].

[43] The 'economic unity of the investment' (or the 'overall operation') approach, which stems from the investment tribunals' jurisprudence, as a name and theory is analyzed in Pecoraro (n 29) 530–71; see also Kleiner and Costamagna (n 29) 315–38.

[44] *SGS Société Générale de Surveillance SA v Republic of the Philippines* (n 42) [102].

[45] For example, the Tribunal in the *CSOB* Award held that '[t]he contractual scheme embodied in the Consolidation Agreement shows, however, that the CSOB loan to the Slovak Collection Company is closely related to and cannot be disassociated from all other transactions involving the restructuring of CSOB'; *CSOB v The Slovak Republic* (Decision on Objections to Jurisdiction of 24 May 1999) ICSID Case No ARB/97/4 [80].

[46] There are also studies that advocate about the application of the 'economic unity of the investment' test in some transboundary activities that are performed in areas where no State can exercise sovereign rights. Such a case is, for example, the extracting activities in high seas and in the Area, which according to the International Law of the Sea has a special status as the common heritage of mankind. If the deep-seabed mining activities operating in the Area constitute an integral part of the investment in the territory of the sponsoring State (the host State), then such activities could qualify as protected investment under the international investment law. These mining activities performed in the Area are usually structured in an interrelated way to the main operation and assets, which

pre-shipment inspection services for exports directed to the host State with the objective of improving the import trade of the Philippines. Such activities were carried out in accordance with the main goal of the investment contract, the improvement of a reliable inspection certificate system, and were not subdivided with the overall services provided within the Philippines, therefore they were classified as investments made in the territory of the host State.[47] In this case, as well as in other cases such as *Deutsche telecom AG v India*[48] and in *Deutsche Bank v Sri Lanka*[49] concerning financial instruments, the Tribunal examined the overall purpose of the investor's activities in order to assess whether the territoriality requirement is fulfilled. It concluded that even if the activities at issue are performed outside the host State or consist of financial instruments, contracts, licences and other agreements or arrangements, which alone do not qualify as an investment, they can still constitute protected investment when they are a substantial and interrelated part of the wider activity that is performed in the territory of the host State.[50] In conclusion, financial instruments, notwithstanding their remoteness from the economic activity or project in the territory of the host State, have to be interconnected with that activity or project in order to qualify as a 'protected investment'.[51]

are localized in the territory of the sponsoring State. See, for example, Pecoraro (n 29) 530–71.

[47] *SGS Société Générale de Surveillance SA v Philippines* (n 42) [101–12]. Similarly, see *SGS Société Générale de Surveillance SA v Pakistan* (Decision on Objections to Jurisdiction of 6 August 2003) ICSID Case No ARB/01/13; *SGS Société Générale de Surveillance SA v Paraguay* (Decision on Jurisdiction of 12 February 2010) ICSID Case No ARB/07/29.

[48] The activity at stake performed outside the host State was related to the delivery of hybrid satellite and terrestrial telecommunication services in the host State; *Deutsche Telekom AG v India* (Interim Award of 13 December 2017) PCA Case No 2014-10.

[49] In this case, although the Tribunal adopted the 'economic benefit' test applied in the *Abaclat* Award, it accepted that the financial instrument at case (a hedging agreement) was interconnected with the main activity taking place in the territory of the host State: '[i]n the present case, it is undisputed that the funds paid by Deutsche Bank in execution of the Hedging Agreement were made available to Sri Lanka, were linked to an activity taking place in Sri Lanka and served to finance its economy which is oil dependent. The Tribunal therefore decides that the condition of a territorial nexus with Sri Lanka is satisfied'. *Deutsche Bank AG v Democratic Socialist Republic of Sri Lanka* (n 32) [292].

[50] So at least, it must be proven that these activities constitute an 'indivisible whole' of an overall operation that is performed in the territory of the host State. See, for example, *Enron Corporation v Argentina* (Decision on Jurisdiction of 14 January 2004) ICSID Case No ARB/01/3 [70].

[51] Arcuri and Violi (n 36) 175.

Otherwise, they would probably be identified as mere cross-border trade transactions.[52]

In this regard, for non-tangible investments to be considered covered investments, arbitral tribunals tend to interpret territoriality by applying two different approaches. The 'economic benefit' approach represents a subjective and investor-centric method, which tends to decouple the investment from the territory of the host State by focusing primarily on the investor's economic gain, rather than on where the core investment activities take place. In contrast, the 'economic unity of the investment' approach applies a more textually and contextually consistent interpretative method, aligning more closely with the object and purpose of territorial clauses in investment treaties – namely, to ensure that treaty protections apply only to investments genuinely linked to the host State's territory and regulatory control. This latter approach supports the tribunal's *ratione materiae* jurisdiction by reinforcing the territorial scope contemplated in both treaties and contracts.

However, this interpretive trend illustrates the increasing prominence of teleological and effectiveness-based reasoning in investment arbitration. Rather than adhering strictly to the ordinary meaning or textual constraints of territorial clauses, some tribunals appear to prioritize the effective realization of the treaty's overarching purpose – such as the promotion and protection of foreign investment – even if this requires stretching the geographic or legal boundaries of what qualifies as a territorial link. In this respect, the investment arbitration jurisprudence may signal a divergence from a holistic approach under Article 31(1) VCLT, which requires that treaty terms be interpreted in good faith according to their ordinary meaning, in context, and in light of their object and purpose. Here, the teleological element seems to assume a driver's seat in the interpretative exercise, sometimes at the expense of textual and contextual fidelity.

In the next section, we examine how arbitral tribunals use a teleological interpretation of the territoriality requirement, not as a condition of BITs to determine a protected investment pursuant to *ratione materiae* jurisdiction but to determine territory when the investment is located in occupied areas over which a State exercises *de facto control.*

[52] See, for example, *Grand River Enterprises Six Nations Ltd v United States of America* (Award of 12 January 2011) Arbitral Tribunal (North American Free Trade Agreement Chapter 11) [23–25]; *Bayview Irrigation District et al v United Mexican States* (Award of 19 June 2007) ICSID Case No ARB(AF)/05/1 [102, 104].

10.3 The Extraterritorial Application of BITs

The term *extraterritorial jurisdiction* traditionally refers to a State's exercise of legal authority over conduct or persons outside its sovereign territory, subject to the limits set by international law. However, in the context of investment arbitration, this term may be misleading. Rather than exercising jurisdiction in a strictly extraterritorial sense, some arbitral tribunals have interpreted BITs as applying to investments located beyond the internationally recognized borders of the host State – such as in occupied territories – so long as the host State exercises effective control over the area. This practice blurs the line between territorial and extraterritorial application, raising important questions about how territorial clauses in BITs are interpreted in light of sovereignty disputes.

Crucially, the question is whether shifts in effective control over a territory may also affect the tribunal's jurisdiction *ratione* loci, as jurisdiction under a BIT often hinges on whether the host State had sufficient authority to extend treaty protections to the investment at the relevant time.[53]

Extraterritorial jurisdiction has been jurisprudentially validated by international courts and tribunals, such as the European Court of Human Rights (ECtHR).[54] Actually, international investment law and international human rights law share foundational principles – such as the protection of individual rights against State interference and access to international adjudication[55] – which allows for meaningful interaction between the two fields.[56] Moreover, observing a growing reference to

[53] D Costelloe, 'Conceptions of State Jurisdiction in the Jurisprudence of the International Court of Justice and the Permanent Court of International Justice' in S Allen et al (eds), *The Oxford Handbook of Jurisdiction in International Law* (Oxford University Press 2019) 455, 455–60.

[54] The ECtHR has repeatedly affirmed the extraterritorial jurisdiction and international responsibility of contracting States for violation of human rights treaty provisions and has recognized state jurisdiction in interpreting the various forms of state power and control. A typical example is the emblematic *Loizidou* Judgement. See *Loizidou v Turkey* [GC] (18 December 1996) Application no 15318/89 [52, 56].

[55] PM Dupuy, 'Unification Rather Than Fragmentation of International Law? The Case of International Investment Law and Human Rights Law' in PM Dupuy, EU Petersmann and F Francioni (eds), *Human Rights in International Investment Law and Arbitration* (Oxford University Press 2009) 45; M Fanou and VP Tzevelekos, 'The Shared Territory of the ECHR and International Investment Law' in Y Radi (ed), *Research Handbook on Human Rights and Investment* (Edward Elgar 2018) 93.

[56] J Coleman, K Cordes and L Johnson, 'Human Rights Law and the Investment Treaty Regime' in S Deva and D Birchall (eds), *Research Handbook on Human Rights and*

human rights in investment arbitration case law, it is interesting to explore whether investment tribunals should take into consideration ECHR and other human rights treaties as relevant rules for the interpretation of their respective investment agreements, according to the customary principle of systemic integration as enshrined in Article 31(3)(c) VCLT.[57]

This section examines the notion of extraterritoriality and the methods of interpretation that arbitral tribunals have used under article 31 VCLT in order to assess the territoriality requirement, and their jurisdiction *ratione loci* to adjudicate a case.[58] For the purpose of this chapter, the extraterritoriality of a BIT refers to its territorial extension applying to investments made in the territory of a State,[59] which is partially occupied by the State that is a contracting party to that BIT. In particular, this chapter explores whether the changes of 'effective control' over the territory[60] affects an arbitral tribunal's jurisdiction under that BIT.[61]

Following the recent developments of international arbitration related to the illegal annexation of the Crimean Peninsula by Russia, this chapter

Business (Edward Elgar 2020) 290; E de Brabandere, 'Human Rights and International Investment Law' in M Krajewski and RT Hoffmann (eds), *Research Handbook on Foreign Direct Investment* (Edward Elgar 2019) 619.

57 TN Papanastasiou, 'The Role of Human Rights in International Investment Arbitration: Arguments Raised by the Parties and Procedural Implications' (2022) 21 LPICT 149, 170–73; N Jansen Calamita, 'International Human Rights and the Interpretation of International Investment Treaties: Constitutional Considerations' in F Baetens (ed), *Investment Law within International Law: Integrationist Perspectives* (Cambridge University Press 2013) 178.

58 This section does not focus on the definition of investment and territoriality requirement of intangible investments that determines the scope *ratione materiae* of most international investment treaties. It is about the interpretation of the term 'territory' and the *ratione loci* application of the international investment treaties when the investment is in a contested or occupied area.

59 Investments that became foreign because of the change of effective control in the territory in question.

60 *Effective control* means the exercise of any jurisdictional function or power over the territory in question, despite the fact that such exercise is illegal under international law. The effective control notion has elaborated by the rich ECtHR's case law. The latest ECtHR's case (*Ukraine and the Netherlands v Russia)*, the effective control of Russia over the occupied territory of Ukraine was confirmed. In this case, the Grand Chamber stated that certain 'areas [of Ukraine] were, from 11 May 2014 and subsequently, under the effective control of the Russian Federation'; *Ukraine and the Netherlands v Russia* [GC] (25 January 2023) App nos 8019/16, 43800/14 and 28525/20 [695].

61 O Kuchmienko, 'To BIT or not to BIT? The Effects of Changes in Effective Control and Temporal Scope on Investment Tribunal Jurisdiction under Ukraine-Russia BIT' (master's thesis, Uppsala University 2019).

uses the Crimean conflict as a case study in exploring whether investments that existed prior to the armed conflict and were damaged, not necessarily by the host State, but rather by another State that occupies part of the host State's territory, can be protected through the BIT framework. On the occasion of the Crimean investment-arbitration cases, this section examines whether international investment treaties apply to occupied territories in view of the *effective* (or *de facto*) control of the aggressor State party over that territory.[62]

Notably, it analyzes the Russia-Ukraine BIT applicability in the territory of Crimea as an investment protection mechanism (in the context of disputed borders), by determining the scope of 'investment' and 'territory', terms that determine the arbitral tribunal's jurisdiction.

10.3.1 The Protection of Foreign Investments in Occupied Territories: The Crimea Investor-State Arbitrations

Following the 2014 annexation, Ukrainian investors that lost their properties or suffered severe damages initiated several *ad hoc* arbitral proceedings against the Russian Federation under the UNCITRAL Arbitration Rules, pursuant to the Russia-Ukraine BIT, considering themselves as foreign investors and Crimea as a territory over which Russia exercises *de facto* control. These proceedings, administered by the Permanent Court of Arbitration (PCA), were seated in Switzerland.

Even though the respondent State (Russia) contested the tribunals' jurisdiction by selecting not to participate in the process,[63] several arbitral awards were rendered affirming the tribunals' jurisdiction and the

[62] For the arbitral tribunal to recognize *effective* (or *de facto*) control of the aggressor State over the territory, this State should demonstrate any of the following behaviours: '1. ability to legislate; 2. substitution of the state authorities; and 3. obtaining a permission of the other state to the wrongdoer's presence in the territory etc'. See O Kuchmiienko, 'The ECHR findings in the Case Ukraine and The Netherlands v Russia' dated 25 January 2023; and Investment Arbitration "Crimean Cases": Any Positive News for Ukrainian Investors?' (*Kluwer Arbitration Blog*, 13 March 2023) <https://arbitrationblog.kluwerarbitration.com/2023/03/13/the-echr-findings-in-the-case-ukraine-and-the-netherlands-v-russia-dated-january-25-2023-andinvestment-arbitration-crimean-cases-any-positive-news-for-ukrainian-investors/> (last accessed 1 June 2025).

[63] This strategy changed after Russia's decision on participation in *PJSC DTEK Krymenergo v the Russian Federation*, PCA Case No 2018-41.

admissibility of the investors' claims.[64] While many of the investor-State arbitrations are at the moment of writing of this chapter still pending, some of the arbitral tribunals proceeded to the adjudication of the dispute on the merits and awarded damages to the claimant, as they found Russia to be in breach of its obligations under the applicable BIT due to unlawful expropriation. Interestingly, the Swiss Federal Supreme Court held public deliberations in two separate appeal proceedings, rejecting Russia's appeal to set aside the interim awards on jurisdiction rendered by the respected arbitral tribunals.[65]

The disputes focused on the territorial scope of the Russia-Ukraine BIT, on whether the BIT extended to Crimea, over which Russia exercised *de facto* control. Arbitral tribunals in this case confirmed that the concept of 'territory' encompasses regions over which a contracting State exercises *de facto* control.[66] Even if BITs do not have any specific explanation for the term 'territory' or any reference to 'effectively controlled'

[64] All awards remain confidential; *Everest Estate LLC et al v Russia ('Everest Estate')* (Decision on Jurisdiction of 20 March 2017) PCA Press Release, 9 August 2016; *Aeroport Belbek LLC and Mr Kolomoisky v Russia ('Aeroport Belbek')* (Interim Award Addressing Certain Issues of Jurisdiction and Admissibility of 24 February 2017) PCA Press Release, 9 March 2017; *JSC CB PrivatBank v Russia ('PrivatBank')* (Interim Award Addressing Certain Issues of Jurisdiction and Admissibility of 24 February 2017) PCA Press Release, 9 March 2017; *PJSC Ukrnafta v Russia ('Ukrnafta')* (Awards on Jurisdiction of 26 June 2017) PCA Press Release, 4 July 2017; *Stabil LLC et al v Russia ('Stabil)* (Awards on Jurisdiction of 26 June 2017) PCA Press Release, 4 July 2017; *Limited Liability Company Lugzor et al v Russia* ('*Lugzor*') (Tribunal's letter dated 29 August 2017) PCA Press Release, 13 December 2017; *Oschadbank v Russia* ('*Oschadbank*') (Judgment of the Paris Court of Appeal dated 30 March 2021); *NJSC Naftogaz of Ukraine, PJSC State Joint Stock Company Chornomornaftogaz, PJSC Ukrgasvydobuvannya and others v The Russian Federation ('Naftogaz')* (Award on Jurisdiction and Liability of 22 February 2019) PCA Case No 2017-16.

[65] The annulment proceedings before the Federal Court in Switzerland were related to the previous arbitration awards on jurisdiction in *PJSC Ukrnafta v Russia* and *Stabil LLC and others v Russia*; see Swiss Federal First Civil Law Court, *Russian Federation v PJSC Ukrnafta* (Judgment of 16 October 2018) 4A_396/2017; Swiss Federal First Civil Law Court, *Russian Federation v Stabil LLC* (Judgment of 16 October 2018) 4A_398/2017.

[66] In fact, Crimean arbitration tribunals have recognized that sovereignty is not a prerequisite for the definition of the term 'territory' under international law, so areas where *effective control* has unlawfully changed are also included in the concept of 'territory' for the purposes of investment protection, unless the BIT provides otherwise. See J Hepburn and R Kabra, 'Investigation: Further Russia Investment Treaty Decisions Uncovered, Offering Broader Window into Arbitrators' Approaches to Crimea Controversy' (*Investment Arbitration Reporter*, 17 November 2017) <https://www.iareporter.com/articles/investigation-further-russia-investment-treaty-decisions-uncovered-offering-broader-window-into-arbitrators-approaches-to-crimea-controversy/> (last accessed 1 June 2025).

areas, arbitral tribunals interpret 'territory' in accordance with Article 31 VCLT. Regarding the term 'territory', the Russia-Ukraine BIT contains wording similar to the majority of BITs,[67] which must be interpreted according to the ordinary meaning under international law and enhance the twofold object and purpose of the BIT as defined in the Treaty's Preamble.[68] Such an interpretative approach was taken in the *Ukrnafta & Stabil* cases taking into consideration the 'useful result' requirement of the BIT's object and purpose, stating that:

> The Appellant rightly does not question that the principles of interpretation of Art. 31 et seq. VCLT are to be observed in interpreting the 1998 Investment Protection Agreement. In particular, according to Art. 31(1) VCLT a treaty is to be interpreted in good faith in accordance with the ordinary meaning to be given to its terms in their context and in light of its object and purpose. Together with interpretation in good faith, a teleological interpretation guarantees the treaty's 'effet utile.' If there are multiple possible interpretations, the term to be interpreted is to be assigned the meaning that guarantees its effective application and does not lead to a result that conflicts with the treaty's object and purpose.[69]

Therefore, a teleological (and grammatical) interpretation (according to Article 31(1) VCLT) supported the fact that the Ukraine-Russia BIT served in its preamble two purposes, the promotion and protection of investments.[70] A broad protection of investments, including investments located in the territory of the Russian Federation only because of subsequent border changes (even if this border change is unlawful), does not

[67] 'Territory' shall denote the territory of the Russian Federation or the territory of the Ukraine and also their respective exclusive economic zone and the continental shelf as defined in conformity with the international law; see Agreement Concerning the Encouragement and Mutual Protection of Investments between Russia and Ukraine (n 19) art 1.4.

[68] It is stated in the Preamble that the Contracting Parties seek 'to create and maintain favorable conditions for mutual investments' and 'to create favorable conditions for the expansion of economic cooperation' among themselves; see Agreement Concerning the Encouragement and Mutual Protection of Investments between Russia and Ukraine (n 19) art 1.4.

[69] *Russian Federation v PJSC Ukrnafta* (n 65) [4.4.2].

[70] ibid; *Russian Federation v Stabil LLC* (n 65) [4.4.3]. See also L Rees-Evans, 'Litigating the Use of Force: Reflections on the Interaction between Investor-State Dispute Settlement and Other Forms of International Dispute Settlement in the Context of the Conflict in Ukraine' in FK Gómez, A Gourgourinis and C Titi (eds), *International Investment Law and the Law of Armed Conflict* (Springer 2019) 173, 187.

contradict the object and purpose of the Ukraine-Russia BIT.[71] The object and purpose of the BIT cannot be restricted just because there is a change in the effective control of the territory in question. Conversely, a narrow interpretation of the term 'territory' due to the *de facto* control of the aggressor State would not only leave investments in the territory at stake unprotected (which would go against the object and purpose of the Treaty) but also allow the aggressor State to benefit from its unlawful action without any responsibility or consequence.[72] Otherwise, a *stricto sensu* interpretation would leave investors in a legal vacuum. A strict interpretation of territorial scope would deprive arbitral tribunals of jurisdiction over such claims, creating a legal vacuum, as harmful acts taken place in occupied territories would be attributable to no State. Therefore, as it is already referred, the Swiss Supreme Court emphasized the principle of effectiveness method of interpretation.[73] The tribunal also concluded that it was unnecessary, for the purpose of applying the Ukraine-Russia BIT, to determine whether the annexation of Crimea was lawful under public international law. From the point of view of the object and purpose of an investment treaty, the important fact is to

[71] R Happ and S Wuschka, 'Horror Vacui: Or Why Investment Treaties Should Apply to Illegally Annexed Territories' (2016) 33(3) JIntArb 245, 245–68.

[72] A similar conclusion was taken in *Sanum Inv Ltd v Lao People's Democratic Republic* (Award on Jurisdiction of 13 December 2013) PCA Case No 2013-13. See also critiques in OG Repousis, 'On Territoriality and International Investment Law: Applying China's Investment Treaties to Hong Kong and Macao' (2015) 37 MichJIntlL 113, 113–90; Y Wang, 'The Fight between Interpretation and Modification: A Critique of Sanum v Laos' (2020) 35(1) ICSID Review – Foreign Investment Law Journal 236, 236–53.

[73] See *Russian Federation v PJSC Ukrnafta* (n 65) [4.4.2]. See also Happ and Wuschka (n 71) 245–68. For views that 'territory' should not be interpreted in such a fashion, see P Dumberry, 'Requiem for Crimea: Why Tribunals Should Have Declined Jurisdiction over the Claims of Ukrainian Investors against Russian under the Ukraine–Russia BIT' (2018) 9(3) JIDS 506. For additional takes on the Crimea Investor-State arbitrations, see indicatively D Tamada, 'War in Ukraine and Implications for International Investment Law' (2024) 26 ICLR 187; GM Vaccaro-Incisa, 'Crimea Investment Disputes: Are Jurisdictional Hurdles Being Overcome Too Easily?' (*EJILTalk!*, 9 May 2018), <https://www.ejiltalk.org/crimea-investment-disputes-are-jurisdictional-hurdles-being-overcome-too-easily/> (last accessed 1 June 2025); E Leikin et al, 'A Decade of Investment Treaty Claims Arising from Russia's Invasion of Ukraine: Lessons and Expectations (Part I)' (*Freshfields Risk & Compliance*, 2024) <https://riskandcompliance.freshfields.com/post/102j57i/a-decade-of-investment-treaty-claims-arising-from-russias-invasion-of-ukraine-l> (last accessed 1 June 2025); A Fouchard Papaefstratiou, 'Crimea as Russian Territory for the Purposes of the Russia-Ukraine BIT: Consent v International Law?' (*Kluwer Arbitration Blog*, 5 February 2023) <https://arbitrationblog.kluwerarbitration.com/2023/02/05/crimea-as-russian-territory-for-the-purposes-of-the-russia-ukraine-bit-consent-v-international-law/> (last accessed 1 June 2025).

ascertain whether the Contracting Party has effective control (authority) over the territory at stake and not whether that control was acquired legally or illegally. While this reasoning might appear to sideline the international law on occupation, it does not necessarily conflict with it. Rather, it reflects a functional approach according to which investment tribunals assess *de facto* control to establish jurisdiction, without making a determination on the legality of that control under the law of armed conflict or occupation.[74]

Even in case of subsequent territorial changes, a treaty remains applicable to the entire territory of each contracting State, without the need for a supplementary agreement (Article 29 VCLT) and therefore the illegality of the annexation of Crimea is irrelevant for the purpose of the application of the Ukraine-Russia BIT. Nevertheless, this does not mean that arbitral tribunals recognize any illegal acquisition of territory as legitimate.[75] On the contrary, the arbitral tribunals emphasized that 'for the assessment of its jurisdiction under Art. 9 IPA 1998, it was not required to address the question of the permissibility of the accession of Crimea into the Russian Federation or the lawfulness of the associated territorial claims'.[76] Therefore, the arbitral tribunals adopted the position of the Ukrainian observations (third party submission) according to which Crimea remained Ukrainian territory, but was temporarily under Russian effective control due to the occupation, exclusively for the purposes of the application of the Russia-Ukraine BIT.[77] Otherwise, such recognition would violate public international law, notably the UN Charter (Article 2 (4)) and would be subject to challenge or annulment.

10.4 Conclusion

This chapter analyzed the interpretation of the territoriality requirement in international investment treaties and investment arbitration in light of customary international law and the Vienna Convention on the Law of Treaties (in particular Article 31). Investigating the extent to which

74 See Hepburn and Kabra (n 66).

75 Regarding the Crimea region, the UN General Assembly adopted a Resolution titled 'Territorial integrity of Ukraine', affirming Ukraine's sovereignty and territorial integrity and calling upon all states not to recognize any change in the status of Crimea region; UNGA, 'Res 68/262: Territorial Integrity of Ukraine' (27 March 2014) UN Doc A/Res/68/262.

76 *Russian Federation v PJSC Ukrnafta* (n 65) [4.2].

77 Rees-Evans (n 70) 188.

special rules and methods have emerged regarding the interpretation process in the field of international investment law, it is found that the notion of territory is conceived in terms of extending investment protection. Arbitral tribunals interpret the territorial requirement based on the intention of the contracting parties to create favourable conditions for the promotion of investments and economic cooperation. Such an interpretive approach creates an expansive tendency of the territorial application of international investment treaties.

The 'economic benefit' approach to the interpretation of territoriality uses one of the BIT's purposes (namely, the economic development of the host State) in contradiction to the wording of the treaty and, therefore, against the interpretation method of Article 31 of the VCLT. More specifically, the text of jurisdiction clauses contained in most BITs and international investment contracts requires a territorial nexus of the investment at stake with the host State and not one of economic benefit. Such method of interpreting the Treaty's purpose over-expands the international investment law's scope of protection, disconnecting the notion of protected investments from the territorial requirement.

On the contrary, the 'economic unity of the investment' approach to the interpretation of territoriality seems to follow the territorial requirement of most jurisdiction clauses, as it requires the connection between a financial transaction or an activity carried outside the host State and the specific investment or project that is localized in the territory of the host State. However, in order to satisfy the territoriality requirement, this approach requires that the activities at stake shall form a substantial and integral part of the overall operation carried out within the territory of the host State.

In addition, the significance of the Tribunals' awards in the Crimea investor-State arbitrations cannot be underestimated, as it was the first time that an arbitral tribunal had found a BIT to be applicable in a territory regarded by the international community as illegally occupied. For the purpose of the application of the Ukraine-Russia BIT, arbitral tribunals found unnecessary to determine the lawfulness of Russia's control over Crimea. Making a teleological interpretation that was supported by the object and purpose of the Ukraine-Russia BIT in its preamble to protect investments, arbitral tribunals confirmed that the concept of 'territory' encompasses regions over which a contracting State exercises *de facto control*. Otherwise, a strict interpretation of the territorial scope of BITs would deprive tribunals of jurisdiction over such claims, leaving foreign investors in a legal vacuum.

Finally, the conclusions of the Crimea investor-State arbitrations could also apply in the midst of complex and overwhelming situations in the international political arena. In light of the object and purpose of international investment treaties, arbitral tribunals could adopt a 'pragmatic approach' in the future by extending the application of the treaty to areas where the aggressor State exercises effective control.

11

Core International Crimes at the Interface

In Search of Unity amidst Diversity in the Interpretation of International Criminal Law

OLYMPIA BEKOU*

11.1 Introduction

In the two decades that have lapsed since the entry into force of the Rome Statute, the field of international criminal law has grown in both vibrancy and reach. Whilst the International Criminal Court (ICC) is at the centre of the system created by the Rome Statute, States are called to play a key role in investigating and prosecuting core international crimes, in accordance with the principle of complementarity.[1] In order to do so, States need to adopt national implementing legislation incorporating the crimes at the domestic level. To date, many States have adopted legislation to implement the Rome Statute[2] and have, therefore, offered their interpretation of the Statute in the process. However, this engagement has often led to divergent approaches, with several States deviating from the Statute. This chapter explores what happens when there is a clash between what is in the Rome Statute and when core international crimes are interpreted differently within and outside the ICC. It further looks into what happens at the interface. Unpicking this interaction not only offers useful insights into the practice and evolution of the core international crimes provisions but may also contribute to a better understanding of the rules of international criminal law interpretation, as well

* I would like to thank Sara Ciucci for her excellent research assistance. All errors and omissions are mine alone.

[1] Rome Statute of the International Criminal Court (adopted 17 July 1998, entered into force 1 July 2002) 2187 UNTS 3, preamble para 10, arts 1, 17 (Rome Statute).

[2] To date, over half of the State Parties (nearly 70) have at least partially adopted implementing legislation; see National Implementing Legislation Database, accessible at <https://demo.hrlc.net/en/> (last accessed 1 June 2025).

as pave the way for possible Rome Statute amendments. Whereas many works have focused on the implementation of the Rome Statute, looking at this interface from the interpretation angle has been overlooked, to date.

This chapter will start with a brief consideration of those institutions that gave rise to international criminal law – namely, the Nuremberg and Tokyo International Military Tribunals (IMTs) and the *ad hoc* Tribunals for the former Yugoslavia and Rwanda. It will consider the influence of customary international law in defining and interpreting core international crimes, as well as its relationship with the principle of legality, a key principle underpinning international criminal justice. Moving then to one of the major instruments of international criminal law of our time – the Rome Statute establishing the ICC – the chapter will discuss to what extent the definitions of crimes contained in Articles 6–8*bis* of the Rome Statute codify customary international law or rather constitute progressive development in the field. Although these categories of crimes can be regarded as largely reflective of customary international law of the time, it is important to note, as recognised under Article 10 of the Statute, that the exclusion of certain crimes from the Rome Statute or the adoption of retrograde definitions must not be read as limiting or precluding the existing customary international law framework or the progressive development of new customary law outside the Statute. Customary international law in this area has considerably developed alongside the Rome Statute, including through the national laws of States. Notably, when adopting domestic implementing legislation, State Parties have often significantly limited or expanded the scope of application of core international crimes enshrined in the Statute. It is, therefore, crucial to consider how different national core crimes provisions can influence the interpretation of the definitions of core international crimes crystallised in the Rome Statute when the ICC is required to step in owing to the national legal system being unwilling or unable genuinely to investigate or prosecute, in line with the principle of complementarity.

This chapter will consider how this potential new state practice and emerging customary law interacts with the treaty provisions and what this means for their interpretation. This chapter will argue that a distinction should be made between creating new substantive law and an interpretation within the scope of existing law. Subsequent practice or customary international law cannot, therefore, be invoked to unacceptably restrict, broaden, or modify the text of the Statute. Nevertheless, ICC judges need to remain cognisant of how core international crimes have been interpreted through implementation at the domestic level.

11.2 The IMTS and *ad hoc* Tribunals: Between Customary International Law and the Principle of Legality

The birth of modern international criminal law can be traced back to the Nuremberg and Tokyo IMTs, established by the victorious Allied Powers following the Second World War.[3] Notably, the definitions of the core crimes in international criminal law – namely, genocide, crimes against humanity, war crimes, and aggression – have been developed at the international level ever since the inception of the field with the creation of these two Tribunals. Core international crimes have since become established categories of crimes in international law, enabling the prosecution of alleged perpetrators at the international level.

At Nuremberg, the Military Tribunal observed that 'the law of war is to be found not only in treaties, but in customs and practices of States which gradually obtained universal recognition' and that 'in many cases, treaties do no more than express and define for more accurate reference the principles of law already existing'.[4] Therefore, the Nuremberg IMT explicitly referred to customary international law in defining the law applicable to the crimes falling within its jurisdiction.[5] Likewise, the Tokyo Tribunal engaged in the practice of determining whether the crimes listed in the Far East Charter constituted customary international law.[6]

It was said at the time that 'the [Nuremberg] Charter is not an arbitrary exercise of power on the part of the victorious nations, but … it is the expression of international law existing at the time of its creation'.[7] Efforts were made to demonstrate respect for the principle

[3] Charter of the International Military Tribunal in Agreement for the Prosecution and Punishment of the Major War Criminals of the European Axis (signed and entered into force 8 August 1945) 82 UNTS 280; Charter of the International Military Tribunal for the Far East (adopted 19 January 1946, amended 26 April 1946) 4 Bevans 20.

[4] *Judgment of the Nuremberg International Military Tribunal of 1 October 1946* (1947) 41 AJIL 172, 219 (*IMT Judgment*).

[5] F Pocar, 'International Criminal Justice and the Unifying Role of Customary Law' (2016) 21(2–3) Uniform LR 171, 171. Specifically, the customary role of war crimes embedded in the Nuremberg Charter was affirmed by referring to treaties such as the 1907 Hague Conventions and the 1929 Geneva Conventions.

[6] L Grover, *Interpreting Crimes in the Rome Statute of the International Criminal Court* (Cambridge University Press 2014) 260.

[7] *IMT Judgment* (n 4) 216.

of *nullum crimen sine lege* – that is, the principle of legality.[8] Nevertheless, the inclusion of certain crimes in the Nuremberg and Tokyo Charters raised concerns about retroactivity and compliance with the principle of legality.[9] Notably, it is questionable whether crimes against peace and crimes against humanity constituted crimes under international law at the time of their occurrence during the Second World War.[10] Therefore, the Nuremberg and Tokyo IMTs have received a great deal of criticism on account of the fact that individuals were prosecuted for crimes that had not existed at the time they were committed.[11] Confronted with such a challenge, the Nuremberg judgment developed a relatively weak conception of the principle of legality, which can operate as a 'principle of justice' rather than as a 'limitation of sovereignty' and can, therefore, be outweighed by considerations of substantive justice.[12]

In response to the so-called victors' justice criticism of the Nuremberg and Tokyo paradigm, and after a long period of inactivity owing to the Cold War,[13] at the time of the establishment of the *ad hoc* Tribunals for the former Yugoslavia (ICTY) and Rwanda (ICTR) in the 1990s, every effort had been made for core crimes definitions enshrined in their Statutes to reflect existing customary international law in the field.[14] The UN Secretary-General's report that preceded the establishment of the ICTY expressly stated that the Tribunal's material jurisdiction is limited to conducts that are, 'beyond any doubt',[15] recognised under

[8] KS Gallant, *The Principle of Legality in International and Comparative Criminal Law* (Cambridge University Press 2009) 68.

[9] T Weigend, '"In General a Principle of Justice": The Debate on the "Crime against Peace" in the Wake of the Nuremberg Judgment' (2012) 10 JICJ 41, 45.

[10] Gallant (n 8) 68.

[11] ibid 44.

[12] *IMT Judgment* (n 4) 217.

[13] At the Nuremberg and Tokyo trials, only the conduct of the citizens of Nazi Germany and Japan were scrutinised, while the acts committed by the victorious Allied Powers were not investigated; see RM Minear, *Victor's Justice: The Tokyo War Crimes Trial* (Princeton University Press 1971).

[14] Sir David Hannay, from the UK delegation, observed that 'the Statute does not, of course, create new law, but reflects existing international law in this field'; UNSC, 'Provisional Verbatim Record of the 3217th meeting' (25 May 1993) UN Doc S/PV 3217, 19.

[15] UNSC, 'Report of the Secretary-General Pursuant to Paragraph 2 of Security Council Resolution 808' (3 May 1993) UN Doc S/25704 [34]. The report explicitly considers as part of customary international law the law embodied in the Geneva Conventions of 1949 for the protection of War Victims; the IV Hague Convention of 1907 and annexed

customary international law, so that 'the problem of adherence of some but not all States to specific conventions does not arise'.[16] However, in the case of the ICTR, the Security Council adopted a more expansive approach to the choice of the applicable law, including within its subject-matter jurisdiction 'international instruments regardless of whether they were considered part of customary international law'.[17]

The UN Secretary-General's report on the ICTY reveals a presumption in favour of customary international law, according to which 'provisions of the Statute defining the crimes within the jurisdiction of the Tribunal should always be interpreted as reflecting customary international law, unless an intention to depart from customary international law is expressed in the terms of the Statute, or from other authoritative sources'.[18] However, concerns were raised at the time on whether breaches of the Geneva Conventions in a non-international armed conflict constituted customary international law,[19] and whether customary international law for crimes against humanity required a nexus with an armed conflict.[20]

regulations; the 1948 Genocide Convention and the 1945 Charter of the International Military Tribunal.

16 ibid [34].

17 UNSC, 'Report of the Secretary-General Pursuant to Paragraph 5 of Security Council Resolution 955' (13 February 1995) UN Doc S/1995/134 [12]. For instance, art 4 of the ICTR Statute includes violations of the Additional Protocol II, 'which has not yet been universally recognized as part of customary international law' and criminalises, for the first time, the acts mentioned in art 3 of the four Geneva Conventions.

18 *Prosecutor v Duško Tadić* (Appeal Judgment) IT-94-1-A (15 July 1999) [296]. Nevertheless, as observed at ibid [287], the presumption of consistency with customary international law is rebuttable and the Security Council could 'explicitly or implicitly depart from general rules of international law'.

19 'The content of customary law applicable to internal armed conflict is debatable'; UNSC, 'Final Report of the Commission of Experts Established Pursuant to Security Council Resolution 780 (1992)' (27 May 1994) UN Doc S/1994/674 [42, 54]. However, the ICTY affirmed that war crimes can also be committed in non-international armed conflict and that this reflects customary international law; see *Prosecutor v Duško Tadić a/k/a/ "Dule"* (Decision on the Defence Motion for Interlocutory Appeal on Jurisdiction) IT-94-1-T (2 October 1995) [134].

20 'Since customary international law no longer requires any nexus between crimes against humanity and armed conflict', the Security Council may have defined the crime in art 5 more narrowly than necessary under customary international law; *Prosecutor v Duško Tadić* (Decision on the Defence Motion) (n 19) [78, 141]. Moreover, crimes against humanity are prohibited 'regardless of whether they are committed in armed conflict, international or internal in character'; UNSC (n 15) [47].

In any case, the primary role played by customary international law in the *ad hoc* international criminal Tribunals' experience has been deemed necessary to comply with the principle of *nullum crimen sine lege* and, specifically, with the prohibition against retroactive application of criminal law. By recognising that 'the tribunal's power to convict an accused of any crime listed in the Statute depends on its existence *qua* custom at the time this crime was allegedly committed',[21] the drafters wanted to avoid risking a possible violation of the principle of legality in the event that a party to the conflict did not ratify a relevant treaty.[22] For the same reason, a few years later, the UN Secretary-General's report on the establishment of a Special Court for Sierra Leone expressly recognised that the international crimes enumerated in the draft statute 'are crimes considered to have had the character of customary international law at the time of the alleged commission of the crime', linking the presumption of interpretation consistent with customary law with the principle of legality and the ban against the retroactive application of the law.[23]

11.3 The Rome Statute Crimes: Codification of Custom or Progressive Development?

The adoption of the Rome Statute of the ICC in 1998 provided a further opportunity for crystallising the customary international law of the time. In developing the definitions of core international crimes,[24] the intention of the drafters at Rome was to limit the Court's jurisdiction to crimes existing under customary international law.[25] To reach the widest possible consensus among States and promote its universal application, it was understood that the Rome Statute was not the 'right place for progressive development of the law into uncertain areas, or for the

[21] See *Prosecutor v Milanovic, Sainovic, Ojdanic* (Decision on Dragoljub Ojdanic's Motion Challenging Jurisdiction – Joint Criminal Enterprise) IT-05-87-PT (21 May 2003) [9].

[22] 'It should be emphasised again that the only reason behind the stated purpose of the drafters that the International Tribunal should apply customary international law was to avoid violating the principle of *nullum crimen sine lege* in the event that a party to the conflict did not adhere to a specific treaty.' *Prosecutor v Tadić* (Decision on the Defence Motion) (n 19) [143].

[23] UNSC 'Report of the Secretary-General on the Establishment of a Special Court for Sierra Leone' (4 October 2000) UN Doc S/2000/915 [12].

[24] Art 5 of the Rome Statute lists genocide, crimes against humanity, war crimes, and aggression as crimes falling under the jurisdiction of the ICC.

[25] R Cryer, 'Of Customs, Treaties, Scholars and the Gavel: The Influence of the International Criminal Tribunals on the ICRC Customary Law Study' (2006) 11(2) JCSL 239, 251.

elaboration of new and uncertain international criminal law'.[26] As stated by Philippe Kirsch, the Court's first president, 'the definitions of crimes in the ICC Statute were to reflect existing customary international law, and not create new law'.[27] Although the Rome Statute does not expressly specify whether the crimes listed in Articles 6–8*bis* are declaratory of custom,[28] these categories of crimes can be regarded as largely reflective of customary international law at the time.[29] This ensures consistency with the principle of legality, as formulated in Article 22 of the Rome Statute.

However, the drafting of an international treaty is always an arduous process. It is hard to hold the narrow line between a pure codification of existing customary law and progressive or retrogressive developments.[30] The Rome Statute was the product of intense multilateral negotiation,[31] which revealed the existence of profound and diverging national positions. The substantive provisions contained in Articles 6–8*bis* 'represent a consensus reached by a large number of States following a lengthy and complex drafting process'.[32] Therefore, the numerous compromises that were made to build consensus among States led to divergence from the then existing content of customary international law.[33]

26 R Cryer, 'The Doctrinal Foundations of International Criminalization' in MC Bassiouni (ed), *International Criminal Law*, Vol 1 (Martinus Nijhoff 2008) 107, 118. At the Preparatory Committee, 'several delegations held the view that the Statute should codify customary international law and not extend to the progressive development of international law'; see UNGA, 'Report of the Preparatory Committee on the Establishment of an International Criminal Court, Volume I' (1996) UN Doc A/51/22 [54].

27 P Kirsch, 'Foreword' in K Dormann (ed), *Elements of War Crimes under the Rome Statute of the International Criminal Court: Sources and Commentary* (Cambridge University Press 2003) xiii.

28 Grover (n 6) 244.

29 GM Danilenko, 'The Statute of the International Criminal Court and Third States' (1999) 21 MichJIntlL 445, 486. The four categories of crimes listed in art 5 of the Rome Statute are generally regarded as *jus cogens* obligations; see LN Sadat and SR Carden, 'The New International Criminal Court: An Uneasy Revolution' (2000) 88(3) Geo LJ 381, 407.

30 GM Danilenko, 'ICC Statute and Third States' in A Cassese, P Gaeta, and JRWD Jones (eds), *The Rome Statute of the International Criminal Court: A Commentary*, Vol 2 (Oxford University Press 2002) 1871, 1891.

31 The international diplomatic conference was held in Rome (Italy) from the 15th of June 1998 to the 17th of July 1998.

32 W Schabas, *The International Criminal Court: A Commentary on the Rome Statute* (2nd edn, Oxford University Press 2016) 336. The Rome Statute was adopted by a non-recorded vote of 120 in favour, 7 against, and 21 abstentions.

33 M Bennouna, 'The Statute's Rules on Crimes and Existing or Developing International Law' in A Cassese, P Gaeta, and JRWD Jones (eds), *The Rome Statute of the International Criminal Court: A Commentary*, Vol 2 (Oxford University Press 2002) 1101, 1102.

While the provisions on genocide,[34] crimes against humanity,[35] war crimes,[36] and aggression[37] are generally considered in line with customary law,[38] the Rome Statute shows, in places, both (limited) progressive development, as well as instances of regression – in particular when looking at the definitions of crimes under Articles 7 and 8 of the Rome Statute. Indeed, as it has been observed by the ICTY in the *Furundžija* case, 'depending on the matter at issue, the Rome Statute may be taken to restate, reflect or clarify customary rules or crystallise them, whereas in some areas it creates new law or modifies existing law'.[39] Therefore, the Rome Statute can be regarded as largely, but not completely, reflective of customary law.[40]

Provisions that have been considered by some authors as going beyond customary international law include, among war crimes, the conscription

[34] Art 6 of the Rome Statute reflects art 2 of the 1948 Convention on the Prevention and Punishment of the Crime of Genocide, which is widely regarded as reflective of custom; see *Reservations to the Convention on Genocide* (Advisory Opinion) [1951] ICJ Rep 15, 23.

[35] The notion of crimes against humanity has been recognised as part of customary international law before the adoption of the Rome Statute. *Prosecutor v Tadić* (Decision on the Defence Motion) (n 19) [141].

[36] Art 8 of the Rome Statute contains most of the provisions of the 1949 Geneva Conventions and Additional Protocol I on 'grave breaches', whose status of norms under customary international law is widely recognised. Although debate arose on whether war crimes committed in non-international armed conflict were declaratory of customary international law, the majority of States supported their inclusion; see T Yudan, *The Rome Statute as Evidence of Customary International Law* (Brill 2021) 69.

[37] The definition of art 8*bis* adopted at Kampala in 2010 has been based on the Nuremberg and Tokyo precedents, as well as on General Assembly Resolution 3314 (UNGA, 'Res 3314 (XXIX): Definition of Aggression' (14 December 1974) UN Doc A/RES/29/3314) and is generally accepted as part of customary international law; see A Cassese et al, *Cassese's International Criminal Law* (Oxford University Press 2013) 142–43.

[38] *Request under Regulation 46(3) of the Regulations of the Court* (Pre-Trial Chamber I, Decision on the 'Prosecution's Request for a Ruling on Jurisdiction under Article 19(3) of the Statute') ICC-RoC46(3)–01/18 (6 September 2018) [45]. Moreover, to the extent that the definitions of crimes in the Rome Statute reflect customary international law, they bind all individuals, regardless of their nationality and where the conduct was committed; Vienna Convention on the Law of Treaties (adopted 23 May 1969, entered into force 27 January 1980) 1155 UNTS 331, art 38 (VCLT).

[39] *Prosecutor v Anto Furundžija* (Judgment) IT-95–17/1-T (10 December 1998) [227]; see also *Prosecutor v Šainović et al* (Appeal Judgment) IT-05–87-A (23 January 2014) [1648]. 'While the ICC Statute may be in many areas regarded as indicative of customary rules, in some areas it creates new law or modifies existing law.'

[40] T Meron, 'Crimes under the Jurisdiction of the ICC' in H von Hebel et al (eds), *Reflections on the International Criminal Court: Essay in Honour of Adrian Bos* (TMC Asser 1999) 47, 48.

or enlistment of children under fifteen years of age into the national armed forces[41] and the indirect transfer by an occupying power of its civilian population into the occupied territory.[42] Moreover, the customary law status of certain acts amounting to crimes against humanity has been called into question, such as forced pregnancy,[43] enforced disappearance and apartheid,[44] as well as the long list of grounds of persecution.[45] Lastly, the policy element required by Article 7(2)(a) of the Rome Statute[46] has also been seen to narrow the customary definition of crimes against humanity.[47] Similar reasoning has been employed regarding the qualification of the concept of persecution as occurring 'in connection with any act or any crime within the jurisdiction of the Court'.[48] However, such progressive definitions, which were not regarded as declaratory of customary international law at the time of the Statute's adoption, are likely to have gradually evolved and crystallised into custom as a result of other international and domestic courts, or domestic implementing legislation, accepting them as 'encapsulating the world community's *opinio juris* on the matter'.[49]

On the other hand, the lack of prohibition on conspiracy to commit genocide constitutes a retrograde deviation from custom.[50] Moreover, in the context of war crimes, the Statute has inadequately codified

[41] Rome Statute, art 8(2)(b)(xxvi). UNSC (n 23) [18]; see also *Prosecutor v Norman* (Decision of Appeals Chamber on Preliminary Motion Based on Lack of Jurisdiction (Child Recruitment) SCSL-2004-14-AR72I (31 May 2004) Dissenting Opinion of Judge Robertson [40–41].

[42] Rome Statute, art 8(2)(a)(viii); see Danilenko (n 30) 1893.

[43] Rome Statute, art 7(1)(g). A Cassese, *International Criminal Law* (2nd edn, Oxford University Press 2008) 126.

[44] Rome Statute, art 7(1)(i), (j). Cassese (n 43) 126.

[45] Rome Statute, art 7(1)(h). Cassese (n 43) 126.

[46] Art 7(2)(a) requires that an 'attack directed against any civilian population' must be committed 'pursuant to or in furtherance of a State or organizational policy to commit such attack'.

[47] Cassese et al (n 37) 107; see also *Prosecutor v Kunarac, Kovac and Vukovic* (Appeals Chamber Judgment) IT-96-23/1-A (12 June 2002) [98].

[48] Rome Statute, art 7(1)(h); see *Prosecutor v Kupreškić et al* (Trial Chamber Judgment) IT-95-16-T (14 January 2000) [580].

[49] Cassese (n 43) 14. For instance, after the adoption of the Rome Statute, several States have incorporated art 7(2)(a) into their national legislation and the element of policy has widely crystallised into customary law; see Grover (n 6) 135 fn 101.

[50] Cassese (n 43) 146. However, it has been observed that this divergence between the ICC Statute and the 1948 Genocide Convention is the result of 'an oversight of exhausted drafters' in Rome. W Schabas, *Genocide in International Law: The Crime of the Crimes* (2nd edn, Cambridge University Press 2009) 315.

prohibited weapons and clearly excluded the legal prohibition on the use of weapons of mass destruction.[51] The Statute also retains some retrograde distinctions between international and non-international armed conflicts, with significantly fewer categories of war crimes included in this latter section. For instance, Article 8(2)(e) lacks a comparable provision to that of Article 8(2)(b)(xx) on the use of weapons that cause superfluous injury and unnecessary suffering, or weapons that are inherently indiscriminate. Other crimes that are not replicated in internal armed conflicts include compelling a prisoner of war or other protected persons to serve in the armed forces of a hostile power;[52] intentionally directing attacks against civilian objects;[53] intentionally launching indiscriminate attacks likely to cause incidental loss of life, injury to civilians or damage to civilian objects, or widespread, long-term, and severe damage to the natural environment;[54] attacking undefended places, which are not military objectives;[55] improper use of flags and markings;[56] use of human shields.[57]

11.4 Temporality of International Criminal Law

Codifying customary international criminal law, as was largely the case with the adoption of the Rome Statute, ensures legal clarity, as well as better consistency and coherence of the law. However, it should be stressed that 'customary law continues to exist and develop alongside treaty law.'[58] International criminal law is a dynamic system. It is not intended to be frozen in time but evolves and develops continuously. As it has been observed by the Nuremberg IMT, 'the laws of the war are not static, but by continual adaptation follow the needs of a changing world'.[59] Concerns have therefore been expressed that the definitions of crimes adopted by the Rome Statute might have 'frozen customary

51 RS Clark, 'Building on Article 8(2)(b)(xx) of the Rome Statute of the International Criminal Court: Weapons and Methods of Warfare' (2009) 12(3) NCLR 366.
52 Rome Statute, art 8(2)(a)(v).
53 ibid, art 8(2)(b)(ii).
54 ibid, art 8(2)(b)(iv).
55 ibid, art 8(2)(b)(v).
56 ibid, art 8(2)(b)(vii).
57 ibid, art 8(2)(b)(xxiii).
58 *Military and Paramilitary Activities in and against Nicaragua (Nicaragua v United States of America)* (Merits) [1986] ICJ Rep 14 [176].
59 *IMT Judgment* (n 4) [445].

definitions in a process of rapid evolution', thus leading to the 'stagnation, if not decline' of the field.[60]

The Rome Statute itself recognises that the ICC does not operate in a vacuum. Indeed, Article 10 stipulates that: 'Nothing in this part shall be interpreted as limiting or prejudicing in any way existing or developing rules for international law for purposes other than this Statute.'[61] This provision, which had been proposed by the late M. Cherif Bassiouni on behalf of the Egyptian delegation and with the strong support of the ICRC,[62] sought to mitigate concerns regarding the codification of some but not all customary international crimes contained in the Statute.[63] Likewise, Article 22(3) of the Statute confirms that the exclusion of criminal liability – in application to the principle of legality – for those conducts not criminalised under the Rome Statute 'shall not affect the characterization of any conduct as criminal under international law independently of this Statute'. Therefore, the exclusion of certain crimes from the Rome Statute, or departure from customary law, is not intended to prejudice the existing customary international law framework or the progressive development of new customary law in the field.[64]

While such provisions are intended to restrict the influence of the Statute on the development of customary law, they are not aimed at determining the role of custom for interpretation purposes. Such an approach is, however, of particular relevance, given that customary international criminal law has further developed alongside the Rome Statute, including through the adoption of national implementing legislation by States.

[60] A Pellet, 'Applicable Law' in A Cassese, P Gaeta, and JRWD Jones (eds), *The Rome Statute of the International Criminal Court: A Commentary*, Vol 2 (Oxford University Press 2002) 1051, 1054.

[61] Although the draft provision originally referred only to the definitions of war crimes, it applies to all the crimes defined in the Statute.

[62] Preparatory Committee on the Establishment of an International Criminal Court, 'Decisions Taken by the Preparatory Committee at its Session Held from 1 to 12 December, Annex I: Report of the Working Group on Definitions and Elements of Crimes' (18 December 1997) UN Doc A/AC.249/1997/L.9/Rev.1; ICRC, 'Statement of 8 July 1998 Relating to the Bureau Discussion Paper in Document A/CONF.183/C.1 / L.53' (8 July 1998) UN Doc A/CONF.183/INF/10 [4].

[63] LN Sadat, 'Custom, Codification and Some Thoughts about the Relationship between the Two: Article 10 of the ICC Statute' (2000) 49(4) DePaul LR 909, 910–1.

[64] A Heinze, 'Article 10' in K Ambos (ed), *Commentary on the Rome Statute of the International Criminal Court* (4th edn, Beck, Hart, Nomos 2022) 756, 773.

11.5 The Adoption of Divergent Domestic Implementing Legislation

With the principle of complementarity being the cornerstone of the Rome system of justice and the ICC operating as a court of last resort,[65] the primary responsibility to investigate and prosecute core international crimes rests with States.[66] The ICC can only intervene when States are 'unwilling' or 'unable' genuinely to do so.[67] To enable States to exercise primary jurisdiction over core international crimes, and investigate and prosecute these crimes domestically, enacting legislation implementing the provisions of the Rome Statute in their respective national legal systems is key. National implementation is indispensable for meeting the 'duty of every State to exercise its criminal jurisdiction over those responsible for international crimes' – as stated in the Preamble of the Rome Statute.[68] Whilst the Rome Statute does not expressly mandate the enactment of national implementing legislation with regard to the Statute crimes, and the decision to implement is left at the discretion of States, over half of the State Parties have so far at least partially adopted domestic implementing legislation with respect to the four core crimes listed under Article 5 of the Statute.[69]

Importantly, the Rome Statute also does not expressly require States to enact domestic implementing legislation incorporating the core crimes in a uniform manner. As such, States are afforded wide discretion when carrying out the implementation task. Substantive differences, therefore, exist in how core international crimes have been interpreted when transposed into national systems. A number of States have replicated the exact wording of the Rome Statute or made explicit reference to its relevant provisions.[70] Other States have instead reformulated, rephrased,

[65] See C Stahn and MM El Zeidy, *The International Criminal Court and Complementarity: From Theory to Practice*, Vol 1 (Cambridge University Press 2012).

[66] Assembly of States Parties, 'Strengthening the International Criminal Court and the Assembly of States Parties' (9 December 2021) ICC-ASP/20/Res.5 [132] <https://asp.icc-cpi.int/sites/asp/files/asp_docs/ASP20/ICC-ASP-20-Res5-AV-ENG.pdf> (last accessed 1 June 2025).

[67] Rome Statute, art 17.

[68] ibid, preamble para 6.

[69] See National Implementing Legislation Database, available at <https://demo.hrlc.net/en/ > (last accessed 1 June 2025).

[70] For instance, Australia, Belgium, Georgia, Kenya, Malta, New Zealand, South Africa, and Trinidad and Tobago have followed the 'replication' method. Austria, Ireland, the Republic of Korea, Uganda, and the United Kingdom have instead embodied the 'reference method'; see Case Matrix Network, 'Implementing the Rome Statute of the

and redrafted the conducts criminalised in the Rome Statute, using different terms from those employed by Articles 6–8*bis* of the Rome Statute in both retrograde or progressive ways.[71]

Some States have adopted narrower definitions of core international crimes – for instance, omitting racial groups or ethnic groups in the domestic definition of genocide,[72] or adopting restrictive definitions of torture or enforced disappearance of persons.[73] Conversely, other States have employed broader definitions based on general international law, other applicable treaties, or new developments in customary international law. Indeed, the implementation task carried out by States is 'not performed in a vacuum' but is necessarily influenced by developments in the field of international criminal law.[74] For instance, several State Parties – such as some Latin American and ex-Soviet countries – have expanded the scope of application of genocide by increasing the number of protected groups[75] or broadening the list of punishable acts to include displacement or deportation.[76] Other States, like Germany, have also included conducts that have been omitted during the negotiations of the Rome Statute – for example, the prohibition on the use of chemical

International Criminal Court' (*ICC Legal Tools Database*, September 2017) 22 <https://www.legal-tools.org/en/doc/e05157/> (last accessed 1 June 2025).

[71] T Hoffmann, 'The Crime of Genocide in its (Nearly) Infinite Domestic Variety' in M Odello and P Lubinski (eds), *The Concept of Genocide in International Criminal Law: Developments After Lemkin* (Routledge 2020) 67, 69.

[72] For instance, Bolivia, Ecuador, Guatemala, Paraguay, and Peru omit racial groups; Costa Rica, El Salvador, and Oman omit ethnic groups; and Nicaragua omits both racial groups and national groups; see Case Matrix Network (n 70) 26; Hoffmann (n 71) 70.

[73] For instance, Germany; see Case Matrix Network (n 70) 35–36.

[74] ICRC, 'Preventing and Repressing International Crimes: Towards an "Integrated" Approach Based on Domestic Practice: Report of the Third Universal Meeting of National Committees for the Implementation of International Humanitarian Law', Vol I (*Czech Red Cross*, 2014) 12 <https://www.cervenykriz.eu/files/files/cz/nsmhp/setkaniNKMHP.pdf> (last accessed 1 June 2025).

[75] The definition of genocide under art 6 of the Rome Statute limits the protected groups to national, ethnic, racial, and religious groups. However, Bangladesh, Colombia, Costa Rica, Ecuador, Ethiopia, Ivory Coast, Nicaragua, Panama, Poland, Togo, and Uruguay include political groups; Estonia, Latvia, Paraguay, Peru, Portugal, and the Philippines include social groups; and Lithuania and Switzerland include both political and social groups; see Case Matrix Network (n 70) 26–27; Hoffmann (n 71) 97. Sixteen other countries, such as Francia and Romania, have undertaken an all-encompassing approach that potentially covers any identifiable group (ibid 84–85).

[76] For instance, Armenia, Bolivia, Ethiopia, Italy, Lithuania, and Spain; see Case Matrix Network (n 70) 30–31.

and biological weapons among their war crimes provision.[77] Moreover, while some States have maintained in their legislation the distinction between international and non-international armed conflicts,[78] this has been blurred by others.[79] A number of States consider direct attacks against civilian objects, disproportionate attacks, and human shields to be war crimes also in non-international armed conflicts, even though the Statute only recognises these as war crimes solely when committed in the course of an international armed conflict.[80]

Whilst provisions of national legislation do not always correspond to the definitions enshrined in the Rome Statute, they purport to criminalise the same conduct. It is, therefore, crucial to consider what happens if national core crimes provisions differ from those found in the Statute – for instance, in a situation case where a State Party conflates international and non-international armed conflicts. Where the ICC is required to step in owing to the national legal system being unwilling or unable genuinely to investigate or prosecute in line with the principle of complementarity, it is at that interface that the interpretation of the national core crime provision in relation to the provision found in the Rome Statute becomes relevant.

11.6 Rules of Interpretation at the ICC

Since its coming into force, ICC judges have been repeatedly tasked with interpreting and applying the Rome Statute.[81] The applicable sources of law to be employed by the ICC are clearly laid down in Article 21 of the Rome Statute, which places primary importance on the text of the

[77] For instance, Argentina, Ecuador, and Germany.

[78] For instance, Lesotho, Lithuania, Malta, Mauritius, Norway, Portugal, Slovenia, South Africa, Timor Leste, Trinidad and Tobago, the Netherlands, the Philippines, Uganda, and the UK; see Case Matrix Network (n 70) 42.

[79] For instance, Albania, Bangladesh, Belgium, Bosnia-Herzegovina, Bulgaria, Canada, Capo Verde, Croatia, Ethiopia, Georgia, Germany, Greece, Montenegro, Serbia, the Republic of Korea, and the Former Yugoslav Republic of Macedonia have all adopted domestic legislation affording war crimes the same coverage regardless of whether committed in international or internal armed conflicts; see Case Matrix Network (n 70) 43–44.

[80] See PS Nagler, 'Research Brief: Harmonizing War Crimes Under the Rome Statute - Geneva Academy Research Brief' (*Geneva Academy*, March 2019) https://geneva-academy.ch/wp-content/uploads/2025/09/Harmonizing-War-Crimes-Under-The-Rome-Statute.pdf (last accessed 1 June 2025).

[81] The Rome Statute expressly refers to the task of 'interpretation' in arts 9(1), 21(3), 22(2). This confirms the role of ICC judges as interpreters and not only appliers of international criminal law. Grover (n 6) 68.

Statute, its Elements of Crimes, and the Rules of Procedure and Evidence.[82] Only residually, and 'where appropriate', judges should apply applicable treaties and principles and rules of international law,[83] as well as general principles of law derived by the Court from national laws, including the national laws of States that would normally exercise jurisdiction over the crime.[84]

While Article 21 of the Rome Statute does not explicitly address the issue of interpretation, the inclusion of a list of applicable sources therein creates a *de facto* framework that guides ICC judges in their interpretative process. In this regard, paragraph 3 of Article 21 explicitly refers to both 'application' and 'interpretation' of the law, acknowledging the intertwined nature of the two processes. Although a distinction exists between application and interpretation,[85] interpretation is the first step in the process of applying the law. Therefore, Article 21 sets out a hierarchy between sources that ICC judges are to apply when interpreting core international crimes[86] and places the definitions contained in the Statute at the top to increase legal certainty and ensure better respect for the principle of legality.[87] Whilst the other sources of law, including

[82] Rome Statute, art 21(1)(a). The role of the Elements of Crimes in assisting ICC judges in the interpretation and application of arts 6–8*bis* is explicitly outlined in art 9(1).

[83] ibid, art 21(1)(b).

[84] ibid, art 21(1)(c).

[85] G Bitti, 'Article 21 of the Statute of the International Criminal Court and the Treatment of Sources of Law in the Jurisprudence of the ICC' in C Stahn and G Sluiter (eds), *The Emerging Practice of the International Criminal Court* (Brill 2009) 281, 303.

[86] The other sources of law provided for in art 21(1)(b) and (1)(c) can only be applied when '(i) there is a lacuna in the written law contained in the Statute, the Elements of Crimes and the Rules; and (ii) such lacuna cannot be filled by the application of the criteria provided for in articles 31 and 32 of the Vienna Convention on the Law of the Treaties and Article 21(3) of the Statute'; see *Prosecutor v Al Bashir* (Pre-Trial Chamber I, Decision on the Prosecution's Application for a Warrant of Arrest against Omar Hassan Ahmad Al Bashir) ICC-02/05-01/09 (4 March 2009) [126]; *Prosecutor v Lubanga Dyilo (Appeals Chamber,* Judgment on the Appeal of Mr Thomas Lubanga Dyilo against the Decision on the Defence Challenge to the Jurisdiction of the Court Pursuant to Article 19 (2)(a) of the Statute of 3 October 2006) ICC-01-04/01-06 (14 December 2006) [34].

[87] Some have pointed out that such a provision was meant as a limitation of the judges' creativity, to discourage judicial law-making; see W Schabas, 'Customary Law or "Judge-Made" Law: Judicial Creativity at the UN Criminal Tribunals' in J Doria et al (eds), *The Legal Regime of the International Criminal Court: Essays in Honour of Professor Igor Blishchenko*, Vol 19 (Martinus Nijhoff 2009) 77.

custom,[88] occupy a subsidiary position,[89] they still have an acknowledged role to filling gaps in the text of the Statute or as an aid for the purposes of interpretation.[90] In any case, these rules of interpretation seem to provide an imperfect solution. They only apply to the Court itself and fail to take into account how States behave within the Rome system of justice created by the Statute, outside it but, in any case, not before the Court.

However, as an international treaty, the Rome Statute is also subject to rules and principles of interpretation codified by the 1969 Vienna Convention on the Law of Treaties (VCLT) – in particular, Articles 31 and 32.[91] As a general principle of interpretation, a treaty shall be interpreted 'in accordance with the ordinary meaning to be given to the terms of the treaty in their context and in the light of its object and purpose'.[92] Moreover, according to Article 31(3) of the Convention, judges are required to take into account subsequent agreements, practice, and law when interpreting a treaty.[93]

The provisions of the ICC Statute on applicable law and the rules set forth by the 1969 VCLT share common ground, yet they are also distinguishable. Both the ICC Statute and the VCLT emphasise the importance of interpreting treaties in accordance with the ordinary meaning of terms, the context, and in light of their object and purpose. Furthermore, Article 31(3) of the VCLT, on the consideration of

[88] Whereas the provision does not explicitly mention 'customary international law', it is widely recognised that this category is clearly encompassed in the generic reference to the 'rules of international law'. F Pocar, 'Transformation of Customary Law Through ICC Practice' (2018) 112 AJIL 182, 183. However, the role of customs, regarded as a secondary source, occupies a less prominent position in the Rome Statute than at the *ad hoc* International Criminal Tribunals.

[89] It has been, however, pointed out that – in practice – all the sources listed in art 21 are helpful to interpret the Rome Statute. Schabas (n 32) 514.

[90] Pocar (n 88) 184; see *Prosecutor v Bemba Gombo* (Judgment Pursuant to Article 74 of the Statute) ICC-01/05-01/08 (21 March 2016) [79].

[91] See *Situation in the Democratic Republic of Congo* (Judgment on the Prosecutor's Application for Extraordinary Review of Pre-Trial Chamber I's 31 March 2006 Decision Denying Leave to Appeal) ICC-01/04-168 (13 July 2006) [33]; *Prosecutor v Lubanga Dyilo* (Decision on the Admissibility of the Appeal of Mr Thomas Lubanga Dyilo against the Decision of Pre-Trial Chamber I entitled 'Décision sur la confirmation des charges of 29 January 2007') ICC-01/04-01/06 (13 June 2007) [8]; *Prosecutor v Katanga* (Judgment Pursuant to Article 74 of the Statute) ICC-01/04-01/07 (7 March 2014) [43].

[92] VCLT, art 31(1); see *Prosecutor v Katanga* (n 91) [55].

[93] ibid, art 31(3).

subsequent agreements, practice, and relevant rules of international law, aligns with the ICC's approach outlined in Article 21. By virtue of this provision, judges are expected to take into account applicable treaties and principles and rules of international law. It could therefore be argued that the ICC Statute is a specialised regime of the VCLT's general principles for treaty interpretation able to meet the specific needs, complexities, and criminal nature of the ICC.

In any case, the interplay between Article 21 ICC Statute and Article 31(3) of the 1969 VCLT, puts ICC judges at the interface: taking into account subsequent agreements, practice and other sources of international law, including custom, when interpreting the Rome Statute. As customary law and general principles of law will continue to evolve beyond the Statute, and new relevant treaties between States will continue to be concluded, the definitions of crimes cannot be considered frozen in time but need to be interpreted in the light of the law existing when the crime is alleged to have been committed.[94]

11.7 The Role of Domestic Implementing Legislation in Interpreting the Rome Statute Crimes

The idea of international criminal law not being static raises questions of how domestic implementing legislation can influence the interpretation of the definitions of core international crimes crystallised in the Rome Statute. This is particularly the case when the Court steps in in light of the principle of complementarity, that is, when national authorities are unwilling or unable to genuinely investigate or prosecute the case. It is, therefore, crucial to understand how potential new State practice and emerging customary international law would interact with the treaty provisions and what this means for their interpretation. The adoption of divergent national legislation on core international crimes does not necessarily have an impact on the interpretation of such crimes.[95] However, a 'systematic, repetitive and concordant' practice of States[96] interpreting and applying the definitions of core international crimes at the domestic level might contribute to the evolution of international customary law alongside the definitions of crimes contained in the

[94] Grover (n 6) 380.
[95] Hoffmann (n 71) 97.
[96] R Gardiner, *Treaty Interpretation* (Oxford University Press 2008) 226.

Rome Statute.[97] If a considerable number of States, both parties and non-parties to the Rome Statute, enacted a particular definition for a crime that departs in some way from Articles 6–8bis of the Statute, it might be argued that a new State practice and possibly opinio juris emerges on the content of the elements of that crime under customary international law. If several States consistently interpret and apply definitions of core international crimes at the domestic level, in a way that departs from the Rome Statute but aligns with one another, this can be perceived as subsequent practice that reflects a common understanding among those States. In this context, the consistent domestic practices might qualify as evidence of the parties' agreement regarding the interpretation of the relevant treaty provisions, falling under Article 31(3)(b) of the 1969 VCLT.[98] Furthermore, even when such consistent State practice does not fully align with the common intention of the parties but reflects general practice among a significant number of States, it could still fall under Article 32 of VCLT, as a supplementary means of interpretation. It could help clarify the treaty provisions in question and confirm the meaning resulting from the application of Article 31.[99]

For instance, with regard to the definition of genocide, a clear trend in State practice towards expanding the list of protected groups to include political and social groups can be identified. To the extent that this evidence of State practice is supported by opinio juris, it could be argued that a larger number of protected groups has crystallised into customary law.[100] Moreover, there is also a growing trend to abandon the distinction between international and non-international armed conflicts among war crimes, which appears in line with customary international law.[101] But does this mean that where a State Party has blurred the distinction between international and non-international armed conflicts – and the ICC steps in owing to complementarity – ICC judges could extend their

97 ICRC (n 74) 25.

98 VCLT, art 31(3)(b).

99 ibid, art 32.

100 However, Hoffmann observed that national differences in the list of protected groups are a sign of dissatisfaction with the international definition but do not represent 'modifications undertaken with the intention of creating a new *opinio juris* and state practice'. Hoffmann (n 71) 97. Similarly, Nersessian pointed out that 'there is no evidence of *opinio juris*' around the inclusion of political groups in domestic law; see DL Nersessian, *Genocide and Political Groups* (Oxford University Press 2010) 128.

101 B McGuckin, 'The Conflict Between Armed Conflicts: Dispensing with the Distinction Between International and Non-International Armed Conflicts' (2018) Durham Global Security Institute Working Paper No 1, 22.

subject matter jurisdiction to war crimes that constitute customary international law but have been excluded from the list of Articles 8(2)(e) of the Rome Statute?

In this regard, it is key to emphasise that the International Criminal Court is bound by the principle of legality. Article 22 provides that no one can be held responsible under the Rome Statute 'unless the conduct in question constitutes, at the time it takes place, a crime within the jurisdiction of the Court'.[102] Moreover, the definition of a crime shall be 'strictly construed'.[103] The goal of the drafters in Rome was to set out all crimes falling under the jurisdiction of the ICC, in as specific and detailed a manner as possible.[104] Therefore, ICC judges are strictly bound by the limits of the Statute's wording when undertaking their interpretative task.[105]

A certain level of flexibility within the Statute's framework is still acceptable 'to avoid excessive rigidity and to keep pace with changing circumstances'.[106] However, whilst the rule of strict construction shall not be intended as curbing the progressive juridical clarification or specification of the content of an offence,[107] the Rome Statute cannot be stretched to create new criminal prohibitions that would then be applied retrospectively. An interpretation based on the object and purpose of the Statute could not be used to create a body of law extraneous to the terms of the treaty or incompatible with the literal reading of the text.[108] It is therefore necessary to distinguish between the creation of new substantive law and an interpretation within the scope of existing law. Whilst a reinterpretation based on subsequent practice or customary international law can be considered acceptable, if it can be reasonably accommodated by the actual text of the Statute, modification of the text under the guise of interpretation is not permissible. A significant departure from the intention of the drafters in order to give effect to a creative

[102] Rome Statute, art 22(1).

[103] ibid, art 22(2).

[104] A Cassese, 'The Statute of the International Criminal Court: Some Preliminary Reflections' (1999) 10(1) EJIL 144, 152.

[105] G Hochmayr, 'Applicable law in Practice and Theory: Interpreting Article 21 of the ICC Statute' (2014) 12(4) JICJ 655, 664.

[106] *Kokkinakis v Greece* (25 May 1993) Application no 14307/88 [40].

[107] B Broomhall, 'Article 22' in K Ambos (ed), *Commentary on the Rome Statute of the International Criminal Court* (4th edn, Beck, Hart, Nomos 2022) 1149, 1162.

[108] *Prosecutor v Katanga* (n 91) [55].

interpretation of the Statute would appear to be 'an inappropriate arrogation of the legislative function by the judiciary'.[109]

The principle of legality, and the primacy of the Statute's text, therefore, prevents judges from expanding the Court's jurisdiction to prosecute crimes that are merely based on subsequent practice or custom but are not clearly defined in the Statute.[110] For instance, ICC judges could not extend their subject matter jurisdiction to the war crime of intentionally directing attacks against civilian objects, as this would broaden the punishable acts beyond Article 8(2)(e) of the Rome Statute. However desirable this may be, and even though a trend is beginning to develop in national legislation to conflate the two, the Statute provision remains abundantly clear. Similarly, finding an accused guilty of political or social genocide before the ICC would clearly constitute a violation of the principle of legality.[111]

Such an approach may seem unduly restrictive, if not conservative. A rigid textual interpretation of the Rome Statute promotes a narrower scope for the definitions of core international crimes.[112] Brave acts of judicial activism have also occurred in a number of instances in the past, including before international tribunals. For instance, in *Tadić*, the ICTY Appeals Chamber held that the nexus with an armed conflict in crimes against humanity was no longer required under customary law.[113] In the *Akayesu* judgment, the ICTR Tribunal expanded the traditionally protected groups under the definition of genocide to include 'any stable and permanent group'.[114] However, although the Rome Statute's provisions offer some flexibility, they are not fully flexible. It is important not to try and stretch them beyond their limits and intended scope.

ICC judges need to be cautious when taking into account subsequent practice and customary international law that significantly narrow or broaden the scope of a crime. Whilst they should be mindful of developments both in State practice and customary law, they must also recognise

109 *Prosecutor v Ruto and Sang* (Judgment on the Appeal of the Prosecutor against the Decision of Trial Chamber V(a) of 18 June 2013 entitled 'Decision on Mr Ruto's Request for Excusal from Continuous Presence at Trial') ICC-01/09-01/11-1066-Anx (25 October 2013) Joint Separate Opinion of Judge Kourula and Judge Ušacka [11].

110 Schabas (n 32) 543; see *Prosecutor v Bemba Gombo* (n 90) [83].

111 Nersessian (n 100) 133.

112 N Jain, 'Interpretive Divergence' (2017) 57(1) VJIL 45, 50.

113 *Prosecutor v Tadić* (Decision on the Defence Motion) (n 19) [141].

114 *Prosecutor v Akayesu* (Trial Chamber I Judgment) ICTR-96-4-T (2 September 1998) [516].

that the Statute is a treaty and that the interpretation and application role of the judiciary must be kept distinct from the law-making role.[115] It is the Assembly of States Parties, as the 'management oversight and legislative body' of the ICC,[116] that can initiate amendments to the Statute following the Article 121 Rome Statute process. For example, a unified approach to war crimes committed in non-international and international armed conflicts could only be taken at the ICC if an amendment were to be made to Article 8(2)(e) of the Rome Statute to incorporate analogous provisions to those found in Article 8(2)(b).[117]

11.8 Concluding Remarks

The chapter has explored what happens at the interface of domestic legal systems having interpreted core international crimes differently from the Rome Statute and the International Criminal Court. Addressing the question of how national implementing legislation can influence the interpretation of the definitions of core crimes crystallised in Articles 6–8*bis* of the Rome Statute provides useful insights into the progressive evolution of international criminal law and sheds some light on the under-explored interaction between implementation and interpretation of the Statute. However, the rules of interpretation laid down in Article 21 of the Rome Statute do not represent an adequate framework to fully unpick this interaction. They only apply to the Court itself and fail to take into account the interpretation of core international crimes provided at the domestic level.

ICC judges ought to be cognisant of how State Parties have implemented core international crimes in their domestic law when engaging in the interpretation of the Rome Statute. Under the 1969 VCLT, judges are required to take into account subsequent agreements, practice, and other

[115] A Ashworth and J Horder, *Principles of Criminal Law* (Oxford University Press 2013) 69.

[116] ICC, 'Assembly of States Parties' (*ICC*, 2025) <https://asp.icc-cpi.int/assembly> (last accessed 1 June 2025).

[117] For instance, an amendment has been adopted on 10 June 2010 granting the Court jurisdiction over the war crime of employing certain poisoned weapons (art 8(2)(b)(xiii)), expanding bullets (art 8(2)(b)(xv), as well as asphyxiating or poisonous gases, and all analogous liquids, materials or devices (art 8(2)(b)(xiv)), when committed in armed conflicts not of an international character; ICC, 'Amendments to Article 8 of the Rome Statute' (10 June 2010) RC/Res.5. More recently, on 6 December 2019, another amendment has been adopted to extend the international use of starvation of civilians as a method of warfare to non-internal armed conflicts.

sources of international law when interpreting a treaty. It may be that some flexibility within the Statute exists, and judicial activism and creativity may be inevitable or even desirable to keep pace with progressive developments in the field. However, it remains necessary to distinguish between an interpretation within the scope of the existing law and modification of the text of a treaty. ICC judges cannot expand the scope of core international crimes' definitions to include new types of conduct or contextual circumstances that are not clearly supported by the text of the Statute. Therefore, where (re)-interpretation based on subsequent State practice cannot be reconciled with the text of a specific provision, formally amending the Statute – following the procedure set forth in Article 121 of the Rome Statute – remains the only available route. Keeping the Rome Statute under review and ensuring its continued evolution in accordance with customary international law would maintain the unity of the international criminal law system and avoid (further) fragmentation.

12

Crimes Against Humanity and Customary International Law

LEILA NADYA SADAT

12.1 Introduction

Crimes against humanity's complicated origin story has generated confusion regarding its modern content and legal foundations. It has nonetheless become a critical component of modern international justice. This chapter explores the development of the crime in the twentieth century, including its evolution in customary international law and its codification in the Rome Statute of the International Criminal Court ('Rome' or 'ICC Statute'). It also takes up the current proposal to re-codify it in a new, specialized, multilateral convention based upon the International Law Commission's (ILC) 2019 Draft Articles on Crimes Against Humanity ('Draft Articles'),[1] a project that 124 States have, thus far, explicitly committed to.[2] It identifies five phases in the crime's development, from its nineteenth-century natural law origins through its codification in the ICC Statute, and finally its possible recodification in a new treaty.

Consistent with the theme of this volume, after exploring the historical genesis and current status of crimes against humanity in customary international law, this chapter evaluates the position of States as regards the unity, evolution, and diversity of their interpretative approach to the ILC Draft Articles and particularly the definition of crimes against humanity in Draft Article 2. Among State supporters of this new treaty, most have embraced the idea of *unity* in approaching the definition of crimes against humanity in the new treaty.[3] By unity, they seem to mean

[1] ILC, 'Draft Articles on Prevention and Punishment of Crimes Against Humanity' (29 April–7 June and 8 July–9 August 2019) UN Doc A/74/10 reproduced in [2019/II – Part Two] YBILC 23 (2019 ILC Draft Articles).

[2] 124 supporters as of November 12, 2024. See also LN Sadat, 'The Forgotten Crime: Forging a Convention for Crimes Against Humanity' (2024) 56 CasWResJIntL 523, 544.

[3] See UNGA, 'Crimes Against Humanity: Report of the Secretary-General' (12 January 2024) UN Doc A/78/717 [9].

that the new treaty should essentially serve as a horizontal 'add-on' to the Rome Statute of the International Criminal Court (ICC), making the two instruments seamlessly consistent as a matter of text and application.

Other States, however, are tempted by the idea of *evolution*, which could adjust the definition to consider developments found in customary international law,[4] such as the prohibition on the slave trade or the emergence of new crimes.[5] Indeed, some States have suggested that the new treaty offers the possibility, consistent with Article 13 of the UN Charter, for progressive development and have proposed the addition of new crimes, including economic crimes,[6] environmental crimes,[7] and the crime of gender apartheid.[8] They agree with taking the Rome Statute definition as the centerpiece of the new treaty but have proposed or accepted modifications they believe will make it a treaty responding to the modern needs of the international community.

Finally, the Draft Articles themselves, like the ICC Statute, have also recognized that there may be a *diversity* of codifications in national legislation, and that customary international law may continue to evolve outside treaty codifications of crimes against humanity. This was the position of the ILC itself, which thus included a 'without prejudice' clause in Draft Article 2(3) to provide States with flexibility in adapting a new treaty to municipal law, so long as the definition they adopt is 'broader'.[9]

4 See Permanent Mission of Romania to the UN, 'Statement Delivered by Ms Alos Lungu, Legal Adviser' (2 April 2024) 2 <https://www.un.org/en/ga/sixth/78/pdfs/statements/cah/40mtg_romania_2.pdf> (last accessed 1 June 2025); Permanent Representative of Denmark to the UN, 'Statement on behalf of the Nordic Countries' (April 2024) 2 <https://www.un.org/en/ga/sixth/78/pdfs/statements/cah/39mtg_nordic_2.pdf> (last accessed 1 June 2025).

5 See Permanent Mission of the Republic of Sierra Leone to the UN, 'Statement by HE Mr Amara S Sowa' (12 October 2023) [9] <https://www.un.org/en/ga/sixth/78/pdfs/statements/cah/11mtg_sierraleone.pdf> (last accessed 1 June 2025); Permanent Mission of the Republic of Cameroon to the UN, 'Declaration du Cameroun faite par NYANID Zacharie Serge Raoul, PhD, Ministre Plénipotentiaire' (October 2023) 2 <https://www.un.org/en/ga/sixth/78/pdfs/statements/cah/10mtg_cameroon.pdf> (last accessed 1 June 2025).

6 See Permanent Mission of the Republic of Sierra Leone to the UN (n 5) [8].

7 See Permanent Mission of the State of Eritrea to the UN, 'Statement Delivered by the Delegation of Eritrea' (11–12 October 2023) 2 <https://www.un.org/en/ga/sixth/78/pdfs/statements/cah/10mtg_eritrea.pdf> (last accessed 1 June 2025).

8 See Permanent Mission of Mexico to the United Nations, 'Intervención de México en el debate sobre el Tema 80: "Crímenes de lesa humanidad"' (11 October 2023) 2 <https://www.un.org/en/ga/sixth/78/pdfs/statements/cah/10mtg_mexico.pdf> (last accessed 1 June 2025).

9 2019 ILC Draft Articles (n 1) art 2(3).

The consequences that might flow from national – or international – variations of the crimes are not spelled out by the Draft Articles, or by the Rome Statute, a point returned to periodically in Sections 12.2, 12.3, and 12.4. Yet, as evidenced by the 2021 judgment of the ICC Appeals Chamber in *Abd-Al-Rahman*, the relationship between treaty codifications of crimes against humanity, including the Rome Statute and customary international law, is important in considering the legality principle with respect to the prosecution of non-Rome Statute State Party nationals for ICC crimes or eventually in universal jurisdiction cases heard by national courts. The purpose of this contribution is not to evaluate these three approaches but to offer some reflections that may be useful to their consideration. This analysis is particularly important given the ongoing negotiations of a new treaty on crimes against humanity.

12.2 Historical Development of Crimes Against Humanity

In the mid-1990s, when the Rome Statute was being negotiated, the international community was experiencing a renaissance in the domain of international law and international lawmaking. Thus, when crises arose, including the collapse of the former Yugoslavia and its descent into war, and the 1994 Rwandan genocide, the response was, in part, to resurrect the project of creating international criminal tribunals and courts to address the commission of atrocities, which had lain fallow since 1945.

But it was not clear what law these new courts and tribunals apply, as the gap between the modern origins of international criminal law at Nürnberg and Tokyo and the efforts, some fifty years later, to enshrine these precedents in modern institutions was considerable. This was particularly true for crimes against humanity, which had no treaty basis prior to its inclusion as Article 6(c) of the Charter of the International Military Tribunal at Nürnberg (IMT Charter)[10] and Article 5(c) of the Charter of the International Military Tribunal for the Far East (IMFTE Charter).[11] Indeed, it was unclear whether the legal basis for crimes against humanity was a treaty, based on the status of the IMT Charter

[10] Agreement for the Prosecution and Punishment of the Major War Criminals of the European Axis (adopted 8 August 1945, entered into force 8 August 1945) 82 UNTS 279 (IMT Statute).

[11] Charter of the International Military Tribunal for the Far East (adopted 19 January 1946, entered into force 19 January 1946) 20 TIAS 1589, art 5(c) (IMFTE)

as a treaty signed by twenty-three States,[12] or a matter of customary international law, as later evidenced by its subsequent adoption by the General Assembly as the Nürnberg Principles of 1950.[13] It was unclear during the period of the crime's emergence, and experts have debated this question for more than seventy years.[14]

The IMT based its interpretation on the Charter it was given, famously noting that, in its view: 'The Charter is not an arbitrary exercise of power on the part of the victorious nations, but [. . .] the expression of international Law existing at the time of its creation; and to that extent is itself a contribution to International Law.'[15] Presumably, the IMT was referencing customary international law. That said, given a dearth of State practice or case law on crimes against humanity, the IMT construed Article 6(c) of its Charter (on crimes against humanity) relatively narrowly. For example, the tribunal required that crimes against humanity have a connection to the other crimes in the Charter (war crimes and/or crimes against peace) to be indictable, which eliminated persecutions committed by the Nazis in the 1930s, prior to the invasion of Poland, from the charges faced by the accused. It also found that the crime of persecution in Article 6(c) was not independent from the other crimes listed in the Charter (murder, extermination, etc.), a limitation later critiqued by scholars.[16]

Nonetheless, three key ideas emerged from the text of the Charter and the Judgment of the Tribunal: (1) crimes against humanity, unlike war crimes, protect all civilians – including a State's own nationals – from widespread or systematic attacks on certain human rights and persecutory campaigns; and (2) neither the accused's official position nor

[12] The IMT Statute was initially signed by the four Allied Powers (France, the Soviet Union, the United States, and the United Kingdom) and later by nineteen other States.

[13] ILC, 'Report of the International Law Commission on the Work of its First Session' (12 April 1949) UN Doc A/CN.4/13 and Corr 1-3 reproduced in [1949/I] YBILC 282.

[14] See MC Bassiouni, *Crimes Against Humanity: Historical Evolution and Contemporary Application* (Cambridge University Press 2011); D Luban, 'A Theory of Crimes Against Humanity' (2004) 29 YaleJIntlL 85; P Sands, *East West Street: On the Origins of Genocide and Crimes Against Humanity* (Orion 2016); E Schwelb, 'Crimes Against Humanity' (1946) 23 BYBIL 178.

[15] *Judgment of the Nuremberg International Military Tribunal of 1 October 1946* (1947) 41 AJIL 172, 224.

[16] RS Clark, 'Crimes Against Humanity' in G Ginsburgs and VN Kudriavtsev (eds), *The Nuremberg Trial and International Law* (Martinus Nijhoff 1990) 177. See also L Sadat Wexler, 'The Interpretation of the Nuremberg Principles by the French Court of Cassation: From *Touvier* to *Barbie* and Back Again' (1994) 32 ColJTransnatlL 289, 306–9.

national law is a defence. Finally, (3) the crimes themselves are particularly egregious, 'characterized either by their seriousness and their savagery [. . .] or by their magnitude, or by the fact that they were part of a system designed to spread terror, or that they were a link in a deliberately-pursued policy against certain groups'.[17]

Because no treaty was ever adopted for crimes against humanity after the war,[18] other than its partial codification in the form of treaties on the crime of genocide (1948), and later apartheid (1974), torture (1984), and enforced disappearance (2006), crimes against humanity persisted in customary international law but without a firm treaty foundation. The ILC had undertaken but not finalized the task of codifying it along with other international crimes. The ILC had also drafted articles to be used in establishing an international criminal court, producing two separate documents in the 1990s, one for a Court in 1994[19] and one for a draft code of crimes in 1996.[20] Both texts referenced crimes against humanity, but neither was ready to serve as the basis of an international criminal court. Instead, when the Security Council established the *ad hoc* international criminal tribunals for the former Yugoslavia (ICTY)[21] and Rwanda (ICTR),[22] it did not rely on the Commission's work but adopted Statutes annexed to Security Council Resolutions adopted under Chapter VII of the United Nations Charter for each of the two entities.

[17] A Cassese, *International Law* (Oxford University Press 2001) 92.

[18] The 1968 Convention on the Non-Applicability of Statutory Limitations to War Crimes and Crimes Against Humanity (adopted 26 November 1968, entered into force 11 November 1970) 754 UNTS 73, adopted the Nürnberg definition by reference in art I(b).

[19] ILC, 'Draft Statute for an International Criminal Court' (2 May–22 July 1994) UN Doc A/49/10 reproduced in [1994/II – Part Two] YBILC 27 (ILC Draft ICC Statute).

[20] The task of preparing a draft code of offences against the peace and security of humankind was entrusted to the International Law Commission in 1947, by General Assembly resolution 177 (II) of 21 November 1947, the same resolution that requested it to formulate the Nürnberg principles. Work was slow and was finally finished in 1996 and adopted by the Commission on second reading. ILC, 'Draft Code of Crimes Against the Peace and Security of Mankind' (6 May–26 July 1966) UN Doc A/51/10 reproduced in [1996/II – Part Two] YBILC 15 [50] (1966 Draft Code of Crimes). See also MC Bassiouni, 'The History of the Draft Code of Crimes Against the Peace and Security of Mankind' (1993) 27 IsraelLR 247.

[21] Established by UNSC, 'Resolution 808 adopted by the Security Council at its 3175th Meeting' (22 February 1993) UN Doc S/Res/808.

[22] Established by UNSC, 'Resolution 955 adopted by the Security Council at its 3453rd Meeting' (8 November 1994) UN Doc S/Res/955 2.

The Secretary-General's Report supporting the establishment of the ICTY[23] stated that the Security Council would not be 'creating or purporting to legislate' but that the ICTY would have the 'task of applying existing international law'.[24] The Report added:

> In the view of the Secretary-General, the application of the principle *nullum crimen sine lege* requires that the international tribunal should apply rule of international humanitarian law which are beyond any doubt part of customary law so that the problem of adherence of some but not all States to specific conventions does not arise.[25]

The Report suggested that the relevant treaties to be applied were the four Geneva Conventions of 12 August 1949, the Hague Convention (IV) Respecting the Laws and Customs of War on Land and the Regulations annexed thereto of 18 October 1907, and the Convention on the Prevention and Punishment of the Crime of Genocide of 9 December 1948, in addition to the Nürnberg Charter.[26]

As for crimes against humanity, the Report noted the absence of a treaty thereon, a *lacuna* that the international community is endeavouring to fill at the present moment,[27] and to which this chapter returns in Section 12.3. Thus, the Report suggested, the Charter and Judgment of the Nürnberg Tribunal and Control Council Law No. 10[28] would be the relevant referents. In addition, the Report observed that '[c]rimes against humanity are aimed at any civilian population and are prohibited regardless of whether they are committed in an armed conflict, international or internal in character'.[29] Despite this, the armed conflict nexus was retained in the *chapeau* of Article 5 when the Statute was finally adopted.[30] Conversely, Article 3 of the ICTY's sister tribunal, the

23 UNSC 'Report of the Secretary-General Pursuant to Paragraph 2 of Security Council Resolution 808' (3 May 1993) UN Doc S/25704.

24 ibid [29].

25 ibid [34].

26 ibid [35].

27 See 2019 ILC Draft Articles (n 1); Sadat (n 2); M Bergsmo and S Tianying (eds), *On the Proposed Crimes Against Humanity Convention* (Torkel Opsahl Academic EPublisher 2014); C Kreß and S Garibian (eds), 'Special Issue: Laying the Foundations for a Convention on Crimes Against Humanity' (2018) 16 JICJ 679; CC Jalloh and LN Sadat (eds), 'Special Issue on the ILC Draft Articles on Prevention and Punishment of Crimes Against Humanity' (2020) 6 African Journal of International Criminal Justice 75.

28 Control Council Law No 10 (20 December 1945).

29 Report of the Secretary General (n 23) [47].

30 UNSC, 'Statute of the International Criminal Tribunal for the former Yugoslavia' (3 May 1993) UN Doc S/25704 art 5 (ICTY Statute).

IICTR excluded the 'armed conflict' element, but included a requirement that the crime be committed 'on national, political, ethnic, racial or religious grounds'.[31] This tendency to codify the crime by adding new material elements depending on the facts of specific conflicts is a problem that persists today. I return to this point in Section 12.2.

Thus instructed, the two *ad hoc* tribunals began adjudicating cases and developing a modern jurisprudence of crimes against humanity as customary international law. Between them, 161 individuals were indicted at the ICTY,[32] and 93 at the ICTR.[33] In a 2013 study, I found that at the ICTY, crimes against humanity represented 40.6 per cent of all indicted offences, and war crimes charges approximately 56.9 per cent. Conviction rates were approximately the same for both the crimes against humanity charges and the war crimes charges (39.3 per cent and 37.5 per cent, respectively). Genocide charges were few, and convictions rare.[34]

In 1999, the ICTY found that under customary international law, crimes against humanity could occur in peace time as well as during armed conflict[35] and rejected the idea that they must be accompanied by discriminatory intent.[36] The *Kunarac* decision also rejected the requirement that crimes against humanity could only be committed pursuant to a State or organizational policy.[37] Some of these important holdings, which, as noted above, were articulated as norms of customary international law, followed and therefore contradicted the earlier *codification* of crimes against humanity in Article 7 of the ICC Statute, which was adopted on July 17, 1998.

Subsequent decisions of both the ICTY and the ICTR also contributed extensively to an understanding of the murder-type crimes and the crime

31 UNSC, 'Statute of the International Criminal Tribunal for Rwanda' (8 November 1994) UN Doc S/RES/955 art 3 (ICTR Statute).

32 See ICTY, 'Infographic: ICTY Facts & Figures' (*International Residual Mechanism for Criminal Tribunals*, 2025) <https://www.icty.org/en/content/infographic-icty-facts-figures> (last accessed 1 June 2025).

33 See ICTR, 'Key Figures of Cases' (*International Residual Mechanism for Criminal Tribunals*, October 2019) <https://unictr.irmct.org/en/cases/key-figures-cases> (last accessed 1 June 2025).

34 LN Sadat, 'Crimes Against Humanity in the Modern Age' (2013) 107 AJIL 334, 343–44.

35 *Prosecutor v Duško Tadić* (Decision on the Defence Motion for Interlocutory Appeal on Jurisdiction) IT-94-1-T (2 October 1995) [141].

36 *Prosecutor v Tadić* (Judgment) IT-94-1-A (15 July 1999) [283].

37 *Prosecutor v Kunarac, Kovac and Vukovic* (Appeals Chamber Judgment) IT-96-23/1-A (12 June 2002) [98].

of persecution and elaborated a comprehensive jurisprudence on sexual and gender based violence as well.[38] As former ICTY Judge Patricia Wald has noted, 'crimes against humanity [became] the growth stock of Tribunal jurisprudence'.[39] Meanwhile, as the *ad hoc* tribunals began their work, the ICC Statute was being negotiated, first in New York during the Preparatory Committee meetings held at the Headquarters of the United Nations and then in Rome during the summer of 1998.

12.3 The Codification and Development of Crimes Against Humanity at the ICC

12.3.1 The Negotiations at Rome

There was little doubt that crimes against humanity would be included in the Rome Statute, given its origins in the Charters of the Nürnberg and Tokyo Tribunals. That said, it had not been included *as such* in the 1991 *Draft Code of Crimes against the Peace and Security of Mankind* produced by the ILC[40] although it was reinserted in the 1996 text and was not within the automatic jurisdiction of the proposed court envisaged by the ILC in 1994.[41] During the Preparatory Committee meetings held prior to the Court's Statute, it was agreed that the definition should reflect the elements of the crime under customary international law.[42]

Yet ascertaining the content of that custom was challenging. Crimes against humanity had originated as *natural law* in the nineteenth century to condemn slavery and the slave trade[43] and King Leopold's atrocities in

[38] See G Mettraux, 'Crimes Against Humanity in the Jurisprudence of the International Criminal Tribunals for the Former Yugoslavia and for Rwanda' (2002) 43 HILJ 237; B Swart, A Zahar and G Sluiter (eds), *The Legacy of the International Criminal Tribunal for the Former Yugoslavia* (Oxford University Press 2011); PM Wald, 'Genocide and Crimes Against Humanity' (2007) 6 WashUGlobalStudLRev 621.

[39] Wald (n 38) 625.

[40] The Draft Code referenced instead 'systematic or mass violations of human rights'. ILC, 'Draft Code of Crimes against the Peace and Security of Mankind. Titles and Texts of Articles Adopted by the Drafting Committee' (5 July 1989) UN Doc A/CN.4/L.459 reproduced in [1991/I] YBILC 186.

[41] ILC Draft ICC Statute (n 19).

[42] UNGA, 'Report of the Preparatory Committee on the Establishment of an International Criminal Court: Volume 2, Compilation of Proposals' (13 September 1996) UN Doc A/51/22 78 [51–54].

[43] See e.g. US Supreme Court, *The Antelope* (1825) 23 US 66, holding that the African slave trade is contrary to the law of nature but is not prohibited by the positive law of nations unless specific treaties have forbidden it. See also B van Schaack, 'Crimes Against

the Congo.[44] In the twentieth century, it began to take shape as *customary international law*, with the judgments of the Nürnberg and Tokyo Tribunals. The texts of the ICTY and the ICTR Statutes were another important source of customary international law, as were judgments from national courts, including the *Barbie*[45] and *Eichmann* cases, from the Supreme Courts of France and Israel, respectively. In *Eichmann*, in particular, the Israeli courts were exercising universal jurisdiction over the accused, as Israel was neither the State or the territory of which the crimes were committed, nor the State of the accused (or the victims) nationality. As the Supreme Court of Israel noted:

> The abhorrent crimes ... [are] crimes which offended the whole of mankind and shocked the conscience of nations are grave offences against the law of nations itself ... in the absence of an International Court, the international law is in need of the judicial and legislative authorities of every country, to give effect to its penal injunctions and to bring criminals to trial. The jurisdiction to try crimes under international law is universal.[46]

Thus, unlike war crimes and genocide, for which treaty texts were available, defining crimes against humanity during the Rome Statute's negotiation required achieving a consensus as to which elements of the crime represented customary international law.[47] This was a considerable challenge in part because unlike the *ad hoc* tribunal statutes, which were drafted after the crimes had already been committed or as they were ongoing, and with a specific crime base in mind, the ICC was drafted for future cases.

Humanity in the 'Western and Other' Group of States: A Continuing Tradition' (2020) 6 African Journal of International Criminal Justice 136; B van Schaack, *Imagining Justice for Syria* (Cambridge University Press 2020).

44 C Gevers, 'African and International Criminal Law' in KJ Heller et al (eds), *The Oxford Handbook of International Criminal Law* (Oxford University Press 2019) 154; ABM Marong, 'The ILC Draft Articles on Crimes Against Humanity, An African Perspective' (2020) 6 African Journal of International Criminal Justice 93.

45 Supreme Court of France, Criminal Law Chamber, *The Prosecutor v Klaus Barbie* (Judgment of 20 December 1985) 86-92714

46 District Court of Jerusalem, *Attorney General of the Government of Israel v Adolf Eichmann* (1968) 36 ILR 18; Israel Supreme Court, *Attorney-General of the Government of Israel v Eichmann* (1962) 36 ILR 277.

47 H von Hebel and D Robinson, 'Crimes within the Jurisdiction of the Court' in RS Lee (ed), *The International Criminal Court: The Making of the Rome Statute* (Kluwer Law International 1999) 79, 90–92.

The link to customary international law was also important because of the potential for worldwide application of the Rome Statute through the vehicle of a Security Council referral of a situation involving the nationals of non-State Parties. For this reason, as several contemporaneous accounts suggest,[48] the negotiators intended the Rome Statute to represent, like the ICTY and ICTR Statutes, customary international law and were not intending to create new law.[49] That said, they included some adaptations that would take into account the fact that a new *court* was being established to prosecute the crimes therein, which would have its own set of jurisdictional limitations and prosecutorial priorities. In the sense of the *North Continental Sea* judgment of the International Court of Justice,[50] there were elements of codification, crystallization, and customary international law creation at Rome as to crimes against humanity.[51] Much of the Statute tracked the Nürnberg definition (codification), some elements that had been debated in prior case law and by scholars were clarified, such as the severing of the link to armed conflict (crystallization), and others, such as the new provisions on sexual and gender-based violence, emerged as new crimes at Rome (creation).

Like other core international crimes, crimes against humanity are composite offences, comprising a material element (an *actus* reus), a mental element (*mens rea*), and a *chapeau* containing context elements that internationalize the crime and distinguish it from ordinary crimes like murder, torture, and crimes of sexual violence, for example. In crafting the *chapeau* containing the context elements of crimes against humanity, the drafters eliminated the element requiring a connection to armed conflict but retained in Article 7(1) the requirement of an 'attack' directed against a civilian population and that the attack on the civilian population be *either* widespread *or* systematic, rejecting the view that the attack must fulfill both requirements under customary international law.

[48] See e.g. P Kirsch, 'Foreword' in K Dormann (ed), *Elements of War Crimes under the Rome Statute of the International Criminal Court: Sources and Commentary* (Cambridge University Press 2003) xiii. Philippe Kirsch chaired the Committee of the Whole at Rome and was elected as the Court's first President.

[49] ibid, xiii.

[50] *North Sea Continental Shelf Cases (Federal Republic of Germany/Netherlands; Federal Republic of Germany/Denmark)* (Judgment) [1969] ICJ Rep 3.

[51] ibid. This chapter does not explore the origins or theoretical basis of customary international law, which has been extensively discussed in other volumes of this series. See e.g. P Merkouris, J Kammerhofer, and N Arajärvi (eds), *The Theory, Practice, and Interpretation of Customary International Law* (Cambridge University Press 2022).

They also eliminated the requirement of discriminatory intent found in the ICTR Statute. However, they added, in Article 7(2)(a), a requirement that the crime be committed 'pursuant to or in furtherance of a state or organizational policy', an element that the ICTY and ICTR had rejected, and which many scholars believe is not required by customary international law.[52]

The eleven offences in Article 7(1)(a) through (k) requires the *actus reus* of the offence be limited to violent attacks upon corporal integrity (and similar offences), tracking the Statutes of the *ad hoc* tribunals, but with important additions. The list of prohibited acts includes murder, extermination, deportation and forcible transfer, imprisonment, torture, rape, and other forms of sexual, gender-based, and reproductive violence, persecution, and a catch-all provision: other inhumane acts. The inclusion of 'other inhumane acts'[53] raises the possibility of new atrocities emerging as crimes against humanity in the future. It has already been used to capture the crime of forced marriage[54] and has been charged in other ICC cases, including the *Abd-Al-Rahman* case, discussed further below. The drafters declined to add environmental and/or economic crimes as certain States had urged during the negotiations of the Rome Statute[55] and as the ILC had discussed during its work on the *Draft Code of Crimes*. This possibility has reappeared in discussions pertaining to the new treaty discussed Section 12.4.

Unlike predecessor tribunals, the ICC operates in real time and with the link to armed conflict explicitly severed in the text of Article 7, it is now understood that crimes against humanity may occur in times of relative peace. Thus, crimes against humanity have emerged as a pivotal

[52] G Mettraux, 'The Definition of Crimes Against Humanity and the Question of a "Policy" Element' in LN Sadat (ed), *Forging a Convention for Crimes Against Humanity* (Cambridge University Press 2011) 142.

[53] Rome Statute of the International Criminal Court (adopted 17 July 1998, entered into force 1 July 2002) 2187 UNTS 3, art 7(1)(k).

[54] *Prosecutor v Dominic Ongwen* (Judgment) ICC-02/04-01/15 (4 February 2021) [2202-88, 2741-53] (factual and legal findings relating to forced marriage).

[55] See LN Sadat, 'Accountability for Environmental Violations and Crimes: Advancing a More Global and Inclusive Approach to International Environmental Law' (UNGA 79 High-Level Week Side Event, New York, September 2024) <https://bpb-us-w2.wpmucdn.com/sites.wustl.edu/dist/b/2004/files/2024/10/Remarks_Crimes-Against-the-Environment_UN-High-Level-Week.pdf> (last accessed 1 June 2025). Environmental Crimes were excluded from the 1996 *Draft Code of Crimes* definition of crimes against humanity by a vote of 9 to 9, with two abstentions, and therefore were not included in art 7 of the Rome Statute, although States raised their inclusion from time to time during the Conference.

offence at the ICC and have been charged or alleged in virtually all the situations referred to the Court to date. In situations involving armed conflict, crimes against humanity charges often track war crimes charges or target persecution or sexual violence. In other situations, crimes against humanity are the only charges that can be brought in the absence of armed conflict (at least at the outset of the referral) and the implausibility of alleging genocide. Given the ubiquity of the crimes against humanity charges at the ICC, we see that the ICC has become, in many ways, a crimes against humanity court.[56]

The early case law of the ICC defined the terms 'widespread' and 'systematic' with relative ease, relying upon jurisprudence from the *ad hoc* international criminal tribunals to do so. It also concluded that the 'attack' against the civilian population need not be a military operation. *Prosecutor v Dominic Ongwen* held that an attack under Article 7 must be 'a course of conduct', by which is meant a 'series or overall flow of events, as opposed to a mere aggregate of random or isolated acts' committed by a State or 'organization'; the latter requiring only that 'the organization has a set of structures or mechanisms, whatever those may be, that are sufficiently efficient to ensure the coordination necessary to carry out an attack directed against a civilian population'.[57]

The meaning of 'State or organizational policy' has presented more difficulties of interpretation as it was not included as a context element at the ICTY or the ICTR. The Court addressed it first in connection with a request to open an investigation into the 2007 post-election violence that took place in Kenya, which the Prosecutor argued constituted a crime against humanity. In considering the Prosecutor's request, a Majority of Pre-Trial Chamber II noted that the policy element was eventually abandoned by the *ad hoc* tribunals but drew upon earlier cases in examining the Rome Statute.[58] Finding that the plan to commit the attack may be inferred from the commission of 'a series of events', including a variety of factors,[59] using classic methods of treaty interpretation, the Majority read 'state or organizational' in Article 7(2)(a) disjunctively, rejecting the notion that only 'State-like organizations may

[56] Sadat (n 34) 377.

[57] *Prosecutor v Dominic Ongwen* (n 54) [2674].

[58] *Situation in the Republic of Kenya* (Decision Pursuant to Article 15 of the Rome Statute of the Authorization of an Investigation into the Situation in the Republic of Kenya) ICC-01/09 (31 March 2010) [86, 89–90]. The Pre-Trial Chamber also referenced the work of commentators to the Rome Statute and consulted the official translations of the text.

[59] ibid [87].

qualify'. Rather, examining its prior decisions, as well as the text of the Statute itself, the jurisprudence of the *ad hoc* Tribunals, and the *travaux préparatoires* including the work of the International Law Commission in elaborating the *1996 Draft Code of Crimes*, it focused upon 'whether a group has the capability to perform acts which infringe on basic human values'. The Chamber added that the organization need not be 'State-like', and that the policy need not have been conceived at the highest level of the State, for 'regional or even local organs of the State could satisfy the requirement of a State policy'.[60] Although Judge Hans-Peter Kaul penned an influential dissent, contending that the organization must be 'State-like' for its policies to fall within the ambit of Article 7, the Majority view has prevailed at the Court.

At the Rome Conference, some delegations wanted to delete the words 'civilian population', arguing that they were imprecise and unnecessary, but this traditional limit on the ambit of crimes against humanity has remained. Thus far, the ICC has followed the ICTY, holding that the definition of 'civilian' in Article 50 of Additional Protocol I to the Geneva Conventions on the laws of war sets forth the relevant standard.[61] That said, as the ICTY has also held, the ICC has found that 'despite the requirement that the attack be directed against a civilian population, there is no requirement that the *individual* victims of crimes against humanity be civilians for the purpose of international humanitarian law (IHL), but may include persons otherwise protected under this body of law'.[62] The Extraordinary Chambers in the Courts of Cambodia (ECCC) has recognized this in its judgments, as well.[63] This is logical: because crimes against humanity, unlike war crimes, can be committed in peacetime, the civilian/combatant distinction may not apply.

The crimes against humanity charged to date have included murder, extermination, torture, deportation or forcible transfer, rape, forced marriage, forced pregnancy, persecution, sexual slavery, and other inhumane acts, among others. The ICC, even with the small number of final judgments achieved to date, is thus generating significant and important jurisprudence setting out the elements for each of these crimes.

60 ibid [89–90].

61 See LN Sadat, 'Putting Peacetime First: Crimes Against Humanity and the Civilian Population Requirement' (2017) 31 Emory IntlLRev 197.

62 *Prosecutor v Bosco Ntaganda* (Judgment) ICC-01/04-02/06 (8 July 2019) [669].

63 *Prosecutor v Kaing Guck Eav alias Duch* (Judgment) 001/18-07-2007/ECCC/TC (26 July 2010).

Of particular significance, the *Ntaganda* and *Ongwen* decisions recognized sexual violence during wartime as a crime against humanity.[64] *Ongwen* added convictions for forced marriage as other inhumane acts under Article 7(1)(k) and forced pregnancy under Article 7(1)(g).[65]

12.3.2 The Status of the ICC's Definition as Customary International Law: The Abd-Al-Rahman *Case*

The Rome Statute exists in a complex international ecosystem. The drafters clearly intended to track customary international law because they intended the Statute to have universal application. While cognizant of the fact that at least in its early years, not all States would become party to the Statute, they nonetheless made ICC law (Rome law) potentially applicable to all persons worldwide through the Security Council referral triggering mechanism for the Court. In addition, under the doctrine of complementarity, the idea is that States would adopt national legislation allowing them to prosecute ICC crimes in order to assume their roles as the primary enforcers of international law. While the assumption may have been that States would 'copy-paste' the text of the Rome Statute into their national legislation, in fact many States have departed from the text of the Rome Statute considerably.[66] Even within the text of the Rome Statute itself, the drafters changed the elements of the crimes slightly and added new crimes, suggesting a certain *evolution* of international criminal law and creating diversity in the field by departing from the statutes of the *ad hoc* international criminal tribunals. Thus, the *unity* of international criminal law, its *evolution*, and its *diversity* were all present at the founding.

Given this evolution and diversity, the question remains whether it is *fair and legal* to apply Rome law to non-State Party nationals. This question arose and was less than satisfactorily addressed by the ICC Appeals Chamber in the *Abd-Al-Rahman* case. The defendant, Abd-Al-Rahman, was a Sudanese national accused of crimes against humanity and war crimes who had surrendered himself to the Court. He challenged the ICC's jurisdiction, *inter alia*, on the basis that since Sudan was not a State Party to the Rome Statute at the time of the Security Council's

[64] *Prosecutor v Bosco Ntaganda* (n 62). See generally J Tridgell, 'Prosecutor v Ntaganda: The End of Impunity for Sexual Violence Against Child Soldiers?' (2017) 23 Aust ILJ 153.
[65] *Prosecutor v Dominic Ongwen* (n 54).
[66] See Chapter 11 by Olympia Bekou.

referral and the events underlying the charges against him, his prosecution violated the principles of *nullum crimen sine lege* and non-retroactivity *ratione personae* in Articles 22(1) and 24(1) of the Statute, unless those crimes were defined either in Sudan's national law or in international treaties and customary international law applicable to Sudan.[67]

The Pre-Trial Chamber made short work of the Defendant's arguments, noting that the purpose of Articles 22 and 24 was to ensure that the Court 'does not deviate from the intention of the drafters that it should apply the statutorily defined crimes, and no others'.[68] Looking to the importance of the Article 13(b) triggering mechanism included in the Statute permitting Security Council referrals, the Chamber reasoned that it would 'call into question the very *raison d'être* of that particular triggering mechanism' to suggest it could only be applied after a searching analysis of the legal obligations expressly accepted or included by the relevant State[69] and declined to examine whether the crimes were prohibited under customary international law.[70]

On appeal, the defence continued to challenge the legality of Mr Abd-Al-Rahman's prosecution. The Prosecutor's appeal brief noted that the 'crimes set out in articles 6, 7, and 8 of the Statute are substantially similar to those in customary international law',[71] and the Appeals Chamber concluded that the charges 'draw upon norms that were recognized globally, including in Sudan, and were fully ascertainable at the time of the conflict in Darfur'.[72] Unlike the Pre-Trial Chamber, however, the Appeals Chamber examined the history of the referral under Security Council Resolution 1593 and noted that the Commission of Inquiry on violations of international humanitarian law and human rights law in Darfur had already reported on the conflict and included, in its reports, an analysis of the 'framework of international human rights and humanitarian laws applicable in Sudan at the time; and found criminal violations

[67] *Prosecutor v Abd-Al-Rahman* (Decision on the Defence 'Exception d'incompétence') ICC-02/05-02/20 (17 May 2021) [12].

[68] ibid [39].

[69] ibid [41].

[70] ibid [42].

[71] *Prosecutor v Abd-Al-Rahman* (Prosecution's Response to the Defence Appeal against the "Decision on the Defence 'Exception d'incompétence') ICC-02/05-02/20 (29 June 2021) [35].

[72] *Prosecutor v Abd-Al-Rahman* (Decision on the Defence Appeal against the "Decision on the Defence 'Exception d'incompétence'") ICC-02/05-02/20 (1 November 2021) [77].

thereof'.[73] Therefore, the Security Council's referral 'encompassed violations of binding international obligations carrying a risk of individual criminal liability'.[74]

Unlike the ICTY and the ICTR, the ICC Appeals Chamber did not seem to agree that the Security Council referral alone solved the *nullum crimen* problem. Instead, it asserted that under the Rome Statute, it must be foreseeable that an accused could have reasonably expect to face prosecution, and the relevant laws must have been ascertainable, in the sense they were sufficiently clear and accessible *to the accused*.[75] The Appeals Chamber then added that the foreseeability test is not met simply because the 'crimes charged can be found in the text of the Statute'. Rather, the Court based the legality of Mr Abd-Al-Rahman's prosecution on the fact that the accused had spent a considerable part of his career as a non-commissioned officer in the military who had actual experience with the application of common Article 3 of the 1949 Geneva Conventions and was personally 'in a position to understand and comply with his obligations in armed conflict under international law'.[76] Only *after* examining the personal familiarity of Mr Abd-Al-Rahman with the laws of war did the Appeals Chamber conclude:

> [T]he Appeals Chamber notes, generally, that the statutory crimes [of the ICC] are a product of a concerted effort to codify the developing state of international law so as to provide the clarity that was lacking in the preceding international tribunals. In principle, the Appeals Chamber considers that the crimes under the Statute were intended to be generally representative of the state of customary international law when the Statute was drafted. *This weighs heavily in favour of the foreseeability of facing prosecution crimes within the jurisdiction of this Court, even in relation to conduct occurring in a State not party to the Statute.*[77]

Thus, the Chamber found that the risk of international criminal liability was 'acute to such a degree that it was foreseeable to an officer of Mr Abd-Al-Rahman's rank'.[78]

The decision of the Appeals Chamber suggesting that non-State Party Nationals are entitled to an individualized determination of whether the

[73] ibid [78].
[74] ibid [79].
[75] ibid [85] (emphasis added).
[76] ibid [88–89].
[77] ibid [89] (emphasis added).
[78] ibid [90].

Rome Statute can be applied to them consistent with the legality principle raises serious conceptual and practical concerns. While certain authors have embraced the decision's restrictive approach,[79] others have noted that it may lead to 'disconcerting results, no sound normative principle supports it, and [it] [...] does not correspond to the design of the creators of the ICC Statute'.[80]

Indeed, it is hard to imagine how the Court will function if the norms in the Statute cannot be applied to individuals hailing from countries that have not joined the Court or whose national legislation does not include ICC crimes. At the present time, the list of non-State party nationals indicted or under investigation by the ICC for crimes committed either in their own jurisdiction (Sudan and Libya) or on the territories of other ICC States Parties or States accepting the jurisdiction of the Court is extensive. It includes the situation in Bangladesh/Myanmar, State of Palestine, and Ukraine, and before the preliminary examinations were dismissed also included the Registered vessels of the Comoros and the Situation in South Korea. It appears that some authors have embraced the notion of a 'Court à la carte' – which was the model rejected at Rome – due to a fundamental misapprehension of the principles underlying the ICC's jurisdiction. A full discussion of this issue is not possible within the confines of this short chapter; however, as I have written elsewhere, jurisdiction is conferred by States upon the ICC, not 'delegated' to them, meaning that they do not transfer bits of their national sovereignty to the Court when they join but instead collectively *confer* power and authority on the ICC as an independent judicial entity.[81] The ICC is an international institution that, like the *ad hoc* tribunals for the former Yugoslavia and Rwanda, exercises the *ius puniendi* of the international community.[82]

[79] See e.g. A Skander Galand, 'The ICC Appeals Judgment on Abd-Al-Rahman Jurisdictional Challenge: A Foreseeable Turn to Substantive Justice?' (*EJILTalk!*, 22 November 2021) <https://www.ejiltalk.org/the-icc-appeals-judgment-on-abd-al-rahman-jurisdictional-challenge-a-foreseeable-turn-to-substantive-justice/> (last accessed 1 June 2025).

[80] M Lemos, 'The Appeals Chamber's Jurisdictional Judgment in *Abd-Al-Rahman* and the Issue of Applicable Law at the International Criminal Court' (2023) 22 Chinese JIL 223, 227.

[81] LN Sadat, 'The Conferred Jurisdiction of the International Criminal Court' (2023) 99 Notre Dame LRev 549.

[82] K Ambos, 'Punishment Without a Sovereign. The *Ius Puniendi* Issue of International Criminal Law: A First Contribution Towards a Consistent Theory of International Criminal Law' (2013) 33 OJLS 293; *Prosecutor v Al-Bashir* (Written Observations of

Crimes against humanity have been identified as crimes that the international community and States have a shared responsibility to protect under paragraphs 138 and 139 of the 2005 World Summit Outcome Document,[83] as *jus cogens* offences by the International Law Commission,[84] and have been included in every international criminal court and tribunal Statute established since the Nürnberg tribunal except for the Special Tribunal for Lebanon. Moreover, Article 7 is increasingly seen by international and national courts and tribunals, including the ICTY, the European Court of Human Rights, the Inter-American Court of Human Rights, US federal courts, and the UK House of Lords, as codifying the customary international law of crimes against humanity.[85] Since there is no treaty on crimes against humanity, many States also have no legislation on crimes against humanity.

The Appeals Chamber's decision in *Abd-Al-Rahman* raises the specter that certain Rome Statute crimes might be opposable vis-a-vis certain accused whereas others would not, depending on the national legislation in force at the time and place the crimes occur. This would mean that the ICC's judges are incorporating through the backdoor by means of judicial *interpretation* arguments raised about the Rome Statute that were rejected during the negotiations. Indeed, the ICC judges were conceptualizing the ICC as if it were a foreign court operating under the principle of universal jurisdiction, where double criminality might indeed pose difficulties. In 2021, a panel of the French *Cour de Cassation* found that a Syrian national could not be tried for crimes against humanity under universal jurisdiction because Syria had not criminalized crimes against humanity, which violated the principle of double criminality.[86] This was reversed by the full Court, which found that the underlying acts of murder, rape, and torture were criminal, and therefore the prosecution could proceed. That holding notwithstanding, the Court noted that

Professor Claus Kreß as *amicus curiae*, with the Assistance of Ms Erin Pobjie, on the Merits of the Legal Questions presented in 'The Hashemite Kingdom of Jordan's Appeal against the "Decision under Article 87(7) of the Rome Statute on the Non-compliance by Jordan with the Request by the Court for the Arrest and Surrender [of] Omar Al-Bashir of 12 March 2018 (ICC-02/05- 01/09-326)"' ICC-02/05-01/09 OA2 (18 June 2018) [11].

83 UNGA, 'Res 60/1: 2005 World Summit Outcome' (16 September 2005) UN Doc A/Res/60/1.

84 2019 ILC Draft Articles (n 1) 24–25.

85 Sadat (n 34) 373.

86 Cour de Cassation of France, *Arrêt du 24 novembre 2021*, Cass Crim, Pourvoi n° 21-81.344, ECLI:FR:CCASS:2021:CR01269 <https://www.courdecassation.fr/en/decision/619de43eb458df69d4022a18> (last accessed 1 June 2025).

certain war crimes and the crime of persecution could not be prosecuted in France under universal jurisdiction.[87] It did not consider the possibility that those crimes could be tried under customary international law.

12.4 The Proposed New Crimes Against Humanity Convention and Its Relationship to Customary International Law

12.4.1 Article 7 of the Rome Statute: Theme and Variations

I have asserted in this chapter that Article 7 of the Rome Statute codified, crystallized, and to a limited extent created a customary international law of crimes against humanity in 1998, and that this body of law can *fairly* and *legally* be applied to the nationals of State and non-States parties by the Court. In one important aspect, it is *narrower* and more restrictive than customary international law in requiring proof of a State or organizational policy. In other limited ways, it is modestly more progressive as a limited number of new crimes were added to the text. It is also evident that the Rome Statute codification is different than the texts of the various *ad hoc* tribunals. Finally, there are variants of crimes against humanity in national legislation. What is to be done about the various iterations of this crime in national and international law?

During the Rome Statute's negotiation, recognizing this, the late Professor M Cherif Bassiouni, who chaired the Drafting Committee at Rome, proposed the inclusion of a provision in the future court's statute to endeavour to preserve the existence of customary international law outside the Rome Statute.[88] It was incorporated as Article 10, which provides that '[n]othing in this Part of the Statute shall be interpreted as limiting or prejudicing in any way existing or developing rules of international law for purposes other than this Statute'.[89] Thus, the ICC Statute itself envisages that, like war crimes, crimes against humanity in the Rome Statute emerged from customary international law, represents a partial codification of customary international law, and remains in

[87] RL Phillips, '2nd Time's the Charm: France's Cour de Cassation Broadens Universal Jurisdiction Law' (*Just Security*, 24 May 2023) <https://www.justsecurity.org/86689/2nd-times-the-charm-frances-cour-de-cassation-broadens-universal-jurisdiction-law/> (last accessed 1 June 2025).

[88] Sadat LN, 'Custom, Codification and Some Thoughts about the Relationship between the Two: Article 10 of the ICC Statute' (2000) 49(4) DePaul LR 909.

[89] Rome Statute (n 53) art 10.

relationship to customary international law, which may continue to develop outside the Rome Statute itself in both national and international courts. The implication of this for the new treaty on crimes against humanity is discussed below.

12.4.2 *Drafting a New Crimes Against Humanity Convention: Unity, Diversity, and Evolution*

Returning to our theme of 'unity, diversity, and evolution', the negotiation of a new multilateral treaty on crimes against humanity has evinced the same trends and instincts manifested during the negotiation of the Rome Statute and its subsequent interpretation by the Court and in academic writings. As noted earlier, States are in the process of discussing a new treaty on crimes against humanity.[90] This conversation has been ongoing ever since the *Crimes Against Humanity Initiative*[91] published a *Proposed Convention on the Prevention and Punishment of Crimes Against Humanity* in 2010.[92] Attention increased after the ILC added 'crimes against humanity'[93] to its long-term programme of work in 2013. In October 2019, the second (final) set of draft articles was taken up by the United Nations General Assembly's Sixth Committee, which considers legal issues.[94] After six years of consistent advocacy by States and civil society, the treaty has finally been sent to negotiations by the UN

[90] LN Sadat, 'Towards a New Treaty on Crimes Against Humanity: Next Steps' (*Just Security*, 13 September 2021) <https://www.justsecurity.org/78063/towards-a-new-treaty-on-crimes-against-humanity-next-steps/> (last accessed 1 June 2025).

[91] Washington University, 'Crimes Against Humanity Initiative' (*Washington University in St Louis*, 2025) <https://sites.wustl.edu/crimesagainsthumanity/> (last accessed 1 June 2025).

[92] Crimes Against Humanity Initiative, 'Proposed International Convention on the Prevention and Punishment of Crimes Against Humanity' (*Washington University in St. Louis*, August 2010) <https://sites.wustl.edu/crimesagainsthumanity/convention-text> (last accessed 1 June 2025).

[93] Support for the idea grew among States over time. LN Sadat, 'A Contextual and Historical Analysis of the International Law Commission's 2017 Draft Articles for a New Global Treaty on Crimes Against Humanity' (2018) 16 JICJ 683. The ILC received a record number of comments (approximately 750) including from 39 States, on its initial set of draft articles authored in 2017. CC Jalloh and LN Sadat, 'Introduction to the Symposium on a Way Forward: Academic and Practitioner Perspectives on the ILC Draft Articles on Prevention and Punishment of Crimes Against Humanity as adopted on Second Reading' (2020) 6 African Journal of International Criminal Justice 79, 87. The comments are summarized in ILC, 'Fourth Report on Crimes Against Humanity, by Sean D Murphy, Special Rapporteur' (18 February 2019) UN Doc A/CN.4/725 [5–7, 15–29].

[94] 2019 ILC Draft Articles (n 1).

General Assembly on the basis of consensus, after significant negotiations occurring during the Fall of 2024.[95] Pursuant to Resolution 79/122, the negotiations will begin in 2026 with the convening of a Preparatory Committee that will meet in two sessions (2026 and 2027), followed by two rounds of treaty negotiations at a UN Diplomatic Conference to take place in 2028 and 2029.[96] During the negotiations in 2024, 124 States voiced support for moving forward,[97] and a declaration supporting the adoption of a new treaty was adopted and circulated by more than 650 civil society organizations and individuals from around the world.[98] Resolution 79/122 was adopted without a vote by the General Assembly and on the basis of consensus by the Sixth Committee; however, the Russian Federation dissociated on both occasions. Given that negotiations on the new treaty will begin in earnest in 2026, the question of how the crime should and will be defined remains on the table.

12.4.2.1 Unity and Evolution

When it adopted a model draft treaty in 2010, the *Crimes Against Humanity Initiative* took the view that the definition of the crime in a new treaty should track the Rome Statute. Most participants in the meetings held in St Louis and The Hague in 2009 were of the view that the 'convention must complement the Rome Statute and do no harm to the ICC'.[99] The International Law Commission took the same position,

[95] A Radhakrishnan et al, 'A Major Breakthrough Towards a Treaty on Crimes Against Humanity' (*Just Security*, 27 November 2024) <https://www.justsecurity.org/105242/podcast-cah-treaty-breakthrough/> (last accessed 1 June 2025); A Radhakrishnan and LN Sadat, 'Key UN Committee Clears Path for Crimes Against Humanity Treaty Negotiations' (*Just Security*, 2 December 2024) <https://www.justsecurity.org/105305/cah-treaty-negotiations-passes-sixth-committee/> (last accessed 1 June 2025).

[96] UNGA, 'Res 79/122: United Nations Conference of Plenipotentiaries on Prevention and Punishment of Crimes against Humanity' (12 December 2024) UN Doc A/Res/79/122.

[97] Author's Unpublished Notes. See also LN Sadat and A Radhakrishnan, 'Justice Delayed Is Justice Denied: Moving Forward with a New Crimes Against Humanity Treaty' (*Just Security*, 23 October 2024) <https://www.justsecurity.org/104188/justice-delayed-denied-crimes-against-humanity-treaty/> (last accessed 1 June 2025).

[98] Global Justice Center, 'Joint Statement in Support of Progress toward a Crimes Against Humanity Treaty' (*Crimes Against Humanity Treaty Now*, 2025) <https://cahtreatynow.org/joint-statement-in-support-of-progress-toward-a-crimes-against-humanity-treaty/> (last accessed 1 June 2025).

[99] LN Sadat, 'A Comprehensive History of the Proposed International Convention on the Prevention and Punishment of Crimes Against Humanity' in LN Sadat (ed), *Forging a Convention for Crimes Against Humanity* (2nd edn, Cambridge University Press 2013) 449.

based upon the large number of States already adhering to the Rome Statute. The Commission also wished to support and promote the harmonization of existing international law.[100] Thus, Draft Article 2(1) and (2) of its text was drawn almost verbatim from Article 7(1) and (2) of the Rome Statute of the Rome Statute, with three exceptions, two of which, the deletion of the definition of gender[101] and the narrowing of the definition of persecution, were substantive.

At the same time, paragraph 2(3) contains a 'without prejudice' clause, making it clear that inclusion of the Rome Statute's definition was without prejudice to broader definitions that may exist in international instruments, customary international law, or national law. Indeed, the ILC, notably, did not see its task as reflecting customary international law in the new treaty's definition. Rather, in the Commission's view:

> While some aspects of these draft articles may reflect customary international law, codification of existing law is not the objective [. . .] rather, the objective is the drafting of provisions that would be both effective and likely acceptable to States, based on provisions often used in widely adhered to treaties addressing crimes, as a basis for a possible future convention. Further, the draft articles are without prejudice to existing customary international law.[102]

Particularly over the last two years, meeting pursuant to a structured meeting schedule and clear rules for debate set forth in Resolution 77/249 and organized by the Bureau of the Sixth Committee, States have debated whether or not a new treaty on crimes against humanity should take Article 7 of the Rome Statute as a given. Delegations have urged caution in amending the existing definition given that it was difficult to achieve consensus on the definition of crimes against humanity at Rome. Thus, the case for 'unity' is a strong one, particularly given the delicate compromise achieved in 1998.

[100] 2019 ILC Draft Articles (n 1) 23 [3], 30–31. In 2023 and 2024, the German Mission to the United Nations hosted intersessional meetings for States and members of civil society that were well-attended and helped to prepare the April Resumed Sessions. The Reports for those meetings are in the records of the UN Sixth Committee. See UNGA, 'Workshop on a Convention on the Prevention and Punishment of Crimes Against Humanity: Notes by Secretariat' (19 April 2023) UN Doc A/C.6/77/INF/3 [12] (2023 Intersessional Workshop Report).

[101] The Commission had retained this language in its first version of the definition adopted in 2017, however, at the second reading stage, an overwhelming number of submissions requested the Commission to delete it on the basis that this definition is now outdated; 2023 Intersessional Workshop Report (n 100) [9(c)].

[102] 2019 ILC Draft Articles (n 1) 23 [3].

At the same time, a trend away from 'strict' unity towards evolution has become evident during the past two years. This seemed particularly true during the April Resumed Session of 2024, held from 1–5 April 2024, during which many States expressed the view that evolution has taken place over the past twenty-five years and minor changes, reflecting the current state of the law, could and should be accommodated.[103] In their view, while the overall goal was a clear, stable, and useful definition of crimes against humanity, the treaty should function as a 'floor', not a 'ceiling', as some States might wish to adapt the definition in their national law by eliminating the policy element, for example, if they believed it was more consistent with customary international law. Many States suggested that this should be particularly so given that elements were added during the Rome Statute's negotiation as jurisdictional filters to avoid overloading the docket of the Court and to reinforce the principle of complementarity. Thus, the preoccupation would not necessarily apply to a crimes against humanity convention implemented directly by States at the horizontal level.[104]

12.4.2.2 Diversity

During the final Resumed Session of the Sixth Committee, which met between 1–11 April 2024, two trends seemed apparent. First, even the large group of States Parties to the Rome Statute, which have been generally supportive of the crimes against humanity treaty, expressed openness to consider a limited number of changes to the text, as discussed above.[105] Another quite small group, led by China, that is not supportive of the treaty, has suggested that the ILC needs to go back and study State practice.[106]

[103] See e.g. UN Sixth Committee, 'Written Comments by the European Union on the International Law Commission's Draft Articles on Prevention and Punishment of Crimes Against Humanity' (*United Nations*, 2023) <https://www.un.org/en/ga/sixth/78/cah/eu_e.pdf> (last accessed 1 June 2025). Noting consensus on the Rome definition but suggesting elements of possible change.

[104] UN Sixth Committee, 'Crimes Against Humanity (agenda item 80): Oral Report of the Co-facilitators Ms Anna Pála Sverrisdóttir (Iceland), Mr Nizhan Faraz Bin Rizal (Malaysia), Mr Edgar Daniel Leal Matta (Guatemala)' (*United Nations*, 5 April 2024) <https://www.un.org/en/ga/sixth/78/pdfs/english/cah_oral_report.pdf> (last accessed 1 June 2025).

[105] ibid.

[106] UN Sixth Committee, 'Comments of the Government of the People's Republic of China Concerning the Draft Articles on Prevention and Punishment of Crimes Against Humanity and the Related Recommendation of the International Law Commission'

In terms of the issues and amendments currently on the table, several are worth noting. These are helpfully summarized by Written Chair Summary of the last two years Resumed Sessions, as well as the Oral Report of the co-Facilitators of the Sixth Committee session.[107] Issues have been raised regarding sexual and gender-based crimes, as well as reproductive violence. Many, but not all, States have expressed support for the Commission's decision to remove the definition of gender in Article 7(3) of the Rome Statute, finding it to be outdated. Other suggestions have been the inclusion of *forced marriage* as a new crime. A proposal has also been advanced to amend *the crime of forced pregnancy and recognize the existence of other forms of reproductive violence.*[108] An amendment to Draft Article (2)(1)(g) has been proposed to add 'sexual *or reproductive* violence' (proposed additional text is italicized) to recognize grave violations of reproductive autonomy that may exist in addition to the two codified crimes. Finally, a proposal is on the table to amend the definition of apartheid in Draft Article 2(1)(j) by adding *gender apartheid* to the text.[109] While the inclusion of forced marriage would be a codification of a customary international law development, given its adjudication by three international criminal courts to date as an 'other inhumane act', the addition of new crimes involving reproductive and sexual violence, and the inclusion of gender apartheid, would involve either the crystallization of an emerging norm or the inclusion of a new norm of international criminal law as these crimes have not yet been accepted as part of existing state practice.

Another set of changes proposes amending the definition of *enforced disappearance* in Draft Article 2(2)(i) to bring it into line with the

(*United Nations*, 28 November 2023) <https://www.un.org/en/ga/sixth/78/cah/china_e.pdf> (last accessed 1 June 2025).

[107] UN Sixth Committee Oral Report (n 104); UNGA, 'Crimes Against Humanity: Draft Written Summary' (11 April 2024) UN Doc A/C.6/78/L.22/Add1.

[108] Regarding draft art 2(2)(f), which like art 7(2)(f) of the Rome Statute, provides that the definition of forced pregnancy shall not be interpreted as 'affecting national laws relating to pregnancy', a proposal to delete this phrase was made, noting that it was the only crime listed in which legality under national law was referenced as a defence to an allegation of crimes against humanity.

[109] UN Sixth Committee Oral Report (n 104) 23. The gender apartheid campaign has issued a legal brief advocating for the amendment of the crime against humanity of apartheid in the draft treaty. See Atlantic Council and Global Justice Center, 'Amending the Crime Against Humanity of Apartheid to Recognize and Encompass Gender Apartheid' (*End Gender Apartheid*, April 2025) <https://endgenderapartheid.today/download/brief/Gender%20Apartheid%20Brief.pdf> (last accessed 1 June 2025)

2006 International Convention for the Protection of All Persons from Enforced Disappearance[110] and another would broaden the definition of persecution in Draft Article 2(1)(h) either by removing the necessity of a linkage between this crime and one of the other crimes entirely or expanding the crimes for which the linkage could be established.[111] A proposal that has received widespread support and is being championed by Sierra Leone is to add the *slave trade* to Draft Article 2(1)(c). Sierra Leone has also tabled a proposal to submit amendments on slavery and the slave trade to Articles 7 (crimes against humanity) and 8 (war crimes) of the Rome Statute. Finally, as mentioned earlier, other possible new offences have been of interest to States including colonialism, starvation of a civilian population, environmental crimes and ecocide,[112] unilateral coercive measures against civilians, terror related acts, use of nuclear weapons, exploitation of natural resources, and crimes against indigenous peoples.[113] While many of these suggestions have not yet been advanced as formal proposals, over the next three years, as the treaty gets negotiated, there will be an opportunity for them to do so.

12.5 Concluding Thoughts

As discussed earlier, crimes against humanity exist in a complex international ecosystem. They emerged first as a natural law objection to slavery and the slave trade that was found legally wanting even if morally compelling. Only later, in the first half of the twentieth century, faced with the horror of the Holocaust, did they find footing in treaty and customary international law. They were then codified and crystallized as treaty law in the guise of the Rome Statute and are now used by national

[110] The 2006 treaty does not include the Rome Statute requirement that the person be disappeared 'with the intention of removing them from the protection of the law for a prolonged period of time'. It has been observed by delegates that that this does not appear in current jurisprudence and that the expression 'prolonged period of time' was vague; 2023 Intersessional Workshop (n 100) [12].

[111] See 2023 Intersessional Workshop (n 100) [13]. Some States that are parties to the Rome Statute, for example, France and Germany, removed this requirement when implementing the Rome Statute. The question of adding other protected categories to art 2(1)(h) arose, including Indigenous peoples and persons with disabilities. In particular, art 11 of the 2006 Convention on the Rights of Persons with Disabilities requires States to protect persons with disabilities in situations of risk, including situations of armed conflict and humanitarian emergencies, which would presumably include crimes against humanity.

[112] Sadat (n 55).

[113] UN Sixth Committee Oral Report (n 104) 20–23.

systems in achieving post-conflict justice and in universal jurisdiction cases[114] and at the ICC. Through judicial development at the *ad hoc* tribunals, national courts, and later at the ICC, the overall contours of this crime now appear to be relatively well-settled although different iterations continue to appear in international law statutes, national legislation, and customary international law. This diversity of text and its application by national and international courts and tribunals has allowed the crime to evolve more freely than, for example, war crimes, which are heavily codified in international treaties, so as to respond to new manifestations of criminality or even highlight long-standing injustices such as colonialism and the slave trade that have historically been condemned but left outside modern texts of international criminal law. The potential expansiveness of this offence, however, has raised questions of legality and fairness to the accused, which have been explored in national and international courts.

What does this mean for the re-codification of this crime in a new treaty? While the ILC largely transplanted the Rome Statute definition of the crime into its draft text, as did our non-governmental project, there now appears to be a certain appetite for change amongst States and members of civil society. This is understandable, for, as Carsten Stahn recently wrote, the Rome Statute is 'still modern, but with growing age, it also gains wrinkles'.[115] Each of these codifications is seen as a 'floor' rather than a ceiling; a minimum 'must have' that States must incorporate in order to comply with their treaty obligations. If the Rome Statute is the current floor, any additions in the new crimes against humanity treaty would presumably not be more restrictive but would potentially add new crimes to the eleven now found in Article 7 of the Rome Statute. At the end of the day, however, States will have to decide how to manage their treaty obligations, and some may not wish to ratify a new treaty that has a different definition than the Rome Statute, particularly if they are required to amend existing national legislation to do so.[116]

114 See e.g. Trial International, 'Universal Jurisdiction Annual Review: Highlights in 2023' (*Trial International*, 14 April 2024) <https://trialinternational.org/latest-post/universal-jurisdiction-annual-review-highlights-in-2023/> (last accessed 1 June 2025), noting an increase of universal jurisdiction prosecutions worldwide.

115 C Stahn, 'The ICC in Its Third Decade: Setting the Scene' in C Stahn and R Braga da Silva (eds), *The International Criminal Court in its Third Decade: Reflecting on Law and Practices* (Brill 2024) 3.

116 The Ljubljana-The Hague Convention on Mutual Legal Assistance did not accept proposals to amend the definition of crimes against humanity other than deleting the definition of gender; see Ljubljana-The Hague Convention on International Cooperation

Of course, a large number of Rome Statute State Parties never incorporated crimes against humanity in their national laws, because the Rome Statute does not actually require them to do so. Instead, the preamble speaks only of a general 'duty' of States to prosecute international crimes.[117] And the sixty-eight or so non-ICC Party States will presumably not find themselves in a conflictual position. The United States, for example, does not currently have national legislation on crimes against humanity, and Ukraine did not until very recently. Thus, it may be both desirable and achievable for States to amend the definition of the crime in negotiating the new treaty. Finally, States are not required to copy-paste either the Rome Statute or the definition of the new treaty into their national law; while they arguably would not be in compliance with the new treaty if they adopted more restrictive provisions than those provided for in the text, Draft Article 2(3) as it currently stands allows them to adopt more expansive definitions, so long as the definition is 'broader'.

In its Draft Articles, the ILC took a positivist approach, suggesting at one point in the *commentaries* that any deviation from the definition would mean that a State could not rely upon the rest of the treaty in terms of cooperation, etc.[118] Yet although modifications of the definition might under some circumstances raise questions under the doctrine of double criminality with respect to mutual legal assistance, assuming the variations are 'material',[119] they are not usually firm impediments to interstate cooperation. This comment by the Commission represents a shift away from the universalist approach of the Rome conference itself,[120] towards a more restrictive approach to even the most serious international crimes.

The preamble of the Draft Articles notes the *jus cogens* status of crimes against humanity. The question of what this means is vitally important

in the Investigation and Prosecution of the Crimes of Genocide, Crimes Against Humanity, War Crimes and Other International Crimes (adopted 26 May 2023, opened for signature on 14 February 2024, not yet in force) art 5(2) <https://www.gov.si/assets/ministrstva/MZEZ/projekti/MLA-pobuda/The-Ljubljana-The-Hague-MLA-Convention.pdf> (last accessed 1 June 2025). It was negotiated outside the United Nations system and has not yet entered into force.

117 Rome Statute (n 53) preamble para 6.

118 2019 ILC Draft Articles (n 1) 26 [46].

119 See e.g. US Court of Appeals, 11th Cir, *US v Belfast* (2010) 611 F.3d 783. Identical language between a treaty and implementing language is not required, rather, legislation implementing a treaty should be a rational relationship to the treaty in that the legislation tracks the treaty's language in all 'material' respects.

120 Sadat (n 88) 919.

for the functioning of this possible new treaty. In the *Furundžija* case, decided during the same period as the Rome Statute's negotiation and adoption, the ICTY found that the peremptory status of the norm against torture meant not only that States had a duty not to commit torture but that they were permitted to try or extradite individuals accused of torture on the basis of universal jurisdiction, could not be subject to any statute of limitations, and were crimes of a 'universal character'.[121] Both the proposed draft treaty and the Rome Statute itself envisage the possibility that States might develop new iterations of crimes against humanity, that may, in turn, create new customary international law. Thus, even with the re-codification of crimes against humanity in a new treaty, the need to consult customary international law both in the interpretation of that instrument and in terms of its continued development, will remain important. In this way, the crime will continue to evolve as a matter of customary international law, and we can expect to see a certain degree of divergence from the Rome Statute and diversity even in national laws on the subject. While mindful of the need for clarity and uniformity to protect to the rights of the accused and ensure that States understand their obligations of prevention and punishment, a certain degree of flexibility – such as we have seen in adjudications of crimes against humanity over the past thirty years – will allow this important category of international crime to remain a critically important legal protection for civilians, in peacetime and during armed conflict, from egregious attacks on their dignity and security.

[121] *Prosecutor v Anto Furundzija* (Judgment) IT-95-17/1-T (10 December 1998) [151–57].

Concluding Observations

13

The Practice of Interpretation in International Law

Unity, Diversity, and Evolution

INETA ZIEMELE*

13.1 Introduction

I am grateful for this invitation and the opportunity to speak to an audience of academics and practitioners on the topic that has preoccupied me in my work as a judge in three different European courts. Let me first of all sketch out the context within which I place the matter of interpreting applicable international law by a relevant court.

First, international law, like any other legal system, must ensure legal certainty. It is especially important for international law in light of the constant criticism advanced towards the nature of this legal system which criticism refers, among others, to consistency of application and enforcement. One of the key tools to ensure legal certainty is a consistent and coherent application of rules based on a generally accepted method of interpretation, where that method serves as the backbone of a court's judgement. The legal system and an act of application of a rule therein gain persuasiveness and legitimacy where the use of the method of interpretation of the rule is consistent from one case to another.

Second, judges are the guarantors of the resilience of law in the sense that it is in their power to ensure its impartial and uniform application, which in turn counters against allegations of inefficiency or bias of that system of law.

These considerations are relevant in ensuring the rule of law in a legal system. Therefore, the general rule of interpretation of treaties is a key element in the international rule of law, as has indeed been argued in

* This contribution is an adjusted transcript from the keynote speech 'The Practice of Interpretation in International Law: Unity, Diversity, and Evolution' given on 1 December 2022 in The Hague.

legal doctrine.[1] All of the actors in this legal system need to be acutely aware of that.

In practice, this is easier said than done, and multiple factors complicate this matter. In this regard, I believe it was Martti Koskenniemi who said that international law has become a discipline for a narrow circle of lawyers.[2] I can confirm from my experience that there is a constant tension as to expectations, on the one hand, on how law will influence international relations and, on the other hand, how much realpolitik gives in to considerations of legal principle. While the judicialisation of international law has made the rule of law in world affairs more visible, there is still a long way to go to ensure that the rule of law paradigm makes indeed a crucial difference beyond the offices of the lawyers in foreign offices and international institutions. Coherence and consistency among the courts in their application of international law are undoubtedly helpful to making the international legal system more resilient and effective, as well as legitimate.

13.2 Use of a General Rule of Interpretation by the European Court of Human Rights and the Court of Justice of the EU

I shall now present the practice of the European Court of Human Rights (EctHR) and the Court of Justice of the EU (ECJ, the Court), which will allow me to share my analysis of the consistency or particularity of the use of a general rule of interpretation of treaties. It is helpful to begin with a general but necessary observation.

The nature of the treaties that these two Courts interpret, based on the object and purpose of these treaties, as disclosed by the Courts in their case-law, has a defining influence on the interpretative work concerned, taking into account the particularities of the legal systems that the Courts are entrusted to safeguard and their respective competences. It seems rather straightforward, but experience shows that it is not. Practice confirms that there has been a fair amount of misunderstanding related to how the Courts apply the object and purpose criterion, as well as the

[1] S Besson, 'General Principles and Customary Law in the EU Legal Order' in S Vogenayer and S Weatherhill (eds), *General Principles of Law: European and Comparative Perspectives* (Hart 2017) 107, 127.

[2] See W Werner, M de Hoon, and A Galán (eds), *The Law of International Lawyers. Reading Martti Koskenniemi* (Cambridge University Press 2017).

good faith criterion. In the international law debate, we at times get lost in translation in absolutely good faith.

I will speak about the object and purpose of the leading European treaties, that is, the European Convention on Human Rights, the Treaty on the European Union (TEU), and the Treaty on the Functioning of the European Union (TFEU), and exemplify how the Courts respectively understand them and what conclusions have been drawn.

13.2.1 European Court of Human Rights

Let me first begin with the European Court of Human Rights. Since its early days, the Court has maintained that its authority to interpret proceeds from an international treaty with a special legal character, that is, a law-making or normative treaty, which has a particular objective and purpose – the protection of human rights in Europe. Already in 1978, the Court's judgment in *Ireland v the United Kingdom* was very clear about the character of the Convention system and indicated a distinct sequitur it drew from it, that is:

> Unlike international treaties of the classic kind, the Convention comprises more than mere reciprocal engagements between Contracting States. It creates, over and above a network of mutual, bilateral undertakings, objective obligations which, in the words of the Preamble benefit from a 'collective enforcement'.[3]

The Court in effect affirms the *erga omnes* character of the ECHR. One of the most powerful consequences the ECtHR has drawn from the special character of the Convention goes back to the *Belilos v Switzerland*[4] and *Loizidou v Turkey* (preliminary objections) case law. In the course of the latter case, the Court had to determine whether Turkey had the right to territorially limit its acceptance of the competence of the Commission and the Court by submitting a declaration that excluded its responsibility over the possible human rights violations in the territory of Northern Cyprus. The Court decided that such a declaration/reservation was invalid and set it aside. In coming to that conclusion, the Court interpreted the relevant articles of the Convention following the general rule of the interpretation of treaties:

[3] *Ireland v the United Kingdom* (19 January 1978) Series A no 25, 90 [239].

[4] *Belilos v Switzerland* (29 April 1988) Series A no 132.

> To determine whether Contracting Parties may impose restrictions on their acceptance of the competence of the Commission and Court [. . .], the Court will seek to ascertain *the ordinary meaning to be given to the terms of these provisions in their context and in the light of their object and purpose* [emphasis added] (see, inter alia, (. . .) and Article 31 para. 1 of the Vienna Convention of 23 May 1969 on the Law of Treaties). It shall also take into account, together with the context, '*any subsequent practice in the application* [emphasis added] of the treaty which establishes the agreement of the parties regarding its interpretation' (see Article 31 para. 3 (b) of the abovementioned Vienna Convention).[5]

The assertion above appears in paragraph 73 of the judgment. It is supported by preceding statements. For example, paragraph 72 affirms that:

> *In addition, the object and purpose* [emphasis added] of the Convention as an instrument for the protection of individual human beings requires that its provisions be interpreted and applied so as to make its safeguards practical and effective.[6]

A point before restates the living instrument doctrine:

> That the Convention is a living instrument which must be interpreted in the light of present-day conditions is firmly rooted in the Court's caselaw (see, inter alia, the Tyrer v. the United Kingdom judgment of 25 April 1978, Series A no. 26, pp. 15–16, para. 31).Such an approach, in the Court's view, is not confined to the substantive provisions of the Convention, but also applies to those provisions, [. . .] which govern the operation of the Convention's enforcement machinery. It follows that *these provisions cannot be interpreted solely in accordance with the intentions of their authors as expressed more than forty years ago* [emphasis added].
>
> Accordingly, even if it had been established, which is not the case, that restrictions, other than those ratione temporis, were considered permissible [. . .] at a time when a minority of the present Contracting Parties adopted the Convention, such *evidence could not be decisive* [emphasis added].[7]

This reasoning can be genuinely understood to mean that there are additional principles to the criterion of the object and purpose of the Convention that impact the interpretation carried out by the Court. Such

[5] *Loizidou v Turkey* (Preliminary Objections) (25 March 1995) Series A no 310 [73].
[6] ibid [72].
[7] ibid [72].

an understanding of the Court's case law is indeed confirmed by the Court itself and by legal doctrine.

It has been suggested that notions such as living instrument, European consensus, and the practical and effective protection of individual rights do not square well with Article 31 of the Vienna Convention on the Law of Treaties (VCLT). However, when examined in detail and in proper context, one begins to wonder whether there is more unity than divergence after all.

The above-quoted *Loizidou* passages bring up the element of time and the special object and purpose of the Convention and juxtapose these notions against State consent expressed forty years earlier. None of that is new to general international law. The International Court of Justice's (ICJ) *Namibia* Advisory opinion on the mandate system, determined as a 'sacred trust for civilization', assumed that the content of the mandate was evolutionary and not static.[8] The Namibia dicta is one of the most important expressions of the intertemporal rule in international law. It confirms the conclusion reached in the International Law Commission (ILC) during the preparation of the VCLT. As put by the Special Rapporteur De Arechaga at the time:

> The intention of the parties should be controlling, and there seemed to be two possibilities as far as the intention was concerned: either they had meant to incorporate in the treaty some legal concepts that would remain unchanged, or if they had no such intention, the legal concept might be subject to change and would then have to be interpreted not only in the context of the instrument, but also within the framework of the entire legal order to which they belong.[9]

In the absence of the intent of the parties to the ECHR to cut it in stone, as it were, it is by definition a living instrument since its object is real human relations, which are evolutive in character, and the purpose of the Convention system is to ensure their effective protection. These observations are helpful in explaining the developments in the Convention's material content over time. There is still a question of the proper

[8] *Legal Consequences for States of the Continued Presence of South Africa in Namibia (South West Africa) Notwithstanding Security Council Resolution 276 (1970)* (Advisory Opinion) [1971] ICJ Rep 16 [45].

[9] ILC, 'Report on the Sixth Session of the Asian-African Legal Consultative Committee (Cairo, February–March 1964) by Eduardo Jiménez de Aréchaga, Observer for the Commission' (21 May 1964) UN Doc A/C N.4/172, reproduced in [1964/II] YBILC 119 [10].

interpretation that detects this evolution, and I will address it after commenting on the competence of the Court.

At this stage, I would like to address the consequences that the ECtHR drew in *Belilos* and *Loizidou* concerning its competence in examining the reservations to the Convention with reference to the Convention's object and purpose, since presuming any automaticity regarding competence of the adjudication body and procedure based in intertemporal rule would indeed be highly delicate. As we know, this question has been present in the international law debate and separate opinions of the ICJ judges since the beginning of the modern era of international law. It has led to extensive work of the ILC on the question of the effects of reservations to treaties with relevant guidelines adopted back in 2011, which resolved most of the misunderstandings.[10] One of the most significant developments in this work was the ILC's recognition that, given their object and purpose, human rights treaties (and a few others) form a set of interdependent, indivisible, and interrelated rights and obligations. Based on such an understanding of the object and purpose, reservations that offend this purpose are impermissible by definition and void *ab initio*. Courts or treaty-monitoring bodies have the competence to determine impermissible reservations, which fall outside the scope of the VCLT. Therefore, the mechanism of reservations and objections is not even applicable. Consequently, it stems from this that the whole law of treaties is based on States entering into their treaty obligation in good faith, and the courts are competent to say when that has not been the case. This approach does not upset the very idea of State consent and does not arbitrarily extend the powers of courts or monitoring committees. In its work on reservations, the ILC in fact provided an explanation of what good faith in the light of object and purpose means.

The paragraphs 75 to 89 of the *Loizidou* judgment regarding preliminary objections serve as a school-book example of how the Court applies a general rule of interpretation of treaties to establish the ordinary meaning of the concept of a 'reservation to the Convention' in view of the object and purpose of this Convention within the context of subsequent practice of States and in view of other relevant rules of international law (in this case, the ICJ Statute and the notion of jurisdiction). After all of the steps, the Court came to the conclusion that:

[10] ILC, 'Report of the International Law Commission on the Work of its Sixty-third Session' (26 April–3 June and 4 July–12 August 2011) UN Doc A/66/10, reproduced in [2011/II] YBILC 1 [75].

> Taking into consideration the character of the Convention, the ordinary meaning of Articles [...] in their context and in the light of their object and purpose and the practice of Contracting Parties, the Court concludes that the restrictions ratione loci attached to Turkey's [...] declarations are invalid.[11]

It still begs the question of whether this method is correct since it arguably limited State consent, which that State expressed when accepting the jurisdiction of a monitoring body. We may still have some unease with Courts and monitoring bodies coming to such bold conclusions, especially in such an area of international law which, as I noted earlier, evolves constantly. Indeed, such case law begs a question whether the States incorporate within the scope of the principle of good faith the understanding that a treaty of a normative character may evolve over time. Various international and national courts have replied in affirmative to this question. State practice largely appears to accept that.

Whatever legal consequences the courts draw within their competence when confronted with different and oftentimes delicate legal questions, the clarity and consistency of the method underpinning the reasoning cannot be underestimated. The tension that comes with teleological interpretation, to which the criterion of the object and purpose of a treaty invites the interpreter to resort to, is inevitable and even more so when applied over time.

In the *Brownlie's Principles of Public International Law*, James Crawford pointed out that '[t]his may involve a judicial implementation of purposes in a fashion not contemplated by the parties. The teleological approach has many pitfalls, not least its overt "legislative" character'.[12] As has been recalled, the evolutive or progressive interpretation is closely linked with the teleological approach and is very much part of the ECtHR's toolbox. Crawford cautioned when noting that the ECtHR 'has preferred an effective and "evolutionary" approach in applying the ECHR'.[13] He pointed out that this approach suffers the defect that 'the ILC did not adopt the principle, considering that as a matter of existing law it was reflected sufficiently in the doctrine of interpretation in good faith in accordance with the ordinary meaning of the text'.[14]

[11] *Loizidou v Turkey* (n 5) [89].
[12] J Crawford, *Brownlie's Principles of Public International Law* (9th edn, Oxford University Press 2019) 365.
[13] ibid 366.
[14] ibid.

Indeed, as noted above with reference to the *Loizidou* case law, the ECtHR disclosed what, in terms of good faith, the acceptance of the competence of the former Commission and the Court by Turkey meant. But in doing so, the Court resorted to notions such as living instrument and the principle of effective rights protection, suggesting an evolutive or teleological interpretation of the Convention. Arguably, it could have arrived at the same result without the need to resort to such notions.

Since the judgment in *Tyrer v the United Kingdom*, we know that the Court will be influenced by 'the developments and commonly accepted standards' in the Member States of the Council of Europe. In other words, the Court searches for European consensus, which consensus prompts the evolutive interpretation of the Convention. The scholarly debate has been coming to grips with this method from different perspectives. Firstly, the lack of 'further details as to its origins, advantages, and disadvantages' of European consensus as grounds for evolutive interpretation has been subjected to the criticism and argument that the Court engages in judicial activism.[15] This indicates the problem attributed to the evolutive interpretation of treaties, that is, the risk of overshadowing State consent, thus giving rise to legitimacy issues, which indeed goes back to Crawford's point referred to earlier.

Secondly, the ECtHR has been criticised for its evolutive interpretation of the Convention because it has allegedly led to casuistic case law. Thirdly, this interpretation has been used as an example within the fragmentation debate.

I have also looked at European consensus in my scholarly work, and the observations I would like to share are the following. The Court's use of the VCLT may suggest that the notions of European consensus and living instrument could be seen as relevant steps, albeit termed differently, within Article 31(3) of the VCLT, which incorporates developments in State practice subsequent to the adoption of a treaty or other relevant rules of international law into a general rule of interpretation of treaties. It is true, however, that not all judgments necessarily use the clearest language as to what subsequent practice is, what other relevant rules are, and in what manner they form part of the Court's interpretation of the Convention. I have come to a few conclusions, based on the language in *Demir and Baykara v Turkey* case,[16] in which the Court

[15] M Forowicz, *The Reception of International Law in the European Court of Human Rights* (Oxford University Press 2010) 12.

[16] *Demir and Baykara v Turkey* [GC] (12 November 2008) Application no 34503/97.

recognised that it may not be too concerned as to whether the State has ratified the treaty or whether the common domestic practices emerge specifically in the application of the European Convention, as the wording of Article 31 (3) would indicate. The Court thus is interested in seeing the common developments and trends relevant to the scope of the European Convention without necessarily identifying the binding character of these developments and practices. In other words, while Article 31 of the VCLT offers a frame of reference for the Court as such, the Court has followed the method of interpretation with certain flexibility.[17]

Naturally, the question that has preoccupied the States and the scholarship is whether such flexibility remains within the scope of a general rule of interpretation of treaties.[18] It is to be noted that the ILC Special Rapporteur Georg Nolte, while generally accepting the Court's approach, nevertheless noted that:

> The European Court of Human Rights mostly limits itself to broad and sometimes rough comparative assessments of the domestic legislation or international positions adopted by States. [. . .] In addition, the character of certain rights sometimes speaks in favour of taking less specific practice into account.[19]

The analysis of Georg Nolte coincides with my own analysis. The broad and rough assessments or flexibility with which the general rule of interpretation of treaties is applied by the EctHR has its risks and the principle of legal certainty should guide the Court as much as the principle of effective protection of rights. The balance is the key.

The Court's case law also entails cases in which the Court does not refer to European consensus and remains purely within the context of Article 31 (3) (c) or (b) of the VCLT, suggesting that European consensus may be something else than the notions contained in points (c) and (b).

In *Hassan v the United Kingdom*, the Court, albeit rather exceptionally, decided to consider subsequent State practice in the application of the

[17] I Ziemele, 'European Consensus and International Law' in A van Aaken and I Motoc (eds), *The European Convention on Human Rights and General International Law* (Oxford University Press 2018) 28.

[18] For a more dynamic reading of art 31 see ME Villiger, *Commentary on the 1969 Vienna Convention on the Law of Treaties* (Martinus Nijhoff 2009) 432–33.

[19] See ILC, 'Second Report on Subsequent Agreements and Subsequent Practice in Relation to the Interpretation of Treaties, by Mr Georg Nolte, Special Rapporteur' (26 March 2014) UN Doc A/CN.4/671 124 [40].

Convention and followed Article 31 (3) (b) of the VCLT. This case was about the deprivation of liberty of a young man by the British armed forces during active hostilities in Iraq following its occupation in 2003. Article 5 of the ECHR does not contain the internment of civilians during armed hostilities among the permitted exceptions from the right to liberty. The Court was faced with a threefold question. First, it had to address the question of the relationship between the ECHR and international humanitarian law (IHL). Secondly, it had to decide whether the Contracting Parties, when exercising their powers under IHL, had to have made a derogation from the ECHR under Article 15 of the Convention. Finally, the Court had to assess whether any subsequent State practice would provide any relevant indications as to the first two issues.[20]

The Court, therefore, had the opportunity to provide its view concerning the impact of subsequent State practice on otherwise a very clear text of Article 5 of the Convention. The Court pronounced as follows:

> In respect of the criterion set out in Article 31 § 3 (b) of the Vienna Convention, the Court has previously stated that a consistent practice on the part of the High Contracting Parties, subsequent to their ratification of the Convention, could be taken as establishing their agreement not only as regards interpretation but even to modify the text of the Convention.[21]

The Court reiterates that subsequent practice of the Convention States is relevant for the evolutive interpretation of the Convention even to the point of establishing the modification of this treaty. This raises the question of whether the Court means an agreement to interpret the existing text or rather a new agreed rule going beyond the treaty. The language of the above passage is somewhat unclear and can appear to go beyond the limits of the general rule of interpretation of treaties, which rule does not open the door for changing the treaty.[22] Such a situation is a reminder of the importance of providing more clarity in the

[20] See further C de Koker, 'Hassan v United Kingdom. The Interaction of Human Rights Law and International Humanitarian Law with regard to the Deprivation of Liberty in Armed Conflicts' (2015) 31(81) Utrecht Journal of International and European Law 90.

[21] See *Hassan v the United Kingdom* [GC] (16 September 2014) Application no 29750/09, ECHR 2014-V1 1 [101] (with references to *Soering v the United Kingdom* (7 July 1989) Series A no 161 and *Al-Saadoon and Mufdhi v the United Kingdom* (2 March 2010) Application no 61498/08, ECHR 2010-IL, 61).

[22] For the same call for careful consideration of subsequent practice and its true meaning, see ILC (n 19) [19].

reasoning based on the general rule of interpretation, which in turn assists in ensuring legal certainty.

The above judicial practice shows that the most difficult part in interpreting an international rule remains the determination of the 'ordinary meaning to be interpreted in good faith'. In other words, one can never really know till the very end of the relevant interpretation how the parties understood the terms and concepts of a legal provision. Therefore, the subsequent practice of the parties and other relevant rules are vital elements for interpretation, providing at least some solid ground to stand on when trying to interpret what the parties really meant, especially after some time has passed. I can also agree with another crucial point made by James Crawford, who argued that 'the doctrine of ordinary meaning involves only a presumption: a meaning other than the ordinary meaning may be established, but the proponent of the special meaning has a burden of proof'.[23]

As I suggested, the issue is not with the method or a general rule as such. Although the ECtHR, over the decades, has felt the need to develop new concepts such as European consensus, the Convention as a living instrument, etc., I do not see that these developments contradict the basic structure and logic of the interpretation of an international treaty that create interdependent obligations among the Constracting Parties. But the Court has to be aware that the risks are there.

13.2.2 The Court of Justice

The ECJ, similar to national constitutional courts, has a somewhat more complex task when it comes to the application of international law, as it stands at a crossroads between international law and EU constitutional law. It may be recalled that, in the words of Joseph HH Weiler: 'Van Gend en Loos not only shaped the legal order; it constituted that order'[24] as 'a new legal order of international law'. The Court of Justice has ever since attempted to live up to the definition provided by *Van Gend en Loos* by trying to disclose and delineate what is new about this

[23] Crawford (n 12) 367 (with reference to a critical comment by H Lauterpacht).

[24] JHH Weiler, 'Revisiting Van Gend en Loos: Subjectifying and Objectifying the Individual' in *50ème Anniversaire de l'Arrêt Van Gend en Loos 1963–2013* (Luxembourg Office des Publications de l'Union Européenne 2013) 11.

autonomous legal order which order too continues to evolve.[25] The general principles, such as autonomy and primacy of the EU legal order, effectiveness or equivalence of the EU law, mutual trust and loyal cooperation, whose source is a mixture of judicial and legislative determination, are essential to the autonomous constitutional character of this legal order.

As the case law of the Court of Justice confirms, this dual character of the EU legal order, that is, international law foundations with constitutional law effects, is crucial to understanding and conceptualising the possibilities and the manner in which synergies with international law take place. It is the proper understanding of the unique character of the EU legal order and the purposes of the Union set forth in the TEU and TFEU that lies at the basis of drawing a distinction between the ECHR system as an integral part of international law and the EU legal order and their relations to international law, respectively.

More specifically, after entering into force, international agreements agreed upon and ratified by the Union with third States or international organisations form 'an integral part of the [Community] legal order'.[26] Nevertheless, such international agreements are subordinate to primary law.[27] As stated by the Court in Opinion 2/15, given the primacy of the TEU and TFEU 'over acts adopted on their basis, those acts, including agreements concluded by the European Union with third States, derive their legitimacy from those Treaties and cannot, (. . .), have an impact on the meaning or scope of the Treaties' provisions'.[28] In other words, international agreements 'cannot "affect" rules of primary EU law or "alter their scope"'.[29]

Such international agreements concluded by the Union must be compatible not only with the Treaties but also with relevant customary

[25] In the so-called conditionality judgments, the Court took note of the stage of the constitutionalisation that the EU legal order has reached. The Court held that: 'The values contained in Article 2 TEU have been identified and are shared by the Member States. They define the very identity of the European Union as a common legal order. Thus, the European Union must be able to defend those values, within the limits of its powers as laid down by the Treaties.' C-156/21, *Hungary v Parliament and Council* (16 February 2022) ECLI:EU:C:2022:97 [127]. See also: C-157/21, *Poland v Parliament and Council* (16 February 2022) ECLI:EU:C:2022:98.

[26] C-1/96, *R v Maff, Ex parte Compassion in World Farming* (19 March 1998) EU.C:1998:113 [1998] ECR 1-1251 [31].

[27] C-181/73, *Haegeman v Belgian State* (30 April 1974) EU:C:1974:41 [1974] ECR 449 [4].

[28] *Opinion 2/15* (16 May 2017) EU:C:2017:376 [2017] OJ C 239/3 (Opinion pursuant to Article 218(11) TFEU) [235].

[29] ibid.

international law and other binding rules of international law. The Court relies in this respect on Article 3(5) TEU, according to which the Union contributes to the strict observance and development of international law.[30] In particular, the Court recalls the Union's obligation to exercise its own powers in compliance with the principles and standards of international law, as well as the rules resulting from international conventions (which are binding on the Union), which involves monitoring the compatibility of agreements concluded by the Union with general international law.[31]

On the basis of Article 216, point 2, TFEU, according to which agreements are binding on the institutions, the Court examines the compatibility of institutions acts with international law.[32] Thus, an appeal for annulment can be brought against an act of secondary law contrary to an international agreement.[33] These features of the EU legal system exemplify that international law is woven into the fabric of EU constitutional law and indeed the principles of the relationship between the EU law and international law speak in favour of a kind of monist outlook.

The concrete impact of international agreements within the judicial order of the European Union is primarily dependent on their 'invocability'. In the judgment in ATAA, the Court indicated that if private persons were to invoke international agreements in support of their subjective rights, they must meet these criteria:

- The Union must be bound by an international agreement;
- the nature and the structure of the international agreement must allow an examination of validity to be challenged;
- 'the provisions of that treaty which are relied upon for the purpose of examining the validity of the act of European Union law appear, as regards to their content, to be unconditional and sufficiently precise'.[34]

[30] C-104/16 P, *Council v Front Polisario* [GC] (21 December 2016) EU:C:2016:973 [2016] OJ C 111.

[31] C-266/16, *Western Sahara Campaign UK* [GC] (27 February 2018) EU:C:2018:118 [2018] OJ C 142/3.

[32] *Joined cases 21 to 24/72 International Fruit Company* (12 December 1972) EU:C:1972:115 [1972] ECR 1219.

[33] C-188/88, *NMB v Commission* (10 March 1992) EU:C:1992:114 [1992] OJ C 81/4.

[34] C-366/10, *Air Transport Association of America (ATAA) and Others* [GC] (21 December 2011) EU:C:2011:864 [2012] OJ C 49/7 [52–54].

In other words, the Court has clarified the concept of a self-executing international treaty for the purposes of the EU legal system through the principle of their invocability. But even in the absence of the invocability and direct effect, the Court has emphasised that 'EU legislation must, so far as possible, be interpreted in a manner that is consistent with international law'.[35] The obligation of interpretation in conformity with applicable international law arises from the primacy of international agreements concluded by the Union and the international conventions entered into by the Union over the secondary law and the EU's loyalty to international law.[36]

The principle of interpretation in conformity with international agreements and conventions is not limited to secondary law and their interpretation by the EU judiciary; it also concerns the national judiciaries in the EU Member States.[37] Accordingly, in the Slovak Brown Bear judgment, the Court evaluated Article 9(3) of the Aarhus Convention, which aims to limit the legal hurdles faced by organisations and individuals working towards environmental protection by making access to information, participation in decision-making, and access to judicial remedies easier. This case reviewed whether the Aarhus Convention could have direct effect also as a matter of EU law. This was not so, but the Court clearly ruled that the Convention requires the Member States to provide for effective procedural arrangements at national levels in the environmental litigation. In this regard, the Court based itself on the necessity to assure effective judicial protection in the areas covered by Union's environmental law. Consequently, national courts must ensure that their interpretation of national law is in conformity with the objectives of Article 9(3) of the Aarhus Convention to the fullest extent possible.[38]

Concerning the methods of interpreting international agreements, the Court emphasises that an international treaty must be interpreted according to the terms in which it was drafted, as well as in the light of its objectives. The Court resorts to Article 31 of the VCLT, specifying that a 'treaty is to be interpreted in good faith in accordance with the ordinary

[35] C-511/13, *Philips Lighting Poland and Philips Lighting v Council* [GC] (8 September 2015) EU:C:2015:553 [2015] OJ C 263/4 [60].

[36] C-188/23, *Conti 11 Container Schiffahrt II* (21 January 2025) EU:C:2025:26.

[37] C-337/95, *Parfums Christian Dior v Evora* (4 November 1997) EU-C:1997:517 [1997] ECR 1-6013.

[38] C-240/09, *Lesoochrandrske zoskupenie (Slovak Brown Bear)* [GC] (8 March 2011) EU: C:2011:125 [2011] ECR I-1255.

meaning to be given to its terms in their context and in the light of its object and purpose'.[39]

The Union is a powerful actor that can support the effectiveness of international law through the interpretation of the EU law in conformity with binding international rules and by taking into account and getting an inspiration from the international legal system to the extent that it is compatible with the objectives of the EU Treaties and the Union's competences.

To sum up, international treaties that the EU as a subject of international law has accepted become part of the EU legal system and, in the hierarchy of legal sources, are above secondary law. These treaties are interpreted based on the general rule of interpretation of international treaties. Moreover, the Court uses among its own methods of interpretation of EU law the contextual interpretation method, which allows the Court to take into account other rules of international law, especially the *ius cogens* rules. The Court also resorts to the principle of interpretation in conformity to mitigate possible backlash if the interpretation of the EU's legal act might indicate issues of invalidity of such an act.

However, there is case law that may appear to jeopardise not only the monist view of the EU legal order but also some of the structures of the international legal system. The obvious cases to be mentioned which have been subject to extensive doctrinal analysis are *Kadi*, Opinion 2/13, and *Achmea* judgments.[40]

First, as it derives from the above, the constitutional order that the EU has constructed is protective of its autonomous character based on its constitutional values, which, as Article 52, paragraph 3, second sentence, of the EU Fundamental Rights Charter in the field of human rights confirms, may indeed be higher than the minimum international standard, including that provided for in the ECHR. It is, therefore, that the *Kadi* case and Opinion 2/13 have to be seen as an ultimate protection of the European view of governance based on indivisibility and inviolability of the rule of law, separation of powers, fair trial, human rights, and democracy. No compromises are permitted within this constitutional

[39] C-344/04, *IATA and ELFAA* [GC] (10 January 2006) EU:C:2006:10 [2006] ECR 1-403 [40].

[40] C-402/05 P and C- 415/05, *P Kadi and Al Barakaat International Foundation v Council and Commission* [GC] (3 September 2008) EU:C:2008:461; *Opinion 2/13 Accession of the EU to the ECHR* (18 December 2014) EU:C:2014:2454; C-284/16, *Achmea* [GC] (6 March 2018) EU:C:2018:158.

order, which ought to be reflected in all EU Member States' constitutional orders. In the *Kadi* context, the Court answered that the enforcement of individual international responsibility couldn't compromise the value of a fair trial. Second, in Opinion 2/13, the Court was concerned about the coherence of its own legal order, which it has the ultimate responsibility for. Again, a normal reaction from a constitutional court wanting to avoid different standards emerging within its legal system through a door over which it has no full control. *Achmea*, in the area of international investment dispute settlement, follows the same logic, even if in this case, both states were EU Member States. However, the dispute settlement body concerned did not qualify under Article 267 TFEU as a tribunal that would be entitled to ask for a preliminary ruling from the Court of Justice. It is, therefore, that following well-established case law with regard to the Benelux Court of Justice or the EFTA Court, the Court of Justice did not accept that adjudication on matters falling within the EU law could be done by a court that is not part of the institutional structure of the EU legal order, as that 'may undermine the autonomy of the [Community] legal order in pursuing its own particular objectives'.[41] It is therefore that the logic of the EU legal order is different from the logic of international legal system. On the one hand, the EU law is open to international law and complies with it as a matter of principle. On the other hand, based on the common values set forth in Article 2 TEU that reflect the very identity of the Union and in view of internal coherence of the rules and mechanisms of the EU, it protects this coherence and clearly impacts the international legal system in return.

However, one of the most prominent examples of how the EU engages with international treaties and other relevant rules of international law concerns the cases regarding the status of the Sahrawi people of Western Sahara and several agreements concluded between the European Union and the Kingdom of Morocco. I would like to briefly comment on the Court's position in the judgment on appeal subsequent to the General Court's judgment, which, upon the application of the Front Polisario, had annulled the association agreement between the EU and Morocco. This agreement did not expressly exclude Western Sahara from its scope and the submission in front of the General Court was that such agreement is contrary to the right to self-determination, Article 73 of the UN Charter, provisions in the Convention on the Law and Sea, the duty of

[41] *Opinion 1/91* (14 December 1991) EU:C:1991:490 [1991] ECR 1-06079 (Opinion pursuant to Article 228 of the EEC Treaty) [30].

the international community to stop 'serious breaches of a peremptory norm of international law, not to recognise and illegal situation resulting from such a breach, and not to provide assistance for the commission of an internationally wrongful act'. The Court recalled that:

> In order to be able to draw correct legal conclusions from the absence of a stipulation excluding Western Sahara from the territorial scope of the Association Agreement, in interpreting that agreement, the General Court was bound not only to observe the rules of good faith interpretation laid down in Article 31(1) of the Vienna Convention but also that laid down in Article 31(3)(c) of that Convention, pursuant to which the interpretation of a treaty must be carried out by taking account of any relevant rules of international law applicable in the relations between the parties.[42]

The Court recognised that the Association Agreement could not extend to include the people of Western Sahara. The Union could not have intended to violate relevant international law. In the case, the Court referenced the ICJ Advisory Opinion on Western Sahara, reaffirming that Western Sahara had a personality that was distinct from the 'territory of the Kingdom of Morocco', and could, therefore, not be 'included within the territorial scope of' neither the Kingdom nor the agreement.[43] Applying Article 31(3)(c) of the VCLT, the Court stipulated that the 'relevant rules of international law applicable in the relations between parties' must be taken into account during the course of interpretation.[44] In this context, the Court recalled that the people of Western Sahara had the right to self-determination. The key issue was the interpretation of the notion of 'territory' in the Association Agreement. The Court pointed out that 'the adjective "its" preceding the term "territory"', that is, 'its territory' refers to a 'geographical space' in which a 'State exercises [its] full powers'. According to the VCLT and international practice, if 'a treaty is intended to apply not only to the territory of a State but also beyond that territory, that treaty expressly provides for it'.[45] Since this did not emanate from the Agreement, this Agreement could not be taken to mean that Western Sahara is part of Morocco's territory. The opposite would be in contradiction to the right to self-determination of the people of Western Sahara. Moreover, '[t]he customary rule codified in Article 29 of the VCLT thus also, a priori, precluded Western Sahara from being

[42] *Council v Front Polisario* (n 30) [86].
[43] ibid [92].
[44] ibid [86].
[45] ibid [95–96].

regarded as coming within the territorial scope of the Association Agreement'.[46]

The Court did diverge with the General Court, stating that 'the principle of the relative effect of treaties had to be taken into account in such an interpretation, since the application to Western Sahara of the Association Agreement, [. . .] would have led to that agreement affecting a "third party" [i.e. the people of Western Sahara]'.[47] Their designation as a 'third party' might have meant that they could be 'incorporated' into the Agreement if they so desired, but the Court proceedings clearly showed a lack of consent from the people of Western Sahara.[48]

In conclusion, the Court states:

> Moreover, the purported intention of the European Union, reflected in subsequent practice and consisting in considering the Association and Liberalisation Agreements to be legally applicable to the territory of Western Sahara, would necessarily have entailed conceding that the European Union intended to implement those agreements in a manner incompatible with the principles of self-determination and of the relative effect of treaties, even though the European Union repeatedly reiterated the need to comply with those principles, as the Commission points out.[49]

The Court maintained in force the EU and Morocco Agreement based on the principle of rational legislator, which is a common principle of constitutional law and which probably, in the case of Agreements with Morocco, translates into a good faith principle. The EU could not be considered to have meant to affect the status of Western Sahara under international law unless it is proven otherwise. But the onus is on the party alleging it. In other words, the trade and other important relations between the Union and Morocco were preserved, while the principles of international law relevant to the rights of the people of Western Sahara were also complied with through the proper use of a general rule of interpretation of a treaty. The object and purpose of the Agreement comprised respect for international law and the context referred to the right to self-determination and consent of being bound by treaties that affect the self-determination entity. This judgment and the line of case law exemplifies the complexity of the ECJ's application of international law.

[46] Ibid [97].
[47] ibid [103, 106].
[48] ibid [106].
[49] ibid [123].

13.3 Concluding Remarks

I will finish my talk by reiterating that the nature of a treaty, determined by the legal relations the treaty is meant to regulate, impacts in important ways the use of a general rule of interpretation of a treaty. Indeed, it is the object and purpose of a treaty that, as discussed in the European context, has a major impact on the evolution of that treaty. There are risks to introducing uncertainty depending on the area of international law or legal regime. At the same time, practice shows that States are acutely aware of the power of courts and carefully follow their case law. Too much liberty may backfire and has backfired in the past. At the end of the day, judges too must be aware of the fine dialectics between State consent and judicial authority and are well advised for reasons of legal certainty and legitimacy to follow the general rule of interpretation.

BIBLIOGRAPHY

Books and Chapters in Edited Volumes

Abi-Saab G, 'The Specificities of Humanitarian Law' in Christophe Swinarski (ed), *Studies and Essays on International Humanitarian Law and Red Cross Principles in Honour of Jean Pictet* (ICRC and Martinus Nijhoff 1984) 265

Adams M and Bomhoff J, 'Comparing Law: Practice and Theory' in M Adams and J Bomhoff (eds), *Practice and Theory in Comparative Law* (Cambridge University Press 2013) 6

Andenas M and Bjorge E, 'Introduction: From Fragmentation to Convergence in International Law' in M Andenas and E Bjorge (eds), *A Farewell to Fragmentation: Reassertion and Convergence in International Law* (Cambridge University Press 2015) 1

Ashworth A and Horder J, *Principles of Criminal Law* (Oxford University Press 2013)

Aust A, *Modern Treaty Law and Practice* (3rd edn, Cambridge University Press 2013)

Baka AI, 'The Logic of Absence in Customary International Law: An Open-System Approach' in P Merkouris, J Kammerhofer and N Arajärvi (eds), *The Theory, Practice, and Interpretation of Customary International Law* (Cambridge University Press 2022) 63

Barral V, 'National Sovereignty over Natural Resources: Environmental Challenges and Sustainable Development' in E Morgera and K Kulovesi (eds), *Research Handbook on Natural Resources and International Law* (Edward Elgar 2016) 3

Bassiouni MC, *Crimes Against Humanity: Historical Evolution and Contemporary Application* (Cambridge University Press 2011)

Bennouna M, 'The Statute's Rules on Crimes and Existing or Developing International Law' in A Cassese, P Gaeta and JRWD Jones (eds), *The Rome Statute of the International Criminal Court: A Commentary*, Vol 2 (Oxford University Press 2002) 1101

Bergsmo M and Tianying S (eds), *On the Proposed Crimes Against Humanity Convention* (Torkel Opsahl Academic EPublisher 2014)

Bernasconi N, Brauch MD and Mann H, 'Civil Society and International Investment Arbitration: Tracing the Evolution of Concern' in T Schultz and F Ortino (eds), *The Oxford Handbook of International Arbitration* (Oxford University Press 2010) 304

Bernaz N, 'Reforming the UN Human Rights Protection Procedures: A Legal Perspective on the Establishment of the Universal Periodic Review Mechanism' in K Boyle (ed), *New Institutions for Human Rights Protection* (Oxford University Press 2009) 75

Besson S, 'General Principles and Customary Law in the EU Legal Order' in S Vogenayer and S Weatherhill (eds), *General Principles of Law: European and Comparative Perspectives* (Hart 2017) 107

Due Diligence in International Law (Brill 2023)

Bianchi A, 'Epistemic Communities in International Arbitration' in F Ortino and T Schultz (eds), *Oxford Handbook of International Arbitration* (Oxford University Press 2017) 569

'Textual Interpretation and (International) Law Reading: The Myth of (In) determinacy and the Genealogy of Meaning' in PHF Bekker, R Dolzer and M Waibel (eds), *Making Transnational Law Work in the Global Economy: Essays in Honour of Detlev Vagts* (Cambridge University Press 2010) 34

Bitti G, 'Article 21 of the Statute of the International Criminal Court and the Treatment of Sources of Law in the Jurisprudence of the ICC' in C Stahn and G Sluiter (eds), *The Emerging Practice of the International Criminal Court* (Brill 2009) 281

Bjorge E, 'The Convergence of the Methods of Treaty Interpretation: Different Regimes, Different Methods of Interpretation?' in M Andenas and E Bjorge (eds), *A Farewell to Fragmentation: Reassertion and Convergence in International Law* (Cambridge University Press 2015) 498

'The Vienna Rules, Evolutionary Interpretation, and the Intentions of the Parties' in A Bianchi, D Peat, and M Windsor (eds), *Interpretation in International Law* (Oxford University Press 2015) 189

'The Vienna Rules, Evolutionary Interpretation, and the Intentions of the Parties' in A Bianchi et al (eds), *Interpretation in International Law* (Oxford University Press 2018) 189

The Evolutionary Interpretation of Treaties (Oxford University Press 2014)

Boisson de Chazournes L and Mbengue MM, 'A "Footnote as a Principle": Mutual Supportiveness in an Era of Fragmentation' in P Holger et al (eds), *Coexistence, Cooperation and Solidarity: Liber Amicorum Rüdiger Wolfrum* (Martinus Nijhoff 2011) 1615

Bouchet-Saulnier F, *The Practical Guide to Humanitarian Law* (3rd edn, Rowman and Littlefield 2014)

Boyle AE and Anderson MR (eds), *Human Rights Approaches to Environmental Protection* (Oxford University Press 1996)

Brölmann C, 'Capturing the Juridical Will of International Organisations' in S Droubi and J d'Aspremont (eds), *International Organizations and Non-State*

Actors in the Formation of Customary International Law (Manchester University Press 2020) 42

'International Organizations and the Disaggregation of Consent' in S Besson (ed), *Consenting to International Law* (Cambridge University Press 2023) 115

'Specialized Rules of Treaty Interpretation: International Organizations' in DB Hollis (ed), *The Oxford Guide to Treaties* (2nd edn, Oxford University Press 2020) 524

The Institutional Veil in Public International Law (Hart 2007) 197

Broomhall B, 'Article 22' in K Ambos (ed), *Commentary on the Rome Statute of the International Criminal Court* (4th edn, Beck, Hart, Nomos 2022) 1149

Brown C, *Commentaries on Selected Model Investment Treaties* (Oxford University Press 2013)

Cassese A et al, *Cassese's International Criminal Law* (Oxford University Press 2013)

International Criminal Law (2nd edn, Oxford University Press 2008)

International Law (Oxford University Press 2001)

Chesterman S, Johnstone I, and Malone DM, *Law and Practice of the United Nations* (2nd edn, Oxford University Press 2016)

Christoffels-DuPlessis A et al, 'Navigating a Sea of Laws: The Quests of Small-scale Fishing Communities in Ghana and South Africa for Protecting Their Customary Rights' in R Bosewell, D O' Kane, and J Hills (eds), *The Palgrave Handbook of Blue Heritage* (Palgrave 2022) 325

Christoffersen J, 'Impact on General Principles of Treaty Interpretation' in MT Kamminga and Martin Scheinin (eds), *The Impact of Human Rights Law on General International Law* (Oxford University Press 2009) 37

Clapham A, *War* (Oxford University Press 2021)

Clark RS, 'Crimes Against Humanity' in G Ginsburgs and VN Kudriavtsev (eds), *The Nuremberg Trial and International Law* (Martinus Nijhoff 1990) 177

Coleman J, Cordes K, and Johnson L, 'Human Rights Law and the Investment Treaty Regime' in S Deva and D Birchall (eds), *Research Handbook on Human Rights and Business* (Edward Elgar 2020) 290

Collins R and Bohm A, 'International Law as Professional Practice: Crafting the Autonomy of International Law' in J d'Aspremont et al (eds), *International Law as a Profession* (Cambridge University Press 2017) 67

Concise Oxford English Dictionary (12th edn, Oxford University Press 2011)

Costelloe D, 'Conceptions of State Jurisdiction in the Jurisprudence of the International Court of Justice and the Permanent Court of International Justice' in S Allen et al (eds), *The Oxford Handbook of Jurisdiction in International Law* (Oxford University Press 2019) 455

Cowell F, 'Identifying Custom in Universal Periodic Review Recommendations 15: Identifying Custom in Universal Periodic Review Recommendations' in

P Merkouris, J Kammerhofer, and N Arajärvi (eds), *The Theory, Practice, and Interpretation of Customary International Law* (Cambridge University Press 2022) 320

Craik N, 'Environmental Impact Assessment' in E Morgera and J Razzaque (eds), *Encyclopedia of Environmental Law: Biodiversity and Nature Protection Law* (Edward Elgar 2017) 431

Crawford J, *Brownlie's Principles of Public International Law* (9th edn Oxford University Press 2019)

Crema L, 'The Interpretative Work of Treaty Bodies: How They Look at Evolutionary Interpretation and How Other Courts Look at Them' in G Abi-Saab et al (eds), *Evolutionary Interpretation and International Law* (Hart 2019) 84

Cryer R, 'The Doctrinal Foundations of International Criminalization' in MC Bassiouni (ed), *International Criminal Law*, Vol 1 (Martinus Nijhoff 2008) 107

D'Aspremont J et al, 'Introduction' in J d'Aspremont et al (eds), *International Law as a Profession* (Cambridge University Press 2017) 1

'The Custom-Making Moment in Customary International Law' in P Merkouris, J Kammerhofer, and N Arajärvi (eds), *The Theory, Practice, and Interpretation of Customary International Law* (Cambridge University Press 2022) 29

Epistemic Forces in International Law (Edward Elgar 2015)

Danilenko GM, 'ICC Statute and Third States' in A Cassese, P Gaeta, and JRWD Jones (eds), *The Rome Statute of the International Criminal Court: A Commentary*, Vol 2 (Oxford University Press 2002) 1871

Darian-Smith E, 'Transnational Legal Education' in P Zumbansen (ed), *The Oxford Handbook of Transnational Law* (Oxford University Press 2021) 1153

David E, *Principes du droit des conflits armés* (4th edn, Bruylant 2008)

De Brabandere E, 'Human Rights and International Investment Law' in M Krajewski and RT Hoffmann (eds), *Research Handbook on Foreign Direct Investment* (Edward Elgar 2019) 619

De Schutter O, 'Human Rights and the Rise of International Organisations: The Logic of Sliding Scales in the Law of International Responsibility' in J Wouters et al (eds), *Accountability for Human Rights Violations by International Organisations* (Intersentia 2010) 51

Delaume GR, 'Consent to ICSID Arbitration' in JJ Norton, M Footer, and M Andenas (eds), *The Changing World of International Law in the Twenty-First Century: A Tribute to the Late Kenneth R. Simmonds* (Kluwer Law International 1998) 155

Des Gouttes P, *La Convention de Genève du 27 juillet 1929: Commentaire* (ICRC 1930)

Di Marco R, 'Customary International Law: Identification versus Interpretation' in P Merkouris, J Kammerhofer, and N Arajärvi (eds) *The Theory, Practice, and Interpretation of Customary International Law* (Cambridge University Press 2022) 416

Domínguez Redondo E, 'Human Rights Through the Backdoor: The Contribution of Special Procedures to the Normative Coherence and Contradictions of International Human Rights Law' in C Buckley, A Donald, and P Leach (eds), *Towards Convergence in Human Rights Law: Approaches of Regional and International Systems* (Brill Nijhoff 2016) 543

Dormann K (ed), *Elements of War Crimes under the Rome Statute of the International Criminal Court: Sources and Commentary* (Cambridge University Press 2003)

Dörr O, 'Article 32' in O Dörr and K Schmalenbach (eds), *Vienna Convention on the Law of Treaties* (2nd edn, Oxford University Press 2018) 627

Douglas Z, 'Property, Investment, and the Scope of Investment Protection Obligations' in Z Douglas, J Pauwelyn, and JE Viñuales (eds), *The Foundations of International Investment Law: Bringing Theory into Practice* (Oxford University Press 2014) 362

Dumberry P, 'The "Minimum Standard of Treatment" in International Investment Law: The Story of the Emergence, the Decline and the Recent Resurrection of a Concept' in K Polackova van der Ploeg, L Pasquet, and L Castellanos-Jankiewicz (eds), *International Law and Time: Narratives and Techniques* (Springer 2022) 381

Dunant H, *A Memory of Solferino* (first published 1862, ICRC 2016)

Dupuy PM, 'Unification Rather Than Fragmentation of International Law? The Case of International Investment Law and Human Rights Law' in PM Dupuy, EU Petersmann, and F Francioni (eds), *Human Rights in International Investment Law and Arbitration* (Oxford University Press 2009) 45

Erinosho B et al, 'Transformative Governance for Ocean Biodiversity' in IJ Visseren-Hamakers and M Kok (eds), *Transforming Biodiversity Governance* (Cambridge University Press 2022) 313

Erwin K et al, '*Lalela uLwandle*: An Experiment in Plural Governance Discussions' in R Bosewell, D O' Kane, and J Hills (eds), *The Palgrave Handbook of Blue Heritage* (Palgrave 2022) 383

Fancioni F and Scovazzi T (eds), *International Responsibility for Environmental Harm* (Kluwer 1991)

Fanou M and Tzevelekos VP, 'The Shared Territory of the ECHR and International Investment Law' in Y Radi (ed), *Research Handbook on Human Rights and Investment* (Edward Elgar 2018) 93

Farrell M, *The Prohibition of Torture in Exceptional Circumstances* (Cambridge University Press 2013)

Fitzmaurice M, 'Interpretation of Human Rights Treaties' in D Shelton (ed), *The Oxford Handbook of International Human Rights Law* (Oxford University Press 2013) 739

Forowicz M, *The Reception of International Law in the European Court of Human Rights* (Oxford University Press 2010)

Fortuna M, 'Different Strings of the Same Harp: Interpretation of Rules of Customary International Law, Their Identification and Treaty Interpretation' in P Merkouris, J Kammerhofer, and N Arajärvi (eds), *The Theory, Practice, and Interpretation of Customary International Law* (Cambridge University Press 2022) 393

Franckx E, 'The Protection of Biodiversity and Fisheries Management: Issues Raised by the Relationship Between CITES and LOSC' in D Freestone, R Barnes, and D Ong (eds), *The Law of the Sea: Progress and Prospects* (Oxford University Press 2006) 210

Gallant KS, *The Principle of Legality in International and Comparative Criminal Law* (Cambridge University Press 2009)

Gardiner R, *Treaty Interpretation* (2nd edn, Oxford University Press 2015)

Treaty Interpretation (Oxford University Press 2008)

Gazzini T and de Brabandere E, *International Investment Law: The Sources of Rights and Obligations* (Brill 2012)

Geiß R and Zimmermann A, 'The International Committee of the Red Cross: A Unique Actor in the Field of International Humanitarian Law Creation and Progressive Development' in R Geiß, A Zimmermann, and S Haumer (eds), *Humanizing the Laws of War: The Red Cross and the Development of International Humanitarian Law* (Cambridge University Press 2017) 222

Gevers C, 'African and International Criminal Law' in KJ Heller et al (eds), *The Oxford Handbook of International Criminal Law* (Oxford University Press 2019) 154

Grossman N, Cohen HG, Follesdal A, and Ulfstein G (eds), *Legitimacy and International Courts* (Cambridge University Press 2018)

Grover L, *Interpreting Crimes in the Rome Statute of the International Criminal Court* (Cambridge University Press 2014)

Harrison J, *Saving the Oceans Through: The International Legal Framework for the Protection of the Marine Environment* (Oxford University Press 2017)

Hart HLA, *The Concept of Law* (3rd edn, Clarendon 2012)

Haynes C and Killander M, 'Universality and the Growth of Regional Systems' in D Shelton (ed) *The Oxford Handbook of International Human Rights Law* (Oxford University Press 2013) 670

Heinsch R, 'The International Committee of the Red Cross and the Geneva Conventions of 1949' in R Geiß, A Zimmermann, and S Haumer (eds), *Humanizing the Laws of War: The Red Cross and the Development of International Humanitarian Law* (Cambridge University Press 2017) 55

Heinze A, 'Article 10' in K Ambos (ed), *Commentary on the Rome Statute of the International Criminal Court* (4th edn, Beck, Hart, Nomos 2022) 756

Henckaerts J-M and Pothelet E, 'The Interpretation of IHL Treaties: Subsequent Practice and Other Salient Issues' in H Krieger and J Püschmann (eds), *Law-Making and Legitimacy in International Humanitarian Law* (Edward Elgar 2021) 150

Henckaerts J-M et al, 'ICRC Perspectives on the Interpretation of the Third Geneva Convention More Than Seventy Years after Its Adoption' in MN Schmitt and CJ Koschnitzky (eds) *Prisoners of War in Contemporary Conflict* (Oxford University Press 2023) 375

Hernandez G, 'The Responsibility of the International Legal Academic: Situating the Grammarian within the "Invisible College"' in J d'Aspremont et al (eds), *International Law as a Profession* (Cambridge University Press 2017) 160

International Law (Oxford University Press 2019)

Higgins R et al, *Oppenheim's International Law: United Nations* (Oxford University Press 2017)

Hoffmann T, 'The Crime of Genocide in Its (Nearly) Infinite Domestic Variety' in M Odello and P Lubinski (eds), *The Concept of Genocide in International Criminal Law: Developments After Lemkin* (Routledge 2020) 67

Hohmann J, 'Principle, Policy and Practice: The Role of the UN Special Rapporteurs on the Right to Adequate Housing in the Development of the Right to Housing in International Law' in A Nolan, R Freedman, and T Murphy (eds), *The United Nations Special Procedures System* (Brill Nijhoff 2017) 275

Hollis DB, 'Sources in Interpretation Theories: An Interdependent Relationship' in S Besson and J d'Aspremont (eds), *The Oxford Handbook on the Sources of International Law* (Oxford University Press 2017) 422

Husa J, 'Research Designs of Comparative Law: Methodology or Heuristics?' in M Adams and D Heirbaut (eds), *The Method and Culture of Comparative Law* (Hart 2014) 64

ICISS, *The Responsibility to Protect: Report of the International Commission on Intervention and State Sovereignty* (International Development Research Centre 2001)

ICRC and the International Federation of Red Cross and Red Crescent Societies, *Handbook of the International Red Cross and Red Crescent Movement* (14th edn, ICRC and the International Federation of Red Cross and Red Crescent Societies 2008) <https://www.rcrc-resilience-southeastasia.org/wp-content/uploads/2017/12/Handbook-RCRC-Movement.pdf>

ICRC, *Commentary on the First Geneva Convention: Convention (I) for the Amelioration of the Condition of the Wounded and Sick in Armed Forces in the Field* (2nd edn, Cambridge University Press 2016)

Commentary on the Second Geneva Convention: Convention (II) for the Amelioration of the Condition of Wounded, Sick and Shipwrecked Members of Armed Forces at Sea (2nd edn, Cambridge University Press 2017)

Commentary on the Third Geneva Convention: Convention (III) Relative to the Treatment of Prisoners of War (2nd edn, Cambridge University Press 2021)

Customary International Humanitarian Law (Cambridge University Press 2005)

International Humanitarian Law: Answers to Your Questions (ICRC 2023)

Ilfe J, *Human Rights from Below* (Cambridge University Press 2012)

Jansen Calamita N, 'International Human Rights and the Interpretation of International Investment Treaties: Constitutional Considerations' in F Baetens (ed), *Investment Law within International Law: Integrationist Perspectives* (Cambridge University Press 2013) 178

Jennings R and Watts A (eds), *Oppenheim's International Law* (9th edn, Oxford University Press 1992)

Joseph S and Kyriakakis J, 'The United Nations and Human Rights' in S Joseph and A McBeth (eds), *Research Handbook on International Human Rights Law* (Edward Elgar 2010) 2

'The United Nations and Human Rights' in S Joseph and A McBeth (eds), *Research Handbook on International Human Rights Law* (Edward Elgar 2010) 21

Kadelbach S, '*Jus Cogens*, Obligations *Erga Omnes* and other Rules: The Identification of Fundamental Norms' in C Tomuschat and JM Thouvenin (eds), *The Fundamental Norms of the International Legal Order: Jus Cogens and Obligations Erga Omnes* (Martinus Nijhoff 2006) 21

Kälin W, 'Examination of State Reports' in H Keller and G Ulfstein (eds), *UN Human Rights Treaty Bodies: Law and Legitimacy* (Cambridge University Press 2012) 32

Keller H and Grover L, 'General Comments of the Human Rights Committee and their Legitimacy' in H Keller and G Ulfstein (eds), *UN Human Rights Bodies: Law and Legitimacy* (Oxford University Press 2012) 118

Kelsen H, *The Law of the United Nations: A Critical Analysis of Its Fundamental Problems* (Stevens 1950)

Kemmerer A, 'Sources in the Meta-Theory of International Law: Hermeneutical Conversations' in S Besson and J d'Aspremont (eds), *The Oxford Handbook on the Sources of International Law* (Oxford University Press 2017) 469

Kirsch P, 'Foreword' in K Dormann (ed), *Elements of War Crimes under the Rome Statute of the International Criminal Court: Sources and Commentary* (Cambridge University Press 2003) xiii

Kolb R and del Mar K, 'Treaties for Armed Conflict' in A Clapham and P Gaeta (eds), *The Oxford Handbook of International Law of Armed Conflict* (Oxford University Press 2014) 79

Kolb R, *Good Faith in International Law* (Hart Publishing 2017)

Koskenniemi M, 'Between Commitment and Cynicism: Outline for a Theory of International Law as Practice' in *Collection of Essays by Legal Advisers of*

States, Legal Advisers of International Organizatios and Practitioners in the Field of International Law (United Nations 1999) 495

Krommendijk J, *The Domestic Impact and Effectiveness of the Process of State Reporting under UN Human Rights Treaties in the Netherlands, New Zealand and Finland: Paper Pushing or Policy Prompting?* (Intersentia 2014)

Kurtz J, *The WTO and International Investment Law: Converging Systems* (Cambridge University Press 2016)

Kysar D, *Regulating from Nowhere: Environmental Law and the Search of Objectivity* (Yale University Press 2010)

Lauterpacht H, *Private Law Sources and Analogies of International Law* (Longmans, Green and Co 1927)

The Function of Law in the International Community (Oxford University Press 1933)

Lawand K and Robinson I, 'Development of Treaties Limiting or Prohibiting the Use of Certain Weapons: The Role of the International Committee of the Red Cross' in R Geiß, A Zimmermann, and S Haumer (eds), *Humanizing the Laws of War: The Red Cross and the Development of International Humanitarian Law* (Cambridge University Press 2017) 141

Le Bouthillier Y, 'Article 32' in O Corten and P Klein (eds), *The Vienna Convention on the Law of Treaties: A Commentary* (Oxford University Press 2011) 841

Leonelli S and Williamson H, 'Introduction: Towards Responsible Plant Data Linkage' in H Williamson and S Leonelli (eds), *Towards Responsible Plant Data Linkage* (Springer, 2023) 1

Lijnzaad L, 'Swimming into Deep Water: Article 91(3) of the Third Geneva Convention and the Successful Escape of Prisoners of War by Sea' in S Marquardt and S Blockmans (eds), *The European Union's Contribution to International Peace and Security: Liber Amicorum in honour of Gert-Jan van Hegelsom* (Brill 2023) 310

Lim CL, '*Inter Arma Silent Leges*? Black Hole Theories of the Laws of War' in VV Ramraj (ed), *Emergencies and the Limits of Legality* (Cambridge University Press 2008) 385

Limon M and Piccone T, *Human Rights Special Procedures: Determinants of Influence* (Foreign Policy at Brookings 2014)

Lo Giacco L, *Judicial Decisions in International Law Argumentation* (Hart 2022)

Loye D, *Commentary on Annex I to Protocol Additional I to the Geneva Conventions of 1949: Regulations concerning Identification, as Amended on 30 November 1993* (ICRC 2002) <https://ihl-databases.icrc.org/en/ihl-treaties/api-amended-annex-i-1993>

Lundmark T, *Charting the Divide Between Common and Civil Law* (Oxford University Press 2012)

Lundy L, *The Rights of Child Human Rights Defenders: Implementation Guide* (Child Rights Connect 2020)

Lupin D and Townsend L, 'The Right to Consultation Is a Right to Be Heard' in D Lupin (ed), *A Research Agenda for Human Rights and the Environment* (Edward Elgar 2023) 103

MacCormick N, *Legal Reasoning and Legal Theory* (Clarendon 1978)

Maljean-Dubois S and Morgera E, 'International Biodiversity Litigation: The Increasing Emphasis on Biodiversity Law before International Courts and Tribunals' in G Futhazar, S Maljean-Dubois, and J Razzaque (eds), *Biodiversity Litigation* (Oxford University Press 2022) 331

Marceau G and Tomazos A, 'Comments on Joost Pauwelyn's Paper: "How to Win a WTO Dispute based on non-WTO Law?"' in S Griller (ed), *At the Crossroads: The World Trading System and the Doha Round* (Springer 2008) 54

Marceau G, 'Balance and Coherence by the WTO Appellate Body: Who Could Do It Better?' in G Sacerdoti, A Yanovich, and J Bohannes (eds), *The WTO at Ten: The Contribution of the Dispute Settlement System* (World Trade Organization 2006) 326

Mattei U, 'Comparative Law and Critical Legal Studies' in M Reimann and R Zimmermann (eds), *The Oxford Handbook of Comparative Law* (Oxford University Press 2006) 815

Maupin JA, 'Differentiating Among International Investment Disputes' in Z Douglas, J Pauwelyn, and JE Vinuales (eds), *The Foundations of International Investment Law: Bringing Theory into Practice* (Oxford University Press 2014) 466

Mayer P, 'Le mythe de l'ordre juridique de base (ou *Grundlegung*)' in P Fouchard, P Kahn, and A Lyon-Caen (eds), *Le droit des relations économiques internationales: Etudes offertes à Berthold Goldman* (Litec 1982) 199

McGarry D, 'When Ancestors Are Included in Ocean and Decision-making' in T Shefer et al (eds), *Hydrofeminist Thinking with Oceans: Political and Scholarly Possibilities* (Routledge 2024) 15

Empathy in the Time of Ecological Apartheid: A Social Sculpture Practice-led Inquiry into Developing Pedagogies for Ecological Citizenship (PhD Thesis, Rhodes University, South Africa 2014)

Melzer N and Kuster E (eds), *International Humanitarian Law: A Comprehensive Introduction* (ICRC 2022)

Melzer N, *Direct Participation in Hostilities* (ICRC 2009)

Merkouris P, 'Interpreting Customary International Law: You'll Never Walk Alone' in P Merkouris, J Kammerhofer, and N Arajärvi (eds), *The Theory, Practice, and Interpretation of Customary International Law* (Cambridge University Press 2022) 347

Interpretation of Customary International Law: Of Methods and Limits (Brill 2024)

Merkouris P, Kammerhofer J, and Arajärvi N (eds), *The Theory, Practice, and Interpretation of Customary International Law* (Cambridge University Press 2022)

Merlin J-B, 'The United Nations Secretariat and Custom' in S Droubi and J d'Aspremont (eds), *International Organizations, Non-State Actors and the Formation of Customary International Law* (Manchester University Press 2019) 261

Meron T, 'Crimes under the Jurisdiction of the ICC' in H von Hebel et al (eds), *Reflections on the International Criminal Court: Essay in Honour of Adrian Bos* (TMC Asser 1999) 47

Mettraux G, 'The Definition of Crimes Against Humanity and the Question of a "Policy" Element' in LN Sadat (ed), *Forging a Convention for Crimes Against Humanity* (Cambridge University Press 2011) 142

Miles CA, 'Indeterminacy' in J d'Aspremont and S Singh (eds), *Concepts for International Law: Contributions to Disciplinary Thought* (Edward Elgar 2019) 447

Mileva N and Fortuna M, 'Environmental Protection as an Object of and Tool for Evolutionary Interpretation' in G Abi-Saab et al (eds), *Evolutionary Interpretation and International Law* (Hart 2019) 123

Minear RM, *Victor's Justice: The Tokyo War Crimes Trial* (Princeton University Press 1971)

Moeckli D, 'Interpretation of the ICESCR: Between Morality and State Consent' in D Moeckli, H Keller, and C Heri (eds), *The Human Rights Covenants at 50: Their Past, Present and Future* (Oxford University Press 2018) 51

Morgera E, 'The Ecosystem Approach and the Precautionary Principle' in E Morgera and J Razzaque (eds), *Encyclopedia of Environmental Law: Biodiversity and Nature Protection Law* (Edward Elgar 2017) 70

'The Progressive Development of International Biodiversity Law: From Nature Conservation to the Biodiversity-Human Rights-Ocean-Climate Nexus' in J Ebbeson and D Langlet (eds), *Fifty Years of International Environmental Law: Developments Since the 1972 Stockholm Conference* (Cambridge University Press 2026)

'The Relevance of the Human Right to Science for the Conservation and Sustainable Use of Marine Biodiversity of Areas Beyond National Jurisdiction: A New Legally Binding Instrument to Support Co-Production of Ocean Knowledge across Scales' in V de Lucia, A Oude Elferink, and L Ngoc Nguyen (eds), *International Law and Marine Areas beyond National Jurisdiction: Reflections on Justice, Space, Knowledge and Power* (Brill 2022) 242

Fair and Equitable Benefit-sharing in International Law (Oxford University Press 2024)

Morgera E and Lennan M, 'Ensuring Mutual Supportiveness of the Paris Agreement with other Multilateral Environmental Agreements: A Focus on Ocean-Based Climate Action' in A Zahar (ed), *Research Handbook on the Law of the Paris Agreement* (Edward Elgar 2024) 362

Morgera E and Nakamura J, 'Shedding a Light on the Human Rights of Small-scale Fisherfolk: Complementarities and Contrasts between the UN Declaration on Peasants' Rights and the Small-Scale Fisheries Guidelines' in M Alabrese et al (eds), *Commentary on the Declaration on the Rights of Peasants* (Routledge 2022) 62

Morgera E, Tsioumani E and Buck M, *Unraveling the Nagoya Protocol: A Commentary of the Protocol on Access and Benefit-Sharing to the Convention on Biological Diversity* (Martinus Nijhoff 2014) 84

Morton T, *Ecology without Nature: Rethinking Environmental Aesthetics* (Harvard University Press 2009)

Mowbray A, 'The European Court of Human Rights' Recourse to External Legal Materials When Interpreting and Applying the Right to Private Life' in C Buckley, A Donald, and P Leach (eds), *Towards Convergence in Human Rights Law: Approaches of Regional and International Systems* (Brill Nijhoff 2016) 131.

Moynier G, *Etude sur la Convention de Genève pour l'amélioration du sort des militaires blessés dans les armées en campagne: 1864 et 1869* (Librarie de J Cherbuliez 1870)

Mührel L, *The Authority of the International Committee of the Red Cross: Determining What International Humanitarian Law Is* (Brill/ Nijhoff, 2024)

Müller F, *Discours de la méthode juridique* (O Jouanjan tr, Presses Universitaires de France 1996)

Nersessian DL, *Genocide and Political Groups* (Oxford University Press 2010)

Nolan A, Freedman R, and Murphy T (eds), *The United Nations Special Procedures System* (Brill Nijhoff 2017)

Nolte G (ed), *Treaties and Subsequent Practice* (Oxford University Press 2013)

O'Connell ME, 'Historical Development and Legal Basis' in D Fleck (ed), *The Handbook of International Humanitarian Law* (4th edn, Oxford University Press 2021) 1

Orakhelashvili A, *The Interpretation of Acts and Rules in Public International Law* (Oxford University Press 2008) 394

Papanastasiou TN, *The Legal Protection of Foreign Investments Against Political Risk. Japanese Business in the Asian Energy Sector* (Quid Pro 2015)

Paparinskis M, *The International Minimum Standard of Treatment and Fair and Equitable Treatment* (Oxford University Press 2013)

Pauwelyn J and Elsig M, 'The Politics of Treaty Interpretation' in JL Dunoff and MA Pollack (eds), *Interdisciplinary Perspectives on International Law and International Relations: The State of the Art* (Cambridge University Press 2013) 445

Pauwelyn J, 'How to Win a WTO Dispute Based on Non-WTO Law? Questions of Jurisdiction and Merits' in S Griller (ed), *At the Crossroads: The World Trading System and the Doha Round* (Springer 2008) 1

Conflict of Norms in Public International Law: How WTO Law Relates to Other Rules of International Law (Cambridge University Press 2009)

Peat D and Winsdor M, 'Playing the Game of Interpretation: On Meaning and Metaphor in International Law' in A Bianchi, D Peat, and M Winsdor (eds), *Interpretation in International Law* (Oxford University Press 2015) 3

Pellet A, 'Applicable Law' in A Cassese, P Gaeta, and JRWD Jones (eds), *The Rome Statute of the International Criminal Court: A Commentary*, Vol 2 (Oxford University Press 2002) 1051

'International Legal Scholarship under Challenge' in J d'Aspremont et al (eds), *International Law as a Profession* (Cambridge University Press 2017) 117

Pictet JS (ed), *The Geneva Conventions of 12 August 1949: Commentary, Vol. I: Geneva Convention for the Amelioration of the Condition of the Wounded and Sick in Armed Forces in the Field* (ICRC 1952)

The Geneva Conventions of 12 August 1949: Commentary, Vol. II: Geneva Convention for the Amelioration of the Condition of Wounded, Sick and Shipwrecked Members of Armed Forces at Sea (ICRC 1960)

The Geneva Conventions of 12 August 1949: Commentary, Vol. III: Geneva Convention relative to the Treatment of Prisoners of War (ICRC 1960)

The Geneva Conventions of 12 August 1949: Commentary, Vol. IV: Geneva Convention relative to the Protection of Civilian Persons in Time of War (ICRC 1958)

Pisillo Mazzeschi R, *'Due Diligence' e Responsabilità Internazionale degli Stati* (Milano, Giuffrè 1989)

Polanco R, *The Return of the Home State to Investor-State Disputes: Bringing Back Diplomatic Protection?* (Cambridge University Press 2019)

Quintin A, *The Nature of International Humanitarian Law: A Permissive or Restrictive Regime?* (Elgar 2020)

Radi Y, *Rules and Practices of International Investment Law and Arbitration* (Cambridge University Press 2020)

Ramcharan B, *The Protection Role and Jurisprudence of the United Nations Human Rights Council* (Brill Nijhoff 2022)

Rees-Evans L, 'Litigating the Use of Force: Reflections on the Interaction Between Investor-State Dispute Settlement and Other Forms of International Dispute Settlement in the Context of the Conflict in Ukraine' in FK Gómez, A Gourgourinis, and C Titi (eds), *International Investment Law and the Law of Armed Conflict* (Springer 2019) 173

Reinisch A, 'Investment Disputes and Their Boundaries' in Société Française pour le Droit International (ed), *Droit des Frontières Internationales: The Law of International Borders* (Pedone 2016) 207

Roberts A, *Is International Law International?* (Oxford University Press 2017)

Rosen M, *Book of Play* (Profile Books 2020)

Rubins N QC, Papanastasiou TN, and Kinsella NS, *International Investment, Political Risk, and Dispute Resolution. A Practitioner's Guide* (2nd edn, Oxford University Press 2020)

Sadat LN, 'A Comprehensive History of the Proposed International Convention on the Prevention and Punishment of Crimes Against Humanity' in LN Sadat (ed), *Forging a Convention for Crimes Against Humanity* (2nd edn, Cambridge University Press 2013) 449

Sandoz Y et al (eds), *Commentary on the Additional Protocols of 8 June 1977 of the Geneva Conventions of 12 August 1949* (Martinus Nijhoff 1987)

Sands P, *East West Street: On the Origins of Genocide and Crimes Against Humanity* (Orion 2016)

Sassòli M, Bouvier AA, and Quintin A, *How Does Law Protect in War? Cases, Documents and Teaching Materials on Contemporary Practice in International Humanitarian Law* (3rd edn, ICRC 2011)

Sassòli M, *International Humanitarian Law: Rules, Controversies and Solutions to Problems Arising in Warfare* (Edward Elgar Publishing 2019)

Schabas W, 'Customary Law or "Judge-Made" Law: Judicial Creativity at the UN Criminal Tribunals' in J Doria et al (eds), *The Legal Regime of the International Criminal Court: Essays in Honour of Professor Igor Blishchenko*, Vol 19 (Martinus Nijhoff 2009) 77

The Customary International Law of Human Rights (Oxford University Press 2021)

The International Criminal Court: A Commentary on the Rome Statute (2nd edn, Oxford University Press 2016)

Scheinin M, 'The Art and Science of Interpretation in Human Rights Law' in B Andreassen, HO Sano, and S McInerney-Lankford (eds), *Research Methods in Human Rights: A Handbook* (Edward Elgar 2017) 17

'The Human Rights Committee's Pronouncements on the Right to an Effective Remedy: An Illustration of the Legal Nature of the Committee's Work under the Optional Protocol' in N Ando (ed), *Towards Implementing Universal Human Rights: Festschrift for the Twenty-Fifth Anniversary of the Human Rights Committee* (Brill Nijhoff 2004) 106

Schermers H and Blokker NM, *International Institutional Law* (6th edn, Martinus Nijhoff 2018)

Schill SW, 'International Investment Law and Comparative Public Law: An Introduction' in SW Schill (ed), *International Investment Law and Comparative Public Law* (Oxford University Press 2010) 29

Schlütter B, 'Aspects of Human Rights Interpretation by the UN Treaty Bodies' in H Keller and G Ulfstein (eds), *UN Human Rights Treaty Bodies: Law and Legitimacy* (Cambridge University Press 2012) 261

Schreuer CH, 'Diversity and Harmonization of Treaty Interpretation in Investment Arbitration' in M Fitzmaurice, O Elias, and P Merkouris (eds), *Treaty Interpretation and the Vienna Convention on the Law of Treaties: 30 Years on* (Brill/Nijhoff 2010) 129

Schreuerand CH et al, *The ICSID Convention: A Commentary* (2nd edn, Cambridge University Press 2010)

Seyersted F, *Common Law of International Organizations* (Brill 2008)

Shelton D, 'The Legal Status of Normative Pronouncements of Human Rights Treaty Bodies' in H Hestermeyer et al (eds), *Coexistence, Cooperation and Solidarity: Liber Amicorum Rüdiger Wolfrum* (Brill 2012) 553

Shihata I, *Legal Treatment of Foreign Investment: The World Bank Guidelines* (Brill 1993)

Sinclair I, *The Vienna Convention on the Law of Treaties* (2nd edn, Manchester University Press 1984)

Sivakumaran S, 'Impact on the Structure of International Obligations' in M Scheinin and M Kamminga (eds), *The Impact of Human Rights Law on General International Law* (Oxford University Press 2009) 146

Sorel J-M and Boré Eveno V, 'Article 31' in O Corten and P Klein (eds), *The Vienna Convention on the Law of Treaties: A Commentary* (Oxford University Press 2011) 804

Sornarajah M, *The International Law on Foreign Investment* (3rd edn, Cambridge University Press 2010)

Stahn C, 'The ICC in Its Third Decade: Setting the Scene' in C Stahn and R Braga da Silva (eds), *The International Criminal Court in its Third Decade: Reflecting on Law and Practices* (Brill 2024) 3

Stahn C and El Zeidy MM, *The International Criminal Court and Complementarity: From Theory to Practice* Vol 1 (Cambridge University Press 2012)

Swart B, Zahar A, and Sluiter G (eds), *The Legacy of the International Criminal Tribunal for the Former Yugoslavia* (Oxford University Press 2011)

Tams C, *Enforcing Obligations Erga Omnes in International Law* (Cambridge University Press 2005)

Tams CJ, Schill S, and Hofmann R, 'Radiating Effects: The Gentle Impact of International Investment Law on General International Law' in CJ Tams, S Schill, and R Hofmann (eds), *International Investment Law and General International Law: Radiating Effects* (Edward Elgar 2023) 2

Tancredi A, 'Some Thoughts on Deterritorialization and Effectiveness in International Law' in A di Stefano (ed), *A Lackland Law? Territory, Effectiveness and Jurisdiction in International and European Law* (Giappichelli 2015) 52

Tindale CW, *The Philosophy of Argument and Audience Reception* (Cambridge University Press 2015)

Trevisanut S, 'The Contribution of UNHCR to Ocean Governance' in DJ Attard, M Fitzmaurice, and A Ntovas (eds), *The IMLI Treatise on Global Ocean Governance*, Vol 2 (Oxford University Press 2018) 243

Ulfstein G, 'Individual Complaints' in H Keller and G Ulfstein (eds), *UN Human Rights Treaty Bodies: Law and Legitimacy* (Oxford University Press 2012) 73

Ünüvar G, 'The Vague Meaning of the Fair and Equitable Treatment Principle in Investment Arbitration and New Generation Clarifications' in AL Kjaer (ed), *Language and Legal Interpretation in International Law* (Oxford University Press 2022) 271

Vadi V, *Analogies in International Investment Law and Arbitration* (Cambridge University Press 2016)

Van Alebeek R and Nollkaemper A, 'The Legal Status of Decisions by Human Rights Treaty Bodies in National Law' in H Keller and G Ulfstein (eds), *UN Human Rights Treaties Bodies: Law and Legitimacy* (Cambridge University Press 2012) 356

Van Damme I, *Treaty Interpretation by the WTO Appellate Body* (Oxford University Press 2009)

Van Schaack B, *Imagining Justice for Syria* (Cambridge University Press 2020)

Venzke I, 'Sources in Interpretation Theories: The International Law-Making Process' in S Besson and J d'Aspremont (eds), *The Oxford Handbook on the Sources of International Law* (OUP 2017) 401

'The Practice of Interpretation in International Law: Strategies of Critique' in J Dunoff and MA Pollack (eds), *International Legal Theory: Foundations and Frontiers* (Cambridge University Press 2022) 305

How Interpretation Makes International Law (Oxford University Press 2012)

How Interpretation Makes International Law: On Semantic Change and Normative Twists (Oxford University Press 2012)

Villiger ME, 'The Rules on Interpretation: Misgivings, Misunderstandings, Miscarriage? The "Crucible" Intended by the International Law Commission' in E Cannizzaro (ed), *The Law of Treaties Beyond the Vienna Convention* (Oxford University Press 2011) 105

Commentary on the 1969 Vienna Convention on the Law of Treaties (Martinus Nijhoff 2009)

Commentary on the 1969 Vienna Convention on the Law of Treaties (Brill 2009)

Viñuales J (ed), *The Rio Declaration on Environment and Development: A Commentary* (Oxford University Press 2015)

Visseren-Hamakers I and Kok M, 'Introduction' in I Visseren-Hamakers and M Kok (eds), *Transforming Biodiversity Governance* (Cambridge University Press 2022) 3

Von Hebel H and Robinson D, 'Crimes within the Jurisdiction of the Court' in RS Lee (ed), *The International Criminal Court: The Making of the Rome Statute* (Kluwer Law International 1999) 79

Waibel M, 'Interpretive Communities in International Law' in A Bianchi, D Peat, and M Windsor (eds), *Interpretation in International Law* (Oxford University Press 2015) 147

Wälde TW and Weiler T, 'Investment Arbitration under the Energy Charter Treaty in the Light of New NAFTA Precedents: Towards a Global Code of

Conduct for Economic Regulation?' in G Kaufmann-Kohler and B Stucki (eds), *Investment Treaties and Arbitration* (Swiss Arbitration Association 2002) 159

Walker N, 'The Gap Between Global Law and Global Justice: A Preliminary Analysis' in N Rougham and A Halpin (eds), *In Pursuit of Pluralist Jurisprudence* (Cambridge University Press 2017) 216

Intimations of Global Law (Cambridge University Press 2014)

Weiler JHH, 'Revisiting Van Gend en Loos: Subjectifying and Objectifying the Individual' in *50ème Anniversaire de l'Arrêt Van Gend en Loos 1963–2013* (Luxembourg Office des Publications de l'Union Européenne 2013) 11

Werner W, de Hoon M, and Galán A (eds), *The Law of International Lawyers. Reading Martti Koskenniemi* (Cambridge University Press 2017)

Yudan T, *The Rome Statute as Evidence of Customary International Law* (Brill 2021)

Zidar A, 'Interpretation and the International Legal Profession: Between Duty and Aspiration' in A Bianchi, D Peat, and M Windsor (eds), *Interpretation in International Law* (Oxford University Press 2015) 133

Ziemele I, 'European Consensus and International Law' in A van Aaken and I Motoc (eds), *The European Convention on Human Rights and General International Law* (Oxford University Press 2018) 28

Zweigert K and Kötz H, *Introduction to Comparative Law* (T Weir tr, 3rd edn, Oxford University Press 1998)

Articles

Aguon J and Hunter J, 'Second Wave Due Diligence: The Case for Incorporating Free, Prior, and Informed Consent into the Deep-Sea Mining Regulatory Regime' (2019) 38 Stanford EnvtlLJ 3

Alvarez J, 'Is Investor-State Arbitration "Public"?' (2016) 7 JIDS 534

'The Return of the State' (2011) 20 Minnesota Journal of International Law 268

Álvarez L and Coolsaet B, 'Decolonizing Environmental Justice Studies: A Latin American Perspective' (2020) 31 Capitalism Nature Socialism 50

Ambos K, 'Punishment without a Sovereign. The *Ius Puniendi* Issue of International Criminal Law: A First Contribution towards a Consistent Theory of International Criminal Law' (2013) 33 OJLS 293

Andenas M and Leiss JR, 'The Systemic Relevance of "Judicial Decisions" in Article 38 of the ICJ Statute' (2017) 77 ZaöRV 907

Annacker C, 'The Legal Régime of Erga Omnes Obligations in International Law' (1993) 46 ZöR 131

Arato J, 'The Private Law Critique of International Investment Law' (2019) 113 AJIL 1

Arcuri A and Violi F, 'Reconfiguring Territoriality in International Economic Law' (2017) 47 NYBIL 175

Arowolo A and Lalude O, '"Their Color Is a Diabolic Die," Colonialism and the State of Environmental Justice in Africa' (2022) 4 Society & Sustainability 1

Azaria D, 'The Legal Significance of Expert Treaty Bodies Pronouncements for the Purpose of the Interpretation of Treaties' (2020) 22(1) ICLR 46

Banakar R, 'Power, Culture and Method in Comparative Law' (2009) 5 International Journal of Law in Context 69

Barnidge RP, 'The Due Diligence Principle in International Law' (2006) 8 ICLR 81

Barros AS and Ryngaert C, 'The Position of Member States in (Autonomous) Institutional Decision-Making: Implications for the Establishment of Responsibility' (2014) 11 IOLR 53

Bartels L, 'Applicable Law in WTO Dispute Settlement Proceedings' (2001) 35(3) JWT 499

Bassiouni MC, 'The History of the Draft Code of Crimes Against the Peace and Security of Mankind' (1993) 27 IsraelLR 247

Basu-Mellish J, 'UN Resolution 1514: The Creation of a New Post-Colonial Sovereignty' (2023) 44 TWQ 1306

Bennett N et al, 'Blue Growth and Blue Justice: Ten Risks and Solutions for the Ocean Economy' (2021) 125 Marine Policy 104387

'Environmental (In)Justice in the Anthropocene Ocean' (2022) 147 Marine Policy 105383

'Ocean Defenders and Human Rights' (2023) 9 Frontiers in Marine Science 1

'Towards a Sustainable and Equitable Blue Economy' (2019) Nature Sustainability 991

Benzing M, 'International Organizations or Institutions, Secondary Law' (2007) MPEPIL 508

Blokker N, 'International Organizations and Customary International Law: Is the International Law Commission Taking International Organizations Seriously?' (2017) 14 IOLR 1

Boyle AE, 'Climate Change, The Paris Agreement and Human Rights' (2018) 67 *ICLQ* 759

'The *Gabčikovo-Nagymaros* Case: Old Law in New Bottles' (1997) 8(1) YBIEL 13

'Globalizing Environmental Liability: The Interplay of National and International Law' (2005) 17(1) JEL 3

'Marine Pollution and the Law of the Sea Convention' (1985) 79(2) AJIL 347

Brölmann C, 'Sustainable Development Goal 6 as a Game Changer for International Water Law' (2018) 7(5) ESIL Reflections 1 <https://esil-sedi.eu/wp-content/uploads/2018/08/ESIL-Reflection-Brolmann.pdf>

Byers M, 'Conceptualising the Relationship Between Jus Cogens and Erga Omnes Rules' (1997) 66 NJIL 211

Calamita J, 'The Principle of Proportionality and the Problem of Indeterminacy in International Investment Treaties' [2014] Yearbook of International Investment Law and Policy 157

Cameron L et al, 'The Updated Commentary on the First Geneva Convention: A New Tool for Generating Respect for International Humanitarian Law' (2015) 97 IRRC 1212

'The ICRC in the First World War: Unwavering Belief in the Power of Law?' (2016) 97 IRRC 1099

Çapar G, 'The Paradox of Global Constitutionalism: Between Sectoral Integration and Legitimacy' (2024) 13(2) Global Constitutionalism 264

Carvin S, 'In Times of War the Law Is Not So Silent' (2008) 12(3) IJHR 471

Cassese A, 'The Statute of the International Criminal Court: Some Preliminary Reflections' (1999) 10(1) EJIL 144

Cassese S, 'Beyond Legal Comparison' [2012] Annuario di Diritto Comparato e di studi legislativi 387

Cavert J, 'Civil Society and Investor-State Dispute Settlement: Assessing the Social Dimensions of Investment Disputes in Latin America' (2018) 23 New Political Economy 46.

Charney JI, 'The Marine Environment and the 1982 United Nations Convention on the Law of the Sea' (1994) 28(4) International Lawyer 879

Churchill RR and Ulfstein G, 'Autonomous Institutional Arrangements in Multilateral Environmental Agreements: A Little-Noticed Phenomenon in International Law' (2000) 94 AJIL 623

Clark RS, 'Building on Article 8(2)(b)(xx) of the Rome Statute of the International Criminal Court: Weapons and Methods of Warfare' (2009) 12(3) NCLR 366

Coomans F, 'Erkenning van het recht op water als mensenrecht' (2009) 34(3) NJCM-B 249

Corkery A, 'The Contribution of the UNHCR Executive Committee to the Development of International Refugee Law' (2006) Aust ILJ 97

Corn GS, 'Principle of Humanity' (2013) MPEPIL 1810.

Crawford J and Keene A, 'Interpretation of the Human Rights Treaties by the International Court of Justice' (2019) 24 IJHR 935

Crawford J, 'Responsibility to the International Community as a Whole' (2001) 8 IJGLS 307

Creamer CD and Simmons BA, 'The Proof Is in the Process: Self-Reporting under International Human Rights Treaties (2020) 114 AJIL 1

Cryer R, 'Of Customs, Treaties, Scholars and the Gavel: The Influence of the International Criminal Tribunals on the ICRC Customary Law Study' (2006) 11(2) JCSL 239

D'Aspremont J, 'Three International Lawyers in A Hall of Mirrors' (2019) 32 LJIL 367

Danilenko GM, 'The Statute of the International Criminal Court and Third States' (1999) 21 MichJIntlL 445

Daugirdas K, 'How and Why International Law Binds International Organizations' (2016) 57 HILJ 325

De Koker C, 'Hassan v United Kingdom. The Interaction of Human Rights Law and International Humanitarian Law with regard to the Deprivation of Liberty in Armed Conflicts' (2015) 31(81) Utrecht Journal of International and European Law 90

De Wet E, 'The International Constitutional Order' (2006) 55 ICLQ 51

Deplano R, 'Assessing the Role of Resolutions in the ILC Draft Conclusions on Identification of Customary International Law' (2017) 14 IOLR 227

Desierto D and Gillespie CE, 'Evolutive Interpretation and Subsequent Practice: Interpretative Communities and Processes in the Optional Protocol to the ICESCR' (2013) 73 ZaöRV 574

Djeffal C, 'Commentaries on the Law of Treaties: A Review Essay Reflecting on the Genre of Commentaries' (2013) 24 EJIL 1223

Domínguez Redondo E, 'Rethinking the Legal Foundations of Control in International Human Rights Law: The Case of Special Procedures' (2011) 29(3) NQHR 261

Downey WG, 'Law of War and Military Necessity' (1953) 47 AJIL 251

Droege C and Giorgou E, 'How International Humanitarian Law Develops' (2022) 104 IRRC 1798

Dumberry P, 'Requiem for Crimea: Why Tribunals Should Have Declined Jurisdiction over the Claims of Ukrainian Investors Against Russian under the Ukraine–Russia BIT' (2018) 9(3) JIDS 506

Dupuy PM, 'L' unité de l' ordre juridique international' (2003) 297 RdC 9

'Reviewing the Difficulties of Codification: On Ago's Classification of Obligations of Means and Obligations of Result in Relation to State Responsibility' (1999) 10 EJIL 371

Eggett C, 'The Role of Principles and General Principles in the "Constitutional Processes" of International Law' (2019) 66 NILR 197

Ellis J, 'General Principles and Comparative Law' (2011) 22 EJIL 949

Etkin B, 'The Changing Rivers of Customary International Law: The Interpretative Process as Flux' (2022) 11(5) ESIL Reflections 1 <https://esil-sedi.eu/wp-content/uploads/2022/11/ESIL-Reflection-Basak-Etkin-FINAL.pdf>

Ferraro T, 'The ICRC's Legal Position on the Notion of Armed Conflict Involving Foreign Intervention and on Determining the IHL Applicable to this Type of Conflict' (2016) 97 IRRC 1227

Fitzmaurice G, 'The Law and Procedure of the International Court of Justice 1951–1954: Treaty Interpretation and Other Treaty Points' (1957) 33 BYBIL 211

Francioni F, 'Equity' [2020] MPEPIL 1399

Frowein J, 'Ius Cogens' (2013) MPEPIL 1437

Gaillard E, 'Thirty Years of *Lex Mercatoria*: Towards the Selective Application of Transnational Rules' (1995) 10 ICSID Review – Foreign Investment Law Journal 208

Garnett R, 'The Defence of State Immunity for Acts of Torture' (1997) 18 Aust YBIL 97

Ghazali Abu Hassan A, 'Military Necessity and the Restriction on Methods and Means of Warfare' (2006) 2 JIS 23

Golay C, Mahon C, and Cismas I, 'The Impact of the UN Special Procedures on the Development and Implementation of Economic, Social and Cultural Rights' (2011) 15 IJHR 299

Guillaume G, 'The Use of Precedent by International Judges and Arbitrators' (2011) 2 JIDS 5

Guzman AT, 'Why LDCs Sign Treaties That Hurt Them: Explaining the Popularity of Bilateral Investment Treaties' (1998) 38 VJIL 639

Hajjar L, 'The Counterterrorism War Paradigm versus International Humanitarian Law: The Legal Contradictions and Global Consequences of the US "War on Terror"' (2019) 44(4) LSI 922

Hamley G, 'The Implications of Seabed Mining in the Area for the Human Right to Health' (2022) 31 RECIEL 389

Handl G, 'International Accountability for Transboundary Environmental Harm Revisited: What Role for 'State Liability'?' (2007) 37(2–3) EP&L 116

'Territorial Sovereignty and the Problem of Transnational Pollution' (1975) 69 AJIL 50

Happ R and Wuschka S, 'Horror Vacui: Or Why Investment Treaties Should Apply to Illegally Annexed Territories' (2016) 33(3) JIntArb 245

Hart HLA, 'Positivism and the Separation of Law and Morals' (1957–58) HLR 593

Helfer LR and Voeten E, 'Walking Back Human Rights in Europe?' (2020) 31(3) EJIL 797

Henckaerts J-M, 'Bringing the Commentaries on the Geneva Conventions and Their Additional Protocols into the Twenty-First Century' (2012) 94 IRRC 1551

Herbet I and Drevon J, 'Engaging Armed Groups at the International Committee of the Red Cross: Challenges, Opportunities and COVID-19' (2020) 102 IRRC 1021

Herdegen M, 'Interpretation in International Law' (2020) MPEPIL 723

Hernández G, 'Law's Determinability: Indeterminacy, Interpretative Authority, and the International Legal System' (2022 69 NILR 191

Hill-Cawthorne L, 'Common Article 1 of the Geneva Conventions and the Method of Treaty Interpretation' (2023) 72 ICLQ 869

Hills J and Maharaj P, 'Designing Transdisciplinarity for Transformative Ocean Governance' (2023) 10 Frontiers in Marine Sciences 1

Hochmayr G, 'Applicable law in Practice and Theory: Interpreting Article 21 of the ICC Statute' (2014) 12(4) JICJ 655

Howse R and Mavroidis PC, 'Europe's Evolving Regulatory Strategy for GMOs: The Issue of Consistency with WTO Law: of Kine and Brine' (2000) 24 Fordham IntlLJ 317

Huneus A and Rask Madsen M, 'Between Universalism and Regional Law and Politics: A Comparative History of American, European, and African Human Rights Systems' (2018) 16(1) International Journal of Constitutional Law 136

ICRC, 'Le Comité international et la Conférence de 1906' (1906) 37 Bulletin 270

'Prof Ernest Röthlisberger: La Nouvelle Convention de Genève' (1908) 39 Bulletin 254

Jacobs FG, 'Varieties of Approach to Treaty Interpretation' (1969) 18(2) ICLQ 318

Jain N, 'Interpretive Divergence' (2017) 57(1) VJIL 45

Jalloh CC and Sadat LN (eds), 'Special Issue on the ILC Draft Articles on Prevention and Punishment of Crimes Against Humanity' (2020) 6 African Journal of International Criminal Justice 75

Jalloh CC and Sadat LN, 'Introduction to the Symposium on a Way Forward: Academic and Practitioner Perspectives on the ILC Draft Articles on Prevention and Punishment of Crimes Against Humanity as adopted on Second Reading' (2020) 6 African Journal of International Criminal Justice 79

Jenks W, 'The Conflict of Law-Making Treaties' (1953) 29 BYBIL 401

Kälin W, 'Human Rights Treaties within the UPR Process: Opportunities and Limits of Intergovernmental Monitoring of Human Rights' (2017) 60 JYBIL 243

Kleiner C and Costamagna F, 'Territoriality in Investment Arbitration: The Case of Financial Instruments' (2018) 9 JIDS 315

Koskenniemi M, 'The Politics of International Law: 20 Years Later' (2009) 20 EJIL 1

Kotzur M, 'Good Faith (Bona Fide)' [2009] MPEPIL 1412

Kozłowski A, 'Systematicity of General Principles of (International) Law: An Outline' (2017) 37 PYBIL 225

Kreß C and Garibian S (eds), 'Special Issue: Laying the Foundations for a Convention on Crimes Against Humanity' (2018) 16 JICJ 679

Kritsiotis D, 'Imagining the International Community' (2002) 13 EJIL 961

Kulovesi K, Mehling M, and Morgera E, 'Global Environmental Law: Context and Theory, Challenge and Promise' (2019) 8 TEL 405

Kupiec JA, 'Returning to Principles of "Fairness and Justice": The Role of Investment-Backed Expectations in Total Regulatory Taking Claims' (2008) 43 Boston College Law Review 865

Lauterpacht H, 'Restrictive Interpretation and the Principle of Effectiveness in the Interpretation of Treaties' (1949) 26 BYBIL 48

Legum B, 'Federalism, NAFTA Chapter Eleven and the Jay Treaty of 1794' (2001) 95 ASIL Proc 202

Lekkas S-I and Merkouris P, 'Interpretation of International Law: Rules, Content, and Evolution' (2022) 69 NILR 183

Lemaire A, 'Le nouveau visage de l' arbitrage entre État et investisseur étranger: le chapitre 11 de l' ALENA' [2001] Revue de l'arbitrage 43

Lemos M, 'The Appeals Chamber's Jurisdictional Judgment in *Abd-Al-Rahman* and the Issue of Applicable Law at the International Criminal Court' (2023) 22 Chinese JIL 223

Lennan M and Morgera E, 'The Glasgow Climate Conference (COP26)' (2022) 37 IJMCL 137

Linderfalk U, 'Is Treaty Interpretation an Art or a Science? International Law and Rational Decision Making' (2015) 26 EJIL 169

Lombard M et al, 'Principles for Transformative Ocean Governance' (2023) Nature Sustainability 1587

Longuet S et al, 'Conference on the ICRC Updated Commentary on the First Geneva Convention: Capturing 60 Years of Practice' (2017–18) 56 MLLWR 1

Luban D, 'A Theory of Crimes Against Humanity' (2004) 29 YaleJIntlL 85

Lubell N, 'Challenges in Applying Human Rights Law to Armed Conflict' (2005) 87 IRRC 737

Lupin Townsend D, 'Silencing, Consultation and Indigenous Descriptions of the World' (2019) 10 JHRE 193

Mačák K and Policinski E, 'In Pursuit of a Treaty's Soul: A Study of the Object and Purpose of the Fourth Geneva Convention' (2024) 73 ICLQ 385

Mackenzie-Gray Scott R, 'Due Diligence as a Secondary Rule of General International Law' (2021) 34 LJIL 343

Marceau G, 'A Call for Coherence in International Law: Praises for the Prohibition Against "Clinical Isolation" WTO Dispute Settlement' (1999) 33(5) JWT 87

'Conflicts of Norms and Conflicts of Jurisdictions: The Relationship Between the WTO Agreement and MEAs and Other Treaties' (2001) 35(6) JWT 1081

'The WTO Dispute Settlement and Human Rights' (2002) 13 EJIL 753

Marceau G and Gonzalez-Calatayud A, 'The Relationship Between Dispute Settlement Mechanisms of Multilateral Environment Agreements (MEAs) and Those of the WTO' (2002) 11(3) RECIEL 275

Marceau G and Trachtman JP, 'A Map of the World Trade Organization Law of Domestic Regulation of Goods: The Technical Barriers to Trade Agreement, the Sanitary and Phytosanitary Measures Agreement, and the General Agreement on Tariffs and Trade' (2014) 48(2) JWT 351

Marong ABM, 'The ILC Draft Articles on Crimes Against Humanity: An African Perspective' (2020) 6 African Journal of International Criminal Justice 93
McCorquodale R, 'An Inclusive International Legal System' (2004) LJIL 477
McDonald N, 'The Role of Due Diligence in International Law' (2019) 68(4) ICLQ 1041
McGrogan D, 'On the Interpretation of Human Rights Treaties and Subsequent Practice' (2014) 32(4) NQHR 352
McLachlan C, 'The Principle of Systemic Integration and Article 31(3)(c) of the Vienna Convention' (2005) 54 ICLQ 279
Mechlem K, 'Treaty Bodies and the Interpretation of Human Rights' (2009) 42 Vanderbilt Journal of Transnational Law 905
Merkouris P, 'Debating Interpretation: On the Road to Ithaca' (2022) 35 LJIL 461
'Interpreting the Customary Rules on Interpretation' (2017) 19 ICLR 126
'The Principle of Systemic Integration' [2021] MPEiPro 2866
Meron T, 'On a Hierarchy of International Human Rights' (1986) 80 AJIL 1
Mettraux G, 'Crimes Against Humanity in the Jurisprudence of the International Criminal Tribunals for the Former Yugoslavia and for Rwanda' (2002) 43 HILJ 237
Mitchell RB et al, 'What we Know and Could Know About International Environmental Agreements' (2020) 20(1) Global Environmental Politics 103
Modirzadeh NK and Lewis DA, 'Humanitarian Values in a Counterterrorism Era' (2022) 103 IRRC 403
Mohr C and Policinski E, 'From the Gilded Age to the Digital Age: The Evolution of ICRC Legal Commentaries' (2022) 104 IRRC 1898
Morgera E and Lennan M, 'Strengthening Intergenerational Equity at the Ocean-Climate Nexus: Reflections on the UNCRC General Comment No 26' (2022) 52 EP&L 445
Morgera E and Lily H, 'Public Participation at the International Seabed Authority: An International Human Rights Law Analysis' (2022) 31 RECIEL 374
Morgera E et al, 'Addressing the Ocean-Climate Nexus in the BBNJ Agreement: Strategic Environmental Assessments, Human Rights and Equity in Ocean Science' (2023) 38 IJMCL 447
'Dawn of a New Day? The Evolving Relationship Between the Convention on Biological Diversity and International Human Rights Law' (2018) 54 Wake Forest Law Review 691
'Global Environmental Law and the Comparative Legal Method(s)' (2015) RECIEL 254
'Justice, Equity and Benefit-Sharing Under the Nagoya Protocol to the Convention on Biological Diversity' (2015) IYBIL 113
'Ocean-based Climate Action and Human Rights Implications under the International Climate Change Regime' (2023) 38 IJMCL 411

'Re-imagining the Future of International Environmental Law Through Children's Human Rights' (2023) 53 EP&L 307

'The Need for an International Legal Concept of Fair and Equitable Benefit-sharing' (2016) 27 EJIL 353

'Under the Radar: The Role of Fair and Equitable Benefit-sharing in Protecting and Realizing Human Rights connected to Natural Resources' (2019) 23 IJHR 1098

Nah A et al, 'A Research Agenda for the Protection of Human Rights Defenders' (2013) 5 JHRP 522

Nakamura J et al, 'International Legal Responses for Protecting Fishers' Fundamental Rights Impacted by a Changing Ocean' (2023) 38 IJMCL 516

Nakamura J, Diz D, and Morgera E, 'International Legal Requirements for Environmental and Socio-cultural Assessments for Large-scale Industrial Fisheries' (2022) 31 RECIEL 336

Niner HJ et al, 'Issues of Context, Capacity and Scale: Essential Conditions and Missing Links for a Sustainable Blue Economy' (2022) 130 Environmental Science and Policy 25

O'Flaherty M, 'The Concluding Observations of the United Nations Human Rights Treaty Bodies' (2006) 27 HRLR 27

Okafor OC, 'The Future of the Human Rights Council: Insights at the Inter-Luminated Juncture of Thought and Experience' (2021) 23 MPYBUNL 40

Okowa P, 'Procedural Obligations in International Environmental Agreements' (1996) 67 BYBIL 275

Ortino F, 'Refining the Content and Role of Investment "Rules" and "Standards": A New Approach to International Investment Treaty Making' (2013) ICSID Review – Foreign Investment Law Journal 152

Palchetti P, 'Making and Enforcing Procedural Law at the International Court of Justice' (2019) 61 QIL 5

Palmieri D, 'An Institution Standing the Test of Time? A Review of 150 Years of the History of the International Committee of the Red Cross' (2012) 94 IRRC 1273

Pan K, 'Difference Between the ICJ and the CERD Committee: A Comment on the *Application of the International Convention on the Elimination of All Forms of Racial Discrimination (Qatar v United Arab Emirates)* Case' (2022) 21 Chinese JIL 195

Papanastasiou TN, 'The Role of Human Rights in International Investment Arbitration: Arguments Raised by the Parties and Procedural Implications' (2022) 21 LPICT 149

Paparinskis M, 'Investment Treaty Arbitration and the (New) Law of State Responsibility' (2013) 24 EJIL 617

Pavoni R, 'Mutual Supportiveness as a Principle of Interpretation and Law-Making: A Watershed for the WTO-and-Competing-Regimes Debate?' (2010) 21 EJIL 649

Peat D, 'Disciplining Rules? Compliance, the Rules of Interpretation, and the Evaluative Dimension of Articles 31 and 32 of the VCLT' (2022) 69 NILR 221

'International Investment Law and the Public Law Analogy: The Fallacies of the General Principles Method' (2018) 9 JIDS 654

Pecoraro A, 'Law of the Sea and Investment Protection in Deep Seabed Mining' (2020) 19 MJIL 530

Pellet A, 'Comments in Response to Christine Chinkin and in Defense of *Jus Cogens* as the Best Bastion against the Excesses of Fragmentation' (2006) 27 FYBIL 83

Pereira T and Erwin K, 'Surfacing Solidarity Praxis in Transdisciplinary Research for Blue Justice' (2023) 19 Ecosystems and People 2260502

Peters A, 'Humanity as the A and Ω of Sovereignty' (2009) 20 EJIL 513

Petit R and Jain N, 'Preserving the Rule of Law in the Age of the "War on Terror": Lessons from the Experience of International Criminal Tribunals' (2008) 39 STLP 67

Plakokefalos I, 'Prevention Obligations in International Environmental Law' (2012) 23(1) YBIEL 3

'Seabed Disputes Chamber of the International Tribunal for the Law of the Sea: Responsibilities and Obligations of States, Sponsoring Persons, and Entities, with Respect to Activities in the Area' (2012) 24(1) JEL 133

Pocar F, 'International Criminal Justice and the Unifying Role of Customary Law' (2016) 21(2–3) Uniform LR 171

'Transformation of Customary Law Through ICC Practice' (2018) 112 AJIL 182

Potestà G, 'Legitimate Expectations in Investment Treaty Law: Understanding the Roots and the Limits of a Controversial Concept' (2013) 28 ICSID Review – Foreign Investment Law Journal 88

Quénivet N, 'Binding the United Nations to Customary (Human Rights) Law' (2020) 17 IOLR 379

Rachovitsa A, 'The Principle of Systemic Integration in International Human Rights Law' (2017) 66 ICLQ 557

Rasulov A, 'Revisiting State Succession to Humanitarian Treaties: Is There a Case for Automaticity?' (2003) 14 EJIL 141

Reitz JC, 'How to Do Comparative Law (1998) 46 AJCL 617

Repousis OG, 'On Territoriality and International Investment Law: Applying China's Investment Treaties to Hong Kong and Macao' (2015) 37 MichJIntlL 113

Rioseco S, 'Conferences of the Parties Beyond International Environmental Law: How COPs Influence the Content and Implementation of their Parent Treaties' (2023) 36 (3) LJIL 699

Roberts A, 'Clash of Paradigms: Actors and Analogies Shaping the Investment Treaty System' (2013) 45 AJIL 45

Robson V, 'The Common Approach to Article 1: The Scope of Each State's Obligation to Ensure Respect for the Geneva Conventions' (2020) 25(1) JCSL 101

Rogers CA, 'Reconceptualizing the Party-Appointed Arbitrator and the Meaning of Impartiality' (2023) 64 HarvILJ 137

Ronen Y, '*Silent Enim Leges Inter Arma* – but Beware the Background Noise: Domestic Courts as Agents of Development of the Law on the Conduct of Hostilities' (2013) 26 LJIL 599

Sadat LN and Carden SR, 'The New International Criminal Court: An Uneasy Revolution' (2000) 88(3) Geo LJ 381

Sadat LN, 'A Contextual and Historical Analysis of the International Law Commission's 2017 Draft Articles for a New Global Treaty on Crimes Against Humanity' (2018) 16 JICJ 683

'Crimes Against Humanity in the Modern Age' (2013) 107 AJIL 334

'Custom, Codification and Some Thoughts About the Relationship Between the Two: Article 10 of the ICC Statute' (2000) 49(4) DePaul LR 909

'Putting Peacetime First: Crimes Against Humanity and the Civilian Population Requirement' (2017) 31 Emory IntlLRev 197

'The Conferred Jurisdiction of the International Criminal Court' (2023) 99 Notre Dame LRev 549

'The Forgotten Crime: Forging a Convention for Crimes Against Humanity' (2024) 56 CasWResJIntL 523

Sadat Wexler L, 'The Interpretation of the Nuremberg Principles by the French Court of Cassation: From *Touvier* to *Barbie* and Back Again' (1994) 32 ColJTransnatlL 289

Salgado Levy C, 'Drafting and Interpreting International Investment Agreements from a Sustainable Development Perspective' (2015) 3(1) GroJIL 59

Salomon ME, 'From NIEO to Now and the Unfinishable Story of Economic Justice' (2013) 62 ICLQ 31

Schachter O, 'The Development of International Law Through the Legal Opinions of the United Nations Secretariat' (1948) 25 BYBIL 91

Scheidel A et al, 'Environmental Conflicts and Defenders: A Global Overview' (2020) 63 Global Environmental Change 102104

Schill SW, 'System-Building in Investment Treaty Arbitration and Lawmaking' (2011) 12 German Law Journal 1083

Schmitt MN and Watts S, 'Common Article 1 and the Duty to "Ensure Respect"' (2020) 96 ILS 674

Schwebel SM, 'The Effect of Resolutions of the UN General Assembly on Customary International Law' in (1979) 73 ASIL Proc 301

Schwelb E, 'Crimes Against Humanity' (1946) 23 BYBIL 178

Sepulveda Amor B, 'The NAFTA and the Claims of Mexican Jurisdiction' (1997) 19 Houston JIntlL 565

Shah S and Sivakumaran S, 'The Use of International Human Rights Law in the Universal Periodic Review' (2021) 21 HRLR 301

Shaw GJ, 'The 2022 ICSID Rules: A Leap Toward Greater Transparency in ICSID Arbitration' (2023) 38 ICSID Review – Foreign Investment Law Journal 54

Shelton D, 'Normative Hierarchy in International Law' (2006) 100 AJIL 291

'Stockholm Declaration (1972) and Rio Declaration (1992)' [2008] MPEPIL 1608

Shields S et al, 'Children's Human Right to be Heard at the Ocean-Climate Nexus' (2023) 38 IJMCL 545

Shirlow E, 'Three Manifestations of Transparency in International Investment Law: A Story of Sources, Stakeholders and Structures' (2017) 8 Gottingen Journal of International Law 73

Sholz W, 'International Regulation of Foreign Direct Investment' (1998) 31 Cornell IntlLJ 485

Sicilianos LA, 'Evolutive Interpretation of the ECHR and Beyond: Recent Developments in the Case-Law of the European Court of Human Rights' (2020) 40 HRLJ 1

Simon-Lledó E et al, 'Biological Effects 26 Years after Simulated Deep-Sea Mining' (2019) 9 Scientific Reports 8040

Singh N, 'Environmental Justice, Degrowth and Post-Capitalist Futures' (2019) 163 Ecological Economics 138

Sohn LB, 'The Stockholm Declaration on Human Environment' (1973) 14(3) HILJ 423

Ssenjonyo M, 'Reflections on State Obligations with Respect to Economic, Social and Cultural Rights in International Human Rights Law' (2011) 25 IJHR 969

Strand M et al, 'Protecting Children's Rights to Development and Culture by Re-imagining "Ocean Literacies"' (2023) 31 International Journal of Children's Rights 941

'Transdisciplinarity in Transformative Ocean Governance Research: Reflections of Early Career Researchers' (2022) 79 ICES Journal of Marine Science 2163

Switzer S, Morgera E, and Webster E, 'Casting the Net Wider? The Transformative Potential of Integrating Human Rights into the Implementation of the WTO Agreement on Fisheries Subsidies' (2022) 31 RECIEL 360

Talmon S, 'Determining Customary International Law: The ICJ's Methodology Between Induction, Deduction and Assertion' (2015) 26(2) EJIL 417

Tamada D, 'War in Ukraine and Implications for International Investment Law' (2024) 26 ICLR 187

Tanaka Y, 'Reflections on Time Elements on the International Law of the Environment' (2013) ZaöRV 139

Telford TG and Ures HA, 'The Role of Incentives in Foreign Direct Investment' (2001) 23(4) Loyola International and Comparative Law Review 605

Temper L, McGarry D, and Weber L, 'From Academic to Political Rigour: Insights from the "Tarot" of Transgressive Research' (2019) 164 Ecological Economics 106379

Titi C, 'Investment Treaty Arbitration Caught in the Public-Private Law Divide' (2024) 45 MichJIntlL 441

Tridgell J, 'Prosecutor v Ntaganda: The End of Impunity for Sexual Violence Against Child Soldiers?' (2017) 23 Aust ILJ 153

Van Schaack B, 'Crimes Against Humanity in the 'Western and Other' Group of States: A Continuing Tradition' (2020) 6 African Journal of International Criminal Justice 136

Venzke I, 'Authoritative interpretation' (2018) MPEPIL 3528

Verdross A, 'Jus Dispositivum and Jus Cogens in International Law' (1966) 60 AJIL 55

Vidmar J, 'Unilateral Revocability in Wightman: Fixing Article 50 with Constitutional Tools' (2019) 15 ECLR 359

Vierdag EW, 'The Time of the "Conclusion" of a Multilateral Treaty: Article 30 of the Vienna Convention on the Law of Treaties and Related Provisions' (1988) 64 BYBIL 100

Waibel M, 'Demystifying the Art of Interpretation' (2011) 22 EJIL 571

Wald PM, 'Genocide and Crimes Against Humanity' (2007) 6 WashUGlobalStudLRev 621

Wälde TW, 'Investment Arbitration under the Energy Charter Treaty' (1996) 12(4) Arbitration International 429

Wang Y, 'The Fight Between Interpretation and Modification: A Critique of Sanum v Laos' (2020) 35(1) ICSID Review – Foreign Investment Law Journal 236

Webb Yackee J, 'Do Bilateral Investment Treaties Promote Foreign Direct Investment? Some Hints from Alternative Evidence' (2010) 51 VJIL 397

Webster E and Morgera E, 'Transformative Capacity Building around a Right to Healthy Environment: What Role for Dignity as a Human Rights Value?' (2021) 9 Griffith Journal of Law and Human Dignity 55

Weigend T, '"In General a Principle of Justice": The Debate on the "Crime Against Peace" in the Wake of the Nuremberg Judgment' (2012) 10 JICJ 41

Weil P, 'Problèmes relatifs aux contrats passés entre un Etat et un particulier' (1969) 128 RdC 94

Weiss T et al, 'The "Third" United Nations' (2009) 15 Global Governance 123.

Werner G, 'Un commentaire du Code des prisonniers de guerre' (1932) 159 Bulletin 199

Werner W, 'Custom as Rewritten Law: The Text and Paratext of Restatement Reports' (2020) 11(3) ESIL Reflections 1 <https://esil-sedi.eu/wp-content/uploads/2022/09/ESIL-Reflection-Wouter-Werner.pdf>

Wilson D, 'European Colonisation, Law, and Indigenous Marine Dispossession: Historical Perspectives on the Construction and Entrenchment of Unequal Marine Governance' (2021) 20 Maritime Studies 387

Wolfrum R, 'General International Law (Principles, Rules and Standards)' [2012] MPEPIL 1408

Worster WT, 'The Divergence Between the ICJ and the Committee on the Elimination of Racial Discrimination regarding Nationality-Based Discrimination' 26(13) ASIL Insights 1 (*ASIL Insights*, 22 November 2022) <https://www.asil.org/insights/volume/26/issue/13>

Wright LHV, Tisdall K, and Moore N, 'Taking Emotions Seriously: Fun and Pride in Participatory Research' (2021) 41 Emotion, Space and Society 100836

Wyborn C et al, 'Imagining Transformative Biodiversity Futures' (2020) 3 Nature Sustainability 670

Zgaga S, 'Military Necessity in International Criminal Law' (2012) 17 Review of Comparative Law 109

Zheng CR, 'The Territoriality Requirement in Investment Treaties: A Constraint on Jurisdictional Expansionism' (2016) 34 SingLR 139

Zwanenburg M, 'The "External Element" of the Obligation to Ensure Respect for the Geneva Conventions: A Matter of Treaty Interpretation' (2021) 97 ILS 621

PhD Theses/Unpublished/Online/Working Paper Series

Eggett C, 'General Principles as Systemic Elements of International Law' (PhD thesis, University of Maastricht 2021)

Hesselman M, 'Human Rights and Access to Modern Energy Services' (PhD thesis, University of Groningen 2023)

Kuchmienko O, 'To BIT or not to BIT? The Effects of Changes in Effective Control and Temporal Scope on Investment Tribunal Jurisdiction under Ukraine-Russia BIT' (master's thesis, Uppsala University 2019)

McGuckin B, 'The Conflict Between Armed Conflicts: Dispensing with the Distinction Between International and Non-international Armed Conflicts' (2018) Durham Global Security Institute Working Paper No 1

Websites

Albar R, 'Common Heritage of Mankind at the Expense of Indigenous People's Rights? BBNJ Treaty and Beyond' (*HHRJ*, 25 October 2023) <https://journals.law.harvard.edu/hrj/2023/10/common-heritage-of-mankind-at-the-expense-of-indigenous-peoples-rights-bbnj-treaty-and-beyond/>

Amann DM, 'Commenting on the ICRC Geneva Commentaries' (*Diane Marie Amann*, 15 March 2016) <https://dianemarieamann.com/2016/03/15/commenting-on-the-icrc-geneva-commentaries-30-march-in-d-c/>

Atlantic Council and Global Justice Center, 'Amending the Crime Against Humanity of Apartheid to Recognize and Encompass Gender Apartheid'

(*End Gender Apartheid*, April 2025) <https://endgenderapartheid.today/download/brief/Gender%20Apartheid%20Brief.pdf.>

Case Matrix Network, 'Implementing the Rome Statute of the International Criminal Court' (*ICC Legal Tools Database*, September 2017) 22 <https://www.legal-tools.org/en/doc/e05157/>

Children's Environmental Rights Initiative, 'Centring Child Rights at COP28: Asks of UNFCCC Party Negotiators' (*Children's Environmental Right Initiative*, 2023) <https://ceri-coalition.org/wp-content/uploads/2023/11/CERI-Policy-Brief_Centring-Child-Rights-at-COP28.pdf>

Cotula L and Webster E, 'COVID-19 and the Sites of Rights Resilience' (*University of Strathclyde Law School Blog*, 2020) <https://www.strath.ac.uk/humanities/lawschool/blog/covid-19andthesitesofrightsresilience/>

Crimes against Humanity Initiative, 'Proposed International Convention on the Prevention and Punishment of Crimes Against Humanity' (*Washington University in St. Louis*, August 2010) <https://sites.wustl.edu/crimesagainsthumanity/convention-text>

Eggett C and Thin S, 'Clarification and Conflation: Obligations Erga Omnes in the Chagos Opinion' (*EJIL: Talk!*, 21 May 2019) <https://www.ejiltalk.org/clarification-and-conflation-obligations-erga-omnes-in-the-chagos-opinion/>

Febrica S, 'Key Messages from the UNEP Winter/Summer School on Human Rights "From Oceans to Taps" (Part: 2) Children, Ocean Defenders, and Plastics" (*One Ocean Hub*, 30 August 2022) <https://oneoceanhub.org/key-messages-from-the-unep-winter-summer-school-on-human-rights-from-oceans-to-taps-part-2-children-ocean-defenders-and-plastics/>

'One Ocean Hub Highlights Role and Needs of Small-scale Fishers at UN Consultations on Environmental Human Rights Defenders' (*One Ocean Hub*, 28 May 2021) <https://oneoceanhub.org/one-ocean-hub-highlights-role-and-needs-of-small-scale-fishers-at-un-consultations-on-environmental-human-rights-defenders/>

'The Food and Agriculture Organization and the One Ocea Hub Co-organized a Workshop on Sustainable Small-Scale Fisheries Law' (*One Ocean Hub*, 28 April 2021) <https://oneoceanhub.org/1939-2/>

Forst M, 'Statement in Support of Ocean Defenders and Protest at Sea' (*Youtube*, 19 March 2024) <https://www.youtube.com/watch?v=AFCnFydWvic>

Fouchard Papaefstratiou A, 'Crimea as Russian Territory for the Purposes of the Russia-Ukraine BIT: Consent v International Law?' (*Kluwer Arbitration Blog*, 5 February 2023) <https://arbitrationblog.kluwerarbitration.com/2023/02/05/crimea-as-russian-territory-for-the-purposes-of-the-russia-ukraine-bit-consent-v-international-law/>

García Escobar G, 'ICJ's Judgment in Ukraine v Russia regarding CERD's Scope of Racial Discrimination: ICJ's Approach to CERD Committee's Views' (*EJILTalk!*, 29 February 2024) <https://www.ejiltalk.org/icjs-judgment-in-

ukraine-v-russia-regarding-cerds-scope-of-racial-discrimination-icjs-approach-to-cerd-committees-views/>

Global Arbitration Review, 'Q&A with Professor Pierre Lalive' <https://cdn.arbitration-icca.org/s3fs-public/document/media_document/media012319104758800008_10_14_gar-pla_interview.pdf>

Global Justice Center, 'Joint Statement in Support of Progress toward a Crimes Against Humanity Treaty' (*Crimes Against Humanity Treaty Now*, 2025) <https://cahtreatynow.org/joint-statement-in-support-of-progress-toward-a-crimes-against-humanity-treaty/>

Global Witness, 'Defending Tomorrow: The Climate Crisis and Threats Against Land and Environmental Defenders' (*Global Witness*, 29 July 2020) <https://www.globalwitness.org/en/campaigns/environmental-activists/defending-tomorrow>

Gourgourinis A, 'The Nature of Investor's Rights under Investment Treaties: A Rejoinder to Martins Paparinskis' (*EJIL:Talk!*, 31 October 2013) <https://www.ejiltalk.org/the-nature-of-investors-rights-under-investment-treaties-a-rejoinder-to-martins-paparinskis/>

Greenwood C, 'Sources of International Law: An Introduction' (*United Nations Treaty Collection*, 2008) <https://legal.un.org/avl/pdf/ls/greenwood_outline.pdf>

Heller KJ, 'First Thoughts from Academia on the Updated GCI Commentary' (*OpinioJuris*, 22 July 2016) <http://opiniojuris.org/2016/07/22/multi-blog-series-first-thoughts-on-the-updated-gci-commentary-from-academia>

Hepburn J and Kabra R, 'Investigation: Further Russia Investment Treaty Decisions Uncovered, Offering Broader Window into Arbitrators' Approaches to Crimea Controversy' (*Investment Arbitration Reporter*, 17 November 2017) <https://www.iareporter.com/articles/investigation-further-russia-investment-treaty-decisions-uncovered-offering-broader-window-into-arbitrators-approaches-to-crimea-controversy/>

ICC, 'Assembly of States Parties' (*ICC*, 2025) <https://asp.icc-cpi.int/assembly>

ICRC, '2013 Arms Trade Treaty' (*ICRC*, 21 April 2021) <https://www.icrc.org/sites/default/files/document/file_list/dp_consult_41_2013_arms_trade_treaty_web_0.pdf>

'Exploring Humanitarian Law (EHL)' (*ICRC*, 5 September 2023) <https://www.icrc.org/en/document/exploring-humanitarian-law-ehl-resource-pack>

'Gendered Impacts of Armed Conflict and Implications for the Application of International Humanitarian Law' (*ICRC*, 29 June 2022) <https://www.icrc.org/fr/publication/4634-gendered-impact-armed-conflict-and-ihl>

'International Humanitarian Law and the Challenges of Contemporary Armed Conflicts: Recommitting to Protection in Armed Conflict on the 70th Anniversary of the Geneva Conventions' (*ICRC*, 22 November 2019) <https://www.icrc.org/en/document/icrc-report-ihl-and-challenges-contemporary-armed-conflicts>

'Legal Review of New Weapons' (*ICRC*, 29 November 2021) <https://www.icrc.org/sites/default/files/document/file_list/dp_consult_12_legal_review_of_new_weapons.pdf>

'National Committees for the Implementation of International Humanitarian Law' (*ICRC*, 21 May 2021) <https://www.icrc.org/sites/default/files/document/file_list/dp_consult_14_national_committees_for_the_implementation_of_ihl.pdf>

ICTR, 'Key Figures of Cases' (*International Residual Mechanism for Criminal Tribunals*, October 2019) <https://unictr.irmct.org/en/cases/key-figures-cases>

ICTY, 'Infographic: ICTY Facts & Figures' (*International Residual Mechanism for Criminal Tribunals*, 2025) <https://www.icty.org/en/content/infographic-icty-facts-figures>

ILC, 'Analytical Guide to the Work of the International Law Commission: Subsequent Agreement and Subsequent Practice in Relation to Interpretation of Treaties' (*ILC*, 5 July 2024) <https://legal.un.org/ilc/guide/1_11.shtml>

Kuchmiienko O, 'The ECHR findings in the Case Ukraine and The Netherlands v Russia' Dated January 25, 2023 and Investment Arbitration "Crimean Cases": Any Positive News for Ukrainian Investors?' (*Kluwer Arbitration Blog*, 13 March 2023) <https://arbitrationblog.kluwerarbitration.com/2023/03/13/the-echr-findings-in-the-case-ukraine-and-the-netherlands-v-russia-dated-january-25-2023-andinvestment-arbitration-crimean-cases-any-positive-news-for-ukrainian-investors/ >

Lapidor E, 'New Developments in ICRC Commentaries to the POW Convention' (*Just Security*, 18 June 2020) <https://www.justsecurity.org/70863/pow-geneva-convention-commentary-highlights-of-new-developments/>

Leikin E et al, 'A Decade of Investment Treaty Claims Arising from Russia's Invasion of Ukraine: Lessons and Expectations (Part I)' (*Freshfields Risk & Compliance*, 2024) <https://riskandcompliance.freshfields.com/post/102j57i/a-decade-of-investment-treaty-claims-arising-from-russias-invasion-of-ukraine-l>

Malinde Lancaster A et al, 'Joint Submission to the Inter-American Court of Human Rights' (*One Ocean Hub*, 18 December 2023) <https://oneoceanhub.org/wp-content/uploads/2024/02/Alana_Lancaster_Final-Updated-Joint-Submission-To-The-Inter-American-Court-Amicii-Of-The-FoL-OOH-RenewTT-GNHRE-Caribbean-ILA-Caribbean_12.02.24.pdf>

McGarry D, Erwin K, and Morgera E, 'What Is Environmental Justice: Understandings from the Global South' (*One Ocean Hub*, 2023) <https://oneoceanhub.org/publications/infosheet-what-is-environmental-justice-understandings-from-the-global-south/>

Meier MW, 'The Updated GCIII Commentary: A Flawed Methodology?' (*Lieber Institute – West Point*, 3 February 2021) <https://lieber.westpoint.edu/updated-gciii-commentary-flawed-methodology>

Millenium Ecosystem Assessment, 'Living Beyond Our Means: Natural Assets and Human Wellbeing' (2005) <https://documents1.worldbank.org/curated/en/366241468134713390/pdf/453520WP0BOX0334087B01PUBLIC1.pdf>

Morgera E and Shields S, 'Policy Brief: Integrating the General Comment 26 on Children's Rights and a Healthy Environment in the Implementation of the FAO Guidelines on Small-scale Fisheries' (*One Ocean Hub*, 5 February 2024) <https://oneoceanhub.org/wp-content/uploads/2024/02/Policy-Brief-integrating-the-general-comment.FAO-Guidelines-on-Small-scale-Fisheries_12.02.24_1.pdf>

'Policy Brief: Integrating the General Comment 26 on Children's Rights and a Healthy Environment in the Implementation of the Global Biodiversity Framework' (*One Ocean Hub*, 5 February 2024) <https://oneoceanhub.org/wp-content/uploads/2024/02/Policy-Brief-integrating-the-General-Comment-26-on-Childrens-Rights-.12.02.24_2-.pdf>

'UN Guidance on Children's Human Right to a Healthy Environment Calls for Protecting Marine Ecosystems, Transforming Industrial Fisheries, and Preventing Marine Pollution' (*One Ocean Hub*, 29 August 2023) <https://oneoceanhub.org/un-guidance-on-childrens-human-right-to-a-healthy-environment-calls-for-protecting-marine-ecosystems-transforming-industrial-fisheries-and-preventing-marine-pollution/>

Morgera E, et al. 'Biodiversity as a Human Right and Its Implications for the EU's External Action' (*European Parliament*, 2020) <https://www.europarl.europa.eu/RegData/etudes/STUD/2020/603491/EXPO_STU(2020)603491_EN.pdf>

'Calling Attention to Children Ocean Defenders' (*One Ocean Hub*, 12 December 2023) <https://oneoceanhub.org/calling-attention-to-children-ocean-defenders/>

'Contributing to the 2025 UN Call for Action on Human Rights with a Focus on Ocean Defenders' (*One Ocean Hub*, 23 October 2023) <https://oneoceanhub.org/contributing-to-the-un-call-for-action-on-human-rights-with-a-focus-on-ocean-defenders/>

'Legal Note: The Request for an Advisory Opinion from the International Court of Justice on the Obligations of States in Respect of Climate Change' (*One Ocean Hub*, 22 March 2024) <https://oneoceanhub.org/publications/legal-note-the-request-for-an-advisory-opinion-from-the-international-court-of-justice-on-the-obligations-of-states-inrespect-of-climate-change/>

'The Ocean Is Included in the Zero Draft of the UN General Comment on Children's Rights to a Healthy Environment' (*One Ocean Hub*, 6 December

2022) <https://oneoceanhub.org/the-ocean-is-included-in-the-zero-draft-of-the-un-general-comment-on-childrens-rights-to-a-healthy-environment/>

'Written Statement of the One Ocean Hub to the International Tribunal for the Law of the Sea' (Statement not submitted Pursuant to Article 138(3) and 133 (3) of the Rules of the Tribunal) (*One Ocean Hub*, 2023) <https://www.itlos.org/fileadmin/itlos/documents/cases/31/written_statements/4/C31-WS-4-10-OOH.pdf>

Mtombheni M et al, 'Deep Sea Decisions Can Consider Indigenous Knowledge' (*360 Info*, 2023) <https://360info.org/deep-sea-decisions-can-consider-indigenous-knowledge/>

Nagler PS, 'Research Brief: Harmonizing War Crimes Under the Rome Statute – Geneva Academy Research Brief' (*Geneva Academy*, March 2019) <https://www.geneva-academy.ch/joomlatools-files/docman-files/Harmonizing%20War%20Crimes%20Under%20The%20Rome%20Statute.pdf>

The Ocean Defenders Project, 'Ocean Defenders at the Forefront of Efforts to Protect the Oceans Against Threats to the Marine Environment and Human Rights' (*The Ocean Defenders Project*, 2023) <https://oceandefendersproject.org>

OHCHR, 'Communication Report and Search' (*OHCHR*, 2025) <https://spcommreports.ohchr.org/>

'Special Procedures of the Human Rights Council: What Are Communications? (*OHCHR*, 2025) <https://www.ohchr.org/en/special-procedures-human-rights-council/what-are-communications>

Okimoto K, 'The United Nations and the Third Geneva Convention' (*EJIL: Talk!*, 26 October 2020) <https://www.ejiltalk.org/the-united-nations-and-the-third-geneva-convention/>

One Ocean Hub, 'About Us' (*One Ocean Hub*, 2024) <https://oneoceanhub.org/>

'Children and Young Peoples' Human Rights to a Healthy Ocean' (*Youtube*, 12 November 2021) <https://www.youtube.com/watch?v=TVoF8hmSpEE&t=414s>

'Contributing Views on Future Work of the Just Transition Work Programme of the UN Climate Change Convention and the 2024 Bonn Ocean-Climate Dialogue' (*One Ocean Hub*, 28 March 2024) < https://oneoceanhub.org/contributing-views-on-future-work-of-the-just-transition-work-programme-of-the-un-climate-change-convention-and-the-2024-bonn-ocean-climate-dialogue/>

'Policy Brief: The Implementation of the WTO Fisheries Subsidies Agreement Should Support the Human Rights of Small-Scale Fisheries' (2023) <https://oneoceanhub.org/wp-content/uploads/2023/10/Policy-Brief-WTO-Fisheries-Subsidies_26.10.23.pdf>

Pereira T, 'Ocean-defending Small-scale Fishers in South Africa Say NO to Seismic Surveys' (*The Ocean Defenders Project*, 2023) <https://oceandefendersproject.org/case-study/no-to-seismic-surveys/>

'Spotlighting Ocean Defenders and the Responsibilities of Marine Conservation Organizations' (*One Ocean Hub*, 12 December 2023) <https://oneoceanhub.org/spotlighting-ocean-defenders-and-the-responsibilities-of-marine-conservation-organizations/>

Phillips RL, '2nd Time's the Charm: France's Cour de Cassation Broadens Universal Jurisdiction Law' (*Just Security*, 24 May 2023) <https://www.justsecurity.org/86689/2nd-times-the-charm-frances-cour-de-cassation-broadens-universal-jurisdiction-law/>

Radhakrishnan A and Sadat LN, 'Key UN Committee Clears Path for Crimes Against Humanity Treaty Negotiations' (*Just Security*, 2 December 2024) <https://www.justsecurity.org/105305/cah-treaty-negotiations-passes-sixth-committee/>

Radhakrishnan A et al, 'A Major Breakthrough Towards a Treaty on Crimes Against Humanity' (*Just Security*, 27 November 2024) <https://www.justsecurity.org/105242/podcast-cah-treaty-breakthrough/>

Sadat LN and Radhakrishnan A, 'Justice Delayed Is Justice Denied: Moving Forward with a New Crimes Against Humanity Treaty' (*Just Security*, 23 October 2024) <https://www.justsecurity.org/104188/justice-delayed-denied-crimes-against-humanity-treaty/>

Sadat LN, 'Accountability for Environmental Violations and Crimes: Advancing a More Global and Inclusive Approach to International Environmental Law' (UNGA 79 High-Level Week Side Event, New York, September 2024) <https://bpb-us-w2.wpmucdn.com/sites.wustl.edu/dist/b/2004/files/2024/10/Remarks_Crimes-Against-the-Environment_UN-High-Level-Week.pdf.>

'Towards a New Treaty on Crimes Against Humanity: Next Steps' (*Just Security*, 13 September 2021) <https://www.justsecurity.org/78063/towards-a-new-treaty-on-crimes-against-humanity-next-steps/>

Sandoz Y, 'The International Committee of the Red Cross as Guardian of International Humanitarian Law' (*ICRC*, 1998) <https://www.icrc.org/en/article/guardian-international-humanitarian-law>

Shields S and Morgera E, 'Policy Brief: What Child Environmental Human Rights Defenders Need to Know to Defend and Protect a Healthy Ocean' (*One Ocean Hub*, 12 December 2023) <https://oneoceanhub.org/wp-content/uploads/2023/12/Policy-Brief-What-child-environmental-human-rights-defenders-need-to-know.12.12.23.pdf>

Skander Galand A, 'The ICC Appeals Judgment on Abd-Al-Rahman Jurisdictional Challenge: A Foreseeable Turn to Substantive Justice?' (*EJILTalk!*, 22 November 2021) <https://www.ejiltalk.org/the-icc-appeals-judgment-on-abd-al-rahman-jurisdictional-challenge-a-foreseeable-turn-to-substantive-justice/>

Stubbins Bates E, 'Geneva Convention III Commentary: Unpacking the Potential of "Ensure Respect" in Common Article 1' (*Just Security*, 30 October 2020)

<https://www.justsecurity.org/73166/geneva-convention-iii-commentary-unpacking-the-potential-of-ensure-respect-in-common-article-1>

Trial International, 'Universal Jurisdiction Annual Review: Highlights in 2023' (*Trial International*, 14 April 2024) <https://trialinternational.org/latest-post/universal-jurisdiction-annual-review-highlights-in-2023/>

UKRI, 'GCRF Global Interdisciplinary Research Hubs' (*UK Research and Innovation*, 13 March 2023) <https://www.ukri.org/publications/gcrf-global-interdisciplinary-research-hubs/>

Ulfstein G, 'Who Is the Final Interpreter in Human Rights: the ICJ v CERD?' (*EJILTalk*, 22 February 2021) <https://www.ejiltalk.org/who-is-the-final-interpreter-in-human-rights-the-icj-v-cerd/>

UN Human Rights – Meetings and Trainings, 'Special Rapporteur on Toxics and Human Rights, Mr Marcos Orellana' (Youtube, 19 March 2024) <https://www.youtube.com/watch?v=ZR5UZcQY6YM>

UN, 'Official Languages' (*UN*, 2025) <https://www.un.org/en/our-work/official-languages>

Vaccaro-Incisa GM, 'Crimea Investment Disputes: Are Jurisdictional Hurdles Being Overcome Too Easily?' (*EJILTalk!*, 9 May 2018), <https://www.ejiltalk.org/crimea-investment-disputes-are-jurisdictional-hurdles-being-overcome-too-easily/>

Washington University, 'Crimes Against Humanity Initiative' (*Washington University in St Louis*, 2025) <https://sites.wustl.edu/crimesagainsthumanity/>

Watson C, 'Parachute Science Falls to Earth' (*Nature Index*, 13 April 2021) <https://www.nature.com/nature-index/news/parachute-science-falls-to-earth>

WTO, 'Glossary' (*WTO*, 2023) <https://www.wto.org/english/thewto_e/glossary_e/glossary_e.htm>

INDEX

Printed in the United Kingdom by TJ Clays Ltd.